D0915578

SAM NUNN

CONGRESSIONAL LEADERS

Burdett A. Loomis
Series Editor

SAM NUNN

STATESMAN OF THE NUCLEAR AGE

Frank Leith Jones

University Press of Kansas

Published by the University Press of Kansas (Lawrence, Kansas 66045), which was organized by the Kansas Board of Regents and is operated and funded by Emporia State University, Fort Hays State University, Kansas State University, Pittsburg State University, the University of Kansas, and Wichita State University.

Publication made possible, in part, by funding from The Dirksen Congressional Center.

Library of Congress Cataloging-in-Publication Data

Names: Jones, Frank L. (Frank Leith), author. Title: Sam Nunn : statesman of the nuclear age / Frank Leith Jones. Other titles: Statesman of the nuclear age
Description: [Lawrence] : University Press of Kansas, [2020] | Series: Congressional leaders | Includes bibliographical references and index.
Identifiers: LCCN 2020011790
ISBN 9780700630127 (cloth)
ISBN 9780700630134 (epub)
Subjects: LCSH: Nunn, Sam. | Nunn, Sam—Influence. | United States. Congress. Senate—Biography. | United States. Congress. Senate. Committee on Armed Services. | Legislators—United States—Biography. | United States—Politics and government—1945–1989. | United States—Politics and government—1989– | National security—United States.
Classification: LCC E748.N86 J66 2020 | DDC 328.73/092 [B]—dc23
LC record available at https://lccn.loc.gov/2020011790.

British Library Cataloguing-in-Publication Data is available.

Printed in the United States of America

10 9 8 7 6 5 4 3 2 1

The paper used in this publication is recycled and contains 30 percent postconsumer waste. It is acid free and meets the minimum requirements of the American National Standard for Permanence of Paper for Printed Library Materials Z39.48-1992.

In memory of my parents

Goldwater was the gunslinger; Nunn, the deliberate statesman.
James R. Locher III

CONTENTS

CONTENTS

SERIES FOREWORD

Congressional leadership comes in many forms. The first book in this series, on Bob Michel, detailed how a man of the minority exerted influence in the House (and beyond) over the arc of a long career. A subsequent volume will flesh out Representative Tom Foley's long rise to leadership in the US House. Both Michel and Foley served as formal party leaders in Congress, which constitutes one clear form of leadership. But it is far from the only path to leadership within the Congress. Margaret Chase Smith (R-ME), for example, led as a strong woman legislator, ahead of her time and unflinching in her opposition to the malevolent tactics of Senator Joe McCarthy (R-WI). Or, through a forty-year career, Representative Henry Waxman (D-CA) demonstrated how a single policy–oriented legislator could exercise great influence on the course of national environmental and energy policies, among other subjects.

Georgia Democratic senator Sam Nunn represents another style of broad policy leadership, one that, while based in the Senate, extended through the whole of American national government and beyond, to affect American and international interests around the world. Frank Jones concludes:

> Senator Nunn's legacy as a strategic leader resulted from his vision of what the United States should do to maintain the international order it preferred, by aligning policy and resources through legislation and other means to promote that vision, and by working within the Senate, but also with the House of Representatives, the executive branch, and internationally, to build consensus and thereby meet the challenges that the nation and its allies and partners confronted for more than two decades.

Very few contemporary US senators have achieved such a status as a "strategic leader"; a short list would include William Fulbright (D-AR), Henry "Scoop" Jackson (D-WA), and perhaps John McCain (R-AZ). Like Nunn, they all enjoyed a long tenure, high committee positions, and formidable expertise.

Nunn's policy leadership flowed from various sources, all overlapping and complementing each other. First, he won election to the Senate in 1972 at age thirty-four and soon became a protégé of the powerful John Stennis (D-MS). He moved up the seniority ladder, expanded his expertise, and chaired the Senate Armed Services Committee from 1987 to 1995. In short, his tenure led to the possibility of great influence when he became committee chair. Second, Nunn became a genuine policy expert on a wide range of defense issues, including arms control; moreover, he understood the defense budget from top to bottom. Beyond that, the Nunn enterprise included several top-flight staffers who could further his agenda.

Third, Nunn's political stance as a moderate Democrat allowed him substantial latitude to make deals with senators from both parties. From conservative Republican Barry Goldwater to liberal Democrat Ted Kennedy, Senate leaders often knew that they could not take his vote for granted and that a Nunn defection would provide cover for other potential defectors. This meant that, even though he was just one of 100 senators, he could wield influence beyond his own vote or even his position as a committee chair.

Finally, the political context of his time as Armed Services Committee chair gave him substantial opportunities to work with Republican presidents Ronald Reagan and George H. W. Bush as the Cold War ended and new geopolitical lines were drawn. By the early 1990s, he knew all the players, both domestic and foreign, and could talk directly with them. To an extent his policy leadership transcended the Congress, extending to the White House, the Defense Department, and beyond. Moreover, when Nunn left the Senate in 1997, his influence continued for more than two decades, most notably on nuclear threat initiatives.

In sum, Sam Nunn led through his policy expertise and his political acumen as he built bridges to and forged alliances with a wide array of political allies and, more than occasionally, adversaries. Not all senators are leaders, but for some, like Nunn, the United States Senate provides great opportunities to lead, if you can grasp them. Without a doubt, he could and did.

—Burdett A. Loomis
Series Editor

ACKNOWLEDGMENTS

This book began with a conversation about the influence the chair of the Senate Armed Services Committee, as a congressional leader, has on US national security policy and strategy. My interlocutor was Jim Locher, who served as a committee staff member as well as an assistant secretary of defense in the George H. W. Bush administration. He is the author of an excellent book on the Goldwater-Nichols Act, which figures prominently in this book. Jim and I discussed a number of potential subjects, but I had only one in mind—Senator Sam Nunn. Jim informed me that Senator Nunn was a private man and was uncertain if he would acquiesce to someone writing about his career, but he considerately introduced me to Cathy Gwin, who served as Senator Nunn's press secretary at one time and is currently the senior director for communications at the Nuclear Threat Initiative (NTI). NTI is a nonprofit, nonpartisan organization that Senator Nunn and the philanthropist Ted Turner founded in 2001 to reduce the likelihood of attacks and accidents involving weapons of mass destruction. Cathy and I met to discuss my interest. She subsequently conveyed my proposal to Senator Nunn, and after a period of consideration, he called me and told me I had his complete support. He gave me access to his personal papers and the oral histories he conducted with his staff just before his retirement from the Senate in 1996, and offered any other help he could render. Without his approval and assistance, the book would not have been possible.

This book is neither a full biography nor an official one; it is a study of Sam Nunn's career as a strategic leader in the US Senate, with explicit attention to his work as a junior member, subcommittee chairman, ranking member, and chairman of the Senate Armed Services Committee. I am particularly grateful to Senator Nunn for the hours he spent responding to my draft chapters by clarifying specific issues, sitting for interviews, and answering innumerable questions about his intentions or thoughts on the various subjects he dealt with in his roles on the committee or, more broadly, the security and foreign policy of the United States. Never once did he intrude upon or interfere with my authorial role.

I want to specifically thank Cathy Gwin for her encouragement, support, and munificent backing. She cleared any barrier I had in obtaining information, whatever the source; provided me copies of Senator Nunn's correspondence, notes, speeches, and other material; and contacted former staff members to assist me with my queries. I am also particularly grateful to the former staff for their time and willingness to respond my questions, especially Robert Bell, Richard Combs, Jim Locher, Roland McElroy, and Arnold Punaro.

A book that examines a senator's lengthy career owes a debt as well to archivists, historians, and librarians. At Emory University's Stuart A. Rose Manuscript, Archives, and Rare Book Library, I was fortunate to have the support of Randy Gue, Susan Potts McDonald, Courtney Chartier, and Kathy Shoemaker. Since Senator Nunn's papers had not been completely processed before my visit to Atlanta, Randy ensured that a preliminary finding aid was created to help me locate relevant files in the collection. I want to thank Brittany Parris and Keith Shuler at the Jimmy Carter Presidential Library; Desiree Butterfield-Nagy at the University of Maine's Fogler Library; Scott Gower at the National Defense University Library's Special Collections; Richard McCulley and Adam Berenbak at the US National Archives and Record Administration's Center for Legislative Archives; Betty Koed, Kate Scott, and Stephen Tull at the US Senate Historical Office; and the librarians and staff at the US Army War College for their expert aid.

Traveling to archives and other sites is an expensive proposition. The visits would not have been possible without a research grant from the Dirksen Congressional Center in Pekin, Illinois. Its generous support of research on congressional leadership and the US Congress made the difference for this project. The center also kindly provided a subvention for this book to be published in the University Press of Kansas's Congressional Leaders series. At the center, I want to thank Frank Mackaman for his personal interest in my scholarship and for recommending I send the manuscript to the University Press of Kansas.

A special thanks to scholars who encouraged my study of Senator Nunn. Harvey Schantz and Harvey Strum furnished me an opportunity to test some of my ideas about Senator Nunn's impact on US foreign policy as a panelist at a conference. Ralph G. Carter and James M. Scott considerately shared their time and expertise on congressional foreign policy entrepreneurs in an exchange of emails. My thanks as well to Ben Guterman, the editor of *Federal History,* the journal of the Society for History in the Federal Government, for publishing an earlier version of chapter 14, "Loose Nukes." The article and the chapter serve as testaments to his guidance and skillful editorship.

Friends and colleagues, former and current, have been generous with their time and counsel. I owe a great deal to Mark Duckenfield, Mike Neiberg, Tami Biddle, Bill Johnsen, Chris Keller, Patrick Bratton, and Gen Lester. Two colleagues, Steve Gerras and the late Charles Van Bebber, read and commented on chapters, for which I am especially appreciative.

David Congdon, acquisitions editor at the University Press of Kansas, put his guiding hand to this project and brought it to fruition, and it was a pleasure to deal with him and his colleagues, especially Mike Kehoe, marketing and sales director, and Colin Tripp, production editor. The press's reviewers, Sean Q Kelly and Douglas B. Harris, contributed valuable comments that sharpened my thinking and identified areas where I could enrich the manuscript. I am grateful as well for Beth Partin's excellent copyedit.

My wife, Sharon, has been my helpmate on this project as she has been on everything I write. She encouraged me, read drafts, corrected errors, offered observations, and assisted in many other ways. I cannot thank her enough for her time and commitment over the years that it took to write this book. I am thankful for everyone mentioned previously and others who helped along the way to hone my views and judgments, but I alone am responsible for any ineptness in style or expression, errors of fact, or any other shortcomings that remain.

INTRODUCTION

Dana Milbank, the *Washington Post* columnist, wrote an opinion piece in 2012 decrying the lack of "giants" in the US Senate, figures of stature, admired by colleagues, "whose authority could transcend party and the usual arithmetic of vote counting." In addition to the revered senators whose portraits hang in the reception room off the Senate floor, Milbank especially noted six esteemed congressional leaders that had served since the 1960s. One of them was Senator Sam Nunn, Democrat of Georgia.[1]

Nunn served four terms in the Senate, twenty-four years, and during his tenure, government officials and journalists, among others, recognized and respected him as the chamber's, and even Congress's, leading expert on defense and national security issues.[2] He not only served at the moment when domestic politics and foreign policy were undergoing far-reaching changes, but he had a vital impact on most of the crucial national security and defense issues of the Cold War era and the "new world order" that followed. These issues included revitalization of the North Atlantic Treaty Organization's (NATO's) military capability, US-Soviet relations, national defense reorganization and reform, the Persian Gulf conflict, and nuclear arms control.

More specifically, Nunn served as chairman of the Senate Armed Services Committee's Subcommittee on Manpower and Personnel (1975–1981), where he enhanced his knowledge of the US military well beyond the subcommittee's immediate jurisdiction, and addressed some of the most significant issues of organization and capability that the post–Vietnam War US military confronted. He assumed this role at a time when, as some experts claim, Congress saw its institutional authority fragmented and subcommittee chairs became prominent power brokers.[3] Most importantly, Nunn served as the Senate Armed Services Committee (SASC) chairman from 1987 to 1994, spanning the end of the Cold War and its immediate aftermath. During the years when he was not holding the committee chairmanship, he served as ranking member (1983–1986 and 1995–1997). In each role, Nunn had a major part in writing and guiding a number of notable pieces of legislation concerning US defense issues into law, but he also helped fashion US foreign policy, especially with respect to arms control treaties and nuclear weapons strategy. His impact transcended the Senate, influencing members of the House of Representatives, senior officials in the Departments of Defense and State, and even the White House. Presidents took note of his power and sway, but also his skills.

Yet, despite this record of accomplishment and proven knowledge, Nunn's senatorial career has not been the subject of any comprehensive study. Instead, he has been one of many figures in books about such topics as defense policy and organization. The principal reason for this neglect is the constraints the Senate's rules impose on access to that institution's papers in the US National Archives. However, another factor is in play. Few scholars and journalists are currently devoting research to the study of the US Congress with respect to the influence that the institution has had on US foreign and defense policy since the Vietnam War. Historian Julian Zelizer pointed out that despite the recent resurgence of interest in Congress, studies of congressional leaders and their impact on US policy have remained decidedly infrequent over the past two decades when compared to the numerous books written about American presidents and other senior government officials. As he also observed, the "political biographies of some of the greatest figures who moved the institution" remain to be written.[4]

The intent of this book is to rectify this deficiency by examining Nunn's leadership as a committee and subcommittee chairman on the Armed Services Committee, and the influence he exerted on defense and national security policy. It serves as a necessary corrective to the tendency among scholars, journalists, and the general public to focus almost entirely on the executive branch in the making of American foreign and national security policy and to ignore the importance of legislators in this regard. In addition, it challenges the conventional view that Congress and the Senate Armed Services Committee are only engaged in activities that affect the defense establishment in one of two ways: budgets and military organization and equipage.[5] In this respect, this book will examine Nunn's leadership in fostering the committee's role in shaping US national security policy and America's post–Cold War defense strategy.

In particular, Nunn played an essential role in the 1970s, constructing the foundation for the successful US defense and foreign policies of the 1980s that helped end the Cold War, along with forging a vision for US national defense in the post–Cold War era. Nunn, as part of a cohort that entered the Senate at the end of US involvement in the Vietnam War, was also the beneficiary of a committee structure that changed dramatically in the 1970s. Political scientist James Lindsay maintains that these changes were most evident in defense policy, and although there have been studies that examine the defense committees, the need for substantial analysis remains.[6] This is especially the case concerning the Senate during the 1970s and 1980s, when the Armed Services Committee overshadowed the Foreign Relations Committee in power and stature.[7]

Moreover, this book examines how a powerful committee chairman, but also a ranking member with a reputation for bipartisanship, can set agendas and fashion policy within the contexts of time, attention, and resource scarcity. In examining his activities through these lenses, this book can reveal Nunn as a "problem solver," sometimes as a partner, and in other cases an independent critic of the executive branch.[8] Thus, a study of Nunn will provide a more complete understanding of the role of a defense committee chairman in the policy-making process, if only to ascertain the conditions under which a chairman decides to undertake significant committee and congressional initiatives in the authorization process, as well as an understanding of the Senate's "advice and consent" function regarding treaties. Pat Towell notes that the importance of these initiatives has been "entirely ignored by students of the defense policy-making process."[9] Nunn's career underscores how a committee chairman's leadership, expertise, and values can be used to negotiate the relationship between the defense establishment and the American public, to articulate military requirements for national defense as well as educate legislative colleagues, and, equally, to ensure not only that the military's programs are acceptable to the American people, but that they are prudently employed for the security of the state.[10]

At times, Nunn was a transactional leader involved in brokering deals between various groups and factions, counting votes, and the like, but he was also a transforming leader, to use the terms James MacGregor Burns coined for these two leadership styles.[11] Thus, his career speaks to the marriage of political acumen and expertise. In several cases, principally through legislation, some of which bears his name, Nunn sought to alter the status quo, renewing American military and strategic culture (reform leadership) and serving as a catalyst of ideas and policies (intellectual leadership). Additionally, as James Locher points out in his study of the Goldwater-Nichols Act, *Victory on the Potomac*, Nunn enjoyed a reputation for moral leadership. The moral dimension of leadership, which Burns believed to be a distinguishing quality of the transforming leader, will also be examined in this book.[12] Assessing Nunn's character in addition to appraising his leadership competencies is essential to comprehending his political success in the Senate and his activities beyond that institution. Such a perspective helps refute the prevalent view that good character and politics are mutually exclusive. Nunn's colleagues respected him for his integrity and his decency, and admired him for his political courage and his willingness to maintain unpopular positions he believed were right, such as his opposition to the Persian Gulf War.

Further, in considering Nunn's leadership, this book must characterize his actions not only in the broader context of twentieth-century American politics, in Georgia and the Democratic Party nationally, but equally important, as an integral part of the post–World War II international order. Although there may have been an American foreign policy consensus during most of the Cold War regarding the Soviet Union as the principal adversary and the threat it posed to US interests, several issues were up for serious debate that had enormous impact on national security policy and defense budgets. His leadership on and knowledge of these issues, and his frequent interaction with foreign leaders in the North Atlantic Treaty Organization, with other allies, and even with Soviet officials such as Mikhail Gorbachev, are indicative of the impact he had on US foreign relations while also advancing US policy aims. Thus, his career provides a valuable means of understanding relationships between the US government and foreign governments and societies, such as in the later Cold War era, when the Soviet Union was collapsing and successor states were emerging.

Lastly, while scholars often contend that members of Congress have three principal motives for legislative activism, which are reelection, partisanship, and personal interest,[13] there is abundant documented evidence that for Nunn, in terms of his internationalist stance, another element prompted his actions: his concern for the broad and long-term interests of the United States. This is not to suggest that the other motives were not involved, such as influence in the chamber, or that these motives do not overlap, only that in numerous instances, he demanded thoughtful deliberation from his colleagues on the fashioning of "good," or more accurately, suitable policy to advance US national interests, regardless of who occupied the Oval Office.[14]

In that regard, a study of his leadership will demonstrate that Nunn acted as a congressional foreign policy entrepreneur, using the broad meaning of foreign policy to include Congress's constitutional powers to declare war, raise and support armies, provide and maintain a navy, regulate naval and land forces, and organize, arm, and call forth the militia. Political scientists Ralph Carter and James Scott have defined congressional foreign policy entrepreneurs as "individuals who initiate action on the *issues* [emphasis added] they care about rather than await administrative action on them," and that entrepreneurship is a "distinct subset of congressional activism and assertiveness." The member undertakes such action because policy does not exist or because the entrepreneur does not agree with the existing policy and seeks to alter it. Nunn's leadership role, most notably as a powerful committee chairman, only served to magnify the number of "avenues of influence" he had and the "impact" he could have on national security issues and strategies in terms of both US foreign policy and internal US government processes, far beyond that of most policy entrepreneurs in Congress. Thus, Nunn acting on his own agenda in the Armed Service Committee or its subcommittees is using his structural position to advance entrepreneurship; whereas if he is acting in response to the administration's agenda, then his activity is more properly characterized as active or assertive leadership.[15] This distinction speaks to the point that Robert Tucker made in *Politics as Leadership*, that leaders influence events, and they do so by diagnosing the situation convincingly, developing a plan of action to resolve the problem, and mobilizing the political community to support the leader's definition of the situation and the plan.[16] Time after time during his senatorial career, Nunn was an "event-maker." Therefore, to have a complete appreciation of Nunn's success as a political leader, it is necessary to trace his career as subcommittee chairman, ranking member, and committee chairman, starting with the formative experiences in the Senate.

Beginning in the early 1970s, as chair of the SASC's Subcommittee on Manpower and Personnel, Nunn, working with Republican colleagues, produced major analyses of the US military's as well as its NATO allies' capacity to defend Western Europe. His 1974 and 1976 reports on the alliance, in particular, spurred the Carter administration toward enhancing NATO's conventional capability. Thus, his investigations and findings strengthened NATO through cooperative programs, led to greater contributions from treaty partners, and ensured US capability to counter the growing power of the Soviet military, which had increased substantially while the United States focused almost entirely on its interests in Southeast Asia.

In the 1980s and early 1990s, during the Reagan and George H. W. Bush administrations, Nunn, as ranking member and later as committee chairman, took the lead in the debates over arms control, particularly with respect to the debate on reinterpreting the Anti–Ballistic Missile Treaty and the ratification of the Intermediate-Range Nuclear Forces Treaty, areas traditionally under the jurisdiction of the Foreign Relations Committee. Whether the ascendancy of the Armed Services Committee during this period, especially during his term as chair, results principally from structural factors (e.g., many major foreign policy issues involve military matters and Armed Services has jurisdiction over the defense budget) or personal ones (e.g., Senator Claiborne Pell's chairmanship of Foreign Relations) is an element worth examining. This is particularly true for this period since a number of the major issues concerned the Senate's constitutional duty to provide advice and consent on these treaties and, in particular, Nunn's prominent role as a cochair of the Senate Arms Control Observer Group. Moreover, during his tenure as ranking member, and particularly during Senator Barry Goldwater's chairmanship of the Arms Services Committee, Nunn held considerable influence over defense issues, to the point at which journalist Sidney Blumenthal observed in a *New Republic* article: "Nunn often adroitly operated as the de facto chairman without Goldwater even aware of his figurehead status."[17] In this period, NATO allies, with the parliamentary system of governance being their frame of reference, often described Nunn as the "shadow secretary of defense."

The 1980s and 1990s are also crucial to understanding Nunn's role in promoting peace. In these decades, he presented initiatives to reduce the risk of accidental nuclear war and, most importantly, the Nunn-Lugar legislation—and its implementation by the Department of Defense, the Cooperative Threat Reduction program—designed to dismantle weapons of mass destruction in the former Soviet Union. For his work in conceiving, legislating, and sustaining this program, Nunn, along with Senator Richard Lugar, the Indiana Republican, twice received a nomination for the Nobel Peace Prize.

In sum, Nunn's leadership provides an opportunity to examine the role of a committee chair over an extended period, a leader mindful of his power but also a maintainer of the Senate's prerogatives, especially with respect to how a senator can shape indirectly the formulation and conduct of national security policy. As political scientist Randall Strahan asserts, individual leaders make a difference in congressional politics when they are willing to assume "political risks to advance goals about which they care deeply."[18] In the case of Nunn, he assumed these risks and brought his expertise and power to bear on US policy, underscoring that both context (in this case, domestic and international environments as well as institutional) and the character-istics of the leader are consequential in studying congressional leadership. Nunn's career also provides a glimpse into how a leader in the legislative branch can set the policy agenda and develop policy through use of the in-stitution's constitutional powers, as well as shape elite and public opinion, and even diplomacy. While these elements have been examined extensively with respect to presidents and other high-level executive branch officials, a similar assessment of a senator's leadership role in these areas is a worthy contribution to a more extensive understanding of how US national security policy and strategy are developed and implemented.

CHAPTER 1

STENNIS'S CADET

A smiling, ebullient Richard Nixon, with his wife Pat at his side, strode into the ballroom at the Shoreham Hotel in Washington, DC, twenty-five minutes after midnight on November 8, 1972. Only minutes before, the incumbent president had delivered his victory speech from the White House Oval Office, thanking those who voted for him on Election Day, and reminding his television audience of the momentous tasks that lay ahead for the nation—peace, prosperity, and progress for all Americans. Now, however, it was a time for celebration. The estimated crowd of 5,000 followers roared their delight as he approached the podium on the platform before them. Their arms waving above their heads, many with four fingers outstretched, chanting wildly and in unison, "Four More Years," again and again. The din muffled the opening bars of "Hail to the Chief." Nixon stepped forward, waved his arm in acknowledgment of their acclamation, and said modestly, "Hi," to which they uttered a cheer, but then quieted. Nixon began to speak in the hushed room, his words occasionally punctuated by ovations and shouts of approval. After thirteen minutes, he concluded his speech by expressing his gratitude to his supporters for making his last campaign "the very best of all."[1]

Nixon's reelection could only be described by the common term—land-slide. Political analyst David Broder declared that it equaled "the greatest of American political history." His Democratic opponent, Senator George

McGovern of South Dakota, suffered "an electoral defeat of historic dimensions." Nixon won 60 percent of the popular vote and carried every state except Massachusetts, as well as the District of Columbia. McGovern had little to show for three months of postconvention campaigning as the party nominee. He had been under attack for his liberal views ever since California's presidential primary in June 1972. One of his critics characterized him as a candidate who favored amnesty for Vietnam War resisters, abortion rights, and decriminalization of marijuana, which they abbreviated as "amnesty, abortion and acid" (lysergic acid diethylamide, or LSD).[2]

In fact, McGovern had largely campaigned on increasing federal spending on US domestic priorities and most importantly, getting the United States out of the war in Vietnam—a conflict the nation had supported or been fighting in for five presidential administrations. It was a sentiment many Americans, disillusioned with the cost of the war in terms of human life and resources, shared. McGovern also articulated the outlook of a number of his Senate colleagues, weary of the leadership role the United States had assumed after World War II; some were convinced that such a role had adverse impacts on other nations, others that US political, economic, and military involvement sullied America's reputation and dishonored its values. McGovern's foreign policy philosophy could be summed up in the three words that defined his campaign, "Come home, America."[3] For its part, the Nixon administration was actively seeking to negotiate a peace settlement with its adversary, North Vietnam. Only a few weeks earlier, at an October 26, 1972, press conference, Nixon's national security advisor, Henry Kissinger, declared, "We believe that peace is at hand in Vietnam," based upon the two parties reaching a general agreement on ending the war. The timing of the event, so close to Election Day, led a suspicious press to dub the announcement the "October Surprise."[4]

For months, pundits never believed that Nixon needed a surprise to win reelection. The outcome was simply an inescapable finale for the underdog McGovern, not only because of his departure from convention on various issues that ended up dividing the Democratic Party, or the power of the presidency that an incumbent enjoys, but also because "electoral demography" favored Nixon. There was no grand realignment, no dramatic shift in voters' behavior, despite eighteen-, nineteen-, and twenty-year-olds being eligible to vote for the first time with the passage of the Twenty-Sixth Amendment. Ultimately, the reason was straightforward, as Republican strategist Kevin Phillips pointed out: "Politics is a numbers game," and Nixon had the numbers.

By August 1972, when Phillips had offered his forecast of a Nixon triumph, McGovern was already down 34 points in national public opinion polls.[5] That figure exemplified the uphill battle the Democratic candidate confronted in challenging a sitting chief executive. That large deficit on Election Day remained, and may have also prompted McGovern to allegedly remark to bystanders when he voted in his boyhood town of Mitchell, South Dakota, "say a little prayer for me."[6]

Nonetheless, while Nixon won the presidency for a second term, and did win in traditional Democratic northern "strongholds" such as New York, Connecticut, and Michigan, as well as making the "Solid South solidly Republican," his party leaders recognized it as a "personal triumph for Mr. Nixon—and not a party triumph." The amount of ticket splitting among voters was substantial, possibly the largest in US political history, with the result that Democrats continued to control both houses of Congress, gaining two seats in the Senate and, in doing so, holding a fourteen-seat majority. In Georgia, Nixon's coattails were just not long enough for the Republican candidate for the US Senate. While thirty-four-year-old Democratic state legislator Sam Nunn appeared to be in trouble of losing the race, that analysis proved faulty. Nunn captured 52 percent of the vote, defeating the Republican, US representative Fletcher Thompson of Atlanta, although Nixon won the state's twelve electoral votes. Touted as one of the "New Democrats" from the South, Nunn's election was a phenomenal outcome for a candidate who had started the race with 2 percent name recognition.[7] Nunn's victory may have appeared unlikely to election experts and pollsters, but to the people of the small Georgia town in which he grew up, it seemed preordained, the product of family connections, talent, hard work, and an ability to seize opportunity.

Samuel Augustus Nunn Jr. was born on September 8, 1938, in Macon, Georgia, and raised in the small town of Perry, the county seat of Houston County, in the middle of the state, about 100 miles south of Atlanta.[8] His only sibling, Harriet Elizabeth, known as Betty, had been born two years earlier. Nunn's family was considered "Southern gentry," part of the town's "social and political aristocracy." His father, Sam Nunn Sr., known locally as "Mr. Sam," was a prosperous landowner, lawyer, and bank officer who served as a state legislator, mayor of Perry, member of the state board of education, and county Democratic Party leader. He was well connected to the governor, Eugene Talmadge, and his son Herman, later a US Senator from the state, and had led the state delegation to the 1932 National Democratic Convention. Nunn's mother, Mary Elizabeth Cannon, was a former schoolteacher from Cordele, Georgia. It was through her that young Sam enjoyed the most important political connection, his boyhood idol, great-uncle Carl Vinson.[9]

Vinson was one of the most powerful members of the House of Representatives, elected in 1914 and, by 1932, chairman of the House Naval Affairs Committee, which after World War II was combined with the Military Affairs Committee to become the Armed Services Committee. He would serve his Georgia district for fifty years, twenty-five consecutive terms, and become known as the "father of the two-ocean Navy" and revered in navy circles as "the Admiral." Vinson dedicated his political career to military affairs. In his role as chairman of the committee dealing with national defense, he shaped the course of US security policy for thirty years, beginning in the 1930s with a vision of how naval and air power would influence American strategy and operations as worldwide conflict loomed. On this point, Admiral Chester Nimitz later remarked, "I do not know where this country would have been after December 7, 1941, if it had not had the ships and the know-how to build more ships fast, for which one Vinson bill after another was responsible."[10]

Vinson was a courtly eccentric. He lived modestly and was self-effacing, but his quiet poise put off guard many an opponent. He appeared to be a "country bumpkin," with his prominent middle Georgia drawl and his spectacles perched at the end of his large nose. In actuality, he was a shrewd political tactician, nicknamed the "Swamp Fox" by his colleagues, with an incisive understanding of the issues, a razor-sharp memory for details, a resolve to rule his committee with firm authority, and a capacity to guide legislation through the House of Representatives and influence the Senate. He was not reluctant to battle with presidents, cabinet secretaries, or senior military officers, but they also respected him, naming an aircraft carrier in his honor while he was still living. President Lyndon Johnson presented him with the highest award available to a civilian, the Presidential Medal of Freedom with special distinction. When he was once considered a contender for appointment as secretary of defense, he allegedly remarked that he would rather "run the Pentagon" from Capitol Hill. Those words were not only the trademark of his power, but also his sense of duty. As he stated in his first speech as a congressman, his principal responsibility was the "Republic's safety" through his duties in Washington; he was known to have traveled outside the continental United States only once. When Congress was in session, he lived in a small residence in Chevy Chase, Maryland, and when it adjourned, he spent the days at his vast 600-acre Baldwin County estate a few miles outside Milledgeville, Georgia, on the Oconee River.[11]

The distance between Milledgeville and Perry is sixty miles, and it was over Thanksgiving dinners at the Nunn household when Congress was not in session that Uncle Carl, Mr. Sam, and Elizabeth discussed the major issues of the day. Other Georgia political luminaries visited the home. For young, impressionable Sam, the meals were the source of an education and a catalyst, forging the attributes that became abundantly clear in his political career. Sam Nunn would grow up in Perry aware of his great-uncle's prestige and his family's prominent place. Equally important, he grew up in a household where hard work, character, and Christianity mattered, prompting him to be a "classic overachiever" that others sought to emulate because of his accomplishments: Eagle Scout, academic success, faithful member of the local Methodist church, and captain of the high school basketball team, leading it to the 1956 state championship. It was also his grittiness that made him an All-State guard, twice. Nunn would later tell a journalist that weak ankles were his physical challenge as a player; his mother wrapped them every day so he could make it through practice. One of his high school teammates recalled a different dimension of Nunn the athlete. When the team was losing the annual state all-star game by five points at half-time, it was not the celebrated successful coach who remained confident, but Nunn with intense, can-do words of encouragement, despite the eventual loss.[12]

Nunn left Perry for Atlanta after high school graduation, entering the Georgia Institute of Technology in 1956, where he played on the freshman basketball team, but transferred to nearby private Emory University after three years. He served in the US Coast Guard for six months, from June 1959 to January 1960, followed by a reserve commitment. Nunn received his undergraduate degree from Emory in 1961, and earned his law degree in 1962. He then joined his great-uncle in Congress after passing the Georgia bar examination, but not before his great-uncle sent one of the House Armed Services Committee staff members to Emory University Law School to interview his professors before offering him a job. Nunn then worked on the House Armed Services Committee staff for a year as counsel on the procurement subcommittee, when Vinson "was at the zenith of his power." The experience Nunn admitted, "had a big effect on me," inducing an urge to run for political office someday. But necessities intervened. He had to make a living, and his next move was more pragmatic. He returned to Perry to practice law because his father had not been well for several years. Back in Perry, Nunn joined his father's law practice, managed the family farm, and married Colleen Ann O'Brien, a Central Intelligence Agency employee, whom he had met in Paris when he was working for Vinson. As president of the local chamber of commerce, he became a member of a group of young community leaders who, after the civil rights legislation of the 1960s, were invested in promoting social harmony among whites and blacks in Perry. Despite the hazards, both personal and professional, of assuming this progressive role, he was elected to the Georgia House of Representatives from Houston County in 1968. Three years later, when the new census figures were available, he offended some of his colleagues by lobbying for the establishment of a new congressional district with his hometown as the hub from which he could run for election as its US representative. He spent months bargaining over district boundaries as a member of the reapportionment committee but failed to obtain the support of Governor Jimmy Carter, whom Nunn had supported in his 1966 and 1970 gubernatorial races. Carter, who won the 1970 election and assumed office in January 1971, preferred a different apportionment plan. In the statehouse, on the day of the redistricting vote, Nunn's detractors posted a painted sign with the words "Bye-bye, Washington" in big letters. The plan was defeated in the Senate. When the vote became known, several legislators stood, pulled out their handkerchiefs, and waved them while mockingly serenading him, "Bye-bye, Sam, bye-bye."[13]

Nunn's luck proved stronger than his hecklers' ill wishes. Richard Russell Jr., the senior US senator from Georgia, died on January 21, 1971, from complications of emphysema while in office. Russell was a giant of the Senate, chairman of the Armed Services Committee, who had forged a strong bond with his fellow Georgian, Vinson, on military affairs. He was a mythic figure in southern politics, but also a vain and overconfident man who sought the Democratic Party's nomination for the presidency in 1952 and was roundly rejected by northern party leaders because of his segregationist views. With his death, Carter surprisingly appointed Atlanta lawyer David Gambrell, chairman of the state Democratic Party who headed Carter's campaign finance committee, to fill the remainder of Russell's term until the November 1972 general election.[14] In the heavily Democratic state, Gambrell's future as a senator seemed predetermined despite his lack of political experience.

The thirty-three-year-old Nunn, who had met Russell a few times while working for Vinson, decided to run for the seat and asked his great-uncle, who had retired from public life seven years earlier, about his chances. According to Nunn, Vinson, like many of the young man's friends, said that he was "crazy to run, that [he] didn't have a chance—mission impossible."

While "Young Sam" respected that opinion, he also believed that he needed to gamble. His great-uncle should not have been surprised by Nunn's youthful resolve; after all, he had been elected to Congress because of a vacant House seat resulting from a death in office, had won election by defeating three moneyed rivals, and had been sworn in as a member of Congress fifteen days before his thirty-first birthday. Despite the view by many friends and family that he was now acting with "foolish irrationality," that inference was unfounded. Nunn was a competitor who believed in himself and was willing to take a risk. One night he sat down with his wife, and drew up a list of reasons why he should run as well as the reasons for not doing so on a yellow legal pad. The reasons against clearly outweighed those in favor. The process, however, settled his mind. If he did not run, he would wonder for the remainder of his life if he had missed a crucial chance. His wife understood and supported his decision. For the next several months, she, his mother, and his sister would canvass the state on his behalf.[15]

Nunn was one of fifteen party hopefuls who sought the seat. When he announced his intention to run in March 1972, a prominent columnist for one of the Atlanta newspapers called it "one of the least significant political events of the year." Undaunted, Nunn began traveling around the state alone in a Pontiac sedan a local car dealer donated, driving down the highways and back roads in the dark, sleeping little, and each day vanquishing his unease about speaking publicly. The pace was unrelenting, and early one morning, he almost crashed into a bridge abutment when he fell asleep at the wheel. After months of this crushing schedule, however, his doggedness and his message secured him the critical endorsement of the *Atlanta Constitution*, and enough votes in the primary to force a runoff with David Gambrell.[16]

Vinson, seeing his great-nephew's determination and amazed by the result, informed his friends and followers he was behind Nunn and helped raise campaign funds. Nunn's campaign was never well-funded, so he bet that Gambrell's appointment had intensified divisions among state Democratic Party blocs. His perspective proved correct. Carter's popularity had nosedived during his first year in office for not being sufficiently conservative, but the governor kept butting into the campaign. Consequently, many of these factions, whose candidates had not been selected for the appointment and had lost in the Democratic primary, solidified as an "anti-Carter coalition" behind Nunn. They formed an unusual mix of groups: those who supported segregationist and former governor Lester Maddox, to the more moderate whites and blacks who had backed the election of African American civil rights leader Julian Bond to the Georgia House of Representatives in 1967.[17]

Nunn fashioned his campaign against Gambrell among rural voters by portraying his foe as an elite, Harvard-educated, big-city lawyer, too liberal, as signified by his support of George McGovern as the party's presidential nominee, and suggesting in a television ad that he had purchased the senatorial seat as payback for financing Carter's election as governor in 1970. It was an accusation Carter found offensive, and their once cordial relationship suffered. Nunn pulled the advertisement at his mother's request, because she abhorred personal attacks. Nunn won the primary narrowly. Vinson then strengthened Nunn's chances of success in the general election by taking him to Washington before the party runoff, to meet with the new chairman of the Senate Armed Services Committee, John Stennis of Mississippi. Nunn and Vinson extracted a promise from his friend Stennis that if Nunn was elected, he would be named to the committee. This gesture solidified Nunn's image as a worthy successor to Russell, where the "tradition of patriotic responsibility and respect for authority" made him heir to the "Georgia heritage," as Nunn called it. Nunn went on to win the general election with state Democratic Party leaders fully behind him. Their support, which included some campaigning with him and a letter from Alabama governor George Wallace, who wished Nunn "every success," helped offset the national party's unpopular presidential candidate. While Nunn stated he did not approve of Wallace's segregationist views, he knew the governor was revered among southern conservatives for his independent streak. Nunn had traveled to Alabama in September to pay his respects, and in turn, Wallace returned the favor a week before the general election. However, Maddox, who supported Nunn in the primary, switched to supporting Nunn's Republican opponent, Fletcher Thompson, in the general election—behind the scenes—after Maddox discovered how much support Nunn had among blacks. One of Thompson's supporters was not above using race-baiting as a campaign tactic, claiming that Nunn and Julian Bond had "teamed up to deceive Georgia voters." But Bond had not endorsed Nunn; he intended to remain neutral. The alleged endorsement was the work of an overzealous African American state senator who had acted without Bond's knowledge. Fortunately for Nunn, he was viewed as being his own candidate, not a national Democratic Party candidate or beholden to any specific group. Instead, he had forged a strong political coalition in a state that was not ready to elect Republicans to statewide offices. Yet, he still fretted. He even feared the rainy, windy weather on Election Day would suppress voter turnout and cost him the election, but it was needless anxiety. He would serve the final months of Russell's term and for six years when the Congress convened its next session. While Carter may not have been pleased that Nunn had challenged his handpicked appointee, in the general election he endorsed Nunn, which likely contributed to the man from Perry's success.[18]

Three weeks after Nunn was formally sworn in as a member of the Ninety-Third Congress on January 3, 1973, Nixon submitted a $267 billion budget for fiscal year 1974. The fight between the president and Congress would not be over the size of the budget, but how those funds would be allocated. Senate majority leader Mike Mansfield, Democrat of Montana, stated that his chamber "should try to work within the ceiling" Nixon had outlined in a budget briefing to congressional leaders of both parties, but emphasized that it would be Congress that had the final say about proposed cuts to social programs, such as health care and education. Mansfield was clear about what he found objectionable in the budget request, remarking that he was "sorry to note" an increase in defense spending, from $75.5 billion in 1973 to $79 billion, a boost for improving salaries and benefits for an all-volunteer army.[19]

As one of the two newest members of the Armed Services Committee, Nunn turned his attention to Mansfield's concerns. Although in his maiden speech in the Senate, on January 26, Nunn called for Congress to adopt new procedures for how the legislative branch decided on funding levels, he was more vocal about the value of an all-volunteer military. In a March interview, Nunn stated he was "dubious about the effectiveness of a volunteer force," adding that the United States must maintain its military strength as a way of preserving peace.[20] Pundits watching the committee under the new leadership of Stennis observed the fifteen members wrestling with how to trim the defense budget but retain US military capability. Most of these outsiders believed that the outcome would be little different than the previous fiscal year's process. There was greater concern, however, among committee members about personnel costs, which were mounting, approaching 60 percent of the defense budget, and squeezing out money for other requirements.[21]

Stennis assumed the chairmanship at a time of deep fissures in American society and in the Senate because of the Vietnam War and the sizable overseas military commitment that the United States maintained. He recognized that even with American troops out of South Vietnam, the committee faced attacks on its jurisdiction in the Senate, a loss of public support for the military, and declining US military power at a time when the Soviet Union had increased its capability. Accordingly, he set about offsetting these trends, especially the inevitable cuts to the defense budget, using every legislative tool at his disposal: subcommittee organizational changes, more professional staff, hearings, review of Defense Department documents, and the requirement for frequent departmental reports on major weapons programs and other high-priced purchases. These actions would demonstrate the committee's increased emphasis on oversight, but equally important, afford defense spending some protection.[22]

The Vietnam War was already less a concern for lawmakers by the spring. On January 27, 1973, the United States, North Vietnam, South Vietnam, and the Provisional Revolutionary Government, which represented the South Vietnamese insurgent groups, had signed the "Agreement on Ending the War and Restoring Peace in Vietnam" in Paris. The accords' provisions called for a cease-fire throughout South Vietnam, and the United States agreed to withdraw its remaining troops and advisors, about 30,000, and dismantle all US bases within sixty days. In return, North Vietnam would release all US prisoners of war.[23]

Eight months later, in mid-September, the nation's attention turned again, this time to the Watergate scandal, a miasma of "bugging, burglary, infiltration, forgeries and lies," as one longtime Democratic maven described it. Nixon stood accused of having a part in the wrongdoings during the 1972 presidential campaign, in which members of his reelection committee and administration officials led a conspiracy that included breaking into the Democratic National Committee headquarters at the Watergate office complex in Washington, DC. The purpose of the break-in was to photograph campaign materials and wiretap telephones. In May 1973, Nixon had appointed a special counsel for the investigation, Archibald Cox, after it was apparent that the administration was attempting to cover up its role. In July, the Senate began investigating the scandal after the media's investigative coverage revealed additional details. The Senate investigation discovered that Nixon had taped discussions in the Oval Office, and the special counsel subpoenaed the tapes. Nixon refused to release them, citing executive privilege, but even after the president asked Cox to drop the subpoena, he refused to do so. The situation only worsened, and in October, Nixon ordered the special counsel fired, which led to another crisis, the "Saturday Night Massacre," wherein Attorney General Elliot Richardson and his deputy resigned rather than carry out the president's order. A new attorney general, Robert Bork, was appointed, and he fired Cox. The public criticism of these actions was enormous. On November 17, at a meeting with more than four hundred Associated Press managing editors in Florida, Nixon claimed the allegations of his being involved in wrongdoing were incorrect. "I am not a crook," he declared. Bork appointed a new special counsel, Leon Jaworski, and the investigation continued.[24]

Meanwhile, the business of government carried on, and Mansfield was serious about cutting defense spending, as he believed that détente between the United States and the Soviet Union signaled an end to the Cold War. He offered an amendment to the Defense Procurement Bill calling for an immediate reduction in the number of US military personnel in Europe. In response, Senator Henry "Scoop" Jackson, a Washington Democrat and a senior member of the Armed Services Committee, and Nunn introduced an alternative. Their amendment, viewed as a compromise, required North Atlantic Treaty Organization (NATO) allies to contribute to the cost of stationing US forces in NATO countries. The president would be obliged to negotiate with the allies direct payments to the United States to offset the annual balance of payments deficit that resulted in part from the cost of stationing those troops overseas. The Defense Department estimated that the annual shortfall was about $1.5 billion for the current fiscal year. Under the amendment's provisions, if the costs for maintaining forces in Europe exceeded 10 percent of the total balance of payments deficits, then the president would have to ask NATO members for contributions equal to the amount of the deficit. Moreover, if NATO allies did not offset the balance of payments deficit to the United States, then its forces would be withdrawn from Western Europe at the equivalent percentage.[25]

At first, the administration opposed the Jackson-Nunn amendment, believing it would damage relations with allies. The State Department considered it an ill-advised precedent, as it would impose a reduction of forces based on balance of payment shortfalls, not a threat assessment. However, the Defense Department under Secretary James Schlesinger later came to view the proposal as providing it leverage with its allies for them to assume a larger share of the cost of maintaining US forces in Europe. Schlesinger used the threat of the amendment at a meeting of NATO defense ministers with some success. The administration's change of view fit with the emerging attitudes on Capitol Hill, as both the House and Senate Armed Services Committees were determined to find a way to solve the balance of payments problem. The amendment passed in the Senate by a resounding majority, 84 to 5 on September 25, and remained essentially intact as reported out by the Senate-House conference on the Defense Procurement Bill. While the amendment addressed an arcane and little noticed topic for anyone not involved in defense and economic issues, it met the needs not only of the defense committees, but the increasing number of members concerned about growing defense budgets and inflation. More importantly, it was Nunn's first major political victory in Congress. Nixon signed the bill into law on November 16.[26] The amendment irritated NATO allies, but by the end of the year, the United States received pledges from them that they would reduce the US balance of payments burden through either purchasing more US arms or assuming the costs themselves.[27]

The success of the "burden-sharing" measure was also indicative of Nunn's relationship with the senior members on the Armed Services Committee, wherein he earned their admiration and support, which Jackson made clear by making Nunn a cosponsor on the amendment. Like Stennis, Jackson treated junior members with respect, and in Nunn he saw someone worth his investment of time and knowledge.[28] Yet, it would be the seventy-one-year-old Stennis that would be Nunn's most valuable benefactor. The elderly legislator, who had been seriously injured by two gunshots wounds during a robbery in front of his District of Columbia residence earlier in the year, realized his travels abroad were at an end. Stennis also wanted to provide Nunn with more opportunities after the chairman returned to the Senate in August after hospitalization. He considered Nunn "very bright" and a "fast learner" who would "make a highly significant contribution" to the committee's work. He appointed Nunn chairman of the newly established Subcommittee on Manpower and Personnel in February 1973. Manpower issues had become increasingly important with the end of the military draft and the establishment of the all-volunteer force.[29]

In February 1974, Stennis directed Nunn to evaluate the impact that the Mansfield Amendment would have on NATO, an opportunity Nunn had reportedly been seeking. Stennis recognized that the majority leader would attempt to raise the issue again during the year. While the war in Vietnam still claimed some congressional attention, Stennis did not want to neglect Europe, where the United States had substantial security and economic interests, and cultural ties.[30] Nunn would be Stennis's "legs and eyes, in effect, in Europe."[31]

Nunn left for Europe with one hundred hours of preparation. He and a committee staff member, Francis Sullivan, spent two weeks on the ground discussing and assessing the state of NATO's military capabilities with US and allied officials, diplomats, and senior military officers, paying particular attention to the status of US and allied forces. In his report to the committee, Nunn underscored that 1974 was the year in which the Nixon administration planned to concentrate on European security matters, dubbing it the "Year of Europe," since it was the twenty-fifth anniversary of the alliance. Nunn suggested that instead, it would be a "Year of Allied and American Acrimony." The change in tone, Nunn offered, resulted from questions about the "continued viability of the alliance and the U.S. commitment to Europe's defense." He believed his report would help inform debate on the alliance and US policy, not only within Congress but among the American public as well.[32]

There were, he noted, a number of critical issues requiring attention that could jeopardize long-term US interests because the Soviet Union and its allies had strengthened their nuclear and conventional capability in Europe and globally. He underscored the deep feelings in NATO countries that the alliance was still crucial to providing the military and political power needed for "offsetting the Soviet challenge" on the continent. Yet, there was also friction that demanded consideration, especially the need for European allies to assume greater responsibility for improving their military capabilities "and to bring about equity in contributions" to the alliance's defense activities. Such a step was necessary to lessen the US share of the conventional burden and provide a long-term footing for an effective European conventional deterrent. This final point was particularly important. Nunn argued the threshold at which the United States would use tactical, and ultimately, strategic nuclear weapons to prevent a Soviet takeover of Western Europe was "quite low" and dangerous. Resorting to nuclear weapons resulted from the alliance's inability to mount an effective conventional defense before being overwhelmed by the Soviets and their Warsaw Pact allies' conventional forces. He also believed that US front line commanders were planning on asking for presidential authority to use nuclear weapons to counter a Warsaw Pact invasion far earlier than US political leaders, including the president, recognized.[33]

Nunn devoted several pages to the alliance's non-nuclear planning and strategy, and offered a critique of the conventional forces balance, stating that in the end, "Achievement of conventional parity [between the two sides] requires a well-thought-out, comprehensive re-ordering of the way in which U.S. and NATO forces are supported and deployed." He then turned his attention to the issues that greatly troubled him and Stennis: the restructuring of US forces in Western Europe and the effect of US troop reductions. Nunn contended that NATO, and especially US forces, needed to be restructured within available financial resources to increase combat power and decrease reliance on early nuclear use, while reducing the number of support troops. He believed US reliance on host nation support could upgrade US combat capability. Such a change, however, would be a major policy decision because US forces would "sacrifice some autonomy." Nonetheless, substantial savings in troops and costs would accrue. The savings could then be used to generate additional combat units, thereby improving conventional capability and elevating the nuclear threshold.[34]

With respect to troop reductions, allied positions varied, but there was a consensus that cuts of 20,000 to 30,000 troops could be managed. However, once the cuts reached 75,000 personnel or more, the US commitment would appear to be declining, and a reduction of 100,000 would "destabilize the overall military posture," undermine the political and psychological value of the alliance, and "could lead to the 'Finlandization' of Europe, and Soviet political dominance" on the continent. Therefore, Nunn observed, the congressional debate on troop levels in Europe needed a different perspective. Mansfield's amendment and likeminded efforts did not tackle the essential issues: the possibility of nuclear war in Europe and how a unilateral withdrawal of US troops affected the nuclear threshold; the long-range US commitment to NATO countries and the level of that commitment as shown by the capability of forces stationed there; the willingness of West Germany to backfill US forces if US troops were withdrawn; and the effect of a unilateral withdrawal of US troops on US-Soviet negotiations regarding mutual and balanced force reductions and strategic arms control. Discussion of these issues was essential not only because of their larger impact on American foreign policy, but because the entire value of the alliance as a longstanding US commitment hung in the balance.[35]

Only weeks before Nunn's report became public, the influence of the Jackson-Nunn amendment became apparent. The Nixon administration became increasingly convinced that its European allies intended to share the costs of maintaining the 315,000 US military personnel in Western Europe, based on a preliminary agreement with West Germany. Bonn had agreed to provide $2.24 billion in payments to offset the deficits caused by stationing troops in that country, taking effect retroactively to mid-1973 and covering those costs through mid-1975. However, unease remained. If the other allies did not cover the remaining deficit, then the administration would be compelled to obey the Jackson-Nunn amendment, and withdraw troops in proportion to the size of the deficit.[36]

After the Armed Services Committee released Nunn's report, the administration became more distressed. Nunn held a press conference on April 8 to present his findings. His comments were viewed as a challenge to the Defense Department's long-standing planning assumption that the United States had adequate combat capability in NATO, giving it sufficient time (ten to twenty days) to deploy by ship forces from the United States. Nunn remarked that this assumption was flawed and the US Army in Europe was "structured on World War II concepts," especially the number of support troops. He complained that the United States had "too much of a long war posture," and agreed generally with the allies' view that NATO should prepare for a short war, calculated in weeks, with the main Warsaw Pact conventional attack toward the Rhine River, designed to sweep across West Germany's northern plains. Reporters were impressed with Nunn's performance. With the report and a single year in office, he was viewed as already "emerging as the military expert among the new generation entering the Senate." While the older members of the committee accepted the Pentagon version perhaps because their perspective had been shaped by World War II experience, Nunn appeared ready to dispute conventional thinking.[37]

A few weeks later, Schlesinger indicated that he was considering a small reduction of about 20,000 army and air force support personnel in Europe. It would be a matter of "streamlining" US forces to achieve "efficiencies," he said when he met with the West German defense minister. He also planned to convert some of these forces into combat units, "beating of fat into swords," as he termed it, hoping to reassure NATO allies. Schlesinger knew, however, that he was in a bind: The armed services feared overall reductions in force numbers now that US involvement in Vietnam had ended and an all-volunteer force was in the making. The European allies' nervousness about a reduced NATO commitment intensified, and US diplomats worried about losing bargaining chips in negotiations with the Soviets. Most importantly, he was under pressure, from both parties and both chambers, to reduce military end strength since the associated costs were considered either unaffordable or the funds could be used for domestic needs.[38]

Schlesinger's concerns were justified, and Stennis proved prescient. On June 9, Mansfield offered an amendment to limit the total number of US troops overseas to 312,000, requiring a reduction of 125,000. Mansfield argued that since the Armed Services Committee recommended an overall reduction in active duty military strength of 49,000, then his proposal required only a further reduction of 76,000.[39]

This time, Nunn led the opposition. He had help from the Nixon administration despite a president with diminishing power because of the Watergate scandal. Schlesinger contacted senators to vote against Mansfield's proposal, and Secretary of State Henry Kissinger wrote to Stennis. In his letter, Kissinger contended that "it is America's strength, both economic and military, that gives weight to our words in the councils of the world." Nunn agreed, stating that a unilateral reduction "would be useful to no one but the Soviets.[40]

That Nunn, a junior senator who had only been in the chamber for twenty months, would take on the majority leader was a bold maneuver. Yet, maneuver he did, using his report as the foundation for his arguments against the Mansfield Amendment during Senate debate. Nunn prudently recognized that Mansfield and his supporters had well-founded arguments about the size and structure of US forces in NATO. In response, Nunn sponsored an Armed Services Committee amendment that required a reduction of 23,000 support troops in Europe, replacing them with combat units, later known as "Nunn Brigades," a move the Ford administration supported and carried out. The House-Senate Conference Committee would ultimately accept his amendment, but reduced the cut to 18,000 support personnel.[41] Nunn had learned this legislative gambit from Jackson, "an acknowledged expert at legislating policy by amendments." Nunn, however, did not stop with this maneuver. He offered another amendment based on his trip findings that required the Pentagon to justify the number, purpose, and security of the 7,000 tactical nuclear weapons it had in Europe, which Democratic senator Stuart Symington of Missouri had investigated during the year, but Nunn successfully moved the issue legislatively.[42]

In the debate over Mansfield's proposal, Nunn vocalized his worries about the nuclear threshold. He was decidedly against Mansfield's position that early reliance on nuclear weapons was acceptable. Mansfield's determination to cut the US force numbers in NATO made early nuclear use inevitable, Nunn asserted. Additionally, the amendment would weaken NATO's conventional defense capability, making US military forces a mere tripwire and lowering the nuclear threshold even further. Nunn insisted that conventional capability should not be diluted and could actually be improved. "With better organization, greater coordination, streamlining, and some change in doctrine, NATO can establish a solid defense and deterrent essentially with present resource levels."[43]

Nunn and his colleagues on the Armed Services Committee were willing to reduce the total end strength of US military forces by 49,000 to show they were not inflexible regarding their opponents' claims. In the view of one analyst, this tactic "reflected a genuine desire for a smaller military establishment, but it "was also a useful political weapon, since it enabled the Committee members to present themselves as moderate reformers and to contrast their carefully considered proposals with the 'meat-axe cuts' desired by Mansfield."[44]

The Mansfield Amendment was ultimately defeated resoundingly, by a vote of 35–54, more than double the 1973 vote.[45] One columnist commented that Nunn had executed "as solid and deft a parliamentary performance in the national security area as the Congress has seen in years, belying the common notion that a legislator must have seniority or 'power' to get something important done." By countering and reframing Mansfield's arguments, Nunn "saved NATO." In victory, Nunn remained modest so as not to offend his more senior colleagues, describing a debate on national security as a matter of determining what is "effective and sensible," and requiring in-depth preparation so one can "get down to the quick."[46] Legislative success in the Senate, he mused years later, was similar to building a legal case. It was a methodical process, a matter of knowing the substance, judging the timing, understanding other members' beliefs and thoughts, and identifying who to consult with before expressing your position publicly and with overwhelming evidence.[47] Additionally, Mansfield made a deep and lasting impression on Nunn regarding leadership and civility by congratulating Nunn on his handling of the opposition. Even with the power he had as majority leader, Nunn remarked, he never retaliated. This was a lesson Nunn never forgot.[48]

For the man at 1600 Pennsylvania Avenue, Richard Nixon, the evidence was piling up against him in the Watergate scandal. By July 1974, the Judiciary Committee of the House of Representatives, which had been investigating the chief executive, recommended three articles of impeachment. On August 5, as required by a Supreme Court ruling, the White House released the transcripts of audiotape that provided concrete evidence that the president was personally involved in the cover-up of the Watergate break-in. With the certainty of impeachment by the House and conviction by the Senate looming, Nixon resigned the presidency effective August 9 with Vice President Gerald Ford assuming the office. The impeachment proceedings ended.[49]

Nunn had not been involved in the Senate Select Committee's Watergate investigation, but like other members he followed the investigation closely. His Armed Services Committee duties demanded considerable time and attention. Stennis remained impressed with Nunn's rapid command of the committee's work and fresh perspective. Although Nunn was the committee's most junior member, Stennis called him "the last but not least" member.[50] Nunn's cadetship was over, but he continued to work diligently and educated himself to become the Senate's foremost expert on defense policy and strategy.

CHAPTER 2

THE EMERGING EXPERT

Ford inherited a disaster. The foreign policy of détente the Nixon administration had painstakingly fashioned had begun to fall apart. In the words of one diplomat, Ford had to put "his own stamp on foreign policy. He was already carrying the political liability of the previous Nixon administration from which he couldn't be totally divorced."[1] The US commitment to South Vietnam was the most immediate and critical issue the new president had to contend with because of his predecessor's secret assurances.

Nixon had made promises to South Vietnamese president Nguyen Van Thieu to overcome his opposition to the Paris Peace Accords, that the United States would help defend his country if the North Vietnamese violated the agreement. In December 1974, the most blatant violation occurred. North Vietnamese forces attacked the South Vietnamese province of Phuoc Long and gained control of the territory. Ford was determined to meet the pledge of his predecessor; however, he had to reckon with a restive Democratic Congress, which had only become less supportive of any assistance to the Thieu regime. The Democratic Party's substantial gain of seats in the House and Senate during the 1974 midterm elections in November signaled the American public's disgust with the Watergate scandal. In addition, Ford's September executive proclamation granting a "full, free, and absolute pardon" to Nixon for any crimes he committed or may have committed during his tenure as president did not help.[2] The Vietnam War remained vastly unpopular among the American public, and congressional opposition to military aid for South Vietnam was intensifying. Nonetheless, sufficient congressional support remained in 1974.[3] The House and Senate Armed Services Committees authorized a fiscal year 1975 amount of $1 billion in military aid for South Vietnam, but in August, Congress appropriated only $700 million. When Ford signed the appropriations bill in October, he complained that the reduced amount did not meet South Vietnam's vital military requirements. It would also embolden its adversaries to conduct further attacks; therefore, it would be essential, the president warned, to reengage with Congress early in 1975 to work out a solution that would meet South Vietnam's needs for the remaining funds.[4]

Ford gave official notice of his intent to secure the additional funding at the end of January when he sent a special message to Congress requesting supplemental assistance of $300 million for Vietnam and $222 million for Cambodia, which was also suffering from a communist onslaught with its survival in question. He justified the request because of North Vietnam's refusal to abide by the Paris Accords and its buildup of forces in the South. US intelligence analysis, the president stated, indicated that the North Vietnamese campaign to impose its will on the South Vietnamese people would be unleashed in the next few months. He reiterated that US military aid was no longer adequate to replace the equipment lost in combat or South Vietnam's depleted ammunition stocks and other supplies. While some members of Congress believed that reducing the US financial commitment would prompt negotiations for a political settlement, the opposite had occurred. A grave situation now existed. Since the United States could not defend South Vietnam, US leaders had pledged to furnish the resources South Vietnam needed to defend itself, as allowed by the agreement. The United States would be judged harshly by allies around the globe if they could not rely on its commitment.[5] Stennis decided to send Nunn to South Vietnam for a firsthand appraisal.

Nunn began the trip as a skeptic of American aid and involvement in South Vietnam and conceded he remained one upon completing his analysis. Like many members, he questioned the value of pouring more money into a government and military that seemed to be on the verge of collapse.[6] In addition to this concern, there were other critical domestic issues that needed attention: a distressed US economy beset by recession and buffeted by inflation, an "energy crisis," and concerns about financial stability.[7]

Over the course of his visit, Nunn held discussions with President Thieu; General Cao Van Vien, chairman of the South Vietnamese Joint General Staff; the US ambassador, Graham Martin; members of his staff; and the Central Intelligence Agency station chief so that he could attain a clear understanding of the political, military, and economic outlook. He concluded that additional US funding alone was not the solution. The Paris Accords had become "merely a piece of paper" and demanded new diplomatic initiatives to overcome the violations. Worse, he found "no one—either for or against American involvement in Vietnam—who [could] advocate a definite action by the United States, and who [could], at the same time, make any convincing projections of the probable outcome resulting from the action." Thus, it became incumbent on him to offer sensible options, recognizing they offered "no guarantee of complete success." He would "formulate a definitive program" for the Armed Services Committee, members of Congress, and ultimately, the American people. "After 13 years of involvement in Vietnam, we owe this to ourselves."[8]

The current military situation was bleak and the prognosis not encouraging. Fighting between North and South Vietnam remained intense. North Vietnamese combat capability had soared, not only because of reduced US aid, but also because there had been a generous growth in Soviet and Chinese support. Consequently, North Vietnamese units were capable of massing against a single objective, while the South Vietnamese had to assume a defensive posture over the entire country.[9]

On the other hand, the US initiative to prepare the regime to fight on its own, "Vietnamization," was a fiasco—the US military had failed to help the South Vietnamese develop the logistics and maintenance processes needed to be self-sufficient. The North had sufficient supplies and equipment in the South to conduct operations for nearly two years. The South, however, was running out of ammunition, spare parts, and gasoline and could not maintain the equipment the United States had provided. In short, South Vietnamese forces did not pose an offensive threat. Instead, the country was fighting for survival, and North Vietnam was on the verge of dealing a death blow. Nunn cautioned that failure was likely if the South Vietnamese government and military lacked "motivation and dedication."[10]

Even with this gloomy appraisal, Nunn believed cutting off aid was not the answer either as it could affect détente with the Soviet Union and China, and the US posture in Asia and globally. Granted, there were few members enthusiastic about providing aid, but the Vietnam problem could not be wished away. Those in Congress who favored a cutoff of aid would have to justify their decision if South Vietnam collapsed and a bloodbath ensued.[11]

Nunn's foremost point was the recognition that military and economic assistance were inseparable, because the economic means underpinned the military resources available to fight. The administration needed to move beyond annual, piecemeal requests, and Congress should take a more comprehensive approach, one that called for coordination among the three Senate committees with jurisdiction: Armed Services, Foreign Relations, and Appropriations. Only one option remained practical: allow for a two-year transition period with the level of US aid based on the estimated amount that China and the Soviet Union were providing North Vietnam. Simultaneously, the United States should negotiate with China and the USSR to reduce their level of assistance to the North. The transition period would provide South Vietnam time to modify its strategy, rebuild its forces, and develop a more appropriate logistics system while also furnishing it sufficient supplies to cope with North Vietnamese aggression. As the South Vietnamese capability strengthened, the US aid package would transition from military purposes to economic and social assistance in the form of humanitarian aid. Yet, Nunn remained down-to-earth. The option would not guarantee a South Vietnamese victory. Money could not substitute for "motivation, effort," and "sacrifice." The United States, he concluded, had to "be willing to accept the possible fall of South Vietnam without reentering the war."[12]

Nunn recognized the acrimonious debate already occurring in Congress and unfavorable public opinion, especially the feelings of "anger" and "frustration" among his constituents; time was running out for South Vietnam. He had become skeptical of the "rosy scenarios" that US and South Vietnamese officials had been offering for a decade since President Lyndon Johnson had "Americanized" the conflict. "This skepticism would stay with him throughout his career whenever military and civilian leaders would suggest an easy fight."[13]

While Nunn's report did not have a direct impact in the Senate, it had the Ford administration's attention. Three days after the Senate released the report, Ford met with Ambassador Martin, who was in Washington for consultations. Ford had not read Nunn's report, so Martin told him that Nunn's findings were consistent with Ford's position that a multiyear appropriation was the best way to support Thieu's government. Martin believed that Congress's decision to reduce the funding request months earlier had shifted the military initiative to the North Vietnamese. Nonetheless, the ambassador remained upbeat. The future depended on US assurance of resupply, which Nunn had noted as the decisive factor.[14]

Martin's optimism was suspect, and Ford knew it. In fact, Nunn had recommended that the president replace Martin as the senator thought he had lost perspective. Ford, however, had other priorities. He had already deflected questions about potential consequences if Congress did not pass the supplemental appropriation he had requested. There was no need, he told reporters, to consider any other options because he trusted in the "good judgment" of Congress. On March 6, 1975, Ford held a nationally televised news conference. The major focus was on Cambodia, where communist forces were close to victory. The president beseeched Congress for an emergency military aid package to prop up the sagging regime. When asked about Ford's speech, Nunn replied that if Congress denied the funds, then the United States was deviating from the stance it had taken since World War II to support pro-US governments from communist takeovers.[15] Within two weeks of the president's speech, North Vietnamese forces launched a major offensive, toppling South Vietnam and achieving their ultimate objective, reunification.

No degree of presidential cajoling could save South Vietnam. On April 30, North Vietnamese tanks smashed through the gates and entered the grounds of the Presidential Palace in Saigon. American involvement in Vietnam was over. The war's end was the beginning of a reappraisal of American military requirements worldwide. Liberals and moderates in the Democratic Party initially believed that a reckoning on defense spending and troop reductions was the next order of business. Yet that did not occur immediately. Those in the center of the Democratic Party worried that such steps would imply that the United States was pulling back, returning to an isolationist past. They also feared the Ford administration would label them weak on defense while the Soviet threat still loomed.

As indications that Democrats were trying to gauge the political winds, Mansfield appeared unlikely to offer a troop reduction amendment this session, and a more modest reduction in the Pentagon budget was forthcoming after liberal Senate Democrats, including new members of the Armed Services Committee who were critics bent on reforming the Defense Department, failed in their attempt to cut defense spending. Senator Walter Mondale, Minnesota Democrat, summed up the centrist position: "It's very important not to signal the Russians and others that we're giving up. The Congress decided against the war in Vietnam. We did not vote to become an isolationist country."[16]

By mid-May, Nunn was leading the Senate debate on the federal government's fiscal year 1976 spending and, in particular, defense. He maintained that the proposed congressional budget resolution's cuts in defense were too deep. The result would be massive layoffs of civilian employees, base closings, and a reduction in military personnel. All of these outcomes would further damage a weak economy.[17] His position was the opening round in a fight over the future of US security policy between liberals and the more conservative members of the Armed Services Committee.

In early June, the Senate began a two-day debate regarding US security in a post–Vietnam War era as it considered the defense authorization bill. It was a broad and far-reaching argument over the basic assumptions that had guided US policy for nearly the past decade. The seriousness of the matter was apparent; dozens of senators from both parties sat at their desks and listened to the case made by liberals, led by Edward "Ted" Kennedy of Massachusetts, and their principal adversaries, Stennis and his Republican ally, Strom Thurmond of South Carolina. Nunn entered the debate by going toe-to-toe with Senator George McGovern over the appropriate balance between nuclear and conventional forces, one of the critical issues. Nunn smoothly outmaneuvered McGovern by defining what the new US overall military strategy should be. He suggested the probability that the United States would fight the Soviets and Chinese simultaneously was no longer valid. The more likely scenario would be a large-scale conventional war in Europe and a smaller conflict elsewhere on the globe. McGovern questioned the requirement for upgraded conventional capability. What difference would it make when the United States and the Soviet Union had such powerful nuclear arsenals, which unleashed would "destroy each other several times over"? Nunn got the better of the argument. "Sane people" Nunn retorted, "would be reluctant to use nuclear weapons in such circumstances." Therefore, the United States needed "conventional parity [with the Soviet Union] as well as nuclear parity." As for détente, Nunn remained skeptical. "The friendly smiles and gestures can disappear in about eight hours." Reporters again marveled at the reputation he was attaining in his third year in the Senate; he was "extremely well informed on military matters."[18]

Nunn continued to press for enhancements in NATO capability, a deficiency that the administration and defense experts in Congress recognized, with the defense of Western Europe once again the primary objective in American military strategy. However, election year politics tended to drown out that concern as former California governor Ronald Reagan, who was challenging Ford for the Republican nomination, claimed that the United States was no longer the number one military power in the world. In fact, during the primary race between Reagan and Ford, Reagan called Nunn and they had a thirty-minute conversation on NATO and its weaknesses. Overall, Nunn expressed disquiet that the complex issues regarding US national security were being oversimplified. Because presidential politics had cheapened a serious debate, Nunn asserted Congress had to push for a larger role in foreign policymaking. He believed the executive branch had forfeited the respect of Congress and the public because of the Vietnam fiasco. Nunn's intellect and his understanding of national security issues drew attention from the press, and he was mentioned as a possible contender, albeit a long shot, in the "secretary of state sweepstakes" should a Democrat win election as president in November.[19] Nunn was advising his fellow Georgian, Jimmy Carter, in his run for the Democratic nomination, though he had waited until Carter won the nomination because Scoop Jackson, Nunn's friend, was also a candidate. His colleagues' opinion of him was changing too. At first, they found him "too stiff, predictably pro-Pentagon in his views, and trying too hard to follow in the path of Senator Russell." In the last year he was seen as an "inquisitive, sometimes critical thinker on military affairs."[20]

While Nunn paid no attention to the media's prognostications, he was sensitive to election year concerns. Nunn and his colleagues on the Armed Services Committee convinced liberal and moderate Democrats to prevent the Republicans from making defense spending a major issue in November by not reducing the defense budget. The House of Representatives followed a similar path. It added $2 billion beyond the requested amount. Even one of the Pentagon's major critics, Democratic representative Patricia Schroeder of Colorado, voted for it. She summed up the outlook on Capitol Hill clearly: "There aren't a great number of profiles in courage up here. The members wanted to get reelected, and they got scared."[21]

With the size of defense budget settled, Nunn turned his attention in the fall to NATO. Behind the scenes, he prodded the army to reassess its strategic assumptions and contingency plans for a war in central Europe. He wanted a comprehensive analysis of whether NATO should prepare itself for a lengthy war lasting months or a short, intense conflict. The US Army chief of staff, General Frederick Weyand, based on Nunn's explicit request, commissioned a classified study of the topic and assigned Lieutenant General James Hollingsworth, a respected and highly decorated combat veteran, to carry it out. Nunn had met Hollingsworth when the general headed US forces in South Korea and was impressed with his leadership. In Nunn's view, the seriousness of the threat to Western Europe meant that a "dose of

Hollingsworth in the NATO bureaucracy" might make a difference in decid-ing the alliance's military preparedness.[22]

Hollingsworth conducted the study and concluded that rather than pre-pare for a protracted war in which NATO traded time for territory, it should concentrate its forces forward, along the West German border, to meet the Warsaw Pact assault. The report substantiated Nunn's position. While the report results and recommendations remained secret, Nunn had access to them because Hollingsworth briefed Nunn and Weyand together. Afterward, Nunn publicly called for a "major revision of NATO strategy and force struc-ture." The Soviet threat and the type of war to be fought had changed be-cause of the overwhelming advantage the Warsaw Pact had in numbers of troops and its achievement of "technological parity" in conventional capabil-ity with the United States. The Warsaw Pact was ready to fight a short war, with little warning, initiated by a massive lightning attack that would crush NATO forces deployed in the center of West Germany, and conclude the con-flict before Western European forces could be reinforced from outside the European theater. NATO needed to be prepared for an intense war only two or three weeks in duration, with a few days' warning, while also "retaining sufficient hedges to deal with a war of extended duration."[23]

As if on cue, US Army general Alexander Haig, commander of NATO forces, announced that the alliance was taking steps to overcome serious readiness problems, including a complacent attitude among troops, which he described as a "garrison mentality." The acknowledgment of deficien-cies stemmed in part, he said, from recognition of "a diminished cushion of warning time" for an imminent Warsaw Pact attack. He did not believe the planning assumptions were flawed and warned against abrupt, prescriptive changes in doctrine from the tactical to the strategic level without careful study. He allowed that NATO was "at something of a watershed." The "utter necessity" was for the Allies to act in concert, which was being "reinforced by a growing awareness of the relentless growth in sheer Soviet military power."[24]

Nunn remained determined to induce a change in NATO strategy. On October 31, 1976, Nunn and a Republican colleague from the Armed Services Committee, Dewey Bartlett of Oklahoma, at Stennis's request, left Washing-ton for Europe to learn firsthand about NATO's ability to fight a conventional war with the Soviet Union. Their chief interests were twofold: US and allied views of the Warsaw Pact threat and NATO readiness to defeat a conven-tional attack with little or no warning. They were accompanied by the Armed

Services Committee staff director, Francis Sullivan; Hollingsworth, retired and now a consultant to the committee; and two personal staff. During their visit, the congressional delegation met with Haig; senior US, British, and West German military officers; West German political leaders; the NATO secretary-general and other alliance officials; as well as the US ambassador to NATO and his staff; and the permanent representatives from the United Kingdom, Belgium, West Germany, and France.[25]

The senators returned on November 14 and issued a preliminary statement, one that they believed would influence the president-elect, Jimmy Carter, who won the election in a close race on November 2. They began by announcing that a revision to NATO's strategy of flexible response "was now open to serious question." They believed "eastward repositioning" of forces and ammunition stocks was crucial to improve readiness and counter an attack by Warsaw Pact forces that might occur with little warning. The applicability of current planning assumptions needed reexamination: it appeared that Soviet forces might be able to initiate an attack from a "standing start," while NATO relied on lengthy warning times to prepare and mobilize. More importantly, NATO forces needed more technologically advanced weaponry to increase their firepower and thereby offset the numerical superiority of the Warsaw Pact. "Should there be another conflict in Europe," they predicted, "militarily it will probably be a 'come-as-you-are' party and the side which arrives 'last with the least' will be condemned to first use of nuclear weapons or conventional defeat."[26]

The senators made their full report to the Armed Services Committee public on January 24, 1977, four days after Carter's inauguration. The timing could not go unnoticed even by those with minimal understanding of the US political climate. The press pounced on the findings. Unnamed sources in the US military, American defense attachés to NATO countries, and general officers in the alliance confided that the Nunn-Bartlett findings were true. The Soviets had increased the number of troops in their satellite counties, improved the destructive capacity and accuracy of their tactical nuclear weapons and delivery systems, and modified their doctrine by emphasizing surprise and escalation to nuclear war if their offensive was stymied. Some NATO leaders worried that the upsurge in Soviet power would result in political pressure on individual allies and, ultimately, intimidate them into neutrality. Others recognized that the military readiness of some allies, especially Great Britain, was suspect. A byzantine argument broke out among experts regarding the methods used to measure NATO's "qualitative advantage" in weaponry. However, this argument was largely stillborn. The Congressional Research Service gave independent confirmation of the report's conclusions: "As it stands, the quantitative balance continues to shift toward the Soviet Union. U.S. qualitative superiority never compensated completely and, in certain respects, is slowly slipping away."[27]

The Nunn-Bartlett report ignited a debate in Congress over military strategy, particularly after the Congressional Budget Office issued a report questioning the army's decision to acquire costly weapon systems. The issue paper noted that the army's conversion of light infantry divisions to mechanized divisions deployed in the United States would be of little value if a short, intense conflict occurred in Europe. It offered some alternatives if the planning assumptions changed.[28] In an interview regarding the claim that NATO was preparing for the "wrong war," Haig contended that it was important "not to become the prisoners of a scenario so extreme that it risks unbalancing our [NATO] force improvement priorities." He continued, "I am not aware that Senators Nunn and Bartlett have postulated such an extreme scenario." He offered that their conclusions were consistent with his own and if their evaluation of deficiencies generated congressional support for improvements, "I warmly welcome that attention."[29]

Whether Carter appreciated such attention was questionable. The Nunn-Bartlett report created a potential problem for Carter, who had campaigned on a pledge to reduce the Pentagon budget by $5–7 billion. The question was, how much would the new president rely on his fellow Georgian's advice concerning defense issues and, in particular, the recommendation that the United States invest in conventional forces to correct apparent weaknesses? The view among the purportedly well-informed was that the relationship between the two was cordial.[30]

Carter believed his relationship with the entire Georgia congressional delegation was based on a "tacit understanding that if I needed them on an issue of importance that I would let them know directly and they would make every effort to support me even though it was damaging for them at home." If he did not need their support, then they were free to vote as they saw fit. He considered Nunn "pre-eminent" on defense issues, and Carter knew Stennis trusted the junior senator's judgment.[31] Others who had worked closely with Nunn had their doubts about the relationship, especially whether the two would agree on defense requirements. James Schlesinger, now Carter's secretary of energy, believed Nunn to be "ambivalent" about Carter and relations between Nunn and his chief advisors "somewhat distant."[32] Nunn's own staff believed that the two were not "on the friendliest terms," a residue of the 1972 primary. There was no question Carter's campaign pledge to cut defense made Nunn uneasy.[33]

Nevertheless, the White House response to the Nunn-Bartlett report was an almost immediate pledge from Vice President Walter Mondale during a trip to Europe that the United States was prepared to augment its commitment to the defense of Western Europe, if the allies did likewise.[34] Less than a month later, Carter directed an assessment of US national security in two parts. The first part would appraise US military force posture and potential military strategies given the current security environment, with reduced emphasis on nuclear weapons. The other was to take a broader review and analyze US capabilities and those of its allies and potential adversaries by examining political, military, economic, and technological developments and capabilities. From this latter assessment, the United States would gain a better grasp of its potential adversaries' policy objectives and strategies and could determine its best options in responding.[35] The Nunn-Bartlett findings figured heavily into this evaluation and in particular, the administration's plans for overhauling NATO's conventional forces and the necessary reallocation of the defense budget to achieve a few instant improvements in conventional capability. It also encouraged two additional assessments dealing with the balance of US-Soviet forces in Europe and an across-the-board examination of US-European relations.[36]

The official reaction from NATO authorities was polite. They did not necessarily share Nunn's views on the defense of NATO's Central Region, but he had made "a valuable contribution to a constructive debate on this aspect of Allied policy."[37] Off the record, some of these leaders admitted that recent NATO war games demonstrated that alliance forces were weak, disorganized, and poorly equipped. Its conventional forces would crumble before a Soviet blitz, possibly before tactical nuclear weapons could be used to halt the advance. Others, such as the chairman of NATO's military committee, declared their views were based on erroneous assumptions, faulty judgment, and a decidedly worst-case scenario and were more counterproductive than helpful by frightening "the hell out of everybody." Yet a month later, he conceded NATO members needed to spend 2–3 percent more as an "insurance premium" to protect Western Europe. In this fractious atmosphere, Harold Brown, the new secretary of defense, offered a tepid response: there was "rough nuclear parity" between the United States and the Soviet Union. A few defense specialists answered that megatonnage was not the issue; the essential element in the balance of power between the two superpowers was their perception of vital interests. In that regard, one analyst noted, NATO had "never been more vulnerable."[38]

Nunn understood Brown's argument, but it was beside the point, especially after General David Jones, the air force chief of staff, and Vice Admiral Robert Long, the navy's deputy chief of naval operations for submarine warfare, testified before the Armed Services Committee that billions of dollars were needed for new strategic weapons if the US forces were to fulfill their assigned deterrent task. Jones indicated that he and the other service chiefs agreed that there was still "rough equivalence" in strategic capabilities between the two superpowers, but that if the Soviet military buildup, both in strategic and conventional forces, was not met with a comparable US effort, then "a significant altered balance" could occur. Nunn spoke for the committee, promising that the hearing was only the beginning of an examination of US strategic capabilities.[39]

By May, Carter had no alternative but to address NATO's perceived military problems directly when he traveled to London to attend the alliance's annual summit. Brown, who accompanied him, knew the political stakes had changed and technical utterances about nuclear parity were not useful. Those who believed NATO incapable of executing its strategy of flexible response were growing in number, and they were prominent, such as retired German general Johannes Steinhoff, the former NATO Military Committee chair, and Philip Goodhart, a leading member of the British House of Commons's military committee.[40]

The day before the summit, Nunn addressed a seminar in Washington emphasizing that the issue was not the concepts underlying the strategy, but the "ability of the alliance to implement" the strategy. NATO leaders must figure out how to streamline the alliance's political decision-making process if a Warsaw Pact attack or unanticipated mobilization took place. He added that war reserve stocks and prepositioned equipment would be paramount in that situation, and described supply conditions of one US corps as "appalling."[41]

The Nunn-Bartlett report was the subject of significant discussion at the summit, and the alliance leaders agreed to take the first step by committing themselves to annual increases in national defense budgets of 3 percent in real terms. However, it would not be until May 1978, after a year of US-led planning, when NATO leaders adopted a more formal approach, the Long-Term Defense Program (LTDP), that Carter had proposed at the summit. The

LTDP formally acknowledged that the alliance needed to resolve its now well-known deficiencies in several key areas of concern, ranging from command and control to readiness and reinforcement capabilities, given the buildup of Warsaw Pact forces.[42]

In August 1977, Carter had signed Presidential Directive 18 (PD/NSC-18), in which he laid out the administration's position on US-Soviet relations and a national strategy based on competition and cooperation. The strategy specified that the United States would seek opportunities to cooperate in areas of mutual concern, such as regional conflicts and arms control. However, the United States would "counterbalance" Soviet military capability, especially in Europe. The principal means of doing so would be to fulfill its commitment to NATO with respect to increasing the level of US defense spending, as Brown testified to at a hearing before the Subcommittee on Manpower and Personnel that Nunn chaired.[43]

Carter soon needed Nunn's help on another, more critical matter—an agreement to relinquish US control of the Panama Canal. Negotiations for a US-Panama treaty began in the Ford administration, but Carter embraced the issue as a top foreign policy goal of his administration. By mid-August 1977, the US negotiators had fashioned a draft pact that would retain the canal's neutrality and another that would turn over the canal and its zone to Panama on December 31, 1999. Two weeks later, on September 7, Carter and Panamanian dictator General Omar Torrijos signed the treaties. There was considerable (mostly Republican) opposition in the Senate, which had to approve the treaties by a two-thirds majority vote before they could take effect. With 1978 a congressional election year, Carter and his advisors recognized that they needed to formulate a strategy to attain the required votes.[44]

Carter invited Nunn, along with several others from both parties, for an initial consultation before the Senate Foreign Relations Committee would begin hearings on the treaties in October. Carter confronted resistance among Democrats. Nunn and the senior senator from Georgia, Herman Talmadge, were among thirty-nine senators who in 1976 had signed an anti-treaty resolution that Thurmond, the Senate's most vocal critic, authored, viewing the issue as an erosion of US sovereignty. Carter concluded that his fellow Georgians would be critical to passage of the treaties. He implored state business leaders and the lawmakers' allies to intervene with Nunn on his behalf. Nunn told the president that "he would try not to embarrass him." He implied that he would follow Talmadge's lead but had already indicated publicly he had significant reservations. Emotions were running high, and

Nunn's constituents were stridently opposed to the treaties. A few Georgia newspaper editorial boards were impatient with Nunn, demanding that he state his position explicitly, but he refused. He wanted to understand both sides of the argument and the evidence before taking a stand, especially on an issue of such import. Majority leader Robert C. Byrd, West Virginia Democrat, had signed the anti-treaty resolution as well, but the White House was now counting him a canal "convert." Byrd, however, refused to twist the arms of his party colleagues, allegedly telling Carter he would have to "sell it" himself.[45] After a series of hearings on the treaties in the Armed Services Committee regarding the impact of the treaties on US national security interests, the probability of Senate approval appeared unpromising. Stennis and several other members opposed the treaties, and used the hearings to provide a forum for retired senior military officers who felt likewise to articulate their unfavorable assessments, which serving officers did their best to offset.[46]

Round one of the debate on the treaties began in mid-February 1978, but the atmosphere was lethargic and routine: days of unceasing talk rather than vigorous argument, a senator napping at his desk at one point, the chamber nearly empty most days; only Senator James Allen, an Alabama Democrat, provided a spark of liveliness by peppering Mondale, the presiding officer, with a volley of parliamentary queries. Capitol Hill correspondents wagered that Carter was only a few votes short of legislative victory, but public support remained weak and conservative, and anti-treaty interest groups were resolute. These opponents counted Nunn among the "doubtful dozen," those who were still testing their constituents' reactions.[47]

Nunn remained quiet regarding his position as February flowed into March when, after four weeks of debate, Byrd finally scheduled a vote on the first of the two treaties, the Neutrality Treaty. In response, the administration intensely lobbied the uncommitted as White House headcounters believed they were still short the two-thirds majority needed for approval. Carter was convinced Nunn was vital to winning several other Democratic senators' votes, especially in the South and among those who trusted Nunn's judgment on military affairs. In fact, Carter's perception was correct. Talmadge and Senator Russell Long, a Louisiana Democrat, told Nunn that they were going to follow his lead on the vote, so Nunn knew his decision would determine two additional votes. Carter invited Nunn to the White House to discuss the treaties and asked for his vote. Nunn assured him that the president would have it. On March 14, Nunn announced his support for the treaties along with his fellow Georgian, Herman Talmadge, and two Republicans.

Talmadge believed, like Nunn, that the value of the canal "was in its use, not the ownership," and that the issue was "vital to a native Georgian who was President of the United States." The number of uncommitted had shrunk to five votes.[48] Nunn explained during the final debate that his decision to support the treaties was based on a risk assessment; in terms of defense, the canal was at greater risk if the Senate did not vote in favor of the resolution of ratification. He maintained that there would be "serious consequences," one of which was that it provided "new opportunities" for the Soviet Union and "its Cuban henchman" to "fan the flames of anti-Americanism throughout Latin America and the Third World." He also worried that failing to ratify the treaties would seriously injure the executive branch's lead role in foreign affairs.[49]

Two days later, at 3:00 p.m., the galleries, press and public, were filled with onlookers. Members of the House of Representatives stood in the back of the public gallery along with dozens of Senate aides. Pages moved briskly around the Senate floor distributing tally sheets. The final, somber hour of debate between supporters and opponents commenced, and then came the vote. Byrd insisted that the senators sit at their desks to vote, as the rules allowed. The roll call began, broadcast nationally on the radio. The senators answered their names with clear responses and then marked the tally sheet in front of them. As the vote progressed, most of the opposition was among members from the South and West, but several Republicans from those regions voted in favor of the treaty. Sixty-seven votes in favor of the treaty were recognized and recorded. Byrd cast the sixty-eighth after passing when his name was first called. The Senate had approved the Neutrality Treaty by a vote of 68 to 32, a one-vote triumph.[50]

The approved resolution of ratification text, however, expressed specific concerns, ones sure to give the Panamanian government problems domestically. Two major amendments and two major reservations had been incorporated into the resolution of ratification. Nunn's support came with a qualification: he introduced one of the reservations, which allowed the United States and Panama to make "agreements of arrangements for stationing of any United States forces or maintenance of defense sites" after Panama officially took control of the canal on December 31, 1999. Carter accepted Nunn's reservation, which had been drafted with the assistance of the Armed Services Committee's general counsel, and the other one that Democratic senator Dennis DeConcini of Arizona and Paul G. Hatfield, a Montana Democrat, introduced, by which the United States could use its military if domestic discord threatened canal operations. The Senate had adopted both by overwhelming majorities. The president understood that the price to be paid for the senators' votes and upholding US credibility in Latin America was concessions and deals. Moreover, Nunn's language reinforced the treaty's defense provisions and the odds of Senate approval.[51] There was a hint of self-protection in Nunn's reservation since he was up for reelection in eight months. This factor prompted Byrd to make him the amendment's principal sponsor. The administration's chief legislative intermediary, Warren Christopher, deputy secretary of state, agreed, and the Panamanians eventually acquiesced to the language. Nunn's vote for the first treaty was not popular in Georgia. His constituents were overwhelmingly against "losing" the canal; opponents had bumper stickers made with the words "Once we had a canal, now we have Nunn." Nonetheless, when the second treaty, which would cede the canal to Panama, came up for a vote in April, he supported the president. Again, Carter's success was contingent on obtaining the support of southern Democrats like Nunn.[52]

Meanwhile, Nunn grew increasingly apprehensive about NATO backsliding on its promise to improve its conventional capabilities, principally in West Germany where Soviet propaganda had been effective. NATO offered a new proposal at its Mutual and Balanced Force Reductions (MBFR) negotiations with the Warsaw Pact in Vienna, which had begun four years earlier. Nunn considered the negotiations notable for their lack of progress. The new proposal, however, sought to break "the four-year deadlock." It required both sides to withdraw equivalent numbers of tanks and personnel, but it allowed the Soviets to remove them from Central Europe, not East Germany. Nunn thought it folly and warned that such a scheme was highly advantageous to the Soviets, because they would select "obsolescent tanks" and "manpower stationed well behind the inter-German border," not their newest armor or elite combat forces deployed along that border. Furthermore, it stripped out of the original NATO proposal the most important demand: "diminution of Warsaw Pact capability to initiate major aggression against Western Europe *with little or no warning*" (emphasis in the original).[53] Nunn was optimistic that his alarm would stiffen NATO's resolve and that it would not fritter away an opportunity to enhance its defenses. It had already adopted many of the recommendations he and Bartlett and had made in their report. His concerns also had an impact on the administration, with Carter requesting his patience on the issue, because an agreement was not going to happen quickly, and the NATO proposal was an initial step. At the president's behest, Brown followed up with assurances. Nunn informed Brown he was unconvinced that Soviet personnel reductions could be verified, and he feared that the Soviets would redeploy them covertly.[54] Brown failed to persuade him otherwise, and the matter ended there. However, Nunn remained at the forefront of other critical elements of the administration's national security policies.

Among knowledgeable Hill watchers, Nunn's role in supporting Carter's ambitious foreign policy agenda was deemed crucial, especially approval of a strategic arms control pact with the Kremlin. If he or a few other prominent Senate Democrats who voted for the Panama Canal Treaties defected, then the likelihood that Carter could build a "solid, loyal bloc of followers in the Senate" was even more unlikely than it was currently. As one keen political observer noted, a victory on the canal treaties based on the president's personal style of bargaining on each issue separately and with individual senators would not translate into a string of further successes in foreign affairs. The impression left by the two close votes was that Congress controlled US foreign policy, not Carter. Nunn summed up the situation succinctly: "Tremendous energy has been consumed by Panama, and the president's supply of political chips is quite limited. This is going to become increasingly evident in the months ahead."[55]

In stark relief, at thirty-nine years old, Nunn's political fortunes were accumulating. He had already been anointed one of the Senate's most influential members, a superb analytical thinker on defense, and "by all accounts, a politically important Senate figure whose power has begun to grow." Even now the expectation among colleagues, think tank experts and political analysts was that because of his diligence, measured approach to issues, and intelligence, he would one day chair the Armed Services Committee, although he was only the seventh-ranking Democrat on the committee. As one specialist noted, "he has parlayed his chairmanship of a once obscure subcommittee on military manpower into headlines as a critic of fellow Georgian Jimmy Carter . . . [and] as an expert on the growing pains of the volunteer Army, the aging pains of NATO," and the future of US-Soviet talks on strategic arms limitations.[56]

As the midterm election approached, Nunn did not shrink from criticizing the administration. In a scorching speech, he stated that the Carter administration would have to expend millions to protect US missiles from Soviet attack, because US negotiators at the arms talks in Geneva had failed to solve this potential problem. He accused the administration of lacking a coherent strategy for attaining a verifiable treaty, expressing his belief that this flaw could provide the "foundation for Soviet superiority." He concluded by reiterating his major concern: there had been a "general deterioration" in the Soviet-US military balance in recent years.[57] Carter helped Nunn make his argument that the administration's defense policy was rudderless by vetoing the defense authorization bill in August, claiming it "cut into the muscle of our military defense." Others interpreted the step as Carter's attempt to wrest control of defense matters from lawmakers bent on dictating US military strategy and its size contrary to the administration's objectives. Nunn responded by warning Carter he was sending the "wrong signals to our friends, our adversaries and the American people."[58] His declaration to work hard to override the veto was popular at home with constituents.

By August, Nunn had captured the Democratic nomination for reelection despite his vote in favor of the Panama Canal treaties. As one confidant remarked, "After six years in the Senate, Nunn's national security credentials were well established and accepted throughout Georgia as among his greatest assets." He had "carefully cultivated" relations with local leaders near the several military installations in the state, and in 1978, his work led to the establishment of the naval submarine base at Kings Bay on the coast of Georgia. He no longer needed the "reputations of Vinson and Russell to lean on."[59]

Nunn won 80 percent of the vote in the primary, crushing his five opponents. He won a second term in the November general election with 83 percent of the vote, a sizable gain over 1972. Although his chances for reelection had been debated among some pundits, their predictions were noticeably wrong. As the lopsided victories underscored, he had no need of coalitions; his constituents viewed him as a person of substance and with an approach to public services they found appealing. Herman Talmadge agreed. He attributed the win to Nunn being a "hard worker," as well as visiting the state often, and paying attention to his constituents, even if he had voted in 1975 for the renewal of the Voting Rights Act of 1965, a stance that was extremely unpopular in Georgia and one he agonized over. Now, Nunn could work on the issues that mattered most.[60] The Carter administration was more concerned about the impending arms control agreement with the Soviet Union. Privately, administration officials believed Nunn's support of the treaty would be essential if the president was to achieve the next priority of his foreign policy agenda, but it required deference to Nunn on other defense issues.[61]

A week after winning a second term, Nunn was in the Soviet Union, joining eleven colleagues from both parties to discuss strategic arms control and other subjects of interest to the two countries. On this first visit to Moscow, he ultimately found the trip educative. But first he had to tolerate the constant propaganda of Soviet foreign policy advisors and four members of the Politburo, including a meeting in the Kremlin with Soviet general secretary Leonid Brezhnev, who in a fifty-minute monologue extolled the impending arms control treaty.[62] Nunn repeatedly asked to have a substantive discussion on arms control with senior military officials, but to no avail. At the last moment, the civilian officials relented, and Nunn met for two hours with Colonel General Mikhail Kozlov, deputy chief of the general staff. This meeting intrigued the press. While Senator Abraham Ribicoff, a Connecticut Democrat, led the delegation, reporters considered Nunn the most important senator in the group. They regarded him the major figure in the Senate debate on the new arms control pact because of his grasp of the complexities of defense strategy and nuclear weapons.[63] They would not be disappointed.

CHAPTER 3

THE PRICE OF SALT

Carter's presidency was already damaged by early 1979. His public approval rating had slipped to 30 percent.[1] As the domestic and international environments changed, his administration's foreign policy appeared to be in disarray, made only worse by the collapse of the shah of Iran's regime on January 16 after months of civil unrest. "In a nutshell," one analyst concluded, "Iran fell through the cracks of the structure of foreign policy-making put together by Jimmy Carter." The distractions of other high-priority foreign policy issues also contributed to the loss of this important "pillar" in the US strategy for the Middle East.[2] Nonetheless, the president and his chief advisors believed the Iran situation could be temporarily set aside as another issue demanded their attention and the expenditure of political capital in their latest campaign—Senate approval of the US-Soviet strategic arms limitation treaty (SALT II). By late 1978, the administration deemed the treaty "essentially complete" because the basic provisions were unlikely to change and the chances of settling the residual issues appeared promising. The treaty would occupy the administration, Senate leadership, and members for much of 1979.[3]

On January 22, Carter presented his fiscal year 1980 defense budget. The request included $145 million to develop a 1,000-mile-range version of the Pershing ballistic missile, the Pershing II. The missile would be able to strike Soviet territory from US missile sites in West Germany. Administration supporters touted the advanced missile as proof that Carter intended to strengthen NATO's nuclear capability.[4] Meanwhile, as the administration negotiated the final points of the SALT II Treaty in Geneva, Switzerland, it was not clear to congressional observers that a defense budget that included funding for the new intermediate-range missile and a new intercontinental ballistic missile (ICBM) would ensure Senate support of the arms control pact. Some presidential assistants reached the same conclusion. On January 23, Frank Moore, who headed the White House congressional relations office, and Zbigniew Brzezinski, Carter's national security advisor, wrote to Carter emphasizing a major point in their legislative strategy: "Nunn is, perhaps the most crucial Senator in the SALT ratification battle."[5] As part of this strategy, Carter aides claimed that the treaty would make it possible to deploy new weapons systems such as the new ICBM and Pershing II, an intermediate-range missile, in the 1980s.[6] For Nunn, the assertion that modernization of nuclear forces alone would boost US defense posture was defective. Nunn knew how to assume a "Stranglovian frame of mind" to understand the numbers and details; nuclear weapons alone were insufficient to counter Soviet power.[7]

One White House wag called the upcoming Senate debate over the arms control treaty the "World Series of world affairs." Early vote counts indicated maybe forty senators would support the treaty, twenty were opposed, and the rest a toss-up. Carter needed sixty-seven votes in favor, and most senators, especially the twenty-four Democrats up for reelection, were measuring the treaty against domestic issues of concern: rising inflation, a rate now over 9 percent; growing energy costs; and sizable unemployment, hovering at nearly 6 percent. The president faced a difficult uphill slog too. While polls indicated the public overwhelmingly supported arms control, he had plenty of naysayers—certainly Republicans, who had abandoned any possibility of bipartisanship, seeing an opportunity to wound the president on his conduct of US-Soviet relations. The schedule for Senate endorsement was another critical factor. Purportedly, the view in the White House was that "time is running out—that the Administration must bring home an initialed treaty by mid-April or risk it getting fatally entangled in the Presidential politics of 1980." Accordingly, Carter's team wanted an early vote and concentrated on uncommitted Democrats it considered bellwethers: Robert C. Byrd, John Stennis, and Nunn. White House strategists believed losing the vote of any two would doom the treaty.[8] Carter had courted Nunn's vote on the treaty from the beginning of his presidency. Within a few weeks after his inauguration, he contacted Nunn about his goals for arms control: "As you know, I will be the monitor and actual negotiator in arms limitation talks, [and] will stay close to you and others."[9]

Nunn's vote would not be won with an assurance. The issue was complicated by his linking of strategic arms control to NATO's increased conventional capability to deter an attack, given that the Warsaw Pact's conventional forces enjoyed a significant advantage in numbers. Consequently, Nunn would remain uncommitted regarding SALT II until he read the treaty language, heard the administration's arguments, and gauged the trade-offs.

Meanwhile, Secretary of State Cyrus Vance and Secretary of Defense Harold Brown began privately negotiating draft treaty language with Nunn.[10] At the end of April, Nunn offered his views of US defense with or without a treaty. His position was blunt: a frontal assault on the president's defense record for the past two years. America's "military margin for error had narrowed," he maintained, because the Soviet Union was vastly outspending the United States on strategic nuclear forces and was on a trajectory to nuclear dominance. It was also "developing forces with growing advantages over NATO superiority." The current trends were unfavorable, and unless the United States and its NATO allies improved their nuclear and conventional forces by investing in them and thereby demonstrating resolve, then the treaty under negotiation and future arms control agreements would "do little more than ratify an emerging Soviet military superiority."[11]

The speech was another signal of Nunn's independence from his fellow Georgian, but more importantly, it highlighted his national prominence on defense, making him not only a "pivotal figure in the SALT debate," but an "heir" apparent to one of the chamber's "Dixie barons," Stennis. Nunn was now seen as one of the new powerful Democrats in the Senate.[12] Carter needed Nunn more than the opposite. As one presidential staff member counseled, Nunn required assurances that the administration realized the security environment was one of US-Soviet competition and that the doctrine of containment was still vital. SALT II, however, was one of the last vestiges of détente, which the administration hoped to keep alive through superpower dialogue on arms control.[13] Brown knew it would be difficult to get agreement in the Senate, and told Carter the same. He believed that senators either intended to gain benefits or obtain concessions that "had nothing to do at all with the SALT II Treaty," or they had fooled themselves into believing their efforts would result in an alternative, "ideal treaty." In reality, the alternative was "no treaty at all." That result would only generate "greater military and political uncertainty," prompt a retreat from improved relations, and stimulate a strategic arms race.[14] For these reasons, he and his staff worked the Senate hard for votes in support, especially Nunn and his "group of influential hawks."[15]

Observers maintained Nunn's attack on the administration's feckless defense program would have enormous impact in the arms control debate, influencing uncommitted senators, many disillusioned by détente, and possibly swaying Stennis. Further, two other prominent senators could still have an effect on the outcome. One was Republican Senate minority leader Howard Baker of Tennessee, who as a candidate for president, was attempting to position himself between the Republican conservatives he needed for party support and electability as the future party nominee. He might act as an honest broker by obtaining concessions in the treaty language acceptable to Republican moderates and conservatives without damaging the agreement. Byrd, the other important member, would set the terms of debate, designate a floor leader, attempt to maintain party unity in favor of it, and endeavor to secure the needed two-thirds majority even if it meant postponing the vote until 1980. While Carter and his advisors might have a different timetable in mind, such a delay would not be calamitous. Carter could portray himself as a seeker of world peace during his campaign and ultimately the victor, if the Senate consented to the treaty.[16]

Then on May 9, Vance, accompanied by Brown, strode into the White House press room and announced a diplomatic breakthrough after five months of intense negotiation between himself and Soviet ambassador Anatoly Dobrynin, who acted as the Kremlin's interlocutor. These meetings resulted in the superpowers reaching an agreement in principle regarding strategic arms limitations. Vance and Brown asserted that the accord would boost US security. Carter remained silent on the issue until the following morning at a meeting with retail merchants, telling them, "I think the single most important achievement that could possibly take place for our nation during my lifetime is the ratification" of the SALT II treaty.[17]

The administration then proceeded to torpedo its strategy to woo Baker and Nunn. Vance warned that Senate amendments to the treaty would unravel a pact beneficial to the United States by limiting the number of strategic forces of the two superpowers through December 1985. He believed there were no changes the Soviets would find acceptable, especially since the United States would not have to dismantle any weapons. Carter had made a misstep by stating that a rejection of the treaty would give the Soviets a propaganda coup by painting the United States as a "warmonger." Nunn retorted that Carter had armed the Soviets for their propaganda campaign with his statement. He added that the Senate might offer amendments that would improve the treaty and he might even support them.[18] Carter and Vance's comments were not only inopportune, but they had visibly drawn the battle lines prematurely, just as the US and Soviet delegations had concluded the treaty. Moreover, with the president scheduled to meet with Leonid Brezhnev at a Vienna summit in mid-June to sign the treaty, they had, as one analyst concluded, ignited "the fiercest ratification struggle since the Senate rejected the Treaty of Versailles 60 years" previously.[19]

Besides this war of words, critics of the eighty-page, nineteen-article treaty packed with "its attendant thicket" of protocols ... and 'common understandings,'" pointed out the areas where they would focus their complaints, ranging from verification measures to ensure the Soviets were complying with the treaty to worries about limitations on future US missile programs and the impact on defending NATO allies, a clear concern in European capitals because of Soviet intermediate-range nuclear weapons aimed at them.[20]

The administration found itself caught between senators allied with the president, contending the treaty was a step toward preventing a nuclear holocaust, and others who believed that the treaty encouraged nuclear war because it failed to reduce the likelihood of a Soviet attack on the United States or nuclear "blackmail" of NATO allies. In the middle were the uncommitted legislators, which included Nunn and a few members of the Armed Services Committee, such as Republicans John Warner of Virginia and William Cohen of Maine, whom Idaho senator Frank Church, the Senate Foreign Relations Committee's Democratic chairman, dubbed "nuclear theologians," members who complicated the discussion when they "'intone' a 'litany' of 'technical terms.'" Nunn's concerns, however, were unambiguous: "Arms control is no substitute for military power." He reminded his colleagues and the public that the "trends in military balance have been adverse to the United States and a continuation of those trends could lead to a decisive military inferiority."[21]

Carter preferred the treaty to be considered on its own merits, but Nunn, Cohen, and Arizona Republican Barry Goldwater, and Ohio Democrat John Glenn, the retired marine and former astronaut, linked their votes to the larger context of defense priorities. They focused attention on the proposed fiscal year 1980 defense budget, which they considered inadequate to meet US security objectives, and a Central Intelligence Agency assessment that the Soviet Union had upgraded the accuracy of the ballistic missiles carrying nuclear warheads so that they could strike US targets within a few hundred yards of their intended aiming point. This enhancement raised the likelihood the Soviets were capable by 1981 of launching a first strike against US land-based missiles, undermining the US nuclear deterrent. To counter this vulnerability, the US Air Force was developing a new ICBM, the "Missile Experimental" (MX), a highly accurate system with multiple, independently targeted nuclear warheads. This program, with a price of more than $25 billion, could match the new generation of Soviet missiles in "silo-busting" capability. Equally important, the missile would be mobile, launched from trucks or rail flatcars. Some political analysts believed White House support for the MX might be traded for approval of the treaty.[22] This analysis was a simplistic reading of the upcoming debate as mere horse trading. Further, as attractive as this deal might be, Nunn wanted proof that the administration had a clear-cut defense strategy that considered the US-Soviet balance in both strategic and conventional capabilities.

The Senate overwhelmingly passed a defense bill on June 13, which included funding for the new MX missile. Five days later, Carter and Brezhnev signed the SALT II Treaty in Vienna. It limited strategic nuclear delivery vehicles (missiles and heavy bombers) for each side, set a limit on the number of multiple independently targetable reentry vehicle (MIRV) missile launchers and heavy bombers with cruise missiles, banned new land-based intercontinental ballistic missile (ICBM) launchers, and limited deployment or testing of new types of strategic offensive weapons through the end of 1981. The treaty was referred to the Senate Foreign Relations Committee and the debate scheduled for fall. Hill insiders believed Nunn remained not only influential, but decisive in the outcome.[23]

Carter was still walking a political tightrope. Liberal senators Mark Hatfield, an Oregon Republican, and Ted Kennedy of Massachusetts scolded Carter for pressing forward with deployment of the MX missile as a concession to hardliners before the meeting with Brezhnev. They viewed the missile program as having a far-reaching, destabilizing effect on US and Soviet nuclear strategies. On the other side, among hardliners, Washington senator Henry "Scoop" Jackson was more vociferous. While his opposition to the treaty was expected, he called the period of détente under Nixon and Ford a "decade of appeasement," and claimed the treaty would give the Soviets nuclear superiority by 1985. Nunn may have shared Jackson's fears, but rather than speaking from Jackson's "Munich script," he restated Brown's report to

Congress that the Soviet Union had been outspending the United States and had swung the military balance in its favor, perhaps decisively. Nunn and Byrd told Brzezinski that without an increase in defense spending, there was no chance of the treaty achieving approval.[24]

By mid-July, with the Foreign Relations Committee holding hearings, the press was describing the White House and Senate positions in military terms, using phrases such as "battle cry" and "uphill battle," and hedging their bets on the administration's success on achieving approval. *Pravda,* the Soviet Communist Party newspaper, unleashed its own campaign to sway senators, stating any tampering with the treaty language would have "dangerous consequences for Soviet-American relations." Carter confirmed this stance by remarking that "to amend any part runs a grave risk of killing the treaty completely," adding that "killer amendments" would lead to "greater uncertainty about the strategic balance" between the two countries. Yet, senators would not buckle. White House aides now believed four senators could facilitate consent; Nunn, Byrd, Baker, and John Glenn were deemed critical.[25]

On July 23, the Armed Services Committee began weeklong hearings on the treaty. Although the committee did not have primary jurisdiction, it had a number of members who were experts on strategic weapons and nuclear doctrine. Brown and the Joint Chiefs of Staff testified that the treaty would limit the Soviet nuclear arsenal. While Jackson and Texas senator John Tower sought to undermine the witnesses' credibility, the hearing did not result in the "argumentative fireworks" many Hill watchers expected. Nunn "gave few hints of how he viewed the pact."[26]

Then, at the next hearing on July 25, Nunn, "with a stroke that may have redrawn the battle lines in the SALT debate," left no doubt of his position. Reading from a prepared statement, he stated that his vote in favor of the treaty, which he believed had merit based on the Joint Chiefs of Staff's testimony, would be contingent upon the president's commitment to increase military spending—real increases of 4–5 percent after inflation in the proposed fiscal year 1980 defense budget and for at least five more years. He could not "in good conscience" vote for the treaty otherwise. With his statement, Nunn carved out a position to which undecided, moderate senators could rally. He argued "only presidential leadership" could change the dangerous trends in Soviet military capability compared to US military power.[27]

One reporter believed that in "parliamentary terms, the Georgia senator's announcement was perhaps the most dramatic development since the Senate committees began formal consideration of the treaty earlier" in the month. Nunn communicated his skepticism that the administration was not committed to a strong defense and, in doing so, linked his support for the treaty to defense spending on conventional forces. Some hard-line Republicans worried that Nunn's position would result in a "new consensus" and obscure the treaty's defects. Liberal Democratic senators did not welcome Nunn's proposal, essentially asking "Carter to alienate the liberal wing of the Democratic Party with an election year coming up."[28] Carter bristled at Nunn's insinuation that his administration had failed to support "adequate" defense budgets. "We don't want to get in an argument with Nunn," he confided to his diary, "but I'm not going to lie down and roll over for him."[29]

Nevertheless, the White House welcomed Nunn's support because he did not criticize the treaty but offered negotiating room, which administration officials scurried to meet. One official, recognizing that an internal fight was likely, believed it could meet Nunn's requirement, "though we may have to break a few bones around here to do it." Lloyd Cutler, whom Carter had appointed special counsel for the treaty that month, was not optimistic. Persuading two-thirds of the Senate to approve the treaty was daunting enough. Additionally, public backing for arms control had waned, and apprehension about Soviet capability was growing. The administration was running out of time.[30]

While Stennis attempted to focus his committee members on the treaty as the reason for the hearings and "not a session on defense authorization," Byrd praised Nunn's position. Carter responded he was not buying Senate votes and doubted Congress would appropriate a substantial increase in defense, but his aides still wanted a win-win deal and were optimistic they could find a figure Nunn might deem reasonable.[31] Pundits speculated that Carter might be able to please two major factions: Nunn and conservatives who viewed the treaty vote as a referendum on waning US military power, and those who favored the treaty on its own merits, viewing it as another positive, incremental step in arms control efforts. The outliers were liberal senators who opposed more military spending as a bargaining chip.[32] They believed Carter's treaty failed to achieve meaningful arms control, and wondered if the treaty was "worth fighting for."[33] If a deal was struck, these liberal members were likely to be displeased, but it was unclear they would vote against the treaty. Carter was far from accomplishing the extravagant promise made in his inaugural address two year earlier: "the elimination of all nuclear weapons from this Earth."[34]

Nunn learned the administration's position when Vance testified before the Armed Services Committee on July 30. The secretary stated Carter would adhere to the pledge he and other NATO leaders made in 1977, a 3 percent increase in military spending. While Vance admitted that inflation and congressional reductions had eroded the administration's commitment, he doubted that an addition of up to 5 percent was required. Nunn made no mention of whether he found the secretary's offer acceptable.[35] Alan Cranston, a California Democrat and the majority whip responsible for vote counting, interpreted Vance's statement as an impediment to "responsible, rational negotiation." Cranston remained optimistic about Senate approval, but sent the White House a clear message. The terms of the debate had changed. Senate consent would be substantially improved if Carter committed to "some increase in defense spending."[36]

A day later, former secretary of state Henry Kissinger testified before the Foreign Relations Committee. The press viewed his endorsement of the treaty as crucial in gaining Republican votes since he had been involved in its negotiation during Ford's tenure as president and was the prime mover behind the SALT I Treaty. The Senate Caucus Room was standing room only when Kissinger sat down before the committee and made his position clear: the Senate should approve the treaty only if Carter agreed to a "binding and urgent commitment to increase military spending." More importantly, the Senate should delay consideration until the next session of Congress, after it and the House passed a supplemental defense appropriation. Unless those steps were taken, he could not endorse the treaty. All the State Department could muster was a feeble reply that it "welcomed" Kissinger's remarks as part of the "constructive debate on these vital foreign policy and defense issues."[37]

The Soviets now offered their official position in a *Pravda* article. Marshal Nikolai Ogarkov chastised senators who opposed the accord, stating that they "unscrupulously manipulate the facts or simply invent them." The Soviet Union would not only adhere to the treaty's provisions but the idea of a "Soviet menace" was a ploy by some senators to blame the Soviets for the "arms race begun by imperialism." Although he did not name Nunn, the marshal argued that "some American leaders intentionally and crudely" misrepresent the "real balance of forces between the U.S.S.R and the U.S.A."[38] Nunn did not react to the article directly, but Ogarkov had fanned the embers. It was going to be a hot month-long break—possibly explosive.

On August 2, Nunn, Jackson and Tower wrote to Carter insisting he furnish a prompt statement of his intentions regarding defense spending for the next five years before the Senate voted on the treaty. The letter's language was unambiguous; the senators would not support the treaty without "real increases of at least 4 to 5 percent" in the defense budget. The price tag for approving SALT II was now $8 billion, according to executive branch estimates. Nunn made no specific demands because he wanted time to review potential programs, but the letter alluded to countering Soviet growth by procuring weapons, ships, and equipment and investing in research and development. Carter appeared ready to talk to the three about specific proposals because his budget director, James McIntyre, told him that no "vital programs" were "going begging."[39] Outside defense experts criticized the lack of specificity in the senators' letter. "Budgets," one critic remarked, "produce the illusion of strength, rather than the reality," especially in an economy experiencing rapid inflation.[40]

The senators' proposal met a serious roadblock when Democrats on the Senate Budget Committee, joined by New Mexico Republican Pete Domenici, voted against raising the congressional budget ceilings that allowed Carter to meet his NATO pledge of a real, 3 percent increase in defense spending, let alone Nunn's demand. The House Appropriations Committee sent a similar signal by reducing Carter's defense budget request. Carter found himself caught in a cross fire between budget cutters and defense spending advocates in both chambers. He also had to contend with twelve liberal senators, ten Democrats and two Republicans, who supported the treaty, but pleaded it not be held "hostage" to the demand for a larger arms budget. Nothing, however, would appease intransigent opponents who found the treaty's provisions fundamentally unacceptable.[41]

Congress may have been in recess, but it was no vacation for Carter. He spent the month weighing how to meet Nunn's call for increased military funding, tasking an interagency group to examine how an increase would affect the economy and developing possible options to meet, at a minimum, the NATO commitment that inflation had ravaged. Publicly, the White House maintained an optimistic stance, claiming that Brown and the Joint Chiefs of Staff had proven that whatever flaws the treaty had, it was still better than no treaty. More importantly, Vance and the Defense Department's "SALT Sellers" believed they had countered opponents' arguments about such esoteric issues as total warhead megatonnage and treaty verification. They held as well that the existing and planned strategic weapons programs maintained the requisite level of deterrence.[42]

The battle over a defense increase continued within administration ranks, with various proposals being floated. One proposal that surfaced, because Nunn and Kissinger's endorsements were viewed as essential, was to add $4 billion to the budget as a down payment to offset higher-than-forecasted inflation, but not make it look like the president gave in to what aides were calling the "Nunn-Kissinger test" or, as others labeled it, the "Sam Nunn blackmail."[43]

With the economy drooping, energy and health care costs rising, the automaker Chrysler Corporation nearing bankruptcy, and inflation running at an annual rate of 13.2 percent, Congress returned in early September faced with domestic woes. The treaty was now intertwined with the larger budget debate and an election year only four months away. Carter held firm—no major increase in defense beyond offsetting inflation. It was a risky decision. The same week, the administration confirmed, through a US intelligence assessment, that a "combat brigade" of 2,000 to 3,000 Soviet troops, beyond the several thousand Soviet advisors who had been in Cuba since 1962, had deployed to the island in recent months. Another obstacle to approval was in place. Carter protested to the Kremlin, but the Soviets said the personnel had a training mission only, refusing to remove them. Subsequently, some senators favored putting off the treaty.[44]

On September 7, in a floor speech, Nunn pushed for Carter to make the "case to the American people" that a substantial increase in defense spending was needed because of "adverse trends" in US military capability. The president's planned request for supplemental defense appropriations to offset inflation was insufficient in view of the military imbalance that Soviet defense spending had created. Narrowing a gap of $60–80 billion demanded "a determined, well-planned, long-term commitment over a 5-to-10 year period."[45] Senator Ernest Hollings, a South Carolina Democrat, supported Nunn. The two planned to work on a resolution to increase the defense spending target by $2.6 billion when the second budget resolution came to a vote in mid-September.[46]

Congress and the White House devoted September to political maneuvering over the budget and the treaty. Carter rejected an increase of 5 percent in defense spending by requesting Congress appropriate an increase of $5 billion to cover inflation. The chairmen of the House and Senate Budget Committees attacked the proposal, and to add to Carter's troubles, several senators, including Nunn, vowed that until the Soviet troops left Cuba, no action should be taken on the treaty. Yet, Nunn remained conciliatory. He stated that while Carter's plan was a "prudent course" for the next fiscal year, he would continue to press for additional growth in succeeding years. In the meantime, he awaited Carter's long-range intentions on that point. In the view of one analyst, both sides might be "edging toward a compromise but had yet to reach common ground."[47]

Common ground was becoming harder to find. Two southern Democrats came out against the treaty as being unverifiable and the presence of Soviet troops in Cuba an indication of Soviet "bad faith." It was a momentous setback for the administration because they had counted on them for support. The US intelligence community's discovery of these troops was causing a major flap, and the administration had handled it badly.[48] The senators' opposition made Nunn's vote more crucial.

At a breakfast meeting at the White House, on September 13, Carter and Nunn squared off. Joining Nunn were Jackson, Hollings, Tower, and Stennis, along with members of Nunn's staff. Mondale, Brown, Brzezinski, a few aides, and a senior Pentagon official joined Carter. Nunn began the discussion and then had two members of his staff, Jeffrey Record and Arnold Punaro, address specific shortfalls in US nuclear and conventional capabilities. The details Punaro presented motivated one startled senior Pentagon official to ask where he got his data. Punaro, who had obtained the information from an army general, replied vaguely, "Friends of conventional forces." Nunn then questioned Brown as to whether a recently completed Pentagon report, which had been leaked to him, verified these findings. Carter turned to Brown and asked if the figures were accurate. Brown admitted they were and suggested that defense spending needed to be increased. With that admission, Nunn said he believed Carter had two options: either support an increase in the defense budget or admit publicly that he had no intention of funding defense at the minimum level needed to protect America's interests. The ultimatum brought complete silence to the room. Carter finally responded, telling Nunn it was not his fault, that defense spending had been cut by his predecessors. He was the one trying to remedy the military deficiencies. "Sam," the president pleaded, "the tremendous cuts were made by the Republicans." Amazed and unconvinced by this appeal since Carter had cut Ford's proposed fiscal year 1978 defense budget by $2.8 billion when he assumed office in 1977, Nunn answered, "Mr. President, you don't seem to understand. If we go to war, we're not going to war with the Republicans."[49] The ultimatum did not end the conversation, but nothing more was accomplished. Hollings told reporters the meeting was a "standoff"; Stennis believed the group had made "some headway." The only positive note was an agreement between Carter and Nunn to meet again later in the day.[50]

Carter could not afford to alienate Nunn. Off the record, the second meeting was an attempt to "convince the Georgian," the "most important single senator in the SALT debate—to be patient and to hold off on any definitive statements about his position on the treaty." Nunn agreed to that request, and refused to discuss the meeting at any length with reporters, remarking that he would await the administration's five-year defense plan before casting his vote. He added that the treaty was stalled to the degree that he predicted it would not come for a vote until the end of the year. Such a delay would give the administration ample time to produce a long-term defense budget. Further, he and Carter agreed that a 3 percent hike, taking inflation into account, was the most the Pentagon could absorb the coming fiscal year, but Nunn emphasized that he expected a 5 percent increase for fiscal years 1981 and 1982. Nunn's resolve on this point stunned the White House in the morning meeting; they had underestimated his fervor. Now, after the second meeting, Carter felt Nunn would be helpful. Brzezinski, who had been meeting with Nunn and Byrd privately to gain their support for the treaty, considered the outcome a "major coup."[51]

Five days later, Carter informed Hollings, hours before the South Carolinian's amendment to the budget resolution came up for a vote, that he would only commit to a 3 percent increase in defense spending for fiscal years 1981 and 1982, but did offer a concession. If a larger increase was warranted, he told Hollings, "I can assure you that I will request it." Senator Gary Hart, a Colorado Democrat, was standing by with a compromise amendment that would support the president's position if Hollings's amendment failed.[52]

In response, the ranking Republican on the Senate Budget Committee, Henry Bellmon of Oklahoma, offered that a vote on the treaty be delayed until the next year. Instead, the Senate should appoint a select committee to review future defense requirements, reasoning that the body needed better information about "where we are and where we are going in U.S. foreign and defense policy." Bellmon's reaction was another blow to the administration because he was viewed as a treaty supporter. Nunn's response was blunt, "It could well be beneficial to the country" if the treaty was defeated, because the Senate concluded that the "overall military trend between the United States and the Soviet Union" was decidedly "unfavorable to the United States."[53]

Once again, Carter misjudged the Senate's mood. Nunn took to the floor to deliver a bleak message. Using statistics derived from administration documents, he informed his colleagues that the Soviet Union had outspent the United States by more than $100 billion in the preceding decade, while inflation made the US defense budget for fiscal year 1980 "less in real dollars than the defense budget of 1965." The administration estimated the Soviet Union was spending 11 percent of its annual gross national product on defense, while the United States spent less than half that. Moscow was on a trajectory to attain military superiority in both strategic and conventional arms, while the United States purchased fewer weapons than it had done fifteen years earlier.[54] His argument, bolstered by the data, proved persuasive.

The same day, the Senate voted 55 to 42 on a Nunn-Hollings proposal to authorize annual increases of 5 percent to the fiscal year 1981 and 1982 defense budgets, in addition to the 3 percent that would be added in fiscal year 1980 that another of their amendments sought. The two amendments added almost $40 billion to defense, with moderate Democrats and Republicans voting in favor. Some pundits speculated that the revelation about Soviet troops in Cuba was the decisive factor. Others maintained that it was easy for senators to vote for the amendment with no political costs. Democratic senator Edmund Muskie of Maine, Budget Committee chairman, decried the vote: the "enemy that has the power to devastate" the nation was not the Soviet Union, he stated, but inflation. Nunn's counterargument was plain. "We in this country have gone to sleep on the assumption that we could end the arms race by slumbering away." It was a costly assumption, as "there is only one country running in the race, and that happens to be the Soviet Union." He added that US forces were unable to meet their worldwide wartime commitments. "Even a five percent growth rate will not be sufficient." He and Hollings proved convincing enough; even if the vote was only symbolic, Nunn's leadership was apparent.[55] The House voted the next day on its proposed budget for fiscal year 1980 and rejected the measure because members could not agree on a figure for defense. The House Budget Committee would have to try again. Nunn's position, however, influenced promilitary House members who shared his concern, but the House Budget Committee chairman said such an increase was unrealistic.[56] The treaty was mired in the fight over the budget in both houses.

The Carter administration now found itself fighting a rearguard action. Brown, who had said that a 5 percent increase was unnecessary to maintain the military balance, informed the Foreign Relations Committee that the administration would not rule out potential increases beyond 3 percent. Some commentators viewed this admission as a reaction to Nunn's statistical display.[57] Indeed, treaty supporters, dwindling in number, believed there was "no way to revive its sagging prospects," after the discovery of the Soviet troops in Cuba and the convincing arguments critics made that the country's defense posture needed shoring up. They argued for postponement of a vote until the troop dispute with the Soviets was resolved or even linking treaty approval to a withdrawal of those troops.[58]

Unnamed sources told a *Washington Post* reporter that Nunn's determined stance resulted from the administration's flip-flopping, which had undermined its credibility with him. He was not alone. Some liberals had lost faith in Carter to the point that Kennedy was contemplating challenging Carter for the party nomination. The one important senator who had not abandoned Carter was Byrd, who had not publicly disclosed his position but was viewed as a committed supporter. At the very least, some speculated, he believed the Senate had an obligation to act rather than postpone a vote until after the 1980 elections.[59]

Over the next few weeks, the administration suffered more setbacks. The Senate Select Committee on Intelligence released a "guardedly favorable" report on the treaty but indicated that while the United States had the technical capability to monitor Soviet military activities, the members could not reach a conclusion as to whether the treaty could be effectively verified. Since the end of the shah's regime, the United States could no longer monitor Soviet missiles tests from listening posts on the Soviet Union-Iran border. Even more importantly, Byrd sided with Nunn by announcing that before he would bring the treaty to a vote, he wanted to see the administration's long-term defense budget plans. Carter said the administration could meet Byrd's demand.[60]

Then the administration changed tactics in October, stating that if the Senate did not approve the treaty, it was likely to undermine the NATO alliance. West German chancellor Helmut Schmidt stated that dismissal would be "a disastrous blow to the necessary leadership of the United States as regards the West as a whole," as well as alliance unity after years of negotiations under three different presidents. Its rejection could also mean that the allies (West Germany, Great Britain, and Italy) would not base cruise missiles and the new US intermediate-range Pershing II missiles in their countries. Carter went further than Schmidt. "Some European countries," Carter warned, "might very well turn toward the Soviet Union . . . and weaken . . . our NATO alliance." On this point, he was largely supported by a Foreign Relations Committee staff report that acknowledged that Schmidt spoke for "all of Allied Europe."[61] Nunn was one of the main targets of the new offensive because of his strong support for the alliance—particularly, the importance of the US conventionally armed cruise missiles for reassuring the allies—and his expertise on Euro-strategic issues. According to General Bernard Rogers, the NATO commander, it appeared that the senator wanted to see the administration's defense budget before making a commitment. Statements of support from NATO allies became part of the campaign. The West German defense minister and the Belgian foreign minister met with Nunn to inform him that their governments supported SALT II and a Senate rejection would lead to a major crisis among the allies, with serious consequences for tactical nuclear forces modernization and arms control.[62]

At a late October hearing before the Armed Services Committee, Brown stated that the allies were linking approval of the treaty to stationing missiles in their countries. Nunn responded, criticizing Carter for his alarmist statement, and challenged the president. "If the Europeans are concerned about their own security, the modernization of theater nuclear forces will go on regardless of what happens to the SALT treaty."[63] Nunn hammered on this point in a speech delivered to a German-American Roundtable in Washington, DC, an event extensively recounted in West German newspapers. He accused the "left wing of the ruling Social Democratic Party" of being a "weak link in NATO's chain on this issue." While he did not address the treaty in length, he argued that "strategic arms negotiations cannot be conducted in a vacuum." The real issue was NATO's "failure to adjust its conventional and theater nuclear force postures to the loss of American strategic nuclear superiority." Consequently, the alliance's most pressing requirement was to ensure a "credible deterrence at the theater nuclear and conventional force levels" since the Soviets had already successfully modernized their theater nuclear forces. The alliance was imperiled if the Soviet Union swayed its leaders to oppose deployment of the new missiles that could strike Soviet and Warsaw Pact territories and credibly threaten their forces. In the long run, basing the new weapons in NATO countries would result in the Soviet Union negotiating a reduction in the number of nuclear warheads deployed in Europe. "Arms control," he contended, "must be the mistress of force planning, not its master." The White House had no comment.[64]

As Thanksgiving Day approached, the pressure on Carter not to bow to Nunn's demands grew. Liberal senators from both parties met with the president and urged him to reject any increase in arms spending. However, the administration suffered another wound when retired Belgian general Robert Close announced that based on his analysis of information available about NATO and Warsaw Pact capabilities, the Soviet Union and its allies could attack and drive across West Germany to seize the Ruhr industrial region in forty-eight hours without employing nuclear weapons. Nunn remarked that Close offered additional proof that Europe's NATO members needed to do more to improve their conventional forces.[65]

By then, Brown had taken charge of negotiations with Nunn and his colleagues on moving defense budget growth toward 5 percent in real terms starting in fiscal year 1981. After he made a deal acceptable to the senators, Brown used polling data to support his plan with the president; recent polls demonstrated that American voters held the same position as Nunn. Sixty percent of voters supported more defense spending; less than 10 percent favored reductions.[66]

In mid-December, Carter announced a five-year increase in the Pentagon budget, 4.5 percent in real terms and further adjusted for inflation if needed, but he would retain his commitment to NATO partners of a 3 percent increase for fiscal year 1980. Speaking at a meeting of an advisory body of prominent business leaders, he stated, "The defense program I am proposing for the next five years will require some sacrifice, but sacrifice we can afford." The same day, NATO leaders approved the deployment of intermediate-range missiles (Pershing II and ground-launched cruise missiles) in Europe. Nunn had no comment when asked about Carter's remarks. He would wait to hear from Brown when he testified.[67]

A day later, Brown found himself before a disbelieving Senate panel. He testified the increase was not designed to gain treaty approval, though he did admit that the budget numbers were based on the arms pact being ratified. Nunn remained skeptical. To counter this doubt, Brown offered that the budget proposals would ensure US leadership in NATO, deter a conventional or nuclear conflict in Europe, and make for a more globally agile force by investing in the navy. He concluded with an admonition, "We must decide now whether we intend to remain the strongest nation in the world. Or we must accept now that we will let ourselves slip into inferiority . . . and that we will become a nation with more of a past than a future. I reject that prospect and I know you do as well."[68]

Nunn and eighteen of his colleagues, five Democrats and thirteen Republicans, not only rejected that prospect, but in a December 17 letter sent a clear message to Carter on how to avoid it. While each of the senators gave different weight to the topics covered in the missive, the letter drafted by Nunn stressed their fears "over the ongoing slippage" in "America's comparative military position," which had "been accentuated by the Senate's deliberations on SALT and by recent international events." This worrisome trend was evident in the erosion of NATO's conventional forces and theater nuclear capabilities. The Soviet navy appeared to be on the verge of challenging the West's supremacy. The senators laid out areas where the administration had failed to develop a "long-range national security strategy" in conjunction with arms control, which the senators agreed was worth pursuing as a means of enhancing US security. They recognized that there might not be sufficient votes to pass a resolution of ratification. If that were the case, then action on the treaty should be delayed until after the elections. The last sentence was a clear message: "Because of our concerns, largely covered by this letter, we are uncommitted as to how we will cast our votes on the SALT II Treaty and the proposed changes."[69]

The letter had its intended effect since the lawmakers represented a decisive voting bloc. Carter replied to each of the senators, underscoring his interest in "achieving a bipartisan consensus" on "these issues of long-range national security strategy, and arms control." He signaled his willingness to consider further concessions. Cranston said that his colleagues had raised "legitimate concerns." There was still the possibility that their concerns could be resolved without them adding amendments to the treaty's provisions that would fatally wound the administration's chance of Senate approval.[70]

Cranston's optimism was misplaced, which became apparent when the White House and Senate leadership agreed to postpone debate until the next year. There were too many other variables in play. As the principal author of the letter to Carter and the "focal point for SALT politics," some senators believed Nunn was demanding too much and had become a publicity seeker. However, the Senate remained in sharp disagreement as to the value of the treaty. Pro-treaty supporters continued to grouse that the pact did not do enough to reduce nuclear arsenals, while opponents believed Nunn had strengthened their position.[71]

The opponents of the treaty proved to be the most adept tacticians. It was not Nunn who engineered the next damaging setback for the administration, but Jackson, Tower, and Goldwater, who forced the issue over Stennis's objections. Their views and that of the Armed Services Committee majority was that the treaty was not in the best interests of US national security, a view expressed in a report the committee released on December 20, by a vote of 10 to 0, with seven voting "present," thereby abstaining and voicing their objection to releasing the report. Nunn, Stennis, and five other Democrats argued the report would undercut the prerogatives of the Foreign Relations

Committee, which had jurisdiction. In November, that committee, after defeating several amendments that would have significantly modified the treaty, had approved it by a vote of 9 to 6, with two Republicans joining seven Democrats, and sent it to the full Senate. Even the committee majority had reservations about the treaty and added comments explaining their reservations and noting their suspicions of the Soviet Union.[72] The Armed Services Committee vote also indicated the waning authority and prominence of the Foreign Relations Committee regarding arms control issues.[73]

Ultimately, the price of a treaty became too steep when Soviet troops invaded Afghanistan on Christmas day. A year earlier, Muslim fundamentalists had overthrown the Afghan communist government and had taken control. Now, the Soviet Union had moved to return its fellow communists to power.[74] On January 3, 1980, Carter wrote Byrd and asked that the treaty not be brought to the floor for a vote but remain on the calendar for potential future action.[75] It was not to happen because Carter was soundly defeated for a second term by Republican Ronald Reagan in November.

As the former president lamented a few days after leaving office, "1980 was pure hell—the Kennedy challenge, Afghanistan, having to put the SALT Treaty on the shelf, the recession, Ronald Reagan. . . . It was always one crisis after another."[76] For Nunn, it was a very good year. His leadership was so prominent that there were reports he was being considered as a potential secretary of defense in Ronald Reagan's cabinet.[77] That his contention that US military preparedness had severely eroded relative to the Soviet Union was now accepted without question gave him the greatest satisfaction.[78] Congress was likeminded; it added $5.2 billion to the president's fiscal year 1981 defense budget request, passing a $159.7 billion appropriations bill. A reluctant Carter signed the bill, now reconciling himself to larger defense spending, despite his campaign pledge to reduce it by $5 billion to $7 billion and balance the budget by 1981.[79]

CHAPTER 4

ARMS AND INFLUENCE

The temperature was unseasonably warm on January 20, 1981, the day of Ronald Reagan's inauguration. Standing behind the podium on the west front of the US Capitol, the president looked out onto the National Mall, and after thanking the various dignitaries sitting behind him on the ceremonial platform, he addressed the American people as "fellow citizens." His first words cast the moment in terms of the orderly transition of power from one official to another, but soon he spoke about the challenges confronting the nation—rampant inflation, unemployment—and he promised that these "economic ills" would eventually recede because of American greatness and his administration's priority commitment to "putting America back to work." In the more than 2,000 words he spoke that day, surprisingly Reagan made little mention of his foreign policy agenda beyond a commitment to allies and a warning to "enemies of freedom" that while Americans' highest desire was for peace, these adversaries should know that "when action is required to preserve our national security, we will act." Those few words about foreign affairs seemed so uncharacteristic of a man who had built his presidential campaign on the argument that America's international stature and power had deteriorated sharply during the preceding decade, and that he would restore American military might and confront its preeminent rival, the Soviet Union, with renewed energy and purpose.[1] He also had as a Republican president, for the first time in two and half decades, a Senate majority that shared his views.

The Ninety-Seventh Congress that convened two weeks earlier was markedly different from its immediate predecessor. Reagan's victory had produced a coattail effect. The Democrats still held the majority in the House, though by a smaller margin, but the Republicans now controlled the Senate. They celebrated this unaccustomed role on January 5, with their new majority leader, Howard Baker, leading the opening ceremonies with gusto and amid bursts of applause from his party colleagues. More importantly, with the change of control, the entire committee leadership was transferred to the Republicans.[2] For Nunn, the loss of the Senate meant he was no longer a subcommittee chairman.

One of Reagan's vows immediately stood out: a substantial military buildup, even if that aim ran contrary to his promise of a balanced budget. As he told his advisors, "Defense is not a budget issue. You spend what you need." With that inflexible position, on March 4 Reagan, with the counsel of his secretary of defense, Caspar Weinberger, requested a considerable increase in Jimmy Carter's fiscal year 1982 defense budget, from $196 billion to $222 billion, the largest peacetime military budget in US history. Furthermore, the administration announced 7 percent increases in defense spending from 1981 to 1985, with the majority of the funds for new weapons, research and development, and enhanced combat readiness. Additionally, the president called for a $.5 billion increase over the $6.3 billion fiscal year 1981 supplemental appropriation his predecessor had requested.[3]

Defense analysts were convinced Reagan was not only committed to a nuclear arms race with the Soviet Union but that he and his advisors were scornful regarding the usefulness of arms control treaties, favoring confrontation over the détente policies of his predecessors Richard Nixon, Gerald Ford, and Carter.[4] Now, it would be the "gospel of peace—through strength" since the invasion of Afghanistan two years earlier had proven the Soviet leadership's treacherous intent and a more antagonistic stance throughout the world.[5]

There was no effective opposition in Congress either to Reagan's defense plans or to his tough rhetoric toward the Soviet Union. The Senate Armed Services Committee approved the 1981 supplemental bill on April 1, authorizing a $6.5 billion increase, and a month later, the committee authorized another $136.2 billion. A little over a week later, after halfhearted debate, the Senate approved the defense authorization bill by a vote of 92 to 1. It was not only a success for Reagan but signaled congressional support for an increase in military spending as the House Armed Services Committee had approved a similar bill. Nonetheless, Nunn was not silent or unfocused with respect to the Senate bill, as his colleagues approved an amendment he offered that required the Defense Department to report to Congress on programs that had substantial cost overruns with an accompanying plan for correction. Moreover, this move indicated the role Nunn and a few of his Senate colleagues and concerned House members would play in the future—reformers. In response to an article by Gary Hart published in the *Wall Street Journal,* a group of pro-defense House and Senate members from both parties formed the Congressional Military Reform Caucus: members who sought to curb wasteful Pentagon spending through procurement reform, and to improve the combat effectiveness of US conventional forces and thereby reduce reliance on nuclear weapons.[6]

Reagan confronted few congressional challenges on national security during his first year in office, but there were two "big fights" as the 1981 legislative session came to end. By late summer, "Reaganomics," the idea of cutting federal spending but increasing the defense budget and reducing taxes, while at the same time balancing the budget, was not having the impact on the economy the president had promised. The projected deficit was now much larger than the administration's estimate, leading to interest rates rocketing and stock prices falling. In response, Reagan stated that the defense budget request would be shaved, but he proposed only an $8 billion reduction in his fiscal year 1982 request. Senate Republican leaders wanted deeper cuts and were joined by the House minority leader, Republican Robert Michel of Illinois. In the end, Reagan prevailed, but Democrats and many Republican were determined that the next session would be different. Even so, Congress approved a $200 billion fiscal year 1982 defense appropriation. Nunn and other Democrats complained the administration was shortchanging the readiness of conventional forces and offered proposals to remedy this deficiency by adding funds. Their amendments were defeated, but it was a clear indication of an emerging coalition of Senate Democrats bent on creating an identifiable Democratic defense agenda that would hold the administration accountable by linking the defense buildup to a comprehensive defense strategy designed to further US foreign policy objectives.[7]

The Democrats' position became increasingly pertinent during the second "big fight": increase US military capabilities in strategic nuclear weapons. Reagan argued that his predecessors had neglected this crucial element of US security and had allowed a "window of vulnerability" to open that the Soviets could exploit with its arsenal of modernized intercontinental ballistic missiles (ICBMs), including the so-called heavy missiles with multiple war-heads. By the time Reagan assumed office, the Soviet Union had gained a sizable advantage in ICBM forces.[8]

To offset this imbalance, Reagan's Strategic Forces Modernization Program focused on the MX missile (named for its original designation, "missile experimental"), as the means of upgrading US strategic deterrence. A highly accurate missile because of its inertial guidance system, it could carry as many as ten multiple independent reentry vehicle (MIRV) nuclear war-heads with an explosive power of 300 kilotons. This explosive power enabled it to put at risk the hardened silos of the Soviet strategic nuclear forces.[9]

However, the MX had a history of political controversy. In the 1970s, air force officials feared that the Soviet Union might use its multiple-warhead missiles in a first strike and destroy US land-based missiles. To prevent this outcome, the air force planned to deploy the MX missile on a mobile trans-porter to make targeting them more difficult for the Soviets. Carter approved the development of the missile in 1979, with deployment in the western United States. The scheme soon ran into opposition from residents in the affected states of Nevada and Utah. The environmental impact and the cost of the proposal worked against it as well as the residents' fear of becoming a more likely target for Soviet missiles, a concern their congressional repre-sentatives shared.[10]

Reagan had campaigned against Carter's mobile version. After months of deliberation, he announced in October his decision to deploy temporarily about three dozen missiles in existing silos that would be further hardened. This interim approach would give his administration until 1984 to develop a superior basing system before they became vulnerable to the more accu-rate Soviet missiles. The decision resulted in the unintended consequence of forming an alliance between Senate Armed Services Committee members who had favored the Carter plan and congressional liberals and anti–nuclear arms activists hostile to Reagan's strategic modernization policy.[11] Nunn be-came the leading representative for the former but fashioned a strategy to appeal to the latter.

In a November 5 hearing before the Armed Services Committee, Nunn derided the administration's "superhardening" proposal as unrealistic and urged Weinberger to develop a long-term basing scheme that incorporated elements of the Carter plan. None of the Republicans on the committee came to the administration's defense.[12] Nunn asserted that the administra-tion's plan not only would be very costly and offer slight protection but, more importantly, could undercut the stability of the nuclear balance by deploying the missiles in such a vulnerable position. The Soviet Union might consider the administration's plan a policy change in which the United States would launch MX missiles before an attack was definitely confirmed. In that case, the Soviets might embrace a comparable policy, which could "dramatically lower the nuclear threshold" and place a "hair trigger on nuclear forces" in both countries.[13] Nunn's position was supported by retired air force general Richard Ellis, the former commander of the Strategic Air Command (SAC), who agreed that for the present, no one knew how to harden the silos to withstand the megatons of power the Soviets would hurl against them.[14]

A week later, Nunn published an op-ed contending that Reagan's arms plans had serious arms control implications that remained unappreciated. Moreover, the administration lacked a long-term strategy for integrating arms control policy with military requirements. Since 1972, arms control policy had focused more on limiting the number of weapons rather than on avoiding or limiting their potential use in a crisis. Nunn revealed that the previous year, he had asked Ellis, then still on active duty, to have the Strategic Air Command study the possibility of a third party, another nation or terrorists, igniting a nuclear exchange between the two superpowers. The SAC assessment showed "real and developing dangers." Nunn stated he was voicing his concerns to underscore the potential for an outbreak of nuclear war as a matter needing greater consideration, given that the proliferation of nuclear weapons was increasing its likelihood. The first step was to devise a mechanism to control or contain these situations quickly and decisively. He urged US and Soviet leaders to cooperate by establishing a military crisis control center for the monitoring and containment of nuclear weapons by third parties and terrorists. This organization could encourage cooperation and build confidence between the rivals, and he exhorted the leaders to begin discussions and negotiations that would avert a crisis and, more importantly, use the center as a mechanism to address other arms control measures that would enhance stability. Arms control policy, he concluded, required clear goals, "long-term continuity and less vulnerability to domestic partisan politics."[15]

Nunn's concerns led him in late November to fashion an amendment to the defense appropriations bill that would halt the administration's $5.6 billion plan to temporarily place forty MX missiles in silos that would not survive a Soviet attack. He was tapping into two major concerns in Congress: the mounting budget deficit, and members who viewed nuclear arms in the wider context of US-Soviet relations and were troubled by Reagan's bellicose anti-Soviet rhetoric.[16]

Republican senator William Cohen agreed with Nunn's assessment. He believed the Defense Department was headed in the "wrong direction" by using the existing silos and wanted to pressure the administration to develop a "basing mode that is survivable, that is acceptable, and that will be adopted."[17] He joined Nunn as a cosponsor of the amendment. Their arguments held sway, and by a vote of 90 to 4, the Senate approved the amendment that denied the Pentagon most of the funds it sought to strengthen the survivability of the existing ICBM silos for the MX. It diverted $334 million of the $354 million for a study to explore alternative basing schemes for the missile. Further, it required Reagan to recommend a long-term alternative to Congress by July 1, 1983. The amendment survived the final appropriations bill, with the House approving an identical amendment.[18]

While Reagan attained his goal of boosting defense spending for the next fiscal year, the debate on the defense appropriations bills suggested that further increases would not be easily achieved. Close observers of Congress detected two important developments in the final days of the session. First, members of both parties on the Armed Services Committee were not going to rubber stamp the administration's requests. Second, the pro-defense reformers had flexed their legislative muscles.[19]

Nunn's charge that the administration had not developed a strategy to chart how it would use the massive increase in defense funding found support among military experts also. John Collins, a defense specialist at the Congressional Research Service, sarcastically remarked, "We've got a national military strategy called M-O-R-E." He added, "We have a request for $1.5 trillion over the next five years with no policy behind it."[20] Collins's criticism accented the reformers' concern that the money might not have been spent effectively. They realized their apprehension was warranted when they heard a senior DOD official admit, "We [DOD] approached the [fiscal year 19]82 budget with what I would call a philosophy, as opposed to a totally articulated strategy."[21]

Nunn, Hart, Cohen, and Republican representatives William Whitehurst of Virginia and Newt Gingrich of Georgia were acknowledged as the informal leaders of the new reform caucus. By December 1981, the group had grown to fifty-five members and its impact was being felt not only on the Hill, with respect to defense spending and procurement improvements, but in the Pentagon. Weinberger understood the power of numbers and the diverse membership—liberals and conservatives, Republicans and Democrats. He met with the group, recognizing its growing influence.[22]

The reformers in both houses began 1982 eager to debate the next defense budget, which the administration would deliver in February. The mood was now noticeably different from a year earlier, when Hart had expressed his concerns about waning US military strength to a nearly empty Senate chamber. Now, he had a group of supporters. In January the reform caucus declared its philosophy. Its first principle set the tone: "First, we are worried that our military can no longer win." They questioned whether the public would continue to support large budgets for a "non-winning military." This decline in capability, measured in personnel numbers, readiness, and strategy, was "the reason military reform" was "urgently needed."[23]

The White House had its own concerns. Despite Reagan's strident anti-Soviet oratory, he was having difficulty translating rhetoric into consistent and coherent foreign policy as the realities of governing interfered. Some pundits suggested that he had largely neglected foreign affairs and his hands-off approach had only generated internal policy disputes. They conceded he had been able to increase the military budget, which most Americans had supported, and strengthen relations with key regional partners through arms sales. The atmosphere in Europe, however, was decidedly different. Publics in the NATO countries worried that the "cowboy President" was ratcheting up hostility with the Soviet Union, threatening to make their nations potential nuclear battlegrounds when he commented on the efficacy of a limited nuclear exchange on the continent. They were not alone; a majority of Americans, according to a survey, expressed concern about a nuclear war breaking out in the next few years. Furthermore, a few NATO leaders preferred détente to confrontation. To prevent a rupture in the alliance and allay American citizens' concerns, Reagan voiced a willingness to engage in arms control talks with the Soviets, and in November 1981, he offered to abandon the deployment of medium-range missiles with nuclear warheads to Western Europe, if the Soviets pulled back their growing force of comparable weapons. The diplomatic stroke caught the Soviets off guard and they rejected the offer, but the proposal appeased many Europeans. There were, however, schisms in the administration between hard-line officials and moderate "multilateralists" who valued maintaining stable relations with NATO partners.[24] It would prove a frustrating year in both branches of government.

Congressional opposition to another huge defense budget materialized as soon as the administration delivered the request to Capitol Hill. Republicans on the Senate Armed Services Committee were particularly uneasy; a sluggish economy and ballooning deficit were the contributors. Nunn, speaking for Democrats, reiterated that the "gap between budget and strategy" remained.[25] His concerns were soon confirmed.

At a February 26 hearing, the service chiefs agreed that President Reagan's planned defense increases over the next few years would not be sufficient for a "reasonable assurance force" to execute the military strategy. Under Secretary of Defense for Policy Fred Iklé confirmed that the resources needed to close the gap between US and Soviet capabilities were larger than originally thought. Nunn pounced on this admission, inquiring of the witnesses the amount of resources they would need in addition to the steep increases already intended. Upon hearing their answers, Nunn summed up their responses: "So all of you are saying even with the increases in the defense budget that we now have, that we are not at the end of the five years in this budget going to have . . . a reasonable assurance force?" Each of the service chiefs nodded. After the hearing, Nunn stated that the hearing only intensified his concerns about a strategy that was "realistic in terms of the resources that will be available." His aides indicated Nunn was concerned that the administration "has spread the nation's military strategy 'too broad' to be affordable and at the same time rectify serious imbalances with the Soviet Union."[26]

With this revelation, other members of Congress, Republicans and Democrats alike in both houses, stated their belief that the administration had failed to justify the need for a large military budget. However, Tower, the Armed Services Committee chairman, declared his opposition to cuts because of his concerns about Soviet military power, despite Congressional Budget Office projections that the defense increase would contribute to an estimated $91.5 billion deficit for fiscal year 1983. Public opinion about the size of the military budget had changed too. A mid-March New York Times/CBS News Poll showed that most Americans favored the defense budget reductions. Hart emphasized Nunn's point that the debate should not be on "how much to spend" but "what it [the defense budget] should be spent for, and why."[27]

The Reagan administration's strategic arms policies were now under attack from a grassroots movement calling for a "freeze" on the number of US and Soviet nuclear weapons. House members supported the idea. Les Aspin, the Wisconsin Democrat who chaired the Armed Services Committee, stated that the "defense consensus of last year" had been "frittered away" by its "casual talk about limited nuclear war" and "by too much greed, trying to put everything into the Pentagon budget, and by poor articulation of a strategy of what we are getting with the money." While Senate liberals supported legislation calling for a freeze, Nunn and Cohen continued to favor linking the strategic weapons programs with arms control initiatives, a stance the Senate Foreign Relations Committee favored. On March 23, the Senate Armed Services Committee's Subcommittee on Strategic and Theater Nuclear Forces voted unanimously to eliminate $2 billion in funding requested in the fiscal year 1983 budget to deploy the first nine MX missiles in existing ICBM silos until Reagan decided on a permanent and survivable basing scheme. A week later, the full committee accepted the subcommittee's report. Supporters and opponents of the program read these actions as a sign that the missile program was finished. The administration found itself on the defensive, inducing Reagan to make a public commitment to arms control negotiations with the Soviets.[28]

In May, Nunn took his next step to force the administration to reduce its appetite for defense spending in view of a missing defense strategy. Again, he chose bipartisanship as the method, leading a collection of senators who favored shrinking the US commitment to NATO. Senator Ted Stevens, an Alaskan Republican and chairman of the Defense Appropriations Subcommittee, expressed annoyance with the NATO allies, insisting that they were flirting with becoming dependent on the USSR by supporting a natural gas pipeline from Siberia. House Republican leaders piled on, asserting that a comprehensive reappraisal of US defense policy was "long overdue." With an anti-alliance attitude emerging and cries for "burden sharing" rampant, Nunn, along with John Glenn and William Roth, a Delaware Republican, introduced a resolution that called upon NATO members to "pool their defense efforts and resources to create, at acceptable costs, a reliable collective conventional force for the defense of the North Atlantic area." In response, senators on the Foreign Relations Committee complained that such a step would injure NATO solidarity.[29]

Reagan, still concerned about the nuclear freeze movement, addressed the prevention of nuclear war and arms reductions when he gave the commencement address at Eureka College in Illinois on May 9. In this speech, he reiterated his commitment to the resumption of arms control negotiations in June 1982, now known as the Strategic Arms Reduction Talks (START). The United States would propose a "practical, phased reduction plan," the first phase focused on reducing the number of ballistic missile warheads. But foremost, Reagan emphasized, he remained committed to strategic nuclear and conventional deterrence in Western Europe, which necessitated increased US and NATO defense expenditures to achieve "a sound East-West military balance."[30] The offer Reagan made was not an opening negotiating position. Instead, the proposal was fashioned to keep the administration's strategic modernization program principally intact, especially the MX missile.[31] Nunn called the speech a "good start," but exhorted Reagan to "seriously consider taking SALT II and then proposing any amendments he thinks necessary."[32] This suggestion was rejected when Secretary of State Alexander Haig informed the Senate Armed Services Committee that SALT II was "dead."[33]

A few days later, on May 13, Nunn took aim at the issue of defense expenditures and the military balance, both nuclear and conventional forces, by submitting a report to the Armed Services Committee titled *NATO: Can the Alliance Be Saved?* In Nunn's exacting analysis, NATO confronted "multiple problems that could destroy the Alliance." He believed that its existing military strategy of flexible response (implied use of tactical and possibly strategic nuclear weapons to repel Soviet and/or Warsaw Pact conventional attacks in Europe that could not be countered with NATO conventional forces) and forward defense had been "severely compromised by profound changes in the global and European military" environments. The alliance was in need of "major repair militarily, politically and economically" if it were to continue to serve as the bulwark of "Western values and interests."[34]

Nunn held that the alliance had become politically fragile because of tensions between the United States and its allies, with a loss of political consensus. The Europeans charged its partner with being more interested in confrontation than in maintaining peace, and they worried about being pulled into war. The United States, for its part, alleged that the Europeans were more interested in trade deals than security and thus subsidized the adversary. Militarily, Nunn argued, the present strategy was obsolete and the US nuclear deterrent undercut, because the Soviet Union had increased its defense expenditures during the 1970s, thereby attaining strategic nuclear parity, fielding superior tactical nuclear forces, and enlarging its conventional capabilities. NATO no longer held the nuclear advantage, which meant that "continued deterrence in Europe" had swung to NATO's inferior and long underfunded conventional forces, which were incapable of "mounting an effective forward defense."[35]

Nevertheless, Nunn believed a capable conventional defense could be created. Although NATO members agreed in principle, altering the strategy was a political problem, and the alliance had no substitute to offer currently because of a belief that the gap between NATO and Soviet conventional capabilities was too large to overcome financially. Consequently, despair had set in. Nunn offered some options that Reagan and the other NATO leaders should consider when they met for the Summit Conference in June.[36]

The essence of the new strategy, Nunn proposed, would be a change in NATO doctrine and an investment in new, advanced technology. The doctrine the US Army and Air Force were developing, known as "AirLand Battle 2000," concentrated on attacking the follow-on, reinforcing Warsaw Pact units, thus preventing them from crossing into West Germany, while simultaneously seizing the initiative by counterattacking the now isolated first echelon Warsaw Pact forces that had succeeded in overrunning NATO territory. Such actions would stop the "momentum of the invasion" and the prospects of a decisive Soviet victory. However, this doctrinal change was insufficient in itself. The new strategy required the outgunned and outnumbered NATO forces to be equipped with technology to offset the Soviets' superior numbers. With these changes and a dedicated alliance-wide effort, a more viable and likewise affordable conventional defense could be created, but it would take reinvigorated political leadership. Nunn did not disregard European anxieties about nuclear war or the powerful attraction of the nuclear freeze movement. He maintained that it would take the combination of a credible conventional defense and arms control measures to reduce the probability of nuclear war. "The conventional horse," he wrote, "must be in front of the nuclear cart."[37]

Nunn would not relent on this point. He continued to focus on the lack of a coherent US defense strategy, calling the administration's approach to national security a "hangover from the Presidential campaign." His suspicions proved correct, as the administration lacked a well-defined national security strategy until Reagan finally approved one on May 20, 1982, the result of a study that Reagan had directed only three and half months earlier.[38]

Nunn remained troubled about the risk of nuclear war, and based on the Strategic Air Command study and his idea of a nuclear risk reduction center, he developed a concrete proposal that the superpowers should form a team that would watch for signs of nuclear weapons development by other nations or terrorists so that if an explosion did occur, the two nations would be able to detect the source promptly. The proposal's other goal was to reduce the possibility of an accidental nuclear confrontation between the superpowers.

Consequently, a rumor soon surfaced that his proposal might even be added as an agenda item for the impending US-Soviet arms control talks in June.[39] The rumor proved to be groundless.

Arguments about defense again gained notice in the fall when Nunn and House Majority Leader Jim Wright, a Texas Democrat, engaged in a televised debate on the topic with Tower and Alabama Representative Jack Edwards, ranking Republican on the House Appropriations Committee's Subcommittee on Defense. The League of Women Voters sponsored the forum, and Ted Koppel of ABC's *Nightline* served as the moderator. Nunn used the opportunity to challenge the administration on the assumptions it used to build its five-year defense program.[40]

The debate highlighted the critical decisions about the fiscal year 1983 defense budget that Congress would soon meet head on. Because of the escalating federal budget deficit, business groups advocated slowing military spending, while liberal Democrats wanted money shifted to fund programs aimed at relieving unemployment. Amid this dispute, on November 10, Leonid Brezhnev, the Soviet Union's leader, died, and Yuri Andropov, former chairman of the KGB, the Soviet security agency, became his successor.[41]

On November 22, Reagan finally responded to Brezhnev's death, and with more than a letter of condolence. He announced that after two years of deliberation and consultations with Congress and technical experts, he would deploy the MX missile, renamed "The Peacekeeper," to maintain America's deterrent capability, and then he outlined his plans for the entire ICBM force. First, as the MX missile's development phase was nearing completion, flight-testing would begin in early 1983. With respect to MX basing, the plan would locate the launch sites much closer together to make them harder for the Soviet missiles to hit because of fratricide. Furthermore, this approach was cost-effective, requiring fewer silos and fewer missiles, and creating a system that would survive current and anticipated Soviet missile advancements. The Soviets would have to invest in technological enhancements to launch a successful surprise attack.[42]

Two weeks later, the chairman of the Joint Chiefs of Staff, US Army general John Vessey, divulged to the Senate Armed Services Committee during a hearing that three of the five service chiefs recommended against proceeding with the plan for closely spaced basing, now known informally as "dense pack," because certain "technical uncertainties" had not been resolved. The disclosure sent a shudder through the Senate, which would soon vote on the program; the House had done so a day earlier, cutting the defense budget proposal to produce only the first five missiles. Skepticism regarding the new plan was rife because of inconsistencies among experts as to whether strengthened silos would improve survivability. Secretary of State George Shultz, who had replaced Haig, went so far as to say that because of the stance of some of the Joint Chiefs of Staff on the dense pack concept, the proposal was "doomed." Nunn summed up the popular view: the administration had made a "fundamental error" in requesting funds to produce the missiles before developing a feasible basing concept.[43]

The Senate did not want to kill the program, but it needed a strong bargaining position when representatives from the two houses met in conference. The Senate leaders had to devise a compromise that would appropriate funds so Reagan could build the MX missile, but restrict spending the funds until a suitable basing system was developed. Nunn was one of the main players seeking a bipartisan compromise that both the Armed Services and Appropriations Committees could accept and that would be satisfactory to the House of Representatives as well.[44]

On December 14, Senate leaders and Reagan reached such a deal, with Reagan announcing that production of the MX missile was contingent on congressional approval of one basing method by the spring of 1983. The final days of the 97th Congress ended with catchall continuing resolutions to avoid a shutdown of the federal government. The defense appropriation was again massive—$232 billion—but $17.6 billion less than Reagan had requested. According to one source, it was "the largest reduction in a president's defense request in decades, but with the exception of the MX missile, it "left the shape of Reagan's planned buildup nearly unchanged."[45] Despite this outcome, Nunn presented a warning as Congress, after an exhausted Senate voted on the last piece of legislation, recessed on the morning of December 23. "The Reagan budget cannot buy all that the president is trying to buy even if it got every dollar."[46] His comment presaged the restrictions Nunn and the other reformers intended to impose in 1983.

CHAPTER 5

ON THE ROAD TO ARMS CONTROL

Senator William Cohen was the perfect partner for Nunn. The lean, photogenic, former college basketball player from Maine made his reputation as a member of the House of Representatives Judiciary Committee during the Watergate scandal, when he abandoned party loyalty and voted to impeach Nixon. Elected to the Senate in 1978, his colleagues judged him a thoughtful, articulate moderate, interested in defense policy as much as he was in writing poetry and novels.[1] As a member of the Armed Services Committee, he shared Nunn's concerns about the Reagan administration's inchoate defense strategy and the nuclear weapons buildup. With an ally like Cohen, Nunn now had, in addition to his bipartisan approach and the formation of the military reform caucus, another avenue to shape legislation while the Democrats remained in the minority for the Ninety-Eighth session beginning in January 1983. As Nunn remarked that month, "I have always tried to approach the national defense arena in an objective, nonpartisan manner, and I hope that I will be able to continue that for as long as I serve in the Senate."[2]

A month earlier, Cohen had approached Nunn with the idea of a build-down approach to US-Soviet arms control in which each side would destroy two nuclear warheads for every new one they deployed in any modernization program. It was not a new subject for Nunn, as the two lawmakers had chatted about such a proposal months earlier, and shared a concern that nuclear war was, ultimately, morally unacceptable because it would result in untold civilian deaths.[3]

As New Year's Day approached, Cohen wrote an op-ed to make his case to the administration and opinion shapers. It appeared in the *Washington Post* on January 3, advocating a "guaranteed arms build-down." Cohen's timing was critical, as he envisioned the proposal as a middle way between the proponents of strategic forces modernization and the nuclear freeze movement's aim of a "mutual verifiable freeze." He did not dismiss the movement contemptuously, as many opponents did; he believed it signaled citizens' genuine fears. However, he held that the movement's goal was not acceptable to the Soviets, because it required allowing the United States to conduct mandatory on-site inspections, which they had rejected historically. He agreed with the administration that a freeze would leave US land-based missile systems vulnerable, and he granted that a build-down was not a cure-all, but it would "raise the nuclear threshold to a higher, safer level" while improving the prospects of lessening tensions, and demonstrate to Americans that its leaders recognized the "peril of nuclear escalation." In short, he argued that nuclear "weapons modernization could be stabilizing and that modernization could and should be combined with nuclear arms reductions." A few hours after the op-ed appeared in the newspaper, Reagan telephoned Cohen and told him that he liked the concept and would be willing to work with him on it.[4]

Cohen met with Nunn throughout January, and in Cohen's words, "He applied his well-known skills as a military policy expert to the task of defining and structuring a legislative build-down resolution." The two men and their staffs conducted studies because they suspected the Pentagon would not be receptive to the idea. Their analysis indicated that the concept would limit the strategic nuclear forces of both sides, but equally crucial, "a plan for reductions paced by modernization could be designed to encourage deployment of stabilizing systems, such as single-warhead ICBMs, and discourage destabilizing weapons," such as multiple warhead missiles. On February 3, they introduced the build-down concept as Senate Resolution 57.[5]

Two days earlier, bipartisanship in a more turbulent form occurred when Secretary of Defense Caspar Weinberger appeared before the Senate Armed Services Committee to justify the administration's $283.6 billion defense budget for fiscal year 1984, $27.9 billion above the current fiscal year. No sooner had he completed his opening statement than members from both parties assailed him with a fusillade of questions. Tower attempted to defend

Reagan's plan, claiming Congress was "caught up in an irrational frenzy" over defense spending, especially after John W. Warner laid into Weinberger. Warner favored a 5–7 percent cut in personnel, instead of the increase the administration wanted. "Nothing is certain but death, taxes and a cut in Congress of defense spending," he replied emphatically, after Weinberger rejected any additional reductions in the Pentagon budget. Nunn, who had publicly stated the administration needed to pay attention to several critical defense issues, especially articulating a clear strategy and priorities, added, but less vehemently than Warner, that while he supported a strong military, Congress intended to trim defense spending substantially, and Weinberger should work with the committee to forestall "foolish" cuts. Democrats Carl Levin of Michigan, and Ted Kennedy, new to the committee, joined him. The former accused Weinberger of "exaggerated rhetoric" and misleading and erroneous information regarding the Soviet threat, while the latter argued with Weinberger to the point that they were talking over each other.[6] As pandemonium periodically broke out, Tower sought to regain control. Yet this hearing before a committee of military proponents suggested that, at least in the opening days, both sides intended to dissect the defense budget request and, where possible, cut it. To attain savings, strategic weapons programs appeared to be the most at risk.

Robert McFarlane, Reagan's deputy national security advisor, fretted over Weinberger's appearance. As McFarlane recalled, "Cap Weinberger's contemptuous attitude toward the Congress made his dealings with that body fractious and troublesome at times." Congress returned the favor. Defense experts in both houses believed Weinberger unqualified for the position, as he lacked the requisite knowledge of the details and seemed incapable of explaining how the president's defense programs were connected to US strategy.[7]

Paul Nitze, special adviser to the president and secretary of state on arms control in the Reagan administration, who knew he needed support from Democrats in the Senate to achieve the administration's arms control objectives, commented years later about a conversation he had with Weinberger. Nitze claimed that Weinberger "had no conception of how an executive branch handles policy and its congressional relations in a period when the opposite party is in control. . . . It is an art, but it can be done." Moreover, Weinberger considered Democrats in Congress the enemy, especially Nunn. Weinberger's position was that "Nunn doesn't understand anything about defense; he's a complete disaster on the floor. I wouldn't think of having anything to do with

Nunn." Nitze coolly noted in response, "This made handling congressional relations in the Reagan administration an almost impossible task."[8]

McFarlane knew firsthand the havoc a cabinet officer's antagonistic attitude could instigate. A former staff member of the Senate Armed Services Committee after he retired from the Marine Corps, McFarlane realized that if Nunn and Warner were calling for sizable reductions in defense spending, then the entire defense budget was in trouble. Aware of the growing force of the nuclear freeze movement, he kept abreast of Senate Resolution 57, which was gaining cosponsors, both liberals and conservatives, and from both parties.[9]

McFarlane was no fan of build-down. His tactic was to "study the plan to death," informing Nunn and Cohen that the administration's START interagency group was considering the concept, but the result was more questions. In frustration, Cohen accused McFarlane of looking for reasons to kill the idea. Cohen then played his trump card, reminding the deputy national security advisor that congressional support for the MX missile remained "eggshell thin."[10] The message was unvarnished: a squabble with Cohen and Nunn would not bode well for the impending decision on MX basing and, ultimately, funding its production.

The previous December, after the "dense pack" proposal had come under fire, Nunn told McFarlane that he believed Weinberger had not been candid in testifying that the Defense Department had comprehensively examined alternative basing modes for the MX missile. Cohen agreed with Nunn's surmise and was even more direct with McFarlane. "You had better put together a bipartisan team of respected analysts to study this issue for you in the next two months, because if the new plan is sent up here in March by Cap Weinberger, it will definitely fail." Party loyalist Tower, who thought the strengthened silo concept meant "just so many more sitting ducks for the Russians to shoot at," agreed.[11]

With congressional concerns paramount and time slipping away, McFarlane took control of managing the MX missile's future without objection from his boss, National Security Advisor William Clark, a longtime Reagan ally who also lacked national security credentials. McFarlane concluded that Cohen's suggestion about a "bipartisan team" had merit. A bipartisan presidential commission composed of renowned foreign policy experts, retired senior military officers, former members of Congress, and highly regarded scientists would be the best course. After compiling a list of proposed members and substituting Brent Scowcroft, a retired air force lieutenant general and former national security advisor to President Gerald Ford, for Henry Kissinger as the commission chair, Reagan approved the membership.[12] With Executive Order 12400, Reagan established the President's Commission on Strategic Forces, also known as the Scowcroft Commission, on January 3. The order authorized the board to "review the strategic modernization program for United States forces, with particular reference to the intercontinental ballistic system and basing alternatives for that system, and provide appropriate advice." It would present its recommendations to the president by February 18, 1983.[13] Four days later, the panel began its work, but not without controversy over its membership, which critics considered skewed in favor of Reagan's defense buildup, or concerns about the short period it had to consider an extremely complicated subject.[14]

The latter proved correct: in mid-February, the White House extended the deadline one month. Meanwhile, the press was able to obtain information about the panel's deliberations. It was reporting that a "fundamental rethinking of US nuclear weapons and strategy" was under way. Nunn offered a guarded response when asked his opinion. "We have so many strategic programs that we are pushed into more and more reliance on nuclear weapons, and we don't have enough money to fund the conventional side."[15] The president struck back when he called upon his fellow citizens to resist "the aggressive impulses of an evil empire," categorizing the nuclear freeze movement as a "very dangerous fraud."[16] He followed this tough talk with a televised briefing in which he showed charts and declassified intelligence photographs that emphasized the growing Soviet threat.[17]

A few weeks later, Nunn delivered a lecture at Georgetown University in Washington, DC, in which he responded to the hard-line stance with a well-thought-out and down-to-earth approach. In the address, he stressed that the administration's stated objective of being "able to meet demands for worldwide war" was not only unrealistic but unaffordable. He offered as an alternative a new, comprehensive military strategy that relied on conventional force improvements in the US active and reserve components, "while maintaining a nuclear deterrent," and increased defense spending by NATO allies along with a buildup in their force levels. He labeled it a matter of "keeping Russian forces in Russia." This objective entailed three actions: first, destroying the Soviet's "tenuous lines of communication" and attacking their rear echelons with "deep aerial strikes" using precision munitions; second, conducting NATO "commando" raids in the bordering Warsaw Pact countries; and last, demolishing and bottling up the Soviet navy and merchant marine worldwide, using US fleets with assistance from Japan in the northern Pacific Ocean. He added that arms control also demanded a strategy that allies and US citizens alike deemed credible and sought reductions that challenged the Soviets to reciprocate or "explain to the European public why they refuse."[18] Forty-three senators from both parties, including many influential freeze supporters such as Gary Hart, were now cosponsors of the build-down concept. Illinois Republican Charles Percy, the Foreign Relations Committee chairman, pronounced it "one of the most innovative and promising arms control proposals to be presented in the Senate in many years."[19]

Arms control had become more expansive than build-down. In late March, fifteen senators, including Nunn, Cohen, and Percy, sent a letter to Reagan advocating a sizable reduction in the number of US tactical nuclear weapons in NATO. The letter was an unambiguous response to Reagan's feeble and contradictory campaign of "hardball" tactics and organized conservative support, designed to lure defense-minded Democrats and moderate Republicans, including House members, from opposing the MX missile to finding a bipartisan compromise to save the program. Democratic representative Les Aspin thought compromise was possible. He had actually been working closely with the commission to forge such a bargain. The commission members had also consulted "Scoop" Jackson and Nunn. Jackson believed the group was fashioning a "realistic package" of proposals. He envisaged Congress supporting the MX but wanting a compromise on the number of missiles to be produced and deployed. Nunn did not dismiss a compromise, but he emphasized that unless the administration developed a new approach to arms control, any MX plan it offered would fail.[20]

Nunn's verdict mattered. Reagan officials stated on background that the Scowcroft Commission's report could presage a "new approach on strategic arms reductions." The commission report, presented to Reagan on April 6, was a compromise document. It examined Soviet military objectives, US strategic forces modernization, and numerous highly technical topics. Nonetheless, the major recommendation was that the United States should deploy the MX as a replacement for the aging Minuteman ICBM and encourage the Soviet Union to negotiate seriously over arms control. It suggested the Defense Department develop a smaller ICBM with a single warhead, the Midgetman, for future deployment. With the report in hand, Reagan informed Congress of his intentions based on the commission's recommendations. He would proceed with the immediate production of the MX missile and deployment of 100 of the missiles in existing Minuteman ICBM silos in Wyoming, which he proposed as the alternate basing plan. Additionally, the administration would begin design of a "small, single warhead ICBM," on a schedule that would make it ready for full-scale development in 1987 and possible deployment in the early 1990s. Lastly, he "reconfirmed" his commitment to "continue to pursue ambitious and objective arms reduction negotiations."[21]

The Joint Chiefs of Staff indicated their unanimous support of Reagan's proposal at a Senate Armed Services Committee hearing in late April, but their unity did not sway Nunn, who responded that he was fashioning a proposal to link deployment of the MX missile with arms control measures. Nunn believed that without such a link, many of his colleagues might not support deployment. Further, he approved of connecting deployment to Soviet behavior and favored confidence-building measures between the two superpowers. Perhaps by deploying only thirty to thirty-five missiles and promising to withhold others, the Americans might convince the Soviets to reduce their strategic arsenal. Nunn believed in a "congressional approach to arms control" to provide policy continuity. "I think it's enormously important," he stated, "for America as a nation to not change arms control positions every time it changes the Administration in power."[22]

Nunn, Cohen, and Percy remained reluctant to support MX deployment in the existing silos. They saw the administration's plan as a "bargaining chip for Congress to elicit action on other strategic issues," specifically, that the missile should become part of the build-down initiative.[23] They sent a letter to Reagan informing him that they would not vote for MX deployment unless he undertook four initiatives: modify the administration's arms control position to reflect the movement toward a single warhead missile; make an immediate start to developing a small and more mobile missile; offer the Soviets a proposal that included the "build-down concept"; and consider formation of a permanent bipartisan commission to advise on arms control and ensure policy continuity when administrations change. Nine House members from both parties sent a similar letter. The countermove got the White House's attention, and the three senators met with James Baker, the White House chief of staff, and Scowcroft to discuss in more detail a possible agreement tying their demands to support of the MX missile plan. Reagan then followed up with a meeting of his advisors, and reports indicated the administration was willing to consider the senators' requirements except for build-down.[24]

Reagan could sense that any advantage he had in the debate was eroding fast. On May 3, 1983, the US Catholic bishops released their pastoral letter on nuclear weapons, a document debated for months and one on which they had consulted with administration officials. In their lengthy and rigorous analysis, the bishops recognized decisions about nuclear weapons had political and military elements, but they also involved moral considerations: "Good ends (defending one's country, protecting freedom, etc.) cannot justify immoral means (the use of weapons which kill indiscriminately and threaten whole societies)." The media paid substantial attention to the letter, and the administration worried that its well-reasoned argument would undermine the defense buildup. While the final draft of the letter made no mention of the MX missile, some of the bishops publicly stated their opposition to the missile as destabilizing.[25]

The MX stayed under assault in Congress. The three senators' stance acquired further support among moderate and conservative Republicans who saw their proposals as a political win-win: supporting the president by voting against the freeze but also lessening US-Soviet tensions. Reagan acknowledged Percy's remark that the administration's plan for the MX "would be in jeopardy" without a change in its arms control position, and with more than forty senators now supporting the build-down resolution, the White House had no trouble counting potential votes. Reagan met with the three senators who reiterated they would not vote for the MX without a well-defined arms control strategy. Behind the scenes, Nunn and Cohen met with Baker to negotiate an agreement. The arrangement, despite Pentagon misgivings, was that Reagan would send a letter to the senators committing to the build-down concept before the Senate Appropriations Committee marked up its defense appropriations bill.[26]

On May 12, in a letter to the three senators, Reagan accepted the senators' propositions and agreed not only that "the principle of mutual build-down . . . would be a useful means to achieve the reduction we all seek," but also that his administration was actively examining how to structure such a proposal for arms reduction talks, which were scheduled for June in Geneva.[27] He sent a similar letter to the nine House members who had written him. As Cohen stated, with Reagan's response in hand, the three senators believed they had an agreement. Nunn understood the compromise as a discrete foreign policy issue shaped by circumstances, and very pragmatic: "when their ox is in the ditch, they'll turn bipartisan to get a hand in hauling it out." Regardless of interpretation, a majority of the Senate Appropriations Committee members voted to release research and development funds for the MX.[28]

A week after the committee vote, Nunn's proposal of a year earlier to reduce the possibility of unintended nuclear war by establishing risk reduction centers received Reagan's formal approval at a Rose Garden ceremony that Nunn attended. After the event, Nunn told reporters that if his proposal was implemented, it "could lead to 'crisis control' centers in both countries and could prevent terrorist groups from being the catalytic agents of a nuclear war." Later in the day, the House approved $625 million for the MX, and the Senate followed a day later, a remarkable turn of events in just five months. Presidential lobbying or flattery aside, Nunn, who voted for the funding despite his doubts about the basing plan, reminded the White House that funding to produce the MX still required congressional approval. "If something doesn't happen on arms control, they could eventually lose the MX. I'll be looking for a good-faith follow-through from the Administration." He later stated, "To be successful in arms control demands a bipartisan approach. We haven't had that for a decade, and the future of arms control is more important than any candidate or party."[29]

Now began the summer of discontent. The president and his national security team were not moving with speed to modify the US negotiating position for talks in Geneva. By early June, they had still not developed a way to include the build-down concept in the American negotiating position. Some senior officials considered it impractical but realized the need to placate Nunn and Cohen. Cohen vented his frustration months later in an op-ed, in which he accused some members of the administration of not "making a positive effort to fulfill the president's pledge."[30] The two decided to seize the initiative.

A week after the MX had its first successful flight test in June, Nunn and Cohen testified before the Senate Foreign Relations Committee on the build-down concept. They distributed to committee members a set of questions and answers designed to respond to criticisms of their scheme. As Cohen related months later, "We had hoped our efforts would be catalytic," but the administration remained silent as to whether it would adopt their plan. Instead, the director of the Arms Control and Disarmament Agency (ACDA), Kenneth Adelman, announced that the United States planned to deploy 100 MX missiles unless the Soviet Union agreed to reduce its arsenal of land-based strategic missiles. Until the Soviets agreed, the administration did not intend to scrap the MX program. Nunn and Cohen responded that the Soviets would not accept such terms, with Nunn adding, "I hope the Administration has a fall-back position. It is going to be very difficult to require the Soviets to completely change their force structure." In Nunn's view, the ACDA director's statement proved the MX was undeniably a bargaining chip. Some moderate Republicans viewed the statement as a repudiation of the deal between the executive and the Congress that had been made in May; others now doubted Reagan's seriousness about arms control.[31]

Cohen voiced his objections in writing to his Republican colleagues on the Armed Services Committee, stating that his "overriding concern has been that we [the United States] are not developing a framework which combines weapons modernization and arms control in a manner which will ultimately improve [nuclear] stability." He reiterated that he had informed the president that his support of the MX missile was contingent on the administration's good faith effort to design such a framework and, equally important, "the development and implementation of a viable build-down proposal." He ended by remarking that the build-down proposal Nunn and he had created and presented to the Senate was an "equitable, negotiable, and verifiable approach to reducing nuclear weapons on both sides." He then laid down his marker. He had no intention of permitting the proposal to become a "meaningless link in the process of procuring the MX missile." Therefore, unless there was a "clear and constructive formulation of a build-down proposal by the Administration," it could not expect his support of the MX program.[32] Nunn followed with telephone calls to McFarlane and Scowcroft, complaining about the lack of progress on the proposal; he was losing patience "shadow-boxing" with the administration.[33]

While Cohen was dismayed with the result of their initiative to gain the administration's acceptance of build-down, it could not move forward on its MX plans either. Adelman's pronouncement had created a fuss in both chambers over the future of the program, and the arms reductions talks in Geneva were going nowhere.[34] By the middle of July, as one journalist wrote, "Public attention these days tends to focus on the MX Missile and superpower arms control talks." Nunn raised the issue of the "nuclear crutch" on which NATO had depended on for years to the neglect of the alliance's conventional forces and questioned the utility of nuclear weapons for defensive purposes. NATO commander US General Bernard Rogers endorsed this position.[35] Nunn's remark signaled that the MX program was in trouble again. He was joined by liberal House members who almost scuttled funding for production of twenty-seven missiles contained in the defense authorization bill, and were powerful enough, with the backing of Majority Leader Jim Wright, to place an indefinite hold on the defense authorization bill. Wright accused Reagan of treating bipartisanship as a "one-way street." Nunn issued another warning. "Our position on the MX has a great deal to do with the arms control position of the Administration." Shortly thereafter, he argued that the administration had still not defined its military strategy. Nunn contended that the administration, with its commitment to "rearming America," needed to convince Congress that the resources it requested were consistent with its objectives and that it had defined its priorities, a point on which many Republicans agreed, outraged by reports of waste and mismanagement.[36]

Although Nunn and Cohen's arms control idea appeared moribund, two stunning events kept it on life support. On September 1, 1983, Jackson, the ranking Democrat on the Armed Services Committee, died in his hometown of Everett, Washington, of a ruptured aorta several hours after holding a press conference in downtown Seattle.[37] Jackson had held the event to condemn the Soviet Union for its purposeful downing of a South Korean airliner carrying 269 passengers, including 63 Americans, and crew when it drifted into Soviet airspace. The Soviet government claimed the airliner was on a spy mission for the United States and a deliberate provocation to test Soviet air defense capabilities. This event had the immediate impact of turning American public opinion against the USSR.[38]

Nunn, who would replace Jackson as the ranking member on the Armed Services Committee, eulogized him on the floor of the Senate, stating that his friend and mentor occupied "the front rank of leaders" in that body, and over time, he would be remembered as a great national leader.[39] Nunn admitted to the emotional impact of Jackson's death, wistfully telling a reporter a few weeks later, "What I'll miss is being able to talk to him on a day to day basis about everything. . . . The impact of his loss is not easy to comprehend."[40]

At the same time, he spoke carefully about the Soviet downing of the Korean airliner and the ensuing acrimony. He expressed concern about the manner in which the administration handled the specifics surrounding the event when it was later disclosed that a US reconnaissance plane had been in the area. A failure to ascertain the facts and to levy inaccurate charges could have grave consequences. Nuclear weapons and their destructive power were prominent in his evaluation. "There's a real obligation of leadership in a crisis, in spite of huge pressures, to try and get as complete a picture as possible before going to the world with charges, particularly in a nuclear age." He solemnly continued that line of thought. "For the first time, you've got a country that can, even by accident, destroy a huge segment of this country."[41]

Considering the heightened tension between the two superpowers,

Nunn, Percy, and Cohen believed arms control needed to be at the top of the agenda. Subsequently, they sent a letter to Scowcroft underscoring that his commission had warned in its report: "Nuclear weapons have sharply raised the stakes and changed the nature of war." In their letter, they noted that the "deplorable Soviet conduct" with respect to the destruction of the Korean airliner had made it "even more essential that President Reagan and the Congress establish a strong united front on our nation's strategic nuclear programs and arms control proposals." The letter stipulated the immediate benefits that the build-down concept would promote by reducing missile warheads by half and added a new, longer-term approach for dealing with the Soviet advantage in "overall destructive capacity" of ballistic missiles (throw-weight) and of bombers and their weapons. The press dubbed the concept "double build-down" because it dealt with reductions to two weapons systems: ballistic missile warheads and bombers.[42]

This new concept had an odd patrimony, a combination of Nunn and Cohen's build-down concept favored by the Senate; Les Aspin and Midgetman missile proponents in the House of Representatives; and the Scowcroft Commission's recommendations, especially Scowcroft's personal consultations with Nunn and Aspin, in addition to the technical expertise of two RAND Corporation analysts, retired air force officers Glenn Kent and Edward Warner, and one of Scowcroft's trusted agents on the commission, R. James Woolsey, a lawyer who had served in the Carter administration. The support of these three political forces was necessary to the Reagan administration if it was to succeed in moving forward with the MX missile and the overall defense buildup. As a result, when they banded together, the administration had no choice but to add the double build-down idea to its arms control proposals in Geneva.[43] It was an amazing outcome, in one commentator's view, "an apotheosis of congressional intervention in the executive branch's conduct of arms control policy; and it came about basically, because there was an almost complete breakdown in congressional confidence in what the Administration was doing."[44] Congress had again pressured a reluctant Reagan administration to engage earnestly in the substance of arms control.

The administration, however, believed nuclear deterrence in Western Europe remained essential because the Soviets had deployed their intermediate-range missile, the SS-20, in 1976, with the capability to target NATO capitals from within Soviet territory. In December 1979, after NATO allies expressed mounting concerns about this threat, the Carter administration and NATO had responded with what became known as the "dual-track" approach. According to US negotiators, this "decision called for US-Soviet arms control negotiations on intermediate-range nuclear forces [INF] with the goal of achieving a balance at the lowest possible levels—the 'arms control' track—while the United States prepared to deploy new INF missile systems in Europe if the negotiations did not obviate the need for that deployment—the 'deployment' track." The United States and the Soviet Union began negotiations on INF in 1981, but after several rounds, the parties could not agree on basic principles. In late 1983, Reagan and NATO leaders agreed to deploy intermediate-range missiles—the US Pershing II missile and ground-launched cruise missile (the so-called Euromissile deployments)—to counter this threat. The Soviet Union had announced previously that it would withdraw from the negotiations if such deployments commenced. The Soviets walked out of the negotiations in November 1983 as the first Pershing II deployments began in West Germany.[45]

Meanwhile, Nunn, Percy, and Cohen remained focused on arms control. The locus of arms control policy was shifting from the executive branch to Congress, using its power to authorize and appropriate, and more specifically, the Armed Services Committees in both chambers were assuming jurisdiction over the issue. They became, as one observer noted, "the central crucibles for working out congressional positions."[46]

The three senators met with three like-minded House Democrats, Les Aspin, Albert Gore of Tennessee, and Norm Dicks of Washington, to produce a comprehensive arms control package that they believed would achieve congressional consensus and that the president could send to US negotiators in Geneva. Nunn and the House members, according to a knowledgeable political pundit, had "stepped into a foreign policy vacuum left by Reagan's inability to move Congress."[47] This "gang of six" thought the Soviets would have no recourse but to negotiate an arms reduction, given this united American stance. They also wanted to give US negotiators sufficient flexibility, so they used the Scowcroft Commission recommendations and incorporated the double build-down concept as part of the agreement. To attain White House backing, they met with Scowcroft and Clark to work out details and, ultimately, to meet and present the results to Reagan. The meeting occurred on October 3, with the president informing them, after some last-minute dickering over the language in the instructions to the US negotiators, that he endorsed their plan, including double build-down, and that it would be proposed in the next round of strategic arms reductions talks scheduled to begin in a few days.[48] Aspin lightheartedly referred to the agreement as the

"Magna Carta," but he and the other five were genuinely serious when they left the Situation Room in the White House to meet with the media on the White House grounds. They each stepped up to the microphones and expressed their satisfaction with the "bipartisan consensus" that had been at long last attained, and remarked that Reagan now had the foundation of an arms control agreement the Senate could accept in its constitutional role of advice and consent.[49]

The cordial meeting and public statements belied the hard bargaining that had gone on for several days between the lawmakers and White House staff, with one presidential aide presenting an ultimatum that led Cohen to state that he would join the opposition if the discussions were over. At another point of friction, Nunn reminded Clark that he and his allies had the votes and could lend the administration support if it would accept the legislators' three-part plan. In addition to a pledge to pursue double build-down, the lawmakers wanted the administration to advance the single-warhead Midgetman and reduce the number of multi-warhead missiles. They also wanted the United States to make concessions in areas where it had an advantage, namely, strategic bombers that carried cruise missiles with nuclear warheads. They asserted that the administration's demand that the Soviets make all the concessions was absurd; no progress could be made in the talks under that condition. The administration would have to offer realistic compromises in areas where the United States had the lead. Lastly, they compelled the administration to add R. James Woolsey, whom the legislators trusted, to the negotiating team to ensure that the build-down proposal was precisely presented to the Soviet and conscientiously addressed in the talks.[50]

Reagan and three of his politically attuned White House aides, James Baker, Staff Secretary Richard Darman, and Kenneth Duberstein, the head of the White House's congressional affairs office, had made their own political calculations, despite objections to the congressional proposal from the Defense Department. They recognized that the members of the gang of six were influential in their respective chambers, thereby increasing the probability of funds being appropriated for the MX missile when it came up for a vote in a few weeks. The White House also knew that the gang of six could hold the missile program hostage. Aside from appeasing Congress on arms control, Shultz and others who supported the congressional proposal convinced Reagan that the administration had demonstrated its mettle by promoting a strong defense, and could now negotiate from a position of strength. With these factors in play, the gang of six had carried out their constitutional responsibility as legislators to reflect public opinion on the issue. Additionally, by their actions, they had also established a major precedent, according to one knowledgeable US official: "growing congressional involvement in the details of U.S. arms control proposals."[51]

While the Soviet reaction was unknown, Reagan held a Rose Garden press conference on October 4 to make his views clear to the Kremlin. With the television cameras capturing his remarks, he told reporters he was sending US chief negotiator Ambassador Edward Rowny to Geneva with a set of proposals that included "building down ballistic warheads and . . . addressing a parallel build-down on bombers." Reagan acknowledged there would have to be "trade-offs," which the United States was prepared to make provided it resulted in "a more stable balance of forces." Now, in this fifth round of talks, the time for Soviet "stonewalling" of US proposals was over, he declared. "The Soviet Union must start negotiating in good faith."[52]

Not every arms control expert or constituent found the proposal favorable, a complaint that Nunn answered head-on in an October op-ed. He defined what was meant by stability: "a condition in which neither side had any incentive to strike first." The most destabilizing nuclear systems were the land-based missiles with multiple warheads that were now susceptible to preemptive attack, an enemy first strike. The build-down concept created "incentives for each side to build" a force consisting of small, mobile ICBMs with a single warhead, because they are more difficult to target and "because two such warheads would be needed to knock out one of the adversary's warheads." Consequently, there would be no incentive to launch a first strike. He contended that if the Soviets agreed to this approach, it would stabilize the nuclear balance, "moving the world a step away from a hair trigger on both sides." The "double build-down," the new part of the proposal, would add to the stability by reducing the destructive power of both sides: the greater destructive power of the Soviets' larger missiles and the American advantage in bomber capability. The formula he, Percy, and Cohen had devised made it possible to accomplish this goal by removing what had become a key impediment to an accord. He finished by saluting the worthy aims of the "nuclear freeze" concept, but it only served to "freeze us into the current, highly unstable balance." Instead, the burden was now on the Soviets to "demonstrate . . . whether or not they are in favor of reaching a fair, equitable, and verifiable agreement that is in the interests of all mankind."[53] In the end, Reagan got his MX missile program, but at the cost of modifying the US negotiating position, which the gang of six demanded in return for their support of the initial production of the missile in the defense appropriations bill. Congress appropriated $2.1 billion for production of the first twenty-one missiles and $2 billion for continued development of the weapon.[54]

As 1983 wound to its end, Nunn turned his attention to another aspect of arms control. He had been working with Warner to refine the idea of "nuclear risk reduction centers" in Washington and Moscow by establishing a working group under their cochairmanship. The group's assessment, an enhancement of the previous Strategic Air Command study, found that the possibility of a third party prompting a full-blown nuclear exchange between the superpowers by accident or miscalculation was distressingly likely, especially if a weapon fell into the hands of a "rogue state or terrorists." The study served to confirm Nunn's belief that the two superpowers could "stumble into accidental nuclear war."[55]

On November 23, Nunn and Warner sent a letter and the working group's report, which they made public, to Reagan, informing him of the results. The report warned that there now existed "an increasing number of scenarios that could precipitate the outbreak of nuclear war that neither side anticipated or intended, possibly involving other nuclear powers or terrorist groups." Establishing the risk reduction centers, staffed by military officers and civilian specialists on duty twenty-four hours a day, with a high-speed communications link between military and political sites in the two capitals, would augment the current teletype "hot line" that only linked the White House and the Kremlin. This report recommended authorization for the military command centers of the two nations to communicate directly, which the current agreement did not allow. Nunn and Warner met with McFarlane to seal the agreement. Afterward, Nunn told reporters that the negotiations on the proposed centers needed to be separate from other arms control efforts. He recognized the challenge ahead: the "negotiations [between the United States and the USSR] would probably be long."[56] His prognosis proved prescient.

Nonetheless, opinion writers and pundits applauded Nunn's several initiatives to reduce the risk of nuclear war. As one noted analyst affirmed, "With the passing of Senator Henry Jackson, the commodore of the loyal defense opposition is now Senator Sam Nunn—whose high reputation assures his access to good counsel on strategic matters."[57] While his proposals on "strategic matters" may have been "unglamorous," they were practical ideas, needed at a time when the public's awareness of the nuclear peril and wishes for a safer world free from extinction intensified. Only three days before Nunn and Warner released their study, the ABC television network aired the movie *The Day After*, a fictional account of a nuclear war between the United States and the Soviet Union that 100 million Americans watched. Nuclear war was no longer a subject Americans or their NATO counterparts could avoid. Tensions were building as the administration continued its hard line to negotiate from a position of military strength. The Bundestag voted to accept deployment of the Pershing II missiles on West German territory the day Nunn and Warner released their study findings. The first nuclear-capable cruise missiles arrived in Great Britain as well, marking the beginning of NATO's intermediate-range nuclear forces deployment. In response, the Soviet Union walked out of the INF talks and, a week later, broke off the START negotiations without indicating a date for their resumption. Soon after, NATO–Warsaw Pact negotiations on Mutual and Balanced Force Reductions, which had begun in Vienna in October 1973, a decade earlier, adjourned. As 1984 approached, the *Bulletin of the Atomic Scientists'* Science and Security Board would move the minute hand of its "Doomsday Clock" to three minutes to midnight, a metaphor for how close the world was to destroying itself with nuclear weapons: the closest to midnight the clock had been since the board's response to the introduction of the hydrogen bomb in 1953.[58]

CHAPTER 6

REDUCING RISKS, SHARING BURDENS

President Reagan remained committed to strategic force modernization and nuclear deterrence despite any setbacks his administration suffered in the first three years of his presidency. He believed that existing government studies, which the defense community had initiated at his direction in early 1983, indicated that a "defense against missile attack might eventually be developed" to augment offensive deterrence but also, crucially, to reduce the risk of nuclear war. On January 6, 1984, nearly ten months after his nationally televised address in which he proposed the development of technology to intercept enemy nuclear missiles, he signed his name to a secret document titled "Strategic Defense Initiative" (SDI). It directed inclusion of the initiative in the fiscal year 1985 defense budget request. Additionally, he ordered that statements regarding the proposed program "should be low key and closely coordinated to ensure that an accurate picture of the nature and scope of this R&D [research and development] effort is presented to the public." Dubbed "Star Wars" by critics in Congress who thought the concept technologically infeasible, SDI would use space-based lasers and other systems to locate, track, intercept, and destroy missiles as they hurtled toward the United States.[1] Reagan intended to make good on this program.

With the new congressional session underway, Nunn, who was running for reelection, fixed his attention on the administration's defense budget request. Nuclear weapons would certainly be of continued concern because of the cost involved, including $250 million the president wanted as a SDI "down payment."[2] When Secretary of Defense Caspar Weinberger testified before the Senate Armed Services Committee regarding the $264.4 billion defense budget request, he informed them that the growth in defense spending could be slowed in fiscal year 1986, provided Congress funded the sizable increase—a 14.5 percent increase over defense spending in the current fiscal year, not adjusting for inflation—that the president wanted in fiscal year 1985. Nunn scoffed at the notion of increased spending, telling the secretary that congressional sentiment indicated otherwise. The cuts made last year would continue, a position that his Democratic colleagues echoed, with Ted Kennedy calling the request "basically irresponsible," and Carl Levin stating that the budget was "being sold to Congress with one-sided charts, misleading, exaggerated, and contradictory statements." Weinberger parried these criticisms with this feeble response: "everyone wants strong defense; nobody wants a strong defense budget."[3]

By March, the battle over the defense budget was raging, with the Armed Services Committee grilling administration witnesses on the cost of SDI. Fred Iklé, the under secretary of defense for policy, told the senators that the high-technology system was needed because the Soviet Union was almost ten years ahead in building a similar system. But Richard DeLaurer, the defense official responsible for research and engineering, could only point to Soviet rocket payload capabilities as the basis for this line of reasoning. The officials conceded the program might not be able to offer the public a "high degree of protection against nuclear missiles," as Reagan had implied. Nonetheless, they contended the system, with a cost of $24 billion over five years, would offer sufficient survival of US missiles to enhance deterrence. Nunn pounded the witnesses on the issue of "population protection," the major point Reagan had stated whereby the protective shield would be so effective it would eventually render "offensive nuclear weapons impotent and obsolete." When he noted that this expectation did not appear in their written statements or testimony, he could only conclude that the technical reality did not match the rhetoric.[4] The admission that the Defense Department had no "silver, gold or platinum bullet" meant that some in the agency wanted to proceed slowly and not oversell the program, but formulate realistic development goals since current knowledge of technical capabilities continued to be "inadequate" and likely remain so into the next decade. Other Pentagon officials admitted confidentially that Reagan's promise of public protection was not likely until the twenty-first century; it was a state-of-the-art project.[5]

Not everyone agreed with the modest approach. A month later, SDI program director and air force lieutenant general James Abrahamson expressed a different outlook. In his first appearance on Capitol Hill, he told the Senate Subcommittee on Strategic and Theater Forces that he envisioned the initiative as having two aspects. It would protect NATO allies from short-range Soviet missiles and the United States against ICBM attacks. Nunn, who was present at the hearing as the committee's ranking member, found his technical argument unconvincing, observing that the general's views exceeded any objectives presented before the Armed Services Committee by other administration officials.[6]

The colossal cost of SDI was also a major concern: 16 percent of the Pentagon's research and development budget by 1989, as Nunn and Representative Les Aspin pointed out, coming at a time when fears about the size of the budget deficit, a slack economy, and rising interest rates troubled many constituents. The struggle over defense spending became a game of chicken between the two branches in early May when Weinberger presented the administration's revised defense budget plan consistent with the three-year deficit reduction plan Reagan and Republican congressional leaders had worked out in March. The deal cut the original request by $13.9 billion, slowing the rate of growth from 13 percent above inflation to 7.8 percent. Aspin stated emphatically that the reduction was insufficient and Congress would slash it further. In response, Reagan sent a letter to Howard Baker that any further reductions were unacceptable, as they would undermine US security interests. He threatened a veto. Aspin derided the intimidation attempt. Nunn was equally undeterred. Congress was looking for substantial decreases, Nunn remarked, an increase of 3 to 5 percent above inflation. To achieve the goal, he predicted the House would kill the MX missile program and the Senate would probably cut it back further. The administration was overinvesting in strategic weapons at the expense of conventional forces, but more importantly, he remained concerned that US military strategy was becoming excessively reliant on nuclear weapons to deter a Warsaw Pact attack.[7] It only heightened the likelihood of nuclear war between the two superpowers by eroding the readiness and sustainability of conventional forces.

John Tower saw the probability of further defense reductions in starker terms; it would damage America's credibility worldwide. Yet, he could not easily dismiss Nunn's argument, because Pentagon reports indicated Nunn was correct about the deterioration of US conventional capability. Consequently, the two agreed that the Defense Department should provide the committee with a report on the preparedness of conventional forces. The report, delivered in mid-May, stated that increased defense spending had resulted in increased capability but additional efforts were still needed. Tower told the press that the report indicated conclusively that capability has increased because of the renewed commitment to defense funding.[8]

Nunn waited patiently and then initiated his assault on the defense budget when debate on the defense authorization bill began in June, after the House had passed its version authorizing $207 billion, $6.5 billion less than the Senate bill. With the Democratic primaries completed and Walter Mondale as its presidential nominee, the party was still sorting out its foreign policy platform, but Nunn was under no such constraints. He broadened the debate in the Senate to arms control. He and other congressional Democrats thought the president's stance might make some Republicans politically vulnerable in the election year. Baker and Charles Percy had the same outlook. The senators appealed to Reagan for regular summit meetings to ease tensions, which the White House rebuffed. The House, dissatisfied by the lack of progress in arms control, had passed its version of the fiscal year 1985 defense authorization bill that restricted MX production to fifteen missiles instead of the forty the administration requested in its fiscal year 1985 defense budget proposal, delayed the Pentagon from beginning production for six months, and authorized spending only if the Soviets did not return to arms control talks in Geneva. Meanwhile, Nunn was working with others to use the Senate version of the authorization bill as the vehicle to reduce the planned deployment of the MX, limit SDI funding, and pass a nonbinding resolution urging Reagan to continue to observe the provisions of the SALT II agreement.[9]

On June 15, Nunn added further to the debate when he spoke in support of S.R. 329, a resolution that he and Warner had fashioned, supporting the establishment of nuclear risk reduction centers. Although they had introduced the resolution in February, momentum in favor of the resolution had been building since early April when Nunn and Warner, together with two members of the working group, testified at a hearing before the Senate Foreign Relations Committee. Percy, the committee chairman, was an avid proponent and a cosponsor of the resolution. The concept had even garnered the State Department's backing the day before the hearing.[10] Now others enthusiastically agreed with Nunn and Warner's goal. With thirty-one cosponsors from both parties, the Senate voted 82 to 0 to approve an amendment to the fiscal year 1985 defense authorization bill incorporating the language of the resolution. Subsequently, in conference with the House, the provision was approved and enacted into law. These final steps underscored the bipartisan spirit on the Hill regarding nuclear weapons, giving credence to Les Aspin's declaration, "This is an arms control year."[11] Nunn and Warner's initiative was another important step in this respect, one that Nunn had been shepherding for three years. However, Nunn caught many of his colleagues and the Reagan administration by surprise a few days later, on June 20, adding another element to the deliberations on the defense authorization bill that no one saw coming. This time he focused on conventional force capability.

"It's shape up or ship out time for NATO," Nunn announced on the Senate floor during continuing debate on the bill. He then began a scorching assault on the alliance's combat readiness, addressing his amendment to compel the allies to increase their contributions to the defense of Western Europe. The message he intended to send the allies was clear. The amendment established a permanent ceiling on US forces at 326,414 personnel. Further, it called for a reduction in the US troop strength by 30,000 annually for three years starting in 1987, unless the allies met one of two conditions: increase defense spending to achieve the alliance's agreed-upon 3 percent goal or meet three other objectives related to improving conventional capabilities that the secretary of defense would have to certify, such as moving toward having a thirty-day supply of munitions in storage, "increasing the number of minimum essential and emergency operating facilities and semi-hardened aircraft shelters" for US fighter airplanes deploying to Western Europe, and making improvements in NATO conventional forces to widen the time between a Soviet attack on a NATO country and the NATO supreme commander's request for the "release and use of nuclear weapons." The magnitude of the troop reductions would be tied to how many of these stipulations were met. If all three were met, then there would be no troop reductions.[12]

Tower rose in opposition, indicating that while the United States was not satisfied with the current level of NATO defense spending, with most member states failing to achieve the alliance's goal of a 3 percent increase in real growth (after inflation), Nunn's "burden-sharing" amendment would only damage relations. While that claim had merit, Nunn's colleagues could not dispute the validity of his argument when he informed them that the United States contributed $90 billion yearly for US forces in Europe, with the additional commitment of reinforcements, which cost another $80 billion, while all the allies combined spent approximately $100 billion. Nunn labeled the allies as "unprepared to fight" while the US taxpayer spent billions to defend them. He quoted US general Bernard Rogers, commander of NATO forces, as saying that the weakness of NATO's conventional forces increased the probability of a nuclear exchange. In essence, Nunn stated, following this line of reasoning, if NATO could not muster a viable non-nuclear defense of Western Europe from Soviet invasion, then NATO conventional forces were no more than a "tripwire" whose annihilation would set off a US nuclear attack to counter the Soviet offensive.[13]

Beyond the military element, Nunn's argument held additional sway with some Republican members for another reason: the principal cosponsor of the amendment was Delaware senator William Roth, a leading fiscal conservative. Roth had recently returned from Luxembourg, where he met with NATO parliamentarians who told him nothing more could be done to improve the alliance's conventional defenses, a contention Roth found infuriating. During the debate, he emphasized the fiscal conservatives' position: US citizens would not "spend large amounts of U.S. tax revenues for the defense of Western Europe if Europe itself is not willing to join in the effort."[14]

With the Reagan defense budget increases, the funding discrepancy between the United States and its allies was becoming conspicuous. The US defense budget was growing in real terms at a rate almost twice as fast as the level agreed to by NATO members; few of the European governments were meeting their promised amount of 3 percent of gross domestic product. As Roth learned firsthand, they were ignoring their collective commitment, or as some governments argued, they were providing support in-kind, a flawed position as the pledge had been to meet direct spending goals for defense.[15]

The increased US spending on defense was also contributing to a budget deficit, another concern of both Republicans and Democrats. Liberal Democrats were equally upset because they feared that assuming an even larger portion of the NATO costs would reallocate funds from the social welfare programs they favored to defense.[16] With Roth's backing, sixteen cosponsors and the Senate's Democratic Caucus, the White House projected Nunn might have enough votes to get his amendment passed.[17] The argument was not over a small amount of money. One estimator determined that NATO's five-year conventional budget totaled nearly $1.4 trillion.[18]

Nunn's decision to make an issue of NATO's conventional capability was not the result of idle thought, hardly the mode of operation for a member who prided himself on knowing "concepts and details." He had articulated his concern on the subject for more than two years. In early 1984,

David Abshire, the US Ambassador to NATO, warned his NATO colleagues of Nunn's determination to motivate the allies to act. He knew Nunn and his staff had been working on various drafts of the amendment for weeks. Abshire believed Nunn's amendment would spur the allies into needed action but urged him to offer the amendment, not ask for a vote. Abshire told Nunn that NATO was reexamining its conventional shortfalls and attitudes in NATO capitals were changing. Additionally, Lord Peter Carrington, the new NATO secretary-general, was coming on board in June and needed time to get established. It would be unfair to present him with a potential time bomb. Nunn offered that he was helping Abshire sell the upgrade in conventional capability and asked if he would be willing to submit a letter for the record that declared the allies had now changed their position on conventional defense capabilities. Abshire demurred. Now, Abshire viewed passage of the amendment "disastrous" for the alliance and urged the few Republican senators he knew to fight to defeat Nunn's proposal. He would later characterize the event as "perhaps the most delicate time in NATO history since the French withdrawal from the military command."[19]

Reagan, recognizing the power and validity of Nunn's argument and with Senate Republican leaders ostensibly unable to rally an ample number of their members to defeat the amendment, weighed in personally. He telephoned Nunn to argue against the amendment. Secretary of State George Shultz lunched with Republican senators and warned that the amendment would result in an unnecessary strain in NATO relations, and Weinberger seconded that belief in personal appeals. Republican leaders, now on the defense, began to fashion an alternate, less damaging amendment that would meet the intent of the Nunn-Roth amendment, but not include a reduction in force size. Nunn responded to press inquiries on a potential modification by remarking he was not averse to compromise; he believed the likely outcome would be rejection of the amendment.[20]

He was right. Reagan's intense lobbying and pleas from NATO leaders led to the amendment's defeat by a vote of 55 to 41 after six hours of debate. Vice President George H. W. Bush presided over the vote in case of a tie because Senate Republicans were unsure of the outcome. The debate became heated at times. Tower asserted that the amendment would "kick our friends in the teeth. It would embarrass," he roared, "the Margaret Thatchers and the Helmut Kohls of the world" who had endured bruising battles in their own countries to support deployment of US Pershing and cruise missiles and withstand a Soviet propaganda campaign. He became so exercised in his exuberance that he stepped out from behind his desk on the floor to "deliver a kick in the air," while exclaiming, "Zap! Take that!"[21] In the end, other than Roth, only three Republicans voted for Nunn's measure; on the Democratic side, six senators voted against, likely considering it an unnecessary slap at the allies. Other Nunn critics found his stance perplexing, some condemning him as a "neo-isolationist," an accusation most found laughable given his staunch support of the alliance in the past.[22]

Nunn had made his point. William Cohen went so far as to state that "when it comes to rattling cages, the Senator from Georgia has already rattled cages" and he had "sent a message to the European alliance." Cohen then proposed an alternative amendment. After Reagan personally called Republicans, the Senate, on a 94 to 3 vote, agreed to the Republican leaders' compromise language, offered by Cohen, that froze US forces at next year's levels unless the secretary of defense certified that NATO allied had "undertaken significant measures" to achieve the goals that Nunn specified in his amendment. The amendment made no mention of US troop reductions, striking the language many senators saw as punitive at a time when the United States was deploying intermediate-range nuclear missiles to Europe. Nunn urged his supporters to vote in favor of Cohen's amendment, as it was better than not achieving any prodding of the allies, but he vowed to continue to offer his amendment on other bills, in this session or the next, until the allies met their commitment. Roth, with Defense Department statistics backing him and Nunn up, added that their amendment "ought to give NATO allies a strong signal that they've got to do more." Even Tower, who would be retiring from the Senate at the end of the session, admitted that the debate and vote alerted the allies that the United States expected improvements; it just did not "need harsh measures to obtain them."[23] As one veteran Capitol Hill watcher observed, likening the floor debate to a heavyweight prize fight: Nunn may have lost a "round," but he had initiated a genuine examination of the issue.[24]

Nunn had help. The issue did not recede quietly. American commentators would not let it, and for weeks the subject occupied the media. Many applauded his amendment; recognizing it as his own particular stamp on US foreign policy. Robert Bowie, a Harvard professor who had served in high-level positions with the State Department and Central Intelligence Agency during the Eisenhower, Johnson, and Carter administrations, viewed Nunn's proposal as a tool for sparking discussion of NATO beyond the burden-sharing equation. While he favored Cohen's alternative, he, like Nunn, found troubling the "heavy reliance on the early use of nuclear weapons to stop a non-nuclear attack." NATO's feeble conventional forces, incapable of carrying on sustained combat, posed a bleak choice—defeat or a resort to nuclear weapons. NATO, Bowie emphasized, urgently needed to improve its conventional capability and shore up NATO's war-fighting strategy.[25]

Editorial writers chimed in. One erudite columnist viewed Nunn as a "latter-day Archimedes" and NATO as an *Ostomachion,* a dissection puzzle, in which the senator was moving a crucial piece of the Atlantic world, using the amendment to force the alliance to meet its fair share of a credible conventional defense to preclude the choice of either surrendering or using nuclear weapons should the Soviets attack and overrun NATO forces. Another viewed the intense lobbying effort as a sign that the issue had embarrassed the Reagan administration after the president had celebrated NATO solidarity at the fortieth anniversary of the Normandy invasion only two weeks earlier. Yet another pointed to the gravity of Nunn's intent. By offering his amendment, the senator had highlighted how important he considered the alliance to US interests and how much he wanted "a military strategy that defends and a political connection that will last." Abshire took issue with that point publicly: NATO had a grand strategy that it was adjusting to the "realities of the 1980s."[26]

Allied leaders could not let the matter rest either. There was genuine anger along with relief, but the focus remained on burden sharing and not the vexing problems of conventional force readiness and the implications of a lowered nuclear threshold. West German defense minister Manfred Wörner, during a visit to Washington in July, took a verbal swing at Nunn, calling the initiative a threat that was "counterproductive," and stating emphatically that the Europeans had assumed "their fair share of the burden." He argued that his country had certainly done so. British leaders asserted the same, and their government, with those of West Germany and Italy as well as NATO officials, had campaigned to defeat Nunn's amendment.[27]

Prominent British defense analysts sided with Nunn, and corroborated the urgency of his concerns despite their government's claims to the contrary.[28] One praised Nunn's amendment as a "shrewd tactical move and as a genuine expression of a sense of grievance with the Allies."[29] It also served as a warning shot aimed at West Germany, which needed to make a larger investment in facilities infrastructure as it had vowed. Lastly, it pressed the allies toward the US position that NATO's military strategy could not rely on US forces to fight alone after its allies had run out of ammunition and supplies, while simultaneously attaining a more evenhanded distribution of the burden-sharing arrangement. Nunn's concern about the escalation from conventional to nuclear weapons was "deeply held and of long standing," but mild nudges had not worked to strengthen conventional deterrence, especially as Warsaw Pact conventional capabilities were increasing while many US military officers and analysts believed NATO's once reliable "technological and qualitative edge" was diminishing. The conventional balance already favored the Warsaw Pact, which had a substantial advantage in weaponry and troops, a massive force of about 1 million personnel compared to NATO's 750,000. Therefore, having flexibility in responding to an attack and reducing the probability of nuclear war between the superpowers were worthwhile political and military objectives, made more likely by credible conventional forces. Now, harsher steps were essential and "legitimate."[30]

Lord Carrington, from his new perch as secretary-general, realized he needed to reduce the rhetorical heat on both sides of the debate. Calm rather than threats became his object. That scarce commodity, political capital, should not be wasted over arguments one way or another, no matter how sophisticated the analysis or the rationale advanced. While Carrington did not agree with Nunn's approach, he unquestionably understood his goal.[31]

Even though Nunn's amendment had not been passed, his supporters in the Senate, including Republicans, would not give in. Ted Stevens, whom Reagan had pressured to vote against the Nunn-Roth amendment, shared Nunn's exasperation. He would ensure the Senate Appropriations Committee report on the fiscal year 1985 defense appropriations included language holding the US Air Force manning levels in NATO at 1984 levels, a small gesture of defiance aimed at the White House. Additionally, in late July, the press learned through a leak that Stevens had commissioned a classified General Accounting Office (GAO) analysis in 1982 of how much the United States was spending on the defense of NATO. The answer was that $122 billion, or 56 percent, of the US defense budget was spent on US forces in Europe, reinforcements from the United States should war occur, and a portion of US strategic nuclear forces.[32]

The study and a recent Defense Department report on US spending in support of NATO only renewed attention to the issue. Not content to let NATO allies be the sole target of his concerns, Nunn used the reports and a GAO study he requested to highlight deficiencies in US combat readiness, to underscore that after a 40 percent increase in the defense budget over the past four years, the Defense Department had not made readiness or the ability to sustain its military forces a priority, but had instead overemphasized expensive new weapon systems. Priorities needed to change, he stressed, to ensure balance between the two major pillars of national defense.[33] This changed tack did not comfort NATO leaders. Still worried about the implications of the Nunn-Roth amendment, representatives from seven member states met in Paris to discuss measures to bolster defense cooperation. However, the drumbeat accusing NATO of not making an adequate contribution continued in the US press well into September.[34]

Cohen's amendment was gaining support in the House as a conference committee wrestled to fashion a final authorization bill in an election year. Nunn took aim at a deal Aspin was attempting to work out with the White House that essentially cut out the Senate. In a stinging floor speech he stated that the culprit was the MX missile and the "victim" was "the national security of this country and the tax-paying citizens who support it." Tower and Aspin could not reach an agreement in conference, and Nunn considered the chance of final action on an authorization bill before Congress adjourned doubtful. Additionally, the defense appropriations bill was hung up in the House Appropriations Committee. By mid-August, the outcome remained indeterminate as the Republican National Convention and Labor Day approached. A continuing resolution was a potential temporary solution, but many Capitol Hill observers thought that an uncommon step in the absence of authorization and appropriations bills. Stevens believed passage of an authorization bill after the Labor Day recess remained realistic, and voiced his opposition to a continuing resolution or a lame duck session. He viewed the problem of passing the authorization bill as an election year nuisance, with the House taking a particularly strident and partisan position on the MX missile.[35]

Stevens proved prescient, but it took the personal intervention of House speaker Thomas P. O'Neill, a Massachusetts Democrat, and Howard Baker to resolve the deadlock on a defense authorization bill. The Baker-O'Neill agreement resolved the MX issue, postponing a decision on the weapon system until March of the next year. Under the terms of the agreement, and specified in both the authorization and appropriations bills, Congress had to pass two resolutions approving production of twenty-one missiles before any funds could be spent. In response to this deal, Nunn claimed that the MX missile was not dead, but it would be a sticking point in the next session. He stated that his vote on the MX missile next year would likely depend on the administration's progress on arms control negotiations. As to conventional force capability, the examination of US and NATO readiness continued. Analysts found Nunn's contention that readiness was suffering to be correct and that the cost of big-ticket, high-technology weapon systems was not only driving the defense budget, but in the words of a former defense official, the United States now had "a big modern fighting force that can fight for a week." The fiscal year 1985 authorization act did not ignore those congressional concerns. Cohen's amendment, which was part of the conference report, required the secretary of defense to continue to submit annual reports on US expenditures for NATO and information on allied improvements and contributions to the alliance, as had been required since the fiscal year 1981 Defense Authorization Act. Congress would continue to scrutinize whether the allies were living up to their previous pledges to maintain the viability of the alliance. Nunn had successfully moved NATO burden sharing to the top of the legislative agenda.[36] On October 19, Reagan signed the fiscal year 1985 Defense Authorization Act into law.[37]

Three weeks later, on November 6, the voters of Georgia, 1.7 million of them, reelected Nunn to a third term in the Senate. He had the endorsements of Senator Mack Mattingly and Congressman Newt Gingrich, the only Republicans in Congress from Georgia. Republican Party leaders in Georgia admitted the futility of running against Nunn. They did not want to spend time and money on a sacrificial candidate. Their position was sensible. Nunn won nearly 80 percent of the vote over his Republican challenger. He carried every county in the state, and his vote total was decisive. For every vote that went to his opponent, four votes went to Nunn. He even offered his supporters a pro rata refund on their contributions to his campaign because he had spent about a third of what he raised.[38] Georgia voters sent Nunn back to Washington confident that his constituents were pleased with his performance. In the presidential contest, however, voters overwhelmingly reelected Reagan with electoral victories in forty-nine states, except for Mondale's home state. Nunn had not endorsed or campaigned for the party's presidential nominee, saying that "the people of Georgia don't need my help in choosing the next president." Despite Reagan spending the week before the election campaigning for Senate Republican candidates, his dramatic win did not translate into a wider margin for his party in the Senate. The Republicans lost two seats; their margin had now shrunk to six. With the Democrats retaining a wide margin in the House of Representatives, Reagan still had to govern with a divided Congress.[39]

Across the Atlantic Ocean, Carrington referred to Nunn's amendment in a speech given to NATO legislators, urging them to build up conventional capabilities to become less reliant on nuclear weapons. Carrington's warning was prompted by his fear that Nunn would revive his amendment and that effort, if successful, would result in a NATO crisis. Roth, who was present as the newly elected vice chairman of the military committee of the NATO Interparliamentary Assembly, left Brussels noting that European colleagues were more positive regarding Carrington's message, but talk was cheap. West German chancellor Helmut Kohl and his advisors, however, had come to the same conclusion as Nunn and Roth. Kohl believed in the criticality of the US nuclear "umbrella," known as extended deterrence, as a hedge against a conventional showdown with the Soviets, but realistically, he also knew that extended deterrence remained viable only if the nuclear threshold was high enough to placate the United States. The German government's understanding of this need for balance between nuclear and conventional capabilities carried over a month later during a visit by Kohl with Reagan at the White House. In a joint communiqué, the leaders stated they would work to strengthen NATO's conventional forces, calling it a "German initiative" rather than an American one to make it appear less heavy-handed, and to reduce the risk of using nuclear weapons. They affirmed that the two nations, working with other NATO members, would seek an arms control agreement with Moscow when talks resumed in January in Geneva. Off the record, a senior administration official noted that Nunn's push to for NATO to improve conventional forces or risk a cutback in the US presence was a catalyst for the language in the joint statement.[40] General Rogers was more blatant, confessing that Nunn as a steadfast champion of NATO "got their attention."[41]

It may have taken a potential crisis in the alliance and US complaints, but in December 1984, the NATO defense ministers agreed to spend $7.85 billion over six years to improve conventional defenses by upgrading a variety of facilities, purchasing advanced weapons, and increasing ammunition stocks to sustain forces for a month. These were the "warstopper" deficiencies Nunn noted; NATO leaders' unease that Nunn would reintroduce what they called his "bad" amendment in the next session of Congress lingered. European officials admitted, "The impact of Nunn's initiative was important because he is widely regarded as a firm supporter of the NATO alliance." They pointed out that Carrington's leadership and the planned funding were tangible demonstrations to America that Europeans were committed to the defense of Western Europe and their treaty obligations. Roth characterized the agreement as an important step and commended Carrington for teaching the "European allies the facts of American political life."[42] Nunn made no comment. He did not have to—NATO had met his demands.

CHAPTER 7

SAM NUNN'S MX MISSILE

Nunn promised that while the MX missile might not be dead, it would be the subject of intense scrutiny. The White House took his promise seriously. One day after the 99th Congress convened its first session, Reagan and Robert McFarlane met with a bipartisan group of congressional leaders, including Nunn. The purpose was to discuss the Pentagon's fiscal year 1986 budget and to make the case for $26 billion in research funding for the Strategic Defense Initiative (SDI), a program Reagan considered "a legitimate subject for research." For his part, McFarlane, now the national security advisor, told the members that the defense buildup and the administration's decision to build the MX missile had prompted the Soviet Union to discuss the possibility of reengaging in arms control talks that they had broken off in 1983. Secretary of State George Shultz would be leaving to meet with Soviet foreign minister Andrei Gromyko in Geneva that evening. The atmosphere after the Oval Office meeting was optimistic. The new Senate majority leader, Kansas Republican Robert Dole, and Robert Byrd, the minority leader, believed, however, that in the current political environment arms control required deeper Senate oversight. One element that was not covered was a novel proposal that Dole and Byrd had fashioned: "a more regular and systematic involvement of the full Senate in the negotiations."[1]

A month earlier Dole, as majority leader–elect, had decided to introduce a resolution that would stress the Senate's deep-seated support for Reagan's arms control efforts. He intended it to be the first substantive act of his leadership by introducing the resolution on the first day of the new Congress, January 3, 1985. Dole reached out to Byrd to obtain Democratic involvement. Byrd, meanwhile, had been working on the formation of a Senate arms control observer group. He had spoken with Reagan about a small, bipartisan delegation of senators being appointed as official observers to any arms control talks that might result from the Shultz-Gromyko meeting. Reagan liked the concept, and Byrd followed up with a written proposal. Soon after, Dole and Byrd discussed their independent initiatives and agreed to introduce a resolution that incorporated both. The State Department not only approved of the plan, but offered full briefings by the US negotiators on any talks, and would attempt to set up meetings between the Soviet delegation and the group on an informal basis. Based on the positive responses, the Senate passed the resolution. Dole and Byrd informed Reagan the group would consist of ten senators, five from each party, with the two leaders in an ex officio capacity. They designated four senators, Nunn, Ted Stevens, Republican senator Richard Lugar of Indiana, the new chairman of the Foreign Relations Committee, and Democratic senator Claiborne Pell of Rhode Island, the ranking member of that committee, as cochairmen.[2] Although the group had no formal function, it provided Nunn with an opportunity to bring his expertise to bear on arms control. Further, because the group had funding, he could, as cochair, shape the group's thinking by selecting experts to educate the members on issues confronting the negotiators. For Nunn, the objective was to "have the Senate fulfill both halves of its constitutional responsibilities, not only the consent half—that's what we've been looking to primarily in the past—but also the advice half."[3]

However, not all the issues surrounding US national security were wine and roses, as Nunn, now working with Barry Goldwater, who assumed the chairmanship of the Armed Services Committee, continued to tell the media about how the defense budget should be cut. A few weeks into January, Nunn reiterated the need to eliminate some programs, particularly in the strategic nuclear area, but said conventional programs needed trimming too. His stance was easy to understand, given that federal budget deficits continued to rage out of control and high-cost programs were budgeted so that their production stretched out over several years. There was no shortage of likely candidates for elimination. Every knowledgeable defense authority had a list, but Hill observers waited to see if Goldwater would agree with Nunn or drag his feet.[4]

Nunn explicitly reproached NATO leaders for their continuing failure to overcome "diminishing confidence" in the members' ability to deter the Warsaw Pact from executing a "lightning conventional attack," a point the NATO commander, General Bernard Rogers, confirmed in testimony before the Senate Armed Services Committee. The United States, Nunn declared, had "kept its part of the bargain," but the allies had not. He warned that unless the allies took steps to remedy this deficiency in conventional forces, he would offer his unsuccessful amendment again. Senator John McCain, Republican from Arizona, agreed and took to the Senate floor to inform his colleagues that he found Nunn's defeated amendment still palatable. "Support for the Nunn amendment was no isolationist fringe," he asserted.[5]

In an interview with *US News & World Report*, Nunn argued that to "make the most efficient use of our defense dollar, we also need to revise our military strategy" because of the mismatch between policy objectives and resources. This balancing of ends and means meant that the Pentagon needed to reappraise its understanding of Soviet capabilities and vulnerabilities.[6] Nunn's thinking was finding favor among the Joint Chiefs of Staff and civilian analysts like Christopher Layne. Layne concurred that the problem stemmed from the administration's lack of a suitable defense strategy, which could be accounted for by a failure to address the imbalance between US "strategic commitments and the resources available to support those commitments." The imbalance between ends and means was a prime example of "strategic over-extension."[7] McCain's statement served as an indicator of an attempt among some Republican legislators to fashion a new foreign policy consensus with Nunn and other Democrats who favored a strong US military, but were equally mindful of the need to bring the deficit under control.

On February 4, Secretary of State Caspar Weinberger and General John Vessey, chairman of the Joint Chiefs of Staff, appeared before the Senate Armed Services Committee to defend Reagan's $317.7 billion defense budget for fiscal year 1986, a 5.9 percent increase after inflation. They got a cool reception. Not only did the Democrats unmistakably declare that the defense budget proposal would be cut, but conservative Republicans now agreed that they confronted a federal budget deficit estimated at $180 billion, hardly a step toward reducing "government red ink," as Reagan had promised. There was no question about Goldwater's position either: defense spending could and would be reduced. Nunn added, "We've got to focus more on what we're getting out of the defense budget. . . . We've got a Pentagon plan that simply cannot be funded." Nuclear weapons programs were "squeezing out" funds for conventional forces. For administration officials, like Office of Management and Budget director David Stockman, the news only got worse, especially when Mark Hatfield, Senate Appropriations Committee chairman, ridiculed the funding scheme, calling it "a fantasy budget conceived in the land of never-ending deficits."[8]

Two weeks later, with the political winds at his back, Nunn moved to broaden the debate on NATO, arguing that its war plans were seriously defective and required revision. His first salvo occurred during a committee hearing with the US Army chief of staff, General John Wickham, as a witness. "If you're a Soviet military man and you thought the U.S. Army could fight 75 days with everybody all around them running out of ammunition in about 12 days, would that add to deterrence?" The US units could not run around the battlefield passing out ammunition to other nations' forces, Nunn asserted. Wickham allowed that in such a "hypothetical" scenario NATO would be better off with more tanks in the opening days of the war rather than more ammunition. Such weaponry might change the course of battle in the first hours or days so that who won or lost would not be determined by who ran out of ammunition first. Nunn then stated the larger issue was whether the United States could airlift sufficient forces and equipment to Europe in time to blunt a Warsaw Pact invasion. Goldwater, a retired US Air Force Reserve general, agreed that the current numbers of transport aircraft in the armed forces were glaringly insufficient to move troops and weapons to Europe quickly, and the likelihood of improving the situation was nil. Given this line of questioning, observers speculated whether Nunn intended to reintroduce his amendment in this session or was lining up an attempt to reallocate money for strategic weapons to conventional forces. Nunn left the question unanswered, but he did remark to Wickham and Secretary of the Army John Marsh: "We are not getting anywhere unless we start behaving as an alliance."[9] But first, there was the matter of the MX missile.

At the end of February, Reagan began a campaign to maintain the viability of the MX missile, rejecting any proposals to delay or compromise. Instead, the strategy was to test Congress's power through a series of votes in mid-March, about a week after the arms control negotiations began in Geneva. The opening round was a rare joint appearance of Weinberger and Shultz before the Senate Armed Services Committee, appealing for support of the missile to enhance the US negotiators' bargaining position. The White House viewed Nunn as the key vote. Although he had voted in favor of the missile in the past, that outcome was not a certainty because of his statement that his support was "getting very, very thin." If he did not see a change in the basing mode, he would, "at some point, vote 'No.'" He repeated that the MX was also related to an arms control regime that limited the number of Soviet nuclear warheads.[10]

While arguments about the MX missile and NATO's conventional force capability swirled around Capitol Hill, Nunn and his colleagues in the Senate Arms Control Observer Group departed for Geneva in March. Before they left, Nunn, Representative Les Aspin, and Representative Jim Wright, the House majority leader, met with Reagan and his negotiating team. Nunn and the others pledged bipartisan support for the negotiations, but refused to endorse continued production of the MX missile, which Reagan had hoped to secure with a vote less than two weeks away.[11]

Two days later, Nunn and his colleagues on the delegation observed the opening session of the renewed arms control meetings with the Soviets, and attended a series of briefings with the US negotiators. Shultz had specifically acknowledged the centrality of Nunn to the administration's strategic arms modernization efforts and the Senate's constitutional role on any arms control treaties. In a letter to the senator, Shultz offered his thoughts on how Nunn and his colleagues could be "most effective as consultants to the Executive Branch" during the negotiations, seeking his counsel as the United States developed its position and as negotiations progressed. Shultz promised to keep him informed on the issues under discussion and any proposed changes in the US position.[12]

On March 12, the observer group held a press conference and issued a joint statement before returning to the United States. As a cochair, Nunn made an opening statement, remarking that the negotiations were "one of the most difficult and complex negotiations that the two countries have ever endeavored to seek agreement on," since they involved three elements: intermediate-range nuclear weapons, strategic weapons, and defense and space weapons. He added that a lot depended on both sides approaching the negotiations "in a constructive attitude," with "creativity and flexibility" to reach an agreement. Nunn became the focal point of reporters' questions attempting to gauge how the trip had affected his views on SDI research, alleged Soviet violations of the 1972 Anti–Ballistic Missile Treaty, the future of the MX missile, and even more telling, the probability of attaining a successful agreement given that in the middle of the negotiations, on March 11, the Soviet Union announced that Premier Konstantin Chernenko had died. Mikhail Gorbachev, the fourth Soviet leader since Reagan had assumed office, had taken power. Nunn dismissed the question about the MX vote out of hand. He responded to the final point by stating he would not speculate on the likelihood of a treaty passing in the Senate. Instead, he underscored that in a period of sadness and difficulty for the Soviets, the Kremlin continued to proceed with the scheduled negotiations. He took that decision, as did the US negotiators, as an encouraging sign of the Soviet Union's "seriousness of purpose."[13] He did not mention that along with a few Senate colleagues and House members, he had already been working on a strategy for linking the future of the Reagan's nuclear weapons to the arms control talks.

In early March, Senate Democrats asked Nunn to develop a strategy aimed at limiting MX missile production in fiscal year 1986. House Democrats made a similar appeal to Aspin and Representative Norm Dicks. On the basis of this plea, Nunn, along with Senator Albert Gore Jr. and Senator William Cohen, developed a proposal that sought a phaseout of MX production in fiscal year 1986, with the intention of giving Reagan only half of the one hundred missiles he sought. Nunn then attained an agreement with Aspin that they would support production of twenty-one MX missiles, in addition to the twenty-one missiles already authorized for production and operational deployment, as a sign of American "good faith" in the arms control negotiations in Geneva. The two lawmakers agreed to slow the production rate of the MX, and possibly reduce the planned deployment of 100 missiles based on their assessment of the situation in Geneva. Nunn would use his position in the observer group to make a determination of the progress in the negotiations. As Nunn told reporters, he intended to vote for the production of twenty-one missiles because he believed it would "put both sides in a mood" to bargain sincerely about reducing their nuclear arsenals. Against the objection of House Speaker Tip O'Neill and other MX opponents, Nunn and Aspin indicated that they did not support killing the program completely.[14] As an alternative, Nunn promoted two goals for the negotiations: flexibility on the part of both parties, but with the Soviets making the opening gesture, and outcomes that would "keep a lid on the arms race," with the Soviets limiting their heavy, land-based missiles and demonstrating that they were not violating the 1972 Anti–Ballistic Missile Treaty. Paul Nitze, now special adviser to the president and secretary of state for arms control, agreed with Nunn on both points. His declaration sent the White House's message to undecided Republicans, pressuring them to vote in favor of MX production. Many of these members consulted with Nunn before the vote, as they found his position tenable.[15]

On March 18, Senate debate on the release of $1.5 billion to produce twenty-one MX missiles began with Dole hopeful he could get the needed votes to support Reagan but admitting the margin was slender. Approval of the release of funds required four votes, two in each chamber, based on the compromise Congress adopted the previous year. Earlier that day, the Senate Armed Services Committee had voted 11 to 6, with Nunn and Mississippi Democrat John C. Stennis joining the nine Republicans to authorize production. The impending Senate vote was so crucial that Reagan made a noontime visit to the Capitol as part of a personal lobbying effort to shore up support among Republicans. On the Senate floor, Nunn bluntly gave notice that while he would vote to support the release of funds for twenty-one missiles, he would not guarantee such a position on future votes. He believed that given the cost-cutting climate in Congress, building the additional MX missiles Reagan wanted was unaffordable and priorities for defense spending would have to shift. His stance convinced a number of Democratic senators who had opposed the missile the previous year to join him. Goldwater spoke in favor of the funding release, but only because a defeat for the president would be "the dangerous thing."[16]

When the first vote came in the Senate, Reagan got his victory by a solid margin, 55 to 45, despite eight Republican defections. Ten Democrats, Nunn, Gore, and Byrd among them, sided with the president but later reaffirmed they would hold fast to their position of limiting deployment of the MX force and slow production, with Nunn emphasizing they would not vote in favor of the additional missiles the administration wanted. The second Senate vote was also favorable. The House followed suit a week later, authorizing release of the production funding, notwithstanding vigorous lobbying by its Democratic leaders. By the end of March, the administration had secured release of the production funds.[17]

The debate, however, was not over. Nunn now moved to the larger issue of pruning the defense budget. "It is a matter of priorities," Nunn claimed. "I believe there are other programs much more important than the MX." Capping the operational deployment of the weapons to fifty would save as much as $2 billion in the fiscal year 1986 defense budget that could be applied to conventional weapons and those strategic systems with better survivability, such as the cruise missile.[18] The bipartisan coalition in both houses was now "noisily unraveling," as Nunn and the other centrist Democrats in the Senate that had forged it announced that they had sufficient supporters to "control the balance" on future MX votes. Nunn's position that continued production would not stabilize the arms race, but rather upset the nuclear balance, was now likely to hold sway among moderate and conservative Democrats, as was Byrd's remark that the MX was a bargaining chip for the Geneva talks. Aspin told his supporters privately that he was now of the mind to produce no further MX missiles with fiscal year funding, beyond the fifty missiles already approved for operational deployment that had begun to be produced in February 1984.[19]

Nunn did not get his way in the Armed Services Committee. In early April, the Republicans agreed to cut the administration's request from forty-eight to twenty-one, based on a compromise devised by Senator John Warner, while Nunn had proposed funding to produce only twelve and slash the planned force deployment to forty instead of the planned 100 missiles to be housed in Minuteman silos near Cheyenne, Wyoming, with the remainder for testing and spares. This proposal lost by a single vote.[20] A few days later, Nunn, together with John Glenn and Stennis, joined the Republicans to approve a smaller defense budget, with Goldwater admitting it was likely to be reduced further by the full Senate. The White House signaled that it would accept the committee's recommended funding level, only a 3 percent increase. Aspin ventured another opinion—deeper cuts by another $8–10 billion.[21] The House Democrats were testing the political winds. When Reagan was elected, polls indicated that 60 percent of Americans wanted defense spending to grow. Four years later, Congress had approved more than $1.1 trillion for the Pentagon. Now, public opinion had shifted; less than 15 percent favored more defense spending because of the rocketing deficit that resulted from no tax increases to pay for such largesse.[22]

Nunn found this change encouraging. In late May, he offered an amendment to the 1986 defense authorization bill that would limit the MX deployment to forty missiles, with fourteen for testing and spares. Senate leaders from both parties believed Nunn had the votes to win this time, which sent the White House into overdrive. Tower, now the chief negotiator of the Strategic Arms Reduction Talks with the Soviet Union in Geneva, and McFarlane rushed to Capitol Hill and met with several senators in the hope of convincing them to defeat Nunn's amendment. They also met with Nunn, seeking a compromise to "freeze," not cap, the number of MX missiles at fifty. Nunn refused to budge, but he was willing to consider other offers. Dole had to intercede for the White House personally to prompt this meeting, appearing on the Senate floor as Nunn was speaking and pleading with him to talk with Reagan's interlocutors. The White House misstep dumbfounded Goldwater, who wondered why Reagan had not acted earlier.[23] Dole's surprising visit to the floor and his appeal signaled an underestimation of Nunn's ability to build a coalition in the changed domestic political environment. Reagan's 1980 campaign pledge no longer had purchase; the bipartisan consensus over defense spending had fractured. In the Senate, a new coalition of moderate Democrats and fiscally conservative Republicans had formed.

The Reagan administration's attempt to find a compromise formula failed, as Nunn rejected the White House offer and no further meetings were scheduled. In its place, debate on his amendment began on May 22. Nunn stood at his desk and began with a story of an old man who was praised for his wisdom. One day, a young man held a bird in his hand and asked the old man whether the bird was alive or dead. If the old man were to say it was alive, then the young man could squeeze it to death, open his hand, and prove him wrong. If the old man said it was dead, the young man could open his hand and release the bird. In the story, the old man tells his questioner that the decision is his to make. Nunn likened Reagan to the young man. He could either accept Nunn's plan and let the MX program live, or he could fight the cap and lose. The decision was his, but the president had no chance to defeat the cap. Shortly after he finished the story, Nunn was called off the floor to answer the telephone. He informed his colleagues he would be willing to address any questions, but first he said, "I have to leave. I'm being called by the fellow with the bird in his hand."[24] Although the Senate Republican majority postponed a vote on the amendment for two days with the additional threat of a filibuster, Reagan decided to let the bird live.

To prevent a highly probable defeat in the Senate, Reagan informed Dole that he would agree to a cap of fifty missiles to be deployed in the existing Minuteman silos, and accepted that fiscal year 1986 funding would be limited to twelve missiles, not the forty-eight the administration wanted. Production of additional missiles would have to wait until Congress considered fiscal year 1987 funding and the administration offered a different basing scheme. Nunn stated that limiting the total operational deployment to fifty "eases the hair-trigger" on nuclear war. The compromise amendment passed the Senate by a vote of 78 to 20, but there were detractors on both sides. Conservatives called it a "sell-out" of US security interests, and liberals complained that the tighter restriction Nunn had first proposed had not been the outcome.[25]

The press considered the result a victory for Nunn, with the *New York Times* stating that the "MX missile, one of the more controversial weapons to lift off the Pentagon drawing boards, took another pounding." The deal the White House accepted was likely to be the best it could get. Nunn observed that the vote had not been the "end of MX," but the "end of the MX in fixed silos." An editorial in the *Washington Post* called the result "The Sam Nunn MX." Nunn "had done a useful and important thing," the editorial claimed. His goal was to ensure that in a crisis, the United States did not strike first to ensure its missiles hit the Soviet missiles in their silos before the Soviets could launch their ICBMs. The MX had become a first-strike weapon and, in effect, inconsistent with America's long-standing nuclear strategy. Further, Nunn's success, including the support of Republican senators, would prompt the administration to accelerate the Midgetman missile, which was less vulnerable to Soviet attack and therefore a retaliatory or second-strike weapon.[26] Nunn was not only signaling to the Soviets that the United States was in a bargaining mood, but he was walking the administration back from the nuclear abyss.

Nunn had spent half the year pointing to the need for a more balanced US military strategy that considered both conventional and nuclear capabilities. He held that NATO capabilities were inextricably tied to both elements of US national security but were often discounted. Too much attention had been spent debating the size of the defense budget, an argument he viewed as "intellectually deficient." Instead, the focus should be on US military objectives and requirements. In this respect, the current military strategy had numerous shortcomings that needed immediate attention. US defense planning was not synchronized with that of NATO allies, to say nothing of their capabilities and war plans. The military goals in the current strategy bore little relationship to the resources available in the future, which were not likely to increase, or current capabilities. The remedies, though difficult to achieve, were clear: US military strategy needed to consider NATO capabilities to a larger extent, and the synchronization of defense planning needed attention.[27]

The good news was that the attention he had caused the year previously with his proposed amendment had proved productive. Rogers, the NATO commander, and David M. Abshire reported that NATO allies were meeting the goal of a 3 percent annual increase in defense spending and increasing their munitions stocks. During a visit to NATO, Nunn told NATO secretary-general Lord Peter Carrington that he was impressed with the alliance's efforts to provide a better return on investment. He informed Abshire he would not raise a troop-withdrawal amendment but, instead, work behind the scenes with him and Defense Department officials on an amendment to improve armaments cooperation among the allies and to add funding for this purpose to the Defense Department budget, provided it harmonized its strategy with NATO's. To make the proposal politically palatable in Congress, the allies would have to invest in this mutual venture too. Nunn gathered sponsorship from Roth and Warner. The proposed legislation applauded NATO for the improvements it had made, but signified there was more to do. Passage of the "good" Nunn amendment, as it was known euphemistically, was, in Abshire's view, "a stroke of sheer creativity seldom seen in the governmental process. [It] helped bring new life to NATO and a new sense of direction. . . . It was an unusual example of congressional and NATO partnership," in keeping with the character that had created the alliance thirty-six years before.[28]

Meanwhile, Nunn continued to push for arms control using strategic weapons modernization as a bargaining tool for US negotiators. His legislative strategy consisted of two elements. First, he and Byrd urged Reagan to continue to observe the provisions of the 1979 SALT II Treaty, which was set to expire by the end of 1985 and was under administration review. To put additional pressure on the White House, Nunn succeeded in pushing through a nonbinding resolution on June 5, by an overwhelming margin of 90 to 5, which offered compromise language that key hard liners and arms control advocates could accept. It recommended that Reagan continue adherence to the treaty provisions, but also gave him approval to take measured steps to respond to Soviet violations of the treaty. After passage of the resolution, Nunn stated categorically that he intended for the Senate to be heard on the subject as the policy was being examined.[29]

The second element of Nunn's legislative strategy concentrated on SDI. Nunn and Warner led a coalition of senators that supported the research program. One columnist, calling Nunn the "Senate's hawkish rabbi on defense," was perplexed by his SDI stance, conceding that the reduction that had occurred in the Armed Services Committee markup, a decrease of $800 million, would not have happened without Nunn's "indispensible concurrence." Senator William Proxmire, a Wisconsin Democrat, perhaps offered the best explanation. Many senators joined Nunn and Warner in supporting some level of funding for SDI research, because they believed wounding the program at this stage could jeopardize the arms control talks. But Proxmire also saw it as bare-knuckle politics: "When you oppose the president of the United States, and when you oppose the Republican leadership and when you have Nunn, who is viewed by most people in our party as the last word on defense, against you, it's pretty hard to get" the votes needed to eliminate the funding.[30] Proxmire was right to single out Nunn. The coalition of liberals and conservatives that he had helped fashion continued to hold. He was part of a swing group of Democrats, including Aspin in the House, who were controlling the pace and focus of the defense debate.

Nunn realized that SDI was a huge bargaining chip. The Soviets wanted the program killed, but he recognized the United States should not curtail the research because it could not verify that the Soviets were conducting new weapons research, which seemed likely. Nunn added that the Soviets might find the United States more willing to consider limiting research if the Soviets stopped "violating arms control treaties." The Soviets also needed to submit proposals that showed a willingness to make deep cuts in their offensive capabilities. Cutting research on strategic defense was "unacceptable." Nunn declared, "The ball is clearly in the Soviets' court."[31]

To underscore that point, in September, during a hiatus in the negotiations and with Reagan scheduled for a November summit meeting with Gorbachev in Geneva, Dole and Byrd led a delegation of seven senators, including Nunn, to Moscow. Their meeting with Gorbachev was viewed as largely unsuccessful. The most optimistic outcome was that the Soviet premier indicated willingness on the part of his government to be more flexible in the negotiations, including on SDI research. Nunn did not view the message as a "substantive breakthrough." He told reporters Gorbachev's definition of basic research was "essentially what you do in the laboratory." He interpreted the allowance as one in which US scientists could think, but "not much more." Nonetheless, Nunn was impressed by Gorbachev as a person. He equated his style with that of a "trial lawyer," with "sharp legal instincts," who would be comfortable in debating issues with Reagan, able to give and take. The Soviet leader dealt in substance. It would be "a serious mistake," Nunn warned, "for the President to go into the summit thinking it will all be resolved by warm personalities." Yet the Kremlin meeting was not without value. Nunn and Warner used it to float the idea of nuclear risk reduction centers with Gorbachev. Nunn handed a paper on the subject directly to the premier, and for five minutes the two senators explained the concept, underscoring that Reagan had personally approved it and, therefore, it represented an official US position. In fact, the Reagan administration had asked Nunn and Warner to raise the topic specifically in anticipation of the first summit between Reagan and Gorbachev, where an agreement on the centers could be seen as a tangible outcome. Gorbachev thought the idea worthy of consideration and promised to see that his government did so, too. The two senators believed that if the Soviets embraced the idea, the concept could become part of the Geneva talks and the impending summit.[32] In a meeting after the Senate delegation's visit to Moscow, Nunn gave Reagan his impression that Gorbachev was a different type of Soviet leader. In speaking to reporters, he said, "I told President Reagan that it was as if Robert Redford came out in lieu of Yassir Arafat as a spokesman for the PLO." The difference was striking.[33]

In the weeks that followed through the autumn, Nunn kept the pressure on Reagan to produce an arms control pact, but the Senate delegation's visit also had an impact. After a six-month logjam, Gorbachev informed Reagan that the Soviets were willing to reduce their nuclear offensive capability substantially, with no mention of the United States halting SDI research. In an October op-ed, Nunn argued that to make the upcoming summit productive, the administration needed a well-conceived agenda with clear and sound proposals on arms control concerning both offensive and defensive systems, and especially fidelity to the 1972 Anti–Ballistic Missile Treaty (ABM Treaty). He believed discussion of risk reduction centers was one topic that both sides could embrace.[34]

As usual, Nunn was able to rally Republican senators to his side to shape the administration's proposals for the impending summit. Cohen supported Nunn by arguing that the Soviets' offer of a 50 percent reduction in their offensive arsenal was only the opening round in the "dance of diplomacy." The two argued that Reagan's counterproposal should be strategically sound and positive, but it should prevent the Soviets from attaining their three major objectives: halting SDI research, dividing the NATO alliance, and undermining congressional and public support for strategic modernization and defense programs. Reagan should focus first on strategic stability by reducing the number of land-based Soviet missiles with multiple independently targetable reentry vehicles (MIRVs), and second, on build-down, which they had advocated in 1983 and which Reagan adopted but had since abandoned. Third, with respect to SDI, Reagan should discuss with the Soviets what development and testing would be allowable under the ABM Treaty. The two were less worried about the superpower leaders reaching an accord and more interested in both presenting good-faith efforts to move forward on the arms control talks.[35]

Nunn used his own bully pulpit to frame the issues of nuclear weapons and arms control and their interrelationship. On November 13, he spoke before the Trilateral Commission, an organization the financier David Rockefeller and other private citizens had founded a decade earlier to encourage dialogue on foreign affairs. Standing in a gallery of the Phillips Collection, an art museum in Washington, Nunn drew attention to a painting by El Greco on one of the walls. He remarked that the painting reminded him of the saying, "Art is the reasoned derangement of the senses." He continued, addressing the arcane subject of his speech: "Well, if you turn to strategic nuclear planning and arms control, it definitely helps to have a derangement of the senses." He then proceeded for several minutes to argue for the strengthening of NATO's conventional forces, contending that bolstering the alliance's deterrent capability was essential in an era of nuclear parity, which only made the nuclear deterrent increasingly less credible.[36]

Turning to arms control and the forthcoming summit as well as the ongoing negotiations, he told the audience that he was "reasonably and cautiously optimistic." He cited three areas where US and Soviet interests aligned, which underpinned his hopefulness. The first was a Soviet economy that was in a tailspin with Gorbachev doing his best to reform it, and a US economy laboring under a huge deficit that now required substantial cuts under the Gramm-Rudman-Hollings Balanced Budget and Emergency Deficit Control Act. The second area was technological: the United States was ahead in space-based defense technology, while the Soviets were able to increase the production rate of several missiles in the short term, giving them an even larger offensive advantage. The third reason was the most critical: stability, that is, both sides "taking the finger off the hair trigger." The reasons for seeking stability were simple: The United States knew its land-based missiles were vulnerable to Soviet attack. The Soviets not only feared that SDI would work but also realized their land-based missiles had become progressively more vulnerable to US systems. Strategic modernization, with the MX, the improved Minuteman III warheads, and the D5 (Trident II) missile launched from US submarines, had made the difference. These new weapons had brought the Soviets to the negotiating table and had given them an incentive to offer reasonable proposals. Now, Nunn concluded, "we have the best opportunity for a significant arms control agreement that we've had in a long time." Two virtues were crucial for President Reagan. The first was patience. The second was timing. The latter depended on Reagan's knowledge of the issues and his ability to discern the best course, Nunn said. "And I think the verdict is still out on that count for the U.S. leadership."[37]

Two days later, Nunn spoke to a large audience at the University of Georgia, summarizing his views on arms control by quoting General Omar Bradley. "Ours is a world of nuclear giants and ethical infants. If we continue to develop our technology without wisdom or prudence, our servant may prove to be our executioner." Nunn deemed the summit to be a defining moment for the administration and its success rested on the president's negotiating skills.[38] The administration was faced with the well-known security dilemma of finding a way to throttle back on the arms race or confront a Soviet Union willing to escalate the tension and undermine stability.

No matter how much it wished to downplay the significance of the summit, the White House took the perspective that it would be the most important one since President John F. Kennedy had faced off with Soviet premier Nikita Khrushchev in 1961. Reagan and Gorbachev were vying for the "moral and political high ground." While the president's advisors stated modest goals for the meeting, one anonymous official involved in summit preparations remarked, "You don't have to convince Shultz and McFarlane that if there's not an arms-control element of some significance coming out of this, the President is going to have some significant public relations problems."[39]

The summit was held November 19 and 20, with the two leaders discussing a range of issues and, in particular, the arms race. The meeting resulted in no agreements on arms control, causing some experts to characterize the meeting as a failure, but Nunn was upbeat. The two leaders had agreed to have experts examine the feasibility of establishing nuclear risk reduction centers. He remained hopeful that the two sides would find a way to produce another arms control treaty.[40] (The two governments finally agreed to establish the centers in September 1987. They remain in operation today.[41])

Although a treaty was unlikely to occur in the next year with the midterm elections in play, Nunn also knew which way the domestic political winds were blowing. "Many candidates will be eager to show their support for budget cutting and for an arms control compromise." He added, "The whole defense budget will be under fiscal pressure in the spring."[42] For months he and Goldwater had been planning how to address the defense budget. After the shocking revelations in the press that the Defense Department paid $400 for hammers and $600 for toilet seats, the two senators would use legislation to reform the Pentagon, reorganizing the Joint Chiefs of Staff and making the department's bureaucratic processes, especially procurement, more efficient. Now "the two most influential 'hawks' in the Senate were demanding changes." As Goldwater aptly put it, the system "is broke and we need to fix it."[43]

CHAPTER 8

THE LONG CRUSADE

By early 1985, supporters of the Congressional Military Reform Caucus had lost confidence in its members improving Pentagon organizational processes, despite multimillion-dollar procurement scandals and recent operational missteps, such as the failed attempt to rescue American hostages in Iran in 1980. Others wondered if the Joint Chiefs of Staff were offering the commander in chief and the secretary of defense their best military advice or were more interested in protecting service equities since, as service chiefs, they resisted any meaningful attempts to attain management efficiencies as long as the dollars flowed into their bureaucracies. Many lawmakers realized that the administration had failed to make its case that throwing money at the military—a 40 percent increase in defense spending, or more than a trillion dollars—had increased national security or military effectiveness. Critics griped that despite the promises of reformers, they could not point to one noteworthy example of reform legislation.[1]

In January 1985, upon assuming the chairmanship of the Armed Services Committee, Senator Barry Goldwater was determined to make defense reorganization his highest priority. As one of Goldwater's aides remarked, "He [Goldwater] saw an opportunity to finally make some changes that would have a significant impact on downstream operations capabilities of the military."[2] He needed and wanted Nunn as a political ally, and the two decided to address the issue head-on as "equal partners," to create an atmosphere of "equality and trust" from the beginning.[3]

Nunn had long waited for this moment. For nearly three years, Republican senator John G. Tower had thwarted him and like-minded senators and House members on reform, feigning interest, conducting meaningless hearings, torpedoing House Armed Services Committee reform proposals in conference, and in due course, ignoring numerous commitments he had made to senators he secretly considered to be "agitating for reform." In Tower's view, there was very little payback to becoming the point man on defense reform.[4]

Goldwater held no such views. In 1984, during floor action on the defense authorization bill, the Arizona senator made a promise of bipartisanship. Regardless of whether he or Nunn became chairman of the Armed Services Committee after the November elections, reorganization was "a subject that is going to receive very deep study, and it is hoped, some resolution, so that our military services not only can perform better in military decisions, but also, just as important to me, perform better in procurement."[5]

As Goldwater later explained, his bipartisan motivation was not to "challenge [the military's] power or trample on its traditions." Instead, he and Nunn sought to revitalize its capabilities, from the advice given to the president to the conduct of combat operations. They recognized that the subject was not one that the public and media would readily understand.[6] The two decided to establish and cochair a small task force of Armed Services Committee members that would assist with drafting legislation, along with staff from the committee who would conduct a comprehensive analysis of the subject. They named committee staff member James R. Locher as the head of the team, joined by Rick Finn and Barbara Brown from the Republican side, and Jeff Smith from the Democratic side. They then announced their plan to study defense organization to committee members in a "Dear Committee Colleague" letter on January 31, 1985.[7]

With these preliminary steps completed, the topic of defense reorganization came to public attention in February when the Center for Strategic and International Studies released its report on military organization at a press conference at Georgetown University in Washington, DC. The report, written by notable defense experts, including Nunn, and winning the endorsement of six former defense secretaries, stated that the Department of Defense needed to correct crucial shortcomings. These included how military leaders advised the president, the formulation of the armed services' budgets, and planning for combat operations. The report argued that service rivalries and deficient coordination among the services had led to wasteful spending and poorly executed military operations, such as the deaths of marines in Lebanon in 1983 and poor coordination among US forces in the 1983 invasion of Grenada. Goldwater had already promised hearings on a potential overhaul of the military and its structure.[8]

The next step was to inform Secretary of Defense Caspar Weinberger formally, which Goldwater and Nunn did on February 4, when they sent him a letter about their objectives and solicited his cooperation. They knew they had a daunting challenge ahead of them. They recognized that it would be difficult to reform the Pentagon from the outside and the resistance from the nation's most senior military officers would be fierce. Weinberger, though he claimed to be open to recommendations, was actually opposed, stating clearly on more than one occasion that he believed the current systems functioned appropriately. In addition, the senators faced resistance on the Armed Services Committee; only two or three other committee members agreed that reorganization was needed.[9] Goldwater understood the odds against their success: it might require overriding a veto from Reagan. "When Nunn and I began to make our move," Goldwater recalled, "I wouldn't have bet more than a sawbuck on our chances of success. History and tradition were against us. Yet I had made up my mind that I would not retire from the Senate without giving reorganization my best shot."[10] In May, they appointed the members of the Task Force on Defense Organization. Goldwater named William Cohen, who was pro-reform, and three Republican anti-reform members: Dan Quayle of Indiana, Pete Wilson of California, and Phil Gramm of Texas. Nunn added Democrats Jeff Bingaman of New Mexico, Carl Levin, and Ted Kennedy.[11]

Nunn was also engaging defense issues on a second front. He and Les Aspin held a forum with Texas Democrats in March to challenge the Reagan administration's defense policy. Nunn knew the political winds were changing nationally, but especially in the South and West. In his view, the national Democratic Party no longer represented conservative Democrats. It had little interest in "wooing the South," believing the region would support the presidential nominee as it had for decades, regardless of ideological inclinations. Moreover, the constituents who elected conservative Democrats felt unwelcome in the party.[12] Consequently, Nunn and other moderate and conservative Democratic elected officials founded the independent and unofficial Democratic Leadership Council (DLC) in February 1985, in defiance of the national party leadership. The DLC's goal was to move the national party to the center and address the concerns of middle-class voters after Reagan trounced Walter Mondale in the 1984 presidential election.[13] Nunn was using his reputation to recast voters' perception that Democrats were weak on national security and to regain the party's credibility on the issue, but he was also being mentioned as a presidential candidate in 1988. At this DLC-sponsored forum, he faulted the administration for not formulating a "coherent military strategy related to the available resources," and argued that it was not spending tax money prudently.[14]

Meanwhile, throughout the spring and summer and into early October, the committee staff team made progress. As their work matured, they uncovered a number of deficiencies in Defense Department operations. However, to prevent undermining their initiative, Goldwater and Nunn brought no public attention to these findings so that opponents could not kill the plan prematurely. Instead, the task force met almost weekly when the Senate was in session, in closed meetings with only the staff team present, to discuss initial findings and to hear from experts on the issues under discussion. Nonetheless, their intent was no secret. The White House was receiving reports on the staff team's work. Hill watchers were intrigued that two of the Senate's leading "hawks" were gunning for changes and together had the muscle to realize their goal. Moreover, their counterparts in the House, led by Democratic representative Bill Nichols of Alabama, with the support of Democratic representative Ike Skelton of Missouri and Aspin, had been battling for change for three years, but had been largely stymied during Tower's chairmanship.[15] Tower knew that favoring reform when the Defense Department bureaucracy saw it as heresy would damage his chances of becoming a future secretary of defense, perhaps in the Reagan administration.

Tower's ambition clouded his judgment and was an obvious obstacle to much-needed reforms. Nunn viewed Weinberger's management of the Pentagon as overly permissive, failing to discipline the services for cost overruns and promoting their services' needs at the expense of a comprehensive military strategy—glaring inefficiencies that occurred as the Defense Department procured too many expensive systems at once and then had to stretch out production. One journalist likened the relationship among the service chiefs to "the heads of big corporations carving up a market, rather than the nation's military leaders hammering out the most impartial, argument-tested advice for the president."[16] Nunn agreed with this assessment. "Basically, it's hands-off. Everybody scratches everybody else's back. . . . I think the last thing we want in the military is to handle the business like a pork barrel bill."[17] Other senators, including Robert Dole and his fellow Republicans, but not those on the Armed Services Committee, were beginning to question Weinberger's stewardship because of the procurement scandals, and by the summer, the secretary's influence with Reagan appeared to be waning. Goldwater had allegedly told White House aides that Weinberger should resign as he was a liability. In June, over Weinberger's initial objections, Reagan appointed the President's Blue Ribbon Commission on Defense Management to examine the organization of the Pentagon, paying particular attention to weapons procurement. With David Packard, chairman of the board of Hewlett-Packard, in charge, it became known as the Packard Commission. Nunn viewed the measure as the president's acknowledgment that there was a "serious problem" in the Pentagon's management.[18] Others saw it as a maneuver to "undermine the reformers and fend off" legislation, but Nunn and the reformers were ready to accept this ploy if the commission's findings suited their ends.[19]

Perhaps sensing a wounded Weinberger, Democrats on the House Armed Services Committee pushed for legislation that would reorganize the Joint Chiefs of Staff and give greater power to the chairman to lessen the parochial interests of the service chiefs by making that position the principal advisor to the president and secretary of defense.[20] In early October, Nunn and Goldwater were ready to reveal the staff study they had been shepherding for the past several months and, ultimately, their own bill that would streamline military processes and promote unity among the services. First, however, they decided to sequester the task force members and the study staff at Fort A. P. Hill, near Fredericksburg, Virginia, on a weekend retreat. Nunn believed that getting the members away from Washington, where they could frankly discuss and debate the completed staff study with several retired military officers and former defense officials, would further the members' knowledge and set their minds at rest that reorganization was not only politically feasible but necessary. Nunn's idea proved to be a master stroke. Although there were contentious moments, by the end of the weekend Goldwater and Nunn believed it had been a fruitful two days, with six of the nine task force members now firmly on the pro-reform side, and two others agreeing with some of the ideas. The pro-reform members were "still underdogs," but the two leaders believed they had improved the odds of success.[21]

Persuaded by the retreat's outcome, Goldwater and Nunn began their assault on Pentagon management with a series of floor speeches, read aloud to an almost empty chamber. Beginning on October 1 and concluding five days later, they characterized the current management situation as wasteful and dangerous, "a confusion of competing factions, quarreling over money in peacetime and tripping over one another in battle." They did not refrain from laying blame on Congress either, castigating the institution for inadequate oversight, poor understanding of the relationship between strategy and resources, and preoccupation with the level of defense spending but little concern, as Goldwater stated, for "what for, why and how well." Nunn commented on a budget fattened by duplicative weapons, and both assailed a Joint Chiefs of Staff system of advising the commander in chief that provided "mushy" advice at best, with Nunn pointing out that Congress was more interested in studying the "feasibility of selling beef, pork and lamb produced in the United States in overseas commissaries" than in how well the Defense Department could meet its military commitments abroad.[22] On October 8, the senators and study staff briefed Weinberger on the staff study. It was a tense, frosty meeting with Nunn and Goldwater jousting with the secretary over the proposed reforms. Weinberger viewed their efforts as a personal jab. Nevertheless, a meeting with the Packard Commission that morning had gone smoothly, aided by the fact that two of the commission members, former New Jersey senator Nicholas Brady and retired army general Paul Gorman, had attended the Fort A. P. Hill retreat and were pro-reform. It appeared Packard was in that camp too, and so was another commission member, Brent Scowcroft, who several times during the study briefing gave Locher a "thumbs up or an okay sign."[23] The commission's response turned out to be more than mere positive signals.

Lending credence to Nunn and Goldwater's assertions, a week later Packard made his first public comments about the commission's findings. He remarked that elemental changes were needed to fix the Pentagon's weapons procurement procedures, which resulted in poor quality, high prices, and long delays in producing weapons. He added that management reforms would not be sufficient to revamp a system that he described as "worse than it was 15 years ago," when he had served as deputy secretary of defense in the Nixon administration. He added, "I think we see at this time that some structural changes are necessary." Although he praised the administration for building up the US military and avoided any criticism of Weinberger, he asserted, "I think the general conclusion is we should have gotten more for our money."[24]

Packard told reporters he had been briefed on the staff study and indicated his commission's views had a lot in common with the forthcoming report. He ended by noting there had been no lack of recommendations on how to improve Pentagon's management in the past four decades. By his count, there had been thirty-five official studies since 1949. The best outcome, he admitted, would be to avoid the fate of its predecessors: the commission's "recommendations ending up on a shelf."[25] Goldwater and Nunn felt the same way about the study they were about to reveal and the legislation they were preparing to present.

On October 16, in Room 562 of the Dirksen Senate Office Building, jammed with onlookers, the two senators unveiled a 645-page staff report criticizing the Defense Department for its internal management problems and its handling of military operations. The report called for sweeping changes to the US military, ninety-one recommendations in all. The most politically explosive recommendation was to abolish the Joint Chiefs of Staff and replace them with a new joint military advisory council. The service chiefs would be responsible solely for managing their services, while the new advisory group would consist of officers from each of the services in their final assignment before retiring so they would be less bound to protect their services' turf. Goldwater and Nunn had no intention of establishing the council. It was a ruse to divert the Pentagon from their principal proposals, made purposely extreme and to which the two senators would grudgingly but graciously surrender. The study also recommended that the regional commanders in chief be given more authority over the forces from the services that they would command in wartime, as well as a larger say in the defense budgeting process. It drew scathing conclusions about the services, rebuking them for parochialism that created "critical gaps in warfighting capabilities, wasted resources through unwarranted duplication, inter-operability problems, inconsistent doctrine, inadequate joint training, and ineffective fighting forces."[26]

A day earlier, the Pentagon spokesperson had insisted that the current system worked fine. He cited as proof a navy operation on October 10 in which its fighters intercepted an Egyptian airliner carrying the four Palestinians responsible for hijacking the cruise ship the *Achille Lauro,* an event that had occurred three days earlier. Weinberger and navy secretary John Lehman took the offensive as well with the report's release, which they had not read, although they had been briefed about its contents. Speaking before the Packard Commission, Weinberger called the criticism exaggerated and Lehman claimed that if it had not been for the increase in the military budget, the navy would not have been able to succeed in the recent intercept mission. Goldwater and Nunn did not waste time arguing with them. On the same day as the report's release, they began hearings on it.[27] While the two senators did not publicly endorse the report, they stated it would be the starting point for a comprehensive reorganization of the Defense Department, the first since Dwight Eisenhower's presidency.

Nunn's criticism of the administration, which he had offered sparingly over the previous four years, struck some Capitol Hill watchers as a major shift. They interpreted his assertiveness as a step toward devising a clear set of Democratic national security policy positions that would challenge Republicans but not appear "soft" on defense. Nonetheless, some of his Democratic colleagues remained skeptical because he had largely supported Reagan on key votes, 66 percent of the time in the current year. Jeffrey Record, a former Nunn aide and now a senior fellow at a Washington think tank, suggested it was a matter of timing. He offered that it had only been in the past six months that Republican solidarity on defense had started to come unglued because of "budget deficits and their deficit phobia."[28] Nunn and Goldwater's plan did not please the Republican members of the Armed Services Committee. Senator John W. Warner said the staff report recommendations constituted unwarranted "open heart surgery on the Department of Defense."[29]

The first incision came at the opening hearing, with Locher as the leadoff witness. He laid out the contents of the report, maintaining that the defense secretary's effectiveness as the head of a vast enterprise was undermined by independent bureaucratic "fiefdoms" and "log-rolling" among the military services so they could protect their budgets and programs. Congress added to the problem by protecting the services on projects that helped their constituencies and by endlessly fiddling with aspects of military programs. The report's recommendations were meant to give the secretary of defense and other senior civilian defense officials more authority to overrule the powerful factions and transfer attention from the minutiae of defense budgets to the services' capabilities to execute critical joint missions, such as nuclear deterrence, defending NATO, or projecting US military power into global hot spots.[30] Warner, who had served as secretary of the navy in the Nixon administration, protested abolishing the current Joints Chiefs of Staff, and specifically objected to the recommendation that the chief of naval operations be replaced as the top maritime advisor to the president and the secretary of defense. "You're stripping his epaulets off right in front of his troops," the lawmaker carped. Phil Gramm contested the claim that the department was badly managed. "The state of readiness is at an all-time high," he asserted, grumbling that critics would use the report's findings "to discredit the progress that has been made."[31]

Within a week, journalists characterized the Pentagon as being "under siege," not only because of the two senators' assault but also because Packard continued to state openly that the Defense Department was "screwed up," and Aspin maintained his pressure for organizational change, indicating that the House would soon have a reform bill for consideration. He chortled that the Senate staff report and its tough line increased his chances of passing the legislation. "We knew [the Pentagon] would think it over once they saw the Senate version. After they hosed all over our bill the last three years, now it looks pretty good by comparison." Weinberger was allegedly calling for a cease-fire, ready to negotiate with the Hill on some of the reform proposals, but as usual he wanted concessions from Congress—no eradication of the Joint Chiefs of Staff was his main sticking point.[32]

On November 14, in a hearing before the Senate Armed Services Committee, Weinberger made his first public appearance since the release of the staff report, and his tone was not conciliatory. Instead, he insisted that sweeping changes to the Pentagon were unnecessary and urged members of Congress to disregard proposals to modify or abolish the Joint Chiefs of Staff. Certainly, no changes should be initiated before the Packard Commission completed its report, though he did admit that about half of the staff report recommendations were sensible. Nonetheless, he found the staff's "assumption" that the service chiefs were too parochial not to be the case based on his experience and added that many of the problems identified in the report had already been rectified or were being addressed, as he had maintained in previous testimony and in his annual report to Congress. Goldwater found the response ridiculous and scolded Weinberger after a heated exchange. "I have to be honest with you—you didn't answer the questions and you haven't approached this thing right," the Arizona Republican declared. "You better go back and read this report."[33]

In a verbal clash with Nunn, Weinberger dismissed the assertion that there had been problems in coordination among the services during the 1983 Grenada invasion, dismissing any problems as the inherent difficulties that always occur in the conduct of large-scale military operations. Nunn responded to this assessment as a "patent absurdity" and referred him to a classified Defense Department report that provided "in vivid detail" the problems encountered during the operation, such as the fact that army and navy radios were not interoperable. He called specific attention to the example of US Army Rangers not being able to communicate with marine units, a problem Nunn had learned about firsthand from army personnel shortly after the operation when he met with members of the ranger unit in Georgia. Nunn brought his point to a close by admonishing the secretary, "You are making unclassified statements that are rebutted by classified material."[34]

Weinberger's arguments had not held up under the senators' withering fire, and within weeks he was waving a white flag, looking to make peace as both houses of Congress began to push for changes in the role of the chairman of the Joint Chiefs of Staff. In a letter to the two senators, he indicated he could accept changes in the structure of the armed forces, including proposals to strengthen the authority of the chairman of the Joint Chiefs of Staff, "provided it is clear that he acts on behalf of the J.C.S." He was not in favor of the staff study recommendation that a joint advisory council of senior military officers be established. Striking a more conciliatory note, he added that "this is not to say that the advice-giving mechanism of the Joint Chiefs of Staff cannot be improved." The press interpreted the letter as an important though unenthusiastic change in the secretary's position. Goldwater and Nunn saw the contents of the letter in a positive light, with Nunn stating it indicated that Defense Department leaders "are approaching this with an open mind and are receptive to some change."[35]

Admiral William J. Crowe Jr., who had been chairman of the Joint Chiefs of Staff for only a few months, testified before the Senate Armed Services Committee a week later regarding his views of the staff study. He was polite but direct. He believed it was severely defective on a number of points. First, it gave too much credence to the opinions of critics. Second, it questioned the chiefs' integrity in carrying out their advisory duties. Third, it failed to give credit to the Joint Chiefs of Staff for their superb role in managing US forces and their operations throughout the world on a daily basis. Lastly, it neglected to note the numerous internal management improvements made in the past three years by the secretary and the Joint Chiefs of Staff. The one recommendation Crowe could not countenance was the one seeking to replace the Joint Chiefs of Staff with a body of advisors. It was adding an unneeded layer to an already sizable bureaucracy. Taking such a step would be a severe error. After stating that he favored the House bill, he proceeded to provide his views on the study's detailed proposals. He was respectful in his disagreement, but in outlining his personal philosophy about reorganization he was clear: "When one addresses reorganization, he is essentially talking about redistributing power, and this fact introduces a great deal of passion into the dialogue." Looking directly at Goldwater and Nunn, he continued, "One of the most difficult tasks your committee faces will be to separate emotional from intellectual arguments." He suggested that incremental steps would be more successfully implemented than "sharp and dramatic reform," not only because of "vested interests" but also because of concerns about "unintended and unpredictable consequences" that could best be remedied as they surfaced. He ended positively, speaking for the other chiefs and himself, saying that they were "determined to work with you in this endeavor."[36] Goldwater and Nunn were relieved to hear peacemaking words from the admiral.

After the congressional recess for the holiday season, Goldwater and Nunn began the next phase of their plan in the Senate, building on the series of hearings they had conducted. The chance of reform became more likely when the House passed a compromise bill on November 20 that elevated the chairman of the Joint Chiefs of Staff by making him the principal military advisor to the president and the secretary of defense. The House vote was a lopsided 383 to 27. With this victory by the bill's sponsors, the "pro–joint movement" leaders Aspin, Nichols, and Skelton, coupled with Goldwater and Nunn's intent to make even deeper reforms, it appeared undeniable that change would occur. As one unidentified defense analyst stated, "You can ignore it [the call for reform] when the think tanks and the college professors say it, but when Goldwater and Nunn both say it, the Pentagon has to listen."[37]

While Weinberger had become more quiescent, Lehman became the chief resister. He maintained that downgrading the role of the service chiefs and empowering the chairman with a large joint staff under his control would lead to the formation of a dreaded "Prussian general staff" that would stifle the military advice of the service chiefs, who would, on occasion, offer useful alternative judgments.[38] This view became even more pointed on February 3, 1986, when Goldwater and Nunn, along with Locher, Finn, and Smith, met with Crowe and the other Joint Chiefs of Staff at the Pentagon in the Joint Chief's conference room, known as "The Tank," for an unexpected discussion. Crowe had named three Republican members of the Armed Services Committee he wanted to attend the meeting, all fierce opponents of reform. Goldwater squelched that idea, and when Crowe stated that the three committee staff members were not needed, Goldwater indicated that their attendance was not a matter for negotiation. Goldwater later remarked about this attempt to add the three senators: "It was obvious that those op-posing military reform were trying to maneuver us into an early, full-blown confrontation—and Nunn and I would have fewer troops." Goldwater knew he and Nunn would face opposition from the four service chiefs; they did not need to have colleagues gang up on them too.[39] Crowe believed Nunn was the main force behind defense reorganization effort. It was he who had "fathered" the bill and Goldwater was merely his instrument, a posi-tion Goldwater would have strongly disputed if Crowe had told him to his face. Goldwater trusted Nunn and viewed him as a "selfless" partner in the endeavor. But in Crowe's view, one shared by some Republican senators, the Georgian had "co-opted" Goldwater, a "brilliant" solution to overcoming po-litical barriers, because Goldwater's standing within the military and his sup-port lent "legitimacy" to Nunn's machinations. Goldwater was susceptible to Nunn's overtures. Because he was about to retire from the Senate after thirty years, Goldwater "wanted to leave some mark that would outlive his own tenure," Crowe asserted.[40]

In the conference room, Crowe sat at the center of the table opposite Goldwater and Nunn. General Charles A. Gabriel, chief of staff of the air force, sat next to him. The other three chiefs, army chief of staff John Wick-ham, Admiral James Watkins, chief of naval operations, and General P. X. Kelley, commandant of the Marine Corps, sat beside the two senators. Crowe began with a prepared statement decrying the proposed legislation, arguing that retaining the current corporate approach remained the best method of ensuring their military advice remained independent. Wickham, Kelley, and Watkins chimed in, and their vehemence was unmistakable. Both senators and their staff were taken aback. It was more than well-argued declarations of opposition; Goldwater found the tone "rancorous" and overwrought. He tried to create a more conciliatory, less confrontational atmosphere with his response, but his words had no effect. The chiefs continued their angry as-sault, with Wickham, Watkins, and Kelley misconstruing Goldwater and Nunn's proposal as making them more subservient to civilian control, which despite Goldwater's attestation, did not settle the matter. Goldwater under-stood it was all about "turf—power" for these three. Goldwater then told the chiefs that the purpose of making the chairman the principal advisor was to enhance the quality of military advice, not undermine it by making it "sub-ject to the control" of civilian secretaries, and pledged to make that clear in the bill's language.[41]

Goldwater and Nunn waited for further attacks, and they came quickly when Wickham, Watkins, and Kelley told the senators that they did not agree with the other major organizational change: the increase in authority that the geographic combatant commanders would have over service component commanders and their forces in their respective regions of responsibility. Goldwater and Nunn believed this change was necessary so that the service components would fight as a joint team. The chiefs argued that the combatant commanders would now be caught up in handling personnel and materiel duties, not combat operations. At this point Nunn spoke up: "In our three years of studying reorganization, no deficiency has been as clearly or painfully demonstrated as the weakness of the unified commanders." He cited several operations that were evidence of failed or poor performance resulting from "the lack of unity of command."[42] To bolster his argument, he explained the planned provisions in detail, neutralizing their contention and justifying the principal objective of the legislation.[43]

The meeting continued for several more minutes, with the group debating other issues of concern to the chiefs. Goldwater would later remark in his no-nonsense manner that the chiefs' position was plainly delivered: "They didn't believe in reorganization, and they were telling us to go to hell." When the meeting ended, Crowe, Gabriel, and Watkins shook hands with the senators; the other two swiftly left the room. Crowe invited Goldwater, Nunn, and the three staff members to his office and extended the courtesy of letting them use it for a private meeting. The conclusion among the five was clear. The chiefs were now a major hurdle to be overcome, especially as their views became public. However, their opposition had also steeled the two senators. Locher wondered out loud if they should examine some other options before the committee began its markup of the proposed bill the next morning. As Goldwater tells it, the two senators "looked at each other. Our answer was clear and certain: Proceed as planned."[44]

When the committee began its markup of the draft bill the next morning, Goldwater and Nunn received stinging letters from the four service chiefs and the three service secretaries criticizing the legislation for the record. Weinberger and Crowe, who had responded to the senators' request for their opinions, remained opposed to the legislation, but they were less heated. The letters became the basis for debate among the committee members. As Nunn and Goldwater expected, the chiefs and their allies were ready for a fight. On the committee, Nunn and Goldwater had eight strong supporters, six Democrats and two Republicans, Strom Thurmond of South Carolina and Cohen. Four Republicans led by Warner, joined by two Democrats, John

Glenn and John C. Stennis, were clearly opposed, with the remaining three Republican members expected to vote with them.[45] A 10 to 9 split indicated the reformers were in a weak position, especially going forward for a floor vote. Now, the hard work of changing minds began, but battle lines had been drawn.

For the next few two weeks, no member changed his position. Bill markup ground on, session after session, with each provision strenuously debated. The nine who opposed the bill began to recognize that they could not sway a pro-reform member to their side. They would have to stick together, modify the language to their advantage where possible, and then convince the full Senate that the legislation should be shelved. It was a tactic that many in the Pentagon supported.[46]

Despite the sizable opposition in the committee, Goldwater and Nunn were committed to an open and fair process, with each member's concerns fully addressed. Warner, while intense in his opposition to the legislation, admitted that this atmosphere made for fruitful debate and bolstered collegiality. "At no time," he would recall, "did the distinguished chair or ranking minority member deny me any privilege under the procedures of the committee to make known my views and the views of those senators working with me." Warner reciprocated in his leadership of the opposition. Both sides admired Goldwater's evenhandedness and willingness to ensure that all views were fairly and completely represented.[47]

Goldwater and Nunn enjoyed one advantage in the composition of the pro-reformers on the committee; they had two superb "lieutenants" in Cohen and Levin. Both had long service on the committee and understood the complicated issues under consideration, and their legal training proved critical in fashioning language when compromise was required or in making arguments that proved instrumental in strengthening the pro-reform position on particular provisions. After a few weeks, the credibility and potency of the pro-reform position became apparent to those members who had decided to keep an open mind. The first anti-reformer to break ranks was Gramm. Over the next several days, others joined him. The opposition was eroding fast and began to buckle.[48]

On February 28, the Armed Services Committee briefly paused in its deliberations so that committee members could hear from Packard regarding his commission's interim report that it would deliver to Reagan that day. The commission had devoted an entire section to military organization and command. More critically, Packard stated, "the portions of the report dealing with defense organization and the committee's bill are consistent and mutually supported." Goldwater and Nunn were ecstatic and expressed the same in a joint press statement after the meeting. Moreover, not only did the commission's position serve as independent affirmation that their pro-reform ideas had merit, but also it convinced other members to join the pro-reform side.[49]

When the committee next met on March 4, only a few members still voiced opposition to the bill's provisions. Most of the other opponents' concerns had been incorporated, but without Goldwater and Nunn surrendering their major initiatives. The debate ultimately had the effect of refining the bill's language to make it stronger and build consensus rather than diluting it. Warner, who had offered more than fifty amendments, had a majority of them included in the final bill. The committee and member staffs speculated on the final vote of the bill, but it would clearly be in favor of the pro-reformers, with maybe two recalcitrant members holding out.[50]

While most of the committee's work was in closed session, the press began to pick up information that it was poised to recommend far-reaching changes to the Defense Department's organization, and especially the military services, despite opposition to some of the provisions by Weinberger and the service chiefs. The vote on the bill was imminent.[51] For most Americans, the topic was too arcane, but for those who followed defense issues, it appeared to be the most colossal shakeup of the military establishment in decades.

March 6 was the next major milestone, when the committee met to vote. Goldwater asked the committee's chief clerk, Chris Cowart, to read the roll. Keeping with past practice, she started with the majority Republicans and their most senior member, Strom Thurmond. His "aye" vote was no surprise. Warner was next, and he voted yes, as did all the other Republicans except one. Jeremiah Denton from Alabama, a retired navy rear admiral, passed. Nunn led off the Democrats with a vote in the affirmative. Stennis voted "aye" as well after explaining his vote based on a lengthy discussion with Goldwater the previous evening that had swayed him. The other Democrats all voted in favor. Goldwater was the last to vote and added to the "ayes." The clerk then asked Denton for his vote. He made it unanimous, 19 to 0.[52]

The outcome of the committee's work was widely and favorably reported in the newspapers as legislation that would enhance cooperation among the military services through joint planning and operations; strengthen the role of the chairman of the Joint Chiefs of Staff as the principal advisor to the president and secretary of defense so they did not receive advice held hostage to service interests; and establish a vice chairman as the sixth member of the Joint Chiefs of Staff to serve as "acting chairman" in the absence of the chairman, instead of the current rotational system. It would also grant additional authority to combatant commanders in the various geographical regions who had responsibility for US military forces stationed there, and create the position of under secretary of defense to oversee the flawed procurement system. In an interview, Nunn called the bill "sweeping and historic," one that would fix problems "that have plagued our national defense for decades," while Goldwater said it was "the most significant piece of defense legislation in the nation's history."[53]

After a month of fourteen exhausting markup sessions, more than one hundred amendments offered for intense debate, and as Goldwater remarked, having "to fight elements of the Pentagon every inch of the way," the partnership of Goldwater and Nunn, along with the committee's unanimous vote and the favorable House bill, had effectively ensured passage of defense reform legislation during this session of Congress. Yet the two senators were not naive enough to believe that enactment of legislation would lead to the fulfillment of their vision. Nunn said as much after the committee vote: "There's no such thing as passing a piece of legislation for a vast organization, and then all of a sudden everybody is adopting it in spirit and marching out and it cures all the problems. . . . It may take five or 10 years for this really to set."[54]

Sensing the momentum behind Goldwater and Nunn's efforts, Reagan stepped in to address defense reforms. On April 1, he signed National Security Decision Directive 219, which approved the initial recommendations of the Packard Commission that could be implemented by executive action. He followed this act four days later with his weekly radio address devoted to defense reform, emphasizing the Packard Commission's work and making no reference to any of the congressional actions to date. He stated that he would soon be sending a message to Congress that would request it to join him in promoting defense reform. The presidential message to Congress arrived on April 24 and again commended the work of the Packard Commission and Congress, but he also noted the constitutional responsibilities of both branches, warned against unnecessary changes, and outlined the few modifications he found acceptable.[55] Vice Admiral John Poindexter, who had been national security advisor for five months, believed the message would receive a chilly reception. Congress would not abandon "years of work" solely on the president's pledge. Poindexter was correct. Goldwater and Nunn rejected the president's appeal, as did their House counterparts. The committees "were convinced that all reforms would require the force of law to guarantee reasonable prospects for meaningful implementation."[56] Nunn began enlisting Senate Democrats to support the bill.[57]

The next major step was to undertake the significant statutory changes Reagan opposed by passing S. 2295, the "Goldwater-Nunn bill," as the press had named it, in the Senate. That moment came at 10:40 a.m. on May 7. As one Pentagon watcher exclaimed, years of "rambling, almost formless discourse" were coming to an end; the issue had transcended partisan politics, becoming a genuine debate over the merits of reorganizing the Defense Department.[58]

Goldwater led off that debate, followed by Nunn, who laid out the key provisions of the legislation in detail, citing deficiency after deficiency the bill was intended to correct, pointing out that the two senators had sought and incorporated Defense Department concerns.[59] Nunn ended the presentation of his evidence, and for more than seven hours the Senate considered the bill. Goldwater and Nunn's speeches proved critical, and there was clear appreciation from members of their regard for the Arizonan as many of the floor speeches delivered were sentiments of esteem. Members stopped by Goldwater's desk to speak with him, shake his hand, or pat his shoulder. They knew the physical pain he was enduring because of the severe arthritis in his hips and knees, as well as the anguish he suffered because of his wife's death five months earlier. Several amendments were offered, but none of them made major changes to the bill. Nunn then offered the final amendment as a tribute to his partner. He recommended that the Senate vote to name the bill "The Barry Goldwater Department of Defense Reorganization Act of 1986." Goldwater rose slowly from his desk on crutches to offer a protest, but then relented; he sat down and cried. The Senate heartily agreed to Nunn's gracious gesture, and at 5:50 p.m., when the clerk finished calling the roll, it had approved the bill 95 to 0, sending a clear signal to Reagan and the Pentagon. The Senate had given the seventy-seven-year-old senator his most satisfying legislative triumph before his retirement at the end of the session, following thirty years of service. Goldwater would have the final say nonetheless, giving credit to his colleague from Georgia. "We [Republicans] better come up with somebody, or I'm going to support this guy for president. He's terrific." Nunn could not reply for a moment, and Goldwater, now seated in a wheelchair, indicated to an aide to roll him out of the chamber.[60]

While the American public did not appreciate the importance of the

Senate's action, journalists who followed defense issues and editorial boards comprehended the implications of the legislation. The Senate had passed the most sweeping changes in the national security apparatus in almost thirty years. The House, anticipating the Goldwater-Nunn victory, had already begun revising its previously passed bill to conform more closely to the Senate version. It soon passed a companion bill named for Congressman Nichols.[61]

The conference committee of the two armed services committee met in mid-August, with Goldwater chairing the proceedings and Nichols as the vice chair. Because the substantive differences in the two bills were extensive, numbering more than two hundred, and there were more than a thousand differences in the language of the provisions, reconciliation of the two bills would not be easy. Goldwater understood the challenge ahead. He requested that the conferees bear four principles in mind: act in the best interests of US national security, keep an open mind by listening to all arguments, consider the issues on their merits, and ensure that the provisions were not ironclad but retained sufficient flexibility for the future. After a grueling month, the conferees completed their work on September 11; the final touch was to name the bill the Goldwater-Nichols Department of Defense Reorganization Act. The Senate passed the conference report on September 15, and the House followed suit the next day, sending it to Reagan for his decision. While some in the Pentagon urged him to veto the bill, such a step would have been futile at this point. He signed the bill on October 1, 1986, and the Goldwater-Nichols Act became law. Out of deference to the Pentagon's hostility to the reform effort, there was no signing ceremony.[62] It was a gratuitous slap at Goldwater, but he was not one to whine. He was satisfied with the outcome and his leading role. "It's the only goddamn thing I've done in the Senate that's worth a damn," he told reporters.[63]

CHAPTER 9

A BATTLE OF WILLS

Sam Nunn assumed the chairmanship of the Senate Armed Services Committee in January 1987 like an Old West gunfighter, pistols drawn. The leadership position was the fulfillment of a longtime ambition. Some observers viewed it as "preplanned and perhaps preordained."[1] After six years of a Republican-dominated Senate, the Democrats now controlled both houses of Congress during the final years of Ronald Reagan's presidency. There were rumors circulating among the political elite that Nunn was now in a position for a possible run for the presidency in 1988, but Nunn shrugged off such matters as he was not interested, and would ultimately announce his decision not to run. He was a conservative Democrat, not likely to do well in Democratic primaries where the liberal wing held sway. Moreover, as he told a confidant on the Democratic Leadership Council, "When I look in the mirror in the morning, I see a chairman of the Armed Services Committee, not a president." He had other, more pressing issues to consider. He immediately announced that for the first session of the 100th Congress, he intended to hold at least a dozen hearings on the US national security strategy.[2] He wanted to shift the attention from the "grains of sand on the beach" to the larger issues of policy and strategy by linking the defense budget to the national security aims. He made rules and procedural changes to the committee, provided the subcommittee chairmen with policy oversight guidance, and directed them to concentrate on specific policy matters. He had the staff analyze the committee's organizational structure, and after consulting with John Warner, the ranking Republican member, directed the formation of new mission-oriented subcommittees with specific policy oversight duties.[3] In the words of the committee's majority staff director, Nunn was in control and provided the staff his "strategic guidance" that set the committee's agenda.[4]

He decided the best approach to improving oversight of defense would be to begin with a complete review of national security strategy and use that as the foundation for examining policies and budgets. As he remarked, "We can't expect the military departments to work jointly if Congress continues to exercise oversight by reviewing the programs of the military departments in isolation." In that regard, he met with Democratic representative Les Aspin to discuss issues of common interest. Lastly, he wanted to improve the committee's ability to relate the budget to national security objectives. In one historian's view, the committee "had never pursued national security strategy so deliberately, systematically, and comprehensively" since its creation in 1947.[5]

Nunn did not neglect party issues related to national security either. Four months earlier, he, along with Aspin and Al Gore, had written a DLC report, "Defending America: Building a Foundation for National Strength," that laid out "cost-effective alternatives" to the administration's policies and positions on research and development for advanced weapons, increased defense burden sharing by NATO allies and Japan, and the future of the SDI program. Their intent was to link foreign policy aims and defense strategy more coherently.[6]

While Nunn would certainly engage the other pressing concern of the Armed Services Committee, defense spending in an era of deficit reduction, an issue of more importance loomed—arms control. The arms control lobby was cautiously optimistic that the 100th Congress would be the bellwether on arms control policy at a time when the administration's policies in this area were a shambles. The lobby supposed the challenge to the president would come from the House and not the Senate, which one writer characterized as continuing to "tiptoe toward any national security/arms control confrontation with Ronald Reagan." The lobby was even less optimistic about the Senate Armed Services Committee, branding it a "conservative stronghold," now headed by Nunn, a "cautious legislator." Then again, as chairman and the party's most respected voice on national security, he would have to consider the views of Democratic committee colleagues, several of whom were promoters of robust arms control measures.[7] Nunn was sensitive to this claim. He and Warner agreed to rename the subcommittee dealing with nuclear forces the Strategic Forces and Nuclear Deterrence Subcommittee, directing the members to develop a bipartisan approach to arms control and strategic forces modernization as well as evaluate and strengthen nuclear deterrence.[8]

Nunn was well aware that the Senate's Democratic leaders planned to add to their legislative agenda two nuclear-testing treaties that had not been acted on by the Republican-led Senate. Nunn informed Robert Byrd, who was once again majority leader, that the president was now adding a reservation regarding verification procedures that broke his commitment to the Senate regarding these ratified treaties. Nunn opposed the reservation: It "will in effect have scuttled a prudent and sensible approach to achieving future limitations on nuclear testing. . . . I also believe the Administration will be buying a bucket full of trouble in both the House and the Senate as we deliberate on arms control amendments this year."[9] However, the Reagan administration soon raised a related issue: the ongoing research and development of the Strategic Defense Initiative. The program remained controversial, nagged by questions regarding its technical feasibility and huge costs. Since 1985 Nunn had been a supporter, voting to approve $3.2 billion for the program in the most recent fiscal year.[10]

On January 12, the Armed Services Committee called Secretary of Defense Caspar Weinberger, its sole witness, to its first of sixteen hearings for the session, and began its comprehensive review of the national security strategy. Nunn admitted that the topic was not "necessarily a terribly interesting subject," but he avowed that "it's at the heart of what we have to do as a beginning point in any kind of rational military process."[11] The new chairman was immediately on the attack. He cast doubt upon the administration's defense strategy, questioning "the clarity, the coherence and the consistency" of its policies, and chiding the administration for misrepresenting comparative US-USSR military strength, which he stated was based on "superficial net assessments."[12] He argued a mismatch existed between the strategy and the funding needed to execute it. He found the administration's plan to fight "3-1/2 wars," in Europe, Asia, and the Persian Gulf, with a potential small conflict somewhere else in the world, to be not merely ambitious but impractical given the budget-cutting mood on Capitol Hill. He also remained skeptical about some aspects of the Pentagon's planning, such as a naval strategy that relied on US aircraft carriers to launch air attacks on the Soviet Union that were vulnerable to Soviet long-range bombers, and insufficient NATO capabilities to counter a Soviet invasion of West Germany.[13]

CHAPTER 9

Committee members eventually raised the SDI project as a topic since the Defense Department had requested $5.3 billion for the program in the fiscal year 1988 budget, having already spent $9 billion on it. In response, Weinberger revealed that it was possible that SDI would be deployed in phases, when each technical component became functional, rather than wait for the entire system to become operational. He told the committee that the government "should never lose sight of" the program's objective: to protect "people and continents," not just critical military targets such as missile bases.[14] Nunn remarked that Weinberger's characterization of the SDI program was confusing because Weinberger's statement seemed contrary to Reagan's contention that the purpose of SDI is "not to enhance deterrence but to replace it."[15] Nunn, as well as many others, including important administration arms control advisors such as Secretary of State George Shultz, was unaware of what journalist Strobe Talbott called Weinberger's "end run."[16]

A month earlier, on December 17, 1986, the defense secretary, joined by Richard Perle, the assistant secretary of defense responsible for arms control, and the SDI program director, Lieutenant General James Abrahamson, had met secretly with the president to discuss the SDI program's status. Weinberger portrayed the program as achieving impressive results, claiming the Pentagon could start building and deploying the SDI's "Phase One" system, kinetic kill vehicles (kinetic energy weapons) in space, by the early 1990s. Weinberger suggested to Reagan in an allegedly "low-key" manner that the program the president wanted to leave as his most significant legacy could be pulled off. Moreover, Weinberger intimated that creating a "partial defense umbrella" to protect US population centers and US strategic missile silos was attainable and worth pursuing.[17]

Then, three weeks after the Weinberger hearing, someone in the administration leaked to the *Washington Times* conversations at a February 3, 1987, White House meeting between Reagan and his advisors, during which Weinberger proposed that to accelerate the SDI program, the United States follow a "permissive" or "broad" interpretation of the 1972 Anti–Ballistic Missile Treaty (ABM), which Weinberger called the "legally correct interpretation." In making this point, Weinberger was harkening back to a "contentious and arcane internal dispute" that began in October 1985 when then national security advisor Robert McFarlane announced that the administration, without advance notice or congressional consultation, was adopting a new interpretation of the treaty based on a preliminary legal opinion by the Department of State's legal adviser, former federal judge Abraham Sofaer. Under this analysis, which dismissed the so-called traditional or narrow interpretation of the treaty that each succeeding administration had upheld since 1972, the Reagan administration, according to McFarlane, could begin unrestricted development and testing of the actual components of a space-based strategic defense system using "exotic technologies," that is, technological advances previously unknown and using "other physical principles" nonexistent at the time the treaty was ratified. The understanding at the time was that Sofaer based his analysis principally on his reading of the treaty text and the negotiating record. In short, using this interpretation would enable the Defense Department's SDI organization to conduct tests that the traditional interpretation prohibited. Shultz, remembering the political furor such an argument had prompted in 1985, and from which embarrassingly the administration had to backtrack under pressure from Congress and allies, recommended that the issue be discussed with the Soviets first. Shultz later claimed, "I knew that if we adopted the 'broad interpretation' at a time when Weinberger was talking up deployment, that would mean a confrontation with Congress and a setback in our ability to get the funds from Congress that the SDI program required."[18]

According to the press account, which senior administration officials confirmed, Reagan allegedly responded, "Why don't we just do this [use the broad interpretation]? Why do we have to make any announcement?" The article quoted the president as stating, "Don't ask the Soviets. Tell them [about the shift]. I see the price tag, and I'm willing to pay." An argument that had been simmering for nearly two years was now heating to a boil.[19] Shultz clearly appreciated how the perception that the administration was chipping away at the treaty and did not care about the Soviet or the Senate's views would be politically disastrous.[20] Richard Burt, a State Department official, was even more forthright about the legal opinion when it first surfaced in 1985. According to Sofaer, Burt came "barging into" his office, bellowing, "What the hell are you doing? Are you crazy?" Sofaer tried to calm Burt down, but Burt remained upset about the opinion: "It's totally insane, like this is the Ten Commandments, the ABM Treaty, the Ten Commandments of American national security and arms control. You have now tried to repeal the Ten Commandments." Sofaer indicated he had merely done his job as a lawyer, but Burt was not done trying to impress upon him the political beehive he had whacked. It was not an issue of analytical quality, integrity, or lawyerly ability, he retorted. "This is a catastrophe for us. You have undermined what was regarded by the arms control community as one of the great documents, one of the great achievements of mankind."[21]

Burt's words were still true two years later. Nunn's reaction to the February 1987 news article was "as angry as his aides had ever seen him." Fired up, he sent a terse letter to Reagan, warning him that the shift in interpretation of the ABM Treaty from the traditional observance that banned the development and testing of space-based ABM systems and components would be costly, risking deeper cuts in the SDI program's funding. The most critical aspect would be a unilateral decision to make such an interpretive change without consulting Congress, which the senator considered a coequal partner in treaty making. Such a step would be a "constitutional confrontation of profound dimensions." He added that if the consultations did not occur, Congress would view the decision as "the end of arms control under your administration." The basis of Nunn's response was his belief that a broad interpretation was not the Senate's understanding of the ABM Treaty when it heard testimony from Nixon administration officials and passed its advice and consent resolution in support of it in 1972. He was conducting an extensive review of his own on the subject, based on congressional access to the ABM record that the two branches had agreed to the previous year. He planned to complete the review in a few weeks.[22]

Nunn was not alone in his consternation. Not only did US allies such as Great Britain, West Germany, and Japan object to this change in interpretation through their ambassadors, British prime minister Margaret Thatcher and West German chancellor Helmut Kohl wrote Reagan to express their displeasure with the potential policy alteration. They saw this precipitous change to support a suspect technological venture as potentially undermining NATO's nuclear deterrence strategy, worsening relations with the Soviets, damaging East-West stability by halting ongoing arms control negotiations, and creating domestic political trouble for them by instigating an arms race and increased military spending. Yuri Dubinin, Soviet ambassador to the United States, informed Shultz that such a step would have a deleterious impact on the strategic arms reductions negotiations in Geneva, a message reiterated by the principal Soviet arms negotiator to his US counterpart, Max Kampelman.[23] US military leaders voiced their reservations about implementation of an initial stage deployment. Admiral William J. Crowe Jr., chairman of the Joint Chiefs of Staff, believed the decision hasty since the "military utility" of a phased deployment remained uncertain. He called the early deployment "premature," a position he had also testified to before the Senate Armed Services Committee on January 21.[24] These reactions to the intended policy change were unambiguous; in response, the Reagan administration hedged, but it also realized consultation with Congress and allies was now vital to counteract the uproar.

In an interview on ABC's *This Week with David Brinkley*, Shultz, based on language worked out with Weinberger and approved by Reagan, stated that he had now come to accept the broad interpretation of the treaty that was needed to ensure realistic testing of SDI components. He believed the negotiating record was ambiguous with respect to testing and developing technologies that were not known in 1972. He added that no decision regarding the interpretive change would occur without first consulting Congress and allies. Nunn, also interviewed by Brinkley, struck back. He declared the first phase that the administration believed would be ready for development and deployment to intercept incoming missiles "could not be tested under any interpretation of the treaty since the technology was known in 1972, and thus fully banned by the pact."[25] Raymond Garthoff, the former executive secretary of the US delegation at the ABM treaty negotiations who had negotiated the provisions under debate, agreed with Nunn. "There is no question," he stated, "that a projectile fired from a satellite is an interceptor based on a familiar physical principle," and thus a known technology in 1972.[26]

Although the administration wanted to present a unified front, opinions differed considerably. Kenneth Adelman, director of the Arms Control and Disarmament Agency, stated that more realistic testing was needed to assure Americans that deployment of the first-phase technology was credible. If not, the United States "would have to abrogate the treaty to do the testing" and thereby assure itself that the SDI program was feasible. However, Adelman added, "no president is going to abrogate the ABM treaty just to do testing."[27] Moreover, while State Department and Arms Control and Disarmament Agency officials concurred with Nunn's assessment that space-based kinetic kill vehicles (KKVs) could not be tested legally since the "KKV was 'based on physical principles' that were well known when the ABM Treaty was signed" in 1972, Pentagon officials contested that viewpoint. This divergence required another meeting with Reagan, with the president stating that no decision would be made until consultations with Congress and the allies occurred. He directed that this process begin immediately. Nunn's letter had put Weinberger's "end run" on hold and postponed the legal bickering.[28]

Behind the scenes, however, conservative Republicans were plotting their future tactics. The Republican "gang of five," who strongly supported SDI and advocated accelerating the program, consisted of Senators Malcolm Wallop of Wyoming, Pete Wilson, and Dan Quayle, along with Representatives Jack Kemp of New York and Jim Courter of New Jersey. They had been pushing for early deployment of a portion of SDI to attain a near-term technical success and ensure the program's political sustainability, especially after Reagan left office.[29]

Conservative columnist George Will, however, believed that Nunn had made the better argument as to the value of the SDI program. Will believed Reagan had oversold the program as developing an "impermeable shield to make nuclear weapons obsolete." Nunn, as Will observed, had contended that creating such a shield was not realistic and that the primary aim of strategic defense was to make deterrence more credible, to cast doubt in the mind of Soviet leaders that they could effectively strike first with nuclear weapons.[30] The scientific community agreed with Nunn too. The nation's leading physicists reported that under the best of circumstances, it would take a decade or more of research to provide the technical knowledge needed for an informed decision about the potential effectiveness and survivability of directed energy weapon systems. This information did not currently exist.[31]

As with every effort Nunn made, he did his homework. Since August 1986, he and the committee's expert on arms control, Robert Bell, had been poring over the ABM Treaty's classified negotiating record after the administration released the documents, but with the stipulation that limited access to members and only six staff members.[32] It was an enormous archive. After five months of painstaking research, Bell completed his review and wrote a draft report numbering more than 250 pages, concluding that the broad interpretation was erroneous. He then turned to Armed Services Committee general counsel, who had been a Department of Defense attorney, and another attorney on Nunn's staff, for a legal review, in which they concurred with his view. Subsequently, Bell and a colleague, after consulting with Congressional Research Service experts on constitutional law and US treaty history, then wrote a legal report for Nunn, with extensive footnotes to support the analysis and lend it scholarly weight.[33]

Nunn's own methodical study of the record and the report resulted in an outline of conclusions he intended to articulate in a series of speeches scheduled for the coming weeks. The first speech would analyze the US Senate's understanding of the treaty's provisions when it voted in August 1972. The second would focus on US and Soviet leaders' behavior with respect to the treaty since its signature. The third would be an assessment of the negotiators' intentions when they fashioned the treaty's provisions.[34] Nunn's investigation, at that moment, placed the "whole world of arms control in his hands," to the point at which his "word will be ABM law."[35]

At Reagan's direction, Pentagon officials made their way to a Capitol Hill meeting with Nunn and other Senate Democratic leaders, assuring them that SDI activities would be consistent with the narrow interpretation until State Department attorneys completed their new evaluation of the legality of the broad interpretation, scheduled for completion in May.[36] Meanwhile, Sofaer, using Nunn's methodology, was conducting a study of how Nixon administration officials understood the disputed provision of the ABM Treaty and how they explained it in their congressional testimony. Additionally, his report would deal with how US and Soviet officials had since portrayed the provision in official communiqués on the agreement. Yet, the administration did not cease its push for accelerating the SDI program, directing Lieutenant General James Abrahamson, the SDI program director, to provide an itemization of tests that could be conducted if the broad interpretation was implemented. As a countermove, Democrats in both chambers planned to introduce legislation that would prohibit any tests that contravened the restrictive interpretation. Jim Wright, now Speaker of the House, warned that if the administration implemented this step, a severe reduction in SDI funding would follow.[37]

On March 11, despite a bad case of laryngitis, Nunn began three consecutive days of speeches on the Senate floor and released the report detailing his and his staff's appraisal. His staff, at the senator's order, had informed the White House that the onslaught was coming. Standing with a microphone in his hand, he stated that the debate over the treaty's interpretation was not a case of whether one is "for or against the ABM Treaty." Furthermore, it should not be approached under the illusion of short-term strategic advantage, patently based on flimsy technical evidence, but instead, with a "decent respect for the long-term interests of the rule of law and the continued integrity of the Constitution." He then proceeded to tackle the first part of his stated methodology, that the 1972 statements from White House and Defense Department officials during the Nixon administration "explicitly" supported the narrow interpretation. He held that the statements, made during the Senate's ratification hearings, were "authoritative," and that they "flatly and unequivocally contradicted" the Reagan administration's claims that the hearing record espoused a broad or more permissive interpretation. Nunn stated that Sofaer's earlier assertions, made in the lawyer's 1985 analysis and subsequently in the June 1986 *Harvard Law Review*, were "inadequate," and that the former judge had undercut the administration's believability by the manner in which he addressed the subject. Nunn pointed to specific comments made by executive branch witnesses during the ratification hearings as evidence. He noted omissions in the legal adviser's appraisal, such as a "crucial" comment a member of the Joint Chiefs of Staff expressed, "that the JCS were aware of the limits on development and testing of [exotic missile defense technologies such as lasers and other futuristic anti-missile defenses and] . . . had agreed to them, and recognized that this was a 'fundamental part of the agreement.'"[38] Moreover, the Senate's leading defense expert at the time, Henry M. "Scoop" Jackson, repeatedly asked executive branch officials about limitations on "exotic space-based weapons" and accepted the Nixon administration's position that only fixed, land-based weapons were permitted, which became the traditional or narrow interpretation.[39] In essence, Nunn argued that the Senate was clearly informed that the development, including testing, and deployment of an "exotic" space-based antimissile system would be prohibited under the ratified treaty. The Reagan administration's reinterpretation was a "fundamental constitutional challenge to the Senate as a whole with respect to its powers and prerogatives" as an "active partner" in treaty making. The treaty was "the law of the land," and the administration was now unilaterally rewriting international law.[40]

The speech transfixed the media.[41] Additionally, the speech forced Frank Carlucci, Reagan's national security advisor, and Howard Baker, now the White House chief of staff, who had only been in his position for a few weeks, to hunt for ways to defuse the situation through compromise. As Carlucci later remarked, the broad interpretation "made sense legally, but politically, it was a disaster, and Congress just blew up . . . so we instantly tangled with Sam Nunn, which is not a good thing to do."[42]

Nunn offered the second part of his analysis reproving the administration's broad interpretation on March 12. Again, his remarks were blistering, this time with respect to the administration's analysis that US and Soviet behavior and official statements since 1972 reinforced its new interpretation based on the record made available to the Senate. In reviewing the record, Nunn maintained that many of the official statements from both governments over the past fourteen years supported the narrow interpretation, and argued that the evidence offered to the contrary was "ambiguous at best, and in some cases, incomplete."[43]

That same day, Perle, the broad interpretation's most vocal advocate, announced his resignation from government. While his decision was not related to the ongoing fracas, the departure of the man known as the "Prince of Darkness" for his hard-line stance against the Soviet Union and an equally accurate reputation for acid-tongued remarks, meant that the chief designer of the administration's strategic arms policies would now be lending his support from the sidelines. Nonetheless, Perle took a final jab at Nunn, calling his legal analysis "profoundly wrong."[44] Perle asserted that the questions Nunn raised had "received little attention" during the hearings and floor debate. He accepted the idea that statements made by Nixon administration officials appeared to defend the narrow interpretation, but he then claimed that they had "misrepresented" the agreement in their testimony. "When you look at the treaty in the record," he maintained, "the statements they made did not reflect the treaty and the negotiating record."[45]

Then, in the midst of the debate, Sofaer acted unilaterally and openly in response to Nunn's stinging indictment in the Senate by sending a letter to the chairman. In the letter, Sofaer seemed to suggest that the Department of State's 1985 legal finding, which justified the administration's broad interpretation, "may have been flawed." This was a stunning admission. He promised that a more comprehensive legal review was ongoing and emphasized he was giving the matter his complete personal attention to ensure that the "analysis we present is complete."[46] White House and State Department officials were apoplectic and vowed they would not have cleared the letter for release.[47]

In response, Nunn coolly gave his third and final speech on the treaty interpretation issue regarding the treaty negotiating record, recognizing there were ambiguities in the record, because it was neither an official transcript of the proceedings nor an official history of the negotiations but a set of documents of "uneven quality." However, he concluded in a raspy voice, they were not "of sufficient magnitude to demonstrate that the Nixon administration reached one agreement with the Soviets and then, presented a different one to the Senate."[48] He added, "I believe it is appropriate at this juncture to pause for a moment and reflect on how the administration could be in such serious error on its position on this very important issue." The administration's procedures were largely to blame. He emphasized the legal disagreements over the interpretation of the negotiating record among agency attorneys, the State Department legal advisor's admission that his staff failed to conduct a rigorous analysis of the Senate's ratification proceedings, and the decision to conduct an interview with only one of the principal US negotiators, Paul H. Nitze, a member of the administration. "Finally, there was no discussion with the Senate, despite the Senate's constitutional responsibilities as a co-guarantor of treaties. Mr. President, to say this is a woefully inadequate foundation for a major policy change is a vast understatement."[49]

The significance of Nunn's speeches and his accompanying report was not lost on his colleagues. The Georgian had captured the interest of both houses on Congress and members of both parties. Warner acknowledged that Nunn's argument presented the most complete "scholarly" study of the issue to date, requiring the administration's pending study to be of the same quality. Kemp admitted that Nunn had essentially undercut the viability of SDI.[50] The press was equally impressed with the speeches' influence. "It was a political event" of consequence, and on the "seemingly arcane issue of treaty interpretation may rest the prospects for Soviet-American relations over the next few years," a *Washington Post* editorial proclaimed.[51]

In the meantime, presidential hopeful Al Gore promoted a bipartisan compromise concerning both the treaty interpretation and SDI funding, which he had worked out in February with Kampelman, Nitze, and Perle. Under the compromise, the administration would not develop or test SDI components that would be in violation of the ABM Treaty. In return, the Senate would support a level of funding for SDI research consistent with the narrow interpretation. Gore discussed the matter with Carlucci and Baker on his return to Washington, but Reagan and Weinberger would not give in. Byrd, Claiborne Pell, and Alan Cranston were supportive of the scheme, but Senate Republicans and their lone Democratic supporter, Ernest "Fritz" Hollings, repudiated the offer, and the proposal gained no traction among House Democrats.[52] Arms control proponents and SDI critics in that chamber, as well as arms control interest groups, had no reason to compromise. They believed Nunn had made their case for them. In fact, the speeches had a cascade effect: Sofaer was summoned before a joint hearing of the Senate Foreign Relations and Judiciary Committees to respond to Nunn's charges.[53] For his part, Nunn kept his own counsel. One aspect was clear—he had reshaped the arms control debate.

By April, a House Armed Services Committee subcommittee recommended the SDI program be cut by $2 billion from the $5.2 billion request, and that the defense authorization bill include language that would legally impose the narrow interpretation on the administration. The full committee agreed with the proposal. Meanwhile, Nunn switched tactics. At an Armed Services Committee hearing on the SDI program that month, he remarked that the interpretation issue was no longer critical, as it was clear that the first-phase tests were based on physical principles well established when the treaty was signed, thereby making testing of them illegal. He based his remarks on a new study that determined the planned deployment was not technologically feasible. The "gang of five" became increasingly vocal, with Kemp announcing his presidential bid and declaring he would make SDI a campaign issue.[54]

For the next two weeks, Republican senators rallied to oppose Nunn on "the key arms control issue of the 100th Congress." However, it was clear that they did not have a coherent strategy. Additionally, some agreed with Nunn; moderates wanted to deescalate the heated rhetoric and prevent any rash actions that could affect the ongoing arms talks with the Soviets in Geneva. The White House talked tough, but cracks were appearing in its position. Although it was clear that the administration did not intend to compromise on SDI, it did want to appear flexible. To that end, Reagan sent Shultz to Moscow to consult with the Soviets and perhaps bargain over a five-year moratorium on deploying strategic defenses and seek some other compromises from the adversary in return. Nitze, reflecting on the House Armed Services Committee's action, warned Reagan that making Nunn an enemy would only result in the chairman taking a similar approach in the Senate.[55]

Meanwhile, Sofaer completed his new study of the broad interpretation of the ABM Treaty, which was leaked to the press on May 1. His conclusion remained the same: the broad, permissive interpretation was justified by the ABM negotiations, and nothing in the ratification hearings was "sufficient to overcome the negotiating history" and undermine the validity of that interpretation.[56] Nunn was irate. "Somebody had better start thinking about where we are going," he said. "We are on a slippery slope here . . . we are on a slippery slope as far as being a nation of laws, and we are on a slippery slope as far as whether America's word can be taken when we enter into an obligation."[57] White House spokesman Marlin Fitzwater commented that Sofaer's study was not the administration's final position on the subject. Another internal review of the ABM Treaty would be completed in June.[58]

Five days later, Nunn maneuvered the Senate into a clash with the administration when the Armed Services Committee voted 12 to 8, with Republican senator William Cohen siding with the Democrats, to restrict SDI development and testing in an amendment to the defense authorization bill. Carl Levin had devised the amendment's original language prohibiting the funding of any activity that would violate the traditional interpretation. However, Nunn offered compromise language so that the Senate would not be legislating the traditional interpretation, which the president would likely veto. Cosponsoring the revised amendment, Nunn's language stipulated that the administration could only spend funds for the SDI program consistent with the budget request it had submitted for fiscal years 1988 and 1989. Nunn could now state that he was merely exercising Congress's power of the purse, ensuring the funds were spent consistent with the purposes for which the administration had requested them. In addition, the bill authorized $4.5 billion for the program, but Nunn warned that could shrink further if the Republicans attempted to block the committee's proposed interpretation provision.[59]

On May 20, Nunn, while addressing the national defense authorization act on the Senate floor, made a fourth speech on the ABM Treaty interpretation issue: an appraisal of Sofaer's recent analysis of the classified negotiating record, which the administration had declassified along with additional documents. Again, Nunn assailed the analysis for inconsistencies or omissions and the use of rhetorical devices to devalue the importance or reliability of certain reports, and he maintained that a "careful review" of the negotiating record refuted the legal advisor's appraisal. The speech was, in the words of one former ABM negotiator, "a devastating rebuttal."[60] In "Johnny-come-lately fashion," the Foreign Relations Committee appeared ready to follow Nunn's lead with a report that supported the narrow interpretation, but Republicans on that committee stymied it.[61] Meanwhile the House acted, passing its version of the defense authorization bill on May 20 with language similar to the Levin-Nunn constraint, which Aspin successfully managed to include in the bill.[62]

The Senate Republicans' strategy now became apparent. They first used a number of parliamentary stalling tactics and eventually a filibuster to prevent debate on the defense authorization bill because of the Levin-Nunn language. The stalemate dragged on from May into July. Nunn and Aspin decided to sidestep the strategy by agreeing to the contents of a defense bill through an informal conference. Aspin collaborated with House Republicans, but he and Nunn circumvented Senate Republicans by agreeing on most issues after Senate Republicans filibustered to prevent the bill from coming to the floor for debate. Consequently, Nunn announced his intention to work with Aspin to finalize an agreement before the August recess that would steer the appropriations committees in both chambers in their formulation of a spending measure for next fiscal year bereft of an approved authorization bill.[63] The recess came and went; the stalemate continued into September. Nitze counted the summer a lost opportunity for bargaining with Nunn, but Weinberger's vehemence remained unabated. He was emphatic that the administration's goal was not to oblige Nunn but to protect Reagan's vision of missile defense.[64]

Nunn redirected his efforts in early September. He sent a letter to the president stating that if the administration did not desist from its ABM re-interpretation relying on the "Sofaer doctrine," then the Senate would be forced to request "all executive branch documents related to the negotia-tion" of the intermediate-range nuclear forces (INF) treaty, which the Soviet Union and the United States planned to conclude before year's end. Nunn stated that the Senate "had no choice" but to request these documents given the administration's position that only the negotiating record provides the authoritative meaning of a treaty, not the testimony of executive branch of-ficials. Therefore, "a reasonably prudent Senate must obtain the entire INF negotiating record if it is not to be derelict" in assessing the pact.[65] Nunn was now linking three arms control measures: the ABM Treaty reinterpretation; the Senate's advice and consent on the forthcoming INF treaty, a treaty the administration considered a diplomatic coup; and congressional concerns about the Reagan administration's deviation from three other arms control practices, which the House defense bill addressed with specific provisions, and with which Nunn and other Senate Democrats agreed. Nunn's standing as chairman and his leadership on arms control made the threat imaginable. In response, the White House's deputy spokesperson told reporters the ad-ministration was studying Nunn's letter and "doing our darnedest to cooper-ate with Congress on the INF treaty."[66]

By mid-September, the Senate's Democratic leadership again tried to break the Republican filibuster led by Senator Jesse Helms, a North Carolina Republican, which was now in its fourth month. Robert Dole of Kansas, who was choreographing the strategy, predicted a cloture vote might occur soon. Hollings had now rejoined his fellow Democrats, and Republican senator Nancy Kassebaum of Kansas had defected. Still unsure of the outcome, Nunn played another trump card, announcing from the floor during debate on the sixth cloture vote that the Senate would not take action on confirming the administration's Supreme Court nominee, Robert Bork, a nomination that had been languishing for more than two months, until the defense bill was completed, a point on which Byrd agreed. The majority leader scheduled a cloture vote for September 15, when Soviet foreign minister Eduard Shevardnadze was in Washington to meet with Shultz on arms control issues and discuss a potential summit meeting later in the year. A Republican defeat on a cloture vote during the visit would potentially embarrass the president.[67]

Whether Nunn's ploy or Byrd's announcement worked is uncertain, but one outcome was clear: on September 11, the Senate began work on the $303 billion defense authorization bill that the Republican filibuster had blocked since May, because they likely no longer had the votes to do so. Moreover, Dole's consultation with Carlucci and Weinberger facilitated the decision to allow the bill to proceed to the floor for consideration; many Republicans doubted the wisdom of further parliamentary maneuvers.[68]

Yet no senator expected the bill to pass unthinkingly. The Levin-Nunn language remained a Republican target. Warner complained that the provision undercut the administration's ability to negotiate with the Soviets on arms control. Nunn's response was biting. Referring to another Virginian, James Madison, Nunn reminded his colleague of that founder's vision of the role the Senate had in treaty making. Speaking directly to Warner, he added, he was certain Warner wanted the Soviets to comprehend "this is a government that has more than one branch and that we are not a monarchy nor are we a dictatorship."[69]

Four days later, on September 15, Republican senators resorted to the filibuster over the Levin-Nunn language itself. Several impassioned exchanges and further wrangling followed, including Nunn again declaring to hold up Bork's confirmation hearing, this time by promising to invoke a Senate rule that would limit the Judiciary Committee's hearings on Bork to two hours at a time, and agreeing he was an obstructionist after the minority whip accused him of it. Byrd then informed his colleagues he would keep the Senate in a round-the-clock session if the filibuster proceeded. With these threats made, Byrd and Dole eventually found a compromise. They agreed to votes on competing Democratic and Republican resolutions that considered the Senate's treaty-making role. The Republican resolution prevented the Senate from legislating on the ABM Treaty interpretation issue during the ongoing US-Soviet negotiations. As expected, the Democratic resolution carried, which affirmed the Senate's role in treaty making by supporting Reagan's arms control negotiations but reserving judgment on treaty provisions until the Senate could scrutinize them.[70] It was a temporary cease-fire.

A few days later, Warner decided to press the treaty interpretation issue by offering a motion to eliminate the Levin-Nunn provision. The motion went down in defeat, 58 to 38, with eight Republicans joining the Democrats and Hollings the only Democrat to side with Warner. It was a major defeat for the president even if the vote demonstrated that the bill might not be veto proof. Nunn played his remaining wild card. He vowed to cut SDI program funding further if Reagan vetoed the bill, realizing that he was in a stronger position since the four senators absent at the time of the vote had previously indicated support of the Levin-Nunn language.[71] Hollings was so angry with the outcome and Nunn's threat that he wrote an opinion piece expressing his outrage with the Democratic leadership for its "politically motivated" efforts to enshrine the narrow interpretation in law, which he believed was incorrect based on his participation in the 1972 ratification debate and his own review of the negotiating record.[72] His Democratic colleagues on the Foreign Relations Committee saw it differently, however, releasing a report, after voting along party lines, condemning the broad interpretation as "the most flagrant abuse of the Constitution's treaty power in 200 years of American history."[73]

Hollings's attack, however, warranted a response. In an op-ed, Nunn challenged Hollings, stating that his colleague's perspective on the issue had been inconsistent and contradictory. At first, Hollings had supported the Defense Department's broad interpretation, and then in his recent testimony on the matter before the Foreign Relations Committee, he had repudiated the department's analysis. Chastising his fellow senator, Nunn hoped that the South Carolinian would continue to deliberate on the subject and, eventually, switch his position and join the "overwhelming majority of former ABM negotiators, senators, House members, and Nixon, Ford and Carter administration officials (including six former secretaries of defense) who stand firmly for the original interpretation."[74] As the *Wall Street Journal* reported, the debate "dealt only fleetingly with defense programs themselves, instead focusing mostly on the extent to which Congress should direct foreign policy —in particular treaty-making with the Soviet Union."[75] On October 2, the Senate, by a vote of 56 to 42, passed the defense authorization bill that rejected the broad interpretation and maintained the Levin-Nunn provision. The bill would now proceed to conference, but since the House version contained similar language, Reagan could only threaten a veto.[76]

The bitterness of the past several months spilled into the media. Columnist Charles Krauthammer accused Nunn, whom he considered "perhaps the ablest and most thoughtful Democrat in the Senate," of "unpardonably putting institutional self-interest above the national interest." Nunn and his Senate colleagues had conducted an irresponsible effort to "legislate the Soviet position of a delicate arms control issue [the narrow interpretation], in the midst of negotiations" in Geneva over strategic arms reductions. In short, Nunn and others were undercutting the US negotiating position, and further weakening a president grievously damaged by the Iran-Contra scandal.[77]

Such protestations, which Nunn had earlier characterized as the White House "shooting itself in both feet," were of little importance. Nunn had proved to be a tough adversary in the "test of wills," and the Senate defense authorization bill demonstrated his power.[78] Looking for a way to take the initiative by asserting a more partisan approach, conservative Republicans in the Senate and White House looked for a scapegoat and found it in Warner. They recognized that Warner had not deserted the party position over the Levin-Nunn language, but they accused him of emasculating its strategy by not dissuading centrist Republicans from supporting the provision on its merits. His vote on October 19 against confirming Robert Bork to the Supreme Court was the breaking point, but he had followed Krauthammer's dictum. "I have always followed the rule up here [on Capitol Hill] that your country is first and politics is second."[79]

By November, only die-hard Republicans like Helms were putting up much of a fight over the defense authorization bill that the House-Senate conferees were completing. In fact, Carlucci, who had been nominated to be secretary of defense, struck a more conciliatory tone during his confirmation hearing before Nunn and the Armed Services Committee on November 12, a week after Weinberger resigned, indicating that he would consult with Congress before making any decisions on pursuing tests that might be construed as flouting the ABM Treaty. Committee members praised him for his willingness to cooperate on this and other issues, and promised a quick confirmation vote.[80] His remarks were decidedly different from those Weinberger uttered at the Pentagon ceremony honoring his departure from office, where he criticized SDI opponents, stating that their antagonism to the defense system was "one of the most dangerous ideas ever to infect our political discourse."[81]

The Senate made good on its promise to confirm Carlucci quickly, but more importantly for the administration, the White House and the conferees, including Nunn, Warner, Aspin, and the ranking Republican on the House Armed Services Committee, William Dickinson, worked out a compromise on the SDI issue that the House and Senate found acceptable and passed. The compromise reduced SDI funding to $3.9 billion, but with the understanding that the Pentagon would limit all SDI tests to those it had previously delineated and certified to Congress through fiscal year 1988, all of which were compliant with the narrow interpretation. A reference to the ABM Treaty did not appear in the bill.[82]

There would be no acceleration of the program as Weinberger had envisioned; there would be no veto. Reagan signed the bill into law on December 4, and the battle over arms control policy that had lasted for six months ended. This provision and the decline in defense funding levels for a third consecutive year were significant gauges that suggested the waning of Reagan's political sway and Nunn's prominent role as committee chairman. As an unnamed Senate Republican aide observed, "This is a different Sam Nunn." Political scientist Norm Ornstein agreed. Nunn reputation as an influential member was long-standing, but now he and other Capitol Hill watchers saw Nunn wielding that influence with the assurance of a "true partisan power broker."[83] Bell best understood Nunn's ardent stance on this issue. It would set an unmistakable example of his ascendancy to a leadership role in the chamber, especially if the Senate's prerogatives were flouted: "Power in the Senate flowed not from losing skirmishes, but from winning them."[84]

CHAPTER 10

DOWN TO ZERO

S ecretary of State George Shultz sat at the witness table, waiting for the proceedings to begin. The hearing room, a vast hall of paneled wood and white marble in the Hart Senate Office Building, dominated its occupants.[1] Seated at the center of the semicircular dais before Shultz was the chairman of the Foreign Relations Committee, Claiborne Pell, the white-haired, courteous but eccentric Democratic legislator. Now in his fifth term of office, Pell, whom President John F. Kennedy once called "the least electable man in America," had a long and abiding interest in international affairs. He had served as a diplomat after his World War II military service, participating in the 1945 San Francisco conference that established the United Nations.[2]

Flanking Pell the morning of January 25, 1988, were sixteen members of the committee waiting for Shultz's testimony on the subject of the hearing, the Intermediate-Range Nuclear Forces Treaty, which Reagan and Mikhail Gorbachev had signed a month earlier.[3] Senate rules required that all treaties, regardless of subject matter, be referred to the Foreign Relations Committee, but in this case, because the accord had military and intelligence ramifications, the Armed Services Committee and the Select Committee on Intelligence were also holding hearings. Senator Robert Byrd and the committee chairmen had established well-defined coordinating procedures for dealing with the treaty. The administration, which was personalizing the pact as "Ronald Reagan's treaty," fretted that the approval process might become unmanageable and possibly fatal, an imaginable consequence given that the Senate had developed the "reputation as a graveyard for nuclear arms control treaties" during the 1970s.[4]

The treaty was of vast importance to the administration and the Soviets. Reagan and Gorbachev had invested significant effort in bringing it to fruition after they nearly agreed to eliminate all strategic nuclear weapons at their 1986 summit in Reykjavik, Iceland. That potential agreement foundered on Reagan's unwillingness to concede to Gorbachev's principal demand, the elimination of the Strategic Defense Initiative (SDI).[5] Despite the failure to reach an accord on strategic nuclear weapons, supporters of the INF Treaty considered it an arms control breakthrough: both parties had approved the destruction of an entire class of nuclear weapons, known as the "zero option," and created a mechanism for verifiable destruction of these weapons through meticulous on-site inspection. Furthermore, it required the Soviets to dismantle more missiles than the United States.[6]

Pell had carefully choreographed the hearing as it placed the Democratic majority in an awkward position during this election year. Democrats heavily favored approving the treaty, a position consistent with opinion polls and the positions of numerous peace and veterans organizations. However, Pell's main concern was the Republicans, who remained divided. A majority supported the president and hoped to benefit from a foreign policy success in the upcoming election, but conservative hard liners believed that either "pragmatists" in his administration had duped Reagan or worse, he had been besotted by the Soviet leader's charm, which they likened to the symptoms of an illness and labeled "Gorby fever."[7] Conservative activists felt the treaty represented another sign of Reagan's abandonment of the principles that earned their support of his presidency. One "New Right" activist claimed the treaty was a "sellout," and called the president a "useful idiot for Kremlin propaganda."[8]

The discord in the Republican ranks would be apparent in the opening minutes of the hearing. As committee chairman, Pell would lead with his introductory remarks. The ranking member, Jesse Helms, the firebrand from North Carolina who was leading opposition to the treaty, would follow.[9] A report had already surfaced in the *New York Times* that Reagan had met with Helms and seven other Senate Republicans in the White House just before Congress began its recess for the holiday season. His aim was to enlist their help in attaining speedy approval of the treaty before a likely summit in Moscow in late May or June. He urged them to pass a "clean" resolution of ratification, not adding any "crippling amendments." In response to this entreaty, Helms responded, "Well, Mr. President, I look around this table and I don't see a yes man. I'm certainly not a yes man." He continued, "I have no intention of being frivolous about it. But if a treaty needs a reservation or an amendment, it's going to be offered in the Senate." According to a witness, Reagan noticeably bristled at this challenge. Still taking the measure of the president, Helms resumed by declaring he had not decided on his position, but he was certain of one point: he would scrutinize the treaty and would remedy any flaws. He ended by advising the president that many of his colleagues would be doing the same so the administration should not expect the Senate to conclude its business swiftly. Helms had fired a warning shot. The anti-Communist right was mobilizing its forces in the Senate and around the country for a battle over the treaty.[10]

The man charged with forging Republican senatorial support for the treaty was Robert Dole of Kansas. As a matter of courtesy, Pell would allow Dole, who was not a committee member, to make opening remarks in support of the treaty from the dais. Dole's appearance had required delicate handling as he had asked to testify as the opening witness, but Pell denied that request, because the purpose of the hearing was to solicit information from the administration, not give the Republicans a forum to tout a potential triumph.[11]

Pell quieted the hearing room with his voice calling for order. It was 10:01 a.m.[12] The treaty's ultimate fate was now to be determined. Arms control experts anticipated trying days ahead, but they judged that after extensive hearings and impassioned debate, the Senate would approve a resolution of advice and consent to the ratification of the treaty. However, no one could predict whether the Senate would attach reservations, amendments, or other conditions, which were in its powers. Amending the treaty would require new negotiations, although such an outcome was rare.[13] The administration was trying to remain confident, a perception Shultz vocalized several minutes into the hearings, when he began to outline the treaty's provisions and contend that its approval was unquestionably consistent with US interests as well as those of NATO allies.[14]

A block away, in the Senate Russell Office Building, Nunn gaveled the Armed Services Committee hearings to order, quieting the crowd of reporters and observers who filled the seats. On the dais, sixteen senators were seated, including Senator Ted Stevens, who served on the Appropriations Committee and was an ex officio member of the committee. His presence indicated continuing interest in seeing the treaty receive approval.[15]

Nunn, generally considered the most "powerful individual personality in the Senate treaty review," began to speak, methodically outlining the hearing's purpose.[16] Of paramount importance was whether the INF Treaty would strengthen or weaken NATO's ability to deter a Soviet attack in Western Europe. Critics of the treaty feared the elimination of the US intermediate-range nuclear missiles (Pershing II missiles and ground-launched cruise missiles) with a range of 500 to 5,500 kilometers would impose an additional burden on NATO's already outnumbered conventional forces. Additionally, the Soviets had deployed intermediate-range missiles (SS-20) targeting NATO bases and installations, which could be launched with little warning. Consequently, treaty opponents, and some supporters including Nunn, suggested that approval of the treaty required a commensurate improvement in the balance of conventional forces in Europe. Tied to this concern were two others: whether NATO's current tactical nuclear weapons, of which there were thousands, would be sufficient to deter such an attack, and whether NATO states should field new nuclear weapons that would not contravene the INF treaty's provisions. There was also a psychological element involved. Nunn and some defense experts wondered if the treaty would damage alliance relations by removing a powerful symbol of the US commitment to Europe's defense. Nunn theorized that the Soviets' strengthened capabilities could allow them to intimidate NATO allies into a position "closer to neutrality, rendering NATO much weaker." Polling in NATO countries indicated that the treaty was highly popular, however, and political leaders had already signaled that disapproval of the treaty or amendments that required its renegotiation would strain relations.[17]

After Nunn framed the issues, other senators' opening remarks consumed several more minutes. Finally, the two witnesses, Secretary of Defense Frank Carlucci and Chairman of the Joint Chiefs of Staff Admiral William J. Crowe Jr., addressed the concerns committee members had raised, especially Republican foes. Carlucci, making his first appearance before the committee since assuming his position two months earlier, went directly to the core issue, arguing that the treaty would enhance NATO security. He underscored that the treaty's provision that called for asymmetrical reductions in the number of weapons between the two foes would serve "as an important precedent for future negotiations in both the strategic nuclear and conventional fields." Crowe was equally brief, but he spent several minutes reviewing NATO security interests and outlining the military advantages attributable to the treaty. He noted that under the treaty's provisions, the Soviets would consent to "asymmetric reductions [in intermediate-range nuclear weapons] by a ratio of 4 to 1." He stated that the treaty was "militarily sufficient and adequately verifiable." He acknowledged the disparity in conventional forces, urging development of more sophisticated weaponry to blunt the Warsaw Pact armor and short-range missile capabilities. However, the two officials' statements were not the only important aspect of the hearing. During a round of questioning, John W. Warner asked Crowe whether any member of the Joint Chiefs of Staff opposed the treaty, Crowe replied that they were unanimous in their support and added that their NATO counterparts were in complete support.[18]

Overall, the Armed Services Committee hearing was a staid and well-mannered affair in comparison to the pyrotechnics at the Foreign Relations Committee hearing, where Helms attacked Shultz's credibility, then proceeded to wave a top-secret document at the secretary, and demanded that he read it as television crews captured the challenge. Allegedly, the document was a new US intelligence assessment of Soviet theater nuclear forces. Shultz adamantly refused to lift the cover sheet and potentially expose the classified information in an open hearing. Ultimately, after an exasperated Shultz asked, "Can I get this document out of my hands?" an aide took the document and returned it to Helms.[19]

Nonetheless, Carlucci and Crowe's testimony did not convince Nunn and his colleagues entirely. Members questioned several issues, including whether the treaty's verification procedures were sufficiently robust to catch any Soviet cheating, whether the Soviets understood that short-range nuclear weapons (those with a range of less than 500 kilometers) could be built and deployed in Europe in the future, and whether the NATO allies were committed to strengthening their conventional forces. Nunn remarked that until he had satisfactory answers to these issues, he would not comment on how he would vote on the pact.[20]

Despite this statement, Nunn was inclined to support the treaty, but he was also going to assure himself that the administration was entirely transparent about its arms control policy. He had already won the first skirmish on this point when the administration agreed before the hearings to provide the Senate with the complete, classified negotiating record (thirty-two volumes and five feet of material). He had demanded access to the record because of the administration's contention the year before that the executive branch could interpret a treaty's provision any way it chose and that executive branch officials' testimony on a treaty might not reflect the true meaning of the accord.[21]

As a consequence, Nunn held that the Senate was "compelled to look at both the treaty and the negotiating record" because the administration's position was tantamount to telling the Senate it could not trust its word as to the meaning of the treaty given in testimony, and that if "something is important or unclear," it was incumbent on the Senate "to flag it."[22] A National Security Council staff member later grumbled that the administration's stand was "counterproductive" because it encumbered Reagan's policy agenda by surfacing a constitutional argument, thereby guaranteeing a fight with Congress.[23]

The remainder of the testimony that week was not controversial. Harold Brown, the former secretary of defense, stated that while he preferred an agreement that allowed the United States to retain some intermediate-range missiles in NATO countries, he believed the treaty to be in US interests. In addition, he pointed out that the president still had the option of using intercontinental ballistic missiles to protect Europe.[24] Dr. Jeanne Kirkpatrick, a steadfast conservative who had recently served as President Reagan's ambassador to the United Nations, followed Brown. She was less enthusiastic about the treaty. Her concerns stemmed from a conviction that the treaty would increase anxieties in NATO about the US commitment. She worried that such a perception would undermine the alliance and result in a more neutral Europe. Yet, she acknowledged that failure to approve the treaty could harm US-European relations, given its popularity among NATO publics. Nunn asked her how the United States should react to evidence of a significant violation of the treaty, such as one in which the Joint Chiefs of Staff considered terminating the entire agreement, because it was plainly detrimental. Kirkpatrick's position was clear: the United States should abandon the pact to show it would not tolerate cheating.[25]

The Armed Services Committee hearings continued into the first week of February, calling upon several who favored the treaty and two detractors. The supporters included the four service chiefs; the US ambassador to West Germany Richard Burt, who had been involved in the diplomatic efforts as an assistant secretary in the State Department; and army general John Galvin, the NATO commander. Galvin supported the treaty, but he argued that the risks involved in withdrawing the missiles required a compensatory measure, namely, improving NATO's conventional forces. Testifying against the treaty were Richard Perle and retired General Bernard Rogers, Galvin's predecessor.[26]

While Galvin and Burt could knowledgeably address the views of NATO military and political leaders, Nunn and a few colleagues decided to learn those positions firsthand when the first set of hearings ended on February 4 and before a weeklong recess began. Nunn, along with Pell and David Boren, the Senate Select Committee on Intelligence chairman, as well as William Cohen, Byrd, and Representative Les Aspin, would attend the Wehrkunde Conference in Munich, the unofficial forum for international security experts, including their NATO counterparts.[27]

However, despite the public appearance over the first two weeks of the hearings of evenhanded and civil discourse regarding the treaty, another issue was playing out in private between Nunn and the administration. Nunn, along with Byrd, had been negotiating with Shultz and other administration officials for weeks on the text of a letter that Shultz would send to Congress stating that executive branch sworn testimony before the Senate on arms control treaties was "authoritative and therefore legally binding in interpreting the scope of treaty provisions."[28] Acceptance of this position would not only have repudiated the administration's current stance, but would also have acquiesced to Nunn's avowed position that a president cannot reinterpret a treaty without Senate concurrence. Nunn and Byrd continued to believe that without this written agreement, the administration could establish a precedent that would erode the Senate's constitutional advice and consent prerogatives.

The issue came to a head on February 5. Shultz, who had agreed to abide by the "narrow interpretation" in a meeting with Nunn and Byrd a few days earlier, now renounced the bargain after meeting with a group of Republican senators who excoriated him for making the deal with the Democrats, thus weakening the administration's case for SDI testing. When Nunn and Byrd learned of Shultz's about-face, they responded with a letter warning him that they would delay a vote on the treaty unless the administration changed its position. They threatened to add language to the treaty that might require its renegotiation or attach various conditions and understandings to it. Additionally, Nunn refused to hold any further Armed Services Committee hearings on the treaty with other administration witnesses until Shultz appeared before the committee to settle this matter. Their price for not disrupting the process was clear-cut. They laid down three principles the administration must adhere to in writing: testimony of all executive branch witnesses and any submissions for the hearing record can be regarded by the Senate as authoritative; the meaning of the treaty as presented can be regarded by the Senate as authoritative, "without the necessity of the Senate's incorporating that testimony and material" in its resolution of ratification through "understandings, reservations, amendments, or other conditions"; and a meaning of the treaty different from that presented to the Senate by the administration cannot be adopted without Senate approval.[29]

Now the administration found itself caught between the Senate Democrats, who formed the majority needed for approval of the treaty, and Republican senators determined not to "surrender" their position on SDI testing. Senator Arlen Specter likened Nunn and Byrd's demand to hostage taking. Thus, while an unidentified White House official railed against the Democrats for threatening to delay treaty approval, administration officials secretly worried about attaining congressional approval, and a State Department spokesperson made mollifying statements, promising that Shultz would be studying the Nunn-Byrd letter thoroughly, certain that the senators' concerns could be addressed to their satisfaction.[30]

The senators' letter propelled Senator Joe Biden, Delaware Democrat, to act as well. He made several statements about devising a means to resolve the issue. On February 9, 1988, he revealed a compromise proposal he believed would prevent the administration from developing and testing the "Star Wars" technology without Senate approval, but also avoid a lengthy fight that would delay the treaty's approval. He called for the Senate to "attach to the new treaty—by majority vote—a statement that bound the administration to the meaning it testified to in asking for Senate ratification." The statement would "establish that, as required by the Constitution, the INF Treaty will be interpreted in accordance with the text of the treaty and the understanding shared by the executive and the Senate at the time of ratification." Further, "any change in that interpretation would require the consent of the Senate."[31] Biden's strategy not only exacerbated the White House's dilemma, but it put Republican senators who favored the treaty in the difficult position of either supporting Reagan unequivocally or acceding to Biden's "compromise" because they did not have the votes to defeat it. Others thought the compromise a sensible approach; however, the entire matter alarmed NATO allies to the point at which the Danish foreign minister publicly castigated Nunn for creating this situation. In response, Byrd offered soothing words while in Munich: the Senate would likely consent to the treaty provided there were not problems concerning its verification regime.[32] Nunn seemed less sanguine.

In his Wehrkunde speech, Nunn emphasized modernizing NATO conventional forces in addition to nuclear weapons not covered in the treaty. He especially addressed West German concerns about short-range missiles such as the Lance missile modernization program, a mobile, surface-to-surface, tactical missile that could provide non-nuclear and nuclear fire support, the first units of which had been deployed to Europe in 1973. The army had decided in 1985 to extend the shelf life of the nuclear Lance. Nunn underscored, however, that a "'nuclear fix' was not the answer to NATO's deterrent woes." He continued, "Let me emphasize this point: our goal is to raise the nuclear threshold in Europe, not to lower it."[33]

While he agreed with Byrd that approval of the INF Treaty would occur eventually, Nunn cautioned, "Misplaced euphoria in the wake of INF could further erode public support of essential force improvements in Europe." He had not forgotten NATO's inability to withstand an overwhelming Warsaw Pact onslaught. In fact, he underlined that point: NATO must surmount its second-rate conventional capability so it would not have to resort to nuclear weapons within days of a Soviet conventional assault.[34] Increasing NATO's conventional capability would raise the nuclear threshold and allow for the rapid reinforcement of NATO lines with units from the United States.[35] Therefore, the NATO summit meeting scheduled for the next month "should be the occasion for a solemn reaffirmation of the U.S. commitment to the alliance in both its nuclear and conventional components."[36]

The political costs of Nunn and Byrd's opposition, buttressed by Biden's and now Pell's promise to move forward by attaching a formal condition to the treaty, ended the standoff. Biden told reporters that a written statement from Shultz was insufficient to remedy the impasse, because it would be binding only on the Reagan administration and not future chief executives.[37] This limitation was unacceptable. The administration backed down. On February 9, Shultz sent a letter to the Senate accepting the three principles Byrd and Nunn stipulated after obtaining the approval of the Senate minority whip, Wyoming senator Alan Simpson. White House press secretary Marlin Fitzwater tried to put a positive gloss on Shultz's letter, stating it only dealt with the INF Treaty and not the ABM Treaty. However, not to undermine Shultz's meaning, he added that he believed the secretary had addressed Nunn and Byrd's concerns.[38]

The assurances in Shultz's letter appeased Nunn and Byrd, and the next day, they dropped their threat to delay hearings.[39] Biden, however, was not satisfied. He did not find Shultz's detailed language adequate, declaring he would block the treaty unless the administration recognized the Senate's constitutional prerogatives.[40] Congress watchers thought the cleavage among Democrats was a sign not only that Nunn had won the skirmish with the administration, but that he had also left the "Democratic majority on the Foreign Relations Committee in disarray."[41] A number of Republicans were infuriated that Shultz had bowed to Nunn's tactics, but several Democrats remained apoplectic that Shultz's letter essentially brushed away the constitutional issue as irrelevant.[42] The institutional power struggle now burst into a public debate over the issues. Constitutional scholars and arms control experts waded in, offering arguments for both sides in opinion pieces, magazine articles, and press interviews.[43]

The battle of words and the political maneuverings sank under the surface as other demands on the Senate's agenda came to the top. Nunn found himself immersed in the details of the defense budget, but this diversion was temporary.[44] His attention returned to the INF Treaty in late February for his committee's next hearings. He had not, however, been sidetracked from his position on the treaty interpretation issue in the interim. When the INF chief negotiator, Ambassador Maynard Glitman, appeared before the committee, Nunn underscored that the witness's testimony, based on Shultz's written promise, constituted an authoritative interpretation of the treaty.[45]

At the beginning of March, with the first round of committee hearings complete, Byrd disclosed his attempt to reduce the perceived power struggle between Democrats on the Armed Services and Foreign Relations Committees. He wanted to intimate to the administration that the Senate would act favorably on the treaty. During the Wehrkunde Conference, Byrd had met with Nunn, Boren, and Pell. They decided that not more than one condition would be attached to the treaty when the Foreign Relations Committee reported it to the Senate floor in late April or early May. Biden, sidelined by surgeries for an intercranial aneurysm discovered in mid-February, seemed to be the odd man out in that his proposed binding language would not be added in committee or on the floor. The agreement did not rule out considering other language on the floor, but the strategy did preclude what the leadership termed the "salad bar" approach to consideration of amendments or other conditions. In essence, it thwarted critics hostile to the treaty, such as Helms, from offering "killer" amendments that would necessitate renegotiation of the treaty.[46]

Soon after Byrd revealed his plans, Nunn and several other senators left for Moscow to meet with Gorbachev. During an extensive, three-hour meeting in the Kremlin, Gorbachev complained to his visitors about the lack of progress on US-Soviet arms negotiations on strategic nuclear weapons and conventional force reductions in Europe. Gorbachev was knowledgeable about the ongoing ABM interpretation debate. He reiterated the Soviet position of strict adherence to the ABM Treaty provisions. After the meeting, Nunn met with reporters, remarking that Gorbachev seemed anxious to sign a strategic arms treaty. He added that while there were still hurdles in negotiating a strategic arms reduction treaty, Nunn and his companions had assured the general secretary that the Senate would approve the INF Treaty.[47]

Biden's proposal, however, proved more attractive than expected. Several Democratic colleagues stated that in his absence, they would offer his understanding either in the committee or on the floor. They believed they had the votes to win acceptance without damaging the Senate's approval. However, if it threatened to derail the resolution of ratification, then they would cease pushing it.[48]

Nunn was having second thoughts too. The meeting with Gorbachev and an attack on his legal interpretation of the ABM Treaty issue in a *Wall Street Journal* op-ed, written by a law professor and a former Reagan administration official, prompted the reassessment. In response to the piece, Nunn pointed out that Charles Cooper, assistant attorney general for the Office of Legal Counsel in the Reagan administration, had reached the same legal conclusion.[49] In addition, Nunn stated he generally supported Biden's reservation. He subsequently met with Byrd, Boren, and Pell, and the four agreed tentatively to introduce Biden's condition during treaty markup.[50]

This decision drew an immediate response from the White House counsel, Arthur Culvahouse Jr., who in a strident letter criticized the Democrats for "an unprecedented arrogation of treaty power" in addition to arguing that Biden's condition obstructed the president's constitutional powers.[51] Nunn refused to back down, and in a letter to Senate Republican leaders, he rebuked Culvahouse's misleading claims and indicated he would support an altered form of Biden's legal condition.[52] Behind the scenes, he was working with Alan Cranston and Richard Lugar to write language that would be acceptable to the Democrats and a majority of Republicans.[53]

On March 22, at the Foreign Relations Committee's final hearing on the treaty, Nunn and Boren reported their panels' preliminary conclusions, the last major hurdles before Pell's committee would finalize its actions. Boren and Cohen, the senior Republican on the Intelligence Committee, stated the United States could monitor and verify Soviet compliance with the treaty and that this belief was unanimous. Nunn and Warner informed the committee that their assessment was incomplete because of the recent testimony of

Glitman, continuing in-depth assessment of the negotiating record, and on-going committee discussion. Nonetheless, they offered several suggestions about future arms control initiatives and addressed the implications of the treaty for a variety of weapons programs. Nunn indicated that he thought the treaty's "positive features" overshadowed any flaws.[54]

The polite atmosphere of the hearing would not prevail. A day later, there was a legislative tussle in the Foreign Relations Committee when Helms and Larry Pressler, a Republican from South Dakota, tried to attach killer amendments to the treaty, but their attempts were defeated by wide margins. Helms then tried to postpone the committee's considerations until Nunn submitted his committee's final report, but to no avail. Helms's delaying tactic was of little consequence, as Nunn reported his committee's findings to the Foreign Relations Committee a few days later. However, Nunn raised a new and "major concern," which had been brought to his attention by Dan Quayle. The administration's testimony regarding whether the treaty allowed or banned futuristic weapons such as lasers or other advanced technologies, rather than conventional warheads, to destroy targets, had been inconsistent. Nunn found Quayle's concerns valid and asserted that clearing up this issue was essential; it must be resolved before the entire Senate could approve the pact. He did not rule out the attachment of an understanding to clarify this point, and he reiterated his concerns about the treaty interpretation issue. Yet despite these reservations, the Armed Services Committee overwhelmingly supported the treaty. Nunn revealed that the committee vote had been 18 in favor against 2 Republican naysayers.[55]

Pell could now bring the treaty to a final vote in the Foreign Relations Committee, which occurred on March 30, when committee Democrats and all but two Republicans voted in favor. This outcome marked the first official step toward approval and sent the treaty to the floor without any killer amendments. The administration remained optimistic that the accord would win final approval before the summit meeting scheduled for late May. Cranston estimated at least 88 votes in favor, easily more than the two-thirds required for final approval. Even so, complications still lay ahead as Helms and his allies promised to carry on their fight against the treaty on the floor, and Nunn repeated his position that the administration still owed a guarantee that futuristic weapons such as lasers would not be prohibited under the treaty. Otherwise, he declared, the Senate might be forced to add a stipulation requiring Soviet concurrence since it could not be demonstrated conclusively that a US-Soviet agreement existed.[56]

The administration took Nunn's message seriously; it recognized that negotiators had not dealt with the issue of what new technologies would be banned under the treaty. State Department officials began to work on language throughout early April, with Glitman assuring senators that this issue would be settled before floor action.[57] It would take more than mere promises. Support for Nunn's stance on futuristic weapons came from two former administration officials, Caspar Weinberger and Kenneth Adelman. The issue also catalyzed interest group opposition. The Conservative Caucus delivered "Neville Chamberlain–style black umbrellas," decorated with slogans that decried the administration's appeasement of the Soviets and its desertion of "America's Troops," to every senator's office. The group's chairman called for a new offensive against a treaty that was pro-Soviet but also suicidal. He vowed to renew caucus efforts to establish anti-treaty coalitions throughout the country.[58]

To address Nunn's apprehensions and calm White House fears about further delays of the treaty's approval, with the summit only a few weeks away, Shultz had Shevardnadze send a letter to him stating that the Soviet Union shared the administration's position that futuristic weapons were prohibited under the INF treaty. The minister's letter affirmed that this was the Soviet Union's definitive position and that the prohibition applied to medium-range and short-range missiles, whether they carried a nuclear warhead or not. Nunn remained unsatisfied, arguing that the letter's language was ambiguous about the treaty's relevance to another group of weapons, unarmed surveillance missiles.[59] This statement incensed Pell, who argued the letter cleared up the issue and negated the need to add a specific understanding. The White House spokesman denounced Nunn's position as an unnecessary impediment, but some senators thought otherwise, most notably Quayle and Pete Wilson. Wilson pointed out that Nunn had checked the negotiating record himself on this issue and found no explicit Soviet agreement on the weapons.[60]

The White House's scolding and a remark from Reagan about the slow pace in approving the pact angered Byrd. He stated that the chamber would not be pushed into accelerating consideration of the treaty to accommodate the White House's "arbitrary deadline." He also backed Nunn completely, to the chagrin of pro-treaty Democrats, stating that he asked the Georgian for a written report on the futuristic weapons issue along with Boren's assessment of how a ban on these weapons could be verified.[61]

Within a few days, the furor died down, Nunn and Byrd backed away from amending the treaty to suggesting that a treaty condition or a side agreement might be sufficient to resolve the ambiguities. However, the treaty seemed jinxed, as no sooner had this issue been surmounted than the Soviets appeared to be backing away from the treaty provisions governing complete inspection of Soviet military facilities to verify compliance. State Department officials and US military inspectors were confident that this issue could be resolved quickly because the treaty language supported such inspections. This spat served only to set off another round of false alarms in Washington.[62]

On April 30, Byrd, joined by Nunn, Pell, and Boren, announced that while he was ready to bring the treaty to the Senate floor on May 11, there were four points that the Intelligence Committee believed the administration needed to resolve, one of which was the latest verification dispute. Nunn believed this issue could be settled, but he warned the Soviets that challenging some of the clearly agreed-to provisions was not helpful.[63] He repeated his view that a side agreement regarding the futuristic weapons issue might be needed. Nonetheless, he remained "cautiously optimistic" about settling the Intelligence Committee concerns. On this point, Boren revealed that the senators had met with Lieutenant General Colin Powell, Reagan's national security advisor. Byrd added that the pertinent committees and the bipartisan leadership would meet to determine if the four issues had been resolved before debate began.[64]

Again, administration officials found themselves in a damage-control posture as Shultz, US negotiator Max Kampelman, Powell, and Glitman traveled to Geneva, Switzerland, to meet with Shevardnadze and fix the technical oversights.[65] A White House aide admitted the administration's lobbying of Congress had been "bungled." In frustration, he observed ruefully, "It never should have gotten this far down the road without these questions being answered." Shultz received most of the blame, though that did not seem justified to knowledgeable onlookers, who noted several executive branch gaffes. Nunn responded to the reproachful exchange in his usual patient, low-key manner.[66] Another storm passed quickly. In two days, after several meetings, some of grueling length, Shultz settled the four issues with his Soviet counterpart. Powell briefed Senate leaders on the results upon his return from Europe, and Nunn spoke for the leaders when he indicated that he had a "positive reaction" but added that he wanted to examine the agreements in detail, which he promised to complete over the weekend. He warned that despite his view that treaty approval could occur in time for the summit meeting, opponents could impede this goal through procedural challenges and amendments during floor consideration.[67]

Nunn's caution proved valid. Movement toward the resolution of ratification stalled several times as senators weighed in on particular issues they believed needed resolution or clarification. Playing odds maker, Nunn offered that the probability of the treaty being approved was "60–40" before the summit. However, he offered an amendment that required the Senate to approve any reinterpretation of the INF pact. The administration opposed the amendment, but Powell, who had become the public face of the administration on the issue and was now playing a prominent role negotiating with Senate leaders and preventing damaging amendments, stayed confident about forging a compromise if that would help expedite Senate action.[68]

Nonetheless, the wrangling over language and parliamentary tactics continued for three more days with Republican opponents, and even some moderates who feared the administration was relinquishing its executive prerogatives, offering amendments, often defeated by ample margins. These roadblocks exasperated Shultz, who in a meeting with Republicans called on them to desist and allow a vote. Byrd was equally frustrated, especially when one amendment Republicans offered was similar to one the Senate had approved a few hours earlier. "If we're going to have Mickey Mouse amendments like this," the majority leader complained, "the President is not going to have this treaty." Nunn became embroiled in an arcane argument over vague wording in the treaty, but he was eventually mollified when Lugar, the Republican floor leader for the treaty, said that the language was indeed "awkward" but that a correction could be made without renegotiating the treaty. Nunn agreed, suggesting the issue could be handled in the resolution or by having the two parties exchange letters of understanding.[69]

Nunn and other Democrats would not be easily dissuaded from their stance on the treaty reinterpretation issue. It remained the principal obstacle, but a breakthrough occurred when Democratic and Republican leaders, without consulting the White House, agreed on compromise language as a condition that would specify how the treaty would be interpreted. The condition, later known as the "Byrd-Biden condition," would be included in the resolution of ratification. The Senate approved the compromise by a vote of 72 to 27.[70] In the aftermath of this vote, the *Wall Street Journal* found it incredible that Senate Republicans would be allies in the "search-and-destroy mission against the vestiges of what was once executive-branch authority over foreign policy."[71] Senate Republicans attempted to downplay the importance of the condition, but Nunn felt the long fight was his to savor. The condition, he asserted, reaffirmed the constitutional principles that had always governed treaty making, bedrock principles that the administration had attempted to undercut by its erroneous interpretation of executive powers.[72]

After dispensing with this issue, the Senate began its vote on the treaty in midafternoon May 27. Nunn and the other committee chairmen, as well as the party leaders, had invested four months of meticulous work in the pact. Pundits and congressional experts were certain that the Senate leaders had the votes needed to pass the resolution of ratification. In a matter of minutes, senators cast their votes in the silent chamber after nine days of hardheaded deliberation and impassioned debate that had often broken into finger pointing and recriminations. When the clerk announced the tally, the result highlighted the often unpredictable nature of politics. The Senate had approved the treaty by a lopsided vote of 93 to 5. Seconds later, one of the spectators in the public galleries began applauding, others followed, and caught up in the moment, some of the members began to applaud as well, an accolade for a historic accomplishment: the first US arms agreement to win approval in the Senate in sixteen years.[73] One commentator noted, "In essence, the INF Treaty served as a referendum on arms control in an administration that had resisted reaching any accommodation with the Soviet Union for seven years."[74]

Flush with victory, Byrd and Dole telephoned Reagan, who had stopped in Finland on his way to Moscow, to inform him of the outcome. The two leaders sat in Byrd's office, flanked by Nunn and others who had played a major role, television cameras recording the moment. Byrd and then Dole spoke in turn with the president, who thanked them for their efforts and invited them to Moscow for the official exchange of the ratification documents the following week. They accepted. The momentous event also lent itself to comedy when one of the telephones the two Senate leaders were using went dead. Nunn then deadpanned that he wanted to assure the bystanders that the one remaining line was not the US-Soviet hotline.[75]

CHAPTER 11

THE TEFLON SENATOR WITH CLOUT

George H. W. Bush, forty-first president of the United States, extended his hand to congressional leaders a day after his 1989 inauguration on an issue of immediate importance: to "build bipartisanship into the conduct of foreign policy." Referring to a letter he received from Senators David Boren and Republican John Danforth of Missouri, Bush stated that he agreed with their suggestion that frequent and extensive consultations with Congress on such issues would reestablish an atmosphere that once been common between World War II and the Vietnam conflict.[1] Many Democrats on Capitol Hill, with their commanding majorities resulting from the November 1988 elections, predicted a measured and cautious start as Bush framed his agenda. Nunn, who had assumed the chairmanship of the Democratic Leadership Council in 1988 because of his prominence on national security and to maintain the council's influence in the party, would be a factor in shaping the opposition's agenda.[2] One member of the Democratic leadership's staff remarked, "We're going to be doing some slow dancing for a while." A reporter noted that since the election, Washington had become a "peaceable kingdom" with vows of bipartisan cooperation.[3] How long these assurances would last was uncertain.

Nonetheless, in keeping with his long-standing interest in international affairs, Bush announced before taking office that the first order of business would be a review of US national security policy, which could take months, maybe a year, given the complex issues involved. Bush and his national security advisor, Brent Scowcroft, wanted meticulous attention paid to US-Soviet relations, especially modernization of land-based missiles such as the MX and the proposed Midgetman missile, and the status of arms control negotiations. Mikhail Gorbachev's ongoing efforts to refashion Soviet foreign policy by restraining growth in military spending and promising substantial conventional force reductions in Eastern Europe in December 1988 had prompted the new administration to recalibrate US assumptions and positions on a number of issues that had driven superpower relations since World War II. A few Bush advisers reasoned that Gorbachev's initiatives had let "the 'genie' of change out of the bottle in the Soviet Union."[4] This view was not shared by Scowcroft, who believed Gorbachev's recent "peace initiatives" were an attempt to play for time to achieve domestic reforms, while "making trouble" for NATO. His position was clear: "I think the Cold War is not over."[5] Amid this speculation about Soviet intentions, Nunn thought Gorbachev's proposition to reduce the number of Soviet troops was helpful, but he too remained skeptical. "Will the reductions be carried out in an honest way?" He avowed that he would have more confidence in the Soviet leader's pledge if the troop reductions involved the withdrawal of a sizable number of units deployed on the East-West border rather than rear-area units.[6] However, Nunn had a more pressing subject to deal with less than a week after Bush's inauguration—the confirmation hearings for John Tower to be secretary of defense. Tower had wanted the job for years, and Bush nominated him before the Federal Bureau of Investigation (FBI) had conducted a background investigation.[7] It would prove to be a rash decision.

On January 25, Nunn brought the Armed Services Committee to order in the vast, chandeliered Senate Caucus Room for the first of several planned hearings on Tower's nomination.[8] At the beginning, it was clear that despite Tower's former chairmanship of the committee, members wanted to erase any impression that he would receive preferential treatment. However, by the end of hearing, one reporter characterized the tone of the hearing as one in which the senators "reciprocated by implying strongly that Tower would be confirmed despite some lawmakers' misgivings" about his previous support of large defense budgets, his criticism of congressional intrusion into national security policy, his recent work as a consultant to defense contractors, and the "allegations of heavy drinking and womanizing." Another reporter described the hearing as "amicable," remarking that the members had become a "cheering section."[9]

Then, on January 31, the nomination hit its first major roadblock. Conservative activist and commentator Paul Weyrich, a leader of the New Right, appeared before the committee and revealed that on numerous occasions he had witnessed Tower drinking and socializing with women other than his spouse just when questions about the nominee's controversial private life seemed to have vanished. Only a few days earlier, many of Tower's former committee colleagues had expressed their sympathy for the intrusive and "unseemly treatment" he had endured. Now they sat in discomfort as Weyrich publicly questioned Tower's moral character and stated that confirmation would be a "national embarrassment." After the hearing, reporters maintained that Weyrich's testimony would not upset the nomination, and senators dismissed the allegations as uncorrelated reports or gossip. Nonetheless, disturbed by the allegations, Nunn and John W. Warner immediately sent a letter to the White House seeking further information about the scores of letters Weyrich claimed the White House had received that contained "specific allegations of moral impropriety." Tower's attorney, Paul Eggers, told reporters that Weyrich's remarks were a stunt to raise funds for the conservative causes he led.[10] For his part, Tower repudiated the allegations and attempted to dispel doubts about his defense industry connections, but Nunn was not mollified. He now publicly expressed concern regarding the appearance of misconduct or indiscretions associated with the nominee's private life and his work with major defense contractors. While the senator did not have misgivings about Tower's knowledge of defense issues, he did have reservations.[11] Further, a closed session on the matter had not resulted in any specific evidence, and C. Boyden Gray, the White House counsel, sent a letter to Nunn and Warner refuting Weyrich's statement about the hundreds of letters sent to the White House regarding Tower's past misconduct.[12]

Then two new allegations surfaced, and on February 2 Nunn decided to postpone the committee vote on Tower's confirmation pending further investigation, a step that the White House approved. Nevertheless, Nunn stated that he still expected Tower to become secretary of defense. He would not detail the allegations, commenting only that they were "serious enough for us to want to check them." Several senators expressed less optimism about Tower's confirmation. For the moment, the White House publicly upheld its support of Tower, but there was growing concern that the nomination was in jeopardy. Some Republican senators shared that belief.[13]

Nunn and Warner remained silent, waiting for the FBI report. Discussion between the two senators and the White House continued, including a private meeting with Bush at which time Nunn, accompanied by Warner, did not encourage the president to withdraw the nomination but explained his concern. Newspapers published gossip, stating that Nunn was angry at the administration for how it had handled the nomination, including leaking information from the investigation to Senate Republicans, and how it had pressured the chairman for a quick committee vote. Nunn's response was terse: "Obviously, there have been some unofficial briefings going on that I as chairman of the committee have not been part of." Some analysts speculated that Nunn was preparing for a presidential run in 1992, but he had already given up the idea, believing the 1988 campaign had been his best chance.[14] Yet it did not take a weathervane to see which way the wind was now blowing.

Senate Republicans, anxious that further allegations would surface, accused the committee of "navel gazing." Newspaper reports hinted Nunn would vote against the nomination, but his response was low-key as usual: "We ought to do something unusual in Washington; we ought to let the facts support the conclusions."[15] Senator J. James Exon, a Nebraska Democrat, indicated that he and Nunn had spoken and it was a "fair characterization" to state that Nunn opposed the nomination despite Bush's attempts to placate him for the White House snub. A Republican senator confirmed Exon's assertion and added that such a step was an "incredible event," putting the nomination in serious jeopardy, although White House officials denied that this outcome was likely. However, Republicans reckoned that even if Tower did receive enough votes to be confirmed, his reputation would be injured irreparably and he would be "useless" as secretary.[16]

A vote on Tower's confirmation would now be postponed for perhaps two weeks, because the FBI would need at least that amount of time to conduct an investigation into an allegation of a financial nature. Nunn refrained from reaching a final judgment on the nomination. He remarked that he had several concerns but would not make a "final decision until all the evidence" was laid out. When pressed further, he admitted that if required to vote at this moment, he would "vote no" because of Tower's history of heavy drinking, a record he found worrisome for a cabinet officer entrusted with such grave matters as military action, especially during a crisis, which demanded "clarity of thought at all times." Nunn was now convinced, as he told a reporter years later, that Tower had a "serious problem with alcohol" whether he acknowledged it or not. This was a particularly sensitive subject to Nunn and Warner, fearful that Tower's problems would set a poor example at a time when the armed forces had serious alcohol and drug abuse issues. Additionally, the two senators had informed the presidential candidates of both parties during the campaign that they had devised specific criteria that the Armed Services Committee would use to assess nominees for senior positions in the Defense Department—a problem with alcohol or drug abuse was one of the factors.[17]

With the nomination process now on hold, Nunn and Warner, along with majority leader George Mitchell, a Maine Democrat, and Robert Dole of Kansas, reached an agreement that the committee would vote on Tower's nomination after its recess concluded on February 21. The leadership agreed as well to expedite consideration of the nomination on the Senate floor as soon as the committee reported out its position. A *Wall Street Journal* editorial accused Nunn of delaying the vote to weaken Tower because the chairman wanted to "run the Pentagon from Capitol Hill." Nunn replied in a letter to the editor that the op-ed writer had made several factually inaccurate statements and, in some cases, absurd suggestions about his conduct and that of the committee and had demonstrated his ignorance of Senate procedures. One veteran Hill analyst asserted that Nunn's standing among his colleagues, on both sides of the aisle, had "coated him with Teflon" and "the allegation of partisanship would not stick." Thomas Mann, a noted political scientist, remarked that Nunn "doesn't need this kind of encounter to enhance his influence." In fact, many rank-and-file Senate Republicans sidestepped the partisan indictment and instead, embraced a "hang tough" mentality, continuing to back the nominee and using appearances on news shows to refute allegations about Tower's drinking habits and promote public support for him.[18]

The debate over Tower's qualifications continued day after day during the recess. The increasingly partisan rift over the nomination was one Bush did not want to widen. Because he was eager to avoid the quarrels that occurred during the Reagan presidency, he invited the chairmen and ranking members of the intelligence and foreign policy committees to the White House to consult on several foreign policy issues during the recess. Nunn was noticeable by his absence, though he received an invitation.[19]

On February 21, the White House delivered to the Armed Services Committee the final section of the FBI's report, which scrutinized Tower's lifestyle and business activities since the 1970s. The agency concluded its report by directly responding to Nunn's concerns about Tower's drinking habits, stating that the former senator "drank excessively" in the 1970s but for the past decade had been a moderate user of alcohol. With respect to Tower's business activities, the report made clear that he did not have any role in the ongoing procurement fraud investigation of the Pentagon, although there had been allegations that he had received illegal campaign contributions during his chairmanship of the Armed Services Committee. However, Nunn stated that he still had doubts about Tower's fitness after spending three hours in a closed committee meeting to discuss the FBI's conclusions.[20]

The hearings were having a physical effect on Nunn. One of his former staff who saw him during this period noticed his worn-down appearance, which Nunn admitted resulted from a lack of sleep and substantial weight loss, but the ordeal was coming to an end. While Nunn wanted to support Tower, the mass of evidence regarding the nominee's womanizing and drinking habits, much of it known for years but documented in the FBI report, outweighed any personal feelings he had.[21]

Three days later, Nunn made his doubts public in a packed hearing room, "With considerable reluctance but with a clear conscience, I will vote no on the Tower nomination," he solemnly pronounced. Immediately thereafter, pundits began to assay his motives, but his friends and colleagues dismissed the importance of such ruminations. Senator Richard Shelby, a Democrat from Alabama, summed up their viewpoint regarding Nunn's conduct: his stature and reputation for doing his "homework over the years" were the chief reasons; no "ulterior motive" was involved. Al From of the DLC added that Nunn believed fervently that the secretary of defense had to be a person "beyond reproach."[22] As Utah Republican senator Orrin Hatch predicted, Nunn's support would be crucial. The committee Democrats joined their leader, rejecting Tower's nomination along party lines, 11 to 9. It was the first time the committee had ever rejected a nominee for secretary of defense. The rejection was not only a rebuff to Bush, but it put the nomination in jeopardy when it came to a floor vote, as Mitchell and Nunn had promised such a step regardless of the committee vote's outcome.[23]

In fact, the committee vote proved climactic, while Senate Republicans strove to save Tower's nomination, they confronted numerous obstacles, namely a Senate with a Democratic majority and months of allegations that had tarnished Tower's reputation. All the same, Republicans hoped to find five Democrats to vote in favor of the nominee and targeted a dozen potential senators to break with their party, while at the same time attacking Nunn for his "blatant partisan politics."[24]

Judgments by columnists and editorial boards suggested that there was division of opinion as to the efficacy of the nomination after the committee vote, with some believing Nunn's statement was filled with "heavy, damning charges," as well as being "extremely elliptical," and that he needed "to come right out and say in plain language what he means" so that the questions about Tower's reliability and integrity would be judged clearly. Others wanted to portray the issue as a partisan knife fight that the president lost.[25]

By early March, Senate Republicans won a delay on a vote until the middle of the month so they could find defectors among the Democrats, but their attacks on Nunn, especially by Dole, served only to bolster the Georgian's support among Democratic members, including conservative southerners. Dole had been calling anyone who opposed the nomination a "Nunn-Partisan." Some of Dole's allies accused Nunn of wanting the position and acting out of resentment. They did not know that Bush, through his campaign chairman James Baker, had offered the job to Nunn shortly after Bush's election. Although he was honored as the offer was an immense compliment, Nunn declined it after considering it for a few days. He wanted to remain in the Senate. However, since the offer had been made in confidence, Nunn refused to reveal this information.[26]

While Nunn took Dole's attacks in stride, they made some GOP members uncomfortable for they knew Nunn to be a person of conviction, a "very moral man," as Arizona Republican John McCain called him. Other Republicans supported him privately, and Nunn's Democratic colleagues came to his defense. Mitchell called him "one of the most respected, if not the most respected, members of the Senate." Bush, in Nunn's view, could not withdraw Tower's nomination without infuriating the conservative wing of the Republican Party, which considered the fight a test of Bush's mettle. However, the president was losing the battle for public opinion. A NBC News poll gauged Americans to oppose the nomination by a 2 to 1 margin, 54 percent to 28 percent; others showed mixed results, but still indicated that in the view of many Americans, Bush had made a poor choice. The majority of Nunn's constituents agreed with this assessment.[27]

In the end, delays and personal attacks carried little weight. The bruising debate over Tower's nomination began on March 2. That morning in a joint meeting of the House and Senate, lawmakers celebrated with speeches, poetry, and pageantry the 200th anniversary of the first Congress convening in New York on March 4, 1789. The festive mood was over by the early afternoon. At 1:00 p.m., after a Senate clerk announced the order of business, a somber Nunn, described as the Democrats' "supreme commander on defense matters," rose to his feet to serve as floor manager in opposition to the nomination. He was acting with a "sense of sorrow" at having to play the role, but he would not shirk his duties, well aware of the ramifications his leading part in opposition to the nomination would have.[28] As a journalist wrote, Nunn, "an acknowledged grandmaster of strategic arms control, is relearning a basic tenet of infantry tactics. The man on the point draws the most fire."[29]

After introductory remarks, Nunn made clear his objection. "The secretary of defense must be a person suited by personal conduct, discretion and judgment to serve second only to the president in the chain of command," Nunn intoned, "to set the highest leadership example . . . and to restore public confidence in the integrity of defense management. . . . Senator Tower cannot meet those standards." As Nunn informed a constituent, "Tower's admitted and substantial history of alcohol abuse" and the appearance of impropriety of using his "public office for private gain" after serving as a top arms control negotiator were Nunn's principal reasons for his lack of support.[30]

Forty-five minutes later, Nunn completed his prepared remarks and with that unleashed from his colleagues volleys of charges and countercharges regarding Tower's fitness and the president's prerogatives as well as various parliamentary maneuvers, some desperate, that would continue until the battle ceased eight days later.[31] Bush's assumption that Tower's nomination would "glide through the Hill" because "Congress is usually kind to its own" and that he was eminently "qualified for the job" was about to be proved disastrously wrong.[32]

The one hundred senators sat solemnly at their desks on the chamber floor the afternoon of March 9. The usual milling around, accompanied by discussions and the occasional jocularity, was absent. Above the legislators, the public gallery was packed with observers, waiting for the voting to begin, sensing that they might be present at an extraordinary moment. In the balance were the new president's authority and prerogatives. After a week of tense, fiery, and confrontational debate, when members dueled with one another regarding motives and personal rectitude, time had arrived for the Senate to decide whether Bush's nominee would be confirmed. The clerk began to read the roll, and with the utterance of the final vote, the result was unmistakable. Nonetheless, Vice President Quayle, the presiding officer, informed the silent assembly, "The nomination of John Tower to be secretary of defense is not confirmed."[33]

By a vote of 53 to 47, for the first time in thirty years and only the ninth time in the history of the Republic, a president's choice of a cabinet member had been rejected. In the immediate aftermath, Dole called the outcome a "hatchet job" and the confirmation process a "hotbed of character assassination"; his colleague, Strom Thurmond, called it a damaging embarrassment that would undermine Bush's standing in the world. Mitchell was quick to assert that the vote should not be interpreted as an effort to harm the president, and Nunn agreed. While Bush praised Tower for maintaining his dignity during the ordeal, within hours after the defeat, the president told reporters that he would nominate Dick Cheney of Wyoming, the second-ranking Republican leader in the House of Representatives, as defense secretary. On learning this news, Nunn and Warner responded that they would begin confirmation hearings the next week, and Mitchell guaranteed "prompt consideration." Unlike Quayle's strong rebuke of the Senate Democrats for letting loose a "new wave of McCarthyism," Bush's remarks in the White House's press briefing room were conciliatory, remarking that his administration needed to "work cooperatively" with Congress on defense issues. He also predicted a swift Senate confirmation.[34] In this instance, he was correct. A week after his nomination of Cheney had been announced, the Armed Services Committee voted unanimously to support confirmation, followed by the entire Senate the next day, again unanimously, making the six-term congressman the Defense Department's seventeenth secretary, and filling a cabinet office that had been vacant for two months.[35]

Meanwhile, the administration had continued with its comprehensive review of US-Soviet relations that the president had formally initiated on February 15, and that he required to be completed within thirty days. He instructed that the analysis be "forward-looking."[36] The assessment, completed on March 14, indicated that while Soviet rhetoric was reason for optimism about future relations between the two nations, the United States needed to maintain its military and economic strength. This period of "transition and uncertainty" required vigilance as the Soviet threat to the United States and its allies had not ended, but the administration would seek to cooperate with the USSR regarding strategic arms control consistent with US defense strategy.[37] However, US defense strategy was the crux of the issue. The icy environment of the Cold War was not merely thawing, but as Paul Wolfowitz, the under secretary of defense for policy, stated, "It had cracked almost completely and we were now in a rushing torrent."[38] Cheney, however, remained wary of quickly reducing military capabilities that might be needed, as he believed Gorbachev's "peace offensive" could be a ruse or, if legitimate, could be internally subverted. There was also the concern that NATO allies might be seduced by the Soviet leader's proposals. Of particular concern was West Germany, where the INF Treaty had already stirred anxieties that the most likely scenario for war between NATO and the Warsaw Pact would involve short-range tactical nuclear weapons (missiles with a range up to 500 kilometers). The West German government of Chancellor Helmut Kohl had reacted to public pressure for nuclear weapons reductions by announcing in February that his government would postpone any decision on the modernization of its Lance surface-to-surface missile, which could carry a nuclear warhead, for at least two years. Kohl implored his NATO allies to commence arms control talks with the Soviets regarding short-range nuclear forces. Given these trends, the Bush administration decided that testing Gorbachev's readiness to decrease conventional force levels in Europe was the best immediate course and in April rejected Kohl's plea for talks, which Cheney called a "dangerous trap" as it could eliminate NATO's nuclear deterrent. Bush, who shared Cheney's skepticism, was more comfortable with retaining the status quo of containment that had worked successfully for four decades.[39] Consequently, there would be no change in US military strategy for the moment.

In fact, the new secretary of defense's immediate concern focused on fighting for Bush's proposed defense budget. There were no problems or burgeoning crises requiring his immediate attention, as Admiral William J. Crowe Jr., chairman of the Joint Chiefs of Staff, informed him days before his confirmation.[40] The final Reagan defense budget, for fiscal year 1990, submitted to the Congress on January 9, 1989, was for $305.6 billion, a 2 percent increase over the previous fiscal year in addition to inflation. However, Bush had made it clear to the Joint Chiefs of Staff during a February meeting that he intended to cut defense spending. The only issue was how quickly it would decline.[41]

On April 14, Bush and congressional leaders from both parties reached a budget agreement that he would cut $9.7 billion and tackle the huge federal deficit of $170 billion.[42] The Soviet threat seemed to be withering, and the issue on the minds of the members of the House and Senate Armed Services Committees was whether several strategic weapons programs begun during Reagan's tenure were still needed. This issue was now prominent because of Gorbachev's December 1988 declaration before the United Nations General Assembly to unilaterally reduce the number of Soviet troops by 500,000 and the number of Soviet tanks by 10,000 in Eastern Europe and the USSR's western military districts within two years.[43] The move had implications for US defense policy and the existing NATO war plan, which was predicated on the assumption that the Soviets and their allies were superior in numbers and would push through Germany and then westward, potentially resulting in the use of US nuclear weapons to stem the onslaught and a Soviet take-over of Western Europe.

Bush chafed under the press coverage that Gorbachev's initiatives and visits in European capitals was having on US-NATO relations, and com-plained that the media accused him of dragging his feet in responding to the Soviet plans. He felt Gorbachev's actions were diminishing US "standing in Europe," but he was not going to react haphazardly despite the perception that the administration lacked policy direction.[44] Further, significant changes were occurring in Eastern Europe, especially in Poland, where an agreement between the communist leadership and Solidarity, the legalized independent labor union, to hold free elections was reached in April. In light of these developments, the media created a public clamor for the president to act quickly in response to Gorbachev's proposals; while among European allies, discontent with Bush administration wariness had begun to expose, accord-ing to one advisor, a "wide transatlantic divide."[45]

Nonetheless, the Bush administration remained circumspect. The first signal of what one State Department official called a "status quo plus" policy approach came on April 20, when Cheney recommended that Bush cancel the truck-borne Midgetman program and proceed with the plan to put MX missiles on railcars because it was a less expensive approach. Nunn then sent a signal of his own, saying, "It is going to be very hard to put together a consensus along that line." Representative Les Aspin agreed, stating the proposal would result in a "political impasse."[46] In response, Bush made his first major national security decision, again indicating his determination to maintain a bipartisan foreign policy consensus that Nunn had emphasized as needed in this instance. The president rejected Cheney's recommenda-tion, stating he believed both missile systems were necessary for US and NATO strategic nuclear deterrence, ending the debate within the adminis-tration, and underscoring a major policy goal: rebuild support for nuclear deterrence, to include extended nuclear deterrence, among Americans and NATO allies. Afterward, Cheney announced quietly that the programs would be started sequentially to manage costs in the short term.[47]

Nunn, who was watching developments in Europe, held a hearing in early May, with Cheney and Crowe as the principal witnesses, to discuss political polarization in NATO, which he thought resulted from NATO's lack of vision that once the INF Treaty went into effect, the short-range missiles would be the next concern. Furthermore, it was evident that NATO lacked a strategy on how to reconcile the conflicting positions of the United States and West Germany concerning these weapons. He believed the alliance was concentrating on "a very narrow part of the problem," missing an opportunity to "correct" the "huge conventional disparity." He suggested that the way to prevent the widening schism between the United States and West Germany would require weaving three elements together. First, the Bush administration should begin negotiations for mutual US-Soviet reductions in short-range nuclear weapons, as West Germany wanted. Second, such negotiations should be conditioned on West Germany agreeing to the planned modernization of Lance missiles. The third component was that a reduction in the number of NATO's short-range missiles, designed to offset the Warsaw Pact's advantages in non-nuclear forces, should not occur until conventional forces on both sides were reduced to an acceptable level.[48]

In response, Cheney expressed his concern that once the negotiations started, NATO allies, bowing to political pressure, would want to "accept the first Soviet offer" to eliminate the weapons. Crowe indicated he had "no problem" with Nunn's "three-track approach," but he doubted the allies would agree to make missile reductions contingent on decreases in conventional forces. With the administration adamant that it would not engage in talks, William Cohen summed up the Arms Services Committee's frustration, "I don't think we can sit back in silence and let the dynamic unfold."[49]

Nunn also had to steer a defense authorization bill through the Senate, so his attention returned to the defense budget the following week when Charles Bowsher, the head of the General Accounting Office (now known as the Government Accountability Office), informed Nunn that despite the defense cuts Cheney had already planned, the Pentagon's five-year defense plan (a forecast of the forces, resources, and programs needed to support Department of Defense operations, now called the "future years defense plan"), would likely exceed even the most optimistic amounts that Congress would appropriate by at least $150 billion. With that conclusion, Nunn called DOD's plan "essentially worthless" because the administration's budget plan and its defense strategy were mismatched.[50]

The critical connection between the defense budget and US defense strategy gained prominence later in the month when Bush attended the NATO summit in Brussels, which he considered his first major foreign policy test.[51] Before the meeting, he indicated that the administration was likely to change course in deciding how to deal with the rapid transformations happening in Eastern Europe and the USSR. After meeting with Kohl, Bush proposed to his NATO counterparts that the dispute over short-range missiles be resolved by accelerating negotiations on a treaty to reduce substantially US and Soviet conventional forces in Europe, and tied negotiation on short-range missiles to "implementation" of an agreement on reducing conventional forces, which he believed could occur in two years. The proposal was well received in Europe and in Moscow. It also received plaudits at home. Nunn pronounced the proposal a "worthy goal" but cautioned that "we should be realistic and not become discouraged if this timetable is not met."[52]

Despite the applause for Bush's bold initiative on conventional weapons and forces, strategic weapons remained a chief concern of Congress given the shifting security environment and the weapons' huge costs. The air force announced in June that it planned to proceed with the B-2 bomber program because it shored up US strategic forces, arguing in an unclassified report released the following month to the Senate Armed Services Committee that the plane's stealth technology rendered Soviet defense systems "largely ineffective." Nunn supported the program because of the technology involved, but he believed that the cost of the bomber, approximately $500–750 million per plane, needed to be considered as well as successful flight testing, a concern shared by other committee members.[53] In a speech at a Washington think tank as strategic arms reduction talks (START) were to be restarted between US and Soviet negotiators, Nunn warned the administration that its two-missile plan faced rejection by Congress because of the expense, and the ICBM modernization plan needed to be tied more visibly to its arms control policy.[54] In turn, Bush met with Nunn and other congressional leaders, promising the administration would not pull a bait and switch by deploying the MX only. He agreed to add almost $1 billion for the Midgetman missile, pleading, "Don't pull the rug out from under us," insisting that he needed the two systems for leverage in negotiations because the Soviets already had two mobile systems deployed, and that the plan would strengthen US deterrence. Nunn later told reporters that Bush's assurances were "very encouraging" and would likely help in obtaining Senate approval for both programs, but that was not guaranteed. Aspin, who also attended, intimated that the additional funding added "credibility" to the administration's assurances about the plan, but he knew from a meeting the day before between Scowcroft and House Democrats that many members opposed the plan because of the stringent budgetary limitations to which the two branches had agreed. Furthermore, Cheney was already axing weapons programs dear to some House constituencies, adding fuel to an already volatile political climate in Washington.[55]

By mid-July, after a week of closed-door sessions, Nunn and his committee approved the Bush administration's $305.6 billion defense budget request with few changes and caveats, satisfied that Cheney had made some difficult choices by eliminating "politically popular weapons programs" in recognition of the budget constraints the Defense Department faced. To shore up the administration's request, Nunn gave the controversial B-2 program his firm backing, emphasizing that it was an essential component of the US nuclear arsenal since the current B-1 bomber could not penetrate Soviet air defenses. He acknowledged that the program's cost prompted "sticker shock" in Congress, including among members of his own committee. As a concession to John Glenn, who favored withholding funding for the B-2 program until it passed flight tests, Nunn and Warner supplied a compromise known as "fly before you buy." The committee laid out conditions that required stringent testing of the plane's airworthiness as well as its ability to elude radar detection that had to be met before funds could be expended. However, Nunn realized that even with these "fences," the program's supporters confronted a substantial challenge in both chambers, especially in the House, where the Armed Services Committee had reduced the program by $800 million. Additionally, the Senate committee had funded continued research for the Strategic Defense Initiative (SDI) at $4.5 billion—another contentious decision that was sure to result in clashes over the authorization bill on the Senate floor and with the House during conference.[56]

Two weeks later, the Senate began consideration of the defense bill. Before taking up the complete bill, Nunn engineered a separate vote specifically on the B-2 bomber program, which the Senate approved by a vote of 98 to 1, affirming the Armed Services Committee's recommendations. Not only was the vote a victory for Bush, who had personally lobbied Congress to provide full funding of the program as essential to US nuclear deterrence, but it gave Nunn and his fellow Senate negotiators leverage in their face-off with the House over the program when the two sides met during conference to shape the defense authorization.[57]

However, the depth of the House's opposition to the Bush defense budget was not readily apparent until its sweeping vote on its version of the bill a day later. It approved a $305.5 billion defense bill by a vote of 261 to 162, but it tore in shreds the administration's plans to promote a range of strategic weapons systems at the expense of conventional arms by severely cutting funding for SDI, rebuffing the two-missile plan (MX and Midgetman), slowing down development of the B-2 bomber, and reinstating funding for two aircraft programs Cheney wanted cancelled but that were economically important to congressional districts in New York, Pennsylvania, and Texas. Furthermore, Aspin's leadership, and that of the ranking Republican on the House committee, was in question because of this full-scale rebellion.

The votes against the White House on the defense bill by House Republicans suggested that they believed the defense budget was inconsistent with the extent and rate of change occurring in the international environment and that the administration was incapable of fashioning realistic US military requirements during a period of confusion and ambiguity, especially in the Soviet Union and its satellites. Further, many members of Congress believed the administration's foreign policy was aimless and that the strategic review it had undertaken provided neither clarity nor a vision of the way ahead.[58]

In the Senate, however, Nunn was fighting for his own version of the bill with success. Collaborating with Warner, he was successful in beating back an amendment to cut SDI funding by a billion dollars, calling the House decision regarding the program "not rational." Although the favorable outcome was by a slim margin, it was the fourth consecutive year Nunn had been victorious on the issue, working cooperatively with a Republican White House and forging a bipartisan coalition of senators.[59] Sensing the mood on the Hill and realizing that the defense budget would be on a downward path for the near term, in early August, Nunn, Warner, and McCain, with the Armed Services Committee's endorsement, introduced three "burden-sharing" proposals. One concentrated on preventing European allies from making precipitous, unilateral troop reductions that would undermine a stable NATO conventional force level. Another proposal prompted Japan to cover fully the cost of the US military presence in that nation; while a third urged consultations with South Korea on a partial, gradual decrease in the number of US forces serving there. Nunn said that the proposals sent a warning to allies that "there can be no free lunches and no free rides."[60] Nunn also fashioned a compromise with his colleagues that led to an agreement that the Pentagon would deploy both the MX and the Midgetman missiles, a further repudiation of the House position. After wrangling over several other amendments to the defense bill and adding the burden-sharing provisions Nunn and his

Republican colleagues had sponsored, the Senate approved the bill by a vote of 95 to 4 on August 2.[61]

It was clear that the large and significant differences between the two versions of the bill set up a potentially combative conference when the negotiators met in September. On September 8, four days after the negotiations began and with the two chambers far from agreement, Nunn addressed the US Chamber of Commerce. While he held the administration accountable for not developing a clear strategy for its strategic arms reduction talks with the Soviets, he stated that the House would bear the blame if the talks were not successful. He maintained that the House's drastic cuts of four major strategic programs had removed any inducement for the Soviets to seek an agreement. "I think the START talks are at stake in the next 30 days," he told the audience. Success would be contingent on a "sensible strategic nuclear program" in which the president and the Joint Chiefs of Staff have confidence.[62]

Nunn's predictions regarding the START talks and their connection to the budget proved prophetic when the Soviets offered to negotiate a treaty that would reduce the number of strategic nuclear weapons without addressing the two parties' disagreement over SDI. While the Bush administration welcomed this offer as an important change that could increase the probability of a treaty in the near term, Nunn, Aspin, and McCain opposed such a deal. They contended that it would be difficult for the Senate to approve a treaty without knowing, as Nunn put it, "what the Soviets consider a breach of the ABM Treaty," while it was also likely to undermine support for SDI. "SDI, in the short term, is already heading downhill—it's a perishable commodity," Nunn asserted. The senators were right to question the worth of the deal as Shevardnadze had indicated only a few days earlier, in a meeting with Secretary of State James Baker, that the USSR would retain the right to pull out of START if it believed the United States had violated the ABM Treaty. Such a position was essentially a "veto over testing" SDI's defensive capabilities, according to Aspin.[63]

With this diplomatic development and the beginning of a new fiscal year only a few days away, the Senate and House conferees considering the defense authorization bill remained far apart on spending for SDI. In response, Nunn, with the support of his committee members and key Senate Appropriations Committee members, made a tactical move by getting the Senate to overturn its earlier decision regarding funding for the Star Wars program with an amendment to the fiscal year 1990 defense appropriations bill. Only two days earlier, the Senate had voted to freeze funding for the program, resulting in what was essentially a $600 million reduction in the amount it had authorized in July. Taking to the Senate floor, Nunn claimed that a reversal of the vote would give him and his colleagues an advantage in the still ongoing authorization conference negotiations with the House. He put the administration on notice as well. During the debate, he criticized it for not clarifying its aims with respect to the system and its relationship to arms control plans, and for devising politically unrealistic defense budgets. A few hours later, the Senate voted 96 to 2 to adopt a final defense appropriations bill that included the additional $600 million in SDI funding.[64] In the end, as had been the case with the Tower nomination, Nunn had revealed his power, influencing the Senate to pass a second defense-related bill that mirrored his priorities and represented 30 percent of the federal budget.[65]

Fast-moving events in the Soviet Union soon recaptured congressional attention as well when Bush agreed to a December "get-acquainted" meeting with Gorbachev in Malta, recognizing that he would have to tread softly in the interim so the United States did not appear to be taking advantage of the USSR's plight, fearful that such a belief might lead to a hostile reaction by hard liners.[66] In fact, labor unrest and food shortages in the USSR had already led some experts to predict a potential uprising against Gorbachev, and with that warning light blinking, on November 2, after almost eight weeks of sometimes-rancorous discussions, House and Senate conferees achieved a compromise regarding the contents of the $305 billion defense authorization bill. They agreed to slice SDI funding substantially, but they decided to continue limited production of the B-2 bomber and authorize the two land-based mobile missiles. However, Nunn told reporters that an additional funding reduction of $8.1 billion was likely because of mandatory budget cuts, which translated into shrinking active-duty military personnel by 10 percent. These troop cuts could be avoided if Congress and the president agreed to a compromise deficit reduction that lowered spending and increased revenues, but that approach seemed unlikely. Bush had only the previous week voiced his belief that the across-the-board budget cuts mandated by the Gramm-Rudman deficit reduction law were needed to discipline the fiscally lenient Congress.[67]

Nunn found Bush's stance perplexing, especially since Cheney had applauded the bill for providing "a strong national defense." Moreover, at a hearing on November 8, Nunn stated that Bush was being unrealistic regarding the damage the automatic cuts would do to the defense budget. In his opening remarks, he dismissed the president's view that the Defense Department could absorb the $8.1 billion impact on its fiscal year 1990 budget without grave ramifications. Sean O'Keefe, the Pentagon comptroller, testifying before the committee, agreed with Nunn's assessment regarding the magnitude of personnel reductions required by the automatic spending cuts. Nunn replied, "We are engaged in the most important arms control negotiations," but the administration appeared tone-deaf to the ramifications that massive troop reductions would have on US commitments. Warner viewed it differently, describing the standoff between the two branches as "the highest stakes poker game I have seen since I've been in the Senate." He believed that Congress and the administration lacked the political courage to make meaningful defense budget reductions in the face of constituent interests.[68] In a matter of a few hours, there would be an entirely new poker game with very different stakes taking place in the divided city of Berlin.

CHAPTER 12

A MANAGEABLE GLIDE-PATH

The Berlin Wall "fell" by accident on November 9, 1989. Less than two years earlier, on a warm spring day, Reagan had stood in front of the Brandenburg Gate in the divided city and addressed a crowd of 200,000, as well as millions more throughout Western Europe by broadcast, pressing Gorbachev to "tear down this wall." However, Reagan's challenge did not catalyze this historic outcome. Ironically, Gorbachev started the process of dismantling the concrete and barbed-wire partition when, over the course of his four years in power, he launched social and political reforms in Soviet-subjugated Eastern Europe, intending to strengthen Communist rule, not abolish it.[1]

East Germans had already been holding massive street protests in major cities in the early days of November, demanding additional freedoms, which the East German Politburo had attempted to appease by issuing minimally revised travel regulations. Now, at 6:00 p.m. on this mid-autumn evening, a member of the Politburo, who had been absent during the leadership's discussion of the "new" rules, erroneously announced at a press conference, in a muddled response to a journalist's question, that border crossing would be allowed for every citizen. Another question immediately followed, asking the official when this change would take effect, and he responded: "Immediately, right away." Tom Brokaw, anchor of NBC's nightly news program, who was fortuitously present at the press conference, felt the atmosphere in the room change palpably.[2] He later recounted, that it was as if "a signal had come from outer space and electrified the room."[3] The bilingual sound technician accompanying Brokaw made an even more astounding appraisal. "It's the end of the Cold War," he whispered to the reporter.[4] Within a few hours, with the Western media reporting the event, crowds of East Germans began to appear at some of the city's border-crossing points. At one station, the guards were quickly outnumbered, and the thousands of people present started demanding they open the gate.[5] West Berliners flocked to the wall as well, drinking beer and champagne and chanting, "Open the gate!" First one gate opened, and then more followed, releasing a deluge of East Germans into West Berlin. Some in the crowd began dancing, creating an impromptu party, and some, dumbfounded by the now unrestrained passage, simply milled about on the streets. However, other Berliners wanted a more symbolic indication that the concrete barrier known as the "Antifascistischer Schutzwall," or "antifascist protective wall," was no more. These euphoric young daredevils clambered to the top of the thirteen-foot-high barrier despite police efforts to stop them; some brought hammers and chisels and began to chip away at it.[6]

For its part, the Bush administration response to the unfolding event was guarded. At an unplanned press conference, the president hailed the opening of the East German borders, stating, "It is clearly a good development in terms of human rights" and a "move toward democracy." Reporters observed a certain restraint in his remarks; his subdued response seemed to indicate that he was not delighted by the news. "I'm elated," he responded, but privately there was a concern among officials that the post–World War II order was tearing apart and a stable replacement was not in place. This uncertainty bred a sense of danger, a fear that events could produce chaos. As one anonymous US policymaker remarked, "What we are dealing with in Eastern Europe, and to a lesser degree in the Soviet Union, is a revolutionary situation. Revolutionary situations have a dynamic of their own." On Capitol Hill, however, members of Congress were less reserved. Senator George Mitchell, speaking for many of his colleagues, was unambiguously enthusiastic; he urged the East German government to destroy the wall, claiming such a step would be one of "lasting substance and meaning."[7]

Nunn had already thought about the enormous changes in the European security environment and their implications for NATO. He was not surprised. On the contrary, he was prepared to deal with them. Two months before the events in East Germany, Nunn had delivered the Alastair Buchan

Memorial Lecture in London. He began his speech by outlining the profound changes that had already occurred. He asked the audience who would have thought possible a decade earlier the economic changes under way, with twelve European nations "on the threshold of realizing the European Economic Community's dream of a single market." He believed these events necessitated a "fundamental restructuring of the European security system." The danger was not that NATO would collapse, but that it would become irrelevant. Moreover, helping to create a stable regional order was not sufficient; the alliance had to be an "instrument for change." NATO had to evolve into an organization that was no longer just a security mechanism.[8]

This transformation, Nunn continued, would entail the challenge of formulating a suitable strategy for responding to the changes occurring in the Soviet Union and Eastern Europe. While he doubted that a return to a more antagonistic Soviet foreign policy was likely in the near term, especially under Gorbachev, such an occurrence could not be dismissed. Thus, the alliance had to deal with such potentialities by considering a set of scenarios, each of which would allow for prudent alterations and flexibility.[9]

Nunn laid out specific aims. First, Western institutions should make the rollback of democratic gains in Poland and Hungary improbable by providing debt relief and investment, not only financial but also intellectual in the form of technical knowledge as well as the exchange of ideas and people. Second, NATO should refrain from giving any form of assistance that did not compel the Soviets to make the hard choices between "guns and butter." Every effort should be made to promote democratic reforms and private enterprise. He also believed that US-Soviet discussions to forestall or thwart terrorist threats, especially those involving weapons of mass destruction, were constructive. This aspect also included arms reduction treaties, both conventional and strategic, which advanced stability and lessened the danger of conflict.[10]

Nunn suggested a two-tier approach to arms control. The first tier entailed the ongoing strategic arms reduction talks (START) and the Conventional Forces in Europe (CFE) negotiations. The second tier would be new, not based on incremental advances, but a "leapfrog" approach beginning with exploratory talks in several areas: land-based multiple warhead systems; anti-satellite systems; nuclear testing limitations beyond current treaty obligations; reductions in the number of short-range nuclear weapons, going ultimately to zero; and even deeper cuts in European conventional forces.[11]

As farsighted as Nunn's vision for NATO was, he recognized the difficulty that lay ahead in fashioning a new Western security structure in view of the profound transformation in progress, for not only the alliance but also the United States. Within weeks of the political turmoil evident in Eastern Europe, many members of Congress vocalized their eagerness to slash the defense budget without assessing the consequences. They claimed a "peace dividend" would result that could be used for domestic purposes. Nunn had no doubt that the military threat to Western Europe had changed, but he warned that before making considerable cutbacks, the administration and Congress had a duty to determine what the threat was. He called upon the administration to conduct a complete assessment of how developments in Europe affected US force structure and, more broadly, obligations to other treaty partners such as South Korea and Japan.[12] In Nunn's view, an overly simplistic response to the altered security environment only made him appreciate even more H. L. Mencken's observation: "There is always an easy solution to every human problem—neat, plausible, and wrong."[13]

The battle over the defense budget began on December 12, 1989, when Tennessee senator James Sasser, chairman of the Budget Committee, held a hearing on the future defense budget. In his opening remarks, Sasser asserted time had come for the "massive expenditures" on defense to be directed toward "the domestic problems facing the country" because military outlays had "diverted us from the enterprise of building a sounder, more productive domestic economy." To counter any moves Nunn and like-minded lawmakers might take to safeguard defense spending, he relied on two former Defense Department officials, Robert S. McNamara and Lawrence Korb, to make the argument for cuts. While both men preferred a measured and efficient decrease, and warned that the administration needed to begin planning a sensible drawdown of US forces, they agreed that perhaps 5 percent, or $15 billion per year, could be pruned over the next decade.[14]

Nunn's strategy to deal with Sasser's conclusions about sizable savings being realized by wholesale reductions in the defense budget was built upon the approach the two former defense officials recommended: a decrease based on sound evidence and reliable judgment. In a lawyerly way, he would build his case through a series of hearings, developing, as he stated, a "conceptual framework or baseline for Congress' review of the Bush administration's foreign policy and national defense budget proposals for fiscal year 1991," given the profound changes occurring in the Soviet Union and Eastern Europe.[15]

The first step was to understand the threat NATO now confronted in

Western Europe. To this end, the Senate Armed Services Committee held its first hearing the same day the Budget Committee was hearing testimony on future defense budgets. For nearly two hours, Nunn and committee members grilled the witnesses, Under Secretary of Defense for Policy Paul Wolfowitz, Central Intelligence Agency official Charles Allen, and air force lieutenant general George Butler, director for strategic plans and policy, J-5, Office of the Joint Chiefs of Staff, on how the Defense Department and the intelligence community were currently assessing the shifting threat environment in Europe, particularly with respect to how much warning time NATO forces would have of a possible Soviet attack.[16]

Based on the information Nunn gleaned from the hearing, he questioned whether the Defense Department's budget proposal had seriously considered the new intelligence estimate that NATO would now have one to three months' warning of an impending Soviet attack, instead of the two weeks that was the current planning assumption. As Nunn saw it, this increase in warning time allowed for less expensive contingency measures. Furthermore, not including this factor in developing the budget was misleading because "warning time drives strategy and strategy drives the budget." Accordingly, the reliability of the proposed budget was now in question. In response, a few annoyed but anonymous Defense Department officials dared members of Congress to propose their own security strategy.[17]

Nunn took his second step in constructing the conceptual framework when he granted the *New York Times* an interview in late December. Nunn informed the military correspondent that he would hold hearings in the third week of January that covered the Defense Department budget proposal for fiscal year 1991, an assessment of the contemporary threats to US national security, and the formulation of a new military strategy. While Nunn refused to address specific programs that were vulnerable to reductions or elimination until his committee was able to hear directly from administration witnesses, he suggested areas that should be scrutinized, as well as intimating to his colleagues a willingness to make sizable reductions in US troop strengths in Europe, by nearly one-third of the current 305,000, and "a partial, gradual draw down" in Asia. He underscored that NATO members and Japan must assume a greater portion of the costs associated with defending the sea lanes that plied these nations with Persian Gulf oil. Yet, he also specified costly programs he would continue to support as crucial, such as the B-2 stealth bomber and a ground-based interceptor system to destroy incoming missiles launched by hostile "third world states" or by accident. Nunn ended the interview by emphasizing that less attention at this point should be given to identifying a certain percentage to be sliced from the defense budget. Instead, he maintained, "We should look at bottom lines on capabilities, not in terms of dollars."[18] The administration received the message, stating that Nunn's proposed decreases in US troop strength in Western Europe would be considered.

The Senate Armed Services Committee opened hearings on January 23, 1990, with CIA director William Webster as the principal witness. Nunn stated that the hearing's purpose was to reexamine the basic assumptions of US defense policy and military budgets for the coming decade by first understanding the intelligence community's assessment of the Warsaw Pact threat. "We've seen the threat change on TV every night," he remarked to underscore the hearing's intent, adding that this changed threat was the basis on which the Congress would build the budget.[19] In response, Webster testified that while the United States should approve of the changes and reforms occurring in the Soviet Union, it was critical to remember that the results in Eastern Europe and the Soviet Union remained "uncertain" and the situation "in flux." Soviet strategic forces remained highly capable, while the Warsaw Pact's conventional force threat to the United States and its NATO allies had declined. He noted that Gorbachev and, for that matter, his successors would have an "even more pressing need than in the past few years to reduce the burden of defense spending and to transfer resources to civilian production." However, he made several cautionary observations regarding other threats. The first concerned transnational terrorism emanating from the Middle East. There were now terrorist groups with the capability to operate in many regions of the world. He equally feared the rising potential for developing nations to build and use weapons of mass destruction while exploiting cutting-edge missile technology. Iran, Iraq, Pakistan, and Libya already had or were close to acquiring nuclear weapons.[20] In response to this last piece of information, Nunn later told reporters that nuclear proliferation was a significant concern, while Warner remarked that the committee would have to consider this newly disclosed information when it reevaluated US military assistance programs.[21]

A week later, the day after Bush delivered his second State of the Union address in which he proposed sharp reductions in the number of US and Soviet military forces in Europe, Nunn's committee held a hearing with Secretary of Defense Dick Cheney and Chairman of the Joint Chiefs of Staff Colin Powell as the witnesses. Nunn believed that fundamental changes in

US defense strategy were also needed to reflect the vanishing East-West friction and the unraveling of the Warsaw Pact's capabilities. "Without a doubt," Nunn counseled Cheney, "fundamental changes and fundamental rethinking are going to have to occur."[22]

In his remarks, Cheney asserted that American troop strength in Europe needed to remain at 225,000, as the president had proposed the night before, because the Soviet Union endured as a superpower capable of destroying the United States, but he also mentioned the need to maintain strong ties with NATO members. Powell supported the administration's troop figure, citing an analysis that the figure the secretary referred to represented the minimum force required to execute the NATO war plan in defense of Western Europe. Nunn offered that the administration should consider deeper cuts if the Soviets withdrew all of their forces from Eastern Europe and a reunified Germany resulted. In reply, Cheney promised to revisit the issue of troop strength in Western Europe if such a spectacular adjustment on the Soviets' part occurred, but the secretary's assent seemed merely an attempt to mollify Nunn. For his part, Nunn remained convinced Soviet troops could be out of East Germany and Czechoslovakia by early 1991 if the CFE talks and progress toward a reunited Germany continued apace, thereby leaving NATO to "face a complete rebuilding of the policy we've been following since 1945."[23]

Another hearing followed the next day, where Nunn sought the views of three former chairmen of the Joint Chiefs of Staff regarding whether the United States should pursue the costly development of both the MX missile and the Midgetman missile. The retired officers testified that the United States could not afford both programs and did not need to deploy both.[24] In raising this issue for consideration, Nunn sought not only to determine programs for potential reduction but to influence the administration's ongoing START negotiations with the Soviets, urging the administration to introduce a new proposal whereby the United States would agree to stop development of the MX missile system if the Soviets would eliminate the mobile version of the SS-24. Some of Bush's advisors agreed with Nunn's proposal, but on Capitol Hill, Joe Biden, who chaired the Senate Foreign Relation Committee's Subcommittee on Europe, pushed back on Nunn's suggestion, underscoring that the parties were on the "verge of completing the first strategic arms agreement in a decade." He wanted to nail down the reductions the talks had achieved. While Nunn certainly supported the goal of decreasing the number of nuclear weapons, he recognized another complicating factor: the influence of domestic politics on the military budget, given the changing threat environment. It was possible that funding for the MX missile could end, he told *Los Angeles Times* editors and reporters at a breakfast session. At best, the program had an even chance of survival. If the program were terminated, then the United States would have lost a bargaining chip to reduce the Soviet capability while working toward the larger goal Nunn had articulated in the Buchan lecture: banning all land-based and multiple-warhead missiles.[25]

Fortified with the information he had garnered from staff analysis and the hearings held over the past two months with administration and former Defense Department officials, active and retired senior military officers, and civilian experts from the United States and allied nations, Nunn now revealed his master plan. On March 22, he delivered a speech on the Senate floor laying into the administration's fiscal year 1991 defense budget and five-year defense plan, asserting that it contained "five big blanks." The Pentagon's figures, he stressed, were based on obsolete assumptions about the threats to US security, and it had failed to develop a new military strategy that responded to the changed environment: those were "the threat and strategy blanks." The proposed defense budget reduction of only 2.6 percent, counting for inflation, was "based on a 1988 threat and a 1988 strategy." Moreover, the department had identified only $70 billion of the $167 billion in defense cuts required to bring defense-spending levels in line with the five-year targets for national defense that the Gramm-Rudman-Hollings Balanced Budget and Emergency Deficit Control Act required, the "dollar blank." The Defense Department had failed to tell Congress what size and structure the military forces should have in the next five years, the "force structure blank," and its review of costly weapons systems was incomplete, the "program blank," which was unfortunate given these other shortcomings influenced decisions regarding whether major programs such as the B-2 bomber, the advanced tactical fighter and others were still needed.[26]

Continuing his remarks, Nunn did not let his fellow Democrats go unscathed. He scolded his colleagues, some of whom had proposed reductions of $20 billion, for seeking deep cuts in defense spending without making the systematic, thoughtful analysis needed to reassess US national security. Such immediate reductions in the budget to achieve instant savings, he observed, would result in severe disruptions to US military personnel and operations.[27]

In concluding his speech, Nunn promised the Senate that the Armed Services Committee would meet its responsibilities in the authorization process, using its best judgment to reach decisions on the FY 1991 defense authorization bill. He then revealed that he had already begun this process, and that over the next few weeks he would present his own views on the changes in the threats, and offer some recommendations on the ways in which the United States should revise its military strategy. He would also highlight revisions to major defense programs and force structure and, ultimately, offer his views on the appropriate level of defense spending that this revised strategy would require. He had one final admonition. He was continually asked by others to provide a "bottom-line defense number." He could not readily supply a figure:

> I don't know of any logical way to arrive at such a figure without analyzing the threat, without determining what changes in our strategy should be made in light of the changes in the threat, and then determining what force structure and weapons we need to carry out this revised strategy. To decide on the size of the defense budget without first going through this process would be little better than pulling a number out of the air.[28]

The response to Nunn's attack was immediate. Sasser retorted that his proposed cuts would cause disruptions, but not of the magnitude that concerned Nunn. Any reduction in spending always created some turbulence. Nunn was masking the most important point. "The issue," Sasser declared, "is whether spending $300 billion annually for defense is justified in a post-cold war world. I think Senator Nunn has laid out a compelling case that it is not." A few days later, Sasser claimed that he would prefer to prepare a defense budget based on an Armed Services Committee assessment, but no help was coming from that quarter.[29] Further, to support his argument for sizable reductions in the budget and active duty forces, Sasser had directed the Congressional Budget Office (CBO) to develop alternative force structures and military strategy for consideration. John Mayer, a senior CBO official, provided the findings in testimony before the Budget Committee in early March, furnishing acceptable alternatives that could reduce the annual defense budget by between $9 billion and $80 billion.[30]

Cheney also rejected Nunn's censure. In an address at the National Press Club in Washington, DC, he informed the attendees that the administration's proposed defense budget was prudent, taking into account the political change in the Soviet Union and Eastern Europe as well as new arms control treaties between the United States and the Soviet Union. Deeper cuts would only heighten the risk during this period of transition. Lawmakers, Cheney protested to the audience in the speech that had been prepared before Nunn vocalized his disapproval, were offering "complaints not solutions." The secretary and Sasser were about to be proven wrong.

Nunn's next step occurred on March 29, when he again took to the Senate floor and challenged the Pentagon's assessment of the Soviet threat based on hearings his committee held with senior intelligence officials, and added his own estimation of how the threat had changed. He proceeded to detail the Warsaw Pact's conventional threat, which he characterized as disintegrating, but offered a different perspective with respect to the Soviet strategic threat. The Soviets persisted in enhancing their strategic nuclear forces, in terms of both offensive capability and defensive forces, where they were making a heavy investment, especially in ballistic missile defense. He concluded that these efforts were a "matter of continued serious concern" and represented "the paramount threat to US national security." Thus, maintaining the US strategic deterrent was necessary, but he acknowledged that the recent turmoil in the Soviet Union made him increasingly worried that its nuclear weapons could be launched by accident or that they could fall into the hands of terrorists or others with malevolent intent. Therefore, both parties should conduct reviews of their nuclear chain of command and fail-safe mechanisms so that they could handle such contingencies and avoid inadvertent nuclear war.[31]

Nunn then stated that while the events occurring in Eastern Europe commanded the most attention, it was imperative for the United States to assess threats in other regions and the numerous risks he saw emerging, such as economic instability and the particular threats posed by radical Islamic fundamentalism. Yet, he also focused on the domestic situation: the weak US economy, a surging national debt, mounting interest payments on that debt, and the growing competitiveness of other industrialized nations at a time when the United States was not investing adequately in a decaying infrastructure, not training the future workforce in mathematics and the sciences, and not maintaining investments in industrial productivity. The major challenge for the remainder of the decade was to distinguish between threats and risks. The United States, he observed, must identify and respond to threats that "directly challenge our vital interests—I mean those threats we are prepared to send our soldiers to die for." It would be up to the United States, working with its allies, to deal with the regional and global risks that, if neglected, could threaten important US interests. Neither of these approaches, he concluded, would be possible without first revising the nation's military strategy.[32]

In the next two weeks, Nunn continued to marshal his arguments to shape the defense budget in line with his strategic vision. Two events helped his efforts. First, a bipartisan group headed by Harold Brown and former secretary of the treasury William Simon and composed of past senior defense officials, retired military officers, and influential lawmakers, including Nunn and Republican senator William Cohen as well as House Democrats and Republicans, released a study differing with administration policy. Using the declining Warsaw Pact threat as its foundation, the study deemed it feasible to cut troop levels in Europe at a rate faster than the administration had forecast. It recommended canceling the administration's planned deployment of the Lance nuclear-armed missile to West Germany and beginning negotiations with the Soviets with the aim of eliminating all short-range nuclear forces in Europe.[33] Second, Cohen dealt a blow to the administration's plans soon thereafter, when he and Senator John McCain released a paper calling for Pentagon spending reductions that were twice as large as the president offered in the budget proposal. Although they favored a cautious approach in making changes to US force posture, they clearly favored less spending on strategic nuclear weapons and, over the next five years, deeper reductions in US forces assigned to defend NATO.[34]

Nunn kept the pressure on the administration, and in mid-April, in response to Cheney's complaint that members of Congress were offering only disapproval of the administration's defense planning, not answers, Nunn presented his version of a US new military strategy. He was addressing his colleagues as much as the Pentagon when he stated that the only prudent way of reducing military spending first required a "sensible military strategy that meets the threats of today and tomorrow." In his tutorial from the floor of the Senate, he stated that he had no disagreement with Bush's report titled *National Security Strategy*, which the administration had released the previous month. That strategy, a statutory requirement, articulated US core and enduring national interests and policy aims. However, the need for a new military strategy remained, one that described how the United States should structure and employ its military forces based on the resources available to support those interests and objectives, as well as any threats to them.[35]

Nunn stated that he shared the circumspect views of his colleagues, Cohen and McCain, and he agreed with their assumptions about the changing strategic environment. Then, he changed course and outlined seven specific military missions that US forces should be expected to carry out. They included deterring attacks on the United States and protecting NATO allies from Soviet conventional aggression, defending treaty partners and other friendly states around the globe, and ensuring the sea lines of communication remained open. He believed that unconventional threats, such as drug trafficking and terrorism, increasingly required attention.[36]

For the next several minutes, he identified and discussed the essential components of a new military strategy, remarking that nuclear deterrence was fundamental to any US military strategy for the projected future. However, reductions in conventional forces could be made consistent with the adjustment in the threat, and more of these forces could be placed in the reserves. He also called for "flexible readiness"—some units would be in a high state of preparedness, others less so. Lastly, he claimed that management of defense resources had to be a focus—savings in procurement and maintenance of weapons, innovative research programs to preserve the US technological advantage, and preservation of a defense industrial base to produce needed weapons and equipment. His prescriptions featured his detailed understanding of defense, as he addressed nuclear doctrine and particular reinforcement strategies. On one point, he was patently clear with respect to contingencies: "Where our vital interests may be threatened, we need to be capable of military intervention. But we should, whenever possible, attempt to manage the threats through diplomatic, economic, and other nonmilitary measures, with the option of increased—and increasingly visible—military presence in the area."[37] Nunn concluded by promising his colleagues that he would next present his views on how best to implement the new military strategy and the level of defense spending needed for the upcoming fiscal year and the next five years consistent with the new strategy.[38]

True to his word, the next day Nunn delivered a floor speech regarding the fiscal year 1991 defense budget; this was his final attempt to frame the critical elements for the chamber's deliberation. He began by stating that he would highlight the policy and budget implications that resulted from the threat assessment and the new military strategy he had proposed previously. He underscored that a new military strategy could not be implemented right away. The immediate savings that would accrue would be relatively small but still worth reaping. Nonetheless, in his judgment, based on the new military strategy he had outlined the day before, the defense budget could be cut by as much as $18 billion below the president's $307 billion request. Over the next five years, he asserted, another $225–255 billion could be saved. He recognized that many in the Senate would not concur with all his specific reductions, but these were issues to grapple with during committee markup and floor debate. He stressed that the suggested reductions were his views only, and that the defense authorization bill would represent the collective assessment of the Armed Services Committee, ultimately modified and approved by the Senate.[39]

Nunn then continued by pointing to specific issues that needed review during congressional deliberations. As examples, he considered continuation of two expensive mobile ICBM programs as unaffordable, and while he supported bomber modernization, he noted that the B-2 stealth bomber program had to be "made more affordable." He expected the Pentagon's major aircraft review, scheduled for completion and presentation to the Armed Services Committee the next week, to address this point. Therefore, he would await the results before making any specific recommendations on the program's funding levels. He favored smaller, more mobile ground forces, identified older, single-purpose weapons that should be retired, and argued for a "constructive competition" for roles and missions among the military services to attain not only efficiencies and foster coordination through integration of capabilities and eradication of redundancy, but also to "break out of a pattern of looking at problems in traditional ways." These propositions and other cost reduction measures, he concluded, exemplified the "first installment on a five-year plan that is consistent with a new military strategy."[40]

In the view of the press, Nunn's speeches served as the point of reference in the impending debate over the future US defense posture. His influential voice on military issues carried weight far beyond the Senate, particularly since he had now outlined a vision for American forces in a changed security environment.[41] Richard Darman, the administration's budget director, who had been Reagan's White House staff secretary, expected that once Congress had defined which specific programs would be cut to meet the deficit target set by law, and the impact on congressional districts and states had become apparent, the infighting would begin. Nunn's final speech had anticipated that reaction. Not only did Sasser want deeper cuts in defense programs, but Nunn knew that Les Aspin confronted a more difficult battle as liberal House Democrats pressured their leadership to carve an additional $3 billion from the Pentagon budget in a plan the House Budget Committee had approved. Nunn called the House cuts unreasonable, but Leon Panetta, the committee chairman, informed reporters that he and the other Democratic leaders consented to the additional decrease just to place themselves in a better bargaining position with Nunn and the Senate.[42]

In May, Sasser made good on his plan to make deeper cuts in defense spending, when the Budget Committee, by a 14 to 9 vote, adopted a $1.2 trillion budget for fiscal year 1991, with a $21 billion reduction in the Pentagon budget. The Budget Committee's decision disappointed Nunn, and he warned the only way to achieve reductions of this magnitude in a single fiscal year was to slash funding for personnel and the accounts for daily operations and maintenance of the forces.[43] However, no progress was forthcoming from either of the two branches of government. Confronted with the requirement to meet the deficit target or accept automatic spending cuts in both domestic and military programs to achieve that legal necessity, administration and congressional leaders agreed to budget talks, seeking a "grand compromise."

In June, Cheney sent the Defense Department's plan to Congress to illustrate, not define, the types of reduction under consideration, indicating where force reductions were feasible without imperiling US security. Some congressional leaders complained that the plan offered too little savings, only $1.3 billion over five years. However, Aspin heralded the plan as a decisive event in the ongoing budget debate, because it indicated that the views of Defense Department officials and knowledgeable lawmakers were converging concerning the size and type of forces required in the future. Nunn shared that opinion: "I think this means there is an emerging consensus on a force structure cut of between 20 and 25 percent."[44]

The sweltering July weather matched the temperature of the negotiations. A heated dispute broke out between White House and congressional budget negotiators over military spending. More critically, there was disagreement among Democrats about where defense reductions should be derived. Nunn found himself in opposition to Democratic colleagues in the House and Senate who sought more drastic reductions than he counseled. Nunn directed his subcommittee chairmen to develop two spending plans: one consistent with his recommended level and the other assuming the larger reduction. This step irritated some Democrats who were suspicious of his motives, believing he would manipulate the numbers to support his position. Sasser made this position clear: "Senator Nunn is not setting the defense numbers for the negotiators." Nunn retorted, "We're going to show that you can get it [defense cuts] out of personnel or procurement." In addressing the trade-off, he asserted that making steep reductions in procurement required even greater cuts in the long term.[45]

Three days later, after a marathon session of nearly seventeen hours to mark up the defense authorization bill, Nunn revealed his committee's recommendations for the 1991 defense budget, approving cuts of $18 billion from the administration's proposal, scaling it back to $289 billion, or by 6 percent. "These are Nunn's numbers," an anonymous committee source acknowledged; the bill was fashioned principally by the chairman. Nunn had set the contours of the debate once again using ideas he articulated in his speeches as the "blueprint for the committee." At a Capitol Hill news conference, Nunn told reporters the committee's plan was a "responsible" and a "manageable glide-path toward restructuring of the military establishment and the way it does business." The committee called for sharp cuts in "Star Wars" technology research and significant curtailment of the Midgetman and MX missile programs, but approved production of two B-2 bombers, while slowing production or eliminating several other major weapons. It also approved a reduction of almost 475,000 personnel over the next five years in addition to the cuts in troop strength for 1991. These measures, Nunn believed, could be taken in view of the drastically diminished Soviet threat.[46]

Nunn's understanding of the new threat environment had precipitated the formulation of his military strategy. While offering substantial reductions to the defense budget to fend off deeper cuts by the White House and congressional negotiators involved in the ongoing budget summit, he was also underscoring the criticality of attaining agreement on a strategy to shape future US global interests rather than allowing a policy vacuum to occur. A Middle East crisis would soon put his judgment on all these matters to the test.

CHAPTER 13

SHIELD AND STORM

At 2:00 a.m. local time on August 2, 1990, lead elements of two Iraqi divisions crossed the adjacent Kuwait border and drove southward, penetrating deeply into the emirate. A third division crossed the border to the west. The nearly 30,000 troops of this opening attack were members of the Iraqi Republican Guard, forces dependably loyal to Iraqi president Saddam Hussein, and combat-tested veterans of the earlier, eight-year war with Iran. Within three hours, the armored divisions' tanks were in the streets of Kuwait City, the capital, and Iraqi soldiers occupied the palace of the emir, who had fled to Saudi Arabia. The Kuwaiti army offered ineffective resistance, while the state radio pleaded with its citizenry to help repel the assault. Early reports from the Kuwaiti embassy in Washington, DC, stated that Kuwaiti casualties were extensive. Meanwhile, US embassy officials in Kuwait City, hearing small arms fire only blocks away from the building, began destroying files as a precautionary measure. Another two hours later, effective opposition ended, and within twelve hours, the entire nation, the size of New Jersey and, more importantly, its rich oilfields, were under Iraqi domination. Iraq had decided to resolve its dispute with Kuwait over oil production and prices by invading.[1]

In Washington, DC, it was 7:00 p.m. on August 1 when the invasion began. Two hours later, National Security Advisor Brent Scowcroft informed President George H. W. Bush of Iraq's action. State Department officials were meeting to discuss potential responses; military officers in the Pentagon's operations center were monitoring the situation. The sole US official announcement came from a White House spokesman who told reporters that the United States condemned the invasion, calling the attack a "blatant use of military aggression," and demanding the "immediate and unconditional withdrawal of all Iraqi forces." There were no explicit promises to come to Kuwait's assistance, and a State Department official summoned the Iraqi ambassador to inform him that "disputes must be settled peacefully."[2] There was no immediate response from Capitol Hill that evening,

The Bush administration now confronted, as one journalist commented, the "sobering reality that despite a longstanding commitment to defend America's vital interests in the Persian Gulf, there was no easy military means to compel Iraq to withdraw its forces from Kuwait."[3] The limited US presence in the region was a factor: the aircraft carrier the USS *Independence* and its battle group were in the Indian Ocean, and a second, the USS *Eisenhower* and its battle group, were steaming to the eastern Mediterranean Sea, prepared to enter the Red Sea. There were no decisions to deploy forces to the region for a land campaign.[4]

At a press conference on August 3, Bush stated that a military response was not imminent, but he did not rule it out. On the NBC program *Today*, Nunn provided his assessment, and expressed what reporters considered the predominant congressional view, that the appropriate response should be diplomatic and economic pressure. Three days later, the United Nations Security Council (UNSC) passed Resolution 661, imposing economic sanctions on Iraq. As part of its diplomatic track and as a means of acquiring international legitimacy, the Bush administration pushed for the resolution, but it was similarly part of its effort to gain domestic support and thereby influence Congress to support the administration's evolving policy.[5]

The Bush administration's actions soon went further than diplomacy. Within the week, the president, citing US interests in the Gulf, dispatched a small number of US Army units to Saudi Arabia to deter an Iraqi incursion into that country and other friendly Arab Gulf states under the operational code name of Desert Shield. The United States also contributed to a fleet of ships enforcing a blockade of Iraq commerce under the UNSC resolution. However, the biggest concern on Capitol Hill was the failure of other nations, especially Arab states, to send ground forces to stand with the US forces. Nunn saw this lack of support as significant.[6]

The commitment of US troops to the Arabian Peninsula was affecting the debate on the defense budget, forcing members' to reconsider deep reductions and altering perceptions about emerging "hot spots" in other parts of the world and the requisite military planning involved. It highlighted insufficiencies in US capabilities for regional conflicts. Nunn capitalized on the moment. The cost of maintaining even a small US defensive force in the Gulf region could cost $2 million to $3 million per day, according to one estimate. Nunn pointed out the larger costs of going to war, while underscoring that the flow of oil from the Persian Gulf had global economic implications; therefore, the United States should not bear the burden alone. Moreover, a war would mean abandoning any attempt to control the budget deficit.[7] The demand for a peace dividend began to fade.[8]

Then, with Congress on summer recess, the president decided to begin a rapid buildup of US forces in the Gulf after a weekend retreat with his principal advisors. The extent of the commitment was not disclosed in a public announcement, but a figure of 250,000 troops was rumored. Only a few congressional leaders were informed of the decision, but Nunn was not one of them.[9] Nunn, who was running for reelection, told the *New York Times* that he believed Congress would favor deploying US forces to protect Saudi Arabia, provided other Arab states contributed too, and he did not expect a combat role for the United States.[10]

A week later, Nunn led the first congressional delegation to Saudi Arabia to visit American troops and assess the situation. At a press conference on August 27, after General Norman Schwarzkopf Jr., the commander of US Central Command and US troops, had briefed the fourteen-member, mostly Republican, Senate delegation, Nunn complained that there was still not sufficient Arab participation. He would bring up the matter with Egyptian president Hosni Mubarak when he met with him in a few days as part of the visit. Nonetheless, Nunn was convinced that the United States had assembled sufficient military capability to deter an Iraqi attack on Saudi Arabia, claiming that it would be "national suicide" on the part of Iraq.[11]

Nunn remained uneasy about the large presence of US troops in the region. He recognized the importance of reassuring the Saudi monarchy, but he expressed concern about the emerging perception that the United States would use the military to attack Iraq or liberate Kuwait. On a Sunday news program, he pressed for the importance of allowing the UN sanctions time to succeed as a means of coercing Iraq forces to depart from Kuwait.[12] Additionally, he expressed concern that the United States had the preponderance of forces in the region, thereby characterizing the Arab forces as "little more than a fig leaf," unless Egypt deployed additional capability to defend Saudi Arabia's northern border.[13]

Throughout September the Bush administration weighed its options, including offensive operations, trying to determine whether economic sanctions were ever going to result in coercing the Iraqis to leave Kuwait. At this point, the military advice Bush received favored using air power and avoiding a land war, provided Iraqi troops did not launch an offensive. If such an attack occurred, US military officials were concerned that the international coalition forces did not have sufficient capability to repel the 265,000 Iraqi troops they would confront and could lose control of some Saudi oilfields, until an air assault on Iraq could stem the tide. Nunn supported the emphasis on air power, but he continued to caution about use of military force.[14]

Not content with merely speaking to reporters and frustrated with the press misconstruing his position on the use of force, Nunn laid out his stance publicly in a letter to the *New York Times*. It consisted of three elements: (1) the United States did have vital interests in the region, (2) the United States had no alternative but to respond to other countries' appeal for assistance to deter further Iraqi aggression, and (3) deterring that aggression and removing Iraqi armed forces from Kuwait was best attained by multilateral measures—diplomatic, economic, and military. His concerns about sustaining a large US presence in Saudi Arabia stemmed from the problems it created "for the Saudi government within its own borders and the Arab world." He favored a "reinforcing strategy," emphasizing US air capabilities. The purpose of US ground forces would be to complement and support Arab forces. If Iraq invaded Saudi Arabia or used chemical weapons, however, then the United States would be forced to "retaliate in a massive way."[15]

On September 21, Bush met with Senate leaders to discuss the situation. The meeting lasted an hour and a half, with the president talking about flash points he thought might lead to war, including terrorist acts and extensive destruction to Kuwait. In response, Nunn offered that if force was necessary, the United States should depend on its air and naval capabilities. He again emphasized the need for more troops from other nations to establish that the United States was not singling out Muslims and Arabs for attack, and to show the American populace that others were willing to fight.[16]

The administration's policy remained largely submerged during the midterm election season, only to resurface as the administration changed the purpose of the mission from resisting aggression by deterring and defending Saudi Arabia to a more bellicose stance of opposing aggression. To underscore its policy change, the administration publicly announced on November 8, two days after the elections, that it was reinforcing US combat troops in Saudi Arabia by almost doubling the number of personnel to 400,000 by the beginning of 1991, an unambiguous signal to the Iraqis that it was prepared for offensive operations.[17] Congressional leaders were not notified of this decision until just before the public announcement. Nunn received a telephone call from Secretary of Defense Dick Cheney at a restaurant in Georgia only an hour or so before the public knew, a slight that irked him, given his role as Armed Services Committee chairman, because the administration had not consulted him or even had the courtesy to keep him informed about its plan for a change in strategy. He insisted that he was bothered more by the decision than the lack of consultation. Privately, he believed the decision to use force had been made. The president's offer to meet with congressional leaders soon and solicit their advice did not placate Nunn or colleagues from either party.[18] Nonetheless, the administration had injured itself with this clumsy move. Bush's approval rating dropped from 75 percent in August to 50 percent. He lost bipartisan backing and allowed those with doubts about whether a political motive or Bush's personalization of the conflict was now involved to challenge the change in strategy.[19]

In response to this new policy, Nunn openly expressed concern that Bush was discarding the more patient approach of letting the UN sanctions have an effect and minimizing the risk to US service members. He criticized the administration's decision to cancel US troop rotations between the Middle East and the United States, terming it a mistake, the first time a prominent Democrat had directly disapproved of Bush's management of the crisis. He was not alone as a chorus of critics from conservative religious leaders to the libertarian Cato Institute questioned US motives or contended that the United States did not have vital interests in the Gulf region that were worth war. However, despite the uproar, congressional leaders were not unanimous in how to respond, with the administration deflecting calls, including some from Republican senators, for a special session of Congress to debate the potential for war, and attempting to calm concerns by stating that the president still wanted a peaceful solution and was only taking prudent steps as commander in chief.[20]

Bush again met with congressional leaders to pacify them, and Nunn expressed his concern about how the United States would respond to other crises in the world, given that it now had a sizable number of troops tied down in the Persian Gulf.[21] He was equally concerned that the administration had no strategic vision regarding US policy objectives in the Gulf region.[22]

In an attempt to examine US Middle East policy more strategically, Nunn wrote an op-ed for the *New York Times* that addressed the point he made to Bush, but he also emphasized that the Persian Gulf crisis and the response to Iraqi aggression concealed issues of greater consequence: the problem of stability of the Middle East after the crisis. Four factors made this a complex and dangerous situation: wide economic disparities among Arab states as measured by per capita income; the burgeoning Arab population that placed extraordinary demands on limited resources; the lack of democracy and regional economic cooperation among Arab countries; and the unresolved Arab-Israeli conflict. None of these issues could be solved easily or quickly, but future US policy should not be one of "benign neglect," but renewed attention to the Arab-Israeli problem, which "polarizes and radicalizes the peoples of the region. It provides cover for militarization and military rule in the area. It fuels an ever more lethal regional arms race." More productively, he believed that the crisis could produce a partnership of Arab nations willing to pursue peace with Israel, which subtle and imaginative US diplomacy could make possible.[23] The same day the newspaper published the editorial, Nunn noted that while Bush had made the case for sending troops to defend Saudi Arabia and to enforce the UN embargo, he had yet to make a convincing argument that liberating Kuwait was a vital US interest, worth American lives, and the burden was on him to do so.[24]

Events moved quickly as the administration sought a UNSC resolution in late November to authorize the use of force against Iraq any time after January 15, 1991. In response, and consistent with his belief that the executive should respect the constitutional role of Congress in such grave matters, Nunn held a series of televised hearings on the crisis, beginning on November 27, to focus the debate on what Senate Democrats viewed as the principal issue, that Bush would go to war without consulting Congress. Moreover, it was another attempt by Nunn to influence administration policy. He opened the first hearing by again doubting the need to initiate combat operations against Iraq, stating that time was on the side of the coalition. The sanctions were likely to be effective means of pressuring Saddam Hussein to remove his forces from Kuwait, despite Iraq's continued defiance. Moreover, he depicted Bush's decision to increase the US force presence in Saudi Arabia as a "fundamental shift" in policy that provoked a "number of serious questions," the most pertinent being whether US interests were furthered by liberating Kuwait using military force.[25]

Nunn then articulated the other "serious questions" that he believed should guide a national debate over the possible use of force; he did not question whether force was justifiable, but asked (1) if "military action" was "wise at this time and in our own national interest." He questioned whether (2) the use of a military force consisting largely of US troops to liberate Kuwait was a US vital interest, and equally important, (3) whether the military objective was to reestablish Kuwaiti sovereignty or something more—the elimination of Iraqi offensive capability, particularly its pursuit of nuclear weapons, an alarm that the administration was now sounding but without concrete intelligence. The remaining questions were more practical: (4) how long could the United States sustain 400,000 US troops in Saudi Arabia, and (5) how sturdy was the coalition?[26]

The first witness, former secretary of defense James Schlesinger, shared Nunn's concerns and supported the view that sanctions could work if the administration gave them sufficient time to succeed. He added that their impact on Iraq was already being felt in the three months they had been in effect, with civilian production down 40 percent and oil production "essentially nil"; export earnings had "dropped correspondingly." The likelihood of accelerating economic debilitation was now greater than expected, and he declared that the "economic pressure can only grow worse." Schlesinger contended that if Hussein understood the US aim to be the elimination of his military's capabilities or his removal from power, then the value of the sanctions would fade. In addition, a US military victory might stir up enmity in the region rather than foster goodwill. While Democrats on the committee largely shared Schlesinger's views, Nunn stated he was not opposed to the administration seeking the resolution to pressure Iraq, but he agreed with Schlesinger's sound advice about potential repercussions from US military action.[27] The *Economist*, a British magazine about current affairs, would later claim that Nunn selected Schlesinger and other witnesses to reinforce his own analysis, demonstrating that his "particular brilliance is to get other men to say what is on his mind."[28] Bush too felt that Nunn had "stacked" the witness list, and while the subsequent and prominent testimony of retired military officers annoyed the president, he knew that Nunn's respected views on national security gave him considerable sway.[29] However, these interpretations were an overstatement since other witnesses believed the time for sanctions to work effectively had passed. Former secretary of state Henry

Kissinger held that reducing Saddam's military power was an opportunity "to restore the balance of offensive capabilities in the area," while Richard Perle, now a resident fellow at the American Enterprise Institute in Washington, DC, contended the time was ripe to move from "buying time to using it for the broader purpose of mobilizing for the destruction of Saddam Hussein's military machine." Perle held that a US military defeat would grievously weaken US standing throughout the world.[30] After five days of hearings, Nunn not only continued to define the contours of the political debate, but he had now underscored the potential geopolitical costs of US military action against an Arab state.[31]

In response, the White House continued to downplay Nunn's hearings, characterizing them as partisan.[32] The administration was certainly doing all it could to nullify Nunn's endeavors and box in Congress. On November 29, the UNSC, by a vote of 12 to 2, with China abstaining, approved Resolution 678, which permitted member states "to use all necessary means" to coerce Iraq to leave Kuwait if Iraq did not withdraw its forces by January 15, 1991. The administration's strategy of vigorous diplomatic activity and its timing, as the United States held the chairmanship of the Security Council for November, were essential in securing the authorization.[33]

A week later, Nunn had an opportunity to question Cheney and General Colin L. Powell, chairman of the Joint Chiefs of Staff, about the movement toward offensive operations. There had been some speculation in the press as to whether Bush had purposely been withholding administration witnesses out of a concern that Nunn's hearings would "send the wrong signal to Saddam Hussein."[34] Befitting this significant occasion, the hearing occurred in a vast room in the Dirksen Senate Office Building to hold the large number of reporters, television crews, and members of the public who would witness the event.[35]

Cheney proved to be a querulous witness, dismissive of the view that economic sanctions would achieve the intended result of forcing Iraqi troops to withdraw from Kuwait. Both officials rebutted the testimony that retired military officers had given the committee, adamant that only military force, specifically the necessity of ground operations, could compel Iraq to comply with the recent UN resolution. In fact, Cheney argued, time was running out. The effects of delaying were already manifest: a weakened global economy, a strengthening of Iraqi defenses in Kuwait and Iraq, and an international coalition that was breaking down. Further, Bush did not need congressional authorization before sending US troops into combat.[36] For his part, Powell believed that he needed to provide a "cold, hard appraisal" of the challenge the coalition faced because Iraq was the "fourth-largest military power in the world," at least on paper. He had "no intention of letting anyone on that committee think it was going to be a cakewalk."[37]

After hours of testimony, Nunn found Cheney and Powell's arguments lacking. He contested their claims that the administration could not allow more time for the sanctions to work. He disagreed with Cheney's contention that the United States should use force to alleviate the economic hardships that several European countries now confronted because of mounting oil prices. Nunn suggested the Saudi Arabians contribute their "windfall profits" to these affected nations, adding that Saudi oil revenues had soared by $30 billion because of the situation.[38] Nunn's Democratic colleagues on the committee were equally skeptical, but the Republican members vocalized their support for the president.[39] The press noted the partisan and sometimes angry exchanges of opinion on the subject in Nunn's committee.[40]

Nonetheless, Nunn had succeeded in his fundamental purpose: he continued to foster a constructive debate and force the administration to explain in detail its policy change and the rationale underpinning it. Haynes Johnson, writing in the *Washington Post,* extolled Nunn for "providing what the nation needs most at this precarious moment: a national forum to air vital war-and-peace questions about the Persian Gulf." He also compared the importance of Nunn's hearings on this "grave national issue" to Senator J. William Fulbright's renowned Vietnam War hearings held more than two decades earlier.[41] As was the case with Fulbright's televised hearings, which earned the Arkansas legislator President Lyndon Johnson's unending enmity, Nunn's purpose was not to mug for the cameras. He wanted to enhance the American public's understanding of the issues and risks involved. Additionally, he used the hearings to point out that Congress shared with the president a significant role in making US foreign policy, and part of that responsibility was to examine the options available to the US government as it wrestled with its next steps. He would not give Bush "carte blanche authority," and the administration, he contended, had not made a convincing case for the military option.[42]

The Vietnam War was on Nunn's mind, but it was his Georgia predecessor, Richard Russell, whom Nunn considered a touchstone, and not Fulbright. "I see the Middle East in some of the same ways that Russell probably saw Vietnam," he said, "a place we would get into and not be able to get out of." While he recognized that the military objective in a potential Gulf war, unlike that in Vietnam, would be unambiguous, he remained unconvinced of the necessity of moving so quickly to the use of force. In his estimation, "It had become vital to get the Iraqis out of there because of the huge commitment of the President's prestige."[43] However, public statements and discreet conversations with senior military officers who expressed their uneasiness about the effect of a war, the cost in American lives, and the belief that time to let the sanctions work was an advantage for the international coalition affected Nunn's viewpoint too.[44] In fact, continued use of economic sanctions had actually been Powell's preferred approach—he labeled it a "strangulation policy"—but the general had reversed course, now believing that the probability of economic pressure attaining the policy objective had waned and was, in fact, unlikely to succeed, as he vocalized at the hearing.[45]

Although some pundits believed political ambition and a run for the presidency in 1992 motivated Nunn, it was clear he had taken his initial position based on a prudent assessment of whether US vital interests were involved at this time. He had indicated that military action was justified to liberate Kuwait, but it was a matter of exploring every other feasible and morally acceptable option before risking American lives. Moreover, he firmly believed that sanctions implemented with patience and persistence could achieve the UNSC resolution's objectives. Support for his position came from an Institute for International Economics report. It stated that because of the Iraqi economy's dependence on oil exports, the sanctions had already reduced Iraq's gross national product almost 50 percent and decimated "virtually all of its hard currency earnings."[46] By taking such a stand, however, he was now on a collision course with the president.

Three days after celebrating the beginning of the New Year, the Congress convened, still uncertain on how to proceed given the UNSC resolution's looming deadline, less than two weeks away. Nonetheless, it began debate on the requirement for a congressional declaration of war and the advisability of the use of force. Most Senate Democrats believed the situation demanded legislation authorizing the use of force, and preferred a continuation of the economic sanctions until military action was absolutely necessary. Nunn stated that the constitutional necessity for congressional action was often a "gray area," given the numerous times Congress had bowed to a president's prerogatives as commander in chief. However, a war with Iraq to liberate Kuwait that involved 400,000 US military personnel was "not a gray area."[47]

On January 8, Bush sent a letter to congressional leaders arguing that the crisis threatened "U.S. vital interests," and specifically asked the two chambers to adopt a resolution that "supports the use of all necessary means to implement" the UNSC resolution. He also indicated that such a resolution would demonstrate US unity with the "international community on the side of law and decency." Such a resolution, he maintained, would send an unmistakable warning to Saddam Hussein to withdraw his forces immediately. The final sentence summed up the administration's position: "This is truly the last best chance for peace."[48] He also dispatched Secretary of State James Baker to Geneva, Switzerland, to meet with the Iraqi foreign minister to make a final attempt to convince Saddam Hussein to withdrawn his forces.

Bush had played his cards well. Scowcroft believed that Baker's final diplomatic mission had "blunted some of the damage done by the Nunn hearings."[49] Furthermore, the president had regained strong approval ratings, hovering around 67 percent according to some polls, but 60 percent believed that Congress should have to vote on a declaration of war before US troops engaged in combat. Bush continued to hold that as commander in chief he had the authority to act given by the UN Security Council.[50] Yet he transmitted a conciliatory message to congressional leaders when he stated at a news conference on January 9: "I don't think it is too late to send a consolidated signal to Saddam Hussein. . . . I think it would be helpful still."[51] Later that same day, Baker, after meeting with the Iraqi foreign minister for more than for six hours, informed the press "regrettably" that there was no indication that Iraq would withdraw from Kuwait, nor any flexibility or new proposals from the Iraqi government.[52] When Nunn heard Baker utter the word "regrettably," he concluded that the probability of defeating a measure authorizing the use of force was vanishing.[53]

In view of this outcome, many on Capitol Hill expected an endorsement of Bush's request for military force, but not without debate and a likely split vote, an outcome the president had hoped to avoid. Majority Leader George Mitchell met with Nunn to discuss language for a Senate resolution, one in which the use of force could be used in due course, but that also included language stating that sanctions should be given additional time to work, and the president would have to request specific authorization from Congress before he could begin offensive operations. In the House, Democratic leaders considered a proposal based on Nunn and Mitchell's language, in addition to one that affirmed Congress alone had the power to decide when the country would go to war.[54] However, Steven Solarz, a New York Democrat who had likened the Persian Gulf crisis to Munich, where the allies appeased Adolf Hitler, and Minority Leader Robert Michel, an Illinois Republican, cosponsored a resolution that authorized the president to use force under the 1973 War Powers Resolution. Bob Dole planned to introduce a similar measure in the Senate.[55]

Nunn believed Congress had an obligation to act expeditiously on Bush's request for the use of force and not drag out the debate beyond a few days. A debate lasting weeks would make the constitutional process look absurd to the American public and the world.[56] In addition, while admitting that Bush would likely prevail on the resolution authorizing force, he decided on one last appeal to mold the forthcoming debate. In a *Washington Post* op-ed, Nunn maintained that Iraq remained vulnerable to the blockade and that this continued pressure would make the country an "economic basket case."[57]

The debate on the proposed measures began in each chamber on January 10, and by the second day, it was apparent that Congress would soon be voting on a resolution to give the president authority to go to war with Iraq since Hussein had rebuffed the administration's final diplomatic effort. Vote counters expected the House to approve the measure easily, but the Senate vote was more difficult to forecast, as there were a number of undecided members. Bush had almost every Republican senator on his side; he needed Democratic support to succeed, and to get that, he called members personally. Democratic senator Joseph Lieberman from Connecticut supported Bush and took on the task of getting his colleagues to vote in favor of the use of force. He informed reporters that eight other Democrats were supportive.[58]

Late on the evening of January 11, in an already long day of debate that would stretch into the next morning, Nunn rose to speak. The gallery surrounding the floor of the Senate was filled with spectators, and his words would be broadcast throughout the world. His position was well known at this point, but he needed to remind all his listeners of the reason he favored continuing the sanctions and opposed the use of force. Many knowledgeable observers viewed his oratory as a major point in the debate, perhaps even having the ability to swing votes to his way of thinking. Before beginning, Nunn informed his colleagues he had a bad cold, and as he spoke, he occasionally sipped water. After framing the issues, he came to his chief observation that the United States too often identified its foreign interests as vital without considering the consequences. "We throw around the word 'vital' very carelessly. When politicians declare an interest vital our men and women in uniform are expected to put their lives at risk to defend that interest." He proceeded to argue against using force at this point, stating, "On balance there is a reasonable expectation that continued economic sanctions backed up by the threat of military force and international isolation can bring about Iraqi withdrawal from Kuwait." Twenty minutes into his speech, a few spectators interrupted his speech by chanting "No blood for oil," but Capitol police rapidly arrested the few demonstrators and then temporarily cleared the visitors' gallery. With order restored, Nunn continued by underscoring to his colleagues that the risk of pursuing the sanctions was considerably less than the "very real risk associated with war and, most importantly, the aftermath of war in a very volatile region of the world." Specifically, it could destabilize the region and unleash "Islamic reaction, anti-Americanism and terrorism." He concluded by ruefully admitting that he and those who shared his position would lose the vote, but he offered these words for Saddam Hussein: "These are the voices of democracy. Don't misread this debate. If war occurs, the constitutional and policy debates will be suspended, and Congress will provide the American troops what they need to prevail. There will be no cutoff of funds for our troops while they engage your forces on the field of battle."[59] Nunn's reading of the situation proved correct. On January 12, the Senate and House rejected the Democratic leaders' proposals to delay military action. The vote in the House was lopsided, but the Senate vote on the Mitchell-Nunn resolution was close at 46 to 53. The second resolution authorizing Bush to use force, though not formally a declaration of war, gained approval first in the Senate by a vote of 52 to 47, and then in the House by 250 to 183, ending three days of somber and often passionate debate.[60]

On January 16, at 7:08 p.m. in Washington, DC, White House spokesman Marlin Fitzwater informed the gathered press corps, "The liberation of Kuwait has begun."[61] Subsequently, Bush made a short, nationally televised address to the nation from the Oval Office, stating that every reasonable effort had been tried to end the crisis peacefully. However, Hussein "met every overture of peace with open contempt."[62] Operations to enforce the UN mandates, now under the code name Desert Storm, commenced with air and cruise missile attacks on Iraq's capital Baghdad and on Iraqi forces.

Nunn's vote against the resolution authorizing force soon became a topic on the minds of his constituents. The first indication of potential displeasure became visible before he cast his vote on the resolution, when a billboard appeared accusing Nunn of "becoming Saddam's best friend." The state's Democratic Party leaders held different views regarding the impact his commitment to continuing the economic sanctions would have on his political future, but there was complaining among some conservative supporters.[63]

However, two weeks later the tone had changed considerably from cautious bellyaching to outright demands for Nunn to explain himself. The *Atlanta Journal-Constitution* reported his vote had ignited an inferno, with numerous letters to the editor stating that they disagreed with his position and doubting his credentials as a reliable conservative.[64] Years later, he would state in an interview that his vote had been based on military and intelligence estimates that the United States would suffer between 10,000 and 20,000 casualties in attempting to liberate Kuwait, which he believed could be reduced by continuing the sanctions and threatening the use of force. He was concerned as well to whether the administration had adequately considered America's enduring interests in the region after the conflict ended.[65]

On January 28, in his first appearance in Georgia after the war began, Nunn jettisoned a speech on the economy, and spent three hours in a question-and-answer session with the audience, explaining not only the tactics and strategy involved in the ongoing conflict and its financial cost, but the rationale for his vote.[66] His understanding of actual events would be limited, however, as the Pentagon allegedly refused to discuss war plans with him, and he would be continuously rebuffed in his attempts to obtain information. Senate Democrats and other Hill watchers remarked that such "cavalier treatment of the Armed Services Committee chairman was unprecedented," and speculated that the maneuver was retaliation for leading the battle to delay the use of force or even his alleged presidential aspirations for a run in 1992, an accusation that the chairman of the Georgia Republican Party advanced. Reportedly, Nunn was "furious at the freeze-out."[67] His popularity took a small dip in Georgia: a nine-point decline to a 63 percent approval rating, most notably among his principal constituency—white, male conservatives. Nunn remained unflustered by this minor drop, stating it was not his goal to "maintain an 80 percent approval rating" with Georgia voters.[68] All the while, Nunn unequivocally stated that he was not a candidate for president. "I cannot visualize any circumstances under which I would run in 1992," he told a Boston television news interviewer, which was reported in an Atlanta newspaper. "Southerners don't like to make Sherman-like statements, but that is pretty close to one."[69]

The war would be over in a matter of weeks, but before the ground phase began and ended, Nunn made a visit to the Gulf to assess the situation firsthand and meet with US military commanders and units. He was heartened by the troops' morale and confident that the coalition forces were combat ready.[70] A day after his return, on February 22, President Bush announced a deadline of 8:00 p.m. February 23 (local time) for Iraqi forces to withdraw from Kuwait, or a ground campaign would commence. Saddam Hussein did not comply, and the ground phase began on February 24. With its forces easily routed by the coalition, the Iraqi government announced it would remove its forces from Kuwait and then the next day stated that it would accept the UN resolutions. A cease-fire between the coalition and Iraqi forces occurred on February 28, ending the so-called 100-hour war, with the emir of Kuwait returning to Kuwait City on March 14. Assessing this military victory, Nunn praised Baker, Cheney, and Scowcroft for successfully managing the delicate coalition, given the tremendous political and military stresses it confronted. He offered that it was now the diplomats' task to secure the peace. Meanwhile, a jubilant Bush welcomed US troops returning to Shaw Air Force Base in South Carolina at the Sumter Memorial Stadium a few days after. While Schwarzkopf and other dignitaries looked on, the president praised them as part of the coalition's victory to liberate Kuwait and stated, in a reference to the Vietnam War, that they had also helped the United States to "liberate itself from old ghosts and doubts."[71]

Georgia Republicans capitalizing on Bush's success now took delight in portraying Nunn as a "national Democrat," willing to abandon the Georgia tradition of "strong, pro-military legislators" to achieve his presidential ambitions.[72] Nunn responded directly to the accusation. "It's frustrating after you've worked on defense issues for 18 years for somebody to think, to put out the word, that you're deciding matters of war and peace on the basis of your presidential desires." He emphatically denied any interest in running for the presidency in 1992, although some in the Democratic Leadership Council and party donors had been pushing for a possible run. Nunn equated running with going on a "quest." More importantly, he reiterated how he calculated his position on the current conflict: "I considered my basic philosophy on war and peace, and that is that you should fight wars only when it's in your vital interest and there's no other reasonable alternative." He added, "And I felt then that there was a reasonable alternative, and I still feel there was a reasonable alternative." He also underscored his view on the purpose of US national security policy: "I believe our goal should be to deter war and have enough strength to not have to fight wars, and I still believe that. I'm not going to jump up from this experience and say, 'Next time you have a war, count me in.'" When asked if he had any regrets, his answer was simply that his "conscience was clear about the way" he had decided, and it remained so now.[73]

Republicans and their supporters, however, characterized the Democrats as a party in shambles over the Gulf crisis; others questioned whether they were sufficiently vigorous enough to protect US interests given they had been wrong on the war.[74] *New York Times* columnist Tom Wicker pointed out that Nunn seemed to be the particular focus of Republican mockery because of his apparently incorrect decision.[75] William McGurn, writing in the conservative magazine *National Review,* was especially rancorous in his assessment. He claimed that Nunn's vote had damaged his standing, and snorted that as chairman of the Armed Services Committee, Nunn could hold hearings and take the defense budget hostage to his liking, but once he cast his vote for "overtly political reasons," he had shown that he was just another partisan hack. The legislator could "not be trusted with the more critical responsibilities of Executive office."[76] Former secretary of defense Caspar Weinberger chimed in, "Sam Nunn has never accepted the fact that he was just a legislator with broad policy powers, like a member of the board, and he has always posed as a leader for strong national security." Perhaps still smarting from old political wounds and demonstrating his ignorance of the legislative branch's functioning, Weinberger took a second swipe: "I always found that he waited until he had a consensus or that the majority had lined up before he committed himself, and I don't consider that strong leadership."[77]

The rhetoric describing Nunn's political prospects were bleak regardless of which anonymous authority, columnist, or Republican political strategist expressed an opinion: his stance on the war had grievously injured him politically, his judgment as a defense expert was now suspect, any future presidential candidacy was ruined, and his power on the Hill was in tatters. Nunn remained unruffled. "Time will tell," he told another interviewer, whether his position on the war had undercut his influence in Congress. He had been through turbulent moments before, after his 1977 vote for the Panama Canal treaties and during the 1989 battle over Bush's nomination of John Tower for secretary of defense, which Nunn had helped crush, and which perhaps, according to some commentators, Bush held against him.[78] Even his constituents could not understand his stance: how could he not support the troops? It worried Georgia's Democratic Party leaders too, fearing long-term effects that might undercut his endorsement of Democrats running for the House of Representatives in 1992.[79] However, these fears proved unfounded, and the arguments for his political demise proved ephemeral. He remained a powerful committee chairman with more pressing issues to worry about.

CHAPTER 14

LOOSE NUKES

For Nunn, the collapse of the Soviet Union started with a telephone call on August 29, 1991. Only a few days earlier, Mikhail Gorbachev, the president of the Soviet Union, had been arrested and then released from his Crimean dacha in a failed coup attempt by hard liners from the military, security services, and Communist Party. Now on the line was Nunn's old friend, Andrei Kokoshin, deputy director of the Institute for US and Canadian Studies, a Soviet think tank. Kokoshin had been attending the same Aspen Institute conference on US-Soviet relations with Nunn in Budapest, Hungary, but when news of the coup became public, he returned to Moscow. He was pleading with Nunn to come to Russia. He kept repeating that it was very important that Nunn witness the change in the political climate and meet the emerging reform leaders. Nunn's political antennae were sensitive to Kokoshin's choice of words: his friend emphasized the word "Russia" repeatedly, not the "Soviet Union." Gorbachev was back in power after the unsuccessful takeover, Kokoshin informed him, but the hero of the moment was Boris Yeltsin. Yeltsin, a political opponent of Gorbachev who had surfaced in the era of perestroika (literally, "restructuring," that is, a restructuring of Soviet political and economic policy), had rallied the people of Moscow with his defiant stance and likely had saved the embryonic democracy movement from an attempt to establish a military dictatorship. In response to Kokoshin's appeal, Nunn offered the excuse that he had no visa to travel to the Soviet Union, but Kokoshin was adamant. He would have the Soviet ambassador to Hungary resolve that issue in a matter of hours, and he was true to his word. The outcome intrigued Nunn, as it spoke volumes about the impending shift in political power, when Kokoshin, who had no official position, could get the Soviet bureaucracy to act with such speed.[1]

The Soviet Union was now in the final stages of unraveling, which had begun two years earlier, in November 1989, with the fall of the Berlin Wall and the subsequent reunification of Germany a year later. Similar scenarios were playing out across Eastern Europe and in the former Soviet republics. The disloyal Soviet officials, who were witnessing the demise of a regime that had been in power for more than seven decades, blamed Gorbachev for the public unrest, the economic turmoil, and the disintegration of the Soviet state. In their view, the Soviet Union was now spiraling out of control, verging on anarchy. Its fragility had been apparent months earlier when the Bush administration provided $2.5 billion in short-term agricultural credit guarantees to the Soviet Union, followed by another $165 million in food aid for thousands of suffering Armenians caught up in the interethnic conflict in Nagorno-Karabakh, and to stem food shortages in the Ural region.[2] As Nunn contemplated these facts, a single question was foremost on his mind: who was in control of Soviet nuclear weapons during the turmoil of the coup? He was alarmed at the notion that the coup perpetrators may have had complete authority over the nuclear weapons.

With his visa problem solved, Nunn traveled from Budapest to Frankfurt by train and then flew to Moscow, where he met with Robert Bell, a member of the Senate Armed Services Committee staff, and Kokoshin.[3] Kokoshin drove Nunn and Bell directly to the Russian White House, the parliament building, where only a few days before, Yeltsin had made his public statement against the coup while standing atop an armored personnel carrier. Nunn was stunned as he surveyed the scene. By his estimate, there were still thousands of people standing outside the building celebrating the result. Nunn, Bell, and Kokoshin forced themselves through the throng and entered the building to meet with Ruslan Khasbulatov, acting chairman of the Supreme Soviet of the Russian Federation, and then outside again so Nunn could converse with General Pavel Grachev, who commanded the Soviet airborne troops. Both men had supported Yeltsin; Grachev had even defied orders from his superiors to arrest the man and instead changed sides. On the steps with people and television camera crews gathering around them, Nunn asked Grachev about the security of the Soviet nuclear weapons, but the general could not answer with any certainty.[4] As Nunn stood there with the Soviet physicist and People's Deputy Roald Sagdeyev, the crowd began hollering at Nunn in Russian, and Nunn noticed that the scientist had removed his parliamentary identification pass. Nunn was perplexed, but Sagdeyev explained. They thought Nunn was a member of the Congress of People's Deputies and were demanding the end of the Soviet Union. "Resign your position! Abolish the Congress!" they scolded. "I wished I had an American flag," Nunn later told a US reporter. "You know, Americans are quite popular there now."[5]

Returning to the building's interior, Nunn spent most of the day listening to the heated and tumultuous debate regarding the future of the Soviet Union. Before Nunn was a diverse array of representatives from across the Soviet Union—including Kazakhstan, Ukraine, and Belarus. Sergey Rogov, a coup opponent also associated with the Institute for US and Canadian Studies, sat beside him interpreting and occasionally editorializing about the speakers' remarks, calling one speaker a "lying SOB." Nunn sensed from Rogov's commentary that Yeltsin's power was increasing and Gorbachev's was on the wane.[6]

The next day, Kokoshin took Nunn and Bell to a dacha outside the city where the Russian would speak to a gathering. Nunn was impressed with the surroundings when they reached their destination, a summerhouse situated in a deep forest. The three entered the building, and before them were "businessmen" from all over the Soviet Union. Men, Nunn surmised, engaged in illegal activity, the underground economy, derisively known as the "Soviet Chamber of Commerce." Nunn imagined that he had traveled back in time, to the 1920s when Al Capone and his lieutenants met, especially after Kokoshin surprised Nunn and Bell by revealing he was armed. The Russian explained that in the wake of the coup attempt, the situation was dangerous. This disclosure of a sidearm impressed Nunn with how volatile the situation was.[7]

Kokoshin spoke for about fifteen minutes and then answered questions for another two hours. The men were respectful, but in the smoke-filled room, Nunn felt ill at ease. He had glimpsed another Russia, the men who ruled legal enterprises combined with illicit ventures. As he would later observe, they were powerful, perhaps even violent men who embodied the future of Russia.[8] The American historian Robert Kagan, another eyewitness to the August events and their immediate aftermath, had a similar impression: the coup had set in motion a "strange blend of democratic revolution, mafia takeover, and cowboy capitalism that would come to characterize the Yeltsin years."[9]

The following day, Kokoshin and Rogov took Nunn to the Kremlin for a meeting with Gorbachev. Nunn was surprised that the president would see him, given the demands of his schedule and the political pressure he was experiencing. Nunn had met Gorbachev several times before in Washington and Moscow. Gorbachev seemed delighted to see Nunn, and the two men exchanged pleasantries and then engaged in a lengthy discussion of the current situation. Gorbachev enthused about forming a new federation of republics, but underscored the need for some form of central authority to preside over what would be the remnants of the Soviet Union. A meeting scheduled for fifteen minutes stretched into an hour. Nunn marveled how collected and calm Gorbachev appeared. Two or three times Nunn rose to leave, but Gorbachev drew him back into conversation. He clearly wanted to continue the discussion.[10] The coup attempt had not cowed him; the situation demanded bold and resolute action. "The country is waiting for decisive steps, for results," he insisted. "But we have to overcome the situation that's resulted from the putsch, not just flap our jaws."[11] Finally, Nunn broached the question about who had been in control of the Soviet nuclear forces when the president had been under house arrest. The president's answer was evasive, and Nunn had the impression that he was uncomfortable. Gorbachev offered reassurances and, recognizing Nunn's stature and reputation, believed that through the senator he could convince the US government that he was still in charge, notwithstanding the coup attempt. His elusive response was actually informative. It confirmed Nunn's suspicions that this period had been one of substantial peril. The experience of the past two days led him to conclude that nuclear proliferation, security risks, and the potential for accidents and miscalculation would be significant issues that the United States would have to confront with the impending dissolution of the Soviet Union.[12]

On Sunday, September 1, Nunn was a guest on CBS's *Face the Nation*, from Moscow. The subject of Soviet control of nuclear weapons surfaced, and Nunn told the viewing audience that the Soviet defense minister, Yevgeny Shaposhnikov, had assured him its nuclear weapons remained "under central government control"; there was no immediate danger to the United States. However, Nunn remarked that the United States and the Soviet Union should discuss new nuclear safeguards, including an agreement to eliminate all tactical nuclear weapons, which he believed were more dangerous than stabilizing. Further, the two countries should consider "self-destruct" devices on missiles to abort an accidental missile launch, and give more attention to risk reduction and nonproliferation activities. He summed up, "And we should make it clear [to the Soviets] we expect central control to be maintained over all of their nuclear weapons, whatever happens in terms of the republics achieving independence. That message has got to come through loud and clear."[13]

During the telecast, Nunn was asked about a plan that Representative Les Aspin, Democrat from Wisconsin and chairman of the House Armed Services Committee, had proposed three days earlier. Aspin called for $1 billion to be taken from the fiscal year 1992 defense budget for humanitarian aid that President George H. W. Bush could use to assist the Soviet people as winter approached. Nunn saw the merits of Aspin's initiative and stated that he was open to using defense funds to convert Soviet military industries to commercial purposes because he believed such a move would lessen the Soviet threat. Left unsaid was Nunn's recognition that a major legislative hurdle existed. The House of Representatives and the Senate had already passed their respective defense authorization bills. Congress was now in its August recess, but soon the two chambers would be in conference to reconcile the differences in the bills. It would be tricky adding new provisions at this late date.[14]

On the flight home, Nunn concluded that the past three days had been the "most unusual 72 hours" he had "ever spent" in his life. He had witnessed the splintering of the Soviet empire, an empire with a massive arsenal of weapons of mass destruction: biological and chemical weapons in addition to nuclear. He was uneasy about two specific groups: the military charged with securing those weapons and the scientists who were knowledgeable about how to develop those weapons. As he visualized the problem, there were three categories of concern. The first category entailed the strategic nuclear weapons targeting the United States that were located on land but also deployed on Soviet submarines. These were the most highly secured weapons. More worrying was the second category, the tactical nuclear weapons: thousands of these battlefield weapons were spread across several time zones. He believed this component to be the principal danger because of the lack of transparency regarding Soviet stockpiles and the difficulty in accounting for all of them. The third category was the fissile materials, enriched uranium and plutonium, that could be used to build nuclear weapons. By one estimate, there was enough material in the Soviet Union to make

50,000 hydrogen bombs. Joining these three problems with existing chemical weapons stockpiles and ongoing biological research programs, a demoralized military, and increasing numbers of unemployed civilians resulted in a dangerous mixture that warranted prompt attention and, ultimately, action. Obviously, neither of the defense authorization bills completed before the coup contained measures to respond to this unfolding situation.[15]

Upon his return to Washington, Nunn met with Aspin to discuss how the United States could help the Soviets maintain control of their weapons of mass destruction. Aspin shared this concern and had expressed it publicly. Nunn reciprocated by stating that he was supportive of Aspin's proposal to provide humanitarian aid but that taking funding for aid from the defense budget was risky. It was likely to be opposed by the Bush administration and by a number of their colleagues. A more fruitful approach would be to use excess military stocks as the source of food and medicine. He also argued there was a much closer relationship between defense and helping the Soviets with controlling their weapons than between defense and humanitarian aid. In the end, the two did not come to an agreement but decided to continue their discussion of potential options.[16]

Aspin's scheme had already run into disapproval. Secretary of Defense Richard Cheney, who remained cautious about defense budget cuts in the aftermath of the failed coup in the Soviet Union and amid fears about a potential civil war, deemed it "a foolish proposal" and "a serious mistake."[17] At a press conference on September 2, President Bush expressed a similar sentiment: "I'm not going to cut into the muscle of defense in this country in a kind of an instant sense of budgetary gratification so that we can go over and help somebody when the needs aren't clear and we have requirements that transcend historic concerns about the Soviet Union."[18] The Cold War mentality was hard to shake. Leading legislators from both parties voiced disapproval as well, arguing against spending money to help the Soviet Union.[19]

Misgivings about the potential for political stability in the Soviet Union were not the only barrier to the plan. House Budget Committee chairman Leon Panetta resisted the proposal because it endangered the budget agreement he, his House colleagues, and Senate counterparts had carefully constructed with Bush in October 1990. The agreement established separate caps on spending for defense, foreign aid, and domestic programs and barred shifting money among those categories. It imposed a pay-as-you-go philosophy to discourage deficit spending.[20]

Yet the Bush administration could no longer dismiss the effect that the deteriorating situation in the Soviet Union could have on control of its nuclear weapons. The US intelligence community had forecast nine months earlier in 1990 that worsening conditions in the Soviet Union would likely—there was at least an even chance—result in a scenario of "deterioration short of anarchy." The analysts gauged that the country's economic, political, ethnic, and social problems would increase at a quickening pace while Gorbachev's power would decline. Although the coup attempt had failed, the estimate's conclusion that more damaging political clashes were likely seemed to be coming true.[21]

At a National Security Council (NSC) meeting on September 5, Bush asked his advisors for their views regarding what policy steps the United States should take, given the uncertain state of affairs in the USSR. After considerable debate, it was evident that there was no agreement about how to proceed. Cheney argued for an approach that would "encourage the breakup of the USSR," while National Security Advisor Brent Scowcroft and Secretary of State James Baker took a cautious line that would make the probability of peaceful change more likely. When Scowcroft raised the issue of the Soviet Union's control of its nuclear weapons, chairman of the Joint Chiefs of Staff General Colin Powell assured the gathering that there was no doubt the "Red Army" was in command in that regard. The subject could not, however, be eliminated from the administration's list of concerns. Ultimately, it added a sixth "principle" to its list of objectives regarding the potential breakup of the USSR: "Central control over nuclear weapons, and safeguards against internal or external proliferation."[22] The administration signaled its concerns about nuclear weapons when Baker remarked during a press conference that day: "We do not want to see the transformation that's taking place in the Soviet Union either create or add to the problems of nuclear weapons proliferation." He informed reporters that he would be traveling to Moscow the following week to discuss progress toward peaceful democratic change.[23] Baker's comments were not just the result of the NSC meeting; during the coup attempt, US intelligence had uncovered several irregular indicators involving the Soviet military's nuclear forces. There were no signs of a nuclear accident or other threat, but Bush asked Baker to pay particular attention to command and control issues when he talked to Gorbachev, Yeltsin, and military leaders.[24]

Nonetheless, the National Security Council meeting was not fruitless. Bush expressed plainly his interest in pursuing deeper cuts in the number of nuclear weapons on both sides while there were still leaders in the

Soviet Union he could work with in the near term. He left no doubt that he wanted "solid proposals," and he asked Scowcroft to work out the details with Cheney about additional arms reductions beyond those Bush and Gorbachev had agreed to in the START signed little over a month earlier.[25] Accordingly, the administration developed a proposal whereby the United States would make unilateral reductions in its nuclear armaments. Bush shared his thoughts in a letter to Gorbachev on September 26, followed by a telephone conversation on the morning of September 27, in which Bush clarified his intentions and Gorbachev was receptive, in principle.[26] Bush then called Yeltsin, who reacted positively and thought that Bush's proposal demonstrated "a new level of trust" between the United States and the Soviet Union.[27]

That evening, on prime-time television, Bush did what appeared to be a political U-turn from his statement at the September 2 press conference. In his speech, he outlined a plan to make substantial reductions in the US and Soviet nuclear arsenals by withdrawing and dismantling tactical nuclear weapons, beginning negotiations to eliminate multiple-warhead intercontinental ballistic missiles, and embarking upon other initiatives to reduce the risk of accidental launches and stem proliferation of weapons of mass destruction and materials. When reporters asked for Nunn's reaction, his response was guardedly positive. He added that he wanted more information about other elements of the plan, but on balance, he believed the president's proposals warranted support.[28]

Bush's announcement to scrap a considerable share of the US nuclear arsenal set off a chain reaction. Within weeks, the budget agreement between the president and Congress began to fray. The defense budget was under additional scrutiny, with some lawmakers clamoring for transferring funding to domestic programs, if as Bush stated, conflict with the Soviets was "no longer a realistic threat." Even Nunn and other Pentagon supporters were questioning why additional defense cuts could not be made.[29] The cry for a "peace dividend" returned.

Meanwhile, in conference, Nunn and Aspin had privately decided to combine their respective proposals into a single amendment to the authorization bill. The first part of the amendment would authorize the use of defense funds to transport humanitarian aid to the Soviet Union. The second would authorize funding for defense conversion, assistance in retraining decommissioned military officers, military-to-military exchanges and the destruction and nonproliferation of weapons of mass destruction.[30]

By late October, when the two committee chairmen were completing the legislation that would oblige Bush to respond to Gorbachev's insistent appeals for an unambiguous US pledge to assist the Soviet Union with its impending humanitarian and economic turmoil, their quiet efforts became public. Writing in the *Washington Post*, Jim Hoagland viewed their plan as "an effort by Democrats to contest Bush's mastery of foreign policy" in the run-up to the presidential election in 1992. As important members of the "centrist group known as Defense Democrats," the two sought to alter "the dovish image" of the party for the same reason.[31]

The consequences went well beyond fine-tuning a political strategy for an upcoming election. Nunn's colleagues on the Armed Services Committee, both Democrats and Republicans, expressed "opposition and indeed outrage" that the Nunn-Aspin amendment was being foisted on them just days before House and Senate conferees were expected to complete work on the authorization bill.[32] Nonetheless, the idea was gaining support among Bush administration officials after weeks of intense and secret discussions between the committee chairmen and influential administration officials, including Cheney, Richard Darman, director of the Office of Management and Budget, and Scowcroft.[33]

Despite the uproar, on November 1 the conferees announced their agreement on a fiscal year 1992 defense budget of $291 billion, making few changes to the Defense Department's proposed budget, as they were reluctant to scuttle the existing budget agreement. Nunn and Aspin were pleased because they had attained their goals after six weeks of negotiation. The authorization bill established a commission, as Nunn had proposed, to help the Soviet Union guide its huge military-industrial enterprise toward a civilian, free market economy. It included a provision that met Aspin's concerns, allowing the Defense Department to spend up to $1 billion to transport and distribute surplus food and medicine, private relief supplies, and other humanitarian aid to the Soviet Union. Spending the funds would be at the discretion of the secretary of defense, but Nunn and Aspin characterized the aid as meeting a valid national security aim: preventing mass starvation and social unrest in a nation with more than 30,000 nuclear weapons. Not all their colleagues shared their perspective. The plan ignited disagreement in the conference's final hours, but Nunn and Aspin succeeded in ramming it through. Republicans on the Senate Armed Services Committee vowed that they would block the measure when it came to a floor vote, but Cheney, speaking for the administration, indicated that it would not oppose the aid provision provided it remained discretionary. In the end, the two Armed Services Committees approved the amendment, adding it to the defense authorization bill, but only after straight party-line votes in both committees.[34] Nunn and Aspin's victory was short-lived, however. A week later, the bill's provision was subjected to withering condemnation in both houses. Republican senators, as promised, assailed the defense bill. Democrats condemned the $1 billion aid provision.[35]

Aspin and his party supporters in the House, including Majority Leader Richard Gephardt, were having an equally difficult time. Representative Newt Gingrich, the House minority whip, judged it an outrage for Aspin and Nunn to add the aid provision at the last minute. Republicans and Democrats on the House Foreign Affairs Committee, who saw the provision as foreign aid and therefore an attempt by Aspin to usurp the committee's authority in foreign policy, worked together to kill the entire defense bill. House speaker Tom Foley, confronting the emerging rebellion, just wanted the controversy to die so the bill could come to the floor for a vote. With the pressure mounting, Aspin signaled that he was willing to drop the contentious plan.[36]

Nunn remained resolute. He admitted the opposition had a legitimate grievance in that the added provision was not in either the House or the Senate versions of the defense bill, but he also felt it was an emergency and, therefore, justified.[37] In defending the provision, Nunn claimed that the aid might be crucial in dealing with pervasive military discontent and civil strife in the Soviet Union. He feared that Soviet nuclear weapons could be sold on the international arms market. Nonetheless, he mollified his critics, suggesting that he would confer with Aspin and Senate colleagues in the next week to preserve, eliminate, or adjust the proposal based on numerous factors, including "tepid and ineffectual White House support." In response, Senator John Warner, Republican from Virginia and Armed Services Committee member, believed that the Bush administration would hold to the position Cheney had stated earlier based on a recent meeting he had with the secretary.[38]

Five days later, on November 13, Nunn and Aspin pulled their proposal, as the opposition from members in both parties was fierce. "We didn't get away with it," Nunn confessed a few years later.[39] In withdrawing the provision because it could derail the entire defense authorization bill, they admitted defeat and suffered an extraordinary political embarrassment. The lack of endorsement from the Bush administration was a critical contributor to the failure. In the view of many in Congress and the media, two powerful legislators, "among the most astute dealmakers and power brokers in Washington," had made a serious blunder by not conferring with their Democratic colleagues sooner and failing to foresee the bipartisan disapproval the plan would generate by aiding the Soviets when many Americans were unemployed because of the deepening recession.[40]

The concerns that had catalyzed Nunn and Aspin to action persisted. Nunn remained troubled by the defeat of a plan his critics characterized as a "giveaway," but he was also angered by his legislative colleagues and the White House's shortsightedness in not recognizing the "great danger that Soviet nuclear weapons would fall into the control of breakaway republics, nationalist groups, even that they would be sold to or stolen by terrorists." As he said in a floor speech the day he pulled the provision from the bill, he would rely on his colleagues to explain to their constituents why they had not voted for the provision when that moment came, especially when the Soviets were asking for US assistance to destroy 15,000 nuclear weapons. For him, it was a commonsense proposition. The United States had spent $4 trillion to contain the Soviet threat for more than four decades; he believed Americans would understand a relatively small investment to substantially reduce the threat.[41]

Nunn was not the only person disquieted by Congress's opposition to aiding the Soviets. Within a week, Robert Strauss, the US ambassador to Moscow, a longtime friend of Bush and a Democrat, added his voice to Nunn's complaint about the US government's imprudence. Strauss was alarmed about the possibility of famine, which caught the attention of two senators: David Boren, an Oklahoma Democrat and a senior member of the Agriculture Committee; and Senator Richard Lugar, an Indiana Republican and the committee's ranking member. They wanted to offer agricultural credit guarantees to the USSR so it could purchase grain from the United States. While the proposition intrigued the White House, the budding proposal appeared doomed. Senate Democrat Patrick Leahy, the Agricultural Committee chairman, viewed it as "playing a deceptive game with American taxpayers," who would bear the ultimate risk of default.[42]

Boren, as chair of the Senate Select Committee on Intelligence, had concerns far beyond food. US intelligence officials apprised him that the situation in the Soviet Union was "very unstable and potentially dangerous." Additionally, former US ambassador to the Soviet Union and career diplomat Jack Matlock, who kept current on Russian affairs, expressed his concerns directly to Boren, and former Oklahoma senator Henry Bellmon, who had recently returned from a visit to the Soviet Union, informed him of dramatically worsening conditions throughout the country.[43]

Nunn was equally committed to his belief that the Soviet Union was "coming apart at the seams," and decided to proceed with a stand-alone bill that would focus principally on dismantling Soviet weapons of mass destruction. He decided to discuss the issue with Lugar, a senior member on the Foreign Relations Committee.[44] Lugar had a long-standing interest in international security and arms control issues, and the two, along with three aides, Robert Bell, Ken Myers, and Richard Combs, started to work on a plan.[45]

Politicians were not the only ones who were concerned about the impending disintegration of a state with nuclear weapons. Dr. Ashton Carter, director of the Center for Science and International Affairs at Harvard University's Kennedy School of Government, and three colleagues had recently completed a study that examined the unprecedented proliferation problem that could result.[46] In Carter's view, there was now the "prospect of an entire continent strewn with nuclear weapons undergoing a convulsive social and political revolution against communism." Their study forecast the end of the Soviet Union and specified the principal threats to reliable custody of more than 27,000 nuclear weapons during that turbulent time. It recommended that the US government establish a comprehensive program to assist the Soviets and the governments of the emergent republics with securing and dismantling their enormous nuclear enterprise, including weapons and material, plants and research programs, and the military and civilian personnel associated with this venture.[47]

To Carter's dismay, when the team presented their findings to Bush administration officials, they received a polite but indifferent reception. However, two important men intervened. One was David Hamburg, president of the Carnegie Corporation of New York, which had funded the study, and the second was William J. Perry, who had served as a high-ranking defense official in President Jimmy Carter's administration, and was now leading a research organization at Stanford University that was examining how the Soviet military-industrial complex could be transformed into a civilian economic engine when the Cold War ceased. Hamburg used his relationship with Nunn and Lugar, who had served as members of the steering committee for the Carnegie Corporation's Prevention of Proliferation Task Force, to set up a meeting between Ashton Carter and the senators.[48]

On November 19, Hamburg, accompanied by Carter and Perry along with John Steinbruner, director of the Foreign Policy Studies Program at the Brookings Institution, met in Lugar's office, where Carter briefed Nunn and Lugar on the study team's findings and recommendations.[49] The impact of the briefing was immediate. It bolstered and corroborated Nunn's belief that it was in the United States' national interest to aid the Soviet Union in securing and controlling its vast stocks of weapons of mass destruction. Lugar was also impressed with the analysis and agreed that they should proceed with restoring the relevant parts of the failed Nunn-Aspin legislation, and fashion a new bill. Nunn and Lugar directed Myers from Lugar's staff, and Bell and Combs from Nunn's staff, to draft the legislation. Combs fashioned the language based on the views of the senators. He coordinated with Representative Aspin's staff on specific provisions and received advice from a member of the House Armed Services Committee. Combs welcomed these recommendations, as one of Nunn and Lugar's goals was to build consensus for the legislation in both houses.[50]

For their part, Nunn and Lugar made a list of senators from both parties who might support the new bill, especially since the issue was receiving prominent attention in other Washington quarters. Carter's briefing occurred during a visit by Viktor Mikhailov, Soviet deputy minister of atomic energy and industry, to the Senate Arms Control Observer Group. Mikhailov described for the legislators his country's problems with storing, destroying, and controlling nuclear weapons. The problem was simple. His country did not have the needed money, about $800 million, to store or dismantle the nuclear weapons Gorbachev had committed to destroy. He pleaded for American help. Sergey Rogov and Andrei Kokoshin, who accompanied him, added to the alarm with a sobering report on nuclear control deficiencies. The three men left their listeners with an unmistakable message: the Soviet Union was coming apart, and the situation required rapid US action.[51] Such messages were received clearly in other Western capitals too. Officials from the leading industrial nations, the Group of Seven (G7), were meeting in Moscow with Gorbachev and representatives from the former Soviet republics, a sign that the central government's power was waning, to determine how they could provide aid but receive assurances that the republics would repay existing debts. In the meantime, Bush announced that the United States would provide almost $1.5 billion in grain and agricultural credits to help the Soviet Union make it through the winter.[52]

Two days later, on November 21, Nunn and Lugar invited a bipartisan group of sixteen senators, chairmen of key committees and other senior members, to a breakfast meeting in a conference room of the Senate Armed Services Committee to hear Carter's briefing. According to Nunn and Lugar, "Once acquainted with Carter's analysis, these colleagues agreed that US domestic political hostility to Soviet aid paled in comparison to the dangers in question." Ultimately, Nunn and Lugar secured the other members' agreement to support a $500 million program to destroy nuclear weapons and a separate $200 million for humanitarian aid. Some of the senators pledged to speak with party colleagues in the Senate, a few others promised to discuss the issue with potentially cooperative members of the House, and still others agreed to engage the administration. The group decided that Senators Boren and Carl Levin, a Michigan Democrat, would take charge of the humanitarian aid effort, while Nunn and Lugar would lead the weapons destruction issue.[53] With this profitable result, Nunn and Lugar were prepared to advance to the next step in their agenda.

The next day, the *Washington Post* published Nunn and Lugar's op-ed in which they characterized the Soviet Union as a nuclear superpower descending into chaos, the signs of which were readily apparent: a plummeting economy, a scarcity of food and other essential goods, a currency growing increasingly worthless, and long-simmering ethnic quarrels exploding into violent clashes. In this moment of turmoil, the United States had an opportunity to foster the largest reduction in weapons of mass destruction in history. They made their appeal sensible and easily understandable to not only their colleagues on Capitol Hill but also the American public. While US assistance could not eradicate the threat that Soviet nuclear, chemical, and biological weapons and technical expertise posed to the United States and its allies, it could catalyze the destruction of a large portion of the arsenal. It would be a significant step in advancing nonproliferation efforts. They emphasized the "importance of preventing the weapons and weapons know-how from being transferred to the Saddam Husseins and the Moammar Gadhafis of the Third World." US assistance would come with a price. Specifically, it would depend on Soviet and republic leaders abiding by all relevant arms control agreements, respecting the human rights of minority groups in the newly sovereign republics, and making clear commitments to demilitarization. They asserted that destroying Soviet weapons of mass destruction made sound economic sense, as the process would lower US defense spending in the future and, consequently, free more funding for domestic priorities. They ended by underscoring that the leaders of the Soviet Union and the republics had requested US help in this project and that Congress needed to act now: "It would be shortsighted and irresponsible to let this opportunity pass." To buttress their claim, that same day they released the Harvard study, whereby a reporter dubbed the weapons proliferation problem as "the frightening possibility of 'loose nukes.'"[54]

The White House agreed with Nunn and Lugar's assessment, but the initiative lay with Capitol Hill. Nunn talked to Scowcroft and discussed the plan with Cheney and Deputy Secretary of Defense Donald Atwood, who had just returned from a trip to Moscow and had heard Soviet appeals for aid directly from Gorbachev and other officials. Along with Boren and Lugar, Nunn attempted to set up a meeting between Bush and Senate leaders to discuss the issue, but Bush refused. Nunn could only assume that while there were administration officials who were "interested individually," no White House endorsement would be forthcoming.[55]

Such a position became more obvious when Under Secretary of Defense for Policy Paul Wolfowitz, speaking at an American Bar Association meeting, stated that he did not believe there was "cause for alarm about who had control over nuclear weapons in the Soviet Union today," but he also hedged that "the future is clearly very uncertain and unpredictable." Nonetheless, he advocated for Washington working with the Soviet Union on measured steps to trim the number of nuclear weapons. A high-level meeting of US and Soviet officials was scheduled the next week to discuss destruction of short-range nuclear missiles.[56]

Nunn and Lugar were not deterred. They built their coalition of cosponsors, now numbering twenty-four, by writing a bill that would win broad backing for the plan and conceivably have the best chance of passage in the closing days of the legislative session. To reassure Senate conservatives, such as Republican minority leader Robert Dole and Jesse Helms, Republican from North Carolina, the bill forbade funds being used to underwrite the Soviet military in any way. The occupational retraining and housing of decommissioned officers from Soviet Strategic Rocket Forces, which had been proposed in the Nunn-Aspin legislation and had been particularly offensive to Republicans on the Senate Armed Services Committee, was eliminated.[57] They addressed other concerns that Senate and House Republicans demanded. In some cases, they made their arguments for a provision based on feasibility rather than political acceptability, such as establishing the Defense Department as the lead agency for the program rather than the Department of State. In other cases, they had to make certain that domestic political concerns were dealt with, such as ensuring that US technology and expertise were used where practicable, including a "Buy American" provision, and requiring prior notification to Congress of the Defense Department's intent to "reprogram," or transfer, funds to the new program. Recipient countries had obligations as well. The most stringent provision established performance criteria that recipient countries were required to fulfill before obtaining Nunn-Lugar funding and that entailed presidential certification. These six criteria or conditions required that recipient entities be "committed" to observing international norms of human rights, abiding by arms control agreements, and enabling US verification that program funds were being used for the purposes on which the United States and the recipient country had agreed: investing their "resources in dismantling and destroying" their nuclear weapons, not using "fissionable and other components of destroyed weapons in new nuclear weapons," and not undertaking "any military modernization program" that exceeded "legitimate defense requirements" as well as "forgoing replacement of destroyed weapons of mass destruction."[58]

When their coalition building was complete, Nunn and Lugar used the Conventional Forces in Europe Treaty Implementation Act as a vehicle, offering an amendment titled the Soviet Nuclear Threat Reduction Act of 1991. The Nunn-Lugar amendment authorized $500 million from the defense budget to help the Soviet Union and its republics solely with destroying nuclear, chemical, and other weapons; transporting, storing, disabling, and safeguarding weapons to be destroyed; and establishing verifiable safeguards against the proliferation of these weapons.[59]

Their attention to their colleagues' concerns and the compromises they made paid off. On November 25, 1991, the Nunn-Lugar bill passed in the Senate. The vote was 86 to 8, supported by fifty-two Democrats and thirty-four Republicans, with eight Republicans voting against the measure. Senator Joe Biden, Delaware Democrat, called the program "the most cost-effective national security expenditure in American history." Others credited Ambassador Strauss's alarms about imminent disorder in the Soviet Union for their support.[60]

While Nunn realized that his partnership with Lugar would strengthen the bill, bringing additional votes to the cause, he marveled at the outcome: "It was the most dramatic reversal of congressional opinion in a two-week period that I've seen, short of something happening like a war. I mean, it was an unbelievable amount of support given how much skepticism there had been." It was a stunning achievement: the ability to connect events occurring in the Soviet Union with the security of the United States.[61] During the debate on the amendment, senators expressed their approval largely because they viewed destroying these weapons as a means of enhancing US security, while others viewed it as a major step toward preventing proliferation.[62]

The Senate Appropriations Committee did not support the proposed funding level the bill's sponsors endorsed, and reduced it to $400 million, without explanation. However, the figure did not add new funding to the Defense Department's budget; instead, it authorized the department to transfer up to $400 million from other categories in its operations and maintenance and working capital accounts to this new program. This discretionary element appeased the White House, which was said to favor the new aid package, and made it more acceptable to members of Congress in both houses, but the Defense Department remained displeased about having to take funding "out of its hide" for a program it considered to be of dubious worth. Still, the proof that Nunn and Lugar had fashioned a politically acceptable bill came a few days later when Les Aspin and House majority leader Richard Gephardt assembled the needed support in the House of Representatives, and the legislation passed that body by acclamation.[63]

Two weeks later, on December 12, Bush signed the defense bill, and Nunn-Lugar became law. The White House press statement only mentioned the Bush administration's commitment to helping the Soviet Union and the republics join "the community of democratic nations," strengthening "a more peaceful and stable international order," and designating several administration officials as responsible for coordinating US assistance. There was no mention of assisting these countries with dismantling nuclear weapons.[64] Moreover, the press paid little attention to another event 185 miles to the north in Princeton, New Jersey. Speaking at Princeton University, Secretary of State Baker voiced no doubt about the matters that concerned him with the end of the Soviet Union. He noted the political and economic issues at stake regarding US relations with the former Soviet Union and the successor states, but a security issue was most troubling: the need to safeguard and destroy the former Soviet Union's vast arsenal of weapons of mass destruction, now under the control of a single authority. The Bush administration was determined to prevent the emergence of new nuclear weapons states from the ongoing transformation of the Soviet Union. In this context, Baker alluded to the Nunn-Lugar amendment. "That's neither charity nor aid," he declared, "that's an investment in a secure future for every American." If not destroyed, he asserted, these weapons might find themselves in the hands of figures like Saddam Hussein or Moammar Gadhafi.[65]

Don Oberdorfer, a *Washington Post* reporter, would not let the event pass unnoticed or unappreciated. He praised the Nunn-Lugar amendment as a beginning step in a drastically altered international environment, judging it the "Senate's foreign policy rescue."[66] It was an eleventh-hour salvage as well. Four days earlier, the presidents of Russia, Ukraine, and Belarus had signed the Belavezha Accords, declaring the Soviet Union dissolved and establishing the Commonwealth of Independent States. By the end of the month, Soviet state institutions stopped operating.[67] As the Central Intelligence Agency had predicted a few months earlier, and Yeltsin underscored in a letter to President Bush in late November, a historic transformation was underway. The old order was dead; an undefined, new political order was being born.[68]

CHAPTER 15

FILLING A POLICY VACUUM

I t took President Bill Clinton less than a week after his January 1993 inauguration to clash with Nunn. Clinton had considered Nunn for the position of secretary of state in the new administration, as well as secretary of defense, but allegedly Nunn's chances for the cabinet position faded because his views on social issues differed considerably from Clinton's.[1] One of those conflicting perspectives prompted the collision—lifting the ban on gays and lesbians to serve openly in the US military. Some commentators immediately saw the disagreement as a sign that Clinton had overrated his political skills and failed to cultivate a relationship with Nunn during the transition.[2]

Clinton's first blunder occurred three days before his inauguration when he met with Secretary of Defense–Designate Les Aspin. The two discussed Aspin's two-phase plan for lifting the prohibition: an interim period of several months to "buy some breathing room," in which the president would direct Aspin to prepare an executive order and fashion Defense Department directives specifying new "standards of sexual conduct." During this period, Aspin would direct the military services to stop asking recruits about their sexual orientation. Additionally, any ongoing proceedings to discharge service members for homosexuality would cease. In due course, the president would issue an executive order revoking the ban.[3]

News of the plan reverberated through the Pentagon, leading to a meeting between Aspin and the Joint Chiefs of Staff. The ninety-minute discussion was less than cordial, with Aspin on the defensive and dithering.[4] The chiefs then demanded an audience with the president, and on January 25, Clinton sat down with General Colin Powell and the officers who headed the four armed services. The meeting was soon intense, with the chiefs worked up, stridently speaking against lifting the ban. Clinton offered his rationale, trying to reduce the friction, agreeing that gays and lesbians' conduct should be proscribed to maintain good order. However, they should be allowed to serve without restriction. He would not relent; he would fulfill his "commitment."[5]

Amid the tempest that lasted two hours, Powell remained a calm presence, stating that such an action would undermine unit morale and cohesion, but that the chiefs would obey the commander in chief despite their personal misgivings. He offered an alternative approach, which he characterized as "stop asking and stop pursuing," that is, no longer asking potential enlistees about their sexual orientation, and no longer investigating service members about the same. Privately, Powell had warned Clinton that issuing an executive order lifting the prohibition would be counterproductive. Congress, which was overwhelmingly against Clinton's initiative, would call the chiefs to testify on the issue, and they were duty bound to offer their personal judgment, thereby expressing their hostility to the presidential policy. Moreover, Congress would likely put the ban into law, with sufficient votes to prevent a presidential veto.[6] Aspin concluded the same after conducting informal soundings on Capitol Hill, that less than 25 percent of the members supported Clinton.[7]

Clinton had the opportunity to hear congressional views directly when he held several meetings with congressional leaders. As Nunn, whose endorsement and support had been critical to Clinton in the primaries, watched the situation unfold, he believed Clinton could have handled the issue more adroitly. In August 1992, when the two met at Pamela Harriman's home in the posh Georgetown section of Washington, DC, Nunn had advised Clinton on the topic. The senator and Democratic nominee discussed crucial defense issues, with Nunn offering his views since he had been instrumental in shaping the national security plank in the party's platform. Finally, they broached the subject Clinton had raised on the campaign trail: that if elected, he would issue an executive order allowing gays to serve.[8]

Nunn told Clinton he differed with him on the subject, and pointed out the likely result of such a step. Once the president issued the order, a member would stand on the Senate floor and offer an amendment to some bill the president considered crucial to his agenda to overturn the chief executive's decision. Nunn continued by stating that Clinton had better have a solid legislative counteroffer because that maneuver would transpire. Nunn believed also that the Republicans would unleash a ferocious attack on Clinton in the media and through television advertisements. Therefore, Clinton needed a strategy to handle the political fallout, and he needed another one to deal with the adverse reaction in the military that would surely happen.[9] Nunn's advice was echoed by two Aspin advisors, who wrote a memorandum in early January suggesting that a clash with Congress on the subject was foreseeable and could be "detrimental . . . to the president's long-term relations with Congress." They recommended Clinton meet with Nunn and Senate majority leader George Mitchell to discuss the topic. The suggestion was purportedly ignored. Mitchell had earlier warned Clinton aides that if Nunn or the Republicans sought to block the president's proposal by codifying the current policy in law, there were not enough votes in the Senate to defeat the bill.[10]

The meeting in the Oval Office between Clinton and the senators commenced with small talk, but it soon shifted to the principal issue. Robert Byrd railed against the president's position by citing Bible verses and underscoring that the military would not accept lifting the ban. Clinton acknowledged the probability of the last point. The arguments continued for several more minutes, with Clinton reiterating the arguments he made to the Joint Chiefs of Staff. Only Ted Kennedy and Virginia senator Charles Robb, a marine veteran and son-in-law of former president Lyndon Johnson, supported the president.[11]

The gathering ended perhaps as expected. Clinton was not backing down, but he was not winning any votes, even from Democrats, whose staff were fielding phone calls from constituents overwhelmingly opposed to Clinton's policy shift. Mitchell told Aspin not to expect more than thirty votes in support if the Senate brought the issue to a vote. Robert Dole and his Indiana colleague, Dan Coats, pledged a legislative challenge. Nunn expressed his belief that Congress should have been consulted on the issue more frequently and voiced his opposition to the proposed change, stating that the decision to do so called for congressional action. Aspin underscored the fact that the key to overcoming congressional resistance and obtaining a successful vote in the legislative branch, if it should come to that, was Nunn's "active leadership," and now the Georgian stood against them.[12]

Actually, that leadership would come in a different form, one in which Nunn was prepared to take the heat for the new president's ineptness by bringing a controversial issue to the forefront so early in his tenure and without first gaining public support. While many analysts saw Nunn's public position as an impediment the newly elected president had to neutralize, other commentators dissected Nunn's words and especially his motives. Innuendo, some of it leaked by White House staff, implied that Nunn was taking revenge on Clinton for not being nominated for a cabinet position, or that it resulted from political jealousy inspired by Nunn's egotistical belief that he should be president, or that Nunn simply enjoyed being the center of attention. Others asserted Nunn's stance was simply the view of a bigot, while some saw it as a matter of deeply held beliefs or principles.[13] Clinton believed Nunn's position derived from the latter. As he recounted years later, Nunn "honored the military culture and saw it as his duty to protect it."[14] Clinton's assessment was correct. Nunn, while certainly sensitive to how the majority of constituents in his conservative state loudly opposed the president's plan, believed he had a responsibility to speak out, to maintain a proper balance between protecting individual rights and safeguarding national security, to which good order and discipline were essential. The military was not civilian society. Further, a constitutional issue was at stake: Congress shared power with the executive regarding how the armed services function. Although some people leveled the charge that Nunn was unsympathetic to gays and lesbians, or worse, homophobic, and had fired two gay staff members several years before, the accusation was false. These former staff members could not obtain security clearances and thus could no longer work on a committee responsible for investigations. Besides, Nunn currently had two gay people on his personal staff.[15]

Mitchell, however, had different concerns as majority leader. He assessed the political damage to Clinton. He wanted Nunn to "conduct hearings and cool the thing off and come up with some compromise." Senate Republicans were threatening to bog down the institution's agenda. The dreaded term "gridlock" had resurfaced. Thus, Nunn appeared publicly as stony-faced and implacable, challenging the president, but he was working on finding a means of meeting Mitchell's request despite becoming the visible target of gay activists and their supporters, including some of his constituents.[16]

Before the Democratic members of the Armed Services Committee met with Clinton, Nunn had already announced that the committee would hold hearings beginning in March. In addition, he informed his colleagues that he had discussed the prohibition with the president and the secretary of defense previously on several occasions, despite press reports to the contrary.

He reiterated that this issue should be discussed with service members at all levels, not just with the Joint Chiefs of Staff, and that the committee would hear from those who supported lifting the ban and those who favored its continuance. He affirmed his view that the subject was one in which Congress shared an interest with the executive branch because of its constitutional responsibilities, and one that demanded thoughtful analysis of numerous questions about the impact of the proposed policy change. Lastly, he requested that his colleagues carefully consider these questions before proposing legislation.[17] The editorial board of the *Atlanta Journal-Constitution*, which opposed abolishing the ban, praised him, calling his position that urged thoughtful public debate a "service to the nation." Hearings were a critical necessity, as was a vote by Congress as representatives of the American people, the editorial board stated, while scolding Mitchell for intimating that a "back-door" deal would settle the matter.[18]

Mitchell's intervention had an effect, and Nunn offered Clinton a lifeline. As Clinton admitted years later, Nunn "first proposed to him the six-month delay to fashion a suitable compromise." Nunn believed it was the only means left for Clinton to refocus the media's attention on the president's foremost agenda items, the economy and health care.[19] Clinton agreed, and at a January 29 news conference with Nunn and Mitchell in attendance, stated he had reached an agreement with the two senators. By July 15, 1993, Aspin would submit a draft executive order, after consulting with military and congressional leaders and other experts, ending the current policy of excluding gay and lesbians from openly serving in the armed forces and, simultaneously, write standards of sexual conduct for all military personnel regardless of orientation. The draft order would also be accompanied by a study conducted over the same period, addressing the practical issues of maintaining unit cohesion and combat readiness that were certain to surface with the policy change.[20] The announcement largely extinguished the firestorm, and Congress watchers believed the president had parried Republican efforts to resolve the issue with legislation that would likely obtain sufficient votes from conservative Democrats. Nunn continued to express his opposition to suspending the ban, but indicated that he would not block the president from taking steps to alter the existing policy.[21] Moreover, Nunn could not help untangle the procedural Republican block without a "don't ask/don't tell" type of substitute.[22] The president followed up with a memorandum to Aspin directing him to take the actions announced at the news conference.[23]

By July 1993, the issue was essentially over, with Clinton's decision to change the policy to the ambiguous language that would remain in effect for nearly two decades and was subsequently codified in law with Clinton's concurrence: "Don't ask; don't tell." The law, addressing the concerns of the Joint Chiefs of Staff, represented an untouched articulation of Nunn's position that included a prohibition against gay conduct deemed prejudicial to good order and discipline.[24]

Many columnists and academics branded the upshot as a political defeat for Clinton. The gay and lesbian community viewed it as a betrayal. Republican members of Congress, conservatives and moderates alike who had opposed the change, saw the compromise as subterfuge, but were generally satisfied with the outcome.[25] Clinton's thoughts, verbalized in his autobiography, encapsulated the entire affair: "In the short run, I got the worst of both worlds—I lost the fight, and the gay community was highly critical of me for the compromise." He believed that Dole had "won big."[26] Nunn had succeeded too, handcuffing Clinton from taking unilateral action on an issue the senator fervently believed demanded a congressional role but was also contrary to his personal beliefs and professional judgment. He had given the new chief executive, in the words of political journalist Elizabeth Drew, "a lesson on power in Washington."[27]

The debate over gay people serving in the military was more than a political humiliation for Clinton; it obscured a number of crucial issues regarding national security policy resulting from nettlesome and complex international crises he had inherited from his predecessor, each of which demanded his attention in the opening days of the administration.[28] However, political damage control and a focus on domestic priorities pushed foreign relations issues to the bottom of the White House's agenda. Consequently, it would be several months before the administration presented its foreign policy vision, and in the interim, it dealt with the ongoing overseas problems in a piecemeal fashion, leading only to more blunders and misjudgments.

In the absence of clear policy direction from the executive branch, Congress stepped in not only to shape the discourse but to develop policy. Yet it too struggled with the US role in the post–Cold War era.[29] The principles and doctrine that had so neatly defined the relationship between the United States and the Soviet Union no longer applied. Long-simmering ethnic, religious, and geopolitical tensions were now boiling in Eastern European countries. Nunn had predicted this problem two years earlier, concerned that if there were not significant improvements in their economies, their citizens would succumb to demagoguery that would inflame cultural and nationalist conflicts.[30]

As he looked at the strategic landscape, Nunn saw that the international marketplace was becoming increasingly competitive. The communist worldview was dead because the world was entering an "age of knowledge and technology and information." Communist countries had not been able to "compete in a world of computers without having some basic freedoms." He believed that human capital; education in science, mathematics, and engineering; investment and savings; and greater productivity were the immediate challenges the United States confronted in the post–Cold War world. It could no longer "live off" its World War II economic, political, and military foundations.[31]

Clinton's defense policy was equally inchoate and undistinguished. The administration and Congress grappled with the purpose of military power now that the Cold War had ended. The expectation that defense spending would be sharply curtailed remained a viable aim for the administration and among many congressional Democrats. The public largely shared this view. In the presidential election year, 1992, there were indications that Americans believed deployment of US forces overseas to deal with calamities (i.e., the United States serving as a "global policeman") was a less attractive policy option, a sentiment Clinton took advantage of in his campaign.[32]

The certainty of further reductions to the defense budget prompted fierce bureaucratic infighting among the military services as they attempted to justify their current missions and personnel levels. Yet, the likelihood of preventing additional cuts was low, because Clinton had to make good on another campaign promise to show how he would reduce the defense budget while preserving US capability to project American power worldwide. On this issue, the president had found his answer in a July 1992 speech Nunn gave in which the Georgia Democrat called for the Defense Department to conduct a "no-holds-barred, everything-on-the-table review" to eliminate "redundancy and duplication" among the armed services. Nunn held that by undertaking such a review, the armed services could identify cuts in the defense budget that could ease the federal government's fiscal crisis resulting from rising deficits and unparalleled national debt. The services could take advantage of the altered international environment and the technological superiority that they had demonstrated so clearly in the Gulf War to reduce their forces.[33] At the same meeting at Harriman's house where the two men discussed defense and foreign policy issues, Clinton had raised the services' roles and missions as the first topic of discussion.[34] In August 1992, the presidential candidate had endorsed Nunn's proposition in a speech in Los Angeles.[35] Now he would use it as the basis for cutting defense costs.

As soon as Clinton assumed office, Nunn made good on his promise that Congress would reassert itself in foreign policy now that the Cold War had ended. "There is the perception that there's more time for decision-making, more time for debate," he avowed, "and that inevitably means that Congress is going to be much more involved."[36] Nunn chaired oversight hearings in January 1993 at which senior military officers briefed the Armed Services Committee on US military operations in Somalia, the former Yugoslavia, and Iraq, carried out under United Nations Security Council (UNSC) resolutions. Nunn expressed concern about these missions, which he characterized as "the slippery slope," involving the United States as the "police force of the world, almost at the direction of the United Nations." He was especially concerned that the operations in Somalia and the Balkans undertaken for humanitarian purposes would escalate into conflicts for which the executive branch had not planned.[37] "If something goes wrong," the American people would be outraged because Congress had been "sitting on its hands," not exercising its constitutional responsibilities in foreign policy while the president committed the United States to these undertakings.[38]

The defense budget proposal the administration submitted in February became the pressing issue. On March 5, Nunn took to the Senate floor to address defense spending as his committee geared up to review the proposal. He was generally supportive of the administration's planned cuts of $122.6 billion over five years, based on holding down federal wage growth and the projected dwindling of inflation. Nonetheless, he questioned several fiscal assumptions on which the reductions and potential cost savings were based, a position supported by a recent General Accounting Office analysis. He argued that the "Pentagon ought to be held harmless against things they have no control over." More importantly, however, he warned his colleagues and the leaders in the House of his opposition to any deeper reductions, convinced that the defense budget had undergone sufficient reductions in recent fiscal years. He had made this position known during conversations and meetings with Clinton and other officials: that he would insist that future Pentagon budgets increase if the expected cost decreases did not transpire; otherwise, the administration's huge spending cuts would result in unplanned reductions in the size of the forces and decreased readiness.[39]

Nunn was confident in staking out such an unwavering position; he knew he could count on Republican support because they were solidly against Clinton's budget plan. Thus, he could demand that the Senate Budget and Appropriations Committees understand that his acceptance of Clinton's defense proposal was not "only a ceiling but a floor," and that he would "be fighting for that view." The potential for a scrap with two powerful chairmen was now in play.[40] However, he knew that many Democrats in the House of Representatives, including Californian Ron Dellums, the new chairman of the Armed Services Committee, sought further cuts in defense spending. Dellums deemed himself a "counterweight" to Nunn.[41]

Later in March, Nunn gave notice that he would not be as pliant regarding the defense cuts as he had earlier intimated. When the Senate Appropriations Committee sent Clinton's $16.3 billion economic stimulus package to the floor for consideration, Nunn introduced nonbinding amendments expressing "the sense of the Senate" that there would be no further defense budget cuts to pay for domestic programs. Further reductions, he contended, should be used to reduce the deficit. His measures did not endear him to the administration or some Democratic colleagues in the Senate.[42] Interviewed on NBC's Meet the Press, Nunn stated that he would secure changes in the president's budget proposal, especially with respect to defense, and he might vote against the overall budget if convinced that it harmed US military capabilities. The administration was not reining in spending growth associated with entitlement programs such as Medicare, Medicaid, and Social Security. On this last point, several other Democrats agreed with him.[43] The Washington Post editorial board supported him too, arguing that he was right to warn that the administration's budget assumptions were overly optimistic. However, he was not without his detractors, even in Georgia, where an editorial claimed he was attempting to preserve defense spending at unnecessary levels.[44]

Nunn was having the impact he wanted: shape the national debate on the broader issue of government spending. The Senate adopted two of his amendments that could restore some Pentagon funding if the economic assumptions proved wrong, over the strong objection of Tennessee senator James Sasser, chairman of the Budget Committee. The amendments were intended as a caution to Appropriations Committee chairman Byrd, who favored increased domestic spending. Nunn wanted to deter Byrd from transferring funds from defense to domestic programs. The Senate did reject, however, his amendment on curbing the growth of entitlement programs, but narrowly, by four votes, an effort that required White House intervention.[45]

The Democrats held together in both the House and Senate, defeating all changes that the Republicans offered to Clinton's economic plan. By month's end, after debate and fervent lobbying from Democratic congressional leaders and the White House, budget resolutions passed in both chambers that were essentially the same, making a compromise on a single budget number easily attainable. It was improbable that Clinton's plan would remain intact during the "reconciliation" process, when congressional committees would specify the spending reductions and tax increases the plan proposed.[46] Nunn spoke directly to this point: "We haven't seen the five-year defense plan. We have been dealing with numbers grabbed out of the air. No one knows where all these cuts are going to come from." Secretary of Defense Aspin admitted he owed details on the defense budget proposal. Critics chimed in that it was not clear how the secretary would relate the spending levels to a defense strategy for the new security environment. Aspin did not foster confidence when he told reporters candidly, "What we're doing is kind of treading water."[47]

With Aspin's remark, Nunn realized he was in a position to shape the defense budget more than he had expected, given Aspin's reputation as a defense expert. Now, the former congressman was confronted with the enormous task of meeting the president's goal to cut billions of dollars in defense spending. The columnist Mary McGrory declared that for the past twelve years, Nunn had been secretary of defense in all but name. The "regular order," that is, his primacy on defense issues, would soon be reestablished, she prophesied.[48] A Democratic staff member on the House Armed Services Committee agreed, and with Aspin's missteps on the budget, a "policy vacuum" existed that Nunn and Dellums would vie to fill.[49]

Nunn demonstrated his capacity to fill the void on April 1, when, at a hearing, he informed Aspin that Congress might not be willing to wait for the Clinton administration to define the fiscal year 1994 defense spending cuts and would make the decisions on its own. Further, the budget had to be responsive to the changed global security environment, Nunn said, noting some "ominous developments," many of which the committee had examined in the previous months, that would influence the US defense posture. Nunn counted himself among those who believed in maintaining a "strong defense," but he chastised the Defense Department for not completing a revised defense strategy and a long-term plan to address the rapidly changing landscape. Given the mood on Capitol Hill, making judicious reductions was imperative, for once made, restoration in the future, short of a war, would be improbable.[50]

Meanwhile, Clinton's foreign policy remained in bad shape, in particular, the administration's stance on the ongoing conflict between Bosnians and Serbs in Bosnia-Herzegovina, a country that had once been part of Yugoslavia until the Bosnians declared independence as a sovereign nation in early 1992. Shortly thereafter, the Bosnian War began among the three ethnic groups that lived in the newly created nation: Bosnia's Muslims, Serbs, and Croats. The Clinton administration planned to help the United Nations assume a more active role in the conflict. On March 31, the UNSC authorized a resolution that called for enforcement of a no-fly zone in Bosnia, which the United States and NATO allies supported.[51] Subsequently, the Clinton administration directed the US military to participate in NATO's Operation Deny Flight, the first armed engagement of American forces in the former Yugoslavia.[52] Nunn was concerned that this decision would embroil the United States in a civil war, one many Americans believed was an issue for Europeans to settle.

Three weeks later, on April 20, Nunn held hearings on the situation in the Balkans, with US Army general John Shalikashvili, the NATO commander, testifying at a time when the Clinton administration was discussing the intensifying fighting in Bosnia and possible options to prevent the Serbs' ethnic cleansing of Bosnian Muslims.[53] While Nunn's hearing was designed to gauge if and how the United States might be involved, the administration itself remained divided on the use of force to end the war.[54]

Over the next several weeks, Nunn became increasingly involved in understanding the Bosnian War, given the tragic consequences the American public was witnessing on nightly news broadcasts. Part of his interest stemmed from the division that existed among his colleagues about what action the United States should take. Senators worried that the United States would find itself mired in another Vietnam War for which it would assume responsibility and from which, thus, it could not easily extricate itself. Others argued that the least the United States could do was to allow the Bosnians to procure the weapons they needed to protect themselves.[55]

In response, the Clinton administration announced its new policy on Bosnia in May as one of "lift and strike": lift the 1991 United Nations arms embargo on Bosnia (UN Security Resolution 713, passed in September 1991, placed an arms embargo on all the territory of the former Yugoslavia) and conduct air strikes against the Serbs. The administration believed that these actions would bring military balance to the conflict, allowing the Bosnians to purchase weapons that would be comparable to Serbian weaponry; airstrikes were designed to thwart Serbian aggression. Few Americans viewed the Bosnian conflict as an important issue at all, with US intervention only occurring when moral issues arose, such as to prevent atrocities or ensure the delivery of aid to vulnerable civilians. Nonetheless, Clinton dispatched Secretary of State Warren Christopher to Europe to seek approval of the policy from NATO allies and the Russians.[56]

Given this state of affairs, Nunn led a senatorial delegation to Moscow to discuss the situation with Russian officials. His talks were held at the same time that Christopher was meeting with Russian president Boris Yeltsin and his foreign minister to discuss how to end the war. Nunn and Christopher alike recognized the difficulty of obtaining a Russian commitment, as it was a longtime ally and patron of the Serbs. Furthermore, Yeltsin had his own domestic troubles, with political foes backing Russian support of Serbia. Russian military officials told Nunn that they viewed airstrikes as ineffective, given the situation on the ground. Christopher had better luck with Yeltsin. The Russian president agreed to deploy troops to Bosnia to help enforce a potential UN peace agreement among Bosnia's three parties, a position Yeltsin had outlined to Nunn when they met. When questioned by the press, Nunn stated that the Christopher-Yeltsin agreement was a "strong signal" that both countries wanted to end the bloodshed.[57]

Nunn made clear to the administration and NATO partners what was at stake in a speech in late May. In the absence of the Clinton administration offering clear US policy aims, Nunn articulated what he believed were US interests regarding the conflict: First, prevent the war from spreading into Kosovo and Macedonia, which would pull Greece and Turkey, NATO allies, into the conflict, but on opposing sides. Second, avoid alienating the Islamic world, which sided with the Bosnian coreligionists. Third, uphold the integrity of NATO and the newfound authority of the United Nations as a peacekeeping institution. Lastly, ensure that any action the United States undertook with respect to the former Yugoslavia would not "abort the quest for democracy in Russia." In any case, the United States should not act unilaterally, but with its NATO allies.[58] Within days of Christopher's return to Washington and because of the unenthusiastic reception Clinton's policy had received from NATO allies, the administration abandoned its "lift and strike" initiative despite public declarations to the contrary.[59]

Bosnia was not the only international crisis where Nunn believed Clinton was misjudging US interests. The situation in the failed state of Somalia, a United Nations mission that Clinton had inherited from his predecessor, which had broadened since its 1991 inception, demanded attention as well. Nunn had held hearings in March to review US military operations designed to establish a secure environment for international famine relief operations that the UN was leading. Nunn believed that the War Powers Resolution applied regarding the participation of US forces, and that Congress was neglecting its constitutional responsibilities. Specifically, Nunn argued that since the deployment was authorized under Chapter VII of the UN Charter where armed force was involved, congressional authorization was needed consistent with US law, the UN Participation Act of 1945. However, in deference to Clinton, Democratic senators did not pursue the topic; neither did congressional Republicans.[60] Three months later, it could not be avoided.

In early June, an armed force associated with the Somali warlord Mohamed Farah Aidid ambushed UN peacekeepers from Pakistan, killing twenty-two and wounding fifty-four.[61] From the UN's perspective, Aidid was attempting to intimidate the peacekeepers and prevent them from carrying out their humanitarian relief mission and gain political power over competing factions. The UNSC responded by unanimously condemning the attack and adopting a resolution that sought the arrest and detention of the perpetrators for prosecution, trial, and punishment.[62] Clinton stated at a news conference that the United States "could not let it go unpunished" and had conducted military operations in response.[63] A week later, on June 24, Nunn held a hearing on the incident, requesting an overall assessment of the UN peacekeeping operations in that failed nation.[64]

As events transpired during the summer, Nunn contended that it was even more crucial to conduct an in-depth review of the Somalia mission. He was not suggesting that US forces be withdrawn immediately, but it was clear that a review was necessary, as the military mission had changed, with US forces now engaged in raids. Some Clinton advisors suggested that the United States keep forces in Somalia until the situation "stabilized," but the meaning of that term was unclear, as was the length of such a commitment.[65]

Nunn's concerns carried weight with Mitchell and Dole. However, Byrd sought more than a review; he wanted US forces withdrawn from Somalia unless Congress specifically authorized the mission. He had not voted to give the US military license to hunt down and disarm Somali warlords and their militias. Regardless of these differences in approach, all concluded the time was right to send a strong message to Clinton. On September 9, Nunn, working with administration officials, Mitchell, Byrd, Dole, and Arizona senator John McCain, reached a compromise. By a vote of 90 to 7, the

Senate passed a nonbinding resolution, proposed as an amendment to the fiscal year 1994 defense authorization bill, that called upon the president to "consult Congress on U.S. policy toward Somalia," report to Congress by October 15 on the administration's objectives, and receive congressional authorization by November 15 in order for US deployments to continue. The measure was not what Byrd had sought, but it served the purpose of urging Clinton to consult with Congress on US policy regarding Somalia.[66]

Bosnia remained a troubling situation. On September 22, Shalikashvili, during his confirmation hearing to be the next chairman of the Joint Chiefs of Staff, revealed to Nunn and the committee members that he would recommend deploying US forces to Bosnia if a legitimate peace settlement was reached. If that occurred, he conceded the United States would likely bear the heaviest burden in terms of troops and funding. The general was less sanguine about Somalia, where he believed the mission now far exceeded its original mandate in securing the delivery of food and relief supplies.[67] As if on cue, two days later, Clinton sent his top national security advisors to Capitol Hill to determine support for sending US troops to Bosnia as part of a NATO operation to implement a cease-fire. Nunn's response to his meeting with the officials was emphatic: "My big question will not be how do we go about it, what our goals are, but do we get out if the parties begin fighting again?" He had more questions than answers at this point, but he was determined that there would be an exit strategy before any commitment of forces.[68] His concerns also signaled his discontent with the lack of strategic planning on the part of the Clinton administration. As Illinois senator Paul Simon pronounced, "When you have a President who is new to foreign affairs and a Secretary of State who is cautious, Congress fills the vacuum."[69]

On October 3, Nunn's worst fears about the Somalia mission transpired. A botched raid on a suspected Aidid stronghold in Mogadishu by US Army Rangers resulted in eighteen US soldiers killed and seventy-nine wounded, with a Somali crowd desecrating the bodies of some American dead and displaying a captured and badly beaten US army helicopter pilot to television cameras. In the aftermath, Clinton and his advisors discussed pulling out US forces immediately, but ultimately believed that chaos would again ensue if it took that step. The congressional response was outrage: House Republicans demanded Clinton withdraw US forces. Byrd proposed a resolution that would end funding for the operation at the end of the year, but Nunn differed.[70] On the Senate floor, he amplified his viewpoint: "We expect our troops in Somalia to remain calm and collected under fire," he said, "and we owe them nothing less than equal composure back here in Washington as we decide what to do next in Somalia."[71]

Nunn held two hearings on the event, at which he not only upbraided the Defense Department for providing information on the incident publicly before briefing Congress, but he expressed his unease with the administration's stunning conclusion that the military mission should remain unchanged.[72] However, Clinton, after consulting with Nunn, Warner, and others, committed to ending the US military deployment by the end of March 1994.[73] The president officially announced this change in strategy to the nation on the evening of October 7, but he had also ordered 1,700 more troops to Somalia to beef up force protection. He vowed that the United States had "started the mission for the right reasons," and the country would "finish it in the right way."[74] In the end, Congress had forced Clinton to accept a deadline and limit the US mission to supporting humanitarian aid, thereby essentially ending US involvement in Somalia.

Nonetheless, as the debate over the US role in Somalia progressed, congressional watchers took note of Nunn's quiet but substantive advisory role, one in which his influence and power was felt. One reporter called it a "quintessential Sam Nunn moment: a difficult question on the use of American force, a restive Congress, a President struggling for consensus." He remained a potent force in foreign policy discussions in both the executive and legislative branches, circumspect in his criticism of the White House, but also not allowing events to stampede him into making careless remarks. An administration official bolstered that image: "I think no Democratic foreign policy is going to get very far, particularly one with a military aspect to it, unless it's blessed by Sam Nunn." His independent mindedness was also on display; he reached his own conclusions after intensive study, not out of deference to a president's wishes.[75]

On October 14, the contest over US foreign policy on Somalia began in earnest, with the president transmitting his policy to Congress. In the Senate, Byrd introduced a resolution to stop funding of US military operations by February 1. His measure restricted US military personnel to defending themselves and securing humanitarian relief supplies in the interim. Nunn, who convened a closed hearing, asked General Joseph Hoar, the commander of US Central Command, responsible for US forces in East Africa, if it was reasonable to withdraw his troops by January 1. Hoar replied that it was, but withdrawing forces would damage the UN mission. Nonetheless, the general supported the president's decision to pull out troops by March 31.[76]

The next day, Senate leaders from both parties achieved the compromise they wanted. The chamber voted, 76 to 23, in favor of an amendment to the defense appropriations bill, which Mitchell, Nunn, and Dole worked out with Byrd, limiting the US troops' role while supporting Clinton's decision to withdraw all US forces no later than March 31. Byrd was gratified with the result. A month later, the Senate compromise became Congress's final position when the House agreed to the provisions in the conference report on the defense appropriations bill. The president signed the bill on November 11, codifying Congress's final verdict on the mission.[77]

The end-of-year victory came at a cost. The congressional criticism of Clinton being incapable of managing US foreign policy, especially involvement in UN peacekeeping operations, did not abate, and his approval rating dipped after the US soldiers died in Mogadishu, but by the end of 1993, his favorability had recovered.[78] Aspin was less fortunate: he became the scapegoat and was pushed out of office. Nunn's name immediately surfaced as a potential replacement, and in January, the White House made him the offer after its first choice withdrew from consideration. Nunn expressed his lack of interest publicly, stating he preferred remaining a senator, where he could "do more for the country."[79]

Yet, the foreign policy issues could not be easily swept away. By late February 1994, the administration, in step with the Russians and several Western European governments, pressured the Bosnian government to make peace with its two adversaries, intimating that the United States would deploy troops to enforce a settlement. Nunn immediately raised caveats, stating that the administration needed to prove it had an exit strategy, with a realistic timetable for withdrawal of forces based on the achievement of specific goals, before Congress should approve such a measure. He underscored that a NATO officer had to be in charge of the operation and the financial cost acceptable.[80]

Nunn's attention, however, soon reverted to the funding debate, but his concerns could not be disconnected from national security policy and strategy, as the new secretary of defense, William Perry, who had replaced Aspin in January, grappled with restructuring the military. Nunn and other lawmakers questioned whether the United States could afford a strategy calling for it to be capable of fighting two regional conflicts nearly simultaneously, in addition to meeting requirements to conduct peacekeeping missions and maintaining an extensive overseas presence. In testimony before the Armed Services Committee in March, Hoar confirmed Nunn's argument when he vocalized that the strategy was infeasible. In his estimation, the demand for transportation assets to deploy US forces would exceed the number of resources available even for a single event. The mismatch between resource levels and the administration's policy objectives was notable, but Perry downplayed the gap, insisting that the strategy was a work in progress, and that a scenario in which US forces had to "fight two wars at once" was "entirely implausible."[81] By June, the arguments had shifted from concepts to arguments over specific capabilities to execute the strategy. Using the administration's analysis of defense requirements, Nunn pointed out inconsistencies between the study and the proposed budget.[82]

Yet, current events continued to intrude when in the same month, the Bosnian vice president, Ejup Granic, implored the United States to lift the arms embargo. Administration officials remained opposed to such a measure; they expressed concern that the move would jeopardize the ongoing peace talks and worsen the fighting. The battle over lifting the embargo had loomed for more than a month; many Republicans, including Dole and McCain, and some Democrats, argued the United States had a moral obligation to allow the Bosnians to defend themselves. They attached an amendment to the defense authorization bill that called for unilateral lifting of the embargo, daring Clinton to veto the defense measure.[83]

In turn, Nunn voiced concerns about this legislative stratagem, arguing that it would undermine NATO solidarity because its members supported the embargo. To prove his point, he held a hearing with officials from NATO member states for their estimate of the consequences of lifting the embargo. They indicated that if such an action transpired, it would throw NATO into disorder, disrupt the fragile cease-fire in place, terminate the humanitarian relief efforts, undermine the peace talks, and expand the conflict. It was a sober event. At one point, while Nunn was speaking, McCain interrupted him, testily pointing out an obvious omission: "Too bad we can't get the view of any of the people getting killed."[84]

The next day, Nunn offered an alternative proposal that endorsed the peace negotiations, but included a provision that if the Serbs did acquiesce to any agreement, then the United States and its NATO allies should seek a repeal of the arms embargo. While the Democratic leadership praised Nunn's effort, his proposal swayed few members. He recognized the validity of his opponents' moral position, but he argued that the United States had to differentiate between moral and vital interests, and as far as he could determine, the Balkans situation was not a vital interest, as no senator was willing to commit US troops.[85]

The two sides remained resolute in their positions. A week later, a Dole-sponsored measure to lift the embargo failed in the Senate on a 50–50 vote. Before that vote, the Senate approved, 52 to 48, a nonbinding amendment sponsored by Nunn and Warner, which the administration championed, that urged Clinton to pursue a multilateral end to the embargo if Serbian forces wrecked attempts at a negotiated peace settlement. Nunn recognized the tenuous nature of the victory, while the Clinton administration saved itself from embarrassment by vigorously lobbying on Capitol Hill. When asked by a reporter if he was satisfied with the outcome, Nunn responded, "Compared to what could have happened, yes." He pointed out that the administration should understand that the overwhelming sentiment in the Senate is that the arms embargo is counterproductive. He recognized another implication of the result: "The Bosnian thing in conference will be very difficult."[86] His perspective underscored the fight ahead. The House version of the defense authorization bill contained a provision calling on Clinton to lift the ban. A few weeks later, Nunn adroitly managed the issue, attaining a conference bill that included language on Bosnia similar to his Senate compromise, which passed the Senate on August 13.[87]

CHAPTER 16

THE LAST TRUE CENTRIST

O n a cold January 3, 1995, Newton Leroy "Newt" Gingrich, Republican congressman from Georgia's Sixth District that included part of suburban Atlanta, fresh from the 1994 midterm elections in which his party gained fifty-two seats in the House of Representatives and the majority, had a message for America. "We will not compromise," he bellowed from the steps of the US Capitol. In fact, Gingrich and more than two hundred of his victorious Republican colleagues had a "Contract with America" to institute his party's wide-ranging policy agenda.[1]

A day later, Gingrich became Speaker of the House. Once in charge, he admitted that the ambitious goals contained in the Contract might be too difficult to implement, but he was determined to make the first one hundred days of his leadership noteworthy. "We may have a more limited success in terms of bills, but the whole language of politics will be in the midst of transformation. We'll be building a bow-wave of change," he informed veteran Washington political journalist Elizabeth Drew.[2] The electoral victory was as much a repudiation of Bill Clinton's handling of the presidency in his first two years and his party's liberal policies as it was a vote of confidence in the Republicans who believed they were now the party of reform. Haley Barbour, chairman of the Republican National Committee, said the success of Republican candidates demonstrated "the mood was not anti-incumbent, or anti-Washington." Instead, voters embraced the Republican Party's philosophy favoring smaller government, lower taxes, "and more individual freedom and personal responsibility, instead of more government power and government responsibility."[3] Regardless of the interpretations being made, there was no question there would be change and, even more likely, confrontation, as Gingrich's declaration threatened. The midterm election was a seismic event that politicians and pundits had not anticipated. Republicans had not controlled the House of Representatives for forty years. No sitting president had suffered such a loss since 1946, when President Harry Truman's Democrats lost fifty-five seats.[4]

While the media made Gingrich the polestar of the "Republican Revolution," Robert Dole became the majority leader in the upper chamber for the second time, when the Republicans captured eight seats, including those of two incumbents. The Republicans' Senate margin increased further after the election, when Democratic senators Richard Shelby of Alabama and Ben Nighthorse Campbell of Colorado switched party affiliation, giving the Republicans a slim four-vote majority. Dole, while taking a more conservative stance over the years in alignment with his party's evolution, also had to mind his own party caucus as it contained several former House members who were Gingrich allies and favored a similar ideological purity. These new members worked together to oust Alan Simpson, a Dole loyalist, as majority whip. They replaced him with Trent Lott of Mississippi, a former congressman who had just completed his first term in the Senate and was one of Gingrich's supporters. Lott believed the midterm elections had established a mandate for change. The Senate needed to fulfill that obligation, and he intended to be an "agent of change."[5] However, Dole recognized that to succeed politically, he needed to maintain good relations with the dozen or so "moderate" or "coalitionist" Republicans in the Senate, who were more prone to fashion bipartisan alliances on issues rather than fighting ideological battles.[6]

Many of the Senate Democrats, still stunned from the electoral bludgeoning, chose Tom Daschle of South Dakota as minority leader by one vote over Connecticut's Christopher Dodd. Daschle had served only a single term as senator and had not held a leadership post before. His name recognition was so obscure that the *New York Times* had to spell his last name phonetically so people would know how to pronounce it. Daschle saw being an unknown as his major qualification for the post because the Democrats needed to "project a new image." However, many veteran senators saw his inexperience as problematic since the role of minority leader demanded "greater skills at combat with the opposing party," which Dodd was believed to have. Nonetheless, Daschle received the benefit of the doubt as a former Mitchell associate, and perhaps an understanding among caucus members that they needed to rebuild the party's strength in the Midwest and West.[7] Moreover, the political and ideological realignment, with its roots in "cultural conservatism," that had been occurring in the South was readily apparent: the majority of southern senators and representatives in both houses were Republicans for the first time since Reconstruction. The party's largest senatorial gains were in the South.[8] "The termites have eaten away at the Democratic Party for quite a while," Nunn remarked. This was especially true in the South, where liberal northern nominees in three presidential elections had failed to win a single state in the region, and the national party had become a liability beginning in the early 1970s. Accordingly, Nunn emphasized the party had to "rebuild, with enduring values and principles, but be willing to take a fresh look at the whole scope of the federal role and of the programmatic and bureaucratic approach."[9] As he had asserted a decade earlier when forming the Democratic Leadership Council (DLC), the Democrats could not afford to be "wedded to the programs of the past" or New Deal thinking; the party needed new ideas.[10]

However, reexamining domestic policy in an era of "tribal politics" would not be sufficient given that foreign policy, in all its dimensions, had taken on a partisan cast also. As one trenchant analyst noted, "deep and bitter political differences over presidential policies on foreign policy" were not new. Senator Arthur Vandenberg's 1947 declaration that "politics stops at the water's edge" was more aphorism than fact.[11]

Nonagenarian Strom Thurmond, who had returned to the Armed Services Committee the previous year, used his seniority to ascend to the chairmanship, but not without concern on the part of some Republican colleagues, who questioned Thurmond's stamina and mental acuity.[12] There was no question that Thurmond's age was affecting his abilities. The relationship between Thurmond and Nunn, however, was positive and strong, so much so that Nunn felt Thurmond was relying on him as his right arm in running the committee. It put Nunn in an awkward position, but he did not want to act as de facto chairman without the power.[13]

The Republicans' agenda on the committee was quickly evident at the first hearing: attack the Clinton administration's "stewardship of military readiness" by questioning whether defense budget reductions were endangering combat capability. The frenzy among conservative and moderate Republicans to argue that preparedness was in peril was obvious when it called marine colonels and navy commanders to the Hill to testify that peacekeeping and humanitarian operations were eroding the military's ability to conduct its principal mission, to fight and win wars. In response to the statements from these officers, an unnamed Pentagon official called their testimony "death by a thousand anecdotes" rather than a systematic analysis of deficiencies. Yet, the hearing placed the administration on the defensive. Edwin Dorn, the under secretary of defense for personnel and readiness, John Hamre, Defense Department comptroller, and Admiral William Owens, vice chairman of the Joint Chiefs of Staff, testified that readiness was the first priority and produced statistics to prove their claim. In the midst of the "heated exchanges" between the Republicans and Pentagon leaders, Nunn calmly asked probing questions about how to measure readiness in the current environment. His questions went largely unanswered in this scene of political theater, but Hamre agreed to the need for a supplemental appropriation to forestall any potential loss in readiness.[14]

By June, the focus shifted from resources to Clinton's policy on Bosnia, an issue on which the president had zigzagged for two years, earning him the moniker "William the Waffler."[15] The United Nations had been engaged in an attempt to end the war and make peace among the warring ethnic groups since early 1992, but its peacekeeping mission (UN Protection Force/UN-PROFOR) was a failure, and many American foreign policy elites blamed the administration for a lack of leadership. Brent Scowcroft, the former national security advisor, mocked Clinton's stance as "peripatetic foreign policy at prey to the whims of the latest balance of forces."[16]

Now, NATO allies, led by Great Britain and France, which had contributed troops to the UN mission, were preparing to deploy a force to protect the withdrawal of approximately 23,000 UN peacekeepers from Bosnia, to which the Clinton administration made a commitment to provide equipment and logistical support. More worrisome to lawmakers was a statement that the administration would possibly deploy US units to assist in the withdrawal. These mixed signals only created more problems for the White House, as Dole, who was positioning himself for a potential run for president in 1996, vowed to introduce a resolution authorizing the president to send ground troops into Bosnia to help with the withdrawal, provided the administration agreed to lift the UN arms embargo.[17]

In a hearing before the Senate Armed Services Committee, members from both parties expressed their concerns and skepticism to administration witnesses, Secretary of Defense William Perry and Joint Chiefs of Staff chairman John Shalikashvili. The committee's common view was that the UN had failed in its mission to deliver humanitarian aid and protect civilians. Some senators called for the UN mission to be scrapped as a step toward lifting the UN arms embargo against the Bosnian government. Democrats expressed frustration when Perry and Shalikashvili struggled to clarify the conditions under which US troops would extract UN peacekeepers from Bosnia. It took Nunn's persistent questioning to elicit from them that the United States might help rescue the beleaguered peacekeepers and NATO allies with a military operation should an emergency occur.[18] Nunn remarked that with NATO allies involved, the United States had an obligation to them as a member of the alliance: "There's a lot more at stake here beyond the tragedy in Bosnia." He was worried that the conflict would spread and if it did, "the United States would, I think, have much more substantial interest involved than purely humanitarian."[19]

Two weeks later, Nunn stated that he favored "one more round of diplomacy to ascertain if there is any possibility for a negotiated peace," but tied to a deadline. If progress had not been made by that date, then UN troops should be withdrawn. He added that US forces should participate in a NATO-led operation to assist in this withdrawal and if needed, rescue allied forces in an emergency. As to the arms embargo, he backed it being lifted once the peacekeepers had been pulled out.[20]

Nunn's remarks about Bosnia signaled his concern about the future of NATO. He did not want to see the alliance he believed was the most "successful in history" devalued in the post–Cold War era, especially when the expectations the United States had regarding its future seemed unsettled. He was mainly worried about the administration's intent to enlarge NATO membership by extending the US security umbrella to former Warsaw Pact states such as Poland, Hungary, and the Czech Republic, a commitment made in late 1993. If these countries were to join the alliance, the United States and the other members would be obligated to come to their defense. However, such a decision would require the Senate, by a two-thirds majority, to approve a revision to the 1949 North Atlantic Treaty. Now, two days after the floor speech, Nunn publicly spoke out against the administration's plans, indicating he was willing to fight a political battle over the issue.[21]

Addressing the Supreme Allied Commander, Atlantic (SACLANT) Seminar in Norfolk, Virginia, on June 22, 1995, Nunn addressed the future of NATO and Russia. After enumerating changes in the European security environment over the past four years, he pointed out that ironically, there was actually less risk but greater instability in the world. He did not dismiss the possibility of a resurgent Russia capable of threatening Western Europe, but the reason for enlarging NATO was not clear. The alliance had announced when and how, but it missed the most important question—why now? The reasons offered depended on the audience, but more importantly, they were contrary to the fundamental reason the alliance existed: "the military power and political intimidation of the Soviet Union." Russia did not pose an immediate threat. In fact, based on his discussions with Russian government officials and Russia specialists, he was convinced that "rapid NATO enlargement" would be "widely misunderstood in Russia" and would have "serious negative impact on political and economic reform in that country."[22]

There were several reasons for this damaging effect. Russian nationalism was mounting, and the reformers were on the defense against a Russian political and military establishment that was demoralized and bitter. For the average Russian, the economic situation was dire and the future unclear. Russian nationalists and demagogues were taking advantage of these feelings of demise and insecurity by claiming NATO enlargement would weaken Russia further and threaten its security. Nunn declared NATO enlargement as envisioned by the administration would only intensify the sense of isolation that democratic and economic reformers already confronted. Moreover, if demagogues and political extremists attained control of the government, it would lead to regional instability, threatening the Baltic countries and Ukraine. "This would set in motion a dangerous action-reaction cycle" at a "volatile and unpredictable moment of Russian history" and declining NATO defense budgets. Nor should anyone forget Russia had an arsenal of nuclear weapons. "This is the stuff that self-fulfilling prophecies, and historic tragedies, are made of," he asserted.[23]

Nunn acknowledged it was easier to criticize than to offer constructive recommendations. He suggested a two-track approach. First, countries that aspired to NATO membership had to develop politically and economically to become eligible first for membership in the European Union in preparation for joining NATO. The second track would be based on Russian behavior. It required Russia to respect the sovereignty of neighboring countries, maintain its commitment to arms control treaties and other obligations, and continue in the direction of democracy and economic reform. This approach required NATO to be vigilant and to react if Russia acted aggressively against its neighbors, violated arms control and other legal obligations that endangered European security, or saw the emergence of a nondemocratic government that suppressed political freedoms. If these developments occurred, NATO should respond, to include expansion eastward based on a genuine threat. "We should not, however, be helping to create the very threat we are trying to guard against."[24]

Administration officials viewed Nunn's speech as a "significant political setback" because of his influence in the Senate, but his speech also targeted another Washington audience. House Republicans favored NATO enlargement, making it part of the Contract with America, followed by the passage of a resolution in February without debate, thereby neglecting the vital issue of how expansion enhanced US interests or discussing how enlargement increased US security commitments. Paradoxically, the House had cut funding to upgrade NATO equipment and facilities as a cost-saving measure. Additionally, Senate Republicans supported enlargement to guard against a resurgent, nationalist Russia they believed harbored new imperial designs. Senator Jesse Helms, chairman of the Foreign Relations Committee, and Mitch McConnell of Kentucky viewed enlargement as the antidote for Clinton's Russia policy, which they characterized as imprudent, one that "bordered on appeasement."[25]

As congressional debate over enlargement got under way in July, Nunn emphasized that "as long as there is no price tag attached to them, resolutions about NATO" would pass easily. He pointed out that they were shortsighted and unrealistic, but few in Congress wanted to take on the well-organized lobbying of groups representing ethnic American voters, particularly Polish Americans. Nunn's concerns began to be recognized, however, as the date for admitting new members grew closer, especially in the Senate, where amending the treaty needed a two-thirds majority. More members recognized that enlargement meant the United States was willing to assume security guarantees for these new members and immense financial obligations, billions of dollars over a ten-year period according to one study, at a time when the US economy was ailing. Additionally, the sixteen current members of the alliance had to agree unanimously to expansion, and that outcome was not clear despite their agreement to study the issue.[26]

US military leaders were adamant that the alliance's capacity not be diluted by adding members that did not contribute to the common defense or could not be integrated effectively with allied forces. Nunn used their alarm to emphasize that the alliance could not become simply a "political and psychological alliance." Otherwise, it would be a "repeat of what happened before World War II, when commitments were made that were not backed up by military capabilities and intentions."[27] His stand encouraged others to speak out. Paul Nitze, the distinguished former presidential advisor and government official, and Jack F. Matlock, a former ambassador to the Soviet Union, along with more than a dozen other noted diplomats, publicly opposed enlargement, agreeing with Nunn that it would aggravate political instability in Europe because the Russians would view it as the West's attempt to "isolate" and "encircle" their country.[28]

For Nunn, the long-term, vital US security interest was a stable Russia that was behaving in a manner consistent with the points he expressed in his Norfolk speech. While the House had sliced $171 million from the administration's budget request of $371 million for the Nunn-Lugar Cooperative Threat Reduction (CTR) program, contending that it was diverting Pentagon funds to a nondefense purpose, Nunn's advocacy lessened the blow. (Begun in fiscal year 1992 through enactment of the Soviet Nuclear Threat Reduction Act of 1991, the Nunn-Lugar amendment to the Conventional Forces in Europe Treaty Implementation Act, the program was renamed the Cooperative Threat Reduction program by the DOD in 1993.) The Senate defense authorization bill cut only $6 million. In the end, after the House and Senate conferees completed their work, the authorization bill cut $71 million from the request. Nunn and Lugar were relieved. Nunn offered that "the danger of proliferation of these destructive capabilities, along with the danger of their unauthorized or accidental use, pose the No. 1 national security challenge facing the United States over the next 10 years and beyond." The threat had not diminished but "remains ominous"; other states such as Iran and North Korea, or terrorist groups, also had nuclear ambitions. Nunn and Lugar realized that in a deficit-conscious Congress, funding for the program would continue to be in jeopardy as long as some viewed the program as foreign aid and not national security.[29]

Despite the administration's embrace of the CTR program and its quest for NATO enlargement, it realized it had to act slowly since there was a relationship between the two issues. The administration's principal policy objective was defining post–Cold War Europe consistent with US interests, particularly the economic and political reforms it had enunciated in its 1994 document, *A National Security Strategy of Engagement and Enlargement*, with respect to Russia. It did not want to jeopardize its principal policy objective by pushing the allies too hard on enlargement. Moreover, the situation in Bosnia diminished the likelihood that the allies would support adding new members to NATO when war was raging nearby.[30] As one analyst noted, the "fratricidal war" in Bosnia was inconsistent with the administration's "vision of a Europe democratic, secure and undivided."[31]

Besides, Dole would not let the war in Bosnia fade. In mid-July he informed the press that he intended to begin debate on a measure to end US participation in the UN arms embargo against the Bosnian government. The White House spokesman expressed the administration's displeasure with the proposed bill as it would induce European allies to quit the peacekeeping mission. Administration officials revealed they were consulting with Nunn to find ways to counter unacceptable aspects of the bill that Dole and Connecticut senator Joseph Lieberman had cosponsored. Lieberman represented many Democrats in the Senate who wanted a change in the US Bosnia policy. A similar sentiment held sway among a large number of House Democrats.[32]

A few days later, Nunn acknowledged in a floor speech that an overwhelming majority of senators supported lifting the embargo. He likewise expressed concern that the bill was incomplete. First, it did not address the administration's commitment of 25,000 US troops to be deployed to support the withdrawal of the peacekeepers from Bosnia. Second, NATO planning for the withdrawal made "no provision for the withdrawal of refugees," and the Senate "must also consider what will happen to the civilian population of Bosnia" if the UN force withdrew. This second point only emphasized the dismal choices the United States confronted concerning the war. Nunn told his colleagues that they "must understand the full consequences of [their] legislation."[33]

Nunn's pronouncement had little effect on delaying debate on the binding resolution. Clinton, worried about NATO's credibility, was more persuasive, convincing Dole to hold off debate for a few days so the president could speak with British and French officials. The consultation made no difference, and on July 25, the Senate began an emotional debate on the measure, with administration officials scampering to Capitol Hill to argue against the resolution. On the Senate floor, Dole criticized the administration's feckless leadership and an incompetent UN. Others argued that the Bosnians had unfairly suffered under the embargo and the United States had a moral obligation to ensure they were adequately armed to defend themselves from their adversary, the Serbs, who had recently overrun the UN "safe area" of Srebrenica.[34]

Nunn took another tack by offering an amendment that would require the administration to "insist" on a United Nations Security Council vote to lift the embargo before the United States acted unilaterally to end its involvement. Nunn stated his rationale: "The embargo should be lifted the way it was imposed, multilaterally, and in the final analysis unilaterally if absolutely necessary." His colleagues agreed. The proposal passed easily, 75 to 23. Republican senator William Cohen proposed a second amendment that would take the matter to the UN General Assembly if any of the other four permanent members of the Security Council vetoed it. It was approved, 57 to 41. The *New York Times* considered these amendments to be "crucial." Nunn's amendment forced the administration to act by introducing a resolution to the Security Council. And Cohen had given the administration a work-around to maintain "international cover" by using an "obscure American-inspired" maneuver, devised in 1950 at the onset of the Korean War, for the General Assembly to deal with a violation of international peace.[35] During the floor debate, Nunn made it clear that he was voting for the Dole-Lieberman bill, but might not vote to override a presidential veto. The administration should not assume Congress would defer to the president as it traditionally did on foreign policy issues. His vote was based on two factors. "It depends," he remarked, "on what happens on the ground. It depends on whether the United Nations and NATO and the United States get an overall policy—that is what I'm going to base my vote on."[36]

For his part, Clinton informed Dole that if his measure passed, he would veto it. It did pass, overwhelmingly, by a bipartisan vote in favor, 69 to 29, just enough to override a veto. Nunn, as promised, voted with the majority, as did nineteen other Democrats. Six days later, on August 1, the House agreed to the Senate's measure by a vote of 298 to 128 and sent it to Clinton for signature or veto. The vote margins clearly indicated Congress could override a veto. As a former National Security Council staff member later observed, the lopsided bipartisan votes were "one more indication that administration policy had reached a dead end and that a fundamental reevaluation of both the aim and the means of the policy was necessary." The votes were also consistent with a recent poll—61 percent of those polled agreed that the embargo should be lifted. Clinton vetoed the resolution. In response, congressional leaders decided to take their four-week recess and did not attempt to override him.[37]

With the Republicans' attempt to drive US Bosnia policy unproductive, Dole and Senate Republican leaders now aimed at defense policy by offering a program that the administration opposed: construction of an anti–ballistic missile defense system. The defense authorization bill for fiscal year

1996, approved by the Armed Services Committee, allocated $300 million for that purpose. It was a direct response, Republicans claimed, to concerns that more countries would have nuclear weapons, and, therefore, a robust missile defense system was needed. Lott went so far as to claim unrealistically about the project, "The "MAD [mutual assured destruction] era is over, thank God." The House had already authorized the project in its version of the authorization bill.[38]

Democratic senators, led by Nunn and Carl Levin of Michigan, opposed the project. These critics wanted to eliminate provisions in the bill that they argued "violated the [ABM] treaty by calling for multiple sites and complained that the measure sought improperly to unilaterally reinterpret its provisions to ban defenses against short-range missiles." Levin contended, "This is a trashing of the ABM Treaty. . . . It is a provocative move to commit ourselves now to deploy an illegal missile defense system." Their determination to strike the provisions was unsuccessful. Yet, not all Senate Republicans agreed with the project. Cohen joined with Nunn to point out that the Senate was not, through its vote, seeking to renegotiate the treaty but to abrogate it, regardless of the bill's language. They cosponsored a resolution that required the president to amend the treaty to allow missile defense systems at multiple sites and, if that failed, consult with the Senate about withdrawing from the pact.[39]

As the debate continued, the administration's position became clear. Clinton would veto the bill. He was not opposed to missile defense; his administration had included funding for pursuing technologies for ground-based systems in the authorization bill, but Secretary of State Warren Christopher told reporters that Cohen and Nunn were correct: the bill would put the United States on "a path to abrogate the ABM Treaty." Perry added that the legislation imperiled implementation of the Strategic Arms Reduction Treaties (START I and II), which were aimed at reducing the US and former Soviet nuclear arsenals. Russia had stated emphatically that its nuclear arms reductions were contingent on adherence to the ABM Treaty.[40]

The threats of a veto and a Democratic filibuster, and with so much at stake regarding arms control, as well as the opposition of Nunn, Levin, and Cohen, meant Senate leaders in both parties sought a compromise. For a week, Warner met with the other three, and when they finished, their compromise language generally followed the proposal Nunn and Cohen had offered. The revised language authorized the Defense Department to begin planning a nationwide missile defense system, but it would not build the network until military requirements, treaty implications, and costs were assessed. The president would also have the authority to negotiate changes in the treaty but would have to obtain congressional approval for any agreement that reduced US defense capabilities. The compromise retained language from the Republicans' original bill that such a system must be operationally capable by 2003, and the funding for the project, $490 million, stayed the same. With the Senate leaders of both parties approving the deal and the White House finding it acceptable, Dole stated that debate on the authorization bill would be delayed until after the August recess.[41]

The center still held with respect to national defense. The Senate approved the bipartisan ABM Treaty compromise when it returned in September by a vote of 85 to 13. It was a win-win outcome. The Republicans achieved their goal of revitalizing ballistic missile defense by renegotiating the ABM Treaty to build a multisite system to protect against incoming missiles, especially in view of rogue states such as North Korea developing ballistic missiles. Senate Democrats were assured the United States would continue to reduce nuclear arsenals and prevent jeopardizing other arms control measures by complying with the treaty until those negotiations failed. Nunn stated that Perry found the compromise language "a dramatic improvement," but the administration still had problems with the bill, and Daschle warned that it was "not anywhere near enactment." However, the Senate approved the full authorization bill, 65 to 34. The appropriations bill had already passed, 62 to 35. Noticeably, both bills fell short of the two-thirds needed to override a veto.[42]

With the bill passed and conference under way, speculation about Nunn's future wormed its way into conversations in Middle Georgia as the summer dragged on and rumors flourished. Six Senate Democrats had already announced they were not seeking reelection. One resident in Nunn's hometown of Perry believed the senator had made a decision but was not ready to reveal it. "Yes, Lord, we're going to miss him," one woman sighed, certain that he was going to retire. Not everyone shared her heartache. A customer at the City Barber Shop, who wished to remain nameless, thought Nunn had been "up there long enough." Georgia state party leaders remained anxious. They knew polls showed him to be immensely popular, with an approval rating of more than 70 percent among Georgia's electorate. He was certainly more popular than Clinton, who was heading up the Democratic ticket. Georgia Republican Party leaders had no candidate to oppose Nunn at the moment. They believed if he retired, then their party would win the seat; meanwhile,

Georgia's congressional delegation, including the nine Republicans, worried his retirement would reduce the state's influence in Washington.[43]

Both Democrats and Republicans in Washington, and especially in the Senate, encouraged him to run for a fifth term. Republican colleagues such as Cohen deemed him a consensus builder, willing to reach across party lines to advance America's national interest. Armed Services Committee members worried that his departure would lessen the panel's status. Thurmond told reporters that he had "urged [Nunn] to stay on." Military leaders worried that they were losing a valuable supporter who understood their institution and culture, as well as the "use of military power as an instrument of foreign policy." Administration officials recognized they would lose a powerful voice, independent but significant: "If Nunn is a no-go, you look around up there and ask, 'Where are the adults?'" His colleagues recognized what twenty-three years of service represented in a single member. One journalist summed up this outpouring of respect by specifying that it was Nunn's approach to issues that made him the legislative glue—"substantive, steeped in expertise, and senatorial prerogatives—and a baronial independence that allows him to range across the political center, serving as a leader in the realm between conservative Republicans and liberal Democrats." To all these pleadings, concerns and assessments of his importance, the only answer the fifty-seven-year-old lawmaker would give publicly was that he would announce his decision soon. Clinton made one last plea for him to seek reelection, but warned Nunn to postpone his announcement for a week, because the verdict of the O. J. Simpson murder trial would be the top story and Nunn deserved more attention, given his service to the nation.[44]

On October 9, Nunn disclosed his plans at a news conference in the State Capitol in Atlanta, where he had begun his political career, before an audience of more than one hundred former colleagues in the state legislature and Congress, elected officials and longtime supporters and friends, as well as potential successors. The event was carried live on CNN with national press present. "After a lot of thought and prayer," he would retire in 1996, after twenty-four "rewarding and fulfilling" years in the Senate. "I know in my heart," he said, "that it is time to follow a new course." He outlined the challenges the country confronted, from international security and the environment to health care and his concern about citizens that were "being left behind as our economy moves from the industrial age to the age of information and knowledge because they lack appropriate education and training." He believed these challenges were "made more difficult because our citizens are increasingly concluding that our political system responds primarily to money and special interests." He then criticized the costs of campaigning, the demands of fundraising, and the growing political extremism in both parties, which imperiled the "common good." A day before, in an interview with the *New York Times*, Nunn had said "he still enjoyed his work in the Senate, but had other things he might want to do." He stated now that he remained optimistic about the future and that he planned to remain involved, but as a "private citizen . . . engaged in the challenges that face our communities and our nation." He maintained that optimistic tone and reiterated his dedication to continued service in his speech. He ended by thanking his family, his friends, staff, colleagues in Congress and Georgia government, Georgia Democrats, and voters for their help and support over the years. The *Atlanta Journal-Constitution* summed up the moment and his service: his decision was "no surprise, but it still is momentous enough to shake the political earth of this state."[45]

However, by the end of the week, Nunn told a reporter that "these next 2 1/2 months [of the current congressional session] are going to seem like a six-year term." A government shutdown loomed as the president and the Republican Congress reached an impasse over the federal budget. Nunn emphasized that this issue would have severe consequences beyond the funding of US agencies. It would erode "confidence in a stable and sensible American government . . . do grave damage to interest rates, to American credibility."[46] Additionally, negotiations over a conference report for the defense authorization bill went on for three months, and when it finally cleared Congress, Clinton vetoed it because of infringements on his constitutional prerogatives as commander in chief regarding operational and tactical control of US forces, and the required deployment of a national missile defense system by 2003, which House Republicans demanded. Nunn, a member of the conference committee, opposed that language, as it was contrary to the compromise he had helped forge in the Senate. The House, however, failed to override the veto, another embarrassing moment for the Republican majorities. They now had to make further concessions in a revised conference report, which Clinton signed into law in February 1996.[47]

Consequential foreign policy issues lingered as well. In late November, Richard Holbrooke, the assistant secretary of state for European and Canadian affairs, had brokered a peace agreement among the Bosnian Muslim, Croatian, and Serbian factions fighting in Bosnia. In response, Clinton informed the nation that he would commit 20,000 US troops, approximately one-third of a NATO-led force, to implement the agreement. The announcement led to substantial congressional opposition, particularly among House Republicans. Few members were persuaded that the United States had a vital national interest in the war worth American lives. Majority Leader Dick Armey said that convincing the House to support the president "would be like pulling teeth through the back of your head." While the administration sought congressional support for the deployment, Clinton stated he would send the forces to the Balkans even if both chambers opposed it.[48]

In the Senate, Dole supported the proposed mission, but several Republican senators were wary of the venture. Thurmond held a committee hearing on November 28. Like many others, he remained unconvinced that "vital US security interests" were "threatened or at stake," but accepted that the United States had an interest in a stable Europe and the viability of NATO. US leadership in NATO was crucial, and therefore he believed the United States should "remain engaged in and show leadership in NATO." Nunn, who cochaired the Senate Democrats' Working Group on Bosnia, was also vocal, expressing concerns about the risks facing US military personnel and their NATO comrades. Yet, he did not discount support, despite a lack of consensus among Democrats, only that there were three pertinent issues that needed to be addressed. He wanted the administration to provide information on the conditions for ending US military involvement and how mission success would be defined, and an assurance that when the implementation force left the region, the Bosnian government would have a favorable balance of forces.[49]

Meanwhile, Dole was having trouble with a dozen Republican senators. Ultimately, he was able to accommodate the naysayers by allowing votes on carefully worded resolutions that indicated opposition to the president's "decision to deploy" US forces, but not the "deployment itself." Secondarily, working with John McCain, Dole offered a resolution that required the United States to lead an effort to train and equip Bosnian fighters so they would achieve military parity with the Serbs by the time the NATO force (known as the Implementation Force) withdrew in December 1996 when its one-year mandate ended. Daschle asked Nunn and several other Democrats to review the draft Dole-McCain resolution. Nunn promised Daschle that he and his colleagues "would have certain constructive suggestions."[50] On December 12, Nunn joined senators from both parties at a White House meeting. Clinton was making a final attempt to "win over those senators who are thought to be opposed to the Bosnia deployment." Clinton invited

Nunn, Levin, and McCain so that the meeting would not be perceived as "an Administration against the naysayers meeting."[51]

On the next night, December 13, at 10:17 p.m., with Vice President Al Gore presiding in case he needed to break a tie, the Senate voted on the Dole-McCain resolution. By the time of the vote, Clinton had already departed for Paris to sign the Dayton peace agreement. The resolution supported the deployment of US troops, but with the condition that the United States would lead a train-and-equip mission so that the Bosnian Muslims would have military capability comparable to their former adversaries. The vote was 69 to 30 in favor. Nunn and other Democrats made the difference: forty-five of them helped Dole obtain the sizable majority. At the same time, the House approved a similar resolution. During the debate, Nunn declared that the Dole-McCain resolution sent a clear message that the Senate might not agree with Clinton's decision-making process for sending troops, but "the commitment of forces is important to prevent the spread of conflict."[52] With those words he captured the principles and the spirit of the Dayton accords, "a settlement to bring an end to the tragic conflict in the region" and "to promote an enduring peace and stability."[53]

CHAPTER 17

AN HONORABLE CAREER

ormer president Jimmy Carter had another job in mind for Nunn after he left the Senate: run for governor. Nunn told reporters he was not interested, but he would not dismiss the idea entirely. It would be three years before the incumbent's second and final term expired.[1] There were other matters that needed his immediate attention, more than the governorship—the dangers posed by the proliferation of weapons of mass destruction (WMD) in a world of changing US-Russian relations.

In early March 1996, an associate director in the General Accounting Office (GAO) testified before the Senate Government Affairs Committee's Permanent Subcommittee on Investigations about a study the agency conducted of nuclear security throughout Russia that the subcommittee had requested. The official informed Nunn, the ranking member, and the other senators present that GAO investigators had identified significant security lapses at civilian and military nuclear storage sites throughout Russia. In one instance, the US personnel wandered onto a site without any identification and discovered a single guard on duty. The overall assessment was that nuclear material was an easy target for terrorists because of lax security. More chilling was the conclusion that the former Soviet republics could not account for a substantial portion of hundreds of tons of weapons-grade uranium and plutonium in their stockpiles, often because of inadequate record keeping. This deficiency, the report stated, represented a "primary national security threat for the United States."[2]

The bad news did not end there. The next day, John Deutch, director of central intelligence, informed Nunn and subcommittee members that the United States was "very poorly" equipped to defend its infrastructure against terrorists with nuclear, chemical, or biological weapons. He claimed there were no indications that terrorists had obtained nuclear material or that "loose nukes" were being sold on the black market. Most of these reports were "bogus." There had been a few cases in which small quantities of weapons-usable material had been transferred to Western Europe, but those amounts were too little for building a nuclear device. Nonetheless, his agency remained concerned about the spread of nuclear material, especially to Iraq, Iran, and to a lesser degree, North Korea and Libya. He did not ease anxieties by remarking that the most significant terrorist threat at the moment was a chemical attack because such a weapon was inexpensive and easy to produce.[3]

These reports only intensified interest among Republicans in constructing a national anti–ballistic missile defense system. On March 21, Kansas senator Robert Dole and Louisiana representative Bob Livingston, chairman of the Appropriations Committee, introduced identical bills, the Defend America Act of 1996, in their respective bodies, requiring the employment of a national defense system by 2003. Dole blamed the administration for vetoing a similar provision in the fiscal year 1996 defense authorization bill, decrying this action as not only denying Americans the protection they needed from such an attack, but also demonstrating a lack of political will and leadership on the part of the White House.[4] In an election year, the Republicans were confident that the issue would show Clinton to be weak on national security and deficient in fulfilling his responsibilities to protect American citizens. They planned to goad Clinton into another veto to emphasize this contention, which would help Republicans win votes in November.[5]

More worrisome reports surfaced in April 1996 that the Russians were constructing a huge underground military complex in the southern Ural Mountain region, employing thousands of workers and consisting of a highway and railroad line as well as residences for the workers. This information, gleaned from US intelligence satellites, Russian parliamentarians, and Russian press reports, did not give any clear indication to US intelligence as to its purpose. It could be a nuclear command post or secret weapons plant or storage location. Regardless, the site was particularly troubling for the administration. It had to certify to Congress that the Russians were not undertaking new military projects except those that met "legitimate defense requirements." Otherwise, the administration could not release Nunn-Lugar funds to the Russians to dismantle its nuclear arsenal. The Russian government refused to provide details, which only compounded unease. However, the administration had already renewed its certification before this information became known in the United States.[6]

Dole, Gingrich, and Republicans inside and outside Congress, along with allies on talk radio and editorial boards, kept attention focused on missile defense, increasingly assured such tactics would move the WMD "threat to the political foreground," in the words of one House Republican. Yet, despite the attention and the House adding funding for the program, the legislation died. Clinton, Secretary of Defense William Perry, and the Joint Chiefs of Staff believed the concept to be misguided and a costly waste. John Shalikashvili, the chairman of the Joint Chiefs of Staff, wrote Nunn in May that he feared the bill would ruin ongoing arms reduction efforts, possibly prompting the Russians to withdraw from the ABM Treaty or to walk away from the Strategic Arms Reduction Treaty (START) negotiations. Such a step would only increase the costs and risks the United States would confront in countering Russian capabilities.[7]

Nunn, along with Democrats from across the party and in both chambers, worked with the administration to nullify the Republicans' argument, focusing again on nonproliferation as the essential component of reducing the probability of an attack on the United States. The administration, Nunn, and his colleagues constructed a policy approach along those lines combining treaties, export controls and economic sanctions as the tools. The Cooperative Threat Reduction (CTR) program was central to the administration's approach. The unity of Democrats in the Senate, the support of military leaders, and a lack of public enthusiasm for the missile defense idea helped doom the Republican legislation. By the end of the summer, Senate proponents of the bill had been routed, despite a favorable vote on the Republicans' House version. Senate Republican John Kyl of Arizona, one of the cosponsors, admitted to having second thoughts: "I've never thought this was a big political winner. It's too complicated, the threat is not easy enough to perceive."[8]

The future of Russia remained a principal concern and, once again, a potential threat. In June, Russians voted in the first round of their presidential election. That event brought additional apprehension among Russian watchers in the United States, especially their worries about the future of

US-Russian relations. Republicans and Democrats remained concerned on this point with the race between Boris Yeltsin, who was running for a second term, and who the administration saw as the candidate most likely to continue economic reforms, and the Communist Party candidate Gennadi A. Zyuganov, who appealed to Russian nationalism, claiming he would return the country to great power status and more state control of the economy. Dole recalled to his colleagues the words President Richard M. Nixon had spoken to him after the Soviet Union disintegrated: "The Soviets have lost the Cold War, but the United States has not yet won it." While leaders in both US political parties favored a "partnership" with the Russians and continued aid, their differences were, as one observer pointed out, matters of "emphasis and degree." Nonetheless, Dole stated that the administration was not paying sufficient attention to US "interests and values." He urged a rapid enlargement of NATO to counter "troubling Russian behavior toward other independent states of the former Soviet Union." For their part, Nunn and Lugar continued to shore up support for funding the CTR program. It irked them that the program was still being perceived as foreign aid. Dole agreed that CTR was a vital component of the key foreign policy issues the United States faced—ensuring nuclear security and disarmament, along with European security and the independence of the states once part of the USSR.[9] Dole's remarks, however, were also a subtle reminder of how US domestic politics and Republican disfavor of foreign aid would likely shape cooperation between the two countries in the near term.

The foreign policy issues that Dole enumerated and the bombing of a US military housing facility (Khobar Towers) in Dhahran, Saudi Arabia, by Islamic terrorists, on June 25, 1996, which killed nineteen American service members and a Saudi citizen and injured hundreds of others, prompted new congressional concerns about terrorist attacks in the United States and the potential use of WMD. Two days later, on June 27, Nunn, Lugar, and Pete Domenici, the Arizona Republican who chaired the Budget Committee, offered an amendment to the defense authorization act aimed at preventing a terrorist attack in the United States using WMD. The amendment included $235 million to counter terrorism, with $61 million dedicated to research on devices to detect and prevent the spread of WMD. The US Customs Service received funds to prevent smuggled weapons and materials from entering the United States and to help the former Soviet states bolster their border control agencies. Additionally, the Departments of Defense and Energy were authorized to respond to a domestic terrorism event where nuclear, biological, or chemical weapons were used. The two departments could spend as much as $80 million to assist local police, fire, and emergency service personnel to prepare for a WMD attack. The amendment added $94 million to expand the scope of the CTR program to include disposal of spent nuclear fuel from Russian warships and reconstruction of some nuclear power plants so they could not produce radioactive material for use in weapons. The Senate passed the measure by a vote of 96 to 0. The amendment, titled the Defense against Weapons of Mass Destruction Act of 1996, but more commonly known as Nunn-Lugar-Domenici, became law when Clinton signed the defense authorization bill in September and was supported with funding in the fiscal year 1997 budget.[10]

In an interview a month after the Senate adopted the amendment, Nunn addressed the growing terrorist threat. He pointed out that the United States had lived under the Soviet nuclear threat for more than four decades. Americans would now have to become accustomed to the idea of an attack within US borders. He believed that increased human intelligence and technology offered the best antidotes to this new threat, including "broader authority on wiretapping." Nunn pointed out the recently enacted Nunn-Lugar-Domenici legislation was aimed at addressing such a threat. He also emphasized that only the Departments of Defense and Energy had the equipment to deal with a WMD event and that state and local governments needed help. Ultimately, protecting against a terrorist attack required a debate in American society about how much security was wanted and the trade-off in time and money. He believed that improvements could be made while protecting constitutional rights.[11]

Speculation about Nunn's future did not abate either. Rumors appeared in the press that if Clinton won a second term, changes in his cabinet were certain. While Nunn was not a front-runner, he was a strong candidate to replace Warren Christopher as secretary of state, should the incumbent decide to leave because of the job's exhausting duties and persistent criticism of his work. Clinton was not pushing Christopher out, but in the coming months, a decision might hinge on the foreign policy goals the president wanted to achieve in a second term. Nunn "had written with real insight about all the big issues—Russia, China and NATO," wrote *New York Times* columnist Tom Friedman. He commanded "genuine respect in the foreign policy community" and was an innovative and visionary thinker, of which Nunn-Lugar was indicative. Yet, his willingness to challenge the president might be a liability, as his recent dismissal of the administration's NATO enlargement plan demonstrated. Nonetheless, on a list of potential candidates, Nunn was near the top. The odds, however, favored those who were already serving in the administration, such as Anthony Lake, Madeleine Albright, and Richard Holbrooke, or steadfast political allies such as George Mitchell.[12]

For some political analysts, Nunn was making a strong case for the job. By mid-September, with Election Day only eight weeks away, Dole, now the Republican presidential nominee for president, remained convinced that he could win overwhelmingly in the South if the midterm election results remained a reliable indicator. The GOP nominee was spending substantial time campaigning in the region. In Georgia, the Clinton campaign had enlisted Nunn as cochair of the president's reelection committee, which surprised some political analysts given how often Nunn had jousted with Clinton on issues early in the president's first term. Clinton, however, needed strong Democratic backing in southern states other than his home state, Arkansas, and that of Vice President Al Gore, Tennessee. Nunn's endorsement was illustrative of Clinton's "changing fortunes." Polls showed that Clinton was ahead in Georgia, which was attributable to the respect Georgians still had for their lame-duck senator.[13]

Domestic politics again gave way to international security concerns, and Nunn continued to write on the "big issues." He joined with Robert Blackwill, a Harvard faculty member, and Arnold Horelick, a professor at the University of California at Los Angeles, to write a RAND paper, *Stopping the Decline in US-Russian Relations*. The three based their analysis on meetings with Russian officials and analysts in Moscow.[14] They believed that relations between the two countries were on a "downward shift toward mutual alienation." NATO enlargement would only serve as an accelerant, and it was likely to undermine important agreements in nuclear and conventional arms control, which they credited as "the legal anchors securing the post–Cold War peace." They feared that friction in relations would undermine nonproliferation cooperation. Their assessment was that the United States had to initiate improvements in the deteriorating relationship, as Yeltsin's "precarious hold on power" precluded his government from taking such action. Improvements in relations would only be successful if US national interests were protected, but US officials had to be equally mindful of Russian perceptions and fears.[15]

The authors argued NATO enlargement required a "soft landing" that included "credible safeguards for Russia's legitimate security" and a recognition of Russia's critical role in the future of European security. A successful outcome would be measured by Russia's tolerance of NATO enlargement. It also meant delinking NATO enlargement from nuclear arms control, especially START II, if there was any hope of the Duma, the lower house of the Federal Assembly of Russia, agreeing to that treaty. Russian security concerns in that agreement required attention and revision. Moreover, the Conventional Armed Forces in Europe (CFE) treaty needed "adaptation or modernization," as it too was integral to the future European security climate because of Russian concerns about the balance of forces tipping against them. Russia would be further reassured if NATO agreed not to deploy nuclear weapons, permanently station forces, or pre-position equipment in new members' territories. In short, NATO enlargement created the possibility of irreparably damaging relations. The authors concluded that to achieve favorable outcomes, the United States and its allies needed to move quickly to address these concerns.[16] Their viewpoint went unheeded.

Yeltsin, after obtaining the majority of votes in the first round of the election process, triumphed in the runoff, winning reelection to the Russian presidency on July 3 by defeating his Communist Party opponent by nearly 14 percent. The next day, July 4, Clinton offered not only his congratulations but declared it an apparent "decisive victory" and another milepost in Russia's development as a democracy and market economy. The president pledged continued support of economic and political reforms in Russia to "complete Russia's integration into the global community."[17] Both the administration and Congress, principally the Republicans, as well as American nongovernmental organizations, especially ethnic interest groups (Polish American and Hungarian American), viewed the reelection results as a signal to push for NATO enlargement.[18]

In the House, Benjamin Gilman, a New York Republican and chairman of the International Relations Committee, had introduced a bill called the NATO Enlargement Facilitation Act of 1996 in early June, with thirty-four cosponsors from both parties. The intent of the bill was to expedite membership in the alliance of fledgling democracies in Central and Eastern Europe by amending the NATO Participation Act of 1994. Poland, Hungary, and the Czech Republic were specifically designated as nations eligible for transition assistance in gaining membership. On July 23, the House passed Gilman's bill by an overwhelming margin, 353 to 65, with 156 Democrats voting "aye."[19]

Dole had introduced an identical bill in the Senate. Some observers wondered whether the chamber would pass it when Dole had only ten cosponsors, all Republicans. Many outsiders believed Nunn's stance would be critical, especially among Democrats, since his earlier public rejection of the concept. On this issue, Nunn and Lugar differed. Lugar had been an avid supporter of NATO expansion since the idea had first surfaced a few years earlier. Administration officials and military leaders in the Defense Department quietly agreed with Nunn that cooperation on nuclear disarmament and nonproliferation was paramount. Other prominent thinkers supported Nunn, including eminent former diplomat George Kennan and several noted scholars, criticizing the idea as a colossal foreign policy misstep.[20]

Two days after the House passed its version, the Senate began debate on its measure. A few Senate staff members and journalists claimed Nunn had not expected the bill to come to floor for a roll-call vote. Further, he did not offer the vigorous opposition to the bill some had expected. One former Clinton White House official believed his impending retirement was a factor. Others alleged Nunn's staff had worked with Senate Republican staff to modify some of the bill's provisions so it would be acceptable to him. Irrespective of these rumors, Nunn initially voted in favor, and when he did, several Democrats joined him. However, before the roll-call vote ended, Nunn switched his vote to "nay," joining fifteen other dissenters. The final tally was 81 in favor to 16 against. On September 30, 1996, Clinton signed into law the Omnibus Appropriations bill (P.L. 104-208), which contained the compromise version of the NATO Enlargement Facilitation Act (H.R. 3564 and S. 1830). Nunn did not let the matter rest. He and other senators were able to amend the defense authorization bill to require the administration to furnish Congress with a report specifying the costs and strategic implications of enlargement. With this maneuver, Nunn signaled that the Senate's advice and consent on amending the North Atlantic Treaty of 1949 to increase the number of the alliance's member states would not be a foregone conclusion after his retirement.[21]

Nunn's last day in the Senate came on October 3, 1996, just before Congress adjourned for the year. A reporter described the scene as an "historic, moving moment." Nunn spoke of his quarter century in the chamber representing Georgia as "the highest honor." His voice trembled occasionally as he thanked his colleagues and his personal staff, as well as the committee and floor staff, who had made his more than a decade as chairman or ranking Democrat on the Armed Services Committee a success.[22]

Yet, Nunn's final floor speech was not simply a farewell. He meant it to be instructive. He enumerated the challenges facing the United States, internationally and domestically. Characteristically, he began with his assessment of US foreign policy and national security in the post–Cold War environment. He stressed his concerns about the proliferation of WMD, especially as part of the increasing threat of terrorism; the fact that US defense information systems were now more vulnerable to computer attacks, particularly the unclassified but sensitive data stored on these networks; and the need to "calibrate" US relations with China, as an emerging power, and Russia, as an "old superpower."[23]

The first challenge demanded strengthened intelligence and law enforcement capabilities, especially preparedness at all levels of government to deal with an attack on the United States. He called for additional attention to computer security, given the tens of thousands of attacks already being directed against Defense Department systems. The private sector had to assume greater responsibilities as well, including protective enhancements to its networks, particularly power transmission and other infrastructure. Cyberspace, he emphasized, brought new problems and demanded different "countermeasures."[24]

As to US relations with China, this might be the most critical issue of them all. "History," he reminded his listeners, "is littered with the uninformed and ineffective responses of an established power toward a rising power." But, he continued, "History teaches us that established powers must provide consistent and credible signals about their expectations and set forth reasonable terms on which they are willing to incorporate the rising power into the international system." The United States needed China's cooperation on many global issues, but both, over the past several years, had been "emphasizing differences" rather than finding "common interests." In that way lay peril, but China also had to bear its share of the "burden" of being a member of the international order, comply with international regimes and agreements, and not simply reap the benefits from its membership in various international institutions.[25]

He noted his continuing concern about NATO enlargement and the crucial need to balance this policy aim with helping Russia continue its advance toward political and economic reform through democratization and the creation of a market economy. NATO enlargement endangered this progress. The Russians had already misinterpreted expansion as a threat, and the premature push fed "paranoia, nationalism, and demagoguery" in its political ranks. The rise of nationalist and extremist elites could occur, which posed a danger to European security. Russia could easily pressure neighboring states such as the Baltic states and Ukraine. Further, if nationalists and extremists gained office, the threat of nuclear war was again all too possible.

Nunn did not end with his discourse on the strategic environment, but underscored that the United States had problems that needed immediate attention: a need to put its "fiscal house in good order," to maintain a strong and growing economy, and to end the constant budget deficits. He also worried about the social fabric unraveling, the loosening of moral standards, and the welfare of American youth. He believed that the political system was not working for most Americans. Partisan politics was undermining meaningful debate, the search for alternatives, compromise, and, ultimately, the main task of government: to find solutions to the nation's problems. The national interest was more important than party dominance. No one party, he contended, could solve these problems. Nonetheless, he would leave Washington, he concluded, convinced that the prospects for a better society lay in the American people.[26]

When he finished, several of his colleagues, Democrats and Republicans, rose from their desks and paid him tribute. Strom Thurmond summed up the feelings of many when he said of Nunn that the Senate was "indebted . . . for all you've done for defense and for this nation and thank you from the bottom of our hearts." In the view of one congressional reporter, Nunn had gained "a reputation as one of the most respected strategic thinkers on Capitol Hill."[27]

Many in the Senate and in Georgia hoped that Nunn would contribute his gifts to public service and remain engaged in public policy issues. He continued to be mentioned in the press as a possible secretary of defense or state, should Clinton win a second term. Nunn told reporters that he had no immediate plans. But three weeks later, Nunn and Lugar were in Ukraine at the invitation of the Ukrainian government, where they, the US ambassador, and a local official turned stainless steel keys in a launch panel. Their action ignited a demolition charge that destroyed a ballistic missile launcher in a nearby, empty SS-19 missile silo. After peering into the hole the dynamite charge left, and with smoke still rising into the hazy morning air, Nunn remarked that this event was representative of what he and Lugar had been intent on accomplishing. "To have played a role in dismantling weapons of mass destruction," he said, "is one of the great high points of my career in the Senate." Later, as he and the other members of the party drove off, he mused aloud about the horror of potential nuclear war between the United States and the Soviet Union and the aftermath of death and destruction for both countries.[28] It was not only nuclear weapons that worried him.

Indeed, he soon was warning about the possibility of a terrorist attack on US soil using biological or chemical weapons, and the nation's lack of preparedness for such a cataclysm. His schedule for the remainder of the year remained full, campaigning for Clinton in Georgia as well as his potential replacement in the Senate, Max Cleland, who had managed the Veteran's Administration during Carter's presidency. When asked about his plans after Election Day, Nunn's spokesperson Cathy O'Brien remarked, "He [is] too busy being a senator."[29]

The election results turned out to be mixed for Democrats. Clinton won a second term, and Cleland was elected to Nunn's vacant seat by a 1 percent margin, but the Republicans retained control of Congress. The near loss of Nunn's seat to a Republican seemed another signal that the South was becoming a GOP stronghold. Nonetheless, with Christopher and Perry deciding not to stay for the second term, Nunn's name again figured prominently as a potential contender for a national security post in the second term.[30]

Nunn was considered a likely cabinet appointment, but he was one of many potential candidates. In his favor, commentators credited him as having the expertise and experience, but also as being someone who could credibly articulate US foreign policy objectives to multiple audiences, foreign and domestic.[31] Yet, there were easily identifiable policy differences between Nunn and Clinton, especially NATO enlargement. Pundits also offered Nunn's independence, prominent stature, and lack of a close relationship with Clinton as factors in why he might not be selected for a position. By the beginning of December, retiring senator William Cohen and US ambassador to the United Nations Madeleine Albright were considered the front-runners to replace Perry and Christopher.[32]

On December 6, the speculation ended; Clinton announced that Cohen and Albright were his picks for secretaries of defense and state. The reasons for Nunn not being selected soon emerged in the press, that he was "too assertive," "not a "team player." However, some experts believed that by choosing Cohen, Clinton was attempting to win over a Republican-led Congress on defense issues. Other observers were less confident in Cohen leading the Pentagon, believing his expertise was slight compared to Nunn's mastery.[33]

It was a mastery that had taken years to achieve, and it would not be easily replaced. His specialized knowledge, in an era when more senators were becoming generalists, resulted from long hours of study and a highly effective capacity to build solid bipartisan coalitions on issues to protect and advance US national interests, attributes Nunn's colleagues respected. They were the hallmarks of Nunn's political leadership, connected to his vision for US national security policy and strategy in his tenure in office during the final two decades of the Cold War and its immediate aftermath.

CONCLUSION

A political career in the US Congress has two essential elements. The first is campaigning and election, and for those who seek to have a long-term effect on legislation and policy, campaigning and reelection. The other major component is governing in Washington, DC.[1] With respect to governing, Nunn's twenty-four-year career can be divided into three major periods of activity for the purpose of understanding his leadership on issues related to US national security policy and strategy. These periods also reflect the significant changes in power, issues, institutional norms, rules, membership, leadership, and committee structure that occurred in the US Senate from the early 1970s until his retirement in 1996, as well as differences in the domestic and international environments.[2]

The first period runs from his election in November 1972 to January 1981. This period can be characterized as his apprenticeship in the Senate, what political scientist Richard Fenno has more aptly called a "period of adjustment."[3] Nunn's adjustment occurs within the larger institution of the Senate and on the Armed Services Committee in particular. However, his apprenticeship is relatively brief for two reasons. First, he is a young man on one of the four most prestigious committees in a Democratic-controlled Senate, the Armed Services Committee, whose members are of an earlier generation and for which the physical demands, especially overseas travel, have an impact. Most of the committee's Democratic members were born at the beginning of the twentieth century. Mississippian John Stennis, the committee chairman, is seventy-one years old; Stuart Symington, President Harry Truman's first secretary of the air force, is also seventy-one; and Senator Sam Ervin from North Carolina is the oldest at seventy-six. Even Henry "Scoop" Jackson is sixty years old. Excluding Nunn, the average age of the Democratic senators on the committee in January 1973, when Nunn is sworn in, is sixty-three years old. Nunn brought youth and vigor to the committee, and he became Stennis's "eyes and legs," especially traveling overseas to investigate issues of importance to the committee.

Nunn's role expanded into Stennis's protégé when Stennis was badly wounded in the robbery attempt outside the chairman's Washington residence. Moreover, Symington, who acted as the interim committee chair, relied on Nunn as well.[4] Nunn was rewarded for his work and growing expertise in the Ninety-Fourth Congress (1975–1976), when Stennis appointed him chairman of the newly established Subcommittee on Manpower and Personnel. While the title of this committee sounds dull, Nunn used his authority and its jurisdiction to extend beyond the usual issues of the armed forces' end strength, the military personnel budget, and recruiting, to explore US military force structure requirements, especially in Western Europe, to assess NATO alliance's conventional capability, and to understand the potential employment of tactical nuclear weapons. Nunn's two reports on NATO for the Armed Services Committee are critical to envisioning the future US role in the alliance with the end of America's direct involvement in the Vietnam War. The 1976 report on NATO, which he wrote with Republican Senator Dewey Bartlett and made public just before President Carter took office, had a major impact in the United States and Western Europe. It initiated the upgrade of NATO's conventional deterrence capability in response to a substantial increase in Soviet military strength while the United States was distracted by its involvement in Southeast Asia.

It was in this formative period that Nunn built his leadership competencies in three areas. The first area was technical competencies in which he, as an emergent leader, learned how to be effective in the Senate as an institution and as a member of the committees to which he was assigned, comprehending the "boundaries of these roles, their demands and constraints, and the expectations of others." Technical competencies included understanding the processes and procedures of the Senate, the role of committee as sources of power and information, the connection between the two congressional chambers, and most importantly, the functional relationship between the executive and legislative branches. This area included developing political and social competence, that is, the ability to participate effectively in the legislative process to determine national interests and, specifically, national security policy objectives and their successful implementation.[5]

The second area was interpersonal competencies. This area included the ability to build consensus, achieving this aim in the Senate and the Armed Services Committee, with external organizations, and even with other nations. Part of achieving consensus was the willingness to compromise, to be sensitive to other stakeholders' needs and concerns. In a political institution like the Senate, exploring ways to achieve agreement that others find acceptable was complex, requiring skills in reasoning, persuasion, collaboration, and negotiation. Negotiation was a critical skill since it relied on the ability to listen actively, to appreciate others' opinions and views, to identify hidden agendas, and to communicate a position while signaling a readiness to compromise or express firmly but respectfully nonnegotiable points. Additionally, the capacity to communicate effectively with members, external audiences, domestic and foreign, and constituents was indispensable.[6]

Nunn used a variety of nonlegislative tools and methods to communicate internally and externally: speeches on the floor of the Senate that dealt with policy issues and constituent concerns, news media interviews, and public speaking engagements.[7] He would not address a topic until he had analyzed an issue comprehensively and understood the perspectives of both sides. He fully understood that the words he chose had an effect well beyond the people hearing them in his immediate surroundings.

The third area was conceptual competencies. The first step was developing a frame of reference, that is, a "complex knowledge structure," a "map" of the strategic environment, formed from experience and self-study. This cognitive activity meant being open to new experiences and information, being a reflective practitioner, and being comfortable with ambiguity and abstract concepts that are inherent in appraising the strategic landscape. It required a capacity to learn, to discern trends and patterns, cause and effect, as well as interdependent relationships, the dynamic nature of events, and the secondary and tertiary impacts of decisions. Nunn was an avid reader of material and, as noted, spent hours preparing for any overseas trip he would take. Additionally, he had to engage in problem management, an understanding of the issues competing for attention on the legislative agenda and the resources needed to remedy or mitigate these problems. The other aspect of this set of competencies was envisioning the future, the capacity to formulate and articulate strategic aims over the long term.[8] As former Armed Services Committee majority staff director Arnold Punaro stated, "Any kind of decision [Nunn] was going to make, or policy he was going to put in place, he was always really looking to the long term. And of course, when it came to legislative strategy . . . he would always be thinking of the fifth and sixth step" before embarking "on the first step."[9]

By the end of this first period, Nunn acquired a reputation among his colleagues in the Senate; leaders of the executive branch, including presidents, senior civilian Defense and State Department officials, and military officers; and the media that covered Capitol Hill and were instrumental in publicizing this reputation. These actors recognized him as an expert on defense issues—that is, he had accrued a record of accomplishments marking the end of the period of adjustment, and the development of a recognizable political style.[10] Moreover, Nunn had become a crucial vote on several key foreign policy issues during this period, most notably the Panama Canal treaties and the Strategic Arms Limitation Treaty (SALT) II, where his competencies in all three areas were evident. Moreover, his votes on the Panama Canal treaties as well as on the extension of the Voting Rights Act are noteworthy because they reflect moral courage, a willingness to support issues in the national interest despite the preferences of his constituents. They did not penalize him at the polls for his votes on these highly charged issues. He won reelection in 1978 with 83 percent of the vote against his Republican challenger, admittedly in a sturdily faithful Democratic state.[11]

The second major period of Nunn's governing activity runs from January 1981 to January 1987, when Ronald Reagan won the 1980 presidential election and Democrats lost the majority in the Senate, with the Republicans gaining twelve seats. Mack Mattingly, chairman of Georgia's Republican Party and the first Republican elected to the Senate from Georgia since Reconstruction, defeated Georgia's senior senator, Herman Talmadge, by a thin margin, less than 28,000 votes out of 1.6 million that were cast.[12]

This was a period of testing for Nunn, but also a time when he made two important contributions. First was Nunn's crucial work on arms control, not an issue of primary jurisdiction for the Armed Services Committee, but one that he believed should be part of US defense policy, along with the more committee-relevant issues of nuclear weapons strategy. Nunn worked in a bipartisan fashion with Republicans John Warner and William Cohen on a number of issues where all three competencies come into play on these arcane subjects, but with a dedication to reducing the likelihood of nuclear war between the two superpowers. The second and more lasting work is his partnership with Republican Barry Goldwater to fashion the legislation known as the Goldwater-Nichols Act of 1986, which reformed the Defense Department's organization. Although Nunn's name does not appear on legislation's title, there is no doubt he was a complete and equal collaborator with Goldwater in this endeavor.

The third period runs from January 1987 to the end of Nunn's political career, but is most important for the eight years he served as chairman of the Senate Armed Services Committee, a period that the *National Journal* called "Sam Nunn, Inc.," because of his power and centralized control.[13] In this period, the pinnacle of his political career, he is the veteran legislator, and a period of "readjustment" occurs when he assumes this new role in governing. Nunn's competencies in the three areas are in full view: the stewardship of the annual national defense authorization bill; pushing the George H. W. Bush administration to adjust the nation's defense strategy in view of a changing security environment with the fall of the Berlin Wall in 1989; and most impressively, his crowning achievement of this period, the Nunn-Lugar Act as the Soviet Union unravels in late 1991. To accomplish these ends within an altered strategic context, he adjusted his frame of reference. He had the vision to see the criticality of controlling and disposing of the former Soviet Union's weapons of mass destruction and their associated infrastructure. Moreover, he had to "fashion a position within a more ideologically diverse committee and then seek passage within an even more diverse Senate" in a rapidly changing international security environment after 1989. This last aspect underscores that leadership is context dependent.[14]

Across more than two decades of Senate service, Nunn's leadership on so many national security issues was apparent, but his leadership reached beyond the common understanding of political leadership; it was an example of strategic leadership. Strategic leadership at the national level is the capacity "to think, to act, and to influence" in such a manner that promotes a "sustainable competitive advantage" for the United States in a global environment marked by threats and opportunities.

David Abshire remarked that Nunn's "importance as a strategic leader was never better demonstrated" than in the early 1980s. "It was then that [Nunn] played a prominent role in the defense transformation that helped end the Cold War." Specifically, Nunn focused "government and public attention in the United States and in Europe, on the critical need to strengthen NATO's conventional forces, thereby reducing the risk of nuclear war." Nunn catalyzed a change in US and allied thinking by "marshalling a cooperative effort," a phenomenal feat, one built on a sound political strategy. Abshire noted, "A key component of a successful strategy is to manipulate and control resources in a way that maximizes their impact on potential opponents. That kind of grand strategic design is hard to achieve in Congress, where the authorization and appropriation processes weave various committees and subcommittees, and multiple players with different agenda compete for influence." He continued by stating that it took a "powerful conceptualist and team builder to bring strategic coherence to that process, and to put his or her mark on the final outcome." It was for these reasons that Abshire considered Nunn a strategic leader.[15]

It was a perspective with which the Pentagon agreed. Secretary of Defense William Perry awarded Nunn the Department of Defense Medal for Distinguished Public Service on July 12, 1996, citing him as "the leading legislative voice on national security issues during a period of extraordinary change and challenge for the Department of Defense." The citation emphasized his "unparalleled knowledge of national defense and foreign policy issues," his "contributions to the security and well being" of the United States, and his bipartisanship. Perry stated that Nunn's "clear and articulate voice" prompted "public debate on defining the vital interests of the United States and promoted a strong defense and peace for future generations."[16]

Senator Nunn's legacy as a strategic leader resulted from his vision of what the United States should do to maintain the international order it preferred, by aligning policy and resources through legislation and other means to promote that vision, and by working within the Senate, but also with the House of Representatives, the executive branch, and internationally, to build consensus and thereby meet the challenges that the nation and its allies and partners confronted for more than two decades.

EPILOGUE

Nunn had promised in his October 1995 speech at the Georgia State Capitol that he would remain engaged in public service and involved in public policy. His chief interest remained arms control and nonproliferation with particular attention to his concerns about accidental nuclear war resulting from miscalculation or misperception of a threat against the United States or its allies.[1] The likelihood of nuclear war had shaped his worldview ever since the Cuban Missile Crisis in October 1962, when he was serving as a staff member of the House Armed Services Committee that his great-uncle chaired. Over the years, that event and others prompted his passion for preventing nuclear war through the establishment of risk reduction centers, the enactment and preservation of critical arms control treaties, and the Nunn-Lugar legislation that initiated the Defense Department's Cooperative Threat Reduction program. As Nunn later remarked regarding that singular event in October 1962, "I made a decision that if I ever had an opportunity to help reduce nuclear dangers and raise the nuclear threshold so that everybody would have more time before they undertook this kind of God-awful, almost planet-ending kind of military response and action, I would try to do it."[2] That sentiment did not end with his retirement from the Senate.

In 2001, he founded the Nuclear Threat Initiative (NTI), a nongovernmental organization, with Ted Turner, the businessman and philanthropist, to reduce the threats from weapons of mass destruction. Nunn became chief executive officer and cochairman, the latter a position he still holds. In the years since its founding, NTI has collaborated with numerous governments and nongovernmental organizations to secure nuclear materials globally, reduce the chance of a dirty bomb attack, raise awareness of nuclear and biological dangers, strengthen nonproliferation efforts, and undertake innovative work on cybersecurity at nuclear facilities.[3]

In January 2007, Nunn, former secretaries of state George Shultz and

Henry Kissinger, and former defense secretary William Perry published an op-ed in the *Wall Street Journal*. The piece, titled "A World Free of Nuclear Weapons," according to the *New York Times,* "sent waves through the global policy establishment." A *Washington Post* columnist later called the essay "revolutionary," as these four "members of the U.S. national security establishment and hawks" had "eventually changed their minds" about the efficacy of nuclear weapons. The elder statesmen called for abolishing nuclear weapons and provided a route to that end. The reaction was extraordinary, not only from editorial boards and columnists, but also academics, scientists, anti-nuclear and peace groups, and others. More concretely, political leaders from more than a dozen countries made statements that mirrored the position the four advocated in the op-ed. The "four horsemen" would pen three more op-eds, one each in 2008, 2010, and 2011, presenting their ideas on nuclear nonproliferation and deterrence; participate in a documentary, *Nuclear Tipping Point,* that NTI produced and that was screened by President Barack Obama at the White House; and become the subjects, along with the physicist Stanley Drell, of Philip Taubman's book *The Partnership: Five Cold Warriors and Their Quest to Ban the Bomb*.[4]

Numerous organizations have recognized and honored Nunn's public service. He was the inaugural recipient in 2011 of the Ivan Allen Jr. Prize for Social Courage for his "service to humanity," established by the Georgia Institute of Technology to honor the former mayor of Atlanta. The same year, the Georgia Historical Society and the Office of the Governor made Nunn a Georgia Trustee, an award to Georgians who contribute to the betterment of the state and the nation. The Historical Society's president, Todd Groce, stated that while Nunn had a noted career in the Senate, the award was for public service: "He [Nunn] stepped onto the world stage, leading the effort to stop nuclear weapons." Similarly, he received the Hessian Peace Prize in 2008 from the Peace Research Institute Frankfurt for his work on nuclear disarmament and for combating nuclear terrorism.[5] In May 2019, the secretary of the navy announced that a new Arleigh Burke–class guided missile destroyer would be named in honor of the former senator. Secretary of the Navy Richard V. Spencer credited Nunn's "leadership in the Senate, specifically as the long-serving chairman of the Senate Armed Services Committee," and noted that his "legacy of service to our nation will continue in the future USS *Sam Nunn*."[6]

Along with Richard Lugar, Nunn received the Chairman's Medal for distinguished lifetime achievement from the Heinz Family Foundation. They were "honored for their visionary leadership to reduce the threat of nuclear chaos and calamity." The award announcement noted: "The courageous leadership of these two global statesmen has helped to significantly diminish the threat of nuclear catastrophe. We—and peaceful nations around the world—are in their debt."[7] Nunn and Lugar's foresight was globally recognized: they were nominated for the Nobel Peace Prize in 2000 and 2001 because of their efforts in furtherance of nuclear disarmament and nonproliferation.[8]

NOTES

Abbreviations Used in Notes

AHP   Alexander Meigs Haig Papers, Library of Congress, Washington, DC

GFL   Gerald Ford Presidential Library, Ann Arbor, MI

GHWBL   George H. W. Bush Presidential Library, College Station, TX

JCL   Jimmy Carter Presidential Library, Atlanta, GA

JLP   James R. Locher III Papers, Special Collections, National Defense University Library, Fort McNair, Washington, DC

MOH   Edmund S. Muskie Oral History Collection, Bates College, Lewiston, ME

NSA-GWU   National Security Archive, George Washington University, Washington, DC

RRL   Ronald Reagan Presidential Library, Simi Valley, CA

SHO   US Senate Historical Office, Washington, DC

SNOH   Sam Nunn Oral History Collection, Stuart A. Rose Manuscript, Archives, and Rare Book Library (MARBL), Emory University, Atlanta, GA

SNP   Sam Nunn Papers, Stuart A. Rose Manuscript, Archives, and Rare Book Library (MARBL), Emory University, Atlanta, GA

SNPP   Sam Nunn Private Papers, Nuclear Threat Initiative offices, Washington, DC

WCP   William S. Cohen Papers, Special Collections, Raymond H. Fogler Library, University of Maine, Orono, ME

Introduction

1. Dana Milbank, "The Missing Giants of the Senate," *Washington Post*, July 10, 2012.
2. Ross K. Baker, *Friend and Foe in the U.S. Senate* (New York: Free Press, 1980), 154, 171; Fred R. Harris, *Deadlock or Decision: The U.S. Senate and the Rise of National Politics* (New York: Oxford University Press, 1993), 92, 101, 161. See also Roger H. Davidson, "Congressional Leaders as Agents of Change," in *Understanding Congressional Leadership*, ed. Frank H. Mackaman (Washington, DC: Congressional Quarterly Press, 1981), 136, 137.

3. Glenn P. Hastedt, *American Foreign Policy, Past, Present, and Future*, 10th ed. (Lanham, MD: Rowman & Littlefield, 2015), 163; Rochelle Jones and Peter Woll, *The Private World of Congress* (New York: Free Press, 1979), 116. See Robert David Johnson, "Congress and U.S. Foreign Policy before 9/11," in *Congress and the Politics of National Security*, ed. David P. Auerswald and Colton C. Campbell (New York: Cambridge University Press, 2012), 33. Roger H. Davidson, "Subcommittee Government: New Channels for Policy Making," in *The New Congress*, ed. Thomas Mann and Norman Ornstein (Washington, DC: American Enterprise Institute, 1981), addresses this point also.

4. Julian E. Zelizer, "Congress Is Back: Scholars Study Its History to Understand Its Problems," *Chronicle Review*, July 17, 2013, B12–B15. The relative lack of attention to congressional leadership as a field of study can be traced to the early 1980s. See Mackaman, introduction to *Understanding Congressional Leadership*, ed. Frank H. Mackaman (Washington, DC: Congressional Quarterly Press, 1981), 3; and Barbara Kellerman, "Leadership as a Political Act," in *Leadership: Multidisciplinary Perspectives* (Englewood Cliffs, NJ: Prentice-Hall, 1984), 63.

5. Pat Towell, "Congress and Defense," in *Congress and the Politics of National Security*, ed. David P. Auerswald and Colton C. Campbell (New York: Cambridge University Press, 2012), 71–72. See also Chuck Cushman, "Defense and the Two Congresses," in *Congress and Civil Military Relations*, ed. Colton C. Campbell and David P. Auerswald (Washington, DC: Georgetown University Press, 2015), 113–115.

6. James Lindsay, *Congress and the Politics of U.S. Foreign Policy* (Baltimore, MD: Johns Hopkins University Press, 1994), 59–61.

7. Robert David Johnson, *Congress and the Cold War* (New York: Cambridge University Press, 2005), 242–286; Cushman, "Defense and the Two Congresses," 116–117.

8. E. Scott Adler and John D. Wilkerson, *Congress and the Politics of Problem Solving* (New York: Cambridge University Press, 2012), 5, 7, 10–11; Dave Mayhew, "Congress as Problem Solver," in *Promoting the General Welfare: New Perspectives on Government Performance*, ed. Alan S. Gerber and Eric M. Patashnik (Washington, DC: Brookings Institution Press, 2006), 220, 223; Harris, *Deadlock or Decision*, 161.

9. Towell, "Congress and Defense," 74.

10. Towell, "Congress and Defense," 86. See Andrée E. Reeves, *Congressional Committee Chairmen: Three Who Made an Evolution* (Lexington: University Press of Kentucky, 1993), 3, 9–10, 15–16, for a discussion of the impact committee chairmen can have on the institution and its outputs.

11. James MacGregor Burns, *Leadership* (New York: Harper and Row, 1978), 19–20.

12. James R. Locher III, *Victory on the Potomac: The Goldwater-Nichols Act Unifies the Pentagon* (College Station: Texas A&M University Press, 2002), 233; Burns, *Leadership*, 170.

13. Barbara Hinckley, *Less than Meets the Eye: Foreign Policy Making and the Myth of the Assertive Congress* (Chicago: University of Chicago Press, 1994), 11–12; Eileen Burgin, "Congress and Foreign Policy: The Misperceptions," in *Congress Reconsidered*, 5th ed., ed. Lawrence C. Dodd and Bruce I. Oppenheimer (Washington,

DC: CQ Press, 1993), 355–356; Robert L. Peabody, "Senate Party Leadership from the 1950s to the 1980s," in *Understanding Congressional Leadership*, ed. Frank H. Mackaman (Washington, DC: Congressional Quarterly Press, 1981), 65–67; David W. Rohde, "Electoral Forces, Political Agendas, and Partisanship in the House and Senate," in *The Postreform Congress*, ed. Roger H. Davidson (New York: St. Martin's Press, 1992), 27–47. See also David Mayhew, *Congress: The Electoral Connection* (New Haven, CT: Yale University Press, 1974); Christopher J. Deering and Steven S. Smith, *Committees in Congress*, 2nd ed. (Washington, DC: CQ Press, 1990); and James M. Lindsay, "Congressional Oversight of the Department of Defense Budget: Reconsidering the Conventional Wisdom," *Armed Forces and Society* 17, no. 1 (Fall 1990): 7–33.

14. Richard F. Fenno Jr., *Congressmen in Committees* (Boston: Little, Brown, 1973), 139; Charles Harman, interview by Tom Chaffin, June 4, 1996, n.p., Sam Nunn Oral History Collection (hereafter cited as SNOH), Stuart A. Rose Manuscript, Archives, and Rare Books Library (hereafter cited as MARBL), Emory University, Atlanta, GA.

15. Ralph G. Carter and James M. Scott, "Taking the Lead: Congressional Foreign Policy Entrepreneurs in U.S. Foreign Policy," *Politics and Policy* 32, no. 1 (March 2004): 38; Carter and Scott, "Setting a Course: Congressional Foreign Policy Entrepreneurs in Post–World War II U.S. Foreign Policy," *International Studies Perspectives* 5, no. 3 (August 2004): 279, 280, 294–296; Carter and Scott, "Understanding Congressional Foreign Policy: Mapping Entrepreneurs and Their Strategies," *Social Science Journal* 47 (2010): 419, 420, 422, 425, 426–427, 428–429; Carter and Scott, *Choosing to Lead: Understanding Congressional Foreign Policy Entrepreneurs* (Durham, NC: Duke University Press, 2009), 11–14; Ralph G. Carter, email message to author, October 7, 2019; James M. Scott, email message to author, October 8, 2019; John W. Kingdon, *Agendas, Alternatives, and Public Policies*, 2nd ed. (New York: Longman, 1995), 180.

16. Robert C. Tucker, *Politics as Leadership* (Columbia: University of Missouri Press, 1981), 31.

17. Sidney Blumenthal, "The Mystique of Sam Nunn," *New Republic*, March 4, 1991, 26.

18. Randall Strahan, *Leading Representatives: The Agency of Leaders in the Politics of the U.S. House* (Baltimore, MD: Johns Hopkins University Press, 2007), 4.

Chapter 1. Stennis's Cadet

1. "Transcript of Nixon's Victory Speech," *New York Times*, November 8, 1972; Richard Nixon Foundation, "President Nixon's Election Victory Speech 1972," accessed February 1, 2020, https://www.youtube.com/watch?v=x7IwUTELcXY.

2. David S. Broder, "Nixon Wins Landslide Victory," *Washington Post*, November 8, 1972; R. W. Apple Jr., "Final Polls Signal Landslide Victory for the President," *New York Times*, November 6, 1972; Interview with Robert D. Novak, *Meet the Press*, MSNBC, July 15, 2007, http://www.nbcnews.com/id/19694666/ns/meet _the_press/t/meet-press-transcript-july/#.WrZ8P4eWyM8.

3. Joshua Muravchik, *The Senate and National Security: A New Mood*, Washington Papers 80 (Beverly Hills, CA: Sage Publications, 1980), 32–34.

4. Gordon Skene, "We Believe . . . Peace Is at Hand—Henry Kissinger—October 26, 1972," *Past Daily* (blog), October 26, 2016, https://pastdaily.com/2016/10/26 /henry-kissinger-october-26-1972/.

5. Kevin Phillips, "How Nixon Will Win," *New York Times*, August 6, 1972; Broder, "Nixon Wins Landslide Victory." See also V. O. Key Jr., "A Theory of Critical Elections," *Journal of Politics* 17, no. 1 (February 1955): 3–18.

6. Broder, "Nixon Wins Landslide Victory."

7. Apple, "Final Polls"; Senate Class II—History, *Our Campaigns*, accessed February 1, 2020, https://www.ourcampaigns.com/ContainerHistory.html?Container ID=111; John Hemphill, "Nunn, a Conservative Democrat, Defeats Rep. Thompson in Georgia Contest for Senate Seat," *New York Times*, November 8, 1972; Warren Weaver Jr., "Democrats Gain 2 Seats and Have 57–43 Majority," *New York Times*, November 9, 1972; Phil Gailey, "Sam Nunn's Rising Star," *New York Times Magazine*, February 4, 1987, 27.

8. Samuel Augustus Nunn, *Biographical Directory of the United States Congress*, accessed February 1, 2020, https://bioguideretro.congress.gov/Home/Member Details?memIndex=n000171; Sam Nunn, Biographical Information and Selected Accomplishments, press release, Office of Sam Nunn, Fall 1996 (in author's possession).

9. Sidney Blumenthal, "The Mystique of Sam Nunn," *New Republic*, March 4, 1991, 23; Gailey, "Sam Nunn's Rising Star," 25; A Conversation with Sam Nunn," *Georgia Tech Alumni Magazine*, Spring 1990, https://issuu.com/gtalumni/docs /1990_66_1; Roland McElroy, *The Best President the Nation Never Had* (Macon, GA: Mercer University Press, 2017), 9, 10, 73.

10. Blumenthal, "The Mystique of Sam Nunn," 23; Andrew Glass, "Rep. Carl Vinson Dies, June 1, 1981," *Politico*, June 1, 2010, https://www.politico.com/story /2010/06/rep-carl-vinson-dies-june-1-1981-037973; "Carl Vinson," *New Georgia Encyclopedia*, accessed February 1, 2020, http://www.georgiaencyclopedia.org /articles/government-politics/carl-vinson-1883–1981.

11. "Carl Vinson," *New Georgia Encyclopedia;* Associated Press, "Carl Vinson, 97, Ex-Congressman Who Was with the House 50 Years, Dies"; Marjorie Hunter, "He Left His Mark on Military," *New York Times*, June 2, 1981; Melvin B. Hill, Jr. and Robert G. Stephens, Jr., "Carl Vinson: A Legend in His Own Time," Carl Vinson Institute of Government, University of Georgia, accessed February 1, 2020, https://georgiainfo.galileo.usg.edu/topics/people/article/political-leaders/carl -vinson.

12. Gailey, "Sam Nunn's Rising Star," 27; Michael Kramer, "Smart, Dull, and Very Powerful," *Time*, March 13, 1989, 28; Timothy Noah, "Born to Be Mild," *Washington Monthly*, December 1989, 11; McElroy, *The Best President*, 9.

13. A Conversation with Sam Nunn"; Blumenthal, "The Mystique of Sam Nunn," 24; Kramer, "Smart, Dull and Very Powerful," 28; Steve Coll, "Sam Nunn, Insider from the Deep Southland," *Washington Post*, February 18, 1986; Noah, "Born to be Mild," 12; Dan Caldwell, *The Dynamics of Domestic Politics and Arms Control:*

The SALT II Treaty Ratification Debate (Columbia: University of South Carolina Press, 1991), 137; McElroy, *The Best President*, 20, 23–24, 31–32; Christopher Langan, "Honor, Respect, Devotion to Duty: Senator Sam Nunn," *Coast Guard Compass* (blog), September 25, 2014, http://coastguard.dodlive.mil/2014/09/honor-respect-devotion-to-duty-senator-sam-nunn/; Cathy Gwin, email message to author, May 23, 2018; Sam Nunn, Oral History, September 30, 1996, Sam Nunn Private Papers (SNPP), Nuclear Threat Initiative offices, Washington, DC.

14. "Richard Russell," *New Georgia Encyclopedia,* accessed February 1, 2020, https://www.georgiaencyclopedia.org/articles/government-politics/richard-b-russell-jr-1897-1971; "David H. Gambrell," *Biographical Directory of the United States Congress,* accessed February 1, 2020, http://bioguide.congress.gov/scripts/biodisplay.pl?index=G000034; Blumenthal, "The Mystique of Sam Nunn," 24; Nunn, Oral History.

15. Blumenthal, "The Mystique of Sam Nunn," 24; Coll, "Sam Nunn"; McElroy, *The Best President*, xi, 7–8, 33, 38–39, 42, 73; Nunn, Oral History; Hill and Stephens, "Carl Vinson: A Legend in His Own Time."

16. WMAZ-TV staff, "Farmer and Statesman Sam Nunn Talks Pecans and Politics," Macon, GA, November 1, 2016, http://www.13wmaz.com/article/news/local/farmer-and-statesman-sam-nunn-talks-pecans-and-politics/93-342320058; Coll, "Sam Nunn"; McElroy, *The Best President*, xii, 71–72, 85, 224.

17. Blumenthal, "The Mystique of Sam Nunn," 24; Kramer, "Smart, Dull, and Very Powerful," 28, 30; McElroy, *The Best President*, 45, 79–81.

18. Coll, "Sam Nunn"; Blumenthal, "The Mystique of Sam Nunn," 24; WMAZ-TV staff, "Farmer and Statesman"; Kramer, "Smart, Dull, and Very Powerful," 28; Susan F. Rasky, "Washington at Work," *New York Times,* May 2, 1990; McElroy, *The Best President*, 79–81, 83–85, 89–90, 96–98, 99–102, 104, 106; Cathy Gwin, email message to author, May 23, 2018; Nunn, Oral History; Philip Taubman, *The Partnership: Five Cold Warriors and Their Quest to Ban the Bomb* (New York: Harper, 2012), 147–148; Roland McElroy, email to author, October 25, 2019.

19. James M. Naughton, "Fight in Prospect," *New York Times,* January 27, 1973.

20. Bruce Cossaboom, "The Armed Services Committee," *Armed Forces Journal International,* March 1973, 49.

21. Cossaboom, "The Armed Services Committee," 49–50.

22. Richard McCulley, *History of the Senate Committee on Armed Services, 1947–1999,* unpublished manuscript, file: Armed Services Committee History, 2000 draft, US Senate Historical Office, Washington, DC (hereafter cited as McCulley MS).

23. US Department of State, "Agreement on Ending the War and Restoring Peace in South Viet-Nam," *Department of State Bulletin,* no. 68, December 20, 1973, 169–188.

24. "Watergate Scandal," *Encyclopedia Britannica Online,* accessed February 1, 2020, https://www.britannica.com/event/Watergate-Scandal; "Watergate Scandal," *New World Encyclopedia,* accessed February 1, 2020, https://www.newworldencyclopedia.org/entry/Watergate_scandal.

25. Congressional Quarterly, *Almanac,* 93rd Cong., 1st Sess., 1973 (Washington, DC: Congressional Quarterly News Features, 1974), 898; John W. Finney, "Senate

Clause Is Used to Prod NATO on Troop Costs," *New York Times,* November 24, 1973; "NATO Allies Assure the U.S. of Aid in Paying Troop Costs," *New York Times,* December 8, 1973; Phil Williams, "Whatever Happened to the Mansfield Amendment?," *Survival* 18, no. 4 (August 1976): 147, 148; Gregory F. Treverton, *The Dollar Drain and American Forces in Germany: Managing the Political Economies of Alliance* (Athens: Ohio University Press, 1978), 47–49.

26. Finney, "Senate Clause"; John Duffield, *Power Rules: The Evolution of NATO's Conventional Force Posture* (Stanford, CA: Stanford University Press, 1995), 203–204; Seymour Weiss, Director, Bureau of Politico-Military Affairs, US Department of State, "Circular Letter," October 26, 1973, Department of State Virtual Reading Room, https://foia.state.gov/Search/results.aspx?searchText=*&begin Date=19731026&endDate=19731027&publishedBeginDate=&publishedEndD ate=&caseNumber=; Department of Defense Appropriation Authorization Act of 1973, 93rd Cong., 1st Sess., Public Law 93-155, sec. 812, November 16, 1973. See also Public Laws, 93rd Cong. (1973–1974), https://www.congress.gov/public -laws/93rd-congress.

27. "NATO Allies Assure the U.S."

28. Robert G. Kaufman, *Henry Jackson: A Life in Politics* (Seattle: University of Washington Press, 2000), 166–167; Phil Williams, *The Senate and U.S. Troops in Europe* (New York: St. Martin's Press, 1985), 243; McElroy, *The Best President,* 126; Rochelle Jones and Peter Woll, *The Private World of Congress* (New York: Free Press, 1979), 116.

29. James T. Wooten, "Stennis Is Shot in Robbery in Front of Home in Capital," *New York Times,* January 31, 1973; "Stennis, Wounded Jan. 30, Returns to Senate Office," New York Times, August 8, 1973; Jones and Woll, *The Private World of Congress,* 115–117; Stennis quote in McCulley MS.

30. Muravchik, 491; Williams, *The Senate and U.S. Troops,* 243; National Archives and Records Administration, Center for Legislative Archives, "A Brief History of the Committee: The Stennis Era, 1969–1980," accessed February 1, 2020, https://www.archives.gov/legislative/finding-aids/reference/senate/armed -services/1969-1980.html; Rocky Rief, interview by Tom Chaffin, October 17, 1996, Box 1, Sam Nunn Oral History (SNOH) collection, Stuart A. Rose Manuscript, Archives, and Rare Book Library, Emory University, Atlanta, GA.

31. Quoted in Taubman, *The Partnership,* 198.

32. Stephen S. Rosenfeld, "Sen. Nunn's NATO Maneuver," *Washington Post,* June 21, 1974; Senate Committee on Armed Services, *Policy, Troops, and the NATO Alliance,* Report of Senator Sam Nunn to the Committee on Armed Services, 93rd Cong., 2nd Sess., 1974, iii–iv, 1.

33. Senate Committee on Armed Services, *Policy, Troops, and the NATO Alliance* iii–iv, 1–3; Arnold Punaro, Box 1, interview by Tom Chaffin, October 15, 1997, McLean, VA, SNOH). See Diego A. Ruiz Palmer, "The NATO-Warsaw Competition in the 1970s and 1980s: A Revolution in Military Affairs in the Making or the End of a Strategic Age?" *Cold War History* 14, no. 4 (2014): 570–571, for a discussion of the deterrent effect of NATO's tactical nuclear weapons and the conditions under which political leaders would authorize use. Ruiz Palmer points out

that the battlefield conditions under which NATO's military commander should make such a request of political leaders were, at this time, ambiguous.

34. Senate Committee on Armed Services, *Policy, Troops, and the NATO Alliance*, 4–9.

35. Senate Committee on Armed Services, *Policy, Troops, and the NATO Alliance*, 9–10; David E. Hoffman, *The Dead Hand: The Untold Story of the Cold War Arms Race and Its Dangerous Legacy* (New York: Doubleday, 2009), 380–381.

36. David Binder, "Bonn Pact Makes U.S. Hopeful NATO Will Share Troop Costs," *New York Times*, March 23, 1974.

37. John W. Finney, "Pentagon Thesis Disputed in Study," *New York Times*, April 9, 1974; Simon Duke, *The Burdensharing Debate: A Reassessment* (New York: St. Martin's Press, 1993), 70.

38. John W. Finney, "U.S. Weighs Trim in Europe Forces," *New York Times*, April 24, 1974; Williams, "Whatever Happened to the Mansfield Amendment?" 147, 148.

39. Congressional Quarterly, *Almanac*, 93rd Cong., 2nd Sess., 1974 (Washington, DC: Congressional Quarterly News Features, 1974), 580.

40. Congressional Quarterly, *Almanac*, 580.

41. Williams, "Whatever Happened to the Mansfield Amendment?," 150–151; Treverton, *The Dollar Drain*, 21; Duffield, *Power Rules*, 210; Nunn, Oral History. See also Barry R. Posen, "Measuring the European Conventional Balance: Coping with Complexity in Threat Assessment," *International Security* 19, no. 3 (Winter 1984–1985): 53n8.

42. Rosenfeld, "Sen. Nunn's NATO Maneuver"; Richard Rhodes, *The Twilight of the Bombs: Recent Challenges, New Dangers, and the Prospects for a World without Nuclear Weapons* (New York, Knopf, 2010), 99; Ambassador James E. Goodby, interview by Charles Stuart Kennedy, December 10, 1990, transcript, Association for Diplomatic Studies and Training Foreign Affairs Oral History Project, Arlington, VA; Nunn, Oral History.

43. Quoted in Williams, "Whatever Happened to the Mansfield Amendment?," 151.

44. Williams, 150, 151.

45. Congressional Quarterly, *Almanac*, 580.

46. Rosenfeld, "Sen. Nunn's NATO Maneuver."

47. Rasky, "Washington at Work."

48. Nunn, email to author, May 23, 2018.

49. "Watergate Scandal," *Encyclopedia Britannica Online*; "Watergate Scandal," *New World Encyclopedia*.

50. McElroy, *The Best President*, 134.

Chapter 2. The Emerging Expert

1. Joseph J. Sisco, "Ford, Kissinger, and the Nixon-Ford Foreign Policy," in *The Ford Presidency: Twenty-Two Intimate Perspectives of Gerald R. Ford*, ed. Kenneth W. Thompson (Lanham, MD: University Press of America, 1988), 327.

2. Gerald Ford, Presidential Proclamation 4311, "Granting Pardon to Richard Nixon," September 8, 1974; Nguyen Tien Hang and Jerrold L. Schecter, *The Pal-

ace File (New York: Harper & Row, 1986), 121–122, 124–125, 150, 161, 163; Jussi Hanhimäki, *The Flawed Architect: Henry Kissinger and American Foreign Policy* (New York: Oxford University Press, 2004), 256, 268.

3. Arnold L. Punaro with David Poyer, *On War and Politics: The Battlefield inside Washington's Beltway* (Annapolis, MD: Naval Institute Press, 2016), 91.

4. Congressional Quarterly, *Almanac*, 94th Cong., 1st Sess., 1975 (Washington, DC: Congressional Quarterly News Features, 1976), 306; Gerald R. Ford, "Statement on Signing the Department of Defense Appropriations Act, 1975," October 9, 1974, online at Gerhard Peters and John T. Woolley, American Presidency Project, https://www.presidency.ucsb.edu/node/255941; http://www.presidency.ucsb.edu/ws/?pid=4439; George C. Herring, "The Executive, Congress, and the Vietnam War, 1965–1975," in *Congress and United States Foreign Policy: Controlling the Use of Force in the Nuclear Age,* ed. Michael Barnhart (Albany: State University of New York Press, 1987), 182–183.

5. Gerald R. Ford, "Special Message to the Congress Requesting Supplemental Assistance for the Republic of Vietnam and Cambodia," January 28, 1975, online by Gerhard Peters and John T. Woolley, American Presidency Project, https://www.presidency.ucsb.edu/node/257175.

6. Nunn, Oral History, September 30, 1996, Sam Nunn Private Papers (SNPP), Nuclear Threat Initiative offices, Washington, DC; Senate Committee on Armed Services, *Vietnam Aid—The Painful Options,* Report of Senator Sam Nunn to the Committee on Armed Services, February 12, 1975, 94th Cong., 1st Sess., v.

7. Bruce K. MacLaury, *The Limping Giant: The American Economy 1974–75,* Federal Reserve Bank of Minneapolis, Annual Report, January 1, 1975, https://www.minneapolisfed.org/publications/annual-reports/the-limping-giant-the-american-economy-197475.

8. Nunn, Oral History; Senate Committee on Armed Services, *Vietnam Aid,* v–vi.

9. Senate Committee on Armed Services, *Vietnam Aid,* 1–4.

10. Senate Committee on Armed Services, *Vietnam Aid,* 4, 5, 6–9.

11. Senate Committee on Armed Services, *Vietnam Aid,* 4, 11–12.

12. Senate Committee on Armed Services, *Vietnam Aid,* 12–13, 15–16.

13. Punaro, *On War and Politics,* 91; Yanek Mieczkowski, *Gerald Ford and the Challenges of the 1970s* (Lexington: University Press of Kentucky, 2005), 292.

14. National Security Adviser, Memorandum of Conversation, Ford, Ambassador Graham Martin (South Vietnam), February 15, 1975, Box 9, Memoranda of Conversations—Ford Administration, Gerald Ford Presidential Library (hereafter cited as GFL), https://www.fordlibrarymuseum.gov/library/document/0314/1552953.pdf.

15. Nunn, email message to author, May 23, 2018; Gerald R. Ford, "The President's News Conference," February 4, 1975, online by Gerhard Peters and John T. Woolley, American Presidency Project, https://www.presidency.ucsb.edu/node/257251; "'If We Abandon Our Allies . . . ' Ford Spells Out His Doctrine," *U.S. News and World Report,* March 17, 1975, 17.

16. Leslie Gelb, "Some in Congress Wary on Arms Cuts," *New York Times,* May 6,

1975; Robert David Johnson, *Congress and the Cold War* (New York: Cambridge University Press, 2005), 209.

17. Eileen Shanahan, "Congress Agrees on a Budget Goal," *New York Times*, May 15, 1975.

18. David E. Rosenbaum, "Senate Opens a Wide-Ranging Debate on the National Military Policy," *New York Times*, June 3, 1975.

19. Leslie H. Gelb, "Congress Likely to Press Its Role in Foreign Policy," *New York Times*, April 19, 1976; Gelb, "The Secretary of State Sweepstakes," *New York Times*, May 23, 1976; Nunn, email message to author, May 23, 2018.

20. John W. Finney, "U.S. Is Reassessing Strategy in Europe," *New York Times*, September 24, 1976; McElroy, email to author, October 25, 2019.

21. Leslie H. Gelb, "Liberal Democrats Retreat on Pentagon's Budget," *New York Times*, June 2, 1976.

22. Sam Nunn, "NATO Strategy," *Survival* 19, no. 1 (January–February 1977): 30–32; NATO Briefing Book 1980, MS106.3.3.5.1, Box 1, Folder 4, William S. Cohen Papers (hereafter cited as WCP), Special Collections, Raymond H. Fogler Library, University of Maine, Orono, ME; Finney, "U.S. Is Reassessing Strategy"; Nunn, interview by author, Washington, DC, May 9, 2018; James H. Willbanks, *Danger 79er: The Life and Times of Lieutenant General James F. Hollingsworth* (College Station: Texas A&M University Press, 2018), xi, 179.

23. Memorandum for the file, Jeff Record, subject: Presentation of General Hollingsworth, July 25, 1976, Subseries 6.5, Box 167, Notes on NATO Trip, Sam Nunn Papers (hereafter cited as SNP), Stuart A. Rose Manuscript, Archives and Rare Book Library, Emory University, Atlanta, Georgia; Memorandum from Lieutenant General E. C. Meyer to General Alexander Haig with Hollingsworth Report attached, undated, Box 62, Edward C. Meyer File, Alexander Meigs Haig Papers (hereafter cited as AHP), Library of Congress, Washington, DC; Finney, "U.S. Is Reassessing Strategy"; Willbanks, *Danger 79er*, 179–180; Senate Committee on Armed Services, *NATO and the New Soviet Threat*, Report of Senator Sam Nunn and Senator Dewey F. Bartlett to the Committee on Armed Services, 95th Cong., 1st Sess., January 24, 1977, iv; Nunn, email message to author, May 23, 2018.

24. John W. Finney, "Haig Reports Readiness Deficiencies and 'a Garrison Mentality,'" *New York Times*, October 14, 1976.

25. US Mission NATO (Brussels) to SECSTATE, Washington, DC, cable (declassified), 111939Z, Nov 76, CODEL Nunn/Bartlett; COMSIXFLT to USCINCEUR, cable (declassified) 110815Z, Nov 76, Report on Visit of Senators Nunn and Bartlett; CINCSOUTH to SACEUR, cable (declassified), 101400Z, Nov 76, Visit of Senators Nunn and Bartlett; BG Bart to SACEUR, cable (declassified), 081458Z, Nov 76, Nunn Delegation Talks, all in Box 85, AHP; Senate Committee on Armed Services, *NATO and the New Soviet Threat*, iii; Nunn, interview by author; Willbanks, *Danger 79er*, 180–181.

26. John W. Finney, "2 Senators Ask Shift in NATO Strategy to Counter Soviet," *New York Times*, November 15, 1976; Senate Committee on Armed Services, *NATO and the New Soviet Threat*, 7–10; Congressional Record—Excerpts from Nunn-

Bartlett Report, Subseries 6.5, Box 168, 1977–1980 (Jeff Record), Envelope US/Senate, SNP.

27. Senate Committee on Armed Services, *NATO and the New Soviet Threat*, 4–6; Drew Middleton, "Anxieties about NATO," *New York Times*, December 10, 1976; Raymond Carroll and Nicholas Proffitt, "Britain's Thin Red Line," *U.S. News & World Report*, December 13, 1976, 49.

28. Congressional Budget Office, *Planning U.S. General Purpose Forces: Army Procurement Issues* (Washington, DC: US Government Printing Office, 1976), xiii–xvi.

29. "Russia's 'Relentless' Arms Buildup," *US News & World Report*, January 17, 1977, 35.

30. Richard J. Madden, "Congress Finds a New Interest in Georgia Bloc," *New York Times*, November 21, 1976.

31. Jimmy Carter, interview by James Sterling Young et al., November 29, 1982, transcript, Carter Presidency Project, Miller Center of Public Affairs, University of Virginia, Charlottesville, VA.

32. James Schlesinger, interview by James Sterling Young et al., July 19–20, 1984, transcript, Carter Presidency Project, Miller Center of Public Affairs, University of Virginia, Charlottesville, VA.

33. Punaro, *On War and Politics*, 93.

34. Arnaud de Borchgrave, "Nightmare for NATO," *Newsweek*, February 7, 1977, 36; Joint Department of State and Department of Defense Briefing Paper, "Vice President's Trip to NATO: Talking Points/Issues," n.d., Jimmy Carter Presidential Library (hereafter cited as JCL), RAC Project Number NLC-133-9-3-1-0. See Vice President Mondale's Meeting with General Alexander M. Haig Jr., Supreme Allied Commander, Europe, January 24, 1977, JCL, RAC Project Number NLC-133-9-11-3-9, for a discussion of the Carter administration's position on NATO preparedness and modernization.

35. Jimmy Carter, Presidential Review Memorandum/NSC-10, subject: Comprehensive Net Assessment and Military Force Posture Review, February 18, 1977.

36. Brian Auten, *Carter's Conversion: The Hardening of American Defense Policy* (Columbia: University of Missouri Press, 2008), 149, 150, 152, 153, 154; Jimmy Carter, Program Review Memorandum/NSC-6, subject: Mutual and Balanced Force Reduction Talks, January 21, 1977; Jimmy Carter, Program Review Memorandum/NSC-9, subject: Comprehensive Review of European Issues, February 1, 1977.

37. Sam Nunn, "Deterring War in Europe: Some Basic Assumptions Need Revising," *NATO Review* 25, no. 1 (February 1977): 5.

38. Borchgrave, "Nightmare for NATO," 36; Michael Getler, "Crack W. German Forces a Key to NATO Strength," *Washington Post*, February 24, 1977; Drew Middleton, "NATO Military Aide Urges Allies to Raise Their Arms Budgets," *New York Times*, March 23, 1977;

39. David Binder, "Pentagon Officials Say Billions in New Strategic Weapons Are Needed," *New York Times*, February 2, 1977; John W. Finney, " . . . But the Army of Volunteers Is Worried," *New York Times*, March 5, 1977.

40. Drew Middleton, "Proposals to Strengthen NATO Focus of Meeting," *New York Times*, May 10, 1977; Harold Brown, with Joyce Winslow, *Star-Spangled Security: Applying Lessons Learned over Six Decades Safeguarding America* (Washington, DC: Brookings Institution Press, 2012), 135.

41. Middleton, "Proposals to Strengthen NATO."

42. Comptroller General of the United States, *NATO's New Defense Program: Issues for Consideration*, ID-79-4A, July 9, 1979, 1–3, 21, https://www.gao.gov/assets/130/127274.pdf.

43. Senate Committee on Armed Services, Subcommittee on Manpower and Personnel, *NATO Posture and Initiatives*, 95th Cong., 1st Sess., 1977, 3–8; Jimmy Carter, Presidential Directive/NSC-18, subject: U.S. National Strategy, August 24, 1977.

44. US Department of State, Office of the Historian, "The Panama Canal and the Torrijos-Carter Treaties," https://history.state.gov/milestones/1977-1980/panama-canal; Angus Deming et al., "The Canal: Time to Go?" *Newsweek*, August 22, 1977, 28.

45. Deming et al., "The Canal: Time to Go?," 28; "Carter in New Bid for Canal Backing," *New York Times*, October 12, 1977; Jimmy Carter, *Keeping Faith: Memoirs of a President* (New York: Bantam Books, 1982), 165, 166; Memorandum from Jeff Record to Nunn, August 30, 1977, subject: The Panama Canal Treaties, Subseries 6.5, Box 167, file: Jeff Record Notebook IV, SNP; Sam Nunn, "Panama Canal Statement," December 1977, Record Group II: US Senate, Subgroup 5: Press relations/media activity, 1972–1996, The Sam Nunn Letter files, 1973–1986, Box 2, SNP; Robert A. Strong, *Decisions and Dilemmas: Case Studies in Presidential Foreign Policy Making Since 1945*, 2nd ed. (Armonk, NY: M.E. Sharpe, 2005), 125; "A Dialogue with Sam Nunn," Senator Howard H. Baker Jr., September 13, 1977, Record Group II: US Senate, subgroup 5: Press relations/media activity, 1972–1996, Subseries 1. "Dialogue with Sam Nunn" files, 1976–1977, 1981, Box 1, folder 20, SNP.

46. Carter, *Keeping Faith*, 163; William L. Furlong, "Negotiations and Ratification of the Panama Canal Treaties," in *Congress, the Presidency and American Foreign Policy*, ed. John Spanier and Joseph Nogee (New York: Pergamon Press, 1981), 189; Jimmy Carter, interview by Tom Chaffin, July 16, 1997, Atlanta, GA, Box 1, Sam Nunn Oral History Collection (SNOH), Stuart A. Rose Manuscript, Archives and Rare Book Library, Emory University, Atlanta, GA.

47. Lynn Langway and Henry W. Hubbard, "The Panama Canal: Round One," *Newsweek*, February 20, 1978, 30.

48. Memorandum, Frank Moore et al., to the President, subject: Panama Treaties—Status, February 27, 1979, JCL, RAC Project Number NLC-126-3-33-1-9; Nunn, Oral History; Herman Talmadge, interview by Tom Chaffin, July 17, 1998, Atlanta, GA, Box 2, SNOH; Adam Clymer, "Canal Pact Support Still Short of Goal," *New York Times*, March 15, 1978; Carter, *Keeping Faith*, 169; Thomas M. Franck and Edward Weisband, *Foreign Policy by Congress* (New York: Oxford University Press, 1979), 278; Johnson, *Congress and the Cold War*, 237; John Opperman, "The Panama Canal Treaties: Legislative Strategy for Advice and Consent," in

Legislating Foreign Policy, ed. Hoyt Purvis and Steven J. Baker (Boulder, CO: Westview Press, 1984), 91–92, 96.

49. Nunn, Oral History; William L. Furlong and Margaret E. Scranton, *The Dynamics of Foreign Policymaking: The President, the Congress, and the Panama Canal Treaties* (Boulder, CO: Westview Press, 1984), 131–132. The quote is found on page 132. See also Johnson, *Congress and the Cold War*, 237.

50. Adam Clymer, "Senate, 68–32, Approves First of 2 Panama Pacts," *New York Times*, March 17, 1978.

51. Clymer, "Senate, 68–32, Approves First of 2 Panama Pacts"; "Tests of Senate Changes in Pact," *New York Times*, March 17, 1978; "Carter's Panama Triumph— What It Cost," *US News & World Report*, March 27, 1978, 27; Carter, *Keeping Faith*, 172; Furlong and Scranton, *The Dynamics of Foreign Policymaking*, 149, 163; William J. Jorden, *Panama Odyssey* (Austin: University of Texas Press, 1984), 519; Punaro, *On War and Politics*, 99.

52. Nunn, Oral History; Hedrick Smith, "After Panama, More Battles," *New York Times*, April 20, 1978; Jorden, *Panama Odyssey*, 535, 537–538, 540–541; Cyrus Vance, *Hard Choices* (New York: Simon & Schuster, 1983), 153; Punaro, *On War and Politics*, 99–100; Roland McElroy, *The Best President the Nation Never Had* (Macon, GA: Mercer University Press, 2017), 172–173.

53. Sam Nunn, "Mutual and Balanced Force Reductions—A Need to Shift Our Focus," *Atlantic Community Quarterly* 16, no. 1 (Spring 1978): 18–21.

54. Edward C. Keefer, *Harold Brown: Offsetting the Soviet Military Challenge, 1977– 1981*, Secretaries of Defense Historical Series, vol. 9 (Washington, DC: Historical Office, Office of the Secretary of Defense, 2017), 445–446. See Memorandum, Zbigniew Brzezinski to President Carter, subject: NSC Weekly Report no. 39, Warning of War in Europe, December 9, 1977, JCL, RAC Project Number NLC-16A-41-89-1-3, for a discussion of the preliminary finding of an ongoing National Intelligence Estimate that resulted from the Nunn-Bartlett report. The new estimate did not support the view that a "full-scale" Warsaw Pact attack would come with "little or no warning."

55. Hedrick Smith, "After Panama, More Battles," *New York Times*, April 20, 1978; "After Carter's Panama Victory," *US News & World Report*, May 1, 1978, 25; Memorandum, Richard Moe to Vice President Mondale et al., subject: SALT, April 10, 1978, JCL, RAC Project Number NLC-133-180-5-4-5.

56. Bernard Weinraub, "Senator Nunn, at 39, Emerging as Expert on Military," *New York Times*, July 1, 1978; Tom Mathews and John J. Lindsay, "Nunn for the Defense," *Newsweek*, July 17, 1978, 35; Nunn, SALT II press release, July 17, 1978, Subseries 6.5, Box 171, New Files, Arms Control, SNP.

57. Sam Nunn, "SALT II," speech to the Air Force Association meeting, Warner Robins, GA, press release, July 17, 1978, Subseries 6.6, Box 171, Arms Control, SNP; Richard Burt, "Nunn Fears Geneva Will Prove Costly," *New York Times*, July 18, 1978.

58. "Behind the Tug of War over Defense Spending," *US News & World Report*, August 28, 1978, 22.

59. McElroy, email to author, October 25, 2019.

60. Weinraub, "Senator Nunn, at 39"; McElroy, *The Best President*, 152, 156, 168, 170–171; Nunn, Oral History; McElroy, email to author, October 25, 2019.

61. Robert G. Kaiser, "Sam Nunn: 'All That Propaganda,'" *Washington Post*, December 24, 1978; Memorandum, Dennis Clift to the Vice President, subject: Foreign Policy Breakfast, June 8, 1978, JCL, RAC Project Number NLC-133-111-1-15-3; Memorandum, Dennis Clift to the Vice President, subject: MFBR Negotiations, July 21, 1978, JCL, RAC Project Number NLC-133-111-2-19-8.

62. Sam Nunn, "Russia: Enigmatic Giant," December 3, 1978, Subseries 6.5, Box 171, file, Trip Reports, SNP; "Group of Senators Starts Soviet Visit," *New York Times*, November 12, 1978; Kim Willenson and David C. Martin, "A New Cuban Missile Crisis?," *Newsweek*, November 27, 1978, 51. See Memorandum, Cyrus Vance to the President, Ribicoff-Soviets, November 24, JCL, RAC Project Number NLC-133-7-2-31-0, for a brief discussion of the atmosphere of the visit.

63. Kaiser, "Sam Nunn: 'All that Propaganda'"; Nunn, "Russia: Enigmatic Giant."

Chapter 3. The Price of SALT

1. Raymond L. Garthoff, *Détente and Confrontation: American-Soviet Relations from Nixon to Reagan*, rev. ed. (Washington, DC: Brookings Institution Press, 1994), 741.

2. Lawrence X. Clifford, "An Examination of the Carter Administration's Selection of Secretary of State and National Security Adviser," in *Jimmy Carter: Foreign Policy and Post-presidential Years*, ed. Herbert D. Rosenbaum and Alexej Ugrinski (Westport, CT: Greenwood Press, 1994), 11.

3. Congressional Quarterly, *Almanac*, 96th Cong., 1st Sess., 1979 (Washington, DC: Congressional Quarterly News Features, 1980), 411; Jan M. Lodal, "SALT II and American Security," *Foreign Affairs* 67, no. 2 (Winter 1978): 245.

4. Congressional Quarterly, *Almanac*, 434.

5. Memorandum, Frank Moore and Zbigniew Brzezinski to the President, Meeting with Senator Sam Nunn, January 23, 1979, Jimmy Carter Presidential Library (JCL), RAC Project Number NLC-126-16-10-1-2; Dan Caldwell, "The Carter Administration, the Senate, and SALT II," in *Carter: Foreign Policy and Post-presidential Years*, ed. Herbert D. Rosenbaum and Alexej Ugrinski (Westport, CT: Greenwood Press, 1994), 342.

6. David Skidmore, *Reversing Course: Carter's Foreign Policy, Domestic Politics, and the Failure of Reform* (Nashville, TN: Vanderbilt University Press, 1996), 142.

7. Tom Mathews and John J. Lindsay, "Nunn for the Defense," *Newsweek*, July 17, 1978, 35.

8. Peter Goldman, with Eleanor Clift, Thomas M. DeFrank, John J. Lindsay, and James Doyle, "The Hard SALT Sell," *Newsweek*, February 19, 1979, 32; James Reston, "Washington," *New York Times*, April 11, 1979; Dan Caldwell, *The Dynamics of Domestic Politics and Arms Control: The SALT II Treaty Ratification Debate* (Columbia: University of South Carolina Press, 1991), 130.

9. Quoted in Caldwell, *The Dynamics of Domestic Politics*, 136–137.

10. Hedrick Smith, "Three-Cornered Arms Talks," *New York Times*, April 14, 1979; J.

Philip Rogers, "The Senate and Arms Control: The SALT Experience," in *Legislating Foreign Policy*, ed. Hoyt Purvis and Steven J. Baker (Boulder, CO: Westview Press, 1984), 174, 176.

11. Nunn, "American Defense With or Without SALT," Address to the National Chamber of Commerce, April 30, 1979, *Atlantic Community Quarterly* 17 (Summer 1979): 155–159; Richard Burt, "Senator Nunn Sees," *New York Times*, May 1, 1979; Robert G. Kaiser, "Carter: SALT Can Be Adequately Verified," *Washington Post*, May 1, 1979.

12. "Heirs to Dixie Barons: New Powers in Senate," *US News & World Report*, May 7, 1979, 62.

13. Brian Auten, *Carter's Conversion: The Hardening of American Defense Policy* (Columbia: University of Missouri Press, 2008), 305–306.

14. Harold Brown, with Joyce Winslow, *Star-Spangled Security: Applying Lessons Learned over Six Decades Safeguarding America* (Washington, DC: Brookings Institution, Press, 2012), 119.

15. Edward C. Keefer, *Harold Brown: Offsetting the Soviet Military Challenge, 1977–1981*, Secretaries of Defense Historical Series, vol. 9 (Washington, DC: Historical Office, Office of the Secretary of Defense, 2017), 168. See Memorandum, Frank Moore and Bob Beckett to the President, subject: SALT II—Senate Update, May 8, 1979, JCL, RAC Project Number NLC-128-11-20-1-5.

16. Memoranda, Zbigniew Brzezinski and Frank Moore to the President, Meeting with Senator Robert C. Byrd, May 9, 1979, and Meeting with Senator Howard H. Baker Jr., JCL, RAC Project Number NLC-133-103-6-2-1 and RAC Project Number NLC-133-103-6-1-2; Robert G. Kaiser, "Next: An Uncertain Senate," *Washington Post*, May 10, 1979; Hedrick Smith, "Congress Worried over Soviets," *New York Times*, May 10, 1979; Tom Mathews, with Eleanor Clift, Lars-Erik Nelson, and Henry W. Hubbard, "On the Offensive," *Newsweek*, May 7, 1979, 30.

17. David Butler, with Lars-Erik Nelson, Eleanor Clift, David C. Martin, John J. Lindsay, and Fred Coleman, "SALT II: And Now for the Battle," *Newsweek*, May 21, 1979, 36; "Texts of Vance and Brown Remarks on Arms Pact," *New York Times*, May 10, 1979; Jimmy Carter, "American Retail Federation Remarks at a White House Breakfast," May 10, 1979, online at Gerhard Peters and John T. Woolley, American Presidency Project, https://www.presidency.ucsb.edu/node/249204.

18. Richard Burt, "Vance Warns That Senate Changes Could Doom Arms-Limitation Pact," *New York Times*, May 14, 1979; Joseph Fromm, "SALT II: Can It End the Arms Race?" *US News & World Report*, May 21, 1979, 21.

19. Fromm, "SALT II: Can It End the Arms Race?" 21; Butler et al., "SALT II: And Now for the Battle," 36.

20. Fromm, "SALT II: Can It End the Arms Race?" 21; Butler et al., "SALT II: And Now for the Battle," 36.

21. "As Battle Shapes Up in Senate," *US News & World Report*, May 28, 1979, 38; George F. Will, "How to Think about SALT," *Newsweek*, May 28, 1979, 104; Arnold L. Punaro, with David Poyer, *On War and Politics: The Battlefield inside Washington's Beltway* (Annapolis, MD: Naval Institute Press, 2016), 93.

22. Richard Burt, "Search for an Invulnerable," *New York Times*, May 27, 1979; "A Battle for SALT Shapes Up," *US News & World Report*, May 28, 1979, 38.

23. Bernard Weinraub, "Senate Delays Debate on Draft Registration and Passes Arms Bill," *New York Times*, June 14, 1979; Charles Mohr, "Arms Pact Faces Senate Challenge in the Fall and an Uncertain Fate," *New York Times*, June 19, 1979; Lawrence J. Korb, "The Role of the Joint Chiefs of Staff in the Strategic Arms Limitations Process: Changing or Constraints?" (paper presented at the National Conference of the Inter-University Seminar on the Armed Forces and Society, Chicago, IL, October 23–25, 1980); US Department of State, Office of the Historian, "Strategic Arms Limitation Talks/Treaty (SALT) I and II," accessed February 1, 2020, https://history.state.gov/milestones/1969-1976/salt; Congressional Quarterly, *Almanac*, 413.

24. David Butler et al., The SALT Summit," *Newsweek*, June 25, 1979, 26; Garthoff, *Détente and Confrontation*, 812; Gaddis Smith, *Morality, Reason, and Power* (New York: Hill and Wang, 1985), 208.

25. Memorandum, Dennis Clift and Ralph Crosby to the Vice President, subject: Senator Sam Nunn and SALT, June 19, 1979, JCL, RAC Project Number NLC-133-114-1-30-3; "SALT—The Real Fight Begins," *Newsweek*, July 2, 1979, 26; Zbigniew Brzezinski, *Power and Principle* (New York: Farrar, Straus and Giroux, 1983), 336–337; Stephen J. Flanagan, "The Domestic Politics of SALT II: Implications for the Foreign Policy Process," in *Congress, the Presidency, and American Foreign Policy*, ed. John Spanier and Joseph Nogee (New York: Pergamon Press, 1981), 67.

26. Charles Mohr, "Senate Armed Services Panel Takes Up Treaty Debate," *New York Times*, July 24, 1979; Mohr, "Joint Chiefs Affirm Support," *New York Times*, July 25, 1979; Korb, "The Role of the Joint Chiefs of Staff."

27. Robert C. Kaiser, "Nunn Ties Vote on SALT to More Defense Spending," *Washington Post*, July 26, 1979; Charles Mohr, "Nunn Links His Support for Pact to Arms Budget Rise," *New York Times*, July 26, 1979; "The World," *New York Times*, July 29, 1979; Stanley J. Heginbotham, "Constraining SALT II: The Role of the Senate," in *Congress and United States Foreign Policy: Controlling the Use of Force in the Nuclear Age*, ed. Michael Barnhart (Albany: State University of New York Press, 1987), 115–116.

28. Mohr, "Nunn Links His Support"; Lloyd Cutler, interview by James S. Young et al., October 23, 1982, transcript, Carter Presidency Project, Miller Center of Public Affairs, University of Virginia, Charlottesville, VA; Robert David Johnson, *Congress and the Cold War* (New York: Cambridge University Press, 2005), 245.

29. Jimmy Carter, *White House Diary* (New York: Farrar, Straus and Giroux, 2010), 348.

30. Kaiser, "Nunn Ties Vote on SALT to More Defense Spending"; Cutler interview; Lloyd N. Cutler and Roger C. Molander, "Is There Life after Death for SALT? *International Security* 6, no. 2 (Fall 1981): 8.

31. Joanne Omang, "Carter Won't Boost Arms Outlays for SALT Votes," *Washington Post*, July 29, 1979; "Arms-Pact Debate: A New Script Has Both Sides Winning," *New York Times*, July 30, 1979.

32. "Arms-Pact Debate"; Burton I. Kaufman and Scott Kaufman, *The Presidency of James Earl Carter*, 2nd ed., rev. (Lawrence: University Press of Kansas, 2006), 188, 189.

33. Donald S. Spencer, *The Carter Implosion* (New York: Praeger, 1988), 116.

34. Jimmy Carter, "Inaugural Address," January 20, 1977, Avalon Project, https://avalon.law.yale.edu/20th_century/carter.asp.

35. Charles Mohr, "Vance Tells Senate 3% Arms-Fund Rise Remains 'Essential,'" *New York Times*, July 31, 1979; Robert G. Kaiser, "Vance Says U.S. Will Seek Rise in '81 Arms Budget," *Washington Post*, July 31, 1979.

36. Charles Mohr, "Cranston Sees 'Room for Negotiation' on Arms Pact," *New York Times*, August 3, 1979.

37. Mohr, "Vance Tells Senate," "Kissinger Suggests Senate Link Treaty to More Arms Funds," *New York Times*, August 1, 1979; Robert Kleiman, "Mr. Kissinger's Artful Recipe," *New York Times*, August 2, 1979.

38. Craig R. Whitney, "Soviet Chief of Staff Charges U.S. Foes of Nuclear Pact Distort the Facts," *New York Times*, August 3, 1979.

39. Charles Mohr, "3 Senators Demand Pledge from Carter on Arms-Fund Rise," *New York Times*, August 3, 1979; George C. Wilson and Walter Pincus, "Embarrassment of Riches for the Pentagon," *Washington Post*, August 3, 1979.

40. Justin Galen, "Curing the Nunn Illusion: Striking a Bargain for SALT," *Armed Forces Journal International*, October 1979, 52.

41. George C. Wilson and Walter Pincus, "Defense Budge War Has Carter in Middle," *Washington Post*, August 4, 1979; Tom Morganthau et al., "The SALT Debate Shifts," *Newsweek*, August 15, 1979, 18; Kaufman and Kaufman, *The Presidency of James Earl Carter*, 188.

42. Charles Mohr, "Arms Pact Debate: New Senate Doubts," *New York Times*, August 6, 1979; Tom Morganthau et al., "The SALT Forces Take the Offensive," *Newsweek*, August 6, 1979, 27; Richard Burt, "President Weighing Five-Year Increase in Military Outlays," *New York Times*, August 10, 1979; Cyrus Vance, *Hard Choices* (New York: Simon & Schuster, 1983), 357; Kaufman and Kaufman, *The Presidency of James Earl Carter*, 188; Memorandum with attachments, Peter Tarnoff to Dennis Clift, subject: Materials for the Vice President on SALT and National Defense, September 6, 1979, JCL, RAC Project Number NLC-133-103-2-4-3.

43. Richard Burt, "The Pentagon Budget Battle," *New York Times*, August 31, 1979; Auten, *Carter's Conversion*, 277.

44. Garland A. Haas, *Jimmy Carter and the Politics of Frustration* (Jefferson, NC: McFarland & Company, 1992), 109; Richard C. Thornton, *The Carter Years: Toward a New Global Order* (New York: Paragon House, 1991), 179; Steven V. Roberts, "Congress Faces Key Spending Decisions as Vacation Ends," *New York Times*, September 2, 1979; Charles Mohr, "Senate to Resume Arms Pact Hearings," *New York Times*, September 2, 1979.

45. Nunn, "SALT II and Defense Spending," copy of floor speech, MS106.3.3.5.3.2, Box 3, Folder 8, Strategic Arms Limitation Talks/Treaty, Memos and Analysis, 1978–79, William S. Cohen Papers, Raymond H. Fogler Library, University of

Maine, Orono, ME; Charles Mohr, "Senator Nunn Bids Carter Push for a Big Rise in Defense Spending," *New York Times,* September 8, 1979.

46. George C. Wilson, "White House Called Two-Faced on Defense Spending," *Washington Post,* September 8, 1979.

47. Steven V. Roberts, "Senate Military Bloc Warms to New Carter Arms Plan," *New York Times,* September 13, 1979.

48. Robert G. Kaiser, "Long Is Opposing SALT Pact, Citing Soviet 'Bad Faith,'" *Washington Post,* September 13, 1979; Gloria Duffy, "Crisis Mangling and the Cuban Brigade," *International Security* 8, no. 1 (Summer 1983): 73–74, 79, 83.

49. Punaro, *On War and Politics,* 95; Muravchik, *The Senate and National Security,* 51–52; Heritage Foundation, "Backgrounder: The Carter Defense Budget," June 21, 1977, 2. For background information on the meeting, see Memorandum, Jim McIntyre and Frank Moore, subject: Meeting with Senate Leaders, September 12, 1979, JCL, RAC Project Number NLC-126-18-10-1-0.

50. Robert G. Kaiser, "White House Moves to Shore Up Support of SALT," *Washington Post,* September 14, 1979; Steven V. Roberts, "Carter and Senators Firm in Dispute on Military Fund," *New York Times,* September 14, 1979; Thornton, 396–397.

51. Kaiser, "White House Moves," *Washington Post*; Brzezinski, *Power and Principle,* 345.

52. Robert G. Kaiser, "New Doubts Raised on SALT Vote," *Washington Post,* September 18, 1979.

53. Kaiser, "New Doubts."

54. Richard Burt, "Differing Views on the Defense Budget Could Affect SALT Agreement," *New York Times,* September 23, 1979.

55. Robert G. Kaiser, "Senate Votes for 5% Defense Increase," *Washington Post,* September 19, 1979; Steven V. Roberts, "Senate Approves Military Budget Larger Than Carter Had Wanted," *New York Times,* September 19, 1979; I. M. Destler, "Trade Consensus, SALT Stalemate: Congress and Foreign Policy in the 1970s," in *The New Congress,* ed. Thomas E. Mann and Norman J. Ornstein (Washington, DC: American Enterprise Institute, 1981), 349.

56. Steven V. Roberts, "House Votes Down Budget Bill," *New York Times,* September 20, 1969.

57. Richard Burt, "Differing Views on the Defense Budget Could Affect SALT Agreement," *New York Times,* September 23, 1979;

58. Robert G. Kaiser, "Soviet Troops in Cuba Treading Heavily on SALT Prospects," *Washington Post,* September 22, 1979; Richard Burt, "Issue and Debate: Serious Trouble Develops for Arms Treaty with Soviets," *New York Times,* September 28, 1979.

59. Kaiser, "Soviet Troops in Cuba."

60. Spencer, *The Carter Implosion,* 116; Robert A. Strong, *Working in the World: Jimmy Carter and the Making of American Foreign Policy* (Baton Rouge: Louisiana State University Press, 2000), 222; Charles Mohr, "Panel in Senate Said to Question Verifying of Pact," *New York Times,* October 5, 1979; Robert G. Kaiser, "Selling SALT: A Defense Plan Preview," *Washington Post,* October 5, 1979; Clark R. Mol-

lenhoff, *The President Who Failed* (New York: Macmillan, 1980), 235; Garthoff, *Détente and Confrontation*, 814.

61. "In Summary: SALT Prospects Are Linked to Missiles for Europe," *New York Times*, October 14, 1979; Joseph Fromm, "Why SALT Can't Be Counted Out Yet," *US News & World Report*, October 22, 1979, 48; Auten, *Carter's Conversion*, 277, 278.

62. Strobe Talbott, *Endgame: The Inside Story of SALT II* (New York: Harper & Row, 1980), 187, 189, 190, 207, 223–224; Memorandum, Zbigniew Brzezinski to President Carter, subject: Daily Report, SALT II Ratification, October 12, 1979, JCL, RAC Project Number NLC-17D-22-5-3-0; Memorandum, Cyrus Vance to President Carter, subject: State Department and ACDA Views on the Cruise Missile Definition, March 7, 1978, JCL, RAC Project Number NLC-7-58-2-19-1; Memorandum, Warren Christopher to President Carter, October 3, 1979, JCL, RAC Project Number NLC-7-22-4-8-8; Memorandum, Zbigniew Brzezinski to Cyrus Vance, October 10, 1979, JCL, RAC Project Number NLC-7-22-4-10-5, A. Bohlen, US Department of State, SALT Ratification, 10/12/79, JCL, RAC Project Number NLC-23-13-6-17-8.

63. "Nunn Warns Against Tying Arms Pact to Missiles," *New York Times*, October 24, 1979.

64. Nunn, "Arms Control and Theater Nuclear Modernization," Speech delivered to a German-American Roundtable, sponsored by the Institute for Foreign Policy Analysis, Washington, DC, October 22, 1979, *Atlantic Community Quarterly* 17 (Winter 1979–1980): 437–444; Walter Pincus, "Nunn Backs Updating Tactical Weapons Force in Europe," *Washington Post*, October 25, 1979.

65. Nunn, floor speech, "SALT and National Security: Where Do We Go from Here?" Subseries 11.3, Box 22, SALT II Hearings/Dec 1979, Sam Nunn Papers, Stuart A. Rose Manuscript, Archives, and Rare Book Library, Emory University, Atlanta, GA; Drew Middleton, "Unprepared? Critics Believe Lapses in NATO's Defence Planning Would Let Russians Reach Germany in 48 Hours," *Globe and Mail* (Toronto, Canada), November 5, 1979; Nunn, foreword to *Europe without Defense? 48 Hours That Could Change the Face of the World*, by Robert Close (New York: Pergamon Press, 1979), vii–x.

66. Keefer, *Harold Brown*, 558.

67. Terence Smith, "President Calls for 4.5% Increases in Military Budgets for Five Years," *New York Times*, December 13, 1979.

68. Martin Tolchin, "Proposed Rises in Military Budget Appear to Aid Drive for Arms Pact," *New York Times*, December 14, 1979.

69. Letter from Nineteen Senators to President Carter, December 17, 1979, *Foreign Relations of the United States, 1969–1976*, vol. 33, SALT II, 1972–1980 (Washington, DC: Government Printing Office, 2013), 968–971; George C. Wilson and Edward Walsh, "Carter to Meet 19 Senators 'Concerned' about SALT," *Washington Post*, December 17, 1979; Destler, "Trade Consensus," 353.

70. Wilson and Walsh, "Carter to Meet 19 Senators"; Jimmy Carter, "Strategic Arms Limitation Treaty Letter to 19 Members of the Senate," December 17, 1979, online at Gerhard Peters and John T. Woolley, American Presidency Project, https://www.presidency.ucsb.edu/node/248288.

71. Robert G. Kaiser, "Latest SALT Maneuvers Lift Administration Hopes but Critics Are Confident," *Washington Post*, December 18, 1979.

72. Haas, *Jimmy Carter*, 109; Richard Burt, "Senate Panel Votes Anti-treaty Report," *New York Times*, December 21, 1979; Smith, *Morality, Reason, and Power*, 213; Caldwell, "The Carter Administration, the Senate, and SALT II," 348; Punaro, *On War and Politics*, 94; Congressional Quarterly, *Almanac*, 427, 428; Richard N. Perle, "The Senator and American Arms Control Policy," in *Staying the Course: Henry M. Jackson and National Security*, ed. Dorothy Fosdick (Seattle: University of Washington Press, 1987), 105, 106.

73. John T. Shaw, *Richard Lugar, Statesman of the Senate: Crafting Foreign Policy from Capitol Hill* (Bloomington: Indiana University Press, 2012), 56–57. See also Johnson, *Congress and the Cold War*, 246.

74. Julian E. Zelizer, *Jimmy Carter* (New York: Times Books, 2010), 103; Carter, *Keeping Faith*, 471–472; Robert M. Gates, *From the Shadows: The Ultimate Insider's View of Five Presidents and How They Won the Cold War* (New York: Simon & Schuster, 1996), 133; Brzezinski, *Power and Principle*, 353.

75. Carter, *Keeping Faith*, 475.

76. Hamilton Jordan, *Crisis: The Last Year of the Carter Presidency* (New York: G. P. Putnam's Sons, 1982), 7.

77. "Washington Whispers," *US News & World Report*, May 12, 1980, 16; Tom Wicker, "In the Nation: Is Ron a Reaganite?" *New York Times*, November 23, 1979.

78. Nunn, "Free World Challenges," Address given at St. Gallen University, Zurich, Switzerland, July 11, 1980, *Atlantic Community Quarterly* 18 (Fall 1980), 272.

79. Congressional Quarterly, *Almanac*, 96th Congress, 2nd session, 1980 (Washington, DC: Congressional Quarterly News Features, 1981), 37, 135.

Chapter 4. Arms and Influence

1. Ronald Reagan, "First Inaugural Address," January 20, 1981, Avalon Project, https://avalon.law.yale.edu/20th_century/reagan1.asp; C-SPAN, President Reagan 1981 Inaugural Address, accessed February 1, 2020, https://www.c-span.org/video/?182163-1/president-reagan-1981-inaugural-address; Library of Congress, US Presidential Inaugurations: Ronald Reagan, accessed February 1, 2020, https://www.loc.gov/rr/program/bib/inaugurations/reagan/index.html; Lou Cannon, "Ronald Reagan: Foreign Affairs," Miller Center of Public Affairs, University of Virginia, accessed February 1, 2020, https://millercenter.org/president/reagan/foreign-affairs; Lou Cannon, "Ronald Reagan: Life in Brief," Miller Center of Public Affairs, University of Virginia, accessed February 1, 2020, https://millercenter.org/president/reagan/life-in-brief.

2. Congressional Quarterly, *Almanac*, 97th Cong., 1st Sess., 1981 (Washington, DC: Congressional Quarterly News Features, 1982), 3, 8.

3. Cannon, "Ronald Reagan: Foreign Affairs"; Congressional Quarterly, *Almanac*, 18, 192.

4. Ronald E. Powaski, *March to Armageddon: The United States and the Nuclear Arms Race, 1939 to Present* (New York: Oxford University Press, 1987), 184.

5. Kenneth Kitts, *Presidential Commissions and National Security: The Politics of Damage Control* (Boulder, CO: Lynne Rienner, 2006), 73.

6. Congressional Quarterly, *Almanac*, 202, 212; "Senate Votes Military Funds in Victory for Reagan," *New York Times*, May 15, 1981; Gary Hart, "The Case for Military Reform," *Wall Street Journal*, January 23, 1981; Gary Hart, "An Agenda for More Military Reform," *New York Times*, May 13, 1986.

7. Congressional Quarterly, *Almanac*, 14, 18, 191, 193–194, 325; Richard McCulley, *History of the Senate Committee on Armed Services, 1947–1999*, unpublished manuscript, file: Armed Services Committee History, 2000 draft, US Senate Historical Office, Washington, DC.

8. Kitts, *Presidential Commissions*, 73, 74; Robert Standish Norris and Thomas B. Cochran, *US-USSR Strategic Offensive Nuclear Forces 1946–1989*, NWD 90-2 (Washington, DC: Natural Resources Defense Council, 1990), n.p., Tables 3 and 4.

9. Ronald Reagan, National Security Decision Directive 12, Strategic Forces Modernization Program, October 1, 1981; US Strategic Command, Fact File: Intercontinental Ballistic Missiles, accessed February 1, 2020, https://web.archive .org/web/20040408091417/http://www.stratcom.mil/FactSheetshtml/ballistic _missiles.htm; Nuclear Weapon Archive, The Peacekeeper (MX) Missile, accessed February 1, 2020, http://nuclearweaponarchive.org/Usa/Weapons/Mx .html.

10. Wade Boese, "United States Retires MX Missile," *Arms Control Today*, n.d., accessed February 1, 2020, https://www.armscontrol.org/act/2005_10/OCT-MX.

11. Congressional Quarterly, *Almanac*, 18–19, 195.

12. Congressional Quarterly, 19, 194, 200.

13. Steven V. Roberts, "Senators Reject Plan for Placing MX Missile in Silos," *New York Times*, December 3, 1981.

14. Stephen Webbe, "Reagan Scorns Senate Rejection of Silo-Based MX Missile Plans," *Christian Science Monitor*, December 4, 1981.

15. Sam Nunn, "Arms Control: What Should We Do," *Washington Post*, November 12, 1981.

16. Congressional Quarterly, *Almanac*, 19, 198; Nunn, Floor Speech: "MX—The Problem of Survivability," December 2, 1981, Subseries 6.5, Box 170, Established Files: MX (3), Sam Nunn Papers, Stuart A. Rose Manuscript, Archives, and Rare Book Library, Emory University, Atlanta, GA.

17. Roberts, "Senators Reject Plan."

18. Senators William Cohen, Sam Nunn, Dan Quayle, and Warren Rudman to Howard Baker, December 3, 1981, MS106.3.3.5.2, Box 3, Folder 8, MX Missile, 1981–83, William S. Cohen Papers, Raymond H. Fogler Library, University of Maine, Orono, ME; Congressional Quarterly, *Almanac*, 196; Webbe, "Reagan Scorns Senate Rejection"; Roberts, "Senators Reject Plan"; Congressional Quarterly, *Congress and the Nation*, vol. 4, 1981–1984 (Washington, DC: Congressional Quarterly, 1985), 208; Lou Cannon, *Reagan* (New York: G. P. Putnam, 1982), 393; James M. Lindsay, *Congress and Nuclear Weapons* (Baltimore, MD: Johns Hopkins University Press, 1991), 65.

19. Steven V. Roberts, "National Desk," *New York Times*, December 5, 1981.
20. Merrill Sheils et al., "Searching for a Strategy," *Newsweek*, June 8, 1981, 30.
21. Sheils et al., "Searching for a Strategy," 30.
22. Brad Knickerbocker, "Defense Reform Group in Congress Tries to Reorder Pentagon Priorities," *Christian Science Monitor*, December 16, 1981.
23. Richard Halloran, "Caucus Challenges Defense Concepts," *New York Times*, January 12, 1982.
24. Hedrick Smith, "Reagan Forced by Events Abroad to Temper His Hard Policies," *New York Times*, January 22, 1982; Brad Knickerbocker, "America's Defense: What Price Security?" *Christian Science Monitor*, January 29, 1982; Knickerbocker, "Reagan Push for Nuclear Arms, Civil Defense Stirs Debate," *Christian Science Monitor*, February 1, 1982.
25. Brad Knickerbocker, "Congress Aims to Cut Defense—but Where?" *Christian Science Monitor*, February 11, 1982; Charles Mohr, "Fears about Deficit Imperil Effort to Improve Weapons Acquisitions," *New York Times*, March 14, 1982.
26. "Greater Outlays on U.S. Arms Urged," *New York Times*, March 9, 1982.
27. Richard Halloran, "Criticism Rises on Reagan's Plan for 5-Year Growth of the Military," *New York Times*, March 22, 1982.
28. Hedrick Smith, "The Nuclear Freeze; News Analysis," *New York Times*, April 1, 1982; Congressional Quarterly, *Almanac*, 97th Cong., 2nd Sess., 1982 (Washington, DC: Congressional Quarterly News Features,1982), 13; Cannon, *Reagan*, 393; "Senate Unit Said to Bar Silo Use for MX Missile," *New York Times*, March 30, 1982; Ronald Reagan, "The President's News Conference," March 31, 1982, online at Gerhard Peters and John T. Woolley, American Presidency Project, https://www.presidency.ucsb.edu/node/244769.
29. Brad Knickerbocker, "New Calls in U.S. to Bring the Boys Home from Europe," *Christian Science Monitor*, May 5, 1982; Stanley Sloan, "Managing the NATO Alliance: Congress and Burdensharing," *Journal of Policy Analysis and Management* 4, no. 3 (Spring 1985): 403.
30. Ronald Reagan, "Address at Commencement Exercises at Eureka College in Illinois," May 9, 1982, online at Gerhard Peters and John T. Woolley, American Presidency Project, https://www.presidency.ucsb.edu/node/245666.
31. Strobe Talbott, "U.S.-Soviet Nuclear Arms Control: Where We Are and How We Got Here," Occasional Paper OPS-001, RAND/UCLA Center for the Study of Soviet International Behavior, January 1985, 6.
32. Quoted in Strobe Talbott, *Deadly Gambits: The Reagan Administration and the Stalemate in Nuclear Arms Control* (New York: Vintage Books, 1985), 273.
33. Talbot, *Deadly Gambits*, 274.
34. Nunn, *NATO: Can the Alliance Be Saved? Report of Senator Sam Nunn to the Committee on Armed Services, United States Senate*, May 13, 1982, *Atlantic Community Quarterly* 20, no. 2 (Summer 1982): 126. Nunn also wrote an article to reach a broader audience that provides his analysis and recommendations. See Sam Nunn, "NATO: Saving the Alliance," *Washington Quarterly* 5, no. 3 (Summer 1982): 19–29.
35. Nunn, *NATO: Can the Alliance Be Saved?*, 126–128.

36. Nunn, 128–129, 132.

37. Nunn, 129–132, 134–136.

38. Leslie H. Gelb, "Weinberger Calls His 'Basic Outlook' Unchanged," *New York Times*, June 16, 1982; Ronald Reagan, National Security Study Directive 1-82, US National Security Strategy, February 5, 1982; Ronald Reagan, National Security Decision Directive 32, US National Security Strategy, May 20, 1982.

39. Eric Gelman, "Nunn's Nuclear Safety Valve," *Newsweek*, June 21, 1982, 15; Barry M. Blechman, "Confidence-Building through Nuclear Risk Reduction Centers," in *Defending Peace and Freedom: Toward Strategic Stability in the Year 2000*, ed. Brent Scowcroft, R. James Woolsey, cochairman, and Thomas H. Etzold, rapporteur (Lanham, MD: University Press of America, 1988), 185; "Democrats Cool to Warhead Plan," *Boston Globe*, May 10, 1982.

40. George C. Wilson, "Congressional Debate about Defense Produces More Accord Than Conflict," *Washington Post*, October 6, 1982; Philip Geyelin, "What National Security Debate?" *Washington Post*, October 15, 1982. For a discussion of the debate topics, see Memorandum, Record to Nunn, Themes for the October defense debate, September 20, 1982: and Memorandum, Jim McGovern to the Majority Staff, subject: Preparation of Senator Tower for a National Security Debate Sponsored by the League of Women Voters, September 23, 1982, Subseries 11.3, Box 1, file, League Debate, SNP.

41. Richard Halloran, "Time Nears for Critical Decisions on Defense," *New York Times*, November 14, 1982; Leslie H. Gelb, "Reagan Plans Speech Monday to Offer Moscow Better Ties," *New York Times*, November 19, 1982.

42. Ronald Reagan, "Statement on Deployment of the MX Missile," November 22, 1982, online by Gerhard Peters and John T. Woolley, American Presidency Project, https://www.presidency.ucsb.edu/node/245689; Ronald Reagan, National Security Decision Directive 69, The M-X Program, November 22, 1982; Curtis Wilkie and Benjamin Taylor, "Reagan Says MX Needed to Deter War," *Boston Globe*, December 12, 1982.

43. Richard Halloran, "3 of 5 Joint Chiefs Asked Delay on MX," *New York Times*, December 9, 1982; George Shultz, *Turmoil and Triumph: My Years as Secretary of State* (New York: Charles Scribner's Sons, 1993), 248.

44. Wilkie and Taylor, "Reagan Says MX Needed"; Steven V. Roberts, "Senators Pursuing a Delicate MX Compromise," *New York Times*, December 14, 1982.

45. Ronald Reagan, "Question-and-Answer Session with Reporters on Production of the MX Missile," December 14, 1982, online by Gerhard Peters and John T. Woolley, American Presidency Project, https://www.presidency.ucsb.edu/node/244794; Steven R. Weisman, "President Agrees to Freeze Money for Building MX," *New York Times*, December 15, 1982; Tom Morganthau et al., "The Games Lame Ducks Play," *Newsweek*, December 27, 1982, 16; Congressional Quarterly, *Almanac*, 13.

46. Melinda Beck et al., "Defending the United States," *Newsweek*, December 20, 1982, 22.

Chapter 5. On the Road to Arms Control

1. "William Sebastian Cohen," *Biographical Directory of the United States Congress,* https://bioguideretro.congress.gov/Home/MemberDetails?memIndex=C000 598; "About William S. Cohen," Raymond H. Fogler Library, University of Maine, Orono, ME, https://library.umaine.edu/cohen/bio/bio2.htm. Both were accessed February 1, 2020.

2. Nunn, "Critical Defense Choices," Southern Center for International Studies, Papers on International Issues no. 4, January 1983, in *Sam Nunn on Arms Control,* ed. Kenneth W. Thompson, vol. 5 (Lanham, MD: University Press of America, 1987), 73.

3. William S. Cohen, "How We Got from There to Here," *Washington Post,* October 9, 1983. For a detailed explanation of the build-down proposal, see Alton Frye, "Strategic Build-Down: A Context for Restraint," *Foreign Affairs* 62, no. 2 (Winter 1983–1984): 292–317.

4. Cohen, "How We Got from There to Here"; Cohen, "A Guaranteed Arms Build-Down," *Washington Post,* January 3, 1983; National Academy of Sciences, Committee on International Security and Arms Control, *Nuclear Arms Control: Background and Issues* (Washington, DC: National Academies Press, 1985), 61.

5. Cohen, "How We Got from There to Here"; "Nuclear Survivability and Stability," Floor Statement, February 3, 1983, and "Cohen and Nunn Introduce Arms 'Build-down Resolution,'" press release, February 3, 1983, Subseries 6.5, Box 170, file, Build-down Proposal, both in Sam Nunn Papers (SNP), Stuart A. Rose Manuscript, Archives, and Rare Book Library, Emory University, Atlanta, GA; Senators Cohen and Nunn, Dear Colleague letter, February 8, 1983, MS 106.3.3.5.3.4, Box 8, Folder 5, Nuclear Freeze, 1983–84, William S. Cohen Papers (WCP), Raymond H. Fogler Library, University of Maine, Orono, ME.

6. Richard Halloran, "Reagan's Arms Budget Assailed at Senate Hearing," *New York Times,* February 2, 1983; David Rogers, "Weinberger, Panel Clash over Cutting Defense Spending," *Boston Globe,* February 2, 1983; Nunn, "Critical Defense Choices," 73–93.

7. Robert McFarlane, with Zofia Smardz, *Special Trust* (New York: Cadell & Davies, 1994), 223.

8. Kenneth W. Thompson, ed., *Foreign Policy in the Reagan Administration,* vol. 3, Miller Center of Public Affairs, Reagan Oral History Series (Lanham, MD: University Press of America, 1993), 39–40.

9. McFarlane, *Special Trust,* 9, 168.

10. Quoted in Strobe Talbott, *Deadly Gambits: The Reagan Administration and the Stalemate in Nuclear Arms Control* (New York: Vintage Books, 1985), 306–307.

11. McFarlane, *Special Trust,* 168, 197, 224; Punaro, *On War and Politics,* 112, 113; Mary McGrory, "Salesman Reagan Is Trying to Unload a Clunker on Congress," *Washington Post,* May 12, 1983.

12. Kenneth Kitts, "The Politics of Armageddon: The Scowcroft Commission and the MX Missile," in *Presidential Commissions and National Security: The Politics of Damage Control* (Boulder, CO: Lynne Rienner, 2006), 78–80.

13. Ronald Reagan, Executive Order 12400, President's Commission on Strategic Forces, January 3, 1983, Ronald Reagan Presidential Library (RRL), https://www.reaganlibrary.gov/research/speeches/10383a.

14. Kitts, "The Politics of Armageddon," 81–82.

15. Brad Knickerbocker, "A Basic Rethinking of Strategy Seen in MX Commission's Hard Look," *Christian Science Monitor,* February 10, 1983; Steven V. Roberts, "Some Defense Committee Members Won't Be Firing Blanks," *New York Times,* February 13, 1983.

16. Ronald Reagan, "Remarks at the Annual Convention of the National Association of Evangelicals in Orlando, Florida," March 8, 1983, RRL, https://www.reaganlibrary.gov/research/speeches/30883b.

17. Hedrick Smith, "Would a Space-Age Defense Ease Tensions or Create Them?" *New York Times,* March 27, 1983.

18. Nunn, "The Need to Reshape Military Strategy," in *Nuclear Arms: Ethics, Strategy, Politics,* ed. R. James Woolsey (San Francisco, CA: ICS Press, 1984), 6, 239–249; Charles Mohr, "2 Senators Urging Arms Policy Shift," *New York Times,* March 21, 1983.

19. William S. Cohen, "Consensus on Arms Control," *New York Times,* March 22, 1983; Douglas C. Waller, *Congress and the Nuclear Freeze: An Inside Look at the Politics of a Mass Movement* (Amherst: University of Massachusetts Press, 1987), 242; Cosponsors of Build down Resolution, MS 106.3.3.5.3.4, Box 2, Folder 6, Build Down, Briefing Book, Tab C, 1983, WCP.

20. Steven V. Roberts, "15 Senators Press Reagan on A-Arms," *New York Times,* March 31, 1983; Hedrick Smith, "Reagan's Tactics on Security Front," *New York Times,* April 7, 1983; Smith, "Officials Say MX Study May Lead to a New Arms-Control Strategy," *New York Times,* April 10, 1983; Kitts, "The Politics of Armageddon," 87–88; Frank Greve, "MX Opponents Hope to Hold Edge, but Defections Have Already Begun," *Philadelphia Inquirer,* April 13, 1983; James M. Lindsay, *Congress and Nuclear Weapons* (Baltimore, MD: Johns Hopkins University Press, 1991), 67.

21. President's Commission on Strategic Forces, *Report of the President's Commission on Strategic Forces* (Washington, DC: The Commission, April 1983), 1–29; Ronald Reagan, "Letter to Congressional Leaders Reporting on the Recommendations in the Report of the President's Commission on Strategic Forces," April 19, 1983, RRL, https://www.reaganlibrary.gov/research/speeches/41983b; George Shultz, *Turmoil and Triumph: My Years as Secretary of State* (New York: Charles Scribner's Sons, 1993), 358.

22. Steven V. Roberts, "Joint Chiefs Back Reagan's MX Plan," *New York Times,* April 22, 1983; Senate Committee on Armed Services, "Senators Comment on DOD Confidence-building Measures," press release, April 12, 1983, Subseries 6.5, Box 170, file: Early Nuclear Risk Reduction, SNP.

23. Cohen, "How We Got from There to Here"; Eric Gelman, "Will Congress 'Build Down' the MX?" *Newsweek,* May 2, 1983, 21.

24. Senators William Cohen, Sam Nunn, and Charles Percy to President Ronald

Reagan, April 29, 1983, MS 106.3.3.5.2, Box 3, Folder 7, Strategic Weapons/MX Missile, 1981–83, WCP; Steven V. Roberts, "Lawmakers Vow to Block the MX unless Reagan Backs Arms Limits," *New York Times*, May 3, 1983; Cohen, "How We Got from There to Here"; Hedrick Smith, "Pressures Build for Arms Control Progress," *New York Times*, May 8, 1983; Smith, "Reagan Calls Meeting on Arms Talks," *New York Times*, May 10, 1983.

25. Strobe Talbott, "Buildup and Breakdown," *Foreign Affairs* 62, no. 3 (Spring 1984): 606–607; National Conference of Catholic Bishops, "The Challenge of Peace: God's Promise and Our Response," Pastoral Letter on War and Peace by the National Conference of Catholic Bishops, May 3, 1983, http://www.usccb.org /upload/challenge-peace-gods-promise-our-response-1983.pdf.

26. Brad Knickerbocker, "US Lawmakers Ask for New Arms Control Initiatives in Exchange for Backing MX," *Christian Science Monitor*, May 11, 1983; McGrory, "Salesman Reagan Is Trying to Unload a Clunker"; Cohen, "How We Got from There to Here"; David M. Alpern et al., "New Push for an Arms Pact," *Newsweek*, May 16, 1983, 24; Barry M. Blechman, "The New Congressional Role in Arms Control," in *A Question of Balance: The President, the Congress, and Foreign Policy*, ed. Thomas E. Mann (Washington, DC: Brookings Institution Press, 1990), 125; "Pentagon's Perle Cautious on 'Build Down' & Arms Commission," *Defense Daily*, May 11, 1983, 59.

27. Ronald Reagan, "Letter to Three Senators Concerning the Strategic Moderniza-tion Program and Nuclear Arms Reduction," May 12, 1983, RRL, https://www .reaganlibrary.gov/research/speeches/51283c.

28. Cohen, "How We Got from There to Here"; Lou Cannon and George C. Wilson, "Reagan Reassures Congress, Is Rewarded with MX Vote," *Washington Post*, May 12, 1983; Steven V. Roberts, "MX Plan Clears Another Hurdle by a 17–11 Vote," *New York Times*, May 13, 1983; Francis X. Clines, "Is It Bipartisanship or Is It Symbiosis?" *New York Times*, May 16, 1983.

29. Francis X. Clines, "Reagan Backs Better Emergency Links with Soviets," *New York Times*, May 25, 1983; Ronald Reagan, "Remarks to Reporters Announcing Endorsement of the Defense Department Recommendations for Direct Com-munication Links between the United States and the Soviet Union," May 24, 1983, RRL, https://www.reaganlibrary.gov/research/speeches/52483b; Steven V. Roberts, "Senate by 59 to 39, Votes $625 Million for Testing MX," *New York Times*, May 26, 1983; Julia Malone, "How Reagan Convinced Congress to Back the MX," *Christian Science Monitor*, May 26, 1983; Steven V. Roberts, "If the MX Is Near, Politics of '84 Can't Be Far Away," *New York Times*, May 27, 1983.

30. Leslie H. Gelb, "Aides Say Reagan Will Modify Plan on Strategic Arms," *New York Times*, June 8, 1983; Cohen, "How We Got from There to Here."

31. Hedrick Smith, "U.S. Presses Soviets for Big Reductions in Its ICBM Force," *New York Times*, June 22, 1983; Cohen, "How We Got from There to Here"; Smith, "Future of MX: Tightrope for Reagan," *New York Times*, June 27, 1983; "This Just In," *New Republic*, July 18, 1983, 9; Nunn, Testimony before Commit-tee on Foreign Relations, June 21, 1983, MS 106.3.3.5.2, Box 2, Folder 4, Build

Down: Analysis, 1983; and Cohen, Statement before the Senate Foreign Relations Committee, June 21, 1983, MS 106.3.3.5.2, Box 2, Folder 6, Build Down, Briefing Book, Tab A: Cohen Testimony to SFRC, 6/21/83, both in WCP.

32. Senate Committee on Armed Services, *Omnibus Defense Authorization Act*, 1984, 98th Cong., 1st Sess., 1983, S. Rep. 98-174, 512–513.

33. Nunn to Cohen, Percy, and staff, Memorandum, June 29, 1983, MS 106.3.3.5.3.4, Box 2, Folder 4, Build Down: Analysis, 1983–84, WCP.

34. Smith, "Future of MX: Tightrope for Reagan."

35. Brad Knickerbocker, "Alternate Deterrents: Trying to Keep NATO from Leaning Too Heavily on Nuclear Weapons," *Christian Science Monitor*, July 21, 1983; Knickerbocker, "Arms Control Talks Reopen," *Christian Science Monitor*, September 15, 1983.

36. B. Drummond Ayres Jr., "MX Proponents in House Bracing for Further Votes on the Missile," *New York Times*, July 22, 1983; Brad Knickerbocker, "Reagan Defense Buildup Prompts Strategy Debate," *Christian Science Monitor*, July 28, 1983.

37. Robert G. Kaufman, *Henry M. Jackson: A Life in Politics* (Seattle: University of Washington Press, 2000), 429–431; David Shribman, "Senator Henry Jackson Is Dead at 71," *New York Times*, September 3, 1983.

38. Paul Szoldra, "There Are Many Parallels between the MH17 Crash and When Russia Shot Down a Civilian Airliner in 1983," *Business Insider*, July 20, 2014, https://www.businessinsider.com.au/ussr-shootdown-korean-air-2014-7.

39. Quoted in Kaufman, *Henry M. Jackson*, 431–432.

40. Bernard Weinraub, "If the Question Is Military, Ask Nunn," *New York Times*, September 20, 1983.

41. Weinraub, "If the Question."

42. Cohen, Nunn, and Percy to Brent Scowcroft, September 9, 1983, MS 106.3.3.5.3. 4, Box 2, Folder 2, Build Down, 1981–83, WCP; Cohen, "How We Got from There to Here"; Martin Tolchin, "3 Senators Propose 2-Step Plan for Cut in Nuclear Weapons," *New York Times*, September 12, 1983; Brad Knickerbocker, "Arms Control Talks Reopen," *Christian Science Monitor*, September 15, 1983; Knickerbocker, "National Security and Nuclear Arms," *Christian Science Monitor*, September 22, 1983; R. James Woolsey, "The Politics of Vulnerability: 1980–83," in *Nuclear Arms: Ethics, Strategy, Politics*, ed. R. James Woolsey (San Francisco: ICS Press, 1984), 264.

43. Strobe Talbott, "U.S.-Soviet Nuclear Arms Control: Where We Are and How We Got Here," Occasional Paper OPS-001, RAND/UCLA Center for the Study of Soviet International Behavior, January 1985, 7, 8; Talbott, *Deadly Gambits*, 334; Talbott, "Buildup and Breakdown."

44. Talbott, "U.S.-Soviet Nuclear Arms Control," 8.

45. Congressional Quarterly, *Almanac*, 98th Cong., 1st Sess., 1983 (Washington, DC: Congressional Quarterly News features, 1984), 120; Kenneth P. Werrell, "The Weapon the US Military Did Not Want: The Modern Strategic Cruise Missile," *Journal of Military History* 53 (October 1989): 430–431, 432; Avis Bohlen, William Burns, Steven Pifer, and John Woolworth, *The Treaty on Intermediate*

Range Nuclear Forces: History and Lessons Learned, Arms Control Series Paper no. 9 (Washington, DC: Brookings Institution, 2012), 1–2, 7, 9–10.

46. Blechman, "The New Congressional Role in Arms Control," 112.

47. Hedrick Smith, *The Power Game: How Washington Works* (New York: Random House, 1987), 17.

48. Cohen, "How We Got from There to Here"; Bernard Gwertzman, "Reagan Approves New Arms Control Offer for Geneva," *New York Times,* October 4, 1983; Smith, *The Power Game,* 548–549; Talbott, *Deadly Gambits,* 337–339.

49. Talbott, *Deadly Gambits,* 339. For an analysis of how the Senate uses its advice and consent power to make foreign policy, see David Auerswald and Forrest Maltzman, "Policymaking through Advice and Consent: Treaty Consideration by the United States Senate," *Journal of Politics* 65, no. 4 (November 2003): 1097–1102, 1106.

50. Smith, *The Power Game,* 547–548; Blechman, "The New Congressional Role in Arms Control," 111; Talbott, *Deadly Gambits,* 338–339.

51. Alton Frye, interviewed by Don Nicoll, April 12, 2001, MOH 268, transcript, Edmund S. Muskie Oral History Collection, Bates College, Lewiston, ME; Daniel Southerland, "Placing Checks on Nuclear Chess," *Christian Science Monitor,* October, 5, 1983; Blechman, "The New Congressional Role in Arms Control," 113; Talbott, *Deadly Gambits,* 337, 338–339.

52. Steven P. Weisman, "Reagan Promotes New Arms Officers," *New York Times,* October 5, 1983; Talbott, "Buildup and Breakdown," 612; Ronald Reagan, "Remarks to Reporters Announcing New United States Initiatives in the Strategic Arms Reduction Talks," October 4, 1983, RRL, https://www.reaganlibrary.gov/research/speeches/100483d; White House, Office of the Press Secretary, fact sheet, Presidential Statement, October 4, 1983, Subseries 6.5, Box 171, file, Arms Control, SNP.

53. Herbert Scoville, "Build-Down (Doom)?" *New York Times,* October 11, 1983; Christopher Paine, "Breakdown on the Build-Down," *Bulletin of the Atomic Scientists,* December 1983, 4–6; Nunn, "Reducing the Nuclear Threat," *Atlanta Journal-Constitution,* October 14, 1983, in *Sam Nunn on Arms Control,* ed. Kenneth W. Thompson (Lanham, MD: University Press of America, 1987), vol. 5, 49–52.

54. Congressional Quarterly, *Almanac,* 204.

55. Nunn, Oral History, September 5, 1996, Sam Nunn Private Papers, Nuclear Threat Initiative offices, Washington, DC; Richard K. Betts, "A Joint Nuclear Risk Reduction Control Center," *Parameters* 15, no. 1 (Spring 1985): 43; Charles Mohr, "Talks Urged for Averting Accidental Nuclear War," *New York Times,* November 25, 1983; "A Nuclear Risk Reduction System: Report of the Nunn/Warner Working Group on Nuclear Risk Reduction," *Survival* 26, no. 3 (May–June 1984): 133–135; David E. Hoffman, *The Dead Hand: The Untold Story of the Cold War Arms Race and Its Dangerous Legacy* (New York: Doubleday, 2009), 382.

56. Nunn, Oral History; Sam Nunn and John W. Warner, "Reducing the Risk of Nuclear War," *Washington Quarterly* 7, no. 2 (Spring 1984), 3–7; John Borawski, "U.S.-Soviet Move toward Risk Reduction," *Bulletin of the Atomic Scientists,* July–August 1987, 17; Charles Mohr, "Talks Urged for Averting Accidental Nuclear

War," *New York Times,* November 25, 1983; Ronald Reagan, "Remarks on Signing the Soviet–United States Nuclear Risk Reduction Center Agreement," September 15, 1987, RRL, https://www.reaganlibrary.gov/research/speeches/091587b.

57. B. Bruce-Briggs, Letter to the editor, *International Security* 9, no. 1 (Summer 1984): 219.

58. Stephen S. Rosenfeld, "Getting Practical about Nuclear Risk," *Washington Post,* November 25, 1983; Robert S. McNamara, "What the U.S. Can Do," *Newsweek,* December 5, 1983, 48; Russell Watson et al., "Can We Cut the Risk?," *Newsweek,* December 5, 1983, 44; North Atlantic Treaty Organization, "NATO Update—1983," http://www.nato.int/docu/update/80-89/1983e.htm; "Arms Control Chronology," *Christian Science Monitor,* November 27, 1984; Doomsday Clock Timeline, 1984, editorial, "Three Minutes to Midnight," *Bulletin of the Atomic Scientists,* https://thebulletin.org/sites/default/files/1984%20Clock%20Statement.pdf.

Chapter 6. Reducing Risks, Sharing Burdens

1. Ronald Reagan, National Security Decision Directive 119, Strategic Defense Initiative, January 6, 1984; Charles Mohr, "Missile Defense: Now a Go-Slow Policy," *New York Times,* March 23, 1984.

2. Richard Halloran, "Democrats Vow to Reduce Pentagon Outlay for 1985," *New York Times,* February 2, 1984; Charles Mohr, "Weinberger Backs $20.5 Billion Bomber Estimate," *New York Times,* February 16, 1984.

3. Halloran, "Democrats Vow."

4. Charles Mohr, "Pentagon Backs Advanced Defense Despite Flaws," *New York Times,* March 9, 1984; "Senator Nunn's Involvement in the Strategic Defense Initiative and Anti-Ballistic Missile Treaty Interpretation Debate," n.d., and "Talking Points on SDI," n.d., Subseries 11.3, Box 23, SDI, Sam Nunn Papers (SNP), Stuart A. Rose Manuscript, Archives, and Rare Book Library, Emory University, Atlanta, GA.

5. Mohr, "Missile Defense."

6. Walter Pincus, "Europe Shielded Too," *Washington Post,* April 25, 1984; "Talking Points on SDI."

7. Steven V. Roberts, "Experts in Congress See More Cuts in Arms Budget Reagan Trimmed," *New York Times,* May 5, 1984; Tom Wicker, "The End of Arms Control," *New York Times,* May 25, 1984; "Senator Nunn's Involvement," Subseries 11.3, Box 23, SDI, SNP.

8. "Senate Panel Cuts Reagan Bid for Less than the House," *Wall Street Journal,* May 18, 1984; Fred Kaplan, "Defense Officials Say Forces Stronger than Four Years Ago," *Boston Globe,* May 16, 1984.

9. "Senate Panel Cuts Reagan Bid"; Hedrick Smith, "Arms Control: Election-Year Pressure on Reagan," *New York Times,* June 13, 1984; Dennis Farney, "Senate Urges Reagan to Observe SALT II as Concern over U.S.-Soviet Ties Grows," *Wall Street Journal,* June 20, 1984.

10. Senate Committee on Foreign Relations, *Hearing before the Committee on Foreign*

Relations on S.Res. 329, 98th Cong., 2nd Sess., April 4, 1984, 1, 6, 68; Letter from Nunn and Warner to Reagan, May 16, 1983, Subseries 6.5, Box 170, file, Early Nuclear Risk Reduction, SNP. See also Roland McElroy, *The Best President the Nation Never Had* (Macon, GA: Mercer University Press, 2017), 189.

11. Smith, "Arms Control"; Sam Nunn, "Nuclear Risk Reduction," in *Sam Nunn on Arms Control,* ed. Kenneth W. Thompson, W. Alton Jones Foundation Series on Arms Control, vol. 5 (Lanham, MD: University Press of America, 1987), 53–57; "Nuclear Safeguard Idea Voted," *New York Times,* June 16, 1984; Sam Nunn and John W. Warner, "US-Soviet Cooperation in Countering Nuclear Terrorism: The Role of Risk Reduction Centers," in *Preventing Nuclear Terrorism: The Report and Papers of the International Task Force on Prevention of Nuclear Terrorism,* ed. Paul Leventhal and Yonah Alexander (Lexington, MA: Lexington Books 1987), 387; Senate Committee on Foreign Relations, *Hearing before the Committee on Foreign Relations on S.Res. 329,* 6, 9.

12. Sam Nunn, "Is the Nunn-Roth Approach to the U.S. Role in NATO Sound?" *Congressional Digest* 63, nos. 8–9 (August–September 1984): 212, 214, 216, 218; S. Amdt. 3268 to S. 2723, *Omnibus Defense Authorization Act for Fiscal Year 1985,* 98th Cong., 2nd Sess., *Congressional Record* 130, no. 85, daily edition (June 20, 1984): S7878; Nunn Amendment, MS 106.3.3.5.3.4, Box 7, Folder 10, North Atlantic Treaty Organization, 1982–86, William S. Cohen Papers (WCP), Raymond H. Fogler Library, University of Maine, Orono, ME. See also John Duffield, *Power Rules: The Evolution of NATO's Conventional Force Posture* (Stanford, CA: Stanford University Press, 1995), 225–226.

13. Martin Tolchin, "Senate Bars Limit on Military Role in Latin America," *New York Times,* June 19, 1984; Helen Dewar, "Reagan Fights Nunn Bid to Cut Troops in Europe," *Washington Post,* June 20, 1984; S. Amdt. 3268 to S. 2723, *Congressional Record.*

14. Roth, quoted in Simon Duke, *The Burdensharing Debate: A Reassessment* (New York: St. Martin's Press, 1993), 78; Nunn and Roth, "Dear Colleague" letter, June 18, 1984, SASC Box 2, Tower Speeches and Nunn Amendment, Nunn Dear Colleague file, Senate Papers of James R. Locher III (JLP), Special Collections, National Defense University Library, Washington, DC.

15. Phil Williams, "The Nunn Amendment, Burden-Sharing, and US Troops in Europe," *Survival* 26, no. 1 (January–February 1985): 4; Richard L. Kugler, *Commitment to Purpose: How Alliance Partnership Won the Cold War* (Santa Monica, CA: RAND, 1993), 425–426.

16. Williams, "The Nunn Amendment," 4.

17. David M. Abshire, *Preventing World War III: A Realistic Grand Strategy* (New York: Harper & Row, 1988), 73; Stanley Sloan, "Managing the NATO Alliance: Congress and Burdensharing," *Journal of Policy Analysis and Management* 4, no. 3 (Spring 1985): 404; Nunn and Roth, "Dear Colleague" letter with Nunn-Roth Amendment attached, June 18, 1984, MS 106.3.3.5.3.4, Box 7, Folder 10, North Atlantic Treaty Organization, 1982–86, WCP.

18. Kugler, *Commitment to Purpose,* 423.

19. Abshire, *Preventing World War III,* 67–68.

20. Nunn, floor speech, NATO Burdensharing Amendment, June 18, 1984, Box 172, ABM-Buy America, SNP; Weinberger to Tower, June 20, 1984, SASC Box 2, Tower Speeches and Nunn Amendment, Letters file, JLP; Helen Dewar, "Reagan Fights Nunn Bid to Cut Troops in Europe," *Washington Post,* June 20, 1984.

21. Congressional Quarterly, *Almanac,* 98th Cong., 2nd Sess., 1984 (Washington, DC: Congressional Quarterly News Features, 1985), 66–67; Dennis Farney, "Senate Defeats Plan Tying U.S. Troops to NATO Spending," *Wall Street Journal,* June 21, 1984.

22. Congressional Quarterly, *Almanac,* 67; Robert Bowie, "Nunn Amendment: NATO Must Do More on Conventional Arms," *Christian Science Monitor,* June 29, 1984.

23. Abshire, *Preventing World War III,* 74; Helen Dewar, "Nunn Loses Bid to Cut U.S. Forces," *Washington Post,* June 21, 1984; Wayne Biddle, "Senate Bars Move to Reduce Troops with NATO Forces," *New York Times,* June 21, 1985; Williams, "The Nunn Amendment," 6.

24. Pat Towell, "Nunn Loses Round on Burden Sharing," *Congressional Quarterly (CQ) Weekly Report,* June 23, 1984, 1480.

25. Bowie, "Nunn Amendment."

26. Stephen S. Rosenfeld, "Putting a Test to Europe," *Washington Post,* June 22, 1984, Hedrick Smith, "Nudging NATO Is a Touchy Issue," *New York Times,* June 24, 1984; Editorial, "Sen. Nunn's Amendment," *Washington Post,* June 25, 1984; David M. Abshire, "Europe: Refitting NATO Strategy for the Future," *Wall Street Journal,* September 12, 1984.

27. Gerald F. Seib, "West Germany, U.S. Sign Accord on Air Defense," *Wall Street Journal,* July 13, 1984; "Around the World," *New York Times,* July 11, 1984; Richard Halloran, "Europe Called Main U.S. Arms Cost," *New York Times,* July 20, 1984; Eugene Kozicharow, "Senate Rejects NATO Troop Reduction," *Aviation Week and Space Technology,* June 25, 1984, 26; William H. Gregory, "Changing Allegiances and NATO," *Aviation Week and Space Technology,* July 30, 1984, 11; "Paying Up," *Time,* December 1984, 58; Bowie, "Nunn Amendment"; British Ambassador Oliver Wright, letter to Cohen, June 18, 1984, MS 106.3.3.5.3.4, Box 7, Folder 10, North Atlantic Treaty Organization, 1982–86, WCP.

28. James Eberle, John Roper, William Wallace, and Phil Williams, "European Security Cooperation and British Interests," *International Affairs* 60, no. 4 (Autumn 1984): 548–549, 559–560.

29. Williams, "The Nunn Amendment," 5, 8.

30. Kugler, *Commitment to Purpose,* 423, 424.

31. Abshire, *Preventing World War III,* 75.

32. Richard Halloran, "Europe Called Main U.S. Arms Cost," *New York Times,* July 20, 1984; Halloran, "Senate Actions Get after NATO Allies on Costs," *New York Times,* August 9, 1984; Hedrick Smith, "Nudging NATO"; Sloan, "Managing the NATO Alliance," 404.

33. Nunn, "Nunn Answers Questions about Combat Readiness," in *Sam Nunn on Arms Control,* ed. Kenneth W. Thompson, vol. 5 (Lanham, MD: University Press of America, 1987), 89–93.

34. Charles Daniel, "NATO Decline: Opportunity for Europe," *Christian Science*

Monitor, August 9, 1984; Drew Middleton, ""Western Defense: Is Europe Doing Enough?" *New York Times,* September 17, 1984.

35. Wayne Biddle, "Pentagon Budget Still Deadlocked," *New York Times,* August 11, 1984; Fred Kaplan, "Compromise Still Eludes MX Antagonists," *Boston Globe,* September 13, 1984.

36. Congressional Quarterly, *Almanac,* 17; Gerald F. Seib, "Defense Spending: Arms Buildup Ordered by Reagan Could Be Less than Meets the Eye," *Wall Street Journal,* October 29, 1984; Sloan, "Managing the NATO Alliance," 404; Bill Keller, "Word of Caution from Senator Nunn May Signal Trouble for MX," *New York Times,* December 23, 1984; Norman Sandler, "'Star Wars' Arms Plan Called Non-negotiable," *Philadelphia Inquirer,* December 24, 1984.

37. Department of Defense Authorization Act for Fiscal Year 1985, H.R. 5167, 98th Cong., 2nd Sess., accessed February 1, 2020, https://www.govtrack.us/congress /bills/98/hr5167; Williams, "The Nunn Amendment," 4.

38. US Election Atlas, 1984 Senatorial General Election Results—Georgia, accessed February 1, 2020, http://uselectionatlas.org/RESULTS/state.php?year=1984 &off=3&elect=0&fips=13&f=0; Lori Santos, "Republicans Picked a Teacher to Send against Sen. Sam Nunn," United Press International, accessed February 1, 2020, http://www.upi.com/Archives/1984/09/05/Georgia-Republicans-picked -a-teacher-to-send-against-Sen/9815463204800/; "Nunn Makes Refund Offer," *New York Times,* April 3, 1985.

39. David Leip, "1984 Presidential General Election Results," accessed February 1, 2020, http://uselectionatlas.org/results/national.php?year=1984; Martin Tolchin, "Reagan Wins by a Landslide," *New York Times,* November 7, 1984; Tolchin, "2-Seat Gain Buoys Senate Democrats," *New York Times,* November 8, 1984; Hedrick Smith, "Reagan Faces Difficult Task in Leading Divided Congress," *New York Times,* November 8, 1984; McElroy, email to author, October 25, 2019.

40. William Drozdiak, "NATO Warned of High-Tech Dazzle," *Washington Post,* November 15, 1984; "Reagan and Kohl Urge Nonnuclear Arms Buildup," *New York Times,* December 1, 1984; William V. Roth, "Sharing the Burden of European Defense," *Christian Science Monitor,* December 3, 1984; Abshire, *Preventing World War III,* 76; Kugler, *Commitment to Purpose,* 428; Ronald Reagan, "Joint Statement Issued at the Conclusion of Meetings with Chancellor Helmut Kohl of the Federal Republic of Germany," November 30, 1984, Reagan Library, https:// www.reaganlibrary.gov/research/speeches/113084b; Reagan, "Remarks of the President and Helmut Kohl of the Federal Republic of Germany Following Their Meetings," November 30, 1984, Reagan Library, https://www.reaganlibrary.gov /research/speeches/113084a.

41. William Beecher, "General Outlines Plan to Avert Nuclear War," *Boston Globe,* December 16, 1984.

42. Richard Slawsky, "Kill the Dog Programmes: An Interview with Senator Sam Nunn," *Jane's Defence Weekly,* April 11, 1987, 641; William Drozdiak, "NATO Agrees on $7.8 billion to Improve Defense," *Washington Post,* December 5, 1984; William V. Roth, "NATO Takes a Good First Step," *Christian Science Monitor,* December 20, 1984; Abshire, *Preventing World War III,* 75–76.

Chapter 7. Sam Nunn's MX Missile

1. James Gerstenzang, "Reagan Calls Hope for Talks Too High," *Los Angeles Times,* January 5, 1985; US Senate, *Report of the Senate Arms Control Observer Group Delegation to the Opening of the Arms Control Negotiations with the Soviet Union in Geneva, Switzerland,* 99th Cong., 1st Sess., 1985, Document 99-7, 2.

2. Senate, *Report of the Senate Arms Control Observer Group,* 2–4.

3. Quoted in Nickolas Roth, "The Evolution of the Senate Arms Control Observer Group," Federation of American Scientists, *Public Interest Report* 67, no. 2 (Spring 2014), https://fas.org/pir-pubs/evolution-senate-arms-control-observer -group/.

4. Editorial, "Where to Cut Defense," *Los Angeles Times,* January 28, 1985; Ernest Conine, "Defense Commitments: Is the U.S. Overextended?" *Los Angeles Times,* January 28, 1985.

5. Sam Nunn, "Improving NATO's Conventional Defenses," in *Sam Nunn on Arms Control,* ed. Kenneth W. Thompson, vol. 5 (Lanham, MD: University Press of America, 1987), 95–96; Tim Carrington, "Some in NATO Fear That 'Star Wars' Proposals Divert Attention from Existing Forces," *Wall Street Journal,* February 12, 1985; Bill Keller, "NATO Chief Finds Conventional Forces Lacking," *New York Times,* March 2, 1985.

6. Sam Nunn, "Cut the Number of Weapons Systems," in *Sam Nunn on Arms Control,* ed. Kenneth W. Thompson, vol. 5 (Lanham, MD: University Press of America, 1987), 98–99.

7. Conine, "Defense Commitments"; Christopher Layne, "Toward German Unification?" *Journal of Contemporary Studies* 7, no. 4 (Fall 1984): 30, 31, 33.

8. James Gerstenzang, "Weinberger Told Budget Will Be Cut," *Los Angeles Times,* February 5, 1985.

9. George C. Wilson, "Nunn to Broaden Debate on NATO by Arguing War Plans Are Flawed," *Washington Post,* February 21, 1985.

10. Bill Keller, "President Mounts Campaign for MX," *New York Times,* February 27, 1985; Nunn, "Cut the Number of Weapons Systems," 99–100.

11. Bill Keller, "Democrats Give Reagan Support on Arms Talks," *New York Times,* March 7, 1985.

12. Senate, *Report of the Senate Arms Control Observer Group,* 5, 15.

13. Senate, *Report,* 21–22, 26–30, 34.

14. Sara Fritz, "MX Funds Seem Assured," *Los Angeles Times,* March 7, 1985; Bill Keller, "Lawmakers Agree on Strategy Tying the MX to Geneva," *New York Times,* March 8, 1985.

15. Sam Nunn, "Back on the Road to Arms Control," in *Sam Nunn on Arms Control,* ed. Kenneth W. Thompson, vol. 5 (Lanham, MD: University Press of America, 1987), 32, 34; Oswald Johnston, "Soviets' Stance Called Absurd," *Los Angeles Times,* March 11, 1985; Steven V. Roberts, "Wavering Senators Feel Pressure as Time Approaches for MX Vote," *New York Times,* March 17, 1985.

16. Steven V. Roberts, "Foes Press to Reverse MX Missile," *New York Times,* March 28, 1985; Roberts, "Dole Says He Expects MX to Survive Vote Today," *New York*

Times, March 19, 1985; David Rogers, "Panel Supports Funding of 21 More MXs," *Wall Street Journal*, March 19, 1985; Sara Fritz, "Panel Approves Funds for MX," *Los Angeles Times*, March 19, 1985; David Alpern et al., "Moscow's Mixed Signals," *Newsweek*, April 1, 1985, 26; Congressional Quarterly, *Almanac:* 99th Cong., 1st Sess., 1985 (Washington, DC: Congressional Quarterly News Features, 1986), 122.

17. Sam Nunn, "The MX," March 26, 1985, MS 106.3.3.5.3.4, Box 6, Folder 7, MX Missile Plan 1985, William S. Cohen Papers (WCP), Raymond H. Fogler Library, University of Maine, Orono, ME; Hedrick Smith, "Reagan's MX Victory: Eye on Audience Overseas," *New York Times*, March 20, 1985; Steven V. Roberts, "Foes Press to Reverse MX Missile"; Roberts, "House Vote Gives Final Approval for Purchase of 21 MX Missiles," *New York Times*, March 29, 1985.

18. Roberts, "Foes Press to Reverse MX Missile"; Roberts, "House Vote Gives Final Approval"; David Rogers and Tim Carrington, "House Votes Final Approval for the MX, but Legislators Warn of Cuts in '86 Funds," *Wall Street Journal*, March 29, 1985.

19. Bill Keller, "MX Debate: It's Not Over," *New York Times*, March 30, 1985; Congressional Quarterly, *Almanac*, 127.

20. "Senate Armed Services Committee Votes for 21 Further MX Missiles," *New York Times*, April 3, 1985; Congressional Quarterly, *Almanac*, 128; Sam Nunn, "The MX," in Edward L. Rowny et al., *Strategic Force Modernization and Arms Control*, National Security Paper no. 6 (Washington, DC: Institute for Foreign Policy Analysis, 1986), 35–40.

21. Bill Keller, "Senate Committee Cuts Reagan Military Budget," *New York Times*, April 5, 1985; James Gerstenzang, "Pentagon Funds Cut $9 Billion by Senate Panel," *Los Angeles Times*, March 5, 1985.

22. Editorial, "What a Trillion Bought," *New York Times*, May 19, 1985.

23. Nunn Amendment to Limit MX Deployment and Procurement, MS 106.3.3.5.3.4, Box 6, Folder 7, MX Missile Plan 1985, WCP; Steven V. Roberts, "President Shifts to an MX Force of 50 for Now," *New York Times*, May 22, 1985; George C. Wilson, "Administration Is Seeking to Avert Senate Approval of Capping the MX," *Washington Post*, May 22, 1985; Congressional Quarterly, *Almanac*, 118.

24. Bob Secter, "Reagan Has No Chance to Defeat MX Cap; Senator Nunn's Rising Influence Reaches White House," *Los Angeles Times*, May 23, 1985.

25. George C. Wilson, "Reagan Halves MX Deployment, Agrees to Base 50 in Silos," *Washington Post*, May 24, 1985; Steven V. Roberts, "Senate in Pact with President, Votes 50 MX's," *New York Times*, May 24, 1985; Sara Fritz, "Senate Sets Limits of 50 Missiles; Reagan Accepts Compromise," *Los Angeles Times*, May 24, 1985; Congressional Quarterly, *Almanac*, 128, 147; James M. Lindsay, *Congress and Nuclear Weapons* (Baltimore, MD: Johns Hopkins University Press, 1991), 69; Reagan to Dole, May 23, 1985, Dole Archives, University of Kansas, Lawrence, KS, http://dolearchivecollections.ku.edu/collections/vip_letters/c020_012_000_071.pdf.

26. "White House Settles for 50 MX's," *New York Times*, May 20, 1985; Editorial, "The Sam Nunn MX," *Washington Post*, May 26, 1985; Paul H. Nitze, with Ann

M. Smith and Steven L. Rearden, *From Hiroshima to Glasnost: At the Center of Decision, a Memoir* (New York: Grove Weidenfeld, 1989), 417.

27. Sam Nunn, "It's Not What We Spend on Defense," in *Sam Nunn on Arms Control,* ed. Kenneth W. Thompson, vol. 5 (Lanham, MD: University Press of America, 1987), 103–106.

28. Editorial, "A Good Year for NATO," *Washington Post,* May 28, 1985; David M. Abshire, *Preventing World War III: A Realistic Grand Strategy* (New York: Harper & Row, 1988), 77–78.

29. Steven V. Roberts, "Senate Vote Urges Backing Arms Pact," *New York Times,* June 6, 1985; Leslie H. Gelb, "Arms Control's Future Is in Doubt, and So Is Its Past," *New York Times,* June 8, 1985; Congressional Quarterly, *Almanac,* 150.

30. George C. Wilson, "Despite Senate Support, SDI's Future Is Cloudy," *Washington Post,* June 9, 1985.

31. Michael Wines and James Gerstenzang, "Use of 'Star Wars' as Bargaining Chip Suggested," *Los Angeles Times,* June 29, 1985; Elizabeth Pond, "Geneva Arms Talks Impasse," *Christian Science Monitor,* July 1, 1985; "Senator Nunn's Involvement," Subseries 11.3, Box 23, SDI, Sam Nunn Papers (SNP), Stuart A. Rose Manuscript, Archives, and Rare Book Library, Emory University.

32. Nunn, Oral History, September 5, 1996, Sam Nunn Private Papers, Nuclear Threat Initiative offices, Washington, DC; Robert Bell, Memorandum for the Record, subject: Nunn/Warner Proposal on Risk Reduction, September 9, 1985, Subseries 6.5, Box 140, file, 1987, SNP; Barry M. Blechman, ed., *Preventing Nuclear War: A Realistic Approach* (Bloomington: Indiana University Press, 1985), 1–6, 167–171; Alan J. Vick, *Building Confidence during Peace and War,* N-2698-CC (Santa Monica, CA: RAND Corporation, 1988), 2; Serge Schmemann, "Gorbachev Hints He Will Be Flexible," *New York Times,* September 4, 1985; Hedrick Smith, "Impressions of M. Gorbachev," *New York Times,* September 12, 1985; Don Oberdorfer, "Reduction of Nuclear Risk Eyed," *Washington Post,* September 16, 1985; "US Lawmakers Size Up Gorbachev," *US News & World Report,* September 16, 1985.

33. Joseph P. Shapiro, with Kathryn Johnson, "How Reagan Prepares for Gorbachev," *US News & World Report,* November 4, 1985; Arnold Punaro, Box 1, interview by Tom Chaffin, October 15, 1997, McLean, VA, Sam Nunn Oral History Collection, Stuart A. Rose Manuscript, Archives, and Rare Book Library, Emory University, Atlanta, GA.

34. Hedrick Smith, "Arms Talks: Soviet Offer May Break Logjam," *New York Times,* September 28, 1985; Sam Nunn, "How to Make the Summit Productive," in *Sam Nunn on Arms Control,* ed. Kenneth W. Thompson, vol. 5 (Lanham, MD: University Press of America, 1987), 43–46.

35. William S. Cohen and Sam Nunn, "Arms Race Breakthrough or Breakdown," in *Sam Nunn on Arms Control,* ed. Kenneth W. Thompson, vol. 5 (Lanham, MD: University Press of America, 1987), 37–40.

36. Sam Nunn, "NATO and Arms Control," in *Sam Nunn on Arms Control,* ed. Kenneth W. Thompson, vol. 5 (Lanham, MD: University Press of America, 1987), 59–60, 66.

37. Nunn, "NATO and Arms Control," 66–69; "Senator Nunn's Involvement in the Strategic Defense Initiative and Anti-Ballistic Missile Treaty Interpretation Debate." For a discussion of the major features of the law Nunn references, see Allen Schick, *Explanation of the Balanced Budget and Emergency Deficit Control Act of 1985—Public Law 99-177 (The Gramm-Rudman-Hollings Act)* (Washington, DC: Congressional Research Service, Library of Congress, 1986), 1–28.

38. Sam Nunn, "The Strategic Defense Initiative," in *Sam Nunn on Arms Control,* ed. Kenneth W. Thompson, vol. 5 (Lanham, MD: University Press of America, 1987), 179–180, 184–185, 187.

39. Hedrick Smith, "Geneva: A Test of Wills," *New York Times,* November 17, 1985.

40. Nunn, Oral History; Bernard Gwertzman, "Summit Finale: Praise from Weinberger," *New York Times,* November 22, 1985; Thomas Graham Jr. and Damien J. LaVera, *Cornerstones of Security: Arms Control Treaties in the Nuclear Age* (Seattle: University of Washington Press, 2003), 503.

41. Senate Committee on Armed Services, "Agreement Signed on Risk Reduction Centers," press release, Subseries 6.5, Box 140, file, 1987, SNP.

42. Mark Whitaker et al., "What's Next for 'Star Wars,'" *Newsweek,* December 2, 1985, 45.

43. Congressional Quarterly, *Almanac,* 172, 174.

Chapter 8. The Long Crusade

1. Jeffrey Record, "The Military Reform Caucus," *Washington Quarterly* 6, no. 2 (Spring 1983): 125–126; Gary Hart, "An Agenda for More Military Reform," *New York Times,* May 13, 1986; John Barry and Tom Morganthau, "Defense: How Much Is Enough?," *Newsweek,* February 3, 1986, 14.

2. Gerald J. Smith, interview by James R. Locher III, May 1994, quoted in Locher, *Victory on the Potomac: The Goldwater-Nichols Act Unifies the Pentagon* (College Station: Texas A&M University Press, 2002), 187.

3. James R. Locher III, "Transformative Leadership on Capitol Hill: The Goldwater-Nichols Defense Reorganization Act," in *Reagan and the World: Leadership and National Security, 1981–1989,* ed. Bradley Lynn Coleman and Kyle Longley (Lexington: University Press of Kentucky, 2017), 88; Barry M. Goldwater, with Jack Casserly, *Goldwater* (New York: Doubleday, 1988), 342; Sam Nunn, interview by James R. Locher III, July 14, 1995, Washington DC, *Victory on the Potomac* Collection, Box 59, Interviews binder, James R. Locher III Papers (JLP), Special Collections, National Defense University Library, Fort Lesley J. McNair, Washington, DC.

4. Locher, *Victory on the Potomac,* 82–83, 92, 186–187, 188–194; Senators Sam Nunn and William Cohen, Congressmen Les Aspin and Samuel Stratton to Phillip Odeen, Recommendations Concerning JCS Reform, September 21, 1984, MS106.3.3.5.2, Box 2, Folder 2, Defense Reorganization, Center for Strategic and International Studies, 1983–1986, William S. Cohen Papers (WCP), Raymond H. Fogler Library, University of Maine, Orono, ME; Sam Nunn, interview by James R. Locher III, September 9, 1996, Washington DC, *Victory on the Potomac* Collection, Box 62, Interviews, Moorer-Smith, Nunn file (Interview), JLP.

5. Quoted in Locher, *Victory on the Potomac*, 186.

6. Goldwater, *Goldwater*, 357–358.

7. Locher, *Victory on the Potomac*, 82–83, 92, 186–187, 220, 221, 222; Sam Nunn, interview by Locher, July 14, 1995, and Sam Nunn, interview by Locher, September 9, 1996, JLP.

8. "Ex-Defense Chiefs Back Military Revamping," *New York Times*, February 20, 1985.

9. "Ex-Defense Chiefs Back Military Revamping"; Locher, *Victory on the Potomac*, 223, 234; Locher, "Transformative Leadership," 88; Letter, Goldwater to Weinberger, March 14, 1986, Box 31, Reagan Library, White House/Senate on DOD Reorganization, Official/Personal Paper Collection, JLP.

10. Goldwater, *Goldwater*, 340; Letter, Goldwater to Reagan, February 24, 1986, Box 31, Reagan Library, White House/Senate on DOD Reorganization, Official/Personal Paper Collection, JLP.

11. Locher, *Victory on the Potomac*, 230, 299; Nunn and Goldwater to Task Force on Defense Organization, MS106.3.3.5.2, Box 1, Folder 16, Defense Organization, Senate Armed Services Committee, 1983–86, WCP.

12. Roland McElroy, email to author, October 25, 2019.

13. Phil Gailey, "Dissidents Defy Top Democrats," *New York Times*, March 1, 1985; Sam Nunn, "Remarks 'Handing Over the Gavel' to Governor Clinton," DLC Convention, New Orleans, March 1990, Sam Nunn Private Papers, Nuclear Threat Initiative offices, Washington, DC; Jon F. Hale, "The Making of the New Democrats," *Political Science Quarterly* 110, no. 2 (Summer 1993): 207; Al From, with Alice McKeon, *The New Democrats and the Return to Power* (New York: Palgrave Macmillan, 2013), 55; Donald W. Beachler, "The South and the Democratic Presidential Nomination, 1972–1992," *Presidential Studies Quarterly* 26, no. 2 (Spring 1996): 413n33.

14. Paul Taylor, "Democrats' New Centrists Preen for '88," *Washington Post*, November 10, 1985; Phil Gailey, "Democrats Assail Reagan Credibility on Military," *New York Times*, March 15, 1986; From, *New Democrats*, 39, 64, 70.

15. Locher, "Transformative Leadership," 92, 96; Arnold L. Punaro, with David Poyer, *On War and Politics: The Battlefield inside Washington's Beltway* (Annapolis, MD: Naval Institute Press, 2016), 131; "The Goldwater-Nichols Defense Reorganization Act," Congressional Quarterly, *Almanac*, 99th Cong., 1st Sess., 1985 (Washington, DC: Congressional Quarterly News Features, 1986), 172–173; Locher, *Victory on the Potomac*, 299–300; Memorandum from Michael Donley to Robert C. McFarlane, subject: Update on SASC DOD Organization Project, Box 31, Reagan Library, White House/Senate on DOD Reorganization, Official/Personal Paper Collection, JLP.

16. Hedrick Smith, *The Power Game: How Washington Works* (New York: Random House, 1987), 201, 213.

17. Nunn, quoted in Smith, *The Power Game*, 201–202.

18. Ronald Reagan, Executive Order 12526, President's Blue Ribbon Commission on Defense Management, July 15, 1985, Ronald Reagan Presidential Library (RRL), https://www.reaganlibrary.gov/research/speeches/71585c; Bill Keller,

"Weinberger under Political Siege, but Few Expect Change of Course," *New York Times*, July 23, 1985.

19. William J. Crowe Jr., with David Chanoff, *The Line of Fire: From Washington to the Gulf, the Politics and Battles of the New Military* (New York: Simon & Schuster, 1993), 152.

20. Congressional Quarterly, *Almanac*, 172.

21. Locher, *Victory on the Potomac*, 335–336, 342–345; Participants in the Weekend Retreat, MS 106.3.3.5.2., Box 1, Folder 2, Defense Organization, Senate Armed Services Committee, 1993–86, WCP; Barry Goldwater, interview by James R. Locher III, Scottsdale, AZ, May 8, 1994, *Victory on the Potomac* Collection, Box 59, Papers, Interviews binder, and Nunn, interview by Locher, September 9, 1996, JLP.

22. Bill Keller, "2 Key Senators Join in Assault on the Military," *New York Times*, October 6, 1985; Locher, *Victory on the Potomac*, 324; Congressional Oversight of National Defense, *Congressional Record*, 99th Cong., 1st Sess., 25348–25352; 25539–25543; 26159–26160; 26346; 26693–26696.

23. Locher, *Victory on the Potomac*, 347, 348, 351–353; Nunn, interview by Locher, September 9, 1996, JLP.

24. Bill Keller, "Panel Set to Propose Major Overhaul for Pentagon," *New York Times*, October 11, 1985.

25. Keller, "Panel Set."

26. Senate Committee on Armed Services, *Defense Organization: The Need for Changes: Staff Report to the Committee on Armed Services*, 99th Cong., 1st Sess., Committee Print, S. Prt. 99-86, October 16, 1985; Tim Carrington, "Study Criticizes Pentagon's Handling of Arms Programs, Military Operations," *Wall Street Journal*, October 16, 1985; Congressional Quarterly, *Almanac*, 174; Punaro, *On War and Politics*, 132; Richard McCulley, *History of the Senate Committee on Armed Services, 1947–1999*, unpublished manuscript, file: Armed Services Committee History, 2000 draft, US Senate Historical Office, Washington, DC.

27. Carrington, "Study Criticizes Pentagon's Handling."

28. James P. Dickenson, "Newly Assertive Nunn Leads the Offense on Defense," *Washington Post*, October 17, 1985.

29. Michael Herron, "The Nation: Plan for Revolution at the Pentagon," *New York Times*, October 20, 1985.

30. Bill Keller, "Proposed Revamping of Military Calls for Disbanding Joint Chiefs," *New York Times*, October 17, 1985.

31. Tim Carrington, "Senators Clash over Proposal to Shift Power at Pentagon away from Services," *Wall Street Journal*, October 17, 1985.

32. Tom Morganthau, Kim Willenson, and John Barry, "The Pentagon under Siege," *Newsweek*, October 28, 1985, 38.

33. "Weinberger Defends Joint Chiefs, *New York Times*, November 15, 1985; Paul Houston, "Weinberger Rejects Disbanding of Joint Chiefs of Staff," *Los Angeles Times*, November 15, 1985; Caspar W. Weinberger, *Annual Report to Congress; Fiscal Year 1987* (Washington, DC: US Department of Defense, 1986), 103–117; Senate Committee on Armed Services, *Reorganization of the Department of Defense*,

Hearings before the Committee on Armed Services, 99th Cong., 1st Sess., 1986, 73–110.

34. "Weinberger Defends Joint Chiefs"; Houston, "Weinberger Rejects Disbanding of Joint Chiefs of Staff"; Locher, *Victory on the Potomac*, 311, 376.

35. Robert Pear, "Weinberger Open to Plan to Revamp Military," *New York Times*, December 5, 1985.

36. William J. Crowe, *Selected Works of William J. Crowe, Jr., USN: Eleventh Chairman of the Joint Chiefs of Staff*, ed. and comp. Julian Burns (Washington, DC: Joint History Office, Office of the Chairman of the Joint Chiefs of Staff, 2013), 14–20.

37. Congressional Quarterly, *Almanac*, 172–174; "Pentagon Command Scrutinized," *Los Angeles Times*, October 17, 1985; Kathleen J. McInnis, *Goldwater-Nichols at 30: Defense Reform and Issues for Congress*, CRS Report 44474 (Washington, DC: Congressional Research Service, 2016), 8.

38. Congressional Quarterly, *Almanac*, 174; William V. Kennedy, "Is the United States Creating a Prussian General Staff?" *Christian Science Monitor*, January 2, 1986.

39. Goldwater, *Goldwater*, 334–335; Locher, *Victory on the Potomac*, 3, 4.

40. Crowe, *The Line of Fire*, 147, 151, 227–229; Goldwater, *Goldwater*, 341–342, 352, 359.

41. Goldwater, *Goldwater*, 336–338; Locher, *Victory on the Potomac*, 5, 7, 8–9; Rick Finn, interview by James R. Locher III, May 2, 1994, and Nunn, interview by Locher, July 14, 1995, JLP.

42. Quoted in Locher, *Victory on the Potomac*, 10.

43. Goldwater, *Goldwater*, 338; Locher, *Victory on the Potomac*, 10.

44. Goldwater, *Goldwater*, 338–339; Locher, *Victory on the Potomac*, 10–12; Nunn, interview by Locher, July 14, 1995, JLP.

45. Goldwater, *Goldwater*, 339; Goldwater, interview by Locher, May 8, 1994, and Nunn, interview by Locher, September 9, 1996, JLP.

46. Locher, "Transformative Leadership," 99–100; Locher, *Victory on the Potomac*, 408–409.

47. Locher, *Victory on the Potomac*, 407.

48. Locher, *Victory on the Potomac*, 408–409; Locher, "Transformative Leadership," 99–100.

49. Locher, *Victory on the Potomac*, 410; President's Blue Ribbon Commission on Defense Management, *An Interim Report to the President* (Washington, DC, February 29, 1986), 9–12.

50. Locher, *Victory on the Potomac*, 408, 410–411.

51. Richard Halloran, "Panel Backs Shift of Military Roles," *New York Times*, February 23, 1986.

52. Locher, *Victory on the* Potomac, 411–412; Goldwater, interview by Locher, Scottsdale, AZ, May 8, 1994, JLP.

53. Fred Hiatt, "Panel Backs Reorganizing the Military," *Washington Post*, March 7, 1986; Hiatt, "Can Congress Quell Rivalry in the Military? Goldwater-Nunn Bill Would Be a Partial Remedy," *Washington Post*, March 8, 1986.

54. Hiatt, "Can Congress Quell Rivalry in the Military?"

55. Ronald Reagan, "Implementation of the Recommendations of the Blue Ribbon Commission on Defense Management," National Security Decision Directive 219, April 1, 1986, RRL, https://www.reaganlibrary.gov/digital-library/nsdds; Reagan, "Radio Address to the Nation on Defense Establishment Reforms," April 5, 1986, RRL, https://www.reaganlibrary.gov/research/speeches/40586a; Reagan, "Message to the Congress Outlining Proposals for Improving the Organization of the Defense Establishment," April 25, 1986, RRL, https://www.reaganlibrary.gov/research/speeches/42486c; Statement of Administration Policy, S. 2295, Department of Defense Reorganization Act of 1986, April 28, 1986, Subseries 11.3, Box 15, file, Goldwater Nichols, April–May 1986, Sam Nunn Papers (SNP), Stuart A. Rose Manuscript, Archives, and Rare Books Library, Emory University, Atlanta, GA.

56. Locher, *Victory on the Potomac*, 408, 418.

57. Nunn to Members of the Democratic Caucus, subject: DOD Reorganization Bill, May 6, 1986, Subseries 11.3, Box 15, file, Goldwater Nichols, April–May 1986, SNP.

58. Locher, *Victory on the Potomac*, 420; Richard Halloran, "Pentagon: Redesigning the Military Command Camel," *New York Times,* May 7, 1986.

59. Sam Nunn, "The Defense Reorganization Act of 1986," in *Sam Nunn on Arms Control,* W. Alton Jones Foundation Series on Arms Control, vol. 5 (Lanham, MD: University Press of America, 1987), 117–144; Crowe, *Line of Fire,* 153.

60. Locher, "Transformative Leadership," 101; "Senate Approves Reorganization of Armed Forces," *Los Angeles Times,* May 8, 1986; George C. Wilson, "Goldwater Is Right, Colleagues Say," *Washington Post,* May 10, 1986; Congressional Quarterly, *Almanac,* 99th Cong., 2nd Sess., 1986 (Washington, DC: Congressional Quarterly News Features, 1987), 458; Locher, *Victory on the Potomac,* 420–421; Goldwater, interview by Locher, Scottsdale, AZ, May 8, 1994, and Nunn, interview by Locher, September 9, 1996, JLP.

61. John H. Cushman, "Senate Approves Military Changes," *New York Times,* May 8, 1986.

62. Senate Committee on Armed Services, "Goldwater and Nunn Announce Conference Agreement on Defense Reorganization Bill," press release, September 11, 1986, MS 106.3.3.5.2, Box 1, Folder 16, Defense Organization, Senate Armed Services Committee, 1983–86, WCP; Locher, "Transformative Leadership," 101; White House, Office of the Press Secretary, Statement by the President, October 1, 1986, Subseries 11.3, Box 15, file, Goldwater Nichols, June-December 1986, SNP.

63. Wilson, "Goldwater Is Right."

Chapter 9. A Battle of Wills

1. Christopher J. Deering, "Decision Making in the Armed Services Committees," in *Congress Resurgent: Foreign and Defense Policy on Capitol Hill,* ed. Randall B. Ripley and James M. Lindsay (Ann Arbor: University of Michigan Press, 1993), 169.

2. Helen Dewar, "Senate Democrats Show They're Back in Charge, Off to Fast Start on Welfare, Trade, Arms," *Washington Post,* January 19, 1987; Phil Gailey, *New York Times Magazine,* "Sam Nunn's Rising Star," February 4, 1987, 25; Roland McElroy, *The Best President the Nation Never Had* (Macon, GA: Mercer University Press, 2017), 197, 198, 199, 201; Al From, with Alice McKeon, *The New Democrats and the Return to Power* (New York: Palgrave Macmillan, 2011), 87–88; Arnold Punaro, interview by Tom Chaffin, October 15, 1997, McLean, VA, Box 1, Sam Nunn Oral History Collection, Stuart A. Rose Manuscript, Archives, and Rare Book Library, Emory University, Atlanta, GA; Bob Bell to Minority Staff, memorandum, subject: Key Issues, December 1, 1986, Senate Papers, SASC Box 4, Strategy Hearings, 1987, Agenda—Major Defense Issues file, James R. Locher III Papers, Special Collections, National Defense University Library, Fort Lesley J. McNair, Washington, DC.

3. Richard McCulley, *History of the Senate Committee on Armed Services, 1947–1999,* unpublished manuscript, file: Armed Services Committee History, 2000 draft, US Senate Historical Office, Washington, DC (McCulley MS); Arnold Punaro, telephone interview by author, January 23, 2020.

4. Arnold Punaro, interview by Tom Chaffin.

5. McCulley MS; Meeting with Rep. Aspin, January 1987, Subseries 11.3, Box 4, file: Committee Organization/General, Sam Nunn Papers (SNP), Stuart A. Rose Manuscript, Archives, and Rare Book Library, Emory University, Atlanta, GA.

6. Paul Taylor, "Military Buildup Faulted by Democratic Centrists," *Washington Post,* September 17, 1986; From, *The New Democrats,* 80.

7. Michael Mawby, "Arms Control Prospects in the 100th Congress," *Arms Control Today,* January–February 1987, 5–6.

8. McCully MS.

9. Ronald Reagan, "Message to the Senate Urging Ratification of Two Treaties Limiting Soviet-United States Nuclear Testing," January 13, 1987, Ronald Reagan Presidential Library, https://www.reaganlibrary.gov/research/speeches/011387a; Letter from Nunn to Robert C. Byrd, February 6, 1987, Subseries 6.5, Box 140, File, "Whites" (Loose material unidentified), SNP.

10. Pat Towell, "Verification Debate Stalls Nuclear Test Pacts," *CQ Weekly,* January 24, 1987, 161; George C. Wilson, "SDI May Be Deployed in Stages, Weinberger Says," *Washington Post,* January 13, 1987; Congressional Quarterly, *Almanac,* 100th Congress, 1st Session, 193.

11. Brian Duffy, with Melissa Healy and Robert Kaylor, "What Weapons Will Work?" *US News & World Report,* January 19, 1987, 18.

12. Gaylord Shaw, "Defense Policy Disappointing, Nunn Says," *Los Angeles Times,* January 13, 1987.

13. Wilson, "SDI May Be Deployed in Stages"; Duffy, with Healy and Kaylor, "What Weapons Will Work?," 18.

14. Senate Committee on Armed Services, *National Security Strategy,* 100th Cong., 1st Sess., 1987, S. Hrg. 100-257, 54, 58–59, 63–64, 70–71; Wilson, "SDI May Be Deployed in Stages"; Duffy, with Healy and Kaylor, "What Weapons Will Work?," 18; US Department of Defense, *Report of Secretary of Defense Caspar W. Wein-*

berger to the Congress on the FY 1988–FY 1989 Budget and FY 1988–92 Defense Programs (Washington, DC: US Government Printing Office, 1987), 282; Strategic Defense Initiative Office, *Report to the Congress on the Strategic Defense Initiative*, April 1987, II-10 to II-13; Caspar Weinberger, *Fighting for Peace: Seven Critical Years in the Pentagon* (New York: Warner Books, 1990), 317, 323–324.

15. "Nunn Assails Confusion on 'Star Wars,' Says Administration Mixes Signals on It and Deterrence," *Los Angeles Times*, January 17, 1987.

16. Strobe Talbott, *The Master of the Game: Paul Nitze and the Nuclear Peace* (New York: Alfred A. Knopf, 1988), 329.

17. Frances FitzGerald, *Way Out There in the Blue: Reagan, Star Wars, and the End of the Cold War* (New York: Simon & Schuster, 2000), 388, 393; Rowland Evans and Robert Novak, "Weinberger's SDI Move," *Washington Post*, January 14, 1987.

18. Shultz, *Turmoil and Triumph: My Years as Secretary of State* (New York: Charles Scribner's Sons, 1993), 871; Raymond L. Garthoff, *Policy versus the Law: The Reinterpretation of the ABM Treaty* (Washington, DC: Brookings Institution Press, 1987), 12–13; Nunn, Oral History, September 5, 1995, Sam Nunn Private Papers (SNPP), Nuclear Threat Initiative offices, Washington, DC; Nunn, "The ABM Reinterpretation Issue," *Washington Quarterly* 10, no. 4 (Autumn 1987): 45–46; Jay Winik, *On the Brink: The Dramatic, Behind-the-Scenes Saga of the Reagan Era and the Men and Women Who Won the Cold War* (New York: Simon & Schuster, 1996), 364, 365, 367; Don Oberdorfer, "ABM Reinterpretation: A Quick Study," *Washington Post*, October 22, 1985.

19. Helen Dewar and R. Jeffrey Smith, "Sen. Nunn Warns Reagan on Shift in Missile Treaty," *Washington Post*, February 7, 1987.

20. Abraham D. Sofaer, interview by Stephen Knott et al., February 7, 2007, Charlottesville, Virginia, Ronald Reagan Oral History Project, Miller Center of Public Affairs, University of Virginia.

21. Sofaer interview.

22. FitzGerald, *Way Out There*, 397; Letter, Nunn to Reagan, February 6, 1987, Subseries 11.3, Box 10, file, ABM Treaty, SNP; Dewar and Smith, "Sen. Nunn Warns Reagan"; Michael R. Gordon, "Reagan Is Warned by Senator Nunn over ABM Treaty," *New York Times*, February 7, 1987.

23. Robert M. Soofer, *Missile Defense and Western European Security: NATO Strategy, Arms Control, and Deterrence* (New York: Greenwood Press, 1988), 76–78, 80–81, 89, 91; Dewar and Smith, "Sen. Nunn Warns Reagan"; Russell Watson, with John Barry, "Speeding Up Star Wars," *Newsweek*, February 16, 1987, 28.

24. Senate Committee on Armed Services, *National Security Strategy*, 434, 437, 454–457; R. Jeffrey Smith, "SDI Decision 'May Be Nearing,'" *Washington Post*, January 23, 1987; Watson, with Barry, "Speeding Up Star Wars," 28; Matthew Bunn and Bruce B. Auster, "Administration Nears Decision on Early Deployment of SDI, Treaty Interpretation," *Arms Control Today*, March 1987, 17.

25. Dusko Doder and R. Jeffrey Smith, "Shultz Accepts Broad View of ABM Treaty," *Washington Post*, February 9, 1987; R. Jeffrey Smith, "Legal Hurdles Remain for Key SDI Tests," *Washington Post*, February 10, 1987; Shultz, *Turmoil and Triumph*, 872.

26. Smith, "Legal Hurdles Remain"; Raymond Garthoff, "Correspondence: On Negotiating with the Russians," *International Security* 2, no. 1 (Summer 1977): 107–109.

27. Smith, "Legal Hurdles Remain."

28. R. Jeffrey Smith, "U.S. Defers Decision on ABM Pact," *Washington Post*, February 11, 1987; Pat Towell, "No Clear Winners, Losers," *CQ Weekly*, February 14, 1987, 271–274; FitzGerald, *Way Out There*, 393–394; Talbott, *Master of the Game*, 329; Mira Duric, *The Strategic Defence Initiative: US Policy and the Soviet Union* (Aldershot, Hampshire, England: Ashgate, 2003), 115.

29. Colin Norman, "Debate over SDI Enters New Phase," *Science* 235, no. 4786 (January 16, 1987): 277, 279; William Durch, *The ABM Treaty and Western Security* (Cambridge, MA: Ballinger Publishing, 1987), 62; Sanford Lakoff and Herbert F. York, *A Shield in Space? Technology, Politics, and the Strategic Defense Initiative* (Berkeley: University of California Press, 1989), 282.

30. George F. Will, "The Deterrence of a Strategic Defense," *Washington Post*, February 12, 1987.

31. N. Bloembergen et al., *Report to the American Physical Society of the Study Group on Science and Technology of Directed Energy Weapons*, reprinted in *Review of Modern Physics* 59, no. 3 (July 1987): S9.

32. Mary McGrory, "Treaty Trashing," *Washington Post*, February 12, 1987; Nunn, Oral History, September 5, 1995, SNPP; Winik, *On the Brink*, 573.

33. Nunn, Oral History; Winik, *On the Brink*, 574, 577.

34. Nunn, Oral History.

35. Mary McGrory, "History Beckons Sam Nunn," *Washington Post*, February 22, 1987.

36. Ronald Reagan, National Security Decision Directive 261, Consultations on the SDI Program, February 18, 1987; Tim Carrington and Jeffrey H. Birnbaum, "Pentagon Slows Its Push for a More Lax Interpretation of the 1972 ABM Treaty," *Wall Street Journal*, February 25, 1987.

37. "Delay Seen in Consultations on SDI," *CQ Weekly*, February 28, 1987, 398; Helen Dewar and R. Jeffrey Smith, "Administration Warned on SDI Testing," *Washington Post*, February 25, 1987.

38. Senator Samuel Augustus Nunn of Georgia, speaking on the Interpretation of the ABM Treaty, Part One: The Senate Ratification Proceedings, on March 11, 1987, 100th Cong., 1st Sess., *Congressional Record* 133, no. 38, S2967–S2968; R. Jeffrey Smith, "Nunn Takes Strict View on ABM," *Washington Post*, March 12, 1987; Michael R. Gordon, "Nunn Says Record on the ABM Treaty Is Being Distorted," *New York Times*, March 12, 1987; Nunn, Oral History; Winik, *On the Brink*, 577.

39. Nunn, speaking on the Interpretation of the ABM Treaty, Part One: The Senate Ratification Proceedings, S2967–S2968; Pat Towell, "Nunn Blasts Administration on ABM Treaty," *CQ Weekly*, March 14, 1987, 457–459; Matthew Bunn, *Foundation for the Future: The ABM Treaty and National Security* (Washington, DC: Arms Control Association, 1990), 68–69; Lakoff and York, *A Shield in Space?*, 183–184.

40. Nunn, speaking on the Interpretation of the ABM Treaty, Part One: The Senate Ratification Proceedings, S2967; Don Oberdorfer, "Sofaer Disavows Portion of ABM Pact Stand," *Washington Post*, March 27, 1987; Punaro interview, by Chaffin.
41. Nunn, Oral History.
42. Frank Carlucci, interview by Stephen Knott, Philip Zelikow, and Don Oberdorfer, August 28, 2001, Charlottesville, Virginia, Ronald Reagan Oral History Project, Miller Center of Public Affairs, University of Virginia.
43. Nunn, speaking on the Interpretation of the ABM Treaty, Part Two: Subsequent Practice under the ABM Treaty, on March 12, 1987, 100th Cong., 1st Sess., *Congressional Record* 133, no. 39, S3090–S3095; Towell, "Nunn Blasts Administration," 457–459.
44. Marjorie Williams, "Perle Resigns Top Arms Policy Post," *Washington Post*, March 13, 1987.
45. Towell, "Nunn Blasts Administration," 457–459.
46. Letter, Sofaer to Nunn, March 9, 1987, Subseries 9.7, Box 30, file: Defense/National Security Subject Files (A-D), SNP; R. Jeffrey Smith, "Nunn Takes Strict View on ABM," *Washington Post*, March 12, 1987.
47. Walter Pincus, "Administration Upset by Adviser's ABM Letter," *Washington Post*, March 17, 1987.
48. Nunn, speaking on the Interpretation of the ABM Treaty, Part Three: The ABM Negotiating Record, on March 13, 1987, 100th Cong., 1st Sess., *Congressional Record* 133, no. 40, S3171–S3173; Towell, "Nunn Blasts Administration," 457–459.
49. Nunn, speaking on the Interpretation of the ABM Treaty, Part Three: The ABM Negotiating Record, S3171–S3173; "For the Record," *Washington Post*, March 17, 1987; American Society of International Law, "The ABM Treaty Resolution," *American Journal of International Law* 82, no. 1 (January 1988): 156; Talbott, *Master of the Game*, 341; Thomas Graham Jr., *Disarmament Sketches: Three Decades of Arms Control and International Law* (Seattle: University of Washington Press, 2002), 155–157.
50. Helen Dewar, "Nunn Reshapes Arms Control Debate," *Washington Post*, March 18, 1987.
51. Editorial, "Sam Nunn and the ABM Treaty," *Washington Post*, March 15, 1987; Lakoff and York, *A Shield in Space?*, 288.
52. Towell, "Nunn Blasts Administration," 457–459; Mary McGrory, "'Star Wars' Heroics," *Washington Post*, March 19, 1987; Helen Dewar, "Hollings Backs Administration on ABM Treaty," *Washington Post*, March 20, 1987; Paul H. Nitze, with Ann M. Smith and Steven L. Rearden, *From Hiroshima to Glasnost: At the Center of Decision: A Memoir* (New York: Grove Weidenfeld, 1989), 438; Talbott, *Master of the Game*, 335; Winik, *On the Brink*, 578–579.
53. Deborah Hart Strober and Gerald S. Strober, *Reagan: The Man and His Presidency* (Boston, MA: Houghton Mifflin, 1998), 238.
54. Pat Towell, "House Panel Deals Setback to SDI Program," *CQ Weekly*, April 4, 1987, 614–615; Helen Dewar, "Hill 'Star Wars' Debate Escalates," *Washington Post*, April 13, 1987; Tamar Jacoby, with John Barry and Robert B. Cullen, "The Moscow Agenda," *Newsweek*, April 20, 1987, 24; Lakoff and York, *A Shield in*

Space?, 283–284; Douglas Waller, James T. Bruce, and Douglas Cook, "SDI: Progress and Challenges, Part II," US Congress, staff report submitted to Senators William Proxmire, J. Bennett Johnston, and Lawton Chiles, Washington, DC, March 17, 1987.

55. Senator Dan Quayle, Dear Colleague Letters, May 14, 20, June 3, 5, 1987, MS106.3.3.5.3.4, Box 1, Folder 1, Anti-Ballistic Missile Reinterpretation, 1986–87, William S. Cohen Papers (WCP), Raymond H. Fogler Library, University of Maine, Orono, ME; Dewar, "Hill 'Star Wars' Debate Escalates"; Jacoby, Barry, and Cullen, "The Moscow Agenda," 24.

56. R. Jeffrey Smith, "Broad ABM-Pact View Justified, Sofaer Asserts," *Washington Post*, May 1, 1987.

57. Sam Nunn, "Should the Nunn-Levin Amendment Be Approved?" *Congressional Digest* 66, no. 11 (November 1987): 272.

58. George de Lama, "Study Backs Reagan on Arms," *Chicago Tribune*, May 14, 1987.

59. De Lama, "Study Backs Reagan"; Nunn, Oral History; Senator Patrick Leahy, Speaking on the Levin-Nunn Language to Limit Testing or Deployment of SDI in Violation of the ABM Treaty, 100th Cong., 1st Sess., *Congressional Record* 133, no. 82, May 20, 1987, S6847.

60. Nunn, speaking on the Interpretation of the ABM Treaty, *National Defense Authorization Act for Fiscal Years 1988 and 1989*, Part Four: An Examination of Judge Sofaer's Analysis of the Negotiating Record, 100th Cong., 1st Sess., *Congressional Record* 133, no. 82, May 20, 1987: S6809–S6831; Garthoff, *Policy versus the Law*, 17.

61. Senate Committee on Foreign Relations, *The ABM Treaty Interpretation Resolution*, Report of the Committee on Foreign Relations, US Senate, together with additional views (Washington, DC: US Government Printing Office, 1987); Senator Dan Quayle, Dear Colleague Letters, May 14, 20, June 3, 5, 1987, MS106.3.3.5.3.4, Box 1, Folder 3, Anti-Ballistic Missile Reinterpretation, 1986–87, WCP; Helen Dewar, "Senate Committee Endorses 'Star Wars' Limits," *Washington Post*, May 6, 1987; Bunn, *Foundation for the Future*, 60.

62. Nunn, Oral History.

63. Helen Dewar, "Democrats Plan End-Run around Defense Spending Filibuster," *Washington Post*, July 18, 1987; Dewar, "Senate GOP Thwarts Arms Control Faceoff," *Washington Post*, July 25, 1987; "Negotiations Prove Fruitless: Defense Stalemate Drags On," *CQ Weekly*, July 25, 1987, 1667.

64. Talbott, *Master of the Game*, 354.

65. Nunn to Reagan, September 1, 1987, MS106.3.3.5.3.4, Box 1, Folder 1, Anti-Ballistic Missile Reinterpretation, 1986–87, WCP; Pat Towell, "Waiting for the INF Treaty: Political Jockeying," *CQ Weekly*, September 5, 1987, 2123; Don Oberdorfer, "Nunn Threatens to Link INF, ABM Treaties," *Washington Post*, September 3, 1987.

66. Lou Cannon, "Reagan Seeks to Avert Treaty Fight with Nunn," *Washington Post*, September 4, 1987.

67. Helen Dewar, "Democrats Targeting 'Star Wars' Filibuster," *Washington Post*, September 11, 1987.

68. Janet Hook, "SDI Limits Still Hotly Contested: Senate Begins Defense Debate as GOP Abandons Filibuster," *CQ Weekly*, September 12, 1987, 2195.

69. Helen Dewar, "GOP Senators End 4-Month Filibuster," *Washington Post*, September 12, 1987.

70. Helen Dewar, "Senate Breaks Another Arms Impasse," *Washington Post*, September 16, 1987.

71. Pat Towell, with Steve Pressman, "Senate Deals Reagan a Major Defeat on SDI," *CQ Weekly*, September 19, 1987, 2228; Helen Dewar, "Senate Votes to Curb SDI Testing," *Washington Post*, September 18, 1987.

72. Ernest Hollings, "Fighting over the ABM Treaty," *Washington Post*, September 29, 1987.

73. American Society of International Law, "The ABM Treaty Resolution," 152, 157.

74. Sam Nunn, "Sen. Nunn Replies," *Washington Post*, October 1, 1987; Bunn, *Foundation for the Future*, 59.

75. Helen Dewar, "Reagan, Hill on Collision Course," *Washington Post*, October 3, 1987; Tim Carrington, "Defense Spending Bill, Passed by Senate after Bitter Dispute," *Wall Street Journal*, October 5, 1987.

76. Pat Towell, "Senate Rebuffs Reagan on Key Defense Issues," *CQ Weekly*, October 3, 1987, 2359.

77. Charles Krauthammer, "Sam Nunn and the Imperial Senate," *Washington Post*, October 6, 1987.

78. Dewar, "Senate Votes to Curb SDI Testing."

79. Pat Towell, "Warner: Seeking Compromise, Finding Criticism," *CQ Weekly*, October 31, 1987, 2675.

80. R. Jeffrey Smith, "Carlucci Vows Cooperation on Defense," *Washington Post*, November 13, 1987; Pat Towell, "Controversy over ABM, SALT," *CQ Weekly*, November 7, 1987, 2722.

81. Quoted in Duric, *The Strategic Defence Initiative*, 117.

82. Helen Dewar, "Senate Defense Bill Sent to White House," *Washington Post*, November 20, 1987; Pat Towell, "Final Amount Depends on Budget Summit," *CQ Weekly*, November 21, 1987, 2865; FitzGerald, *Way Out There*, 393.

83. Congressional Quarterly, *Almanac*, 100th Cong., 1st Sess., 193, 207; Sara Fritz, "Opting Out of the Race, Nunn Emerges as Tough Partisan," *Los Angeles Times*, October 4, 1987.

84. Bell, quoted in Winik, *On the Brink*, 573.

Chapter 10. Down to Zero

1. Susan F. Rasky, "Reporter's Notebook: Arms Debate," *New York Times*, February 1, 1988.

2. William H. Honan, "Claiborne Pell, Ex-Senator, Dies at 90," *New York Times*, January 1, 2009; Scott MacKay, "The Life and Times of an Uncommon Man: Sen. Claiborne Pell," Rhode Island Public Radio, October 20, 2011, https://wrnipoliticsblog.wordpress.com/2011/10/20/the-life-and-times-of-an-uncommon-man-sen-claiborne-pell/.

3. Senate Committee on Foreign Relations, *Hearing, INF Treaty,* 100th Cong., 2nd Sess., Part 1, January 25, 1988, 1; "Soviet Union–United States Summit in Washington, DC," joint statement, December 10, 1987, *Presidential Documents,* vol. 23 (December 12, 1987), 1494.

4. Letter, Byrd to Nunn, December 2, 1986; Letter, Nunn to Byrd, December, 2, 1987; and Leadership Coordinating Fact Sheet on INF Treaty, December 4, 1987, all in Subseries 11.3, Box 6, file, INF Hearings, Sam Nunn Papers (SNP), Stuart A. Rose Manuscript, Archives, and Rare Book Library, Emory University, Atlanta, GA; Julie Johnson, "Washington Talk: Congress; Arms Pact: Next Hurdle Is Senate 'Graveyard,'" *New York Times,* January 12, 1988; Janne E. Nolan, "The INF Treaty," in *The Politics of Arms Control Treaty Ratification,* ed. Michael Krepon and Dan Caldwell (New York: St. Martin's Press, 1991), 373.

5. Condoleezza Rice, "U.S.-Soviet Relations," in *Looking Back on the Reagan Presidency,* ed. Larry Berman (Baltimore, MD: Johns Hopkins University Press, 1990), 81.

6. Raymond L. Garthoff, *The Great Transition: American-Soviet Relations and the End of the Cold War* (Washington, DC: Brookings, 1994), 326–327; James Voorhees, *Dialogue Sustained: The Multilevel Peace Process and the Dartmouth Conference* (Washington, DC: United States Institute of Peace Press, 2002), 194–195; William E. Pemberton, *Exit with Honor: The Life and Presidency of Ronald Reagan* (Armonk, NY: M. E. Sharpe, 1997), 195; David Hoffman, "NATO Is Halting Deployment," *Washington Post,* November 26, 1987; William E. Kline, "The INF Treaty," Case Program, C-16-89-887, Kennedy School of Government, Harvard University, 1989, 1, 4.

7. Senate Committee on Foreign Relations, *Hearing, INF Treaty,* Part 1, 3–9; Garthoff, *The Great Transition,* 327, 334; Pemberton, *Exit with Honor,* 195. See also David T. Jones, interviewed by Charles Stuart Kennedy, March 16, 1999, Association for Diplomatic Studies and Training, Foreign Affairs Oral History Project.

8. Howard Phillips, "The Treaty: Another Sellout," *New York Times,* December 11, 1987; E. J. Dionne Jr., "Leaderless Conservatives Approach '88 in Splinters," *New York Times,* December 13, 1987.

9. Senate Committee on Foreign Relations, *Hearing, INF Treaty,* Part 1, 3–5.

10. Hedrick Smith, "The Right Against Reagan," *New York Times,* January 17, 1988; Frederick Kempe and Tim Carrington, "Senate Opens Debate on Missile Treaty as Politics Promises to Lengthen Process," *Wall Street Journal,* January 26, 1988.

11. Senate Committee on Foreign Relations, *Hearing, INF Treaty,* Part 1, 5–9; Susan Rasky, "Senate Hearings on Missile Treaty a Test for Reagan," *New York Times,* January 24, 1988.

12. Senate, Committee on Foreign Relations, *Hearing, INF Treaty,* Part 1, 1.

13. Johnson, "Next Hurdle Is Senate 'Graveyard.'"

14. Senate Committee on Foreign Relations, *Hearing, INF Treaty,* Part 1, 9–29; George Shultz, "The INF Treaty: Strengthening U.S. Security," *Current Policy,* no. 1038, US Department of State, Bureau of Public Affairs, Washington, DC.

15. Senate Committee on Armed Services, *Hearing, NATO Defense and the INF Treaty,* 100th Cong., 2nd Sess., Part 1, January 25, 1988, 1, 3, 27; Robert Bell,

email message to author, February 22, 2015; John T. Shaw, *Richard Lugar, States-*
man of the Senate: Crafting Foreign Policy from Capitol Hill (Bloomington: Indiana
University Press, 2012), 178–179; Letter, Nunn and Warner to Stevens, December 10, 1987, Subseries 11.3, Box 16, INF Treaty, SNP.

16. David T. Jones, *The Senate and INF Ratification* (Carlisle, PA: US Army War College, Strategic Studies Institute, 1992), 12.

17. Senate Committee on Armed Services, *Hearing, NATO Defense and the INF*
Treaty, Part 1, 1–3; Nunn, Oral History, September 5, 1996, SNPP; "Reducing
Missiles in Europe," *New York Times*, January 24, 1988; Rasky, "Senate Hear-
ings on Missile Treaty a Test for Reagan." See also Context for Researchers on
SASC Consideration of INF Treaty file, Senate Papers, SASC Box 6, Intermedi-
ate Nuclear Forces Treaty, James R. Locher III Papers (JLP), Special Collections,
National Defense University Library, Fort Lesley J. McNair, Washington, DC.

18. Senate Committee on Armed Services, *Hearing, NATO Defense and the INF*
Treaty, Part 1, 29–31, 38–43, 61; Helen Dewar, "INF Treaty Bolsters Security,"
Washington Post, January 26, 1988. See William J. Crowe Jr., with David Chanoff,
The Line of Fire: From Washington to the Gulf, the Politics and Battles of the New
Military (New York: Simon & Schuster, 1993), 310; and Secretary of Defense
Frank C. Carlucci, US Department of Defense, *Support of NATO Strategy in the*
1990s: A Report to the United States Congress in Compliance with Public Law 100-
180, January 25, 1988, Senate Papers, SASC Box 6, Intermediate Nuclear Forces
Treaty, JLP.

19. Dewar, "INF Treaty Bolsters Security."

20. Senate Committee on Armed Services, *Hearing, NATO Defense and the INF*
Treaty, Part 1, 63–83, 86–132; Dewar, "INF Treaty Bolsters Security"; Memorandum, Bell to Nunn, subject: Final Verification Details in INF, Subseries 11.3, Box
6, file, INF Treaty, and Memorandum, Bell and Locher to Nunn, subject: Recap
of Carlucci/Crowe Hearing, January 25, Box16, INF Treaty, SNP.

21. Jones, *The Senate and INF Ratification*, 9–10; Memorandum, Smith, Effron, Bell,
and Goodman to Nunn, subject: Effect of the Sofaer doctrine on the relationship
between the negotiating record and ratification proceedings on the INF Treaty,
December 15, 1987, with attachments, Subseries 11.3, Box 17, INF Treaty, SNP.

22. Rasky, "Senate Hearings on Missile Treaty a Test for Reagan"; R. Jeffrey Smith,
"Girding for Battle on the INF Treaty," *Washington Post*, January 24, 1988.

23. Rice, "U.S.-Soviet Relations," 87.

24. Senate Committee on Armed Services, *Hearing, NATO Defense and the INF*
Treaty, 100th Cong., 2nd Sess., Part 2, January 29, 1988, 2–63.

25. Senate Committee on Armed Services, *Hearing, NATO Defense and the INF*
Treaty, Part 2, 66–93.

26. Senate Committee on Armed Services, *Hearing, NATO Defense and the INF*
Treaty, Part 2, February 1–2, 1988, 100–158, 160–211, 215–247; *Hearing, NATO*
Defense and the INF Treaty, Part 3, February 4, 1988, 82–176.

27. "Briefing; High-Level Gathering," *New York Times*, February 5, 1988.

28. R. Jeffrey Smith, "Dispute Threatens INF Treaty," *Washington Post*, February 6,
1988.

29. Nunn and Robert Byrd, letter to Shultz, February 5, 1988, Senate Papers, SASC Box 6, Intermediate Nuclear Forces Treaty, INF—Shultz Letter file, JLP; Smith, "Dispute Threatens INF Treaty"; Michael R. Gordon, "Key Democrats Threaten to Stall Missile Treaty over ABM Dispute," *New York Times*, February 6, 1988.

30. Michael R. Gordon, "White House Criticizes Democrats for Threatening Arms Pact Delay," *New York Times*, February 7, 1988; Rudy Abramson, "Threat to Stall Nuclear Treaty Called Political," *Los Angeles Times*, February 9, 1988; Memorandum, National Security Planning Group Meeting, February 9, 1988, subject: US Options for Arms Control Summit, Ronald Reagan Presidential Library, https://www.thereaganfiles.com/880209.pdf.

31. Joe Biden, *Promises to Keep: On Life and Politics* (New York: Random House, 2007), 216.

32. Editorial, "Sound Way Out of the Treaty Trap," *New York Times*, February 9, 1988; Howell Raines, "Senators Soothe Europe on Arms Pacts," *New York Times*, February 9, 1988; Robert Bell, email message to author, February 22, 2015.

33. "Lance," US Army Aviation and Missile Life Cycle Management Command, https://history.redstone.army.mil/miss-lance.html; James M. Markham, "Carlucci Calls for New Tactical Missiles," *New York Times*, February 8, 1988; Sam Nunn, "The American/Soviet Disarmament Negotiations and their Consequences for NATO," Speech to the Wehrkunde Conference, February 7, 1988, Senate Papers, SASC Box 6, Intermediate Nuclear Forces Treaty, Wehrkunde Speech—Senator Nunn—Feb 1988 file, JLP; Nunn, Wehrkunde Conference speech, "INF Treaty: Implications for NATO," Feb. 7, 1988, Subseries 6.5, Box 140, File: 1988, SNP.

34. Rudy Abramson, "Pact Delay Threatened by Senators: Nunn, Byrd Seek Pledge on White House INF Views," *Los Angeles Times*, February 7, 1988; Tim Carrington, "Kohl Stance on Nuclear Arms Intensified Allied Concerns about European Defense," *Wall Street Journal*, February 8, 1988.

35. Nunn, telephone interview by author, May 1, 2015.

36. William Tuohy, "Carlucci Warns Europe of U.S. Pullout on Arms Issue," *Los Angeles Times*, February 8, 1988.

37. R. Jeffrey Smith, "INF Rift Widens as Biden and Pell Up the Ante," *Washington Post*, February 9, 1988.

38. Shultz, letter to Nunn, February 9, 1988, Senate Papers, SASC Box 6, Intermediate Nuclear Forces Treaty, INF—Shultz Letter file, JLP; R. Jeffrey Smith, "Shultz Signs Letter Accepting Democrats' Demand in INF Dispute," *Washington Post*, February 10, 1988; "Shultz Tells Senate to Consider INF Testimony Authoritative," *Los Angeles Times*, February 10, 1988.

39. Michael R. Gordon, "2 Senate Democrats End Threat to Delay Pact," *New York Times*, February 11, 1988.

40. R. Jeffrey Smith, "Shultz INF Letter Soothes 2 Senators, Angers 3rd," *Washington Post*, February 11, 1988.

41. Helen Dewar, "INF Debate Turns into Partisan Power Struggle," *Washington Post*, February 11, 1988.

42. R. Jeffrey Smith, "When Treaty Interpretations Differ, Who Has the Last Word?" *Washington Post,* February 17, 1988.

43. Smith, "When Treaty Interpretations Differ"; John M. Broder and Rudy Abramson, "Administration Yields in Arms Treaty Dispute," *Los Angeles Times,* February 11, 1988; Editorial, "The INF Ballet," *Wall Street Journal,* February 11, 1988; Edwin M. Yoder Jr., "What's in a Treaty?" *Washington Post,* February 15, 1988; Robert F. Turner, "Beware the Tyranny of the Senate," *Wall Street Journal,* February 22, 1988.

44. John H. Cushman, Jr., "$299-Billion Military Budget Drops Weapons and People," *New York Times,* February 19, 1988.

45. Hearing, *NATO Defense and the INF Treaty,* 100th Cong., 2nd Sess., Part 4, February 22–23, 1988, 339–490.

46. Helen Dewar, "Byrd, Allies Agree to Smooth Way for INF Pact," *Washington Post,* March 1, 1988; Jules Witcover, *Joe Biden: A Life of Trial and Redemption* (New York: William Morrow, 2010), 236.

47. Gary Lee, "Gorbachev Sees Pact on Arms by Summit," *Washington Post,* March 12, 1988.

48. Helen Dewar, "Byrd, Allies Agree to Smooth Way for INF Pact": Witcover, *Joe Biden,* 238, 239; R. Jeffrey Smith, "White House Opposes Conditions Democrats Seeking for INF Treaty," *Washington Post,* March 19, 1988; Rudy Abramson, "Administration Opposes Senators' Demand on Pact," *Los Angeles Times,* March 19, 1988.

49. Robert F. Turner, "Beware the Tyranny of the Senate," *Wall Street Journal,* February 22, 1988; Nunn, Letter to the Editor, *Wall Street Journal,* March 15, 1988.

50. Smith, "White House Opposes Conditions"; Abramson, "Administration Opposes Senators' Demand on Pact."

51. Michael R. Gordon, "Democrats Clash with Reagan over Arms Treaty," *New York Times,* March 20, 1988; Culvahouse to Lugar, March 17, 1988, and March 22, 1988, Subscrics, 6.5, Box 140, file, "Whites" (loose material unidentified), SNP.

52. R. Jeffrey Smith, "U.S. Can Verify Soviet INF Pact Compliance, Panel Says," *Washington Post,* March 23, 1988.

53. Rudy Abramson, "Senators Reject Missile Treaty 'Killers,'" *Los Angeles Times,* March 24, 1988.

54. R. Jeffrey Smith, "U.S. Can Verify Soviet INF Pact Compliance"; Jones, *The Senate and INF Ratification,* 16–17; Nunn, Prepared Statement, testimony before Foreign Relations Committee, March 22, 1988, Subseries 6.5, Box 140, File: 1988, SNP.

55. Senate Committee on Armed Services, *NATO Defense and INF Treaty,* Report 100-312 (Washington, DC: US Government Printing Office, April 1988); Helen Dewar, "INF Treaty Called Unclear on Futuristic Weapons," *Washington Post,* March 29, 1988; Robert Bell, email message to author, February 22, 2015.

56. Helen Dewar, "Senate Unit Approves INF Treaty," *Washington Post,* March 31, 1988.

57. Dewar, "Senate Unit"; Lucy Howard, "An INF Snag," *Newsweek,* April 4, 1988, 7; Letter Nunn and Warner to Carlucci with attachment ("Additional Questions on

the INF Treaty & Future Weapons"), April 11, 1988, Subseries 11.3, Box 16, file, INF Treaty, SNP.

58. Helen Dewar, "Discord Rises over INF Coverage," *Washington Post*, April 15, 1988.

59. Susan F. Rasky, "Nunn Says Arms Treaty May Need Amendment on Future Weapons," *New York Times*, April 20, 1988.

60. Helen Dewar, "Byrd: Senate Won't 'Rush' on INF Pact," *Washington Post*, April 22, 1988; Pete Wilson, Letter to the Editor, *Washington Post*, May 7, 1988.

61. Dewar, "Byrd: Senate Won't 'Rush' on INF Pact."

62. Helen Dewar, "Senate Prodded on INF Pact Approval," *Washington Post*, April 26, 1988; R. Jeffrey Smith, "U.S., Soviets Dispute INF Verification," *Washington Post*, April 29, 1988; Susan F. Rasky, "Arms Pact Debate Is Tentatively Set," *New York Times*, April 30, 1988.

63. Helen Dewar, "Senate Plans INF Pact Debate May 11," *Washington Post*, April 30, 1988.

64. Rudy Abramson, "Key Senate Democrats Want 4 INF Pact Issues Clarified," *Los Angeles Times*, April 30, 1988.

65. Maynard Glitman, *The Last Battle of the Cold War: An Inside Account of Negotiating the Intermediate Range Nuclear Forces Treaty* (New York: Palgrave Macmillan, 2006), 230; Garthoff, *The Great Transition*, 335, 347.

66. Susan F. Rasky, "Bedeviling an Arms Pact: The Details," *New York Times*, May 11, 1988.

67. Glitman, *The Last Battle of the Cold War*, 230–231; Susan F. Rasky, "Tone in the Senate Turns Upbeat as Obstacles to Arms Treaty Fade," *New York Times*, May 14, 1988.

68. Josh Getlin, "Nunn Says Odds Favor INF Pact OK by Summit Time," *Los Angeles Times*, May 23, 1988; Jack F. Matlock Jr., *Reagan and Gorbachev: How the Cold War Ended* (New York: Random House, 2004), 247.

69. Helen Dewar, "Shultz, Dole Ask End to INF Delays," *Washington Post*, May 24, 1988; Susan F. Rasky, "Toward the Summit," *New York Times*, May 27, 1988; Rudy Abramson, "Dole Threatens to End Debate on Arms Pact," *Los Angeles Times*, May 24, 1988; David T. Jones, interview.

70. Senate Amendment 2302 to Treaty 100-11; Susan F. Rasky, "Toward the Summit," *New York Times*, May 27, 1988; David A. Koplow, "When Is an Amendment Not an Amendment? Modification of Arms Control Agreements without the Senate," *University of Chicago Law Review* 59, no. 3 (Summer 1992): 886n6; Frances FitzGerald, *Way Out There in the Blue: Reagan, Star Wars, and the End of the Cold War* (New York: Simon & Schuster, 2000), 442; Letter, Nunn to Biden, May 27, 1988, Subseries 11.3, Box 16, File, INF Treaty, SNP.

71. Editorial, "INF's Killer Condition," *Wall Street Journal*, May 27, 1988.

72. Rasky, "Toward the Summit."

73. Glitman, *The Last Battle of the Cold War*, 232; Helen Dewar, "Senate Approves Historic INF Treaty," *Washington Post*, May 28, 1988.

74. Nolan, "The INF Treaty," 358.

75. Dewar, "Senate Approves Historic INF Treaty."

Chapter 11. The Teflon Senator with Clout

1. Ann Devroy, "Bush Sends Signals to Congress," *Washington Post,* January 22, 1989. Bush reiterated this goal at his first press conference as president on January 27, 1989, AP Archive, https://www.youtube.com/watch?v=KRwL2Zy6R-w.

2. Al From, with Alice McKeon, *The New Democrats and the Return to Power* (New York: Palgrave Macmillan, 2011), 96.

3. Robin Toner, "Transition in Washington," *New York Times,* January 19, 1989.

4. Don Oberdorfer, "Bush Teams Plans Early Review of Military," *Washington Post,* January 17, 1989; Gerald M. Boyd, "Bush Aides Plan Review of Policy toward Russians," *New York Times,* January 15, 1989.

5. David Hoffman, "Gorbachev Seen as Trying to Buy Time for Reform," *Washington Post,* January 23, 1989.

6. Michael R. Gordon, "Soviet Limit Their Quick-Strike Ability," *New York Times,* January 26, 1989.

7. Bob Schieffer, *This Just In: What I Couldn't Tell You on TV* (New York: G. P. Putnam's Sons, 2003), 315, 318.

8. Senate Committee on Armed Services, *Nomination of John G. Tower to Be Secretary of Defense,* 101st Cong., 1st Sess., 1989, 1–2, 5–7.

9. Helen Dewar, "Tower Says He'd Accept Hill Budget Constraints," *Washington Post,* January 26, 1989; Dan Balz, "Senate Panel Amicable in Questioning of Tower," *Washington Post,* January 27, 1989.

10. Senate Committee on Armed Services, *Nomination of John G. Tower,* 240–253; Mary McGrory, "Sweet Babble of Tower," *Washington Post,* January 29, 1989; Helen Dewar, "Tower's Moral Character Questioned," *Washington Post,* February 1, 1989.

11. Senate Committee on Armed Services, *Nomination of John G. Tower,* 289–339; Helen Dewar, "Tower Tries to Allay Senators' Doubts," *Washington Post,* February 2, 1989; Schieffer, *This Just In,* 315.

12. Alison Pytte, "Questions of Conduct Delay Vote on Tower," *CQ Weekly,* February 4, 1989, 222.

13. Pytte, "Questions of Conduct," 222; Helen Dewar, "New Probe Delays Vote on Tower," *Washington Post,* February 3, 1989.

14. John J. Fialka and Andy Pasztor, "Tower Nomination as Defense Secretary Faces Growing Trouble on Senate Panel," *Wall Street Journal,* February 8, 1989; Timothy Noah, "Born to Be Mild," *Washington Monthly,* December 1989, 11, 16; Sam A. Nunn Jr., interview by Myron A. Farber, June 3, 2013, Session no. 1, transcript, Carnegie Corporation of New York Oral History Project, Columbia Center for Oral History, Columbia University, New York, NY.

15. Helen Dewar, "New Charge Snags Vote on Tower," *Washington Post,* February 8, 1989.

16. Andrew Rosenthal, "2 Top Democrats Ready to Oppose Tower Nomination," *New York Times,* February 8, 1989.

17. Helen Dewar, "Tower Vote Delayed for at Least 2 Weeks," *Washington Post,* February 9, 1989; Schieffer, *This Just In,* 315–316; Arnold Punaro, telephone interview by author, January 23, 2020.

18. Helen Dewar, "Nunn Sees White House Inconsistency on Tower," *Washington Post*, February 10, 1989; Pat Towell, "Financial Dealings Examined: Vote on Nomination of Tower Delayed," *CQ Weekly*, February 11, 1989, 259; Helen Dewar and Ann Devroy, "Senate Panel May Vote on Tower Thursday," *Washington Post*, February 22, 1989; Nunn, Letter to the Editor, *Wall Street Journal*, February 23, 1989; Chuck Alston, "The Teflon Senator Slugs It Out," *CQ Weekly*, March 4, 1989, 462.

19. David Hoffman, "President, Lawmakers Probe How to Avoid Rifts," *Washington Post*, February 12, 1989.

20. Ann Devroy and Helen Dewar, "FBI Offers No Evidence Tower 'Unfit,' Aide Says," *Washington Post*, February 21, 1989.

21. Roland McElroy, *The Best President the Nation Never Had* (Macon, GA: Mercer University Press, 2017), 174–176.

22. Senate Committee on Armed Services, "Statement of Senator Nunn on Tower Nomination," Press Release, February 23, 1989, Subseries 9.7, Box 42, file 1982–1994 (2 of 2), Press Room 315, Sam Nunn Papers (SNP), Stuart A. Rose Manuscript, Archives, and Rare Book Library, Emory University, Atlanta, GA; Robin Toner, "Pivotal Southerner Votes Thumbs Down on Tower," *New York Times*, February 24, 1989.

23. Helen Dewar, "Nunn, a Fellow Southerner, Is Crucial to Tower's Chances," *Washington Post*, February 21, 1989; Senate Committee on Armed Services, *Nomination of John G. Tower*, 1, 341–390; Helen Dewar and Tom Kenworthy, "Senate Panel Rejects Tower's Pentagon Nomination," *Washington Post*, February 24, 1989; Senate Committee on Armed Services, Report with minority views, *Consideration of the Honorable John G. Tower to be Secretary of Defense*, February 28, 1989, Subseries 9.7, Box 20, SNP.

24. Robin Toner, "G.O.P. Leaders in Senate Striving to Keep Tower Nomination Alive," *New York Times*, February 25, 1989; Helen Dewar, "GOP Fights to Save Tower Nomination," *Washington Post*, February 25, 1989; R. W. Apple Jr., "Tower Effort: Skirmish, Not a War," *New York Times*, February 27, 1989; Charles Harman, interview by Tom Chaffin, June 4, 1996, Atlanta, GA, Box 1, Sam Nunn Oral History Collection, Stuart A. Rose Manuscript, Archives, and Rare Book Library, Emory University, Atlanta, GA.

25. Editorial, "The Tower Fight," *Washington Post*, February 28, 1989; Dan Balz, "Fast Transition from Bipartisanship to Arm Twisting," *Washington Post*, February 28, 1989.

26. McElroy, *The Best President*, 175; Schieffer, *This Just In*, 316, 318–319, Nunn, interview by author, Washington, DC, May 9, 2018.

27. McElroy, *The Best President*, 176; David Rogers, "GOP Arranges Delay in Vote on Tower," *Wall Street Journal*, March 2, 1989; David Lauter, "Democrats Appear to Rally 'Round Nunn," *Los Angeles Times*, March 2, 1989; Dewar, "Nunn, a Fellow Southerner"; Schieffer, *This Just In*, 317, 318, 318; Fred R. Harris, *Deadlock or Decision: The U.S. Senate and the Rise of National Politics* (New York: Oxford University Press, 1993), 160–163; Memo from Rocky Rief to Arnold Punaro, re: Letters regarding Tower Nomination and Memo from Rief to Nunn, March 10,

1989, Reaction to Your Vote on Tower Nomination in Subseries 6.5, Box 140, file, Tower Nomination, SNP, and Memo from Lyles, Bell, and Effron to Nunn, *Washington Post* article "Tracing the Steps of Tower's Downfall," March 29, 1989, Subseries 9.7, Box 20, John Tower Confirmation Files, SNP.

28. Mary McGrory, "An Easy One for Democrats," *Washington Post,* March 2, 1989; Robin Toner, "Senators Mark Congress's Rich Past before Facing the Painful Present," *New York Times,* March 3, 1989.

29. Alston, "The Teflon Senator Slugs It Out," 462.

30. Letter from Nunn to Oliver Bateman, May 18, 1989, Subseries 6.5, Box 140, File, "Whites" (loose material unidentified), SNP.

31. Pat Towell, "Senate Wages Partisan Duel on Fitness, Prerogatives," *CQ Weekly,* March 4, 1989, 461; David S. Broder, "It's Showtime, George," *Washington Post,* March 12, 1989.

32. George H. W. Bush, *All the Best, George Bush: My Life in Letters and Other Writings* (New York: Scribner, 2013), 414.

33. Helen Dewar, "Senate Kills Tower's Nomination as Defense Chief, 53–47," *Washington Post,* March 10, 1989; Michael Oreskes, "Senate Rejects Tower, 53–47," *New York Times,* March 10, 1989.

34. Helen Dewar, "Senate Kills Tower's Nomination"; Oreskes, "Senate Rejects Tower"; David Hoffman, "Rep. Cheney Chosen as Defense Nominee," *Washington Post,* March 11, 1989; George Bush, "The President's News Conference," March 10, 1989, online at Gerhard Peters and John T. Woolley, American Presidency Project, https://www.presidency.ucsb.edu/node/248446.

35. George Bush and Brent Scowcroft, *A World Transformed* (New York: Alfred A. Knopf, 1998), 23; Senate Committee on Armed Services, *Nominations Before the Senate Armed Services Committee,* 101st Cong., 1st Sess., 1989, 1–12, 22, 26, 29–30, 33–34, 37, 41–42, 44, 47–49, 52–53, 56–58, 61; Andrew Rosenthal, "Cheney Gets Warm Reception in Senate Hearing," *New York Times,* March 15, 1989; Helen Dewar, "Panel Approves Cheney Nomination," *Washington Post,* March 17, 1989; Melissa Healy, "Senators Vote 92–0 for Cheney Confirmation," *Los Angeles Times,* March 18, 1989; Department of Defense, 101st Cong., 1st Sess., Congressional Record 135, no. 31, March 17, 1989: S2994, in the *Congressional ProQuest,* accessed February 3, 2020.

36. Raymond L. Garthoff, *The Great Transition: American-Soviet Relations and the End of the Cold War* (Washington, DC: Brookings Institution Press, 1994), 376; George Bush, National Security Review 3, Comprehensive Review of US-Soviet Relations, February 15, 1989, George H. W. Bush Presidential Library (GHWBL), https://bush41library.tamu.edu/files/nsr/nsr3.pdf.

37. Garthoff, *The Great Transition,* 377; George Bush, National Security Directive 23, United States Relations with the Soviet Union, September 22, 1989, GHWBL, https://bush41library.tamu.edu/files/nsd/nsd23.pdf; Dick Cheney, *In My Time: A Personal and Political Memoir* (New York: Threshold Editions, 2011), 158.

38. Paul Wolfowitz, "Shaping the Future: Planning at the Pentagon, 1989–93," in *In Uncertain Times: American Foreign Policy after the Berlin Wall and 9/11,* ed. Melvin P. Leffler and Jeffrey W. Legro (Ithaca, NY: Cornell University Press, 2011), 45.

39. Richard A. Melanson, "George Bush's Search for a Post–Cold War Grand Strategy," in *The Bush Presidency: Ten Intimate Perspectives of George Bush*, ed. Kenneth W. Thompson (Lanham, MD: University Press of America, 1998), 155; Wolfowitz, "Shaping the Future," 46, 47; Robert L. Hutchings, *American Diplomacy and the End of the Cold War: An Insider's Account of U.S. Policy in Europe, 1989–1992* (Baltimore, MD: Johns Hopkins University Press, 1997), 28; Ronald E. Powaski, *The Entangling Alliance: The United States and European Security, 1950–1993* (Westport, CT: Greenwood Press, 1994), 163.

40. Bob Woodward, *The Commanders* (New York: Simon & Schuster, 1991), 69.

41. Don M. Snider, *Strategy, Forces and Budgets: Dominant Influences in Executive Decision Making, Post–Cold War, 1989–91* (Carlisle, PA: US Army War College, Strategic Studies Institute, 1993), 13–14.

42. Pat Towell, "Defense Spending Decisions Sure to Stir Controversy," *CQ Weekly*, April 22, 1989, 915.

43. Powaski, *The Entangling Alliance*, 163; Hutchings, *American Diplomacy and the End of the Cold War*, 8–9.

44. Bush, *All the Best*, 418.

45. Hutchings, *American Diplomacy and the End of the Cold War*, 9, 10, 11.

46. Michael R. Gordon, "Pentagon Chief Urges Cancelling Midgetman Plan," *New York Times*, April 20, 1989; Don Oberdorfer, *From the Cold War to a New Era: The United States and the Soviet Union, 1983–1991*, updated ed. (Baltimore, MD: Johns Hopkins University Press, 1999), 347.

47. R. Jeffrey Smith, "Missiles for Roads and Rails," *Washington Post*, April 24, 1989; Mary McGrory, "Bush Picks 'All of the Above,'" *Washington Post*, April 25, 1989; Hutchings, *American Diplomacy and the End of the Cold War*, 28.

48. Senate Committee on Armed Services, Department of Defense Authorization for Appropriations for Fiscal Years 1990 and 1991, 101st Cong., 1st Sess., 1989, 54–60; George C. Wilson, "NATO 'Shooting Itself in the Foot,'" *Washington Post*, May 4, 1989.

49. Senate Committee on Armed Services, Department of Defense Authorization for Appropriations for Fiscal Years 1990 and 1991, 54–60; Wilson, "NATO 'Shooting Itself in the Foot'"; Don Oberdorfer, "President Adamant on Missile Talks," *Washington Post*, May 4, 1989.

50. Senate Committee on Armed Services, Department of Defense Authorization for Appropriations for Fiscal Years 1990 and 1991, 286–296, 310–312; Andrew Rosenthal, "Pentagon Off Target by $150 Billion," *New York Times*, May 11, 1989.

51. Bush, *All the Best*, 426.

52. R. Jeffrey Smith, "Bipartisan Praise Greets Bush Proposal," *Washington Post*, May 31, 1989; Oberdorfer, *From the Cold War*, 346–350; Garthoff, *The Great Transition*, 380–381; George Bush, "Remarks Announcing a Conventional Arms Control Initiative and a Question-and-Answer Session with Reporters in Brussels," May 29, 1989, GHWBL, https://bush41library.tamu.edu/archives/public-papers/464.

53. Richard Halloran, "Stealth Bomber Is Given Go-Ahead," *New York Times*, June 10, 1989; "B-2 Is Key to U.S. Defense Strategy," *Los Angeles Times*, July 12, 1989.

54. Helen Dewar, "Missile Plan in Peril," *Washington Post*, June 14, 1989; Dewar, "Bush's 'Two-Missile' Proposal Jeopardized," *Washington Post*, June 19, 1989.

55. Helen Dewar, "Bush Pledges Major Increase in Midgetman Missile Funds," *Washington Post*, June 21, 1989; Pat Towell, "Bolstering the 2-Missile Strategy," *CQ Weekly*, June 24, 1989, 1559.

56. Senate Committee on Armed Services, *National Defense Authorization Act for Fiscal Year 1991*, 101st Cong., 1st Sess., 1989, S. Rep. 101-385, 68–70, 125–131; Sara Fritz, "Defense Budget OKd but Panel Wants B-2 Test," *Los Angeles Times*, July 15, 1989; Andrew Rosenthal, "Senate Committee Approves Cheney's '90 Military Plan," *New York Times*, July 15, 1989; Pat Towell, "Senate Committee Affirms Cheney's Weapons Cuts," *CQ Weekly*, July 15, 1989, 1809.

57. "Bush Seeks Full Funding for Stealth," *Los Angeles Times*, July 24, 1989; Sara Fritz, "Senate Backs Funding of Stealth Bomber," *Los Angeles Times*, July 29, 1989; Pamela Fessler and Pat Towell, "Senate Defense Measure Sticks Closer to Bush Blueprint," *CQ Weekly*, July 29, 1989, 1979; *National Defense Authorization Act for Fiscal Years 1990 and 1991*, 101st Cong., 1st Sess., *Congressional Record* 135, no. 102, July 27, 1989: S8948, in the *Congressional ProQuest*, accessed February 3, 2020.

58. Tom Kenworthy, "House Defense Bill Rejects Bush's Goals," *Washington Post*, July 28, 1989; Pat Towell, "After Setbacks in the House, Bush Playing Catch-Up," *CQ Weekly*, July 29, 1989, 1972.

59. Kenworthy, "House Defense Bill Rejects Bush's Goals"; Towell, "After Setbacks in the House," 1972.

60. Helen Dewar, "Senate Would Penalize Firms for B-2 Defects," *Washington Post*, August 1, 1989; Sam Nunn and John McCain, "U.S. Allies: No More Free Rides," *Washington Post*, August 13, 1989.

61. Andrew Rosenthal, "Senate Gives Bush a Missiles Victory," *New York Times*, August 2, 1989; Helen Dewar, "Senate Clears $305 Billion Defense Bill," *Washington Post*, August 3, 1989.

62. Sara Fritz," Defense Dispute Perils Arms Talks, Nunn Says," *Los Angeles Times*, September 15, 1989.

63. Sara Fritz, "Key Lawmakers Discount Soviet Shift on Arms," *Los Angeles Times*, September 26, 1989.

64. Susan F. Rasky, "Senate Votes More Money for Anti-Missile Program," *New York Times*, September 29, 1989; Sara Fritz, "Senate Uses Ploy to Boost Funding for Star Wars," *Los Angeles Times*, September 29, 1989; Helen Dewar, "Senate Reverses, Adds Funds for Star Wars," *Washington Post*, September 29, 1989; Pat Towell, "With an Eye to Conference, Senate Zigzags on SDI," *CQ Weekly*, September 30, 1989, 2571.

65. Noah, "Born to be Mild," 10–11, 14.

66. Michael R. Beschloss and Strobe Talbott, *At the Highest Levels: The Inside Story of the End of the Cold War* (Boston: Little, Brown, 1993), 143.

67. Hobart Rowen, "Racing the Clock in Eastern Europe," *Washington Post*, October 26, 1989; Helen Dewar, "Panel Votes $305 Billion Defense Bill," *Washington Post*, November 3, 1989; John Broder, "Conferees Agree on Defense Budget,"

Los Angeles Times, November 3, 1989; Melissa Healy, "Law May Force 10% Cut in Active-Duty Troops," *Los Angeles Times,* November 9, 1989; George Bush: "Statement on Deficit Reduction in Fiscal Year 1990," November 2, 1989, online at Gerhard Peters and John T. Woolley, American Presidency Project, https://www.presidency.ucsb.edu/node/264501.

68. Senate Committee on Armed Services, *Impacts of a Sequester on the Department of Defense in Fiscal Year 1990 and Fiscal Year 1991,* 101st Cong., 1st Sess., 1989, 1–7, 9–17, 26, 28–31, 40–41, 48–49; John Broder, "Conferees Agree on Defense Budget"; Patrick E. Tyler, "Pentagon Says Troop Strength Might Decline by 10 Percent," *Washington Post,* November 9, 1989.

Chapter 12. A Manageable Glide-Path

1. Mary Elise Sarotte, "How the Berlin Wall Really Fell," *New York Times,* November 8, 2014; Gerald M. Boyd, "Raze Berlin Wall, Reagan Urges Soviets," *New York Times,* June 13, 1987.
2. Sarotte, "How It Went Down," *Washington Post,* November 1, 2009.
3. Quoted in Sarotte, "How It Went Down."
4. Quoted in Mary Elise Sarotte, *The Collapse: The Accidental Opening of the Berlin Wall* (New York: Basic Books, 2014), 117.
5. Sarotte, "How It Went Down."
6. Tom Shales, "The Day the Wall Cracked," *Washington Post,* November 10, 1989; Robert McCartney, "East Germany Opens Berlin Wall and Borders," *Washington Post,* November 10, 1989; Serge Schmemann, "East Germany Opens Frontier to the West," *New York Times,* November 10, 1989.
7. Thomas L. Friedman, "U.S. Worry Rises over Europe's Stability," *New York Times,* November 10, 1989.
8. Nunn, "Challenges to NATO in the 1990s," *Survival* 32, no. 1 (January–February 1990): 6–8. Nunn originally presented the lecture on September 4, 1989.
9. Nunn, "Challenges to NATO," 6–8.
10. Nunn, 6–8.
11. Nunn, 9–10.
12. Susan F. Rasky, "Lawmakers Say Pentagon Hasn't Thought Through Its Cuts," *New York Times,* November 27, 1989.
13. H. L. Mencken, "The Divine Afflatus," in *A Mencken Chrestomathy* (New York: Alfred A. Knopf, 1949), 443.
14. Senate Committee on the Budget, *After the Thaw: National Security Objectives in the Post Cold-War Era,* 101st Cong., 1st Sess., 1989, 3, 7, 10–14, 20, 35–37, 45–50; David E. Rosenbaum, "Spending Can Be Cut in Half, Former Defense Officials Say," *New York Times,* December 13, 1989.
15. Senate Committee on Armed Services, *Threat Assessment: Military Strategy and Operational Requirements,* 101st Cong., 1st Sess., 1989, 2.
16. Senate Committee on Armed Services, *Threat Assessment,* 1–43.
17. Michael R. Gordon, "President Rejects Plan to Ground Nuclear Airborne Command Post," *New York Times,* December 16, 1989; Gordon, "Nunn Says U.S.

Should Negotiate Deeper Cuts," *New York Times*, January 1, 1990; Patrick E. Tyler, "Nunn Calls Defense Plan Flawed," *Washington Post*, December 13, 1990.

18. Gordon, "Nunn Says U.S. Should Negotiate Deeper Cuts."

19. Senate Committee on Armed Services, *Threat Assessment*, 46, 47–49, 56–57.

20. Senate Committee on Armed Services, *Threat Assessment*, 57–61.

21. Michael Wines, "U.S. Policy: Congress Starts Review of U.S. Military Posture," *New York Times*, January 24, 1990.

22. Congressional Quarterly, *Almanac*, 101st Cong., 2nd Sess. (Washington, DC: Congressional Quarterly News Features, 1991), 672.

23. Senate Committee on Armed Services, *Department of Defense Authorization for Appropriations for FY91*, 101st Cong., 2nd Sess., 1990, 9, 13, 139–140, 142, 162, 165–167, 201–204; R. W. Apple Jr. "Bush's Quandary on Forces in Europe," *New York Times*, February 2, 1990.

24. Senate Committee on Armed Services, *Threat Assessment: Military Strategy and Operational Requirements*, 101st Cong., 2nd Sess., 1990, 348–350, 357–359, 364–365, 368–370.

25. Michael R. Gordon, "Arms Control," *New York Times*, February 14, 1990; R. Jeffrey Smith, "Scowcroft Seeking Ban on Some Mobile Missiles," *Washington Post*, January 15, 1990; Paul Houston, "Missile Systems May Face Ax," *Los Angeles Times*, February 10, 1990.

26. Memo, McCord to Nunn, subject: Background for 2nd meeting with Sasser/Byrd/Bentsen, March 21, 1990, Subseries 11.3, Box 14, file FYXX, Sam Nunn Papers (SNP), Stuart A. Rose Manuscript, Archives, and Rare Book Library, Emory University, Atlanta, GA; Sam Nunn, "Defense Budget Blanks, March 22, 1990," in *Nunn 1990: A New Military Strategy*, Significant Issues Series, vol. 12, no. 5 (Washington, DC: Center for Strategic and International Studies, 1990), 1–9. See also Christopher J. Deering and Steven S. Smith, *Committees in Congress*, 2nd ed. (Washington, DC: CQ Press, 1990), 240–242, 245.

27. Nunn, "Defense Budget Blanks," 11–14; Michael R. Gordon, "Nunn Opens a Double Attack in Military Spending Debate," *New York Times*, March 23, 1990.

28. Nunn, "Defense Budget Blanks," 14–15; Nunn, "Floor Speech on ABM Treaty Reinterpretation," March 1987, Subseries 9.7, Box 30, Defense/National Security Subject Files (A-D), ABM Treaty Reinterpretation 1987, 2/87–6/87, SNP.

29. Gordon, "Nunn Opens a Double Attack"; David E. Rosenbaum, "No Long-Term Plan on Military Savings," *New York Times*, March 25, 1990.

30. John D. Mayer, Deputy Assistant Director, National Security Division, Congressional Budget Office, testimony before the Committee on the Budget, United States Senate, March 8, 1990, 1–3, 30; Dan Morgan, "Sasser Backs $12 Billion Defense Cut," *Washington Post*, March 9, 1990.

31. Nunn, "The Changed Threat Environment of the 1990s, March 29, 1990," in *Nunn 1990: A New Military Strategy*, Significant Issues Series, vol. 12, no. 5 (Washington, DC: Center for Strategic and International Studies, 1990), 16–33.

32. Nunn, "The Changed Threat Environment," 33–40.

33. Michael R. Gordon, "Study Proposes Deeper U.S. Troop Cuts in Europe," *New York Times*, April 2, 1990.

34. Michael R. Gordon, "2 G.O.P. Senators Would Double Military Cuts," *New York Times*, April 6, 1990; "Position Paper on National Defense," Subseries 11.3, Box 19, Military Strategies no. 3, SNP; Nunn, "A New Military Strategy, April 19, 1990," in *Nunn 1990: A New Military Strategy*, Significant Issues Series, vol. 12, no. 5 (Washington, DC: Center for Strategic and International Studies, 1990), 43.

35. Nunn, "A New Military Strategy," 41–43.

36. Nunn, 43–44.

37. Nunn, 44–52.

38. Nunn, 60.

39. Nunn, "Implementing a New Military Strategy: The Budget Decisions, April 20, 1990," in *Nunn 1990: A New Military Strategy*, Significant Issues Series, vol. 12, no. 5 (Washington, DC: Center for Strategic and International Studies, 1990), 61–64.

40. Nunn, "Implementing," 64–82.

41. Michael R. Gordon, "Nunn Proposes Sharp U.S. Military Cuts in Europe," *New York Times*, April 20, 1990. See also Don M. Snider, *Strategy, Forces, and Budgets: Dominant Influences in Executive Decision Making, Post–Cold War, 1989–91* (Carlisle, PA: US Army War College, Strategic Studies Institute, 1993), 26–27.

42. Susan F. Rasky, "Nunn Urges Cutting Bush Budget for Military," *New York Times*, April 21, 1990.

43. Rasky, "Senators Seek Military Budget Leaner than Bush's," *New York Times*, May 3, 1990; Paul Houston, "Senate Tops House in Defense Budget Cuts," *Los Angeles Times*, May 3, 1980.

44. Michael R. Gordon, "Cheney Gives Plan to Reduce Forces," *New York Times*, June 20, 1990.

45. Susan F. Rasky, "Budget Talks Resume Amid Brewing Dispute," *New York Times*, July 11, 1990.

46. Eric Schmitt, "Nunn Panel Cuts Pentagon $18 Billion," *New York Times*, July 14, 1990; Congressional Quarterly, *Almanac*, 676; Molly Moore, "Senate Committee Cuts Pentagon Troops," *Washington Post*, July 14, 1990; John M. Broder, "Senate Panel Urges Cutting Military Ranks," *Los Angeles Times*, July 11, 1990; "Senate Panel OKs Troop Cuts," *Los Angeles Times*, July 13, 1990.

Chapter 13. Shield and Storm

1. Jean Edward Smith, *George Bush's War* (New York: Henry Holt, 1992), 16; US Department of Defense, *Conduct of the Persian Gulf War: Final Report to Congress* (Washington, DC: US Department of Defense, 1992), 3; Michael R. Gordon, "Iraqi Army Invades Capital of Kuwait," *New York Times*, August 2, 1990; "Situation in Brief," *Washington Post*, August 3, 1990.

2. Gordon, "Iraqi Army Invades Capital."

3. Michael R. Gordon, "The Iraqi Invasion," *New York Times*, August 3, 1990.

4. Department of Defense, *Conduct of the Persian Gulf War*, 19.

5. UN Security Council, Resolution 661, Iraq-Kuwait, S/RES/661 (August 6,

1990), http://www.refworld.org/docid/3b00f16b24.html; James A. Baker III, with Thomas M. DeFrank, *The Politics of Diplomacy: Revolution, War, and Peace, 1989–1992* (New York: G. P. Putnam's Sons, 1995), 332–333.

6. R. W. Apple Jr., "U.S. Set to Blockade Baghdad's Shipping," *New York Times*, August 10, 1990; George Bush, National Security Directive 45, U.S. Policy in Response to the Iraqi Invasion of Kuwait, August 20, 1990.

7. Susan F. Rasky, "New Deployment in Gulf May Slow Drive for Deep Cuts in Military Budget," *New York Times*, August 12, 1990.

8. Richard L. Berke, "Peace Dividend: Casualty in the Gulf?" *New York Times*, August 30, 1990.

9. Michael Wines, "Largest Force since Vietnam Committed in 15-Day Flurry," *New York Times*, August 19, 1990; Smith, *George Bush's War*, 102.

10. Smith, *George Bush's War*, 102–103.

11. R. W. Apple Jr., "Bush Facing Scrutiny by Congress on His Policy in the Persian Gulf," *New York Times*, August 28, 1990; Eric Schmitt, "Lawmakers Touring Persian Gulf Stressing Sanctions," *New York Times*, September 4, 1990; David B. Ottaway, "Senator Calls for More Arab Troops," *Washington Post*, August 28, 1990.

12. Schmitt, "Lawmakers Touring Persian Gulf."

13. Michael R. Gordon, "Combined Force in Saudi Arabia Is Light on Arabs," *New York Times*, September 5, 1990.

14. R. W. Apple Jr., "As Forces Build, U.S. Weighs Its Options," *New York Times*, September 7, 1990.

15. Nunn, letter to the editor, *New York Times*, September 9, 1990.

16. George Bush and Brent Scowcroft, *A World Transformed* (New York: Alfred A. Knopf, 1998), 372; David Hoffman, "U.S. Approach in Gulf Clouded by Uncertainty," *Washington Post*, September 30, 1990.

17. Dilip Hiro, *Desert Shield to Desert Storm: The Second Gulf War* (New York: Routledge, 1992), 237.

18. Tom Mathews, "The Road to War," *Newsweek*, January 28, 1991, 54; James A. Baker III, with Thomas M. DeFrank, *The Politics of Diplomacy: Revolution, War, and Peace, 1989–1992* (New York: G. P. Putnam's Sons, 1995), 335; Sidney Blumenthal, "The Mystique of Sam Nunn," *New Republic*, March 4, 1991, 27; David S. Broder, "Sen. Nunn: Democrats' Shadow Commander," *Washington Post*, December 16, 1990; David S. Broder, interview with Nunn, December 12, 1990, Subseries 9.7, Box 21, Persian Gulf Research Files, Sam Nunn Papers (SNP), Stuart A. Rose Manuscript, Archives, and Rare Book Library, Emory University, Atlanta, GA; Senator Sam Nunn, Oral History, September 4, 1996, Sam Nunn Private Papers, Nuclear Threat Initiative offices, Washington, DC.

19. Lawrence Freedman and Efraim Karsh, *The Gulf Conflict, 1990–1991: Diplomacy and War in the New World Order* (Princeton, NJ: Princeton University Press, 1993), 211; Nunn, Oral History, September 4, 1996.

20. Michael Oreskes, "A Debate Unfolds over Going to War against the Iraqis," *New York Times*, November 12, 1990; Michael R. Gordon, "When to Threaten Iraq?," *New York Times*, November 13, 1990; Andrew Rosenthal, "Senators Asking Presi-

dent to Call Session over Gulf," *New York Times*, November 14, 1990; Helen Dewar, "Key GOP Senators Seek Vote on Gulf," *Washington Post*, November 14, 1990; Smith, *George Bush's War*, 204.

21. Bush and Scowcroft, *A World Transformed*, 401.

22. Nunn, Oral History; "Interview with Senator Sam Nunn," CNN, *The World Today*, January 14, 1989, Transcript ID: 671089, Subseries 9.7, Box 21, file: Persian Gulf Research Files, SNP.

23. Sam Nunn, "The Gulf Isn't the Only Crisis," *New York Times*, November 18, 1990.

24. Susan F. Rasky, "Congress Asks What It Should Do in the Gulf," *New York Times*, November 18, 1990.

25. Senate Committee on Armed Services, *Crisis in the Persian Gulf Region: U.S. Policy Options and Implications*, 101st Cong., 2nd Sess., 1990, 107–108.

26. Senate Committee on Armed Services, *Crisis in the Persian Gulf*, 109.

27. Senate Committee on Armed Services, 113–120, 125, 126, 130–132, 136–138, 143–145, 147–150, 153, 156, 158–161, 162–165, 166–168, 169, 170.

28. *The Economist* is quoted in R. W. Apple Jr., "Remaking of Sam Nunn with '92 in the Distance," Washington Talk, *New York Times*, December 20, 1990.

29. George Bush and Brent Scowcroft, *A World Transformed* (New York: Alfred A. Knopf, 1998), 417, 418; John M. Sununu, interviewed by James S. Young et al., Charlottesville, VA, June 8–9, 2000, George H. W. Bush Oral History Project, Miller Center of Public Affairs, University of Virginia, https://millercenter.org /the-presidency/presidential-oral-histories/john-h-sununu-oral-history-062000.

30. Senate Committee on Armed Services, *Crisis in the Persian Gulf Region*, 279, 326–328, 361.

31. Pat Towell, "Aspin's Political Clout Grows as Nunn's Leverage Is Questioned," *CQ Weekly*, March 23, 1991, 756, 757.

32. Smith, *George Bush's War*, 213–214; Richard Rhodes, *The Twilight of the Bombs: Recent Challenges, New Dangers, and the Prospects for a World without Nuclear Weapons* (New York: Knopf, 2010), 35.

33. Smith, *George Bush's War*, 216; Richard B. Cheney, interviewed by Philip Zelikow et al., Dallas, TX, March 16–17, 2000, George H. W. Bush Oral History Project, Miller Center of Public Affairs, University of Virginia, https://millercenter.org /the-presidency/presidential-oral-histories/richard-b-cheney-oral-history; UN Security Council, Resolution 678, Iraq-Kuwait, S/RES/678 (November 29, 1990), http://www.refworld.org/docid/3b00f16760.html.

34. Mary McGrory, "An Important Moment," *Washington Post*, November 29, 1990.

35. Michael R. Gordon and Bernard E. Trainor, *The Generals' War: The Inside Story of the Conflict in the Gulf* (Boston: Little, Brown, 1995), 179.

36. Senate Committee on Armed Services, *Crisis in the Persian Gulf*, 638–650, 659–665; Gordon and Trainor, *The Generals' War*, 179; Michael R. Gordon, "Cheney Sees Need to Act Militarily," *New York Times*, December 4, 1990.

37. Colin L. Powell, with Joseph E. Persico, *My American Journey* (New York: Random House, 1995), 493.

38. Senate Committee on Armed Services, *Crisis in the Persian Gulf*, 681–682.

39. Senate Committee on Armed Services, 683–731.

40. Michael R. Gordon, "Cheney Sees Need to Act Militarily"; Susan F. Rasky, "Democrats Say Iraqi Moves Won't Turn Debate," *New York Times*, December 8, 1990.

41. Haynes Johnson, "Putting Iraq on Hold," *Washington Post*, November 30, 1990.

42. Ann Devroy and Tom Kenworthy, "No Plans for Recalling Congress," *Washington Post*, November 30, 1990.

43. Blumenthal, "The Mystique of Sam Nunn," 27.

44. David Gergen, "The Democrats Go-Slow Gulf Policy," *US News & World Report*, December 10, 1990; R. Jeffrey Smith, "Iraq Sanctions Seen Working Slowly," *Washington Post*, November 24, 1990; Lawrence Freedman and Efraim Karsh, "How Kuwait Was Won: Strategy in the Gulf War," *International Security* 16, no. 2 (Fall 1991): 8n7. General Schwarzkopf's reservations are quoted in Sam Nunn, "The Persian Gulf Crisis," *Vital Speeches of the Day* 57, no. 8, February 1, 1991, 241. (Nunn gave the speech on January 10, 1991, and it was published in February.)

45. Gordon, and Trainor, *The Generals' War*, 156; Hiro, *Desert Shield and Desert Storm*, 266.

46. Letter, Nunn to Rep. Steven Solarz, January 3, 1991, Subseries 11.3, Box 22, file, Persian Gulf War no. 2, SNP; Broder, "Sam Nunn: Democrats' Shadow Commander."

47. Richard McCulley, *History of the Senate Committee on Armed Services, 1947–1999*, unpublished manuscript, file: Armed Services Committee History, 2000 draft, US Senate Historical Office, Washington, DC.

48. George H. W. Bush, Letter to Congressional Leaders on the Persian Gulf Crisis, January 8, 1991, George H. W. Bush Presidential Library (GHWBL), http://bush41library.tamu.edu/archives/public-papers/2599.

49. Bush and Scowcroft, *A World Transformed*, 421.

50. Adam Clymer, "Bush Asks Congress to Back the Use of Force If Iraq Defies Deadline," *New York Times*, January 9, 1991; Freedman and Karsh, *The Gulf Conflict*, 291.

51. The President's News Conference on the Persian Gulf Crisis, January 9, 1991, GHWBL, http://bush41library.tamu.edu/archives/public-papers/2605.

52. Baker, *The Politics of Diplomacy*, 364; William Thomas Allison, *The Gulf War, 1990–91* (New York: Palgrave Macmillan, 2012), 88–89.

53. Baker, *The Politics of Diplomacy*, 364.

54. Clymer, "Bush Asks Congress to Back the Use of Force"; "Excerpts from Gulf Resolutions before the Congress," *New York Times*, January 12, 1991; Walter Pincus, "Debate in Congress Reshuffles Disparate Democrats," *Washington Post*, January 11, 1991.

55. "Congressional Resolutions," *Washington Post*, January 11, 1991; Sara Fritz and William J. Eaton, "Congress Authorizes Gulf War," *Los Angeles Times*, January 13, 1991.

56. Tom Kenworthy, "Hill Set to Open Debate on Gulf War," *Washington Post*, January 5, 1991.

57. Tom Kenworthy and John E. Yang, "Support of Bush Authority to Act Seen En-

hanced by Iraqi Rebuff," *Washington Post,* January 10, 1991; Haynes Johnson, "Good Wars and Bad," *Washington Post,* January 11, 1991.

58. Bush and Scowcroft, *A World Transformed,* 443; Adam Clymer, "Baker Warns of Fast Strike If Kuwait Deadline Passes," *New York Times,* January 12, 1991.

59. Clymer, "Baker Warns of Fast Strike"; C-SPAN Senate Session, January 11, 1991, http://www.c-span.org/video/?15652–1/senate-session; Nunn, Oral History; Nunn, "Floor Speech," January 11, 1991, and "Closing Statement on Resolution," January 12, 1991, Subseries 9.7, Box 21, Persian Gulf Research Files, SN Statements on Persian Gulf, SNP.

60. Tom Kenworthy and Helen Dewar, "Divided Congress Grants President Authority to Wage War," *Washington Post,* January 13, 1991; Congressional Quarterly, *Almanac,* 102nd Congress, 1st Session, 1991 (Washington, DC: Congressional Quarterly News Features, 1992), 442.

61. "Statement on Allied Military Action in the Persian Gulf," January 16, 1991, GHWBL, http://bush41library.tamu.edu/archives/public-papers/2624.

62. "Address to the Nation Announcing Allied Military Action in the Persian Gulf," January 16, 1991, GHWBL, http://bush41library.tamu.edu/archives/public-papers/2625.

63. A. L. May, "Nunn Walks Tightwire as He Opposes Bush on Gulf," *Atlanta Journal-Constitution,* January 11, 1991.

64. Dick Williams, "Of Stars Wars and Victory and Mr. Noodnik Nunn," *Atlanta Journal-Constitution,* January 22, 1990.

65. David Pace, "Georgia Senator Regrets Vote against Gulf War," *Milwaukee Journal-Sentinel,* December 26, 1996; Daniel R. Heimbach, "The Bush Just War Doctrine: Genesis and Application of the President's Moral Leadership in the Persian Gulf War," in *From Cold War to New World Order: The Foreign Policy of George H. W. Bush,* ed. Meena Bose and Rosanna Perotti (Westport, CT: Greenwood Press, 2002), 449; Roland McElroy, *The Best President the Nation Never Had* (Macon, GA: Mercer University Press, 2017), 177, 178.

66. Adam Clymer, "Explaining War Votes Back in Home Districts," *New York Times,* January 28, 1990; A. L. May, "War in the Middle East," *Atlanta Journal-Constitution,* January 23, 1991.

67. "Shutting Out Sam Nunn," *Newsweek,* February 4, 1991; Barton Gelman and R. Jeffrey Smith, "Iraq's Modest Response to Attack Brings Hope, Caution," *Washington Post,* January 18, 1991; McElroy, *The Best President,* 177; Sam Nunn, interview by Sidney Blumenthal for *New Republic,* transcript of remarks, January 17, 1991, Washington, DC, Subseries 9.7, Box 2, Persian Gulf Research Files, SNP.

68. A. L. May, "War Stance Costs Nunn Popularity," *Atlanta Journal-Constitution,* February 2, 1991; Memo to File, Linda M. Matthews, Feb. 11, 1990, Subseries 9.7, Box 21, Persian Gulf Research Files (Personal Notes/Memos 1991), SNP.

69. A. L. May, "Taking a Presidential Pose, Nunn Charges Social Needs Unmet," *Atlanta Journal-Constitution,* February 25, 1991; May, "Nunn Seems to Rule Out White House Bid," *Atlanta Journal-Constitution,* March 5, 1991.

70. Mike Christensen, "Nunn Hopes Iraqis Will Give Up before Ground War Necessary," *Atlanta Journal-Constitution,* February 21, 1991.

71. George Bush, "Remarks at the Community Welcome Home for Returning Troops in Sumter, South Carolina," March 17, 1991, GHWBL, https://bush411i brary.tamu.edu/archives/public-papers/2800; John E. Yang and Dana Priest, "Lawmakers Acclaim Call for Cease-Fire, Restraint on Saddam," *Washington Post,* February 28, 1991.

72. Robin Toner, "For First Time, Nunn's in Fray for Opposing One," *New York Times,* March 13, 1991.

73. Toner, "For First Time"; Nunn, transcript, interview by Robin Toner, March 9, 1991, Denver, Colorado, Subseries 9.7, Box 21, Persian Gulf Research Files, Gulf War Clippings, etc., SNP; Al From, with Alice McKeon, *The New Democrats and the Return to Power* (New York: Palgrave Macmillan, 2011), 136–137.

74. Jack Fowler, "Democrats in Disarray," *National Review,* January 28, 1991, 27–28; Leslie Gelb, "Foreign Affairs; A Party Derided," *New York Times,* March 10, 1991.

75. Tom Wicker, "Winner and Losers," In the Nation, *New York Times,* March 16, 1991.

76. William McGurn, "Beltway Battles," *National Review,* February 25, 1991, 34–36.

77. Quoted in McGurn, "Beltway Battles," 34–36. For a study of how committee chairs assume various leadership styles because of the dispersion of power in Congress and the type of committees they lead, see Christine DeGregorio, "Leadership Styles in Congressional Committee Hearings," *Western Political Quarterly* 45, no. 4 (December 1992): 971–983.

78. A. L. May, "Nunn's Tough Vote against War Brings Tough Times," *Atlanta Journal-Constitution,* March 10, 1991; Eleanor Clift, "Mr. Defense Loses His Luster," *Newsweek,* March 18, 1991, 40; William F. Buckley Jr., "The Politics of Victory," On the Right, *National Review,* April 15, 1991, 62. See also R. W. Apple Jr., "Remaking of Sam Nunn."

79. Bob Hurt, interview by Tom Chaffin, Washington, DC, October 16, 1996, Box 1, Sam Nunn Oral History Collection, Stuart A. Rose Manuscript, Archives, and Rare Book Library, Emory University, Atlanta, GA.

Chapter 14. Loose Nukes

1. Sam Nunn, Oral History, September 5, 1996, Washington, DC, Sam Nunn Private Papers (SNPP), Nuclear Threat Initiative offices, Washington, DC; Sam Nunn, telephone interview by author, March 20, 2015.

2. Sam Nunn and Richard Lugar, "The Nunn-Lugar Initiative: Cooperative Demilitarization of the Former Soviet Union," in *The Diplomatic Record, 1992–1993,* ed. Allan E. Goodman (Boulder, CO: Westview Press, 1995), 141. The republics declaring independence before, during, and shortly after the August coup attempt as well as during Nunn's visit were Lithuania, Estonia, Latvia, Georgia, Ukraine, Belarus, Moldova, Kyrgyzstan, and Uzbekistan.

3. Nunn, Oral History; Nunn, telephone interview by author; Robert Bell, email message to the author, April 7, 2015.

4. Nunn, Oral History; Nunn, telephone interview by author; Robert Bell, notes from Senator Nunn's Trip to Moscow, August 30–September 3, 1991, SNPP.

5. Nunn, quoted in Deborah Scroggins, "Nunn Urging Central Control of Soviet Arms," *Atlanta Journal-Constitution*, September 5, 1991; Nunn, telephone interview by author.

6. Nunn, Oral History; Mikhail Gorbachev, *Memoirs* (New York: Doubleday, 1996), 649; Nunn, telephone interview by author.

7. Nunn, Oral History; Nunn, telephone interview by author; Bell, email message to the author.

8. Nunn, Oral History; Nunn, telephone interview by author.

9. Robert Kagan, "A Front-Row Seat for the Russian Coup of '91," *Washington Post*, August 18, 2011.

10. Nunn, Oral History; Cable Network News, Interview with Senator Sam Nunn, transcript, September 2, 1991; Cable, US Embassy Moscow to Secretary of State, subject: Senator Nunn's Meeting with Gorbachev, September 2, 1991; Nunn's personal notes from meeting with Gorbachev, September 2, 1991, all in SNPP.

11. Anatoly S. Chernyaev, *My Six Years with Gorbachev* (University Park: Pennsylvania State University Press, 2000), 381.

12. Nunn, Oral History; Scroggins, "Nunn Urging Central Control"; Bell, email message to the author; Cable, US Embassy Moscow to Secretary of State.

13. Helen Dewar, "Sen. Nunn Reassured on Soviet Arms," *Washington Post*, September 2, 1991; ABC, *Good Morning America*, Interview with Senator Sam Nunn, transcript, September 4, 1991, SNPP; Nunn, Oral History; Richard Bradee, "Aspin's Plan to Deal with Arms Threat," *Milwaukee Sentinel*, August 29, 1991.

14. Nunn, Oral History; Nunn and Lugar, "The Nunn-Lugar Initiative," 142; Scroggins, "Nunn Urging Central Control."

15. "Beyond Fear: America's Role in an Uncertain World," Radio Documentary, Interview with Senator Sam Nunn, Stanley Foundation with KQED Public Radio, March 2007; Nunn and Lugar, "The Nunn-Lugar Initiative," 142.

16. Nunn, Oral History; Bradee, "Aspin's Plan"; Nunn, telephone interview by author.

17. John Lancaster and Barton Gellman, "Citing Soviet Strife, Cheney Resists Cuts," *Washington Post*, August 30, 1991.

18. George H. W. Bush, "The President's News Conference in Kennebunkport, Maine," September 2, 1991, George H. W. Bush Presidential Library, https://bush41library.tamu.edu/archives/public-papers/3334.

19. Paul I. Bernstein and Jason D. Wood, *The Origins of Nunn-Lugar and Cooperative Threat Reduction*, Case Study 3, Center for the Study of Weapons of Mass Destruction (Washington, DC: National Defense University, 2010), 4.

20. Nunn and Lugar, "The Nunn-Lugar Initiative," 142–143; Eric Pianin, "The Budget Pact: Worst of Both Worlds?" *Washington Post*, October 1, 1991.

21. Director of Central Intelligence, National Intelligence Estimate (NIE) 11–18–90, November 1990, v, https://www.cia.gov/library/readingroom/docs/19901101.pdf.

22. George Bush and Brent Scowcroft, *A World Transformed* (New York: Alfred A. Knopf, 1998), 540–542, 544.

23. Scroggins, "Nunn Urging Central Control."

24. James A. Baker III, with Thomas M. DeFrank, *The Politics of Diplomacy: Revolution, War, and Peace, 1989–1992* (New York: G. P. Putnam's Sons, 1995), 526.

25. Bush and Scowcroft, *A World Transformed*, 544–45; Powell, *My American Journey*, 241; Michael R. Beschloss and Strobe Talbott, *At the Highest Levels: The Inside Story of the End of the Cold War* (Boston: Little, Brown, 1993), 445–446.

26. Memorandum of Telephone Conversation, subject: Telecon with Mikhail Gorbachev, President of the USSR, September 27, 1991, National Security Archive, George Washington University, Washington, DC (hereinafter cited as NSA-GWU).

27. Memorandum of Telephone Conversation, subject: Telecon with Yeltsin, President of the Republic of Russia, September 27, 1991, NSA-GWU.

28. Helen Dewar, "Hill Leaders Show Solid Support for Bush's Arms Cuts Proposal," *Washington Post*, September 28, 1991.

29. David E. Rosenbaum, "Cashing In the Bomb," *New York Times*, October 6, 1991; Andy Pasztor and Peter Gumbel, "Soviet Response Surpasses U.S. Arms Cut Plan," *Wall Street Journal*, October 7, 1991; Memorandum of Telephone Conversation, subject: Telecon with Gorbachev, President of the USSR, October 5, 1991, NSA-GWU.

30. Nunn, Oral History.

31. Jim Hoagland, "The Democrats' Audacious Take on Soviet Aid," *Washington Post*, October 31, 1991.

32. Nunn, Oral History.

33. Eric Schmitt, "Pentagon May Give Moscow $1 Billion," *New York Times*, November 1, 1991; Paul Houston, "$1-Billion Aid Plan for Soviets Proposed Defense," *Los Angeles Times*, November 2, 1991.

34. John Lancaster, "Defense Bill Includes Soviet Aid," *Washington Post*, November 2, 1991; Eric Schmitt, "Soviet Upheaval Has Little Impact on Spending Bill," *New York Times*, November 2, 1991; Andy Pasztor, "House, Senate Hammer Out Defense Bill," *Wall Street Journal*, November 3, 1991; Richard Combs, "U.S. Domestic Politics and the Nunn-Lugar Program," in *Dismantling the Cold War: U.S. and NIS Perspectives on the Nunn-Lugar Cooperative Threat Reduction Program*, ed. John M. Shields and William C. Potter (Cambridge, MA: MIT Press, 1997), 43.

35. Helen Dewar, "Plan to Spend Defense on Soviets May Die," *Washington Post*, November 8, 1991.

36. Dewar, "Plan to Spend Defense"; Richard Bradee, "Plan to Aid USSR May Stall Bill," *Milwaukee Sentinel*, November 8, 1991; Paul Houston, "Democrats Warn They May Drop Soviet Aid Package," *Los Angeles Times*, November 8, 1991.

37. Sam Nunn, "Remarks," Session 3, "Using Science and Technology to Meet New Defense and Arms Control Needs," Fifth Panel Discussion, White House Forum on the Role of Science and Technology in Promoting National Security and Global Stability, March 29–30, 1995.

38. Dewar, "Plan to Spend Defense"; Bradee, "Plan to Aid USSR"; Houston, "Democrats Warn."

39. Nunn, "Changing Threats in the Post–Cold War World," speech, Monterey Institute for International Studies, Monterey, CA, August 25, 1995.

40. Eric Schmitt, "Moscow Aid Plan Dying in Congress," *New York Times*, November 13, 1991.

41. "Pentagon Money Will Not Go to USSR," *All Things Considered*, National Public Radio, Washington, DC, November 13, 1991; Helen Dewar, "Lawmakers Drop Aid for Soviets," *Washington Post*, November 14, 1991.

42. Robert D. Hershey Jr., "2 Senators Seek to Revive Plan to Divert Pentagon Funds," *New York Times*, November 20, 1991.

43. Don Oberdorfer, "First Aid for Moscow," *Washington Post*, December 1, 1991.

44. Nunn, Oral History.

45. Ashton Carter and William J. Perry, *Preventive Defense: A New Security Strategy for America* (Washington, DC: Brookings Institution Press, 1999), 71–72.

46.. Ashton B. Carter, Kurt Campbell, Steven Miller, and Charles Zraket, *Soviet Nuclear Fission: Control of the Nuclear Arsenal in a Disintegrating Soviet Union* (Cambridge, MA: Center for Science and International Affairs, Harvard University, 1991).

47. Ashton Carter, "Origins of the Nunn-Lugar Program," Presentation to the Presidential Conference on William Jefferson Clinton: The "New Democrat from Hope," Hofstra University, November 2005; Carter, Campbell, Miller, and Zraket, *Soviet Nuclear Fission*, i–iv.

48. Richard Combs, telephone interview by author, February 5, 2015; David A. Hamburg, *A Perspective on Carnegie Corporation's Program, 1983–1997* (New York: Carnegie Corporation of New York, 1997), 19; Carter, "Origins of the Nunn-Lugar Program"; Carter and Perry, *Preventive Defense*, 71–72; Bernstein and Wood, *The Origins of Nunn-Lugar and Cooperative Threat Reduction*, 6.

49. Combs, "U.S. Domestic Politics and the Nunn-Lugar Program," 43–44.

50. Combs, telephone interview by author; Richard Combs, email message to author, February 2, 2015, with attachment (Richard Combs, "Origins of the Nunn-Lugar Legislation"), June 24, 2013; Combs, "U.S. Domestic Politics and the Nunn-Lugar Program," 44; Bernstein and Wood, *The Origins of Nunn-Lugar and Cooperative Threat Reduction*, 7.

51. Nunn and Lugar, "The Nunn-Lugar Initiative," 144; Bernstein and Wood, *The Origins of Nunn-Lugar and Cooperative Threat Reduction*, 46n30; Oberdorfer, "First Aid for Moscow."

52. "Soviet Talks on G-7 Help Hit New Snags," *Wall Street Journal*, November 21, 1991; "U.S. Government Offers More Aid to Soviet Republics," *Morning Edition*, National Public Radio, Washington, DC, November 21, 1991. By November 1991, all the Soviet republics had declared their sovereignty.

53. Nunn and Lugar, "The Nunn-Lugar Initiative," 144; Carter and Perry, *Preventive Defense*, 71–72; Don Oberdorfer and R. Jeffrey Smith, "Senators Back Aid to Soviets for Arms Cuts," *Washington Post*, November 22, 1991; Oberdorfer, "First Aid for Moscow."

54. Sam Nunn and Richard Lugar, "Dismantling the Soviet Arsenal: We've Got to Get Involved," *Washington Post*, November 22, 1991; Robert C. Toth, "Funds Sought to Control Soviet 'Loose Nukes,'" *Los Angeles Times*, November 22, 1991.

55. Oberdorfer, "First Aid for Moscow"; George Bush, "Address to the Nation on Re-

ducing United States and Soviet Nuclear Weapons," September 27, 1991, online at Gerhard Peters and John T. Woolley, American Presidency Project, https://www.presidency.ucsb.edu/node/266636.

56. Oberdorfer and Smith, "Senators Back Aid to Soviets."

57. Oberdorfer and Smith, "Senators Back Aid to Soviets"; Nunn and Lugar, "The Nunn-Lugar Initiative," 144; Combs, "U.S. Domestic Politics and the Nunn-Lugar Program," 42–44; Nunn, telephone interview by author.

58. Combs, "U.S. Domestic Politics and the Nunn-Lugar Program," 45; Bernstein and Wood, *The Origins of Nunn-Lugar and Cooperative Threat Reduction*, 8; Soviet Nuclear Threat Reduction Act of 1991, Public Law 102-228, 102nd Cong., 1st Sess. (December 12, 1991), sec. 211.

59. Theodore Galdi, *The Nunn-Lugar Program for Soviet Weapons Dismantlement: Background and Implementation* (Washington, DC: Congressional Research Service, 1995), 3–4.

60. Don Oberdorfer and Helen Dewar, "Senate Votes to Assist Soviet Nuclear Cutbacks," *Washington Post*, November 26, 1991; Eric Schmitt, "Senate Votes Aid to Soviets to Scrap Atomic Arms," *New York Times*, November 26, 1991; Conventional Forces in Europe Treaty Implementation Act of 1991, H.R. 3807, 102nd Cong., 1st Sess., *Congressional Record* (November 25, 1991), Senate Vote no. 274.

61. Nunn, Oral History.

62. Galdi, *The Nunn-Lugar Program*, 4; *Congressional Record* 137, no. 176, daily edition, 102nd Cong., 1st Sess. (November 25, 1991): S18001, S18018, S18038.

63. Combs, "U.S. Domestic Politics and the Nunn-Lugar Program," 44; Bernstein and Wood, *The Origins of Nunn-Lugar and Cooperative Threat Reduction*, 8, 14n35; Nunn and Lugar, "The Nunn-Lugar Initiative," 145; Michael Ross, "Senate Votes $700 Million for Soviet Aid," *Los Angeles Times*, November 26, 1991.

64. George H. W. Bush, "Statement by Press Secretary Fitzwater on Assistance to the Soviet Union and the Republics," December 12, 1991, George H. W. Bush Presidential Library, https://bush41library.tamu.edu/archives/public-papers/3737.

65. James Baker, "America and the Collapse of the Soviet Empire: What Has to Be Done," Address at Princeton University, Princeton, NJ, December 12, 1991, *U.S. Department of State Dispatch* 2, no. 50, December 16, 1991, 887, 888–890.

66. Oberdorfer, "First Aid for Moscow."

67. Bernstein and Wood, *The Origins of Nunn-Lugar and Cooperative Threat Reduction*, 8, 14 n33.

68. Central Intelligence Agency, Directorate of Intelligence Paper, "Gorbachev's Future," May 23, 1991, NSA-GWU; Letter from Yeltsin to Bush, undated, NSA-GWU. Russian foreign minister Andrey Kozyrev handed this letter to President Bush on November 26, 1991.

Chapter 15. Filling a Policy Vacuum

1. David Halberstam, *War in a Time of Peace: Bush, Clinton, and the Generals* (New York: Scribner, 2001), 172–173; Elizabeth Drew, *On the Edge: The Clinton Presi-*

dency (New York: Simon & Schuster, 1994), 27; Nunn, interview by author, Washington, DC, May 9, 2018.

2. Fred I. Greenstein, "Political Style and Political Leadership: The Case of Bill Clinton," in *The Clinton Presidency: Campaigning, Governing, and the Psychology of Leadership,* ed. Stanley A. Renshon (Boulder, CO: Westview Press, 1995), 143.

3. Barton Gellman, "Clinton Sets 2-Phase Plan to Allow Gays in Military," *Washington Post,* January 22, 1993; John F. Harris, *The Survivor: Bill Clinton in the White House* (New York: Random House, 2005), 16; Bill Clinton, *My Life* (New York: Alfred A. Knopf, 2004), 483.

4. Gellman, "Clinton Sets 2-Phase Plan"; Harris, *The Survivor,* 16.

5. Harris, *The Survivor,* 17; Ann Devroy, "Joint Chiefs Voice Concern to Clinton on Lifting Gay Ban," *Washington Post,* January 26, 1993; Clinton, *My Life,* 483; George Stephanopoulos, *All Too Human: A Political Education* (Boston, MA: Little, Brown, 1999), 123.

6. Harris, *The Survivor,* 17; Taylor Branch, *The Clinton Tapes: Wrestling History with the President* (New York: Simon & Schuster, 2009), 6; Devroy, "Joint Chiefs Voice Concern"; Stephanopoulos, *All Too Human,* 123.

7. Stephen Barr, "Hill Backs Gay Ban, Aspin Says," *Washington Post,* January 25, 1993; Branch, *The Clinton Tapes,* 5.

8. Bob Hurt, interview by Tom Chaffin, Washington, DC, October 16, 1996, Box 1, Sam Nunn Oral History Collection, Stuart A. Rose Manuscript, Archives, and Rare Book Library, Emory University, Atlanta, GA; Transcript, "NBC Today" Interview of Senator Sam Nunn by Katherine Couric, February 3, 1993, Box 41, Series 9.6, Beth Solomon files, Sam Nunn Papers (SNP), Stuart A. Rose Manuscript, Archives, and Rare Book Library, Emory University, Atlanta, GA; Jon F. Hale, "The Making of the New Democrats," *Political Science Quarterly* 110, no. 2 (Summer 1993): 226, 227.

9. Hurt interview.

10. Dan Balz, "A Promise That Held Inevitable Collision," *Washington Post,* January 28, 1993; Drew, *On the Edge,* 44.

11. Branch, *The Clinton Tapes,* 5–6; Clinton, *My Life,* 484; Denise M. Bostdorff, "Clinton's Characteristic Issue Management Style: Caution, Conciliation, and Conflict Avoidance in the Case of Gays in the Military," in *The Clinton Presidency: Images, Issues, and Communication Strategies* (Westport, CT: Praeger, 1996), 197.

12. Thomas E. Ricks, "Clinton Reiterates He'll End Military's Ban on Homosexuals," *Wall Street Journal,* January 26, 1993.

13. Dilys M. Hill, "The Clinton Presidency: The Man and his Times," in *The Clinton Presidency: The First Term, 1992–96,* ed. Paul S. Herrnson and Dilys M. Hill (New York: St. Martin's Press, 1999), 6; Branch, *The Clinton Tapes,* 7; Barbara Sinclair, "Trying to Govern Positively in a Negative Era: Clinton and the 103rd Congress," in *The Clinton Presidency: First Appraisals,* ed. Colin Campbell and Bert A. Rockman (Chatham, NJ: Chatham House, 1996), 101; Gloria Borger, "Who's the Newest Democrat of Them All?," *US News & World Report,* July 26, 1993, 37; James MacGregor Burns and Georgia J. Sorenson, *Dead Center: Clinton-Gore Leadership and the Perils of Moderation* (New York: Scribner, 1999), 98; Stepha-

nopoulos, *All Too Human*, 126; Bob Dart, "Nunn Called 'Old-Fashioned Bigot,'" *Palm Beach Post*, March 27, 1993; Laurence Jolidon, "Nunn Plays the Enemy Within, Ga. Democrat Is a Thorn in Clinton's Side," *USA Today*, March 31, 1993.

14. Branch, *The Clinton Tapes*, 7; Clinton, *My Life*, 484.

15. Interview of Nunn by Couric; Hurt interview; Steven V. Roberts, "Senator Nunn's Little Mutiny," *US News & World Report*, February 8, 1993, 40; Sinclair, 101; Nunn, email message to author, June 2, 2016.

16. Hurt interview; Shirley L. Smith, "Gays Bash Nunn on Military Ban . . . but Rally Leaders to Accept Delay in Changing Rules," *Atlanta Journal-Constitution*, February 14, 1993; Chuck Alston, "Clinton's Rough Start with the Hill: Minor Slip or Serious Flaw?" *CQ Weekly*, January 30, 1993, 203; Stephanopoulos, *All Too Human*, 126; Mary McGrory, "For Whom the Phone Tolls," *Washington Post*, January 31, 1993; Transcript, "NBC Today," Interview of Nunn by Couric.

17. Sam Nunn, Hearings on the Department of Defense Policy Excluding Homosexuals from Service in the Armed Forces, S. 755, *Congressional Record* 139, no. 9, 103rd Cong., 1st Sess., January 27, 1993.

18. Editorial, "Lifting of Gay Ban Ought to Involve Congress Debate," *Atlanta Journal-Constitution*, January 27, 1993.

19. Clinton, *My Life*, 7; Alston, "Clinton's Rough Start," 203; Transcript, "NBC Today," Nunn interview by Couric.

20. William J. Clinton, "The President's News Conference," January 29, 1993, online at Gerhard Peters and John T. Woolley, American Presidency Project, https://www.presidency.ucsb.edu/node/220052.

21. Pat Towell, "Campaign Promise, Social Debate Collide on Military Battlefield," *CQ Weekly*, January 30, 1993, 226.

22. Nunn, email to author, June 2, 2016.

23. William J. Clinton, Memorandum for the Secretary of Defense, "Ending Discrimination on the Basis of Sexual Orientation in the Armed Forces," January 29, 1993.

24. Kitty Cunningham, "The Senate's Last Word on Gays," *CQ Weekly*, September 11, 1993, 2401; Bostdorff, "Clinton's Characteristic Issue Management Style," 190, 198, 212; Nunn, "Gays and Lesbians in the Armed Forces," S. 8876, *Congressional Record* 139, no. 99, 103rd Cong., 1st Sess., July 16, 1993; 10 U.S.C. § 654, Policy Concerning Homosexuality in the Armed Forces, *JUSTIA US Law*, https://law.justia.com/codes/us/2010/title10/subtitlea/partii/chap37/sec654.

25. Towell, "Campaign Promise, Social Debate," 226; Stephanopoulos, *All Too Human*, 128–129; Helen Dewar, "Panel Acts to Codify Gay Policy," *Washington Post*, July 24, 1993; Paul J. Quirk and Joseph Hinchliffe, "Domestic Policy: The Trials of a Centrist Democrat," in *The Clinton Presidency: First Appraisals*, ed. Colin Campbell and Bert A. Rockman (Chatham, NJ: Chatham House, 1996), 223; Harris, *The Survivor*, 18.

26. Clinton, *My Life*, 486.

27. Drew, *On the Edge*, 47.

28. Congressional Quarterly, *Congress and the Nation*, vol. 9: 1993–1996 (Washington, DC: Congressional Quarterly, 1997), 187.

29. Congressional Quarterly, *Congress and the Nation*, vol. 9, 191.
30. "A Conversation with Sam Nunn," *Georgia Tech Alumni Magazine* (Spring 1990).
31. "A Conversation with Sam Nunn," *Georgia Tech Alumni Magazine*.
32. George H. Quester, "Defense Policy," in *The Clinton Presidency: The First Term, 1992–96*, ed. Paul S. Herrnson and Dilys M. Hill (New York: St. Martin's Press, 1999), 143.
33. Sam Nunn, "The Defense Department Must Thoroughly Overhaul the Services' Roles and Missions," Subseries 9.6, Box 42, files: Germany—Roles and Missions, SNP; Barton Gellman, "Services Moving to Protect Turf," *Washington Post*, January 28, 1993.
34. Jeffrey R. Smith, Memorandum of Conversation, subject: Meeting between Governor Clinton and Senator Nunn, August 6, 1992, Box 11, Anthony Lake Papers, Library of Congress, Washington, DC.
35. Nunn, "The Defense Department Must."
36. John Dumbrell, *Clinton's Foreign Policy: Between the Bushes, 1992–2000* (New York: Routledge, 2009), 36.
37. Senate Committee on Armed Services, *Joint Chiefs of Staff Briefing on Current Military Operations in Somalia, Iraq, and Yugoslavia*, 103rd Cong., 1st Sess., 1993, 104; "Broad Foreign Policy/National Security Framework," Meet the Press Briefing Book, September 1993, Subseries 11.3, Box 7, SNP.
38. Ryan C. Hendrickson, *The Clinton Wars: The Constitution, Congress, and War Powers* (Nashville, TN: Vanderbilt University Press, 2002), 26; Senate Committee on Armed Services, *Joint Chiefs of Staff Briefing on Current Military Operations in Somalia, Iraq, and Yugoslavia*, 20.
39. Pat Towell, "Nunn Says Cuts Are Reasonable but Wants Pentagon Protected," *CQ Weekly*, March 6, 1993, 531; John Lancaster, "Nunn Warns Against Defense Cut Plan," *Washington Post*, March 6, 1993; Letter, Nunn to Clinton, February 13, 1993, Subseries 11.3, Box 14, FY94 Defense Budget, SNP.
40. Towell, "Nunn Says Cuts Are Reasonable"; Lancaster, "Nunn Warns against Defense Cut Plan"; US General Accounting Office, "Major Issues Facing a New Congress and a New Administration," Statement of Charles A. Bowsher, Comptroller General of the United States, before the Committee on Governmental Affairs, US Senate, January 8, 1993, GAO/T-OCG-93-1, 4–6.
41. Barton Gellman, "Witness Aspin Encounters Flak Back at Home," *Washington Post*, March 31, 1993.
42. Sam Nunn, "Is Clinton Cutting Twice as Much from Defense?" *Aviation Week & Space Technology*, March 22, 1993, 64; Ernie Freda, "Nunn Asks Senate to Limit Defense Cuts," *Atlanta Journal-Constitution*, March 23, 1993; Eric Pianin, "Senate Appropriations Panel Sends Economic Stimulus Plan to Floor," *Washington Post*, March 24, 1993.
43. "Senator Nunn to Seek Changes in Clinton's Defense Budget," *Washington Post*, March 22, 1993.
44. "Sam Nunn on the Defense Budget," *Washington Post*, March 25, 1993.
45. Pat Towell, "Autonomous Ally," *CQ Weekly*, March 27, 1993, 732.

46. George Hager, "Senate Democrats Close Ranks, Endorse Clinton Budget," *CQ Weekly*, March 27, 1993, 731.

47. Barton Gellman, "Defense Budget 'Treading Water,'" *Washington Post*, March 28, 1993.

48. Mary McGrory, "Cmdr. Nunn Calls the Shots," *Washington Post*, March 30, 1993.

49. Barton Gellman, "Witness Aspin Encounters Flak."

50. Senate Committee on Armed Services, *Department of Defense Authorization for Appropriations for Fiscal Year 1994 and the Future Years Defense Program*, Part I, 103rd Cong., 1st Sess., 1993, 2–4, 52.

51. UN Security Council, Resolution 816, Bosnia and Herzegovina, S/RES/816 (March 31, 1993), http://unscr.com/en/resolutions/816; North Atlantic Treaty Organization, "Peace Support Operations in Bosnia and Herzegovina," accessed February 2, 2020, https://www.nato.int/cps/en/natohq/topics_52122.htm?selectedLocale=en.

52. Dean Simmons et al., "Air Operations over Bosnia," *Proceedings Magazine*, May 1997, 58–63.

53. Michael R. Gordon, "NATO General Is Reticent about Air Strikes in Bosnia," *New York Times*, April 21, 1993; Senate Committee on Armed Services, *Department of Defense Authorization for Appropriations for Fiscal Year 1994*, Part I, 125–126; Ambassador Madeleine K. Albright, memorandum for National Security Adviser, subject: Options for Bosnia, April 14, 1993, CIA FOIA Electronic Reading Room, https://www.cia.gov/library/readingroom/docs/1993-04-14.pdf.

54. Gordon, "NATO General Is Reticent"; Senate Committee on Armed Services, *Department of Defense Authorization for Appropriations for Fiscal Year 1994*, Part I, 221–223.

55. Stephen Engleberg, "What to Do in Bosnia? Three Hard Choices," *New York Times*, April 29, 1993; Bruce B. Auster, "The Commander and Chiefs," *US News & World Report*, February 8, 1993, 37, 39; Senator Joseph R. Biden Jr., *To Stand against Aggression: Milosevic, the Bosnian Republic and the Conscience of the West*, report to the Committee on Foreign Relations, US Senate (Washington, DC: Government Printing Office, 1993), 2–8; Elaine Sciolino, "In Congress, Urgent Calls for Action against Serbs," *New York Times*, April 20, 1993.

56. UN Security Council, Resolution 713, Socialist Federal Rep. of Yugoslavia, S/RES/713 (September 25, 1991); Stockholm International Peace Research Institute, "EU Arms Embargo on the Former SFR of Yugoslavia (Bosnia and Herzegovina)," https://www.sipri.org/databases/embargoes/eu_arms_embargoes/bosnia; Andrew Bacevich, *American Empire: The Realities and Consequences of U.S. Diplomacy* (Cambridge, MA: Harvard University Press, 2002), 92; Richard Sobel, "U.S. and European Attitudes toward Intervention in the Former Yugoslavia: *Mourir pour la Bosnie?*" in *The World and Yugoslavia's Wars*, ed. Richard H. Ullman (New York: Council on Foreign Relations, 1996), 146.

57. Daniel Williams, "Russia Vows Bosnia Peace Role," *Washington Post*, May 6, 1993.

58. Sam Nunn, "U.S. National Security Interests: Challenges and Priorities," Remarks at the Richard Russell Foundation Symposium on National Security, May

24, 1993, University of Georgia, Athens, GA, Subseries 11.3, Box 7, Briefing Book (3-ring binder), SNP; Randal Ashley, "No Easy Answers on Bosnia," *Atlanta Journal-Constitution*, May 25, 1993; Sam Nunn, Compromise on Bosnian Arms Embargo, Press Release, May 12, 1994, LexisNexis.

59. Laura Silber and Allan Little, *Yugoslavia: Death of a Nation* (New York: TV Books, 1996), 287; Ivo Daalder, *Getting to Dayton: The Making of America's Bosnia Policy* (Washington, DC: Brookings Institution Press, 2000), 18.

60. Senate Committee on Armed Services, *Current Military Operations in Somalia*, 103rd Cong., 1st Sess., 1993, 19–22, 27–31; Harry Johnson and Ted Dagne, "Congress and the Somalia Crisis," in *Learning from Somalia: The Lessons of Armed Humanitarian Intervention*, ed. Walter Clarke and Jeffrey Herbst (Boulder, CO: Westview Press, 1997), 196.

61. Paul Lewis, "U.N. Asks Arrests of Somali Killers," *New York Times*, June 7, 1993.

62. UN Security Council, Resolution 837, Somalia, S/RES/837 (June 6, 1993), http://unscr.com/en/resolutions/837.

63. William J. Clinton, "The President's News Conference," June 17, 1993, online at Gerhard Peters and John T. Woolley, American Presidency Project, https://www.presidency.ucsb.edu/node/220478.

64. Senate Committee on Armed Services, *Joint Chiefs of Staff Briefing on Current Military Operations in Somalia, Iraq, and Yugoslavia*, 1993, 2–25.

65. "Mediator Sees Bosnia Pact within Days," *Atlanta Journal-Constitution*, September 1, 1993; John L. Hirsch and Robert B. Oakley, *Somalia and Operation Restore Hope: Reflections on Peacemaking and Peacekeeping* (Washington, DC: United States Institute of Peace Press, 1995), 124–125.

66. Helen Dewar and Barton Gellman, "Senate Asks Clinton to Get Approval for Continued Troops Deployment," *Washington Post*, September 10, 1993; Congressional Quarterly, *Almanac*, 103rd Cong., 1st Sess., 1993 (Washington, DC: Congressional Quarterly News Features, 1994), 56-C; Johnson and Dagne, "Congress and the Somalia Crisis," 197–198, 199–200.

67. John Lancaster, "Shalikashvili Indicates a Will to Send Troops to Police Bosnia," *Washington Post*, September 23, 1993; Senate Committee on Armed Services, *Nominations before the Senate Armed Services Committee*, 103rd Cong., 1st Sess., 1993, 1151–1221, especially 1178; Congressional Quarterly, *Almanac*, 1993, 479.

68. Elaine Sciolino, "Nunn Says He Wants Exit Strategy Before U.S. Troops Go to Bosnia," *New York Times*, September 24, 1993.

69. Clifford Krauss, "Every New President Gets a Rematch," *New York Times*, September 26, 1993.

70. John H. Cushman Jr., "5 G.I.'s Are Killed as Somalis Down 2 U.S. Helicopters," *New York Times*, October 4, 1993; Congressional Quarterly, *Almanac*, 1993, 490, 491.

71. Quoted in Congressional Quarterly, *Almanac*, 1993, 490, 491.

72. Senate Committee on Armed Services, *Current Military Operations in Somalia*, 1993, 75–77.

73. Clifford Krauss, "The Somalia Mission: Congress; Clinton Gathers Congress Support," *New York Times*, October 8, 1993.

74. William J. Clinton, "Address to the Nation on Somalia," October 7, 1993, online at Gerhard Peters and John T. Woolley, American Presidency Project, https://www.presidency.ucsb.edu/node/218391https://www.presidency.ucsb.edu/node/218391.

75. Robin Toner, "Respected but Sometimes Unpopular, Nunn Relishes Pivotal Advisory Role," *New York Times*, October 12, 1993.

76. Clifford Krauss, "Clinton Resists Earlier Somalia Pullout," *New York Times*, October 14, 1993; Senate Committee on Armed Services, *Current Military Operations in Somalia*, 1993, 144–155, especially 148–149 and 154–155.

77. Congressional Quarterly, *Almanac*, 1993, 490, 492, 576.

78. Jim Hoagland, "Hung Up on Appearances," *Washington Post*, January 23, 1994; Gallup, "Presidential Approval Ratings—Bill Clinton," accessed February 2, 2020, https://news.gallup.com/poll/116584/presidential-approval-ratings-bill-clinton.aspx.

79. Eric Schmitt, "A Nominee's Withdrawal; Nunn Spurned a Clinton Offer of Defense Job," *New York Times*, January 20, 1994; Susan Lacetti, "Who's Tossing Hat in Pentagon Ring? Not Me, Says Nunn," *Atlanta Journal-Constitution*, January 20, 1994.

80. Elaine Sciolino, "Republicans Say Congress Could Balk on Bosnia Force," *New York Times*, February 24, 1994.

81. Eric Schmitt, "Cost-Minded Lawmakers Are Challenging a 2-War Doctrine," *New York Times*, March 10, 1994; Senate Committee on Armed Services, *Department of Defense Authorization for Appropriations for Fiscal Year 1995 and the Future Years Defense Program*, 103rd Cong., 2nd Sess., 1994, 344–345; John D. Morrocco, "U.S. Facing Shortfalls in Two-War Strategy," *Aviation Week & Space Technology*, May 2, 1994, 59.

82. Pat Towell, "Defense Authorization: Senate Panel Gives Clinton B-2 Funds He Didn't Seek," *CQ Weekly*, June 11, 1994, 1537; John D. Morrocco, "Showdown Looms on Bomber Force," *Aviation Week & Space Technology*, June 20, 1994, 25.

83. Katherine Q. Seelye, "Clinton Tries to Head Off Senate on Bosnia Embargo," *New York Times*, June 24, 1994.

84. Seelye, "Clinton Tries to Head Off Senate"; Senate Committee on Armed Services, *Impact of Unilateral U.S. Lifting of the Arms Embargo on the Government of Bosnia-Herzegovina*, 103rd Cong., 2nd Sess., 1994, 5–26, 28–38.

85. Senate Committee on Armed Services, *Impact of Unilateral U.S. Lifting of the Arms Embargo*, 5–26, 28–38.

86. Katherine Q. Seelye, "Senate Fails to Lift Bosnia Arms Embargo," *New York Times*, July 2, 1994; Congressional Quarterly, *Almanac*, 103rd Cong., 2nd Sess., 1994 (Washington, DC: Congressional Quarterly News Features, 1995), 425.

87. Pat Towell, "Defense Authorization: Conferees Finesse Decisions on Bosnia and Bomber," *CQ Weekly*, August 13, 1994, 2368; Carroll J. Doherty, "Senate Puts Clinton on Zigzag Course toward Ending Bosnia Arms Embargo," *CQ Weekly*, August 13, 1994, 2.

Chapter 16. The Last True Centrist

1. Roland McElroy, *The Best President the Nation Never Had* (Macon, GA: Mercer University Press, 2017), 208; James A. Thurber and Roger H. Davidson, eds., preface to *Remaking Congress: Change and Stability in the 1990s* (Washington, DC: Congressional Quarterly, 1995), xiv.

2. Elizabeth Drew, *Showdown: The Struggle between the Gingrich Congress and the Clinton White House* (New York: Simon & Schuster, 1996), 14.

3. Adam Clymer, "Committee Chairmanships Are Sure Spoils of Victory," *New York Times*, November 10, 1994; Alfred J. Tuchfarber et al., "The Republican Tidal Wave of 1994: Testing Hypotheses about Realignment, Restructuring, and Rebellion," *PS: Political Science and Politics* 28, no. 4 (December 1995): 694; Andrew E. Busch, "Political Science and the 1994 Elections: An Exploratory Essay," *PS: Political Science and Politics* 28, no. 4 (December 1995): 708–710.

4. James A. Thurber, "Remaking Congress after the Electoral Earthquake of 1994," in *Remaking Congress: Change and Stability in the 1990s*, ed. James A. Thurber and Roger H. Davidson (Washington, DC: Congressional Quarterly, 1995), 1; Norman J. Ornstein and Amy L. Schenkenberg, "The 1995 Congress: The First Hundred Days and Beyond," *Political Science Quarterly* 110, no. 2 (Summer 1995): 184.

5. Drew, *Showdown*, 17–18; Paul Kane, "The 4 Most Important Whip Races in Congressional History," *Washington Post*, June 19, 2014.

6. Ornstein and Schenkenberg, "The 1995 Congress," 198–199.

7. Drew, *Showdown*, 19; Adam Clymer, "Two Senators Vie to Lead Minority," *New York Times*, November 25, 1994.

8. Thurber, "Remaking Congress," 2; James E. Campbell, "The Presidential Pulse and the 1994 Midterm Congressional Election," *Journal of Politics* 59, no. 3 (August 1997): 852–853; Ornstein and Schenkenberg, "The 1995 Congress," 184–186.

9. "Sam Nunn in His Own Words," *Atlanta Journal-Constitution*, October 15, 1995; Donald W. Beachler, "The South and the Democratic Presidential Nomination, 1972–1992," *Presidential Studies Quarterly* 26, no. 2 (Spring 1996): 402; Phil Gailey, "Dissidents Defy Top Democrats," *New York Times*, March 1, 1985; Jon F. Hale, "The Making of the New Democrats," *Political Science Quarterly* 110, no. 2 (Summer 1993): 213.

10. Paul Kane, "What Democrats Can Learn from the Centrists Who Got Bill Clinton to the White House," *Washington Post*, January 4, 2018; Hale, "The Making of the New Democrats," 220.

11. Norm Ornstein, "Losing the Senate," *Argument* (blog), *Foreign Policy*, March 29, 2013, http://foreignpolicy.com/2013/03/29/losing-the-senate/.

12. "Power Play Failed, Thurmond Says," *New York Times*, February 5, 1995.

13. Nunn, interview by author, May 9, 2018, Washington, DC.

14. Eric Schmitt, "Congressional Roundup: Military Readiness," *New York Times*, January 20, 1995.

15. Larry Berman and Emily O. Goldman, "Clinton's Foreign Policy at Midterm," in

The Clinton Presidency, ed. Colin Campbell and Bert A. Rockman, (Chatham, NJ: Chatham House, 1996), 291.

16. Quoted in Berman and Goldman, "Clinton's Foreign Policy at Midterm," 291.
17. Elaine Sciolino, "Clinton's Policy on Bosnia Draws Criticism in Congress," *New York Times,* June 8, 1995; Ivo Daalder, *Getting to Dayton: The Making of America's Bosnia Policy* (Washington, DC: Brookings Institution Press, 2000), 61–62.
18. Sciolino, "Clinton's Policy on Bosnia."
19. "For the Record," *Washington Post,* June 9, 1995.
20. "For the Record," *Washington Post,* June 9, 1995; "Nunn Seeks Deadline," *Washington Post,* June 20, 1995.
21. Michael Dobbs, "Nunn Breaks Ranks on NATO Expansion," *Washington Post,* June 23, 1995.
22. Sam Nunn, "The Future of NATO in an Uncertain World," speech delivered before the SACLANT Seminar 95, Norfolk, VA, June 22, 1995, Sam Nunn Private Papers, Nuclear Threat Initiative offices, Washington, DC.
23. Nunn, "The Future of NATO."
24. Nunn.
25. Michael Dobbs, "Enthusiasm for Wider Alliance Is Marked by Contradictions," *Washington Post,* July 7, 1995; Ronald D. Asmus, *Opening NATO's Door: How the Alliance Remade Itself for a New Era* (New York: Columbia University Press, 2002), 118–121; Strobe Talbott, "Why NATO Should Grow," *New York Review of Books,* August 10, 1995, n1, http://www.nybooks.com/articles/1995/08/10/why -nato-should-grow/.
26. Dobbs, "Enthusiasm for Wider Alliance."
27. Dobbs.
28. Dobbs; Asmus, *Opening NATO's Door,* 121, 122.
29. Congressional Quarterly, *Almanac,* 104th Cong., 1st Sess., 1995 (Washington, DC: Congressional Quarterly News Features, 1996), 9-4, 9-10, 9-15; Bob Deans, "Keeping the Genie in Its Bottle—A Do-or-Die Global Power Struggle," *Atlanta Journal-Constitution,* May 10, 1995; Committee on Strengthening and Expanding the Department of Defense Cooperative Threat Program, National Academy of Sciences, *Global Security Engagement: A New Model for Cooperative Threat Reduction* (Washington, DC: National Academies Press, 2009), 21–24.
30. James M. Goldgeier, "The U.S. Decision to Enlarge: How, When, Why, and What Next?" *Brookings Review* 17, no. 3 (Summer 1999): 20; John Dumbrell, *Clinton's Foreign Policy: Between the Bushes, 1992–2000* (London: Routledge, 2009), 87; Joyce P. Kaufman, "A Challenge to European Security and Alliance Unity," *World Affairs* 161, no. 1 (Summer 1998): 22, 24.
31. Asmus, *Opening NATO's Door,* 124.
32. Alison Mitchell, "Conflict in the Balkans: The Policy," *New York Times,* July 15, 1995; Daalder, *Getting to Dayton,* 62–63; Helen Dewar, "Senate Votes to Lift Bosnia Arms Ban," *Washington Post,* July 27, 1995.
33. "Nunn Lays Out Grim Choices in Bosnian War," *Atlanta Journal-Constitution,* July 19, 1995; Michael Dobbs, "U.S. Favors 'Aggressive' NATO Airstrikes in Bosnia," *Washington Post,* July 19, 1995.

34. Dumbrell, *Clinton's Foreign Policy*, 87; Elaine Sciolino, "Senate Debates Arms Ban," *New York Times*, July 26, 1995; Sciolino, "Defiant Senators Vote to Override Bosnian Arms Ban," *New York Times*, July 27, 1995; Sciolino, "Senate Vote to End Embargo May Prove a Pyrrhic Victory," *New York Times*, July 28, 1995; Dewar, "Senate Votes to Lift Bosnia Arms Ban."

35. Sciolino, "Senate Debates Arms Ban"; Sciolino, "Defiant Senators Vote to Override"; Dewar, "Senate Votes to Lift Bosnia Arms Ban."

36. Congressional Quarterly, *Almanac*, 1995, 10–12.

37. Sciolino, "Senate Debates Arms Ban"; Dewar, "Senate Votes to Lift Bosnia Arms Ban"; Daalder, *Getting to Dayton*, 63–64; Ryan C. Hendrickson, "War Powers, Bosnia, and the 104th Congress," *Political Science Quarterly* 113, no. 2 (Summer 1998): 249.

38. Helen Dewar, "Senate Backs Missile Defense Network," *Washington Post*, August 4, 1995.

39. Dewar, "Senate Backs Missile Defense."

40. Dewar.

41. "Senators Offer Missile Defense Compromise," *Washington Post*, August 12, 1995. This issue was widely covered in the press. The Republicans, who controlled the Senate, wanted to build a multisite, national anti–ballistic missile system. They emphasized that the system was not a return to SDI (a space-based system), but a ground-based system designed to protect the United States from an "accidental launch," "limited strike," or "an attack from a rogue state such as North Korea." See as an example, Associated Press, "Senators Set out Compromise on Plan for Missile Defense," *St. Louis Post-Dispatch*, August 12, 1995.

42. Bradley Graham, "Congress to Push for a National Missile Defense," *Washington Post*, September 5, 1995; Helen Dewar, "Senate Backs Missile Plan," *Washington Post*, September 7, 1995.

43. Jill Vejnoska, "The Talk of Perry," *Atlanta Journal-Constitution*, September 9, 1995; Ken Fosken, "What If Nunn Doesn't Run?" *Atlanta Journal-Constitution*, September 10, 1995; Eric Schmitt, "Even G.O.P. Asking Nunn Not to Retire from Senate," *New York Times*, October 2, 1995.

44. Schmitt, "Even G.O.P. Asking Nunn Not to Retire."

45. Sam Nunn, untitled (speech transcript), October 9, 1995, George State Capitol building, in author's possession; Kevin Sack, "Nunn Looks at His Future," *New York Times*, October 8, 1995; Mike Christensen and Mark Sherman, "End of an Era: Nunn to Retire from Senate," *Atlanta Journal-Constitution*, October 9, 1995; "Sam Nunn Retires," *Atlanta Journal-Constitution*, October 10, 1995.

46. Tom Baxter, "Relaxed, Revealing Nunn Says Climate Stormy for Politics," *Atlanta Journal-Constitution*, October 15, 1995.

47. Congressional Quarterly, *Almanac*, 1995, 9-3, 9-13, 9-14; William J. Clinton, "Statement on Signing the National Defense Authorization Act for Fiscal Year 1996," February 10, 1996, online at Gerhard Peters and John T. Woolley, American Presidency Project, https://www.presidency.ucsb.edu/node/222768.

48. Kaufman, "A Challenge to European Security," 27–28; William J. Clinton, "Address to the Nation on Implementation of the Peace Agreement in Bosnia-

Herzegovina," November 27, 1995, online at Gerhard Peters and John T. Woolley, American Presidency Project, https://www.presidency.ucsb.edu/node/220919; Katherine Q. Seelye, "Legislators Get Plea by Clinton on Bosnia Force," *New York Times*, November 29, 1995.

49. Seelye, "Legislators Get Plea by Clinton"; Memorandum, DeBobes to Nunn, subject: Bosnia Working Group Meeting, November 28, 1995, Subseries 11. 3, Box 11, file, Bosnia, Sam Nunn Papers (SNP), Stuart A. Rose Manuscript, Archives, and Rare Book Library, Emory University, Atlanta, GA.

50. Francis X. Clines, "Balkans 101: Not with a 10-Foot Pole," *New York Times*, November 29, 1995; Katherine Q. Seelye, "Nearly Half of House Members Sign Letter Opposing Bosnia Deployment," *New York Times*, December 8, 1995.

51. Memorandum, DeBobes to Nunn, subject: White House meeting, December 12, 1995, Subseries 11. 3, Box 11, file, Bosnia, SNP.

52. Katherine Q. Seelye, "Anguished, Senators Vote to Support Bosnia Mission," *New York Times*, December 14, 1995.

53. US Department of State, *Dayton Accords*, November 21, 1995, https://2001-2009 .state.gov/p/eur/rt/balkans/c16265.htm.

Chapter 17. An Honorable Career

1. Matthew S. Quinn, "Carter to Nunn: Run for Governor Next," *Atlanta Journal-Constitution*, November 10, 1995.

2. Senate Committee on Governmental Affairs, Permanent Subcommittee on Investigations, *Global Proliferation of Weapons of Mass Destruction*, Part II, 104th Cong., 2nd Sess., 1996, 1–7, 17–21; Philip Shenon, "Ex-Soviet A-Bomb Fuel an Easy Target for Terrorists," *New York Times*, March 13, 1996; Philip Taubman, *The Partnership: Five Cold Warriors and Their Quest to Ban the Bomb* (New York: Harper, 2012), 276.

3. Senate Committee on Governmental Affairs, Permanent Subcommittee on Investigations, *Global Proliferation*, Part II, 73–89; Tim Weiner, "U.S. Vulnerable to Terrorist Chemical Weapons," *New York Times*, March 21, 1996.

4. Defend America Act of 1996, S. 1635, 104th Cong., 2nd Sess., https://www.con gress.gov/bill/104th-congress/senate-bill/1635; Defend America Act of 1996, H.R. 3144, 104th Cong., 2nd Sess., https://www.congress.gov/bill/104th-con gress/house-bill/3144; see also *Congressional Record* 142, no. 40, 104th Cong., 2nd Sess., 1996, S2651–S2652.

5. Joseph Cirinione, "Why the Right Lost the Missile Defense Debate," *Foreign Policy* 106 (Spring 1997): 39–41.

6. Michael R. Gordon, "Despite Cold War's End, Russia Keeps Building a Secret Complex," *New York Times*, April 16, 1996.

7. Cirinione, "Why the Right Lost," 41, 49.

8. Cirinione, 52–53.

9. Steven Erlanger, "Russia—Watchers in U.S. Feel Bipartisan Anxiety," *New York Times*, June 17, 1996; John T. Shaw, *Richard Lugar, Statesman of the Senate: Crafting Foreign Policy from Capitol Hill* (Bloomington: Indiana University Press,

2012), 65–66. See Ashton Carter and William J. Perry, *Preventive Defense: A New Security Strategy for America* (Washington, DC: Brookings Institution Press, 1999), 74–75, for a discussion of congressional vacillation regarding implementation of the Nunn-Lugar Cooperative Threat Reduction program.

10. Congressional Quarterly, *Almanac*, 104th Cong., 2nd Sess., 1996 (Washington, DC: Congressional Quarterly News Features, 1997), chap. 8, p. 7; John F. Sopko, "The Changing Proliferation Threat," *Foreign Policy* 105 (Winter 1996–1997): 18; Bill Summary (final), Defense against Weapons of Mass Destruction Act of 1996, in author's possession; Letter, Nunn, Lugar, and Domenici to Inouye, September 19, 1996, Subseries 11.3, Box 12, file, Counter-proliferation (Nunn-Lugar), Sam Nunn Papers, Stuart A. Rose Manuscript, Archives, and Rare Book Library, Emory University, Atlanta, GA; Richard Davis, General Accounting Office, Testimony before the Subcommittee on National Security, International Affairs, and Criminal Justice, Committee on Government Reform and Oversight, House of Representatives, *Observations on the Nunn-Lugar-Domenici Domestic Preparedness Program*, GAO/T-NSIAD-99-16, October 2, 1998, 2.

11. Rhonda Cook, "Targeting Terrorism," *Atlanta Journal-Constitution*, July 30, 1996.

12. Thomas L. Friedman, "Help Wanted?" *New York Times*, August 28, 1996; Bob Deans, "Washington Speculates on the Next Secretary of State," *Atlanta Journal-Constitution*, September 22, 1996.

13. Richard L. Berke, "If Clinton Sees Votes in South, He's Not Just Whistling Dixie," *New York Times*, September 13, 1996.

14. Robert Blackwill, Arnold Horelick, and Sam Nunn, *Stopping the Decline in US-Russian Relations*, P-7986, RAND Corporation, Santa Monica, CA, 1996, 1.

15. Blackwill, Horelick and Nunn, *Stopping the Decline*, 1.

16. Blackwill, Horelick and Nunn, 1–2, 7–9.

17. William J. Clinton, "Statement on the Russian Presidential Election, July 4, 1996," online at Gerhard Peters and John T. Woolley, American Presidency Project, https://www.presidency.ucsb.edu/node/222718.

18. Charles Gati, "NATO Enlargement: Who, Why, and How?" *SAIS Review* 19, no. 2 (Summer–Fall 1999): 213–214; Frank Ksozorus Jr., *Hungary's Accession to NATO: An Expanded Report* (Washington, DC: American Hungarian Federation of Metropolitan Washington, DC, 2007), accessed February 2, 2020, http://www.americanhungarianfederation.org/docs/AHFDC_NATO_Expansion_Report.pdf.

19. House of Representatives, NATO Enlargement Facilitation Act of 1996, H.R. 3564, 104th Cong., 2nd Sess., accessed February 2, 2020, https://www.govtrack.us/congress/bills/104/hr3564; Senate, NATO Enlargement Facilitation Act of 1996, S. 1830, 104th Cong., 2nd Sess., accessed February 2, 2020, https://www.govtrack.us/congress/bills/104/s1830.

20. Senate, NATO Enlargement Facilitation Act of 1996; James M. Goldgeier, *Not Whether but When: The U.S. Decision to Enlarge NATO* (Washington, DC: Brookings Institution Press, 1999), 104–105; Carter and Perry, *Preventive Defense*, 29–32, 58; Gati, "NATO Enlargement," 215, 216; Strobe Talbott, "Why NATO Should Grow," *New York Review of Books*, August 10, 1995, http://www.nybooks

.com/articles/1995/08/10/why-nato-should-grow/; Dan Reiter, "Why NATO Enlargement Does Not Spread Democracy," *International Security* 25, no. 4 (Spring 2001): 48.

21. Senate, NATO Enlargement Facilitation Act of 1996; Goldgeier, *Not Whether but When*, 104–105; Jeremy D. Rosner, "The American Public, Congress and NATO Enlargement," *NATO Review* 45, no. 1 (January 1997): 12–14; Commission on Security and Cooperation in Europe, *Report on Human Rights and the Process of NATO Enlargement* (Washington, DC: Commission on Security and Cooperation in Europe, 1997), 7.

22. Bob Deans, "Nunn's Last Day on the Hill Is Historic, Moving Moment," *Atlanta Journal-Constitution*, October 4, 1996.

23. Nunn, "Farewell Address," in *Lessons and Legacies: Farewell Addresses from the Senate*, ed. Norman J. Ornstein (New York: Perseus Publishing, 1997), 122–124.

24. Nunn, "Farewell Address," 124–129.

25. Nunn, 130–132.

26. Nunn, 135–142.

27. *Congressional Record*, 104th Cong., 2nd Sess., 1996, S12254–S12255, S12279, S12273–A12274, S12298–S122300.

28. Joseph Albright, "Nunn Helps Destroy Nuclear Arms in Ukraine," *Atlanta Journal-Constitution*, October 24, 1996.

29. Mark Sherman, "Terrorist Attacks a Major U.S. Risk, Nunn Warns," *Atlanta Journal-Constitution*, October 31, 1996; Elaine Sciolino, "14 Senators Retire: Some to Write, One to Marry," *New York Times*, October 27, 1996.

30. David E. Rosenbaum, "Democrats Fail to Reverse Right's Capitol Hill Gains," *New York Times*, November 6, 1996; "South," *New York Times*, November 6, 1996; Todd S. Purdum, "Same Star, but Supporting Cast to Change," *New York Times*, November 7, 1996.

31. Steven Erlanger, "Clinton May Be Pressured to Act on Global Stage," *New York Times*, November 11, 1996.

32. Alison Mitchell, "Maine Republican Is Seen as Leading for Defense," *New York Times*, November 15, 1996; John F. Harris, "Clinton Mulls National Security Choices," *Washington Post*, December 4, 1996.

33. Alison Mitchell, "Albright to Head State Dept.; Republican in Top Defense Job," *New York Times*, December 6, 1996; Todd S. Purdum, "Top Nominees Were Most Likely Candidates All Along," *New York Times*, December 6, 1996; R. W. Apple Jr., "National Security Team Must Fill in the Blanks," *New York Times*, December 6, 1996.

Conclusion

1. Richard F. Fenno Jr., *The Emergence of a Senate Leader: Pete Domenici and the Reagan Budget* (Washington, DC: CQ Press, 1991), xii.

2. Norman J. Ornstein, Robert L. Peabody, and David W. Rohde, "The U.S. Senate in an Era of Change," in *Congress Reconsidered*, 5th ed., ed. Lawrence C. Dodd and Bruce I. Oppenheimer (Washington, DC: CQ Press, 1993), 13–38; Frank H.

Mackaman, preface to *Understanding Congressional Leadership* (Washington, DC: Congressional Quarterly Press, 1981), vi.

3. Fenno, *The Emergence of a Senate Leader,* xii. See Mackaman, introduction to *Understanding Congressional Leadership* (Washington, DC: Congressional Quarterly Press, 1981), 5.

4. Rochelle Jones and Peter Woll, *The Private World of Congress* (New York: Free Press, 1979), 115–116.

5. Stephen J. Gerras, ed., *Strategic Leadership Primer,* 3rd ed. (Carlisle, PA: Department of Command, Leadership, and Management, US Army War College, 2010), 31–32; Rocky Rief, interview by Tom Chaffin, n.p., October 17, 1996, Box 1, Sam Nunn Oral History Collection (SNOH), Stuart A. Rose Manuscript, Archives, and Rare Book Library, Emory University, Atlanta, GA. For a discussion of how leadership based on principles, values, norms, expertise, culture, and traditions affects institutions and political choice, see Erwin Hargrove, "Two Conceptions of Institutional Leadership," *in Leadership and Politics: New Perspectives in Political Science,* ed. Bryan D. Jones (Lawrence: University Press of Kansas, 1989), 57–59, 63–64, 66–68.

6. Gerras, *Strategic Leadership Primer,* 33. See Mackaman, introduction to *Understanding Congressional Leadership,* 5–6.

7. Eileen Burgin, "Congress and Foreign Policy: The Misperceptions," In *Congress Reconsidered,* 5th ed., ed. Lawrence C. Dodd and Bruce I. Oppenheimer (Washington, DC: CQ Press, 1993), 338–341.

8. Gerras, *Strategic Leadership Primer,* 28–31. For an insightful discussion of the role of cognitive skills in legislating, see David Mayhew, "Lawmaking as a Cognitive Enterprise," in *Living Legislation: Durability, Change, and the Politics of American Lawmaking,* ed. Jeffrey A. Jenkins and Eric M. Patashnik (Chicago, IL: University of Chicago Press, 2012), 255–264.

9. Arnold Punaro, Box 1, interview by Tom Chaffin, October 15, 1997, McLean, VA, SNOH.

10. Fenno, *The Emergence of a Senate Leader,* xii; Bernard Weinraub, "Sam Nunn, at 39, Emerging as Expert on Military," *New York Times,* July 1, 1978; Fred R. Harris, *Deadlock or Decision: The U.S. Senate and the Rise of National Politics* (New York: Oxford University Press, 1993), 92, 101, 161; Jones and Woll, *The Private World of Congress,* 114–122.

11. "Georgia, US Senate," Ourcampaigns.com, accessed February 5, 2020, https://www.ourcampaigns.com/RaceDetail.html?RaceID=5326; Wayne King, "Busbee and Nunn Easily Capture Nominations in Georgia Primary," *New York Times,* August 9, 1978.

12. Clerk of the US House of Representatives, *Statistics of the President and Congressional Election of November 4, 1980* (Washington, DC: Government Printing Office, 1981), 14, 73–73; Art Harris, "The End of the Talmadge Legend," *Washington Post,* November 18, 1980.

13. Christopher J. Deering, "Decision Making in the Armed Services Committees," in *Congress Resurgent: Foreign and Defense Policy on Capitol Hill,* ed. Randall B. Ripley and James M. Lindsay (Ann Arbor: University of Michigan Press, 1993),

169, 172; David C. Morrison, "Sam Nunn Inc.," *National Journal* 23 (1991): 1483–1486.

14. Deering, "Decision Making in the Armed Services Committees," 174, 181; Archie Brown, *The Myth of the Strong Leader: Political Leadership in Modern Politics* (New York: Basic Books, 2014), 25; Barbara Kellerman, "Leadership—It's a System, Not a Person!" *Daedalus* 145, no. 3 (Summer 2016): 91–93.

15. David M. Abshire, "Sam Nunn: Strategic Leadership," in *Triumphs and Tragedies of the Modern Congress: Case Studies on Legislative Leadership,* ed. Maximilian Angerholzer III, James Kitfield, Christopher P. Lu, and Norman Ornstein (Santa Barbara, CA: Praeger, 2014), 102–103, 108.

16. "Full Honor Review and Award Ceremony for Senator Sam Nunn," Subseries 11.3, Box 16, File, Historical Interest Awards, Sam Nunn Papers, Stuart A. Rose Manuscript, Archives, and Rare Book Library, Emory University, Atlanta, GA.

Epilogue

1. David E. Hoffman, *The Dead Hand: The Untold Story of the Cold War Arms Race and Its Dangerous Legacy* (New York: Doubleday, 2009), 380, 382.

2. Quoted in Roland McElroy, *The Best President the Nation Never Had* (Macon, GA: Mercer University Press, 2017), 20.

3. Nuclear Threat Initiative, *Annual Report* (Washington, DC: Nuclear Threat Initiative, 2018), 1–29.

4. George P. Shultz, William J. Perry, Henry A. Kissinger, and Sam Nunn, "A World Free of Nuclear Weapons," *Wall Street Journal,* January 4, 2007; Amanda Erickson, "These Cold War Hawks Are Now Championing an End to Nuclear Weapons," *Washington Post,* October 6, 2017; Nuclear Threat Initiative, *Innovation and Action for a Secure World* (Washington, DC: Nuclear Threat Initiative, 2015), 5, 21.

5. Georgia Trend, "Georgia's New Trustees," February 2011, accessed February 3, 2020, http://www.georgiatrend.com/February-2011/Georgias-New-Trustees/; Peace Research Institute Frankfurt, "Awardees of the Hessian Peace Prize," accessed February 4, 2020, https://www.hsfk.de/en/the-peace-research-institute/awards/awardees-of-the-hessian-peace-prize/;

6. Secretary of the Navy Public Affairs, "SECNAV Names New Destroyer in Honor of US Senator from Georgia," story number: NNS190506–01, release date: 5/6/2019, accessed February 3, 2020, https://www.navy.mil/submit/display.asp?story_id=109469.

7. Heinz Family Foundation, The Heinz Awards, 10th award, Chairman's Medal category, "Richard Lugar + Sam Nunn," accessed February 4, 2020, http://www.heinzawards.net/recipients/richard-lugar-sam-nunn.

8. *Encyclopedia Britannica Online,* s.v. "Sam Nunn," accessed February 4, 2020, https://www.britannica.com/biography/Sam-Nunn.

BIBLIOGRAPHY

Archives and Other Repositories

Association for Diplomatic Studies and Training. Foreign Affairs Oral History Project. Arlington, VA. https://adst.org/oral-history/oral-history-interviews/.

Bush, George H. W. Papers. George H. W. Bush Presidential Library, College Station, TX. https://bush41library.tamu.edu/archives/nsd.

Bush, George H. W. Presidency Project. Miller Center of Public Affairs, University of Virginia, Charlottesville, VA. https://millercenter.org/the-presidency/presidential-oral-histories/george-h-w-bush.

Carnegie Corporation of New York Oral History Project. Columbia Center for Oral History, Columbia University, New York.

Carter, Jimmy. Papers. Jimmy Carter Presidential Library, Atlanta, GA.

Carter, Jimmy. Presidency Project. Miller Center of Public Affairs, University of Virginia, Charlottesville, VA. https://millercenter.org/president/carter.

Central Intelligence Agency. FOIA Electronic Reading Room, Washington, DC. https://www.cia.gov/library/readingroom/home.

Cohen, William S. Papers. Raymond H. Fogler Library, University of Maine, Orono, ME.

Dole, Robert, and Elizabeth Dole. Archive and Special Collection. University of Kansas, Lawrence. https://dolearchives.ku.edu/.

Ford, Gerald R. Papers (Digital Collections). Gerald Ford Presidential Library, Grand Rapids, MI. https://www.fordlibrarymuseum.gov/collections-digital.aspx.

Haig, Alexander Meigs. Papers. Library of Congress, Washington, DC.

Lake, Anthony. Papers. Library of Congress, Washington, DC.

Locher, James R., III. Papers. Special Collections, National Defense University Library, Fort Lesley J. McNair, Washington, DC.

Muskie, Edmund S. Oral History Collection. Bates College, Lewiston, ME. https://scarab.bates.edu/muskie_oh/.

National Archives and Records Administration, Center for Legislative Archives, Washington, DC.

National Security Archive. George Washington University, Washington, DC. https://nsarchive.gwu.edu/digital-national-security-archive.

Nunn, Sam. Oral History Collection. Stuart A. Rose Manuscript, Archives, and Rare Book Library, Emory University, Atlanta, GA.

Nunn, Sam. Papers. Stuart A. Rose Manuscript, Archives and Rare Book Library, Emory University, Atlanta, GA.

Nunn, Sam. Private Papers. Nuclear Threat Initiative offices, Washington, DC.

Reagan, Ronald. Papers. Ronald Reagan Presidential Library, Simi Valley, CA.

Reagan, Ronald. Presidency Project. Miller Center of Public Affairs, University of Virginia, Charlottesville, VA. https://millercenter.org/president/reagan.

US Department of State. Virtual Reading Room, Washington, DC. https://foia.state .gov/Search/Library.aspx.

US Senate. Historical Office, Washington, DC.

Books and Monographs

Abshire, David M. *Preventing World War III: A Realistic Grand Strategy.* New York: Harper & Row, 1988.

Adler, E. Scott, and John D. Wilkerson. *Congress and the Politics of Problem Solving.* New York: Cambridge University Press, 2012.

Allison, William Thomas. *The Gulf War, 1990–91.* New York: Palgrave Macmillan, 2012.

Angerholzer, Maximilian, III, James Kitfield, Christopher P. Lu, and Norman Ornstein, eds. *Triumphs and Tragedies of the Modern Congress: Case Studies on Legislative Leadership.* Santa Barbara, CA: Praeger, 2014.

Asmus, Ronald D. *Opening NATO's Door: How the Alliance Remade Itself for a New Era.* New York: Columbia University Press, 2002.

Auerswald, David P., and Colton C. Campbell, eds. *Congress and the Politics of National Security.* New York: Cambridge University Press, 2012.

Auten, Brian. *Carter's Conversion: The Hardening of American Defense Policy.* Columbia: University of Missouri Press, 2008.

Bacevich, Andrew. *American Empire: The Realities and Consequences of U.S. Diplomacy.* Cambridge, MA: Harvard University Press, 2002.

Baker, James A., III, with Thomas M. DeFrank. *The Politics of Diplomacy: Revolution, War, and Peace, 1989–1992.* New York: G. P. Putnam's Sons, 1995.

Baker, Ross, K. *Friend and Foe in the U.S. Senate.* New York: Free Press, 1980.

Barnhart, Michael, ed. *Congress and United States Foreign Policy: Controlling the Use of Force in the Nuclear Age.* Albany: State University of New York Press, 1987.

Berman, Larry, ed. *Looking Back on the Reagan Presidency.* Baltimore, MD: Johns Hopkins University Press, 1990.

Bernstein, Paul I., and Jason D. Wood. *The Origins of Nunn-Lugar and Cooperative Threat Reduction.* Case Study 3, Center for the Study of Weapons of Mass Destruction. Washington, DC: National Defense University, 2010.

Beschloss, Michael R., and Strobe Talbott. *At the Highest Levels: The Inside Story of the End of the Cold War.* Boston: Little, Brown, 1993.

Biden, Joe. *Promises to Keep: On Life and Politics.* New York: Random House, 2007.

Blackwill, Robert, Arnold Horelick, and Sam Nunn. *Stopping the Decline in US-Russian Relations.* P-7986. RAND Corporation, Santa Monica, CA, 1996.

Blechman, Barry M., ed. *Preventing Nuclear War: A Realistic Approach.* Bloomington: Indiana University Press, 1985.

Bohlen, Avis, William Burns, Steven Pifer, and John Woolworth. *The Treaty on Intermediate Range Nuclear Forces: History and Lessons Learned.* Arms Control Series Paper no. 9. Washington, DC: Brookings Institution, 2012.

Bose, Meena, and Rosanna Perotti, eds. *From Cold War to New World Order: The Foreign Policy of George H. W. Bush.* Westport, CT: Greenwood Press, 2002.

Branch, Taylor. *The Clinton Tapes: Wrestling History with the President.* New York: Simon & Schuster, 2009.

Brown, Archie. *The Myth of the Strong Leader: Political Leadership in Modern Politics.* New York: Basic Books, 2014.

Brown, Harold, with Joyce Winslow. *Star-Spangled Security: Applying Lessons Learned over Six Decades Safeguarding America.* Washington, DC: Brookings Institution, Press, 2012.

Brzezinski, Zbigniew. *Power and Principle.* New York: Farrar, Straus and Giroux, 1983.

Bunn, Matthew. *Foundation for the Future: The ABM Treaty and National Security.* Washington, DC: Arms Control Association, 1990.

Burns, James MacGregor. *Leadership.* New York: Harper and Row, 1978.

Burns, James MacGregor, and Georgia J. Sorenson. *Dead Center: Clinton-Gore Leadership and the Perils of Moderation.* New York: Scribner, 1999.

Bush, George H. W. *All the Best, George Bush: My Life in Letters and Other Writings.* New York: Scribner, 2013.

Bush, George H. W., and Brent Scowcroft. *A World Transformed.* New York: Alfred A. Knopf, 1998.

Caldwell, Dan. *The Dynamics of Domestic Politics and Arms Control: The SALT II Treaty Ratification Debate.* Columbia: University of South Carolina Press, 1991.

Campbell, Colin, and Bert A. Rockman, eds. *The Clinton Presidency: First Appraisals.* Chatham, NJ: Chatham House, 1996.

Campbell, Colton C., and David P. Auerswald, eds. *Congress and Civil Military Relations.* Washington, DC: Georgetown University Press, 2015.

Cannon, Lou. *Reagan.* New York: G. P. Putnam, 1982.

Carter, Ashton B., Kurt Campbell, Steven Miller, and Charles Zraket. *Soviet Nuclear Fission: Control of the Nuclear Arsenal in a Disintegrating Soviet Union.* Cambridge, MA: Center for Science and International Affairs, Harvard University, 1991.

Carter, Ashton, and William J. Perry. *Preventive Defense: A New Security Strategy for America.* Washington, DC: Brookings Institution Press, 1999.

Carter, Jimmy. *Keeping Faith: Memoirs of a President.* New York: Bantam Books, 1982.

———. *White House Diary.* New York: Farrar, Straus and Giroux, 2010.

Carter, Ralph G., and James M. Scott. *Choosing to Lead: Understanding Congressional Foreign Policy Entrepreneurs.* Durham, NC: Duke University Press, 2009.

Cheney, Dick. *In My Time: A Personal and Political Memoir.* New York: Threshold Editions, 2011.

Chernyaev, Anatoly S. *My Six Years with Gorbachev.* University Park: Pennsylvania State University Press, 2000.

Clarke, Walter, and Jeffrey Herbst, eds. *Learning from Somalia: The Lessons of Armed Humanitarian Intervention.* Boulder, CO: Westview Press, 1997.

Clinton, Bill. *My Life.* New York: Alfred A. Knopf, 2004.

Coleman, Bradley Lynn, and Kyle Longley, eds. *Reagan and the World: Leadership and National Security, 1981–1989.* Lexington: University Press of Kentucky, 2017.

Committee on Strengthening and Expanding the Department of Defense Cooperative Threat Program. National Academy of Sciences. *Global Security Engagement: A New Model for Cooperative Threat Reduction.* Washington, DC: National Academies Press, 2009.

Congressional Quarterly. *Almanac.* 93rd Cong., 1st Sess., 1973. Washington, DC: Congressional Quarterly News Features, 1974.

———. *Almanac.* 93rd Cong., 2nd Sess., 1974. Washington, DC: Congressional Quarterly News Features, 1974.

———. *Almanac.* 94th Cong., 1st Sess., 1975. Washington, DC: Congressional Quarterly News Features, 1976.

———. *Almanac.* 96th Cong., 1st Sess., 1979. Washington, DC: Congressional Quarterly News Features, 1980.

———. *Almanac.* 96th Cong., 2nd Sess., 1980. Washington, DC: Congressional Quarterly News Features, 1981.

———. *Almanac.* 97th Cong., 1st Sess., 1981. Washington, DC: Congressional Quarterly News Features, 1982.

———. *Almanac.* 97th Cong., 2nd Sess., 1982. Washington, DC: Congressional Quarterly News Features, 1982.

———. *Almanac.* 98th Cong., 1st Sess., 1983. Washington, DC: Congressional Quarterly News Features, 1984.

———. *Almanac.* 98th Cong., 2nd Sess., 1984. Washington, DC: Congressional Quarterly News Features, 1985.

———. *Almanac.* 99th Cong., 1st Sess., 1985. Washington, DC: Congressional Quarterly News Features, 1986.

———. *Almanac.* 99th Cong., 2nd Sess., 1986. Washington, DC: Congressional Quarterly News Features, 1987.

———. *Almanac.* 100th Cong., 1st Sess., 1987. Washington, DC: Congressional Quarterly News Features, 1988.

———. *Almanac.* 103rd Cong., 1st Sess., 1993. Washington, DC: Congressional Quarterly News Features, 1994.

———. *Almanac.* 103rd Cong., 2nd Sess., 1994. Washington, DC: Congressional Quarterly News Features, 1995.

———. *Almanac.* 104th Cong., 1st Sess., 1995. Washington, DC: Congressional Quarterly News Features, 1996.

———. *Almanac.* 104th Cong., 2nd Sess., 1996. Washington, DC: Congressional Quarterly News Features, 1997.

———. *Congress and the Nation.* Vol. 4: 1981–1984. Washington, DC: Congressional Quarterly, 1985.

———. *Congress and the Nation.* Vol. 9: 1993–1996. Washington, DC: Congressional Quarterly, 1997.

Crowe, William J., Jr. *Selected Works of William J. Crowe, Jr., USN: Eleventh Chairman of the Joint Chiefs of Staff.* Ed. and comp. Julian Burns. Washington, DC: Joint History Office, Office of the Chairman of the Joint Chiefs of Staff, 2013.

Crowe, William J., Jr., with David Chanoff. *The Line of Fire: From Washington to the Gulf, the Politics and Battles of the New Military.* New York: Simon & Schuster, 1993.

Daalder, Ivo. *Getting to Dayton: The Making of America's Bosnia Policy.* Washington, DC: Brookings Institution Press, 2000.

Davidson, Roger H., ed. *The Postreform Congress.* New York: St. Martin's Press, 1992.

Deering, Christopher J., and Steven S. Smith. *Committees in Congress,* 2nd ed. Washington, DC: CQ Press, 1990.

Denton, Robert E., and Rachel L. Holloway. *The Clinton Presidency: Images, Issues, and Communication Strategies.* Westport, CT: Praeger, 1996.

Dodd, Lawrence C., and Bruce I. Oppenheimer, eds. *Congress Reconsidered,* 5th ed. Washington, DC: CQ Press, 1993.

Drew, Elizabeth. *On the Edge: The Clinton Presidency.* New York: Simon & Schuster, 1994.

———. *Showdown: The Struggle between the Gingrich Congress and the Clinton White House.* New York: Simon & Schuster, 1996.

Duffield, John. *Power Rules: The Evolution of NATO's Conventional Force Posture.* Stanford, CA: Stanford University Press, 1995.

Duke, Simon. *The Burdensharing Debate: A Reassessment.* New York: St. Martin's Press, 1993.

Dumbrell, John. *Clinton's Foreign Policy: Between the Bushes, 1992–2000.* London: Routledge, 2009.

Durch, William. *The ABM Treaty and Western Security.* Cambridge, MA: Ballinger Publishing, 1987.

Duric, Mira. *The Strategic Defence Initiative: US Policy and the Soviet Union.* Aldershot, Hampshire, England: Ashgate, 2003.

Fenno, Richard F., Jr. *Congressmen in Committees.* Boston: Little, Brown, 1973.

———. *The Emergence of a Senate Leader: Pete Domenici and the Reagan Budget.* Washington, DC: CQ Press, 1991.

FitzGerald, Frances. *Way Out There in the Blue: Reagan, Star Wars, and the End of the Cold War.* New York: Simon & Schuster, 2000.

Fosdick, Dorothy, ed. *Staying the Course: Henry M. Jackson and National Security.* Seattle: University of Washington Press, 1987.

Franck, Thomas M., and Edward Weisband. *Foreign Policy by Congress.* New York: Oxford University Press, 1979.

Freedman, Lawrence, and Efraim Karsh. *The Gulf Conflict, 1990–1991: Diplomacy and War in the New World Order.* Princeton, NJ: Princeton University Press, 1993.

From, Al, with Alice McKeon. *The New Democrats and the Return to Power.* New York: Palgrave Macmillan, 2013.

Furlong, William L., and Margaret E. Scranton. *The Dynamics of Foreign Policymaking:*

The President, the Congress, and the Panama Canal Treaties. Boulder, CO: Westview Press, 1984.

Garthoff, Raymond L. *Détente and Confrontation: American-Soviet Relations from Nixon to Reagan,* rev. ed. Washington, DC: Brookings Institution Press, 1994.

———. *The Great Transition: American-Soviet Relations and the End of the Cold War.* Washington, DC: Brookings Institution Press, 1994.

———. *Policy versus the Law: The Reinterpretation of the ABM Treaty.* Washington, DC: Brookings Institution Press, 1987.

Gates, Robert M. *From the Shadows: The Ultimate Insider's View of Five Presidents and How They Won the Cold War.* New York: Simon & Schuster, 1996.

Gerber, Alan S., and Eric M. Patashnik, eds. *Promoting the General Welfare: New Perspectives on Government Performance.* Washington, DC: Brookings Institution Press, 2006.

Gerras, Stephen J., ed. *Strategic Leadership Primer,* 3rd ed. Carlisle, PA: Department of Command, Leadership, and Management, US Army War College, 2010.

Glitman, Maynard. *The Last Battle of the Cold War: An Inside Account of Negotiating the Intermediate Range Nuclear Forces Treaty.* New York: Palgrave Macmillan, 2006.

Goldgeier, James M. *Not Whether but When: The U.S. Decision to Enlarge NATO.* Washington, DC: Brookings Institution Press, 1999.

Goldwater, Barry M., with Jack Casserly. *Goldwater.* New York: Doubleday, 1988.

Goodman, Allen E., ed. *The Diplomatic Record, 1992–1993.* Boulder, CO: Westview Press, 1995.

Gorbachev, Mikhail. *Memoirs.* New York: Doubleday, 1996.

Gordon, Michael R., and Bernard E. Trainor. *The Generals' War: The Inside Story of the Conflict in the Gulf.* Boston: Little, Brown, 1995.

Graham, Thomas, Jr. *Disarmament Sketches: Three Decades of Arms Control and International Law.* Seattle: University of Washington Press, 2002.

Graham, Thomas, Jr., and Damien J. LaVera. *Cornerstones of Security: Arms Control Treaties in the Nuclear Age.* Seattle: University of Washington Press, 2003.

Haas, Garland A. *Jimmy Carter and the Politics of Frustration.* Jefferson, NC: McFarland, 1992.

Halberstam, David. *War in a Time of Peace: Bush, Clinton, and the Generals.* New York: Scribner, 2001.

Hamburg, David A. *A Perspective on Carnegie Corporation's Program, 1983–1997.* New York: Carnegie Corporation of New York, 1997.

Hanhimäki, Jussi. *The Flawed Architect: Henry Kissinger and American Foreign Policy.* New York: Oxford University Press, 2004.

Harris, Fred R. *Deadlock or Decision: The U.S. Senate and the Rise of National Politics.* New York: Oxford University Press, 1993.

Harris, John F. *The Survivor: Bill Clinton in the White House.* New York: Random House, 2005.

Hastedt, Glenn P. *American Foreign Policy, Past, Present, and Future,* 10th ed. Lanham, MD: Rowman & Littlefield, 2015.

Hendrickson, Ryan C. *The Clinton Wars: The Constitution, Congress, and War Powers.* Nashville, TN: Vanderbilt University Press, 2002.

Hernnson, Paul S., and Dilys M. Hill, eds. *The Clinton Presidency: The First Term, 1992–96.* New York: St. Martin's Press, 1999.

Hinckley, Barbara. *Less than Meets the Eye: Foreign Policy Making and the Myth of the Assertive Congress.* Chicago: University of Chicago Press, 1994.

Hiro, Dilip. *Desert Shield to Desert Storm: The Second Gulf War.* New York: Routledge, 1992.

Hirsch, John L., and Robert B. Oakley. *Somalia and Operation Restore Hope: Reflections on Peacemaking and Peacekeeping.* Washington, DC: United States Institute of Peace Press, 1995.

Hoffman, David E. *The Dead Hand: The Untold Story of the Cold War Arms Race and Its Dangerous Legacy.* New York: Doubleday, 2009.

Hutchings, Robert L. *American Diplomacy and the End of the Cold War: An Insider's Account of U.S. Policy in Europe, 1989–1992.* Baltimore, MD: Johns Hopkins University Press, 1997.

Jenkins, Jeffrey A., and Eric M. Patashnik, eds. *Living Legislation: Durability, Change and the Politics of American Lawmaking.* Chicago: University of Chicago Press, 2012.

Johnson, Robert David. *Congress and the Cold War.* New York: Cambridge University Press, 2005.

Jones, Bryan, ed. *Leadership and Politics: New Perspectives in Political Science.* Lawrence: University Press of Kansas, 1989.

Jones, David T. *The Senate and INF Ratification.* Carlisle, PA: US Army War College, Strategic Studies Institute, 1992.

Jones, Rochelle, and Peter Woll. *The Private World of Congress.* New York: Free Press, 1979.

Jordan, Hamilton. *Crisis: The Last Year of the Carter Presidency.* New York: G. P. Putnam's Sons, 1982.

Jorden, William J. *Panama Odyssey.* Austin: University of Texas Press, 1984.

Kaufman, Burton I., and Scott Kaufman. *The Presidency of James Earl Carter,* 2nd ed., rev. Lawrence: University Press of Kansas, 2006.

Kaufman, Robert G. *Henry M. Jackson: A Life in Politics.* Seattle: University of Washington Press, 2000.

Keefer, Edward C. *Harold Brown: Offsetting the Soviet Military Challenge, 1977–1981.* Secretaries of Defense Historical Series, vol. 9. Washington, DC: Historical Office, Office of the Secretary of Defense, 2017.

Kellerman, Barbara. *Leadership: Multidisciplinary Perspectives.* Englewood Cliffs, NJ: Prentice-Hall, 1984.

Kingdon, John W. *Agendas, Alternatives, and Public Policies,* 2nd ed. New York: Longman, 2009.

Kitts, Kenneth. *Presidential Commissions and National Security: The Politics of Damage Control.* Boulder, CO: Lynne Rienner, 2006.

Kline, William E. *The INF Treaty.* Case Program, C-16-89-887, Kennedy School of Government, Harvard University, 1989.

Krepon, Michael, and Dan Caldwell, eds. *The Politics of Arms Control Treaty Ratification.* New York: St. Martin's Press, 1991.

Ksozorus, Frank, Jr. *Hungary's Accession to NATO: An Expanded Report*. Washington, DC: American Hungarian Federation of Metropolitan Washington, DC, 2007.

Kugler, Richard L. *Commitment to Purpose: How Alliance Partnership Won the Cold War*. Santa Monica, CA: RAND, 1993.

Lakoff, Sanford, and Herbert F. York. *A Shield in Space? Technology, Politics, and the Strategic Defense Initiative*. Berkeley: University of California Press 1989.

Leffler, Melvin P., and Jeffrey W. Legro, eds. *In Uncertain Times: American Foreign Policy after the Berlin Wall and 9/11*. Ithaca, NY: Cornell University Press, 2011.

Leventhal, Paul, and Yonah Alexander, eds. *Preventing Nuclear Terrorism: The Report and Papers of the International Task Force on Prevention of Nuclear Terrorism*. Lexington, MA: Lexington Books 1987.

Lindsay, James M. *Congress and Nuclear Weapons*. Baltimore, MD: Johns Hopkins University Press, 1991.

———. *Congress and the Politics of U.S. Foreign Policy*. Baltimore, MD: Johns Hopkins University Press, 1994.

Locher, James R., III. *Victory on the Potomac: The Goldwater-Nichols Act Unifies the Pentagon*. College Station: Texas A&M University Press, 2002.

Mackaman, Frank H., ed. *Understanding Congressional Leadership*. Washington, DC: Congressional Quarterly Press, 1981.

Mann, Thomas, ed. *A Question of Balance: The President, the Congress, and Foreign Policy*. Washington, DC: Brookings Institution Press, 1990.

Mann, Thomas, and Norman Ornstein, eds. *The New Congress*. Washington, DC: American Enterprise Institute, 1981.

Matlock, Jack F., Jr. *Reagan and Gorbachev: How the Cold War Ended*. New York: Random House, 2004.

Mayhew, David. *Congress: The Electoral Connection*. New Haven, CT: Yale University Press, 1974.

McElroy, Roland. *The Best President the Nation Never Had*. Macon, GA: Mercer University Press, 2017.

McFarlane, Robert, with Zofia Smardz. *Special Trust*. New York: Cadell & Davies, 1994.

Mencken, H. L. *A Mencken Chrestomathy*. New York: Alfred A. Knopf, 1949.

Mieczkowski, Yanek. *Gerald Ford and the Challenges of the 1970s*. Lexington: University Press of Kentucky, 2005.

Mollenhoff, Clark R. *The President Who Failed*. New York: Macmillan, 1980.

Muravchik, Joshua. *The Senate and National Security: A New Mood*. Washington Papers 80. Beverly Hills, CA: Sage Publications, 1980.

National Academies of Sciences, Committee on International Security and Arms Control. *Nuclear Arms Control: Background and Issues*. Washington, DC: National Academies Press, 1985.

Nguyen, Tien Hang, and Jerrold L. Schecter. *The Palace File*. New York: Harper & Row, 1986.

Nitze, Paul H., with Ann M. Smith and Steven L. Rearden. *From Hiroshima to Glasnost: At the Center of Decision: A Memoir*. New York: Grove Weidenfeld, 1989.

Norris, Robert, and Thomas B. Cochran. *US-USSR Strategic Offensive Nuclear Forces*,

1946–1989. NWD 90-2. Washington, DC: Natural Resources Defense Council, 1990.

Nuclear Threat Initiative. *Annual Report.* Washington, DC: Nuclear Threat Initiative, 2018.

——. *Innovation and Action for a Secure World.* Washington, DC: Nuclear Threat Initiative, 2015.

Nunn, Sam. *Nunn 1990: A New Military Strategy.* Significant Issues Series, vol. 12, no. 5. Washington, DC: Center for Strategic and International Studies, 1990.

Oberdorfer, Don. *From the Cold War to a New Era: The United States and the Soviet Union, 1983–1991,* updated ed. Baltimore, MD: Johns Hopkins University Press, 1999.

Ornstein, Norman J., ed. *Lessons and Legacies: Farewell Addresses from the Senate.* New York: Perseus Publishing, 1997.

Pemberton William E. *Exit with Honor: The Life and Presidency of Ronald Reagan.* Armonk, NY: M. E. Sharpe, 1997.

Powaski, Ronald E. *The Entangling Alliance: The United States and European Security, 1950–1993.* Westport, CT: Greenwood Press, 1994.

——. *March to Armageddon: The United States and the Nuclear Arms Race, 1939 to Present.* New York: Oxford University Press, 1987.

Powell, Colin L., with Joseph E. Persico. *My American Journey.* New York: Random House, 1995.

Punaro, Arnold L., with David Poyer. *On War and Politics: The Battlefield inside Washington's Beltway.* Annapolis, MD: Naval Institute Press, 2016.

Purvis, Hoyt, and Steven J. Baker, eds. *Legislating Foreign Policy.* Boulder, CO: Westview Press, 1984.

Renshon, Stanley A., ed. *The Clinton Presidency: Campaigning, Governing, and the Psychology of Leadership.* Boulder, CO: Westview Press, 1995.

Rhodes, Richard. *The Twilight of the Bombs: Recent Challenges, New Dangers, and the Prospects for a World without Nuclear Weapons.* New York: Knopf, 2010.

Ripley, Randall B., and James M. Lindsay, eds. *Congress Resurgent: Foreign and Defense Policy on Capitol Hill.* Ann Arbor: University of Michigan Press, 1993.

Rosenbaum, Herbert D., and Alexej Ugrinski, eds. *Jimmy Carter: Foreign Policy and Post-presidential Years.* Westport, CT: Greenwood Press, 1994.

Rowny, Edward L., et al. *Strategic Force Modernization and Arms Control.* National Security Paper no. 6. Washington, DC: Institute for Foreign Policy Analysis, 1986.

Sarotte, Mary Elise. *The Collapse: The Accidental Opening of the Berlin Wall.* New York: Basic Books, 2014.

Schieffer, Bob. *This Just In: What I Couldn't Tell You on TV.* New York: G. P. Putnam's Sons, 2003.

Scowcroft, Brent, and R. James Woolsey, cochairman, and Thomas H. Etzold, rapporteur. *Defending Peace and Freedom: Toward Strategic Stability in the Year 2000.* Lanham, MD: University Press of America, 1988.

Shaw, John T. *Richard Lugar, Statesman of the Senate: Crafting Foreign Policy from Capitol Hill.* Bloomington: Indiana University Press, 2012.

Shields, John M., and William C. Potter, eds. *Dismantling the Cold War: U.S. and NIS*

Perspectives on the Nunn-Lugar Cooperative Threat Reduction Program. Cambridge, MA: MIT Press, 1997.

Shultz, George. *Turmoil and Triumph: My Years as Secretary of State.* New York: Charles Scribner's Sons, 1993.

Silber, Laura, and Allan Little. *Yugoslavia: Death of a Nation.* New York: TV Books, 1996.

Skidmore, David. *Reversing Course: Carter's Foreign Policy, Domestic Politics, and the Failure of Reform.* Nashville, TN: Vanderbilt University Press, 1996.

Smith, Gaddis. *Morality, Reason, and Power.* New York: Hill and Wang, 1985.

Smith, Hedrick. *The Power Game: How Washington Works.* New York: Random House, 1987.

Smith, Jean Edward. *George Bush's War.* New York: Henry Holt, 1992.

Snider, Don M. *Strategy, Forces, and Budgets: Dominant Influences in Executive Decision Making, Post–Cold War, 1989–91.* Carlisle, PA: US Army War College, Strategic Studies Institute, 1993.

Soofer, Robert M. *Missile Defense and Western European Security: NATO Strategy, Arms Control, and Deterrence.* New York: Greenwood Press, 1988.

Spanier, John, and Joseph Nogee, eds. *Congress, the Presidency, and American Foreign Policy.* New York: Pergamon Press, 1981.

Spencer, Donald S. *The Carter Implosion.* New York: Praeger, 1988.

Stephanopoulos, George. *All Too Human: A Political Education.* Boston, MA: Little, Brown, 1999.

Strahan, Randall. *Leading Representatives: The Agency of Leaders in the Politics of the U.S. House.* Baltimore, MD: Johns Hopkins University Press, 2007.

Strober, Deborah Hart, and Gerald S. Strober. *Reagan: The Man and His Presidency.* Boston, MA: Houghton Mifflin, 1998.

Strong, Robert A. *Decisions and Dilemmas: Case Studies in Presidential Foreign Policy Making Since 1945,* 2nd ed. Armonk, NY: M. E. Sharpe, 2005.

———. *Working in the World: Jimmy Carter and the Making of American Foreign Policy.* Baton Rouge: Louisiana State University Press, 2000.

Talbott, Strobe. *Deadly Gambits: The Reagan Administration and the Stalemate in Nuclear Arms Control.* New York: Vintage Books, 1985.

———. *Endgame: The Inside Story of SALT II.* New York: Harper & Row, 1980.

———. *The Master of the Game: Paul Nitze and the Nuclear Peace.* New York: Alfred A. Knopf, 1988.

Taubman, Philip. *The Partnership: Five Cold Warriors and Their Quest to Ban the Bomb.* New York: Harper, 2012.

Thompson, Kenneth W., ed. *The Bush Presidency: Ten Intimate Perspectives of George Bush.* Lanham, MD: University Press of America, 1998.

———. *The Ford Presidency: Twenty-Two Intimate Perspectives of Gerald R. Ford.* Lanham, MD: University Press of America, 1988.

———. *Foreign Policy in the Reagan Administration.* Miller Center Reagan Oral History Series, vol. 3. Lanham, MD: University Press of America, 1993.

———. *Sam Nunn on Arms Control.* W. Alton Jones Foundation Series on Arms Control, vol. 5. Lanham, MD: University Press of America, 1987.

Thornton, Richard C. *The Carter Years: Toward a New Global Order.* New York: Paragon House, 1991.

Thurber, James A., and Roger H. Davidson, eds. *Remaking Congress: Change and Stability in the 1990s.* Washington, DC: Congressional Quarterly, 1995.

Treverton, Gregory F. *The Dollar Drain and American Forces in Germany: Managing the Political Economies of Alliance.* Athens: Ohio University Press, 1978.

Tucker, Robert C. *Politics as Leadership.* Columbia: University of Missouri Press, 1981.

Ullman, Richard H., ed. *The World and Yugoslavia's Wars.* New York: Council on Foreign Relations, 1996.

Vance, Cyrus. *Hard Choices.* New York: Simon & Schuster, 1983.

Vick, Alan J. *Building Confidence during Peace and War.* N-2698-CC. Santa Monica, CA: RAND Corporation, 1988.

Voorhees, James. *Dialogue Sustained: The Multilevel Peace Process and the Dartmouth Conference.* Washington, DC: United States Institute of Peace Press, 2002.

Waller, Douglas C. *Congress and the Nuclear Freeze: An Inside Look at the Politics of a Mass Movement.* Amherst: University of Massachusetts Press, 1987.

Weinberger, Caspar. *Fighting for Peace: Seven Critical Years in the Pentagon.* New York: Warner Books, 1990.

Willbanks, James H. *Danger 79er: The Life and Times of Lieutenant General James F. Hollingsworth.* College Station: Texas A&M University Press, 2018.

Williams, David A., ed. *Case Studies in Policy Making & Implementation,* 6th ed. Newport, RI: Naval War College, 2002.

Williams, Phil. *The Senate and U.S. Troops in Europe.* New York: St. Martin's Press, 1985.

Winik, Jay. *On the Brink: The Dramatic, Behind-the-Scenes Saga of the Reagan Era and the Men and Women Who Won the Cold War.* New York: Simon & Schuster, 1996.

Witcover, Jules. *Joe Biden: A Life of Trial and Redemption.* New York: William Morrow, 2010.

Woodward, Bob. *The Commanders.* New York: Simon & Schuster, 1991.

Woolsey, R. James, ed. *Nuclear Arms: Ethics, Strategy, Politics.* San Francisco: ICS Press, 1984.

Zelizer, Julian E. *Jimmy Carter.* New York: Times Books, 2010.

Journal Articles and Book Chapters

Abshire, David M. "Sam Nunn: Strategic Leadership." In *Triumphs and Tragedies of the Modern Congress: Case Studies on Legislative Leadership,* ed. Maximilian Angerholzer III, James Kitfield, Christopher P. Lu, and Norman Ornstein, 102–107. Santa Barbara, CA: Praeger, 2014.

American Society of International Law. "The ABM Treaty Resolution." *The American Journal of International Law* 82, no. 1 (January 1988): 151–165.

Auerswald, David, and Forrest Maltzman. "Policymaking through Advice and Consent: Treaty Consideration by the United States Senate." *Journal of Politics* 65, no. 4 (November 2003): 1097–1110.

Beachler, Donald W. "The South and the Democratic Presidential Nomination, 1972–1992." *Presidential Studies Quarterly* 26, no. 2 (Spring 1996): 402–414.

Berman, Larry, and Emily O. Goldman. "Clinton's Foreign Policy at Midterm." In *The Clinton Presidency*, ed. Colin Campbell and Bert A. Rockman, 290–324. Chatham, NJ: Chatham House, 1996.

Betts, Richard K. "A Joint Nuclear Risk Reduction Control Center." *Parameters* 15, no. 1 (Spring 1985): 39–51.

Blechman, Barry M. "Confidence-Building through Nuclear Risk Reduction Centers." In *Defending Peace and Freedom: Toward Strategic Stability in the Year 2000*, ed. Brent Scowcroft and R. James Woolsey, 181–194. Lanham, MD: University Press of America, 1988.

———. "The New Congressional Role in Arms Control." In *A Question of Balance: The President, the Congress, and Foreign Policy*, ed. Thomas E. Mann, 109–145. Washington, DC: Brookings Institution Press, 1990.

Bloembergen, N., et al. *Report to the American Physical Society of the Study Group on Science and Technology of Directed Energy Weapons*. Reprinted in *Review of Modern Physics* 59, no. 3 (July 1987): S1. https://journals.aps.org/rmp/pdf/10.1103/Rev ModPhys.59.S1.

Bostdorff, Denise M. "Clinton's Characteristic Issue Management Style: Caution, Conciliation, and Conflict Avoidance in the Case of Gays in the Military." In *The Clinton Presidency: Images, Issues, and Communication Strategies*, ed. Robert E. Denton Jr. and Rachel L. Holloway, 189–224. Westport, CT: Praeger, 1996.

Bruce-Briggs, B. Letter to the editor. *International Security* 9, no. 1 (Summer 1984): 219.

Burgin, Eileen. "Congress and Foreign Policy: The Misperceptions." In *Congress Reconsidered*, 5th ed., ed. Lawrence C. Dodd and Bruce I. Oppenheimer, 333–363. Washington, DC: CQ Press, 1993.

Busch, Andrew E. "Political Science and the 1994 Elections: An Exploratory Essay." *PS: Political Science and Politics* 28, no. 4 (December 1995): 708–710.

Caldwell, Dan. "The Carter Administration, the Senate, and SALT II." In *Jimmy Carter: Foreign Policy and Post-presidential Years*, ed. Herbert D. Rosenbaum and Alexej Ugrinski, 331–355. Westport, CT: Greenwood Press, 1994.

Campbell, James E. "The Presidential Pulse and the 1994 Midterm Congressional Election." *Journal of Politics* 59, no. 3 (August 1997): 830–857.

Carter, Ralph G., and James M. Scott. "Setting a Course: Congressional Foreign Policy Entrepreneurs in Post–World War II U.S. Foreign Policy." *International Studies Perspectives* 5, no. 3 (August 2004): 278–299.

———. "Taking the Lead: Congressional Foreign Policy Entrepreneurs in U.S. Foreign Policy." *Politics and Policy* 32, no. 1 (March 2004): 34–70.

———. "Understanding Congressional Foreign Policy: Mapping Entrepreneurs and Their Strategies." *Social Science Journal* 47 (2010): 418–438.

Cirinione, Joseph. "Why the Right Lost the Missile Defense Debate." *Foreign Policy* 106 (Spring 1997): 38–55.

Clifford, Lawrence X. "An Examination of the Carter Administration's Selection of Secretary of State and National Security Adviser." In *Jimmy Carter: Foreign Policy and Post-presidential Years,* ed. Herbert D. Rosenbaum and Alexej Ugrinski, 5–17. Westport, CT: Greenwood Press, 1994.

Cohen, William S., and Sam Nunn. "Arms Race Breakthrough or Breakdown." In *Sam Nunn on Arms Control,* ed. Kenneth W. Thompson, 37–40. Vol. 5. Lanham, MD: University Press of America, 1987.

Combs, Richard. "U.S. Domestic Politics and the Nunn-Lugar Program." In *Dismantling the Cold War: U.S. and NIS Perspectives on the Nunn-Lugar Cooperative Threat Reduction Program,* ed. John M. Shields and William C. Potter, 41–60. Cambridge, MA: MIT Press, 1997.

Cushman, Chuck. "Defense and the Two Congresses." In *Congress and Civil Military Relations,* ed. Colton C. Campbell and David P. Auerswald, 113–126. Washington, DC: Georgetown University Press, 2015.

Cutler, Lloyd N., and Roger C. Molander. "Is There Life after Death for SALT?" *International Security* 6, no. 2 (Fall 1981): 3–20.

Davidson, Roger H. "Congressional Leaders as Agents of Change." In *Understanding Congressional Leadership,* ed. Frank H. Mackaman, 135–156. Washington, DC: Congressional Quarterly Press, 1981.

———. "Subcommittee Government: New Channels for Policy Making." In *The New Congress,* ed. Thomas Mann and Norman Ornstein, 99–133. Washington, DC: American Enterprise Institute, 1981.

Deering, Christopher J. "Decision Making in the Armed Services Committees." In *Congress Resurgent: Foreign and Defense Policy on Capitol Hill,* ed. Randall B. Ripley and James M. Lindsay, 155–182. Ann Arbor: University of Michigan Press, 1993.

DeGregorio, Christine. "Leadership Styles in Congressional Committee Hearings." *Western Political Quarterly* 45, no. 4 (December 1992): 971–983.

Destler, I. M. "Trade Consensus, SALT Stalemate: Congress and Foreign Policy in the 1970s." In *The New Congress,* ed. Thomas E. Mann and Norman J. Ornstein, 329–359. Washington, DC: American Enterprise Institute for Public Policy Research, 1981.

Duffy, Gloria. "Crisis Mangling and the Cuban Brigade." *International Security* 8, no. 1 (Summer 1983): 67–87.

Eberle, James, John Roper, William Wallace, and Phil Williams. "European Security Cooperation and British Interests." *International Affairs* 60, no. 4 (Autumn 1984): 545–560.

Flanagan, Stephen J. "The Domestic Politics of SALT II: Implications for the Foreign Policy Process." In *Congress, the Presidency, and American Foreign Policy,* ed. John Spanier and Joseph Nogee, 44–76. New York: Pergamon Press, 1981.

Freedman, Lawrence, and Efraim Karsh. "How Kuwait Was Won: Strategy in the Gulf War." *International Security* 16, no. 2 (Fall 1991): 5–41.

Frye, Alton. "Strategic Build-Down: A Context for Restraint." *Foreign Affairs* 62, no. 2 (Winter 1983–1984): 292–317.

Furlong, William L. "Negotiations and Ratification of the Panama Canal Treaties." In *Congress, the Presidency, and American Foreign Policy,* ed. John Spanier and Joseph Nogee, 77–106. New York: Pergamon Press, 1981.

Garthoff, Raymond. "Correspondence: On Negotiating with the Russians." *International Security* 2, no. 1 (Summer 1977): 107–109.

Gati, Charles. "NATO Enlargement: Who, Why, and How?" *SAIS Review* 19, no. 2 (Summer–Fall 1999): 211–217.

Goldgeier, James M. "The U.S. Decision to Enlarge: How, When, Why, and What Next?" *Brookings Review* 17, no. 3 (Summer 1999): 18–21.

Greenstein, Fred I. "Political Style and Political Leadership: The Case of Bill Clinton." In *The Clinton Presidency: Campaigning, Governing, and the Psychology of Leadership,* ed. Stanley A. Renshon, 137–147. Boulder, CO: Westview Press, 1995.

Hale, Jon F. "The Making of the New Democrats." *Political Science Quarterly* 110, no. 2 (Summer 1993): 207–232.

Hargrove, Erwin. "Two Conceptions of Institutional Leadership." In *Leadership and Politics: New Perspectives in Political Science,* ed. Bryan D. Jones, 57–83. Lawrence: University Press of Kansas, 1989.

Heginbotham, Stanley J. "Constraining SALT II: The Role of the Senate." In *Congress and United States Foreign Policy: Controlling the Use of Force in the Nuclear Age,* ed. Michael Barnhart, 98–121. Albany: State University of New York Press, 1987.

Heimbach, Daniel R. "The Bush Just War Doctrine: Genesis and Application of the President's Moral Leadership in the Persian Gulf War." In *From Cold War to New World Order: The Foreign Policy of George H. W. Bush,* ed. Meena Bose and Rosanna Perotti, 441–464. Westport, CT: Greenwood Press, 2002.

Hendrickson, Ryan C. "War Powers, Bosnia, and the 104th Congress." *Political Science Quarterly* 113, no. 2 (Summer 1998): 241–258.

Herring, George C. "The Executive, Congress, and the Vietnam War, 1965–1975." In *Congress and United States Foreign Policy: Controlling the Use of Force in the Nuclear Age,* ed. Michael Barnhart, 176–186. Albany: State University of New York Press, 1987.

Hill, Dilys M. "The Clinton Presidency: The Man and his Times." In *The Clinton Presidency: The First Term, 1992–96,* ed. Paul S. Herrnson and Dilys M. Hill, 1–21. New York: St. Martin's Press, 1999.

Johnson, Harry, and Ted Dagne. "Congress and the Somalia Crisis." In *Learning from Somalia: The Lessons of Armed Humanitarian Intervention,* ed. Walter Clarke and Jeffrey Herbst, 191–204. Boulder, CO: Westview Press, 1997.

Johnson, Robert David. "Congress and U.S. Foreign Policy before 9/11." In *Congress and the Politics of National Security,* ed. David P. Auerswald and Colton C. Campbell, 18–44. New York: Cambridge University Press, 2012.

Kaufman, Joyce P. "A Challenge to European Security and Alliance Unity." *World Affairs* 161, no. 1 (Summer 1998): 22–32.

Kellerman, Barbara. "Leadership as a Political Act." In *Leadership: Multidisciplinary Perspectives,* 53–89. Englewood Cliffs, NJ: Prentice-Hall, 1984.

———. "Leadership—It's a System, Not a Person!" *Daedalus* 145, no. 3 (Summer 2016): 83–94.

Key, V. O., Jr. "A Theory of Critical Elections." *Journal of Politics* 17, no. 1 (February 1955): 3–18.

Kitts, Kenneth. "The Politics of Armageddon: The Scowcroft Commission and the

MX Missile." In *Presidential Commissions and National Security: The Politics of Damage Control*, 73–99. Boulder, CO: Lynne Rienner, 2006.

Koplow, David A. "When Is an Amendment Not an Amendment? Modification of Arms Control Agreements without the Senate." *University of Chicago Law Review* 59, no. 3 (Summer 1992): 981–1072.

Layne, Christopher. "Toward German Unification?" *Journal of Contemporary Studies* 7, no. 4 (Fall 1984): 7–37.

Lindsay, James M. "Congressional Oversight of the Department of Defense Budget: Reconsidering the Conventional Wisdom." *Armed Forces and Society* 17, no. 1 (Fall 1990): 7–33.

Locher, James R., III. "Transformative Leadership on Capitol Hill: The Goldwater-Nichols Defense Reorganization Act." In *Reagan and the World: Leadership and National Security, 1981–1989*, ed. Bradley Lynn Coleman and Kyle Longley, 81–107. Lexington: University Press of Kentucky, 2017.

Lodal, Jan M. "SALT II and American Security." *Foreign Affairs* 67, no. 2 (Winter 1978): 245–268.

Mackaman, Frank H. Introduction to *Understanding Congressional Leadership*, 1–21. Washington, DC: Congressional Quarterly Press, 1981.

———. Preface to *Understanding Congressional Leadership*, v–viii. Washington, DC: Congressional Quarterly Press, 1981.

Mayhew, David. "Congress as Problem Solver." In *Promoting the General Welfare: New Perspectives on Government Performance*, ed. Alan S. Gerber and Eric M. Patashnik, 219–236. Washington, DC: Brookings Institution Press, 2006.

———. "Lawmaking as a Cognitive Enterprise." In *Living Legislation: Durability, Change, and the Politics of American Lawmaking*, ed. Jeffrey A. Jenkins and Eric M. Patashnik, 255–264. Chicago, IL: University of Chicago Press, 2012.

Melanson, Richard A. "George Bush's Search for a Post–Cold War Grand Strategy." In *The Bush Presidency: Ten Intimate Perspective of George Bush*, ed. Kenneth W. Thompson, 151–166. Lanham, MD: University Press of America, 1998.

Morrison, David C. "Sam Nunn Inc." *National Journal* 23 (1991): 1483–1486.

Nolan, Janne E. "The INF Treaty." In *The Politics of Arms Control Treaty Ratification*, ed. Michael Krepon and Dan Caldwell, 355–397. New York: St. Martin's Press, 1991.

Norman, Colin. "Debate over SDI Enters New Phase." *Science* 235, no. 4786 (January 16, 1987): 277–290.

"A Nuclear Risk Reduction System: Report of the Nunn/Warner Working Group on Nuclear Risk Reduction." *Survival* 26, no. 3 (May–June 1984): 133–135.

Nunn, Sam. "The ABM Reinterpretation Issue." *Washington Quarterly* 10, no. 4 (Autumn 1987): 45–46.

———. "American Defense with or without SALT." Address to the National Chamber of Commerce, April 30, 1979. *Atlantic Community Quarterly* 17 (Summer 1979): 155–159.

———. "Arms Control and Theater Nuclear Modernization." Speech delivered to a German-American Roundtable, sponsored by the Institute for Foreign Policy Analysis, Washington, DC, October 22, 1979. *Atlantic Community Quarterly* 17 (Winter 1979–1980): 437–444.

———. "Back on the Road to Arms Control." In *Sam Nunn on Arms Control*, ed. Kenneth W. Thompson, 31–35. Vol. 5. Lanham, MD: University Press of America, 1987.

———. "Challenges to NATO in the 1990s." *Survival* 32, no. 1 (January–February 1990): 6–8.

———. "The Changed Threat Environment of the 1990s, March 29, 1990." In *Nunn 1990: A New Military Strategy*, 16–40. Significant Issues Series, vol. 12, no. 5. Washington, DC: Center for Strategic and International Studies, 1990.

———. "Critical Defense Choices." Southern Center for International Studies, Papers on International Issues no. 4, January 1983. In *Sam Nunn on Arms Control*, ed. Kenneth W. Thompson, 73–88. Vol. 5. Lanham, MD: University Press of America, 1987.

———. "Cut the Number of Weapons Systems." In *Sam Nunn on Arms Control*, ed. Kenneth W. Thompson, 97–102. Vol. 5. Lanham, MD: University Press of America, 1987.

———. "Defense Budget Blanks, March 22, 1990." In *Nunn 1990: A New Military Strategy*, 1–15. Significant Issues Series, vol. 12, no. 5. Washington, DC: Center for Strategic and International Studies, 1990.

———. "The Defense Reorganization Act of 1986." In *Sam Nunn on Arms Control*, ed. Kenneth W. Thompson, 117–144. Vol. 5. Lanham, MD: University Press of America, 1987.

———. "Deterring War in Europe: Some Basic Assumptions Need Revising." *NATO Review* 25, no. 1 (February 1977): 4–7.

———. "Farewell Address." In *Lessons and Legacies: Farewell Addresses from the Senate*, ed. Norman J. Ornstein, 122–142. New York: Perseus Publishing, 1997.

———. Foreword to *Europe without Defense? 48 Hours That Could Change the Face of the World*, by Robert Close, vii–x. New York: Pergamon Press, 1979.

———. "Free World Challenges." Address given at St. Gallen University, Zurich, Switzerland, July 11, 1980. *Atlantic Community Quarterly* 18 (Fall 1980): 268–274.

———. "How to Make the Summit Productive." In *Sam Nunn on Arms Control*, ed. Kenneth W. Thompson, 43–46. Vol. 5. Lanham, MD: University Press of America, 1987.

———. "Implementing a New Military Strategy: The Budget Decisions, April 20, 1990." In *Nunn 1990: A New Military Strategy*, 61–82. Significant Issues Series, vol. 12, no. 5. Washington, DC: Center for Strategic and International Studies, 1990.

———. "Improving NATO's Conventional Defenses." In *Sam Nunn on Arms Control*, ed. Kenneth W. Thompson, 95–96. Vol. 5. Lanham, MD: University Press of America, 1987.

———. "Is the Nunn-Roth Approach to the U.S. Role in NATO Sound?" *Congressional Digest* 63, nos. 8–9 (August–September 1984): 212, 214, 216, and 218.

———. "It's Not What We Spend on Defense." In *Sam Nunn on Arms Control*, ed. Kenneth W. Thompson, 103–106. Vol. 5. Lanham, MD: University Press of America, 1987.

———. "Mutual and Balanced Force Reductions—A Need to Shift Our Focus." *Atlantic Community Quarterly* 16, no. 1 (Spring 1978): 18–21.

———. "The MX." In *Strategic Force Modernization and Arms Control* by Edward L. Rowny et al. National Security Paper no. 6, 35–40. Washington, DC: Institute for Foreign Policy Analysis, 1986.

———. "NATO and Arms Control." In *Sam Nunn on Arms Control*, ed. Kenneth W. Thompson, 59–69. Vol. 5. Lanham, MD: University Press of America, 1987.

———. *NATO: Can the Alliance Be Saved?* Report of Senator Sam Nunn to the Committee on Armed Services, United States Senate, May 13, 1982. *Atlantic Community Quarterly* 20, no. 2 (Summer 1982): 126–132.

———. "NATO: Saving the Alliance." *Washington Quarterly* 5, no. 3 (Summer 1982): 19–29.

———. "NATO Strategy." *Survival* 19, no. 1 (January–February 1977): 30–32.

———. "The Need to Reshape Military Strategy." In *Nuclear Arms: Ethics, Strategy, Politics*, ed. R. James Woolsey, 239–249. San Francisco: ICS Press, 1984.

———. "A New Military Strategy, April 19, 1990." In *Nunn 1990: A New Military Strategy*, 41–60. Significant Issues Series, vol. 12, no. 5. Washington, DC: Center for Strategic and International Studies, 1990.

———. "The New Terror: Nutcakes with Nukes." *New Perspectives Quarterly* 13, no. 1 (Winter 1996): 32–35.

———. "Nuclear Risk Reduction." In *Sam Nunn on Arms Control*, ed. Kenneth W. Thompson, 53–57. Lanham, MD: University Press of America, 1987.

———. "Nunn Answers Questions about Combat Readiness." In *Sam Nunn on Arms Control*, ed. Kenneth W. Thompson, 89–93. Vol. 5. Lanham, MD: University Press of America, 1987.

———. "Reducing the Nuclear Threat." *Atlanta Journal-Constitution*, October 14, 1983. In *Sam Nunn on Arms Control*, ed. Kenneth W. Thompson, 49–52. Vol. 5. Lanham, MD: University Press of America, 1987.

———. "Should the Nunn-Levin Amendment Be Approved?" *Congressional Digest* 66, no. 11 (November 1987): 264, 266, 268, 270, 272, and 274.

———. "The Strategic Defense Initiative." In *Sam Nunn on Arms Control*, ed. Kenneth W. Thompson, 179–194. Vol. 5. Lanham, MD: University Press of America, 1987.

Nunn, Sam, and Richard Lugar. "The Nunn-Lugar Initiative: Cooperative Demilitarization of the Former Soviet Union." In *The Diplomatic Record, 1992–1993*, ed. Allan E. Goodman, 139–156. Boulder, CO: Westview Press, 1995.

Nunn, Sam, and John W. Warner. "Reducing the Risk of Nuclear War." *Washington Quarterly* 7, no. 2 (Spring 1984): 3–7.

———. "US-Soviet Cooperation in Countering Nuclear Terrorism: The Role of Risk Reduction Centers." In *Preventing Nuclear Terrorism: The Report and Papers of the International Task Force on Prevention of Nuclear Terrorism*, ed. Paul Leventhal and Yonah Alexander, 381–393. Lexington, MA: Lexington Books, 1987.

Opperman, John. "The Panama Canal Treaties: Legislative Strategy for Advice and Consent." In *Legislating Foreign Policy*, ed. Hoyt Purvis and Steven J. Baker, 77–105. Boulder, CO: Westview Press, 1984.

397

Ornstein, Norman J. "Losing the Senate." *Argument* (blog). *Foreign Policy*, March 29, 2013, http://foreignpolicy.com/2013/03/29/losing-the-senate/.

Ornstein, Norman J., Robert L. Peabody, and David W. Rohde. "The U.S. Senate in an Era of Change." In *Congress Reconsidered*, 5th ed., ed. Lawrence C. Dodd and Bruce I. Oppenheimer, 13–38. Washington, DC: CQ Press, 1993.

Ornstein, Norman J., and Amy L. Schenkenberg. "The 1995 Congress: The First Hundred Days and Beyond." *Political Science Quarterly* 110, no. 2 (Summer 1995): 183–206.

Peabody, Robert L. "Senate Party Leadership from the 1950s to the 1980s." In *Understanding Congressional Leadership*, ed. Frank H. Mackaman, 51–115. Washington, DC: Congressional Quarterly Press, 1981.

Perle, Richard N. "The Senator and American Arms Control Policy." In *Staying the Course: Henry M. Jackson and National Security*, ed. Dorothy Fosdick, 85–107. Seattle: University of Washington Press, 1987.

Posen, Barry R. "Measuring the European Conventional Balance: Coping with Complexity in Threat Assessment." *International Security* 19, no. 3 (Winter 1984–1985): 47–88.

Quester, George H. "Defense Policy." In *The Clinton Presidency: The First Term, 1992–96*, ed. Paul S. Herrnson and Dilys M. Hill, 142–163. New York: St. Martin's Press, 1999.

Quirk, Paul J., and Joseph Hinchliffe. "Domestic Policy: The Trials of a Centrist Democrat." In *The Clinton Presidency: First Appraisals*, ed. Colin Campbell and Bert A. Rockman, 262–289. Chatham, NJ: Chatham House, 1996.

Record, Jeffrey. "The Military Reform Caucus." *Washington Quarterly* 6, no. 2 (Spring 1983): 125–129.

Reiter, Dan. "Why NATO Enlargement Does Not Spread Democracy." *International Security* 25, no. 4 (Spring 2001): 41–67.

Rice, Condoleezza. "U.S.-Soviet Relations." In *Looking Back on the Reagan Presidency*, ed. Larry Berman, 71–92. Baltimore, MD: Johns Hopkins University Press, 1990.

Rogers, J. Philip. "The Senate and Arms Control: The SALT Experience." In *Legislating Foreign Policy*, ed. Hoyt Purvis and Steven J. Baker, 160–195. Boulder, CO: Westview Press, 1984.

Rohde, David W. "Electoral Forces, Political Agendas, and Partisanship in the House and Senate." In *The Postreform Congress*, ed. Roger H. Davidson, 27–47. New York: St. Martin's Press, 1992.

Rosner, Jeremy D. "The American Public, Congress, and NATO Enlargement." *NATO Review* 45, no. 1 (January 1997): 12–14.

Roth, Nickolas. "The Evolution of the Senate Arms Control Observer Group." Federation of American Scientists, *Public Interest Report* 67, no. 2 (Spring 2014). https://fas.org/pir- pubs/evolution-senate-arms-control-observer-group/.

Ruiz Palmer, Diego A. "The NATO-Warsaw Competition in the 1970s and 1980s: A Revolution in Military Affairs in the Making or the End of a Strategic Age?" *Cold War History* 14, no. 4 (2014): 533–573.

Sinclair, Barbara. "Trying to Govern Positively in a Negative Era: Clinton and the

103rd Congress." In *The Clinton Presidency: First Appraisals*, ed. Colin Campbell and Bert A. Rockman, 88–125. Chatham, NJ: Chatham House, 1996.

Sisco, Joseph J. "Ford, Kissinger, and the Nixon-Ford Foreign Policy." In *The Ford Presidency: Twenty-Two Intimate Perspectives of Gerald R. Ford*, ed. Kenneth W. Thompson, 319–332. Lanham, MD: University Press of America, 1988.

Skene, Gordon. "We Believe . . . Peace Is at Hand—Henry Kissinger—October 26, 1972." *Past Daily* (blog), October 26, 2016, https://pastdaily.com/2016/10/26/henry-kissinger-october-26-1972/.

Sloan, Stanley. "Managing the NATO Alliance: Congress and Burdensharing." *Journal of Policy Analysis and Management* 4, no. 3 (Spring 1985): 396–406.

Sobel, Richard. "U.S. and European Attitudes toward Intervention in the Former Yugoslavia: *Mourir pour la Bosnie?*" In *The World and Yugoslavia's Wars*, ed. Richard H. Ullman, 145–182. New York: Council on Foreign Relations, 1996.

Sopko, John F. "The Changing Proliferation Threat." *Foreign Policy* 105 (Winter 1996–1997): 3–20.

Stockholm International Peace Research Institute. "EU Arms Embargo on the former SFR of Yugoslavia (Bosnia and Herzegovina)." https://www.sipri.org/databases/embargoes/eu_arms_embargoes/bosnia.

Talbott, Strobe. "Buildup and Breakdown." *Foreign Affairs* 62, no. 3 (Spring 1984): 587–615.

Thurber, James A. "Remaking Congress after the Electoral Earthquake of 1994." In *Remaking Congress: Change and Stability in the 1990s*, ed. James A. Thurber and Roger H. Davidson, 1–8. Washington, DC: Congressional Quarterly, 1995.

Thurber, James A., and Roger H. Davidson, eds. Preface to *Remaking Congress: Change and Stability in the 1990s*, xiii–xvi. Washington, DC: Congressional Quarterly, 1995.

Towell, Pat. "Congress and Defense." In *Congress and the Politics of National Security*, ed. David P. Auerswald and Colton C. Campbell, 71–99. New York: Cambridge University Press, 2012.

Tuchfarber, Alfred J., et al. "The Republican Tidal Wave of 1994: Testing Hypotheses about Realignment, Restructuring, and Rebellion." *PS: Political Science and Politics* 28, no. 4 (December 1995): 689–696.

Werrell, Kenneth P. "The Weapon the US Military Did Not Want: The Modern Strategic Cruise Missile." *Journal of Military History* 53 (October 1989): 419–438.

Williams, Phil. "The Nunn Amendment, Burden-Sharing, and US Troops in Europe." *Survival* 26, no. 1 (January–February 1985): 2–10.

———. "Whatever Happened to the Mansfield Amendment?" *Survival* 18, no. 4 (August 1976): 146–153.

Wolfowitz, Paul. "Shaping the Future: Planning at the Pentagon, 1989–93." In *In Uncertain Times: American Foreign Policy after the Berlin Wall and 9/11*, ed. Melvin P. Leffler and Jeffrey W. Legro, 44–62. Ithaca, NY: Cornell University Press, 2011.

Woolsey, R. James. "The Politics of Vulnerability: 1980–83." In *Nuclear Arms: Ethics, Strategy, Politics*, 251–266. San Francisco: ICS Press, 1984.

Zelizer, Julian E. "Congress Is Back: Scholars Study Its History to Understand Its Problems." *Chronicle Review*, July 17, 2013, B12–B15.

Magazine Articles

"After Carter's Panama Victory." *U.S. News and World Report*, May 1, 1978.

Alpern, David, et al. "Moscow's Mixed Signals." *Newsweek*, April 1, 1985.

———. "New Push for an Arms Pact." *Newsweek*, May 16, 1983.

Alston, Chuck. "Clinton's Rough Start with the Hill: Minor Slip or Serious Flaw?" *CQ Weekly*, January 30, 1993.

———. "The Teflon Senator Slugs It Out." *CQ Weekly*, March 4, 1989.

"As Battle Shapes Up in Senate." *U.S. News and World Report*, May 28, 1979.

Auster, Bruce B. "The Commander and Chiefs." *U.S. News & World Report*, February 8, 1993.

Barry, John, and Tom Morganthau. "Defense: How Much Is Enough?" *Newsweek*, February 3, 1986.

"A Battle for SALT Shapes Up." *U.S. News and World Report*, May 28, 1979.

Beck, Melinda, et al. "Defending the United States." *Newsweek*, December 20, 1982.

"Behind the Tug of War over Defense Spending." *U.S. News and World Report*, August 28, 1978.

Blumenthal, Sidney. "The Mystique of Sam Nunn." *New Republic*, March 4, 1991.

Boese, Wade. "United States Retires MX Missile." *Arms Control Today*, n.d., accessed February 1, 2020, https://www.armscontrol.org/act/2005_10/OCT-MX.

Borawski, John. "U.S.-Soviet Move toward Risk Reduction." *Bulletin of Atomic Scientists*, July–August 1987.

Borchgrave, Arnaud de. "Nightmare for NATO." *Newsweek*, February 7, 1977.

Borger, Gloria. "Who's the Newest Democrat of Them All?" *U.S. News and World Report*, July 26, 1993.

Buckley, William F., Jr. "The Politics of Victory." On the Right column. *National Review*, April 15, 1991.

Bunn, Matthew, and Bruce B. Auster. "Administration Nears Decision on Early Deployment of SDI, Treaty Interpretation." *Arms Control Today*, March 1987.

Butler, David, with Thomas M. DeFrank, Fred Coleman, Lars-Erik Nelson, and Kim Willenson. "The SALT Summit." *Newsweek*, June 25, 1979.

Butler, David, with Lars-Erik Nelson, Eleanor Clift, David C. Martin, John J. Lindsay, and Fred Coleman. "SALT II: And Now for the Battle." *Newsweek*, May 21, 1979.

Carroll, Raymond, and Nicholas Proffitt. "Britain's Thin Red Line." *U.S. News and World Report*, December 13, 1976.

"Carter's Panama Triumph—What It Cost." *U.S. News and World Report*, March 27, 1978.

Clift, Eleanor. "Mr. Defense Loses His Luster." *Newsweek*, March 18, 1991.

"A Conversation with Sam Nunn." *Georgia Tech Alumni Magazine* (Spring 1990).

Cunningham, Kitty. "The Senate's Last Word on Gays." *CQ Weekly*, September 11, 1993.

"Delay Seen in Consultations on SDI." *CQ Weekly*, February 28, 1987.

Deming, Angus, et al. "The Canal: Time to Go?" *Newsweek*, August 22, 1977.

Doherty, Carroll J. "Senate Puts Clinton on Zigzag Course toward Ending Bosnia Arms Embargo." *CQ Weekly*, August 13, 1994.

Duffy, Brian, with Melissa Healy and Robert Kaylor. "What Weapons Will Work?" *U.S. News and World Report,* January 19, 1987.

Fessler, Pamela, and Pat Towell. "Senate Defense Measure Sticks Closer to Bush Blueprint." *CQ Weekly,* July 29, 1989.

Fowler, Jack. "Democrats in Disarray." *National Review,* January 28, 1991.

Fromm, Joseph. "SALT II: Can It End the Arms Race?" *U.S. News and World Report,* May 21, 1979.

———. "Why SALT Can't be Counted Out Yet." *U.S. News and World Report,* October 22, 1979.

Gailey, Phil. "Sam Nunn's Rising Star." *New York Times Magazine,* February 4, 1987.

Galen, Justin. "Curing the Nunn Illusion: Striking a Bargain for SALT." *Armed Forces Journal International,* October 1979.

Gelman, Eric. "Nunn's Nuclear Safety Valve." *Newsweek,* June 21, 1982.

———. "Will Congress 'Build Down' the MX?" *Newsweek,* May 2, 1983.

Gergen, David. "The Democrats' Go-Slow Gulf Policy." *U.S. News and World Report,* December 10, 1990.

Glass, Andrew. "Rep. Carl Vinson Dies, June 1, 1981." *Politico,* June 1, 2010, https://www.politico.com/story/2010/06/rep-carl-vinson-dies-june-1-1981-037973.

Goldman, Peter, with Eleanor Clift, Thomas M. DeFrank, John J. Lindsay, and James Doyle. "The Hard SALT Sell." *Newsweek,* February 19, 1979.

Gregory, William H. "Changing Allegiances and NATO." *Aviation Week & Space Technology,* July 30, 1984.

Hager, George. "Senate Democrats Close Ranks, Endorse Clinton Budget." *CQ Weekly,* March 27, 1993.

"Heirs to Dixie Barons: New Powers in Senate." *U.S. News and World Report,* May 7, 1979.

Hook, Janet. "SDI Limits Still Hotly Contested: Senate Begins Defense Debate as GOP Abandons Filibuster." *CQ Weekly,* September 12, 1987.

Howard, Lucy. "An INF Snag." *Newsweek,* April 4, 1988.

"'If We Abandon Our Allies' . . . Ford Spells Out His Doctrine." *U.S. News and World Report,* March 17, 1975.

Jacoby, Tamar, with John Barry and Robert B. Cullen. "The Moscow Agenda." *Newsweek,* April 20, 1987.

Kozicharow, Eugene. "Senate Rejects NATO Troop Reduction." *Aviation Week & Space Technology,* June 25, 1984.

Kramer, Michael. "Smart, Dull, and Very Powerful." *Time,* March 13, 1989.

Langway, Lynn, and Henry W. Hubbard. "The Panama Canal: Round One." *Newsweek,* February 20, 1978.

Mathews, Tom. "The Road to War." *Newsweek,* January 28, 1991.

Mathews, Tom, with Eleanor Clift, Lars-Erik Nelson, and Henry W. Hubbard. "On the Offensive." *Newsweek,* May 7, 1979.

Mathews, Tom, and John J. Lindsay. "Nunn for the Defense." *Newsweek,* July 17, 1978.

Mawby, Michael. "Arms Control Prospects in the 100th Congress." *Arms Control Today,* January–February 1987.

McGurn, William. "Beltway Battles." *National Review,* February 25, 1991.

McNamara, Robert S. "What the U.S. Can Do." *Newsweek*, December 5, 1983.

Morganthau, Tom, with Howard Fineman, Gloria Borger, and Thomas M. DeFrank. "The Games Lame Ducks Play." *Newsweek*, December 27, 1982.

Morganthau, Tom, with John J. Lindsay and David Martin. "The SALT Forces Take the Offensive." *Newsweek*, August 6, 1979.

Morganthau, Tom, with Lars-Erik Nelson, John J. Lindsay, David Martin and Eleanor Clift. "The SALT Debate Shifts." *Newsweek*, August 15, 1979.

Morganthau, Tom, with Kim Willenson and John Barry. "The Pentagon under Siege." *Newsweek*, October 28, 1985.

Morrocco, John D. "Showdown Looms on Bomber Force." *Aviation Week & Space Technology*, June 20, 1994.

———. "U.S. Facing Shortfalls in Two-War Strategy." *Aviation Week & Space Technology*, May 2, 1994.

National Conference of Catholic Bishops. "The Challenge of Peace: God's Promise and Our Response." Pastoral Letter on War and Peace by the National Conference of Catholic Bishops. May 3, 1983. http://www.usccb.org/upload/challenge -peace-gods-promise-our-response-1983.pdf.

"Negotiations Prove Fruitless: Defense Stalemate Drags On; Nunn Threatens to Drop Bill." *CQ Weekly*, July 25, 1987.

Noah, Timothy. "Born to Be Mild." *Washington Monthly*, December 1989.

Nunn, Sam. "Is Clinton Cutting Twice as Much from Defense?" *Aviation Week & Space Technology*, March 22, 1993.

———. "The Persian Gulf Crisis." *Vital Speeches of the Day*, February 1, 1991.

Paine, Christopher. "Breakdown on the Build-Down." *Bulletin of the Atomic Scientists*, December 1983.

"Paying Up." *Time*. December 1984.

"Pentagon's Perle Cautious on 'Build Down' & Arms Commission." *Defense Daily*, May 11, 1983.

Pytte, Alison. "Questions of Conduct Delay Vote on Tower." *CQ Weekly*, February 4, 1989.

Roberts, Steven V. "Senator Nunn's Little Mutiny." *U.S. News and World Report*, February 8, 1993.

"Russia's 'Relentless' Arms Buildup." *U.S. News and World Report*, January 17, 1977.

"SALT—The Real Fight Begins." *Newsweek*, July 2, 1979.

Shapiro, Joseph P., with Kathryn Johnson. "How Reagan Prepares for Gorbachev." *US News and World Report*, November 4, 1985.

Sheils, Merrill, et al. "Searching for a Strategy." *Newsweek*, June 8, 1981.

"Shutting Out Sam Nunn." *Newsweek*, February 4, 1991.

Simmons, Dean, Phillip Gould, Verena Vomastic, and Philip Walsh. "Air Operations over Bosnia." *Proceedings Magazine*, May 1997.

Slawsky, Richard. "Kill the Dog Programmes: An Interview with Senator Sam Nunn." *Jane's Defence Weekly*, April 11, 1987.

Talbott, Strobe. "Why NATO Should Grow." *New York Review of Books*, August 10, 1995, http://www.nybooks.com/articles/1995/08/10/why-nato-should-grow/.

"This Just In." *New Republic.* July 18, 1983.

Towell, Pat. "After Setbacks in the House, Bush Playing Catch-Up." *CQ Weekly,* July 29, 1989.

———. "Aspin's Political Clout Grows as Nunn's Leverage Is Questioned." *Congressional Quarterly Weekly,* March 23, 1991.

———. "Autonomous Ally." *CQ Weekly,* March 27, 1993.

———. "Bolstering the 2-Missile Strategy." *CQ Weekly,* June 24, 1989.

———. "Campaign Promise, Social Debate Collide on Military Battlefield." *CQ Weekly,* January 30, 1993.

———. "Controversy over ABM, SALT: White House, Conferees Near Deal on Arms Control." *CQ Weekly,* November 7, 1987.

———. "Defense Authorization: Conferees Finesse Decisions on Bosnia and Bomber." *CQ Weekly,* August 13, 1994.

———. "Defense Authorization: Senate Panel Gives Clinton B-2 Funds He Didn't Seek." *CQ Weekly,* June 11, 1994.

———. "Defense Spending Decisions Sure to Stir Controversy." *CQ Weekly,* April 22, 1989.

———. "Final Amount Depends on Budget Summit." *CQ Weekly,* November 21, 1987.

———. "Financial Dealings Examined: Vote on Nomination of Tower Delayed by New Allegations." *CQ Weekly,* February 11, 1989.

———. "House Panel Deals Setback to SDI Program." *CQ Weekly,* April 4, 1987.

———. "No Clear Winners, Losers: Administration, Hill Revisit Debate over ABM Pact, SDI." *CQ Weekly,* February 14, 1987.

———. "Nunn Blasts Administration on ABM Treaty." *CQ Weekly,* March 14, 1987.

———. "Nunn Loses Round on Burden Sharing . . . but Starts Serious Debate on the Issue." *Congressional Quarterly Weekly Report,* June 23, 1984.

———. "Nunn Says Cuts Are Reasonable but Wants Pentagon Protected." *CQ Weekly,* March 6, 1993.

———. "Senate Committee Affirms Cheney's Weapons Cuts." *CQ Weekly,* July 15, 1989.

———. "Senate Rebuffs Reagan on Key Defense Issues." *CQ Weekly,* October 3, 1987.

———. "Senate Wages Partisan Duel on Fitness, Prerogatives." *CQ Weekly,* March 4, 1989.

———. "Verification Debate Stalls Nuclear Test Pacts." *CQ Weekly,* January 24, 1987.

———. "Waiting for the INF Treaty: Political Jockeying." *CQ Weekly,* September 5, 1987.

———. "Warner: Seeking Compromise, Finding Criticism." *CQ Weekly,* October 31, 1987.

———. "With an Eye to Conference, Senate Zigzags on SDI." *CQ Weekly,* September 30, 1989.

Towell, Pat, with Steve Pressman. "Senate Deals Reagan a Major Defeat on SDI." *CQ Weekly,* September 19, 1987.

"US Lawmakers Size Up Gorbachev." *U.S. News and World Report,* September 16, 1985.

Watson, Russell, et al. "Can We Cut the Risk?" *Newsweek*, December 5, 1983.

Watson, Russell, with John Barry. "Speeding Up Star Wars." *Newsweek*, February 16, 1987.

Whitaker, Mark, et al. "What's Next for 'Star Wars.'" *Newsweek*, December 2, 1985.

Will, George F. "How to Think about SALT." *Newsweek*, May 28, 1979.

Willenson, Kim, and David C. Martin. "A New Cuban Missile Crisis?" *Newsweek*, November 27, 1978.

Newspapers, Wire Services, and News Media

American Broadcasting Corporation

Associated Press

Atlanta Journal-Constitution

Boston Globe

Business Insider

Chicago Tribune

Christian Science Monitor

C-SPAN

Globe and Mail (Toronto, Canada)

Los Angeles Times

Milwaukee Journal-Sentinel

Milwaukee Sentinel

MSNBC

National Broadcasting Corporation

National Public Radio

New York Times

Palm Beach Post

Philadelphia Inquirer

United Press International

USA Today

Wall Street Journal

Washington Post

Publications of International Bodies

Commission on Security and Cooperation in Europe. *Report on Human Rights and the Process of NATO Enlargement*. Washington, DC: Commission on Security and Cooperation in Europe, 1997.

North Atlantic Treaty Organization. "NATO Update—1983." http://www.nato.int/docu/update/80–89/1983e.htm.

North Atlantic Treaty Organization. "Peace Support Operations in Bosnia and Herzegovina." https://www.nato.int/cps/en/natohq/topics_52122.htm?selectedLocale=en.

UN Security Council. Resolution 661. Iraq-Kuwait, S/RES/661 (August 6, 1990). http://www.refworld.org/docid/3b00f16b24.html.

———. Resolution 678. Iraq-Kuwait. S/RES/678 (November 29, 1990). http://www
.refworld.org/docid/3b00f16760.html.

———. Resolution 713. Socialist Federal Rep. of Yugoslavia. S/RES/713 (September
25, 1991). http://unscr.com/en/resolutions/713.

———. Resolution 816. Bosnia and Herzegovina. S/RES/816 (March 31, 1993).
http://unscr.com/en/resolutions/816.

———. Resolution 837. Somalia. S/RES/837 (June 6, 1993). http://unscr.com/en
/resolutions/837.

Unpublished Sources

Korb, Lawrence J. "The Role of the Joint Chiefs of Staff in the Strategic Arms Limi-
tations Process: Changing or Constraints?" Paper presented at the National
Conference of the Inter-University Seminar on the Armed Forces and Society,
Chicago, IL, October 23–25, 1980.

McCulley, Richard. *History of the Senate Committee on Armed Services, 1947–1999*.
Washington, DC: US Senate Historical Office, 2000 draft.

Nunn, Sam. "Changing Threats in the Post–Cold War World." Speech given at the
Monterey Institute for International Studies, Monterey, CA, August 25, 1995.

Talbott, Strobe. "U.S.-Soviet Nuclear Arms Control: Where We Are and How We Got
Here." Occasional Paper OPS-001. RAND/UCLA Center for the Study of Soviet
International Behavior, January 1985.

US Government Publications

Executive Branch

Army Aviation and Missile Life Cycle Management Command. "Lance." https://his
tory.redstone.army.mil/miss-lance.html.

Baker, James. "America and the Collapse of the Soviet Empire: What Has to Be Done."
Address at Princeton University, Princeton, NJ, December 12, 1991. *U.S. Department of State Dispatch* 2, no. 50, December 16, 1991, 887, 888–890.

Department of Defense. *Conduct of the Persian Gulf War: Final Report to Congress*.
Washington, DC: US Department of Defense, 1992.

———. *Report of Secretary of Defense Caspar W. Weinberger to the Congress on the FY
1988–FY 1989 Budget and FY 1988–92 Defense Programs*. Washington, DC: US
Government Printing Office, 1987.

Department of State. "Agreement on Ending the War and Restoring Peace in
South Viet-Nam." *Department of State Bulletin*, no. 68, December 20, 1973,
169–188.

———. *Dayton Accords*, November 21, 1995, https://www.state.gov/p/eur/rls/or/day
ton/.

———. *Foreign Relations of the United States, 1969–1976*. Vol. 33, SALT II, 1972–1980.
Washington, DC: Government Printing Office, 2013.

———, Office of the Historian. "The Panama Canal and the Torrijos-Carter Treaties."
https://history.state.gov/milestones/1977–1980/panama-canal.

———, Office of the Historian. "Strategic Arms Limitation Talks/Treaty (SALT) I and II." https://history.state.gov/milestones/1969–1976/salt.

———, Office of the Historian. "The War in Bosnia, 1993–1995." http://history.state.gov/milestones/1993–2000/bosnia.

Director of Central Intelligence. National Intelligence Estimate (NIE) 11–18–90, November 1990, https://www.cia.gov/library/readingroom/docs/19901101.pdf.

MacLaury, Bruce K. *The Limping Giant: The American Economy 1974–75.* Federal Reserve Bank of Minneapolis, Annual Report, January 1, 1975, https://www.minneapolisfed.org/publications/annual-reports/the-limping-giant-the-american-economy-197475.

National Security Planning Group. "US Options for Arms Control Summit." Memorandum, February 9, 1988. http://www.thereaganfiles.com/document-collections/national-security-council.html.

Nunn, Sam. "Remarks." Session 3, "Using Science and Technology to Meet New Defense and Arms Control Needs." Fifth Panel Discussion, White House Forum on the Role of Science and Technology in Promoting National Security and Global Stability. March 29–30, 1995, https://clintonwhitehouse3.archives.gov/WH/EOP/OSTP/forum/html/ses3.html.

Schultz, George. "The INF Treaty: Strengthening U.S. Security." *Current Policy*, no. 1038. US Department of State, Bureau of Public Affairs, Washington, DC.

Strategic Defense Initiative Office. *Report to the Congress on the Strategic Defense Initiative*, April 1987.

Weinberger, Caspar W. *Annual Report to Congress: Fiscal Year 1987.* Washington, DC: US Department of Defense, 1986.

Presidential Documents

Bush, George H. W. "Address to the Nation Announcing Allied Military Action in the Persian Gulf," January 16, 1991. George H. W. Bush Presidential Library, https://bush41library.tamu.edu/archives/public-papers/2625.

———. "Address to the Nation on Reducing United States and Soviet Nuclear Weapons," September 27, 1991. George H. W. Bush Presidential Library, https://bush41library.tamu.edu/archives/public-papers/3438.

———. National Security Directive 23. United States Relations with the Soviet Union, September 22, 1989. George H. W. Bush Presidential Library, https://bush41library.tamu.edu/files/nsd/nsd23.pdf.

———. National Security Directive 45. U.S. Policy in Response to the Iraqi Invasion of Kuwait. August 20, 1990, George H. W. Bush Presidential Library, https://bush41library.tamu.edu/files/nsd/nsd45.pdf.

———. National Security Review 3, Comprehensive Review of US-Soviet Relations, February 15, 1989. George H. W. Bush Presidential Library, https://bush41library.tamu.edu/files/nsr/nsr3.pdf.

———. "The President's News Conference," March 10, 1989. George H. W. Bush Presidential Library, https://bush41library.tamu.edu/archives/public-papers/156.

———. "The President's News Conference in Kennebunkport, Maine," September 2,

1991. George H. W. Bush Presidential Library. https://bush41library.tamu.edu/archives/public-papers/3334.

———. "The President's News Conference on the Persian Gulf Crisis," January 9, 1991. George Bush Presidential Library, http://bush41library.tamu.edu/archives/public-papers/2605.

———. "Remarks at the Community Welcome Home for Returning Troops in Sumter, South Carolina," March 17, 2001. George H. W. Bush Presidential Library, http://bush41library.tamu.edu/archives/public-papers/2800.

———. "Statement by Press Secretary Fitzwater on Assistance to the Soviet Union and the Republics," December 12, 1991. George H. W. Bush Presidential Library, https://bush41library.tamu.edu/archives/public-papers/3737.

———. "Statement on Allied Military Action in the Persian Gulf," January 16, 1991. George H. W. Bush Presidential Library, http://bush41library.tamu.edu/archives/public-papers/2624.

———. "Statement on Deficit Reduction in Fiscal Year 1990," November 2, 1989. George H. W. Bush Presidential Library, https://bush41library.tamu.edu/archives/public-papers/1135.

Carter, Jimmy. Presidential Directive/NSC-18. U.S. National Strategy, August 24, 1977. Jimmy Carter Presidential Library, https://www.jimmycarterlibrary.gov/assets/documents/directives/pd18.pdf.

———. Program Review Memorandum/NSC-6. Mutual and Balanced Force Reduction Talks, January 21, 1977. Jimmy Carter Presidential Library, https://www.jimmycarterlibrary.gov/assets/documents/memorandums/prm06.pdf.

———. Program Review Memorandum/NSC-9. Comprehensive Review of European Issues, February 1, 1977. Jimmy Carter Presidential Library, https://www.jimmycarterlibrary.gov/assets/documents/memorandums/prm09.pdf.

———. Program Review Memorandum/NSC-10. Comprehensive Net Assessment and Military Force Posture Review, February 18, 1977. Jimmy Carter Presidential Library, https://www.jimmycarterlibrary.gov/assets/documents/memorandums/prm10.pdf.

Clinton, William J. "Address to the Nation on Implementation of the Peace Agreement in Bosnia-Herzegovina," November 27, 1995. Online at Gerhard Peters and John T. Woolley, American Presidency Project, https://www.presidency.ucsb.edu/node/220919.

———. "Address to the Nation on Somalia," October 7, 1993. Online at Gerhard Peters and John T. Woolley, American Presidency Project, https://www.presidency.ucsb.edu/node/218391.

———. Memorandum for the Secretary of Defense. "Ending Discrimination on the Basis of Sexual Orientation in the Armed Forces," January 29, 1993.

———. A National Security Strategy of Engagement and Enlargement. Washington, DC: White House, 1994.

———. "The President's News Conference," June 17, 1993. Online at Gerhard Peters and John T. Woolley, American Presidency Project, https://www.presidency.ucsb.edu/node/220478.

———. "The President's News Conference." January 29, 1993. Online at Gerhard Pe-

ters and John T. Woolley, American Presidency Project, https://www.presidency
.ucsb.edu/node/220052.

———. "Statement on Signing the National Defense Authorization Act for Fiscal
Year 1996," February 10, 1996. Online at Gerhard Peters and John T. Woolley, American Presidency Project, https://www.presidency.ucsb.edu/node
/222768.

———. "Statement on the Russian Presidential Election, July 4, 1996." Online at
Gerhard Peters and John T. Woolley, American Presidency Project, https://www
.presidency.ucsb.edu/ws/pid=53303.

Ford, Gerald R. Presidential Proclamation 4311. Granting Pardon to Richard Nixon,
September 8, 1974. Gerald R. Ford Presidential Library, https://www.fordlibrary
museum.gov/library/speeches/740060.asp.

———. "The President's News Conference," February 4, 1975. Online at Gerhard Peters and John T. Woolley, American Presidency Project, https://www.presidency
.ucsb.edu/node/257251.

———. "Special Message to the Congress Requesting Supplemental Assistance for
the Republic of Vietnam and Cambodia," January 28, 1975. Online at Gerhard
Peters and John T. Woolley, American Presidency Project, https://www.presi
dency.ucsb.edu/node/257175.

———. "Statement on Signing the Department of Defense Appropriations Act,
1975," October 9, 1974. Online at Gerhard Peters and John T. Woolley, American
Presidency Project, http://www.presidency.ucsb.edu/ws/?pid=4439.

President's Blue Ribbon Commission on Defense Management. *An Interim Report to
the President.* Washington, DC, February 29, 1986.

President's Commission on Strategic Forces. *Report of the President's Commission on
Strategic Forces.* Washington, DC, April 1983.

Reagan, Ronald. Executive Order 12400. President's Commission on Strategic
Forces, January 3, 1983. Ronald Reagan Presidential Library, https://reaganli
brary.archives.gov/archives/speeches/1983/10383a.html.

———. Executive Order 12526. President's Blue Ribbon Commission on Defense
Management, July 15, 1985. Ronald Reagan Presidential Library, https://www
.reaganlibrary.gov/research/speeches/71585c.

———. "Message to the Congress Outlining Proposals for Improving the Organization of the Defense Establishment," April 25, 1986. Ronald Reagan Presidential
Library, https://www.reaganlibrary.gov/research/speeches/42486c.

———. National Security Decision Directive 12. Strategic Forces Modernization Program, October 1, 1981. Ronald Reagan Presidential Library, https://www.reagan
library.gov/sites/default/files/archives/reference/scanned-nsdds/nsdd12.pdf.

———. National Security Decision Directive 32. U.S. National Security Strategy, May
20, 1982. Ronald Reagan Presidential Library, https://www.reaganlibrary.gov
/sites/default/files/archives/reference/scanned-nsdds/nsdd32.pdf.

———. National Security Decision Directive 69. The M-X Program, November 22,
1982. Ronald Reagan Presidential Library, https://www.reaganlibrary.gov/sites
/default/files/archives/reference/scanned-nsdds/nsdd69.pdf.

———. National Security Decision Directive 119. Strategic Defense Initiative, Janu-

ary 6, 1984. Ronald Reagan Presidential Library, https://www.reaganlibrary.gov
/sites/default/files/archives/reference/scanned-nsdds/nsdd119.pdf.

———. National Security Decision Directive 219. Implementation of the Recommendations of the Blue Ribbon Commission on Defense Management, April 1,
1986. Ronald Reagan Presidential Library, https://www.reaganlibrary.gov/sites
/default/files/archives/reference/scanned-nsdds/nsdd219.pdf.

———. National Security Decision Directive 261. Consultations on the SDI Program,
February 18, 1987. Ronald Reagan Presidential Library, https://www.reaganli
brary.gov/sites/default/files/archives/reference/scanned-nsdds/nsdd261.pdf.

———. National Security Study Directive 1-82. U.S. National Security Strategy, February 5, 1982. Ronald Reagan Presidential Library, https://www.reaganlibrary
.gov/sites/default/files/archives/reference/scanned-nssds/nssd1-82.pdf.

———. "Radio Address to the Nation on Defense Establishment Reforms," April
5, 1986. Ronald Reagan Presidential Library, https://www.reaganlibrary.gov/re
search/speeches/40586a.

———. "Remarks at the Annual Convention of the National Association of Evangelicals in Orlando, Florida," March 8, 1983. Ronald Reagan Presidential Library,
https://www.reaganlibrary.gov/research/speeches/30883b.

———. "Remarks on Signing the Soviet–United States Nuclear Risk Reduction
Center Agreement," September 15, 1987. Ronald Reagan Presidential Library,
https://www.reaganlibrary.gov/research/speeches/091587b.

———. "Remarks to Reporters Announcing Endorsement of the Defense Department Recommendations for Direct Communication Links between the United
States and the Soviet Union," May 24, 1983. Ronald Reagan Presidential Library,
https://www.reaganlibrary.gov/research/speeches/52483b.

———. "Remarks to Reporters Announcing New United States Initiatives in the
Strategic Arms Reduction Talks," October 4, 1983. Ronald Reagan Presidential
Library, https://www.reaganlibrary.gov/research/speeches/100483d.

———. "Soviet Union–United States Summit in Washington, DC." Joint statement,
December 10, 1987. Ronald Reagan Presidential Library, https://www.reaganli
brary.gov/research/speeches/121087a.

Congressional Publications

Bills and Resolutions

House of Representatives. Defend America Act of 1996. H.R. 3144, 104th Cong., 2nd
Sess., https://www.congress.gov/bill/104th-congress/house-bill/3144.

———. Department of Defense Authorization Act for Fiscal Year 1985. H.R. 5167,
98th Cong., 2nd Sess., https://www.govtrack.us/congress/bills/98/hr5167.

———. NATO Enlargement Facilitation Act of 1996. H.R. 3564, 104th Cong., 2nd
Sess., https://www.govtrack.us/congress/bills/104/hr3564.

Senate. Defend America Act of 1996. S. 1635. 104th Cong., 2nd Sess., https://www
.congress.gov/bill/104th-congress/senate-bill/1635.

———. NATO Enlargement Facilitation Act of 1996. S. 1830, 104th Cong., 2nd Sess.,
https://www.govtrack.us/congress/bills/104/s1830.

Senate Committee on Armed Services. Department of Defense Authorization for Appropriations for Fiscal Years 1990 and 1991. 101st Cong., 1st Sess., 1989.

Debates

Congressional Oversight of National Defense. *Congressional Record,* 99th Cong., 1st Sess., 25348–25352; 25539–25543; 26159–26160; 26346; 26693–26696.

Conventional Forces in Europe Treaty Implementation Act of 1991. H.R. 3807. 102nd Cong., 1st Sess., *Congressional Record* (November 25, 1991), Senate Vote no. 274.

The Defend America Act of 1996. *Congressional Record* 142, no. 40, 104th Cong., 2nd Sess., 1996. S2651–S2652.

Gays and Lesbians in the Armed Forces. S. 8876. *Congressional Record* 139, no. 99. 103rd Cong., 1st Sess., July 16, 1993.

Levin-Nunn Language to Limit Testing or Deployment of SDI in Violation of the ABM Treaty. *Congressional Record* 133, no. 82. 100th Cong. 1st Sess., May 20, 1987.

National Defense Act for Fiscal Years 1990 and 1991. S8948. *Congressional Record* 135, no. 102. 101st Cong., 1st Sess., July 27, 1989.

Nunn, speaking on the Interpretation of the ABM Treaty, *National Defense Authorization Act for Fiscal Years 1988 and 1989*, Part Four: An Examination of Judge Sofaer's Analysis of the Negotiating Record, 100th Cong., 1st Sess., *Congressional Record* 133, no. 82, May 20, 1987

Part One: The Senate Ratification Proceedings. *Congressional Record* 133, no. 38. 100th Cong., 1st Sess., March 11, 1987.

Part Two: Subsequent Practice under the ABM Treaty. *Congressional Record* 133, no. 39. 100th Cong., 1st Sess., March 12, 1987.

Part Three: The ABM Negotiating Record. *Congressional Record* 133, no. 40. 100th Cong., 1st Sess., March 13, 1987.

Senate Amdt. 3268 to S. 2723, *Omnibus Defense Authorization Act for Fiscal Year 1985. Congressional Record* 130, no. 85, daily edition, 98th Cong., 2nd Sess., June 20, 1984. https://www.congress.gov/amendment/98th-congress/senate-amendment/3268?r=30.

Hearings

General Accounting Office. "Major Issues Facing a New Congress and a New Administration." Statement of Charles A. Bowsher, Comptroller General of the United States, before the Committee on Governmental Affairs, US Senate, January 8, 1993, GAO/T-OCG-93-1.

———. Testimony before the Subcommittee on National Security, International Affairs, and Criminal Justice, Committee on Government Reform and Oversight, House of Representatives. *Observations on the Nunn-Lugar-Domenici Domestic Preparedness Program*, GAO/T-NSIAD-99-16, October 2, 1998.

Hearings on the Department of Defense Policy Excluding Homosexuals from Service in the Armed Forces. S. 755. *Congressional Record* 139, no. 9. 103rd Cong., 1st Sess., January 27, 1993.

Mayer, John D., Deputy Assistant Director, National Security Division, Congressional Budget Office. Testimony before the Committee on the Budget. US Senate, March 8, 1990.

Senate Committee on Armed Services. *Crisis in the Persian Gulf Region: U.S. Policy Options and Implications.* 101st Cong., 2nd Sess., 1990.

———. *Current Military Operations in Somalia.* 103rd Cong., 1st Sess., 1993.

———. *Department of Defense Authorization for Appropriations for Fiscal Year 1991.* 101st Cong., 2nd Sess., 1990.

———. *Department of Defense Authorization for Appropriations for Fiscal Year 1994 and the Future Years Defense Program,* Part I. 103rd Cong., 1st Sess., 1993.

———. *Department of Defense Authorization for Appropriations for Fiscal Year 1995 and the Future Years Defense Program.* 103rd Cong., 2nd Sess., 1994.

———. *Hearing, NATO Defense and the INF Treaty.* 100th Cong., 2nd Sess., Part 1, January 25, 26, 27, 1988.

———. *Hearing, NATO Defense and the INF Treaty.* 100th Cong., 2nd Sess., Part 2, January 28, 29; February 1–2, 1988.

———. *Hearing, NATO Defense and the INF Treaty.* 100th Cong., 2nd Sess., Part 3, February 3–4, 16, 1988.

———. *Hearing, NATO Defense and the INF Treaty.* 100th Cong., 2nd Sess., Part 4, February 22–23, 1988.

———. *Impact of Unilateral U.S. Lifting of the Arms Embargo on the Government of Bosnia-Herzegovina.* 103rd Cong., 2nd Sess., 1994.

———. *Impacts of a Sequester on the Department of Defense in Fiscal Year 1990 and Fiscal Year 1991.* 101st Cong., 1st Sess., 1989.

———. *Joint Chiefs of Staff Briefing on Current Military Operations in Somalia, Iraq, and Yugoslavia.* 103rd Cong., 1st Sess., 1993.

———. *National Security Strategy.* 100th Cong., 1st Sess., January 12 and 27, 1987, S. Hrg. 100-257.

———. *Nomination of John G. Tower to Be Secretary of Defense.* 101st Cong., 1st Sess., 1989.

———. *Nominations before the Senate Armed Services Committee.* 101st Cong., 1st Sess., 1989.

———. *Nominations before the Senate Armed Services Committee.* 103rd Cong., 1st Sess., 1993.

———. *Reorganization of the Department of Defense, Hearings before the Committee on Armed Services.* 99th Cong., 1st. Sess., 1986.

———, Subcommittee on Manpower and Personnel. *NATO Posture and Initiatives.* 95th Cong., 1st Sess., 1977.

———. *Threat Assessment: Military Strategy and Operational Requirements.* 101st Cong., 1st Sess., 1989.

———. *Threat Assessment: Military Strategy and Operational Requirements.* 101st Cong., 2nd Sess., 1990.

Senate Committee on Foreign Relations. *The ABM Treaty Interpretation Resolution.* Report of the Committee on Foreign Relations, United States Senate, together with additional views. Washington, DC: US Government Printing Office, 1987.

———. *Hearing, INF Treaty.* 100th Cong., 2nd Sess., Part 1, January 25, 1988.

————. *Hearing before the Committee on Foreign Relations on S. Res. 329.* 98th Cong., 2nd Sess., April 4, 1984.

Senate Committee on Government Affairs, Permanent Subcommittee on Investigations. *Global Proliferation of Weapons of Mass Destruction,* Part I. 104th Cong., 1st Sess., 1995, 1–730.

————. *Global Proliferation of Weapons of Mass Destruction,* Part II. 104th Cong., 2nd Sess., 1996.

————. *Global Proliferation of Weapons of Mass Destruction,* Part III. 104th Cong., 2nd Sess., 1996.

Senate Committee on the Budget. *After the Thaw: National Security Objectives in the Post Cold-War Era.* 101st Cong., 1st Sess., 1989.

Reports and Documents

Biden, Joseph R., Jr. *To Stand against Aggression: Milosevic, the Bosnian Republic and the Conscience of the West.* Report to the Committee on Foreign Relations, US Senate. Washington, DC: Government Printing Office, 1993.

Clerk of the US House of Representatives. *Statistics of the President and Congressional Election of November 4, 1980.* Washington, DC: Government Printing Office, 1981.

Comptroller General of the United States. *NATO's New Defense Program: Issues for Consideration,* ID-79-4A. Washington, DC: General Accounting Office, July 9, 1979. https://www.gao.gov/assets/130/127274.pdf.

Congressional Budget Office. *Planning U.S. General Purpose Forces: Army Procurement Issues.* Budget Issue Paper. Washington, DC: US Government Printing Office, 1976.

Galdi, Theodore. *The Nunn-Lugar Program for Soviet Weapons Dismantlement: Background and Implementation.* Washington, DC: Congressional Research Service, 1995.

McInnis, Kathleen J. *Goldwater-Nichols at 30: Defense Reform and Issues for Congress,* CRS Report 44474. Washington, DC: Congressional Research Service, 2016.

Schick, Allen. *Explanation of the Balanced Budget and Emergency Deficit Control Act of 1985—Public Law 99-177 (The Gramm-Rudman-Hollings Act).* Washington, DC: Congressional Research Service, Library of Congress, 1986.

Senate. *Report of the Senate Arms Control Observer Group Delegation to the Opening of the Arms Control Negotiations with the Soviet Union in Geneva, Switzerland.* 99th Cong., 1st Sess., 1985, Document 99-7.

Senate Committee on Armed Services. *Defense Organization: The Need for Changes.* Staff Report to the Committee on Armed Services, 99th Cong., 1st Sess., Committee Print, S. Prt. 99-86, October 16, 1985.

————. Department of Defense Authorization for Appropriations for Fiscal Year 1994 and the Future Years Defense Program, Part I. 103rd Cong., 1st Sess., 1993.

————. *National Defense Authorization Act for Fiscal Year 1991,* 101st Cong., 1st Sess., 1989, S. Rep. 101-385.

————. *NATO and the New Soviet Threat.* Report of Senator Sam Nunn and Senator

Dewey F. Bartlett to the Committee on Armed Services, US Senate, 95th Cong., 1st Sess., January 24, 1977.

———. *NATO Defense and the INF Treaty.* Report 100-312. Washington, DC: US Government Printing Office, April 1988.

———. *Omnibus Defense Authorization Act,* 1984, 98th Cong., 1st Sess., 1983, S. Rep. 98-174.

———. *Policy, Troops, and the NATO Alliance.* Report of Senator Sam Nunn to the Committee on Armed Services, US Senate, 93rd Cong., 2nd Sess., 1974.

———. *Vietnam Aid—The Painful Options.* Report of Senator Sam Nunn to the Committee on Armed Services, US Senate, 94th Cong., 1st Sess., February 12, 1975.

Waller, Douglas, James T. Bruce, and Douglas Cook. "SDI: Progress and Challenges, Part II." US Congress staff report submitted to Senators William Proxmire, J. Bennett Johnston, and Lawton Chiles. Washington, DC, March 17, 1987.

Treaties

Treaty Between the United States of America and the Union of Soviet Socialist Republics on the Elimination of their Intermediate-Range and Shorter-Range Missiles. Treaties, 100th Cong. (1987–1988), 100-111.

INDEX

INDEX